Edited by John Rodden

# Lionel Trilling
## and the Critics

## Opposing Selves

Foreword by Morris Dickstein

University of Nebraska Press

Lincoln and London

Acknowledgments for the use of copyrighted
materials appear on pages 477–81, which
constitute an extension of the copyright page.
Foreword © 1999 by Morris Dickstein
© 1999 by the University of Nebraska Press
Manufactured in the United States of America
∞
Library of Congress Cataloging-in-Publication Data
Lionel Trilling and the critics: opposing
selves / edited by John Rodden;
foreword by Morris Dickstein.
    p.   cm.
Includes bibliographical references and index.
ISBN 0-8032-3922-X (cloth : alk. paper).—
ISBN 0-8032-8974-X (pbk. : alk. paper)
1. Trilling, Lionel, 1905–1975—Criticism
and interpretation.   2. Criticism—United
States—History—20th century.    3. Culture—
Historiography.    I. Rodden, John.
PS3539.R56Z86    1999
818'.5209—dc21        98–53491
CIP

# Lionel Trilling and the Critics

# Contents

## E. M. Forster (1943)

## The Middle of the Journey (1947)

## The Liberal Imagination (1950)

**The Opposing Self (1955)**

**A Gathering of Fugitives (1956)**

**Beyond Culture (1965)**

## Illustrations

*Foreword*

*A Man Nobody Knew:*

*Lionel Trilling Remembered*

**Morris Dickstein**

In recent years the climate of opinion surrounding a writer has come in for almost as much attention as the work itself; indeed, for some who see the meaning of literary texts as prismatic and unstable, this shifting spectrum *is* the work itself, the sum of how it has been perceived, assimilated, and reimagined. Since the 1960s, collections of articles devoted to individual writers have multiplied as teaching and research tools but their purpose has changed. Once focused on close reading, they now reflect the historical interests of teachers and scholars. Books like this show us how a writer's reputation evolved but also serve as lessons in the time-bound nature of interpretation, documenting how received ideas, cultural assumptions, and subjective preferences color our understanding of all we read. *Lionel Trilling and the Critics: Opposing Selves*, edited by John Rodden, is almost unique because its subject is not a poet or novelist but a critic, Lionel Trilling, who only occasionally tried his hand at imaginative writing. Neither Edmund Wilson, whom Trilling warmly admired, nor F. R. Leavis, with whom he shared many literary assumptions, has as yet been the subject of such a historical record, though Wilson's work was more wide ranging and Leavis's more controversial than Trilling's.

One reason is that Wilson, with the famous transparency of his writing, and even Leavis, with his far knottier, more Jamesian manner, always made clear exactly what they wanted to say. Trilling, on the other hand, despite the uncommon grace and felicity of his style, was often seen as elusive, even enigmatic, and his essays evoked a broader range of critical response. This perplexing quality of Trilling's work, especially its uncertain political thrust, drew the attention of some outstanding literary minds, from R. P.

Blackmur, R. W. B. Lewis, and Joseph Frank to Denis Donoghue, Lewis Simpson, and Irving Howe. Nearly all their reviews deal with Trilling's books, not with the person behind them; they dance around an enigma, a felt need for explanation. "Part of the pleasure of seeing Mr. Trilling's essays brought together surely consists in finding out what he has been up to all along," wrote Blackmur in 1950. But Trilling himself was seen by many friends, colleagues, and students as someone hard to pin down, genial but detached, in spite of the familiar personal tone he deployed so well. Even the reminiscences published after his death are remarkably free of revealing detail, as if answering to his own lifelong reticence. The private man eluded his friends as much as the essays puzzled many of his readers.

This wall of privacy began to crumble in 1979 when his widow, Diana Trilling, published an account of his ordeal in gaining tenure as a Jew teaching English at Columbia in the 1930s. Then in *Partisan Review* in 1984 came a selection from his journals, and finally in 1993 Mrs. Trilling brought out *The Beginning of the Journey*, a vinegary memoir of the first decades of their marriage. It was written with a kind of tough love, as if only an absolute fidelity to the truth could be faithful to his memory. Despite her bracing force and clarity, all the more remarkable in a writer approaching ninety, Mrs. Trilling could fall into pettiness, recalling minor slights and settling old scores sixty years later. (She describes complaining to her analyst of her husband's "repeated failure to remember to put out the garbage.") She understates her own disabling problems and the burden they must have placed on Trilling. But the book also disclosed that a man whom many had seen as the very soul of civility could also be depressive, alcoholic, abusive to his wife, and inhumanly remote to his students.

Diana Trilling's book was part tribute, part revelation, part declaration of independence by someone who felt she had dwelled too long in her husband's shadow. But it was also a loving portrait that made the man more complex and interesting than he had ever seemed, while it shattered the facade that, by her own account, he had spent a lifetime shoring up. Mrs. Trilling presented her husband as someone riven by sharp inner conflicts, at times beset by depression and rage, yet shielded from friends and colleagues by a wall of discretion and restraint. It seems safe to say that though *The Beginning of the Journey* will scarcely be the last word, anything written about Trilling in the future will undoubtedly take more account of the man himself. This has been true of the modern writers in general as biographies and personal letters and time itself have sharply altered our sense of who they were.

To the students of my generation who studied with him at Columbia in the late fifties and early sixties, a decade after *The Liberal Imagination* had made him famous, Trilling was already something of a legendary figure, the intellectual conscience of the undergraduate English Department, the entrepreneur of distinguished book clubs, a link to the turbulent world of the New York intellectuals, and above all a teacher and critic who was dangerous to emulate and virtually impossible to please. Trilling's soft voice, twinkling ironic manner, and elaborate politeness cloaked a demanding toughness that all his students quickly encountered. His face had a perpetually worried look; the furrowed brow and dark shadows around his eyes seemed to speak of the agonies and responsibilities of the intellectual life. His demeanor, which was exactly the same in public and private, combined lightness and *gravitas*, and he could make a joke even about his deepest concerns. He has sometimes been castigated as a spokesman for middle-class values, but once, when asked by a wide-eyed David Susskind on public television if there was one thing in the culture we could do without, he said wryly, "the middle class."

Trilling was especially concerned that teaching literature, especially modern literature, would reduce its exigency to a pedagogical routine. In his lecture course on modern writers in the spring of 1960, he announced to us right at the beginning that he was heartily sick of undergraduate critical writing, tired of all the gestures of existential urgency that went into it. In disgust he had thought of asking each of us to write a straight biographical report on one of the authors—to be graded on style alone. In an atmosphere that prized critical thinking over all things, this was a calculated insult, however genially delivered. He didn't follow through, of course: it was only a shock tactic to bring home his demand that we take these writers more personally, take their presumed assault on us to heart.

When his famous essay on the teaching of modern literature appeared in *Partisan Review* six months later, we were irate to find ourselves held up to ridicule as examples of benign insensitivity. There was no mention here of writing biographical sketches of the modern writers, only of rising to their spiritual challenge, which we manifestly failed to do. "When the term-essays come in, it is plain to me that almost none of the students have been taken aback by what they have read: they have wholly contained the attack. . . . I asked them to look into the Abyss, and, both dutifully and gladly, they have looked into the Abyss, and the Abyss has greeted them with the grave courtesy of all objects of serious study, saying: 'Interesting, am I not? And *exciting* . . .'" He had hauled the moderns into the classroom, but there was no way to convince him that far from taking them in stride, we found them as thrilling and problematic as they had seemed to his own generation, some forty years earlier. I've now read enough undergraduate writing to appreciate the exasperation that can come from poring over too many routine, even competent accounts of serious subjects. But this hardly explains why a famous professor would satirize his students for the convenience of a literary argument.

Our vanity, our cocky sense of our own brilliance, was wounded by this skewed report of what had actually taken place in the classroom. Yet we respected him hugely for his crankiness, his impossible standards, his refusal to be merely nice. Trilling seemed impervious to the kind of showy undergraduate cleverness that impressed some of our other teachers. But he himself was not at his best in a lecture course, where the pressure he felt to say something fresh and spontaneous conflicted with the rhetorical demands of reaching a large audience.

He was no performer, but he did not spare himself for failing to rise to the occasion. Once, in what seemed like a wholly improvised lecture on Kafka, he began musing about how difficult it was to talk about *The Trial*. He described approaching each of his colleagues in turn, asking them for something to say about this elusive novel. They had a great deal to say, he reported, and much of it was quite brilliant, but somehow it was not what *he* wanted to say, not exactly the right thing. Perhaps, he implied, no critical language, no display of analytical energy could quite measure up to it. Perhaps an appalled and silent awe, or some sense of horror, was the right response to such an unsettling work. On that day at least, we heard the genuine sound of silence in the casual flow of his associations, his lecture about not being able to lecture.

But that day was the exception. Generally, Trilling needed the give and take of a small class to bring out what was best in him. He seemed bored by his own ideas, tired of the sound of his own voice; he needed something unexpected to react to, some angle he hadn't anticipated. This was rarely possible in the formal setting of the lecture room. Still, we admired even the *Partisan Review* essay for the way it projected Trilling's ideal course on modern writers, the one we missed having.

As a teacher, Trilling had no body of knowledge to convey, no methodology. By and large he saved his ideas for his writing, where he exercised an exquisite tact that emerged only sporadically in the classroom. Like his own teacher, Mark Van Doren, who had just retired, he taught by example, not precept. What meant most to him was to be possessed by a book, to be disoriented and changed by it. His quarrel with the New Critics and with academic scholars was that they saw literature, even modern literature, as an object of knowledge, not as a source of power, a verbal enactment of will and desire. To Trilling, the writer was someone determined to impose himself, to make something happen; as a critic, Trilling's inclination was to pay attention "to the poet's social and personal will . . . to what the poet *wants*."

The one reservation in his tribute to Edmund Wilson is that while the older critic admires many writers, "he is never astonished by them, or led to surrender himself to them." After Trilling's death Irving Howe wrote about the edginess of Trilling's engagement with literature, how he would "circle a work with his fond, nervous wariness, as if in the presence of some force, some living energy, which could not always be kept under proper control— indeed, as if he were approaching an elemental power." Trilling talked about books as if they might rise up and attack him; he was especially fond of quoting Auden's remark that books read us as much as we read them.

Trilling opened himself to books in ways he found hard to expose himself to actual human beings. His considerable demeanor and limpid ingratiating prose disguised more than they revealed. Trilling once brought down on his head the wrath of the cultural guardians when he tried to penetrate the disguises of Robert Frost, to look behind his public mask. Frost himself was pleased to be taken seriously, though he once wrote to his friend Sidney Cox, "I have written to keep the over-curious out of the secret places of my mind both in my verse and in my letters to such as you." In a Blakean couplet Trilling quoted to justify his unusual birthday tribute to the poet, Frost put this even better:

> We dance round in a ring and suppose,
> But the Secret sits in the middle and knows.

Diana Trilling's memoir makes a great issue of Trilling's own acts of concealment. She portrays him as a man nobody knew, bowed down by heavy burdens of family responsibility, conflicted and often depressed in private, kindly but self-protective in company. Though closely identified with Freud—to the extent that the *New York Times Book Review* commissioned him to review each of the three volumes of Ernest Jones's biography—he "made a point of not mentioning his own analysis at college or anywhere. . . . [H]e had a public image to protect, perhaps especially at Columbia." She describes how he became a symbolic figure for his students, a "moral exemplar" who was a focus of their fantasies and ambitions, as Mark Van Doren had been for Trilling's generation. "Lionel did not create or encourage this image. Consciously he scorned it. Yet unconsciously he conspired in it. . . . Like a father who instinctively conceals his shortcomings from his offspring lest their respect for him be diminished, he was at pains not to reveal human fallibilities which had sent him into analysis."

Mrs. Trilling's own fallibilities were virtually impossible to conceal; her phobias must have placed great demands on those around her. But she was also more downright and direct in her response to people: invariably blunt yet closely attentive to everyone she met, she was prone to tell them exactly what she thought. Trilling, on the other hand, seemed distant, genial, and ironic. He could be very caring with his best and flakiest students; he might encourage and take a special interest in them, as he did with Allen Ginsberg, or with the fictional Tertan in his 1943 story "Of This Time, Of That Place." But his standards were so severe that some writers who had been his students (such as Ivan Gold) found his patronage unnerving, as if his critical eye were always peering over their shoulder. Even established writers such as Saul Bellow and John O'Hara would be unnerved as he alternately bestowed and withheld his approval of their work. There was a genuine anguish behind this caprice: I sensed that Trilling lived in fear of pronouncing a wrong judgment or perpetrating a bad sentence.

In later years he turned more lofty, and Mrs. Trilling berates him for allowing his students to see him as invulnerable. When a former student, now a colleague, comes by to confess his fears about approaching fatherhood, Trilling remains graciously remote, as if he himself had never experienced such cares. "When the young man left, I turned on Lionel in a fury. Who was he to allow such a distinction between himself and the rest of the world?"

This recollection struck home with me since I too had been a student and then a colleague who, at an impressionable point in my life, had seen Trilling as a role model and a mentor, someone who demonstrated the kind of power and eloquence and public reach a literary critic could have. I wouldn't have dreamed of consulting him about a personal problem, or showing him my own vulnerability. Instead I took his remoteness as some kind of rejection, and gradually learned not to expect his blessing, but rather to look to myself and to close friends for direction. The one painful episode I had with Trilling came in my first year of teaching at Columbia. I had just submitted a thesis on Keats to the Yale English faculty and, in a moment of spontaneous generosity, Trilling asked if he could read it. Keats was a special passion of his, the subject of his longest and richest essay. It was natural that he should be curious to read it but equally natural, for him at least, that he proved unable to do so, even after it appeared as a book.

I must have sealed my fate when I mentioned that one of my Yale readers—I think it was Cleanth Brooks—had called it "Trillingesque." (It was not at all clear that he meant it as a compliment.) There were other influences that were more important—if anything, the book carried on a covert argument with Trilling's essay—but it was too late to take back what I had tactlessly reported to him. When it became clear that he was *not* going to read it, I tried, politely but insistently, to relieve him of the burden, but he adamantly refused to let it go. Was it self-absorption, ambivalence, or a subtle form of aggression that kept him from either reading or relinquishing it? Each time we met he would assure me in the strongest terms that there was nothing he wanted to read more, especially as he himself was somehow in it. I had foolishly tried to give him a selfish reason to be interested in what I had done. Unfortunately, it seemed, to examine his reflection in someone else's work was more than he could bear, and for years it created a barrier that made other conversation difficult. At each encounter there was an elephant in the room: the mild guilt feelings he felt obliged to express, the keen disappointment I somehow failed to conceal.

Our long acquaintance, always cordial, settled into a series of missed connections. I only got his full attention when I criticized him, as when I praised in passing a Delmore Schwartz essay that had attacked him, or when I wrote to him to question his description of Whittaker Chambers as a "man of honor," to which he replied with a carefully argued letter, almost lawyerly in tone, that was clearly meant to be part of the ultimate public record. As fame multiplied the demands on him, his protective shell hardened. But his discretion and reserve must have preceded the time he had a public image to sustain. Some of his detachment was admirable, and contributed to his stature. He rarely allowed himself to be sucked into the quarrels of the New York intellectuals or the intense backbiting on the Columbia campus. He resisted signing petitions, and generally took the long view, especially where politics was concerned.

His Arnoldian detachment, his need to examine every side of the question, gave him purchase as a critic but took its toll on him as a person. By temperament he was prone to second thoughts and hesitations, and this left him ineffective in faculty deliberations. Because he held so much back, I knew him better from his books than from his considerable presence. As students we had all imagined that "Lionel Trilling," which sounded so euphoniously English, was a constructed personality, though we wrongly assumed he had changed his name, as had other New York Jewish intellectuals who felt burdened by their modest origins. We knew nothing of his early explorations of Jewish identity in numerous stories and reviews for the *Menorah Journal* in the 1920s.

I learned from a later essay (his tribute to Robert Warshow) that he had sparked resentment by refusing to associate himself with *Commentary* when it started in 1945, though his friend and mentor Elliot Cohen was its founding editor. Trilling may have been trying to separate himself as much from Cohen's overbearing influence—he could be an intrusive, domineering editor—as from any overtly Jewish institution. But just a year earlier, in *Commentary*'s predecessor publication, the *Contemporary Jewish Record*, Trilling had responded to a symposium of writers under forty by distancing himself even more dramatically from any institutional Jewish culture. "I do not think of myself as a 'Jewish writer,'" he wrote. "I do not have it in mind to serve by my writing any Jewish purpose. I should resent it if a critic of my work were to discover in it either faults or virtues which he called Jewish." Trilling conceded that his position showed "a certain gracelessness—if only because millions of Jews are suffering simply because they have the heritage that I so minimize in my own intellectual life." Resisting the tribal claims of "the unimaginable sufferings of masses of men," Trilling could hardly acknowledge what was happening to the Jews of Europe in 1944. As he saw it, any self-consciously Jewish writer only intensified his own exclusion from "the general life" and showed "a willingness to be provincial and parochial."

In bracketing the Jewish themes that had engaged him in his early work, Trilling was determined above all to become an *American* writer, to join the mainstream and participate in the common life. But this was exactly the moment when American literature was being ethnicized, when writers like Richard Wright, Saul Bellow, Ralph Ellison, James Baldwin, Bernard Malamud, and Alfred Kazin were taking a hyphenated path *into* the mainstream, leaving the Anglophile manner behind. Behind these writers lay Kafka, Dostoevsky, Mark Twain, even Sholom Aleichem rather than Trilling's beloved English models. By comparison with these new ethnically accented but scarcely parochial books, Trilling's 1947 *roman à these*, *The Middle of the Journey*, feels abstract and dislocated, as Robert Warshow pointed out with some harshness in one of the best essays ever written on Trilling.

The urbanity to which Trilling aspired was the style of the city, the style of the center. It was worldly and cosmopolitan, rather than local; like E. M. Forster, Trilling was drawn to the abstract dilemmas of the moral life, not the embodied, situated identities of particular lives. But the culture of the city had changed—it was growing polycentric—and Trilling paid the price for his detachment, as he had feared from the outset of his career. The emotional sources that might have nourished a career in fiction were blocked. In his journals we see his ambivalence writ large. He broods over the freewheeling lives of writers like Hemingway and the young Kerouac, identifying art with adventure, narcissism, and even criminality. But even as his acute self-consciousness hobbled his fiction, his ambivalence gave power to his criticism.

Trilling's awareness of his need for concealment was as great as Frost's. His first contribution to the *Menorah Journal*, "Impediments," published before he turned twenty, was a precocious story with implications that rippled out over his next fifty years. Indeed, it may have been the most self-revealing thing he ever wrote. Little more than a slight undergraduate anecdote, it describes a dormitory encounter between the cynical, supercilious narrator and his earnest friend Hettner, "a scrubby little Jew" who is trying to break through his crust of witty sarcasm. "I did not like the fellow," the narrator admits. Though Hettner makes no overt demands on him and gives no sign of wanting to further their "slight acquaintance," the narrator tries to keep their talk as impersonal as possible: "I felt always defensive against some attempt Hettner might make to break down the convenient barrier I was erecting against men who were too much of my own race and against men who were not of my own race and hated it. I feared he would attempt to win into the not-too-strong tower I had built myself, a tower of contemptible ivory perhaps, but very useful. . . . [T]here was a straining eagerness about him, an uncertain fugitive air that put me on my guard lest he come to me for a refuge I did not want to give." The narrator's problem with Hettner is not simply that the man is too Jewish and too eager, or that he grew up poor and doesn't dress very well—we're told that his "untidy blue serge gives him the look of a shop assistant"—or that he is too widely read, too immersed in ideas, too obviously an intellectual; his problem is that Hettner may reveal himself to him, may force "obnoxious" confidences on him, and in the process show how much alike they are: "Hettner had come in for what he would call an intelligent and serious conversation; that is, he wanted to talk about himself, to give me hints as to what he really was, to tell me things about his soul. I could see that easily. Now, I do not want to know about people's souls; I want people quite entirely dressed; I want no display of fruity scabs and luscious sores. I like people's outsides, not their insides, and I was particularly reluctant to see this man's insides; they would be, probably, too much like mine." Finally the narrator's impregnable sarcasm and distance, his cold propriety, deflect Hettner; invincible in his tower, the narrator parries every thrust, "and I, whose victories were few enough, smiled at that victory of mine." But Hettner, as he turns to leave, wins the last round. "What a miserable dog you are," he says, not very loud, as a parting shot.

Though Mrs. Trilling identifies the protagonist of the story with Trilling and Hettner with a friend of his, Henry Rosenthal, who later became a rabbi and then a teacher of philosophy, it would be unwise to take the off-putting narrator, who dares us to dislike him, simply as the young Trilling. Rather, like Eliot's Prufrock, he is the kind of persona on whom the modernist writer projects his own most ambiguous qualities, in this case his defensiveness, his fear of experience, the barriers he erects against other people. Hettner, in turn, is that other modernist figure, the secret sharer, the despised and threatening double, who embodies the more ethnic Jewishness, the neediness and vulnerability that the narrator instinctively resists. And Hettner's parting shot is yet another modern device, the twist that turns the story upon itself, recoiling against its own point of view. This ironic reversal would become a specialty of later Jewish-American writers, including Norman Mailer in "The Time of Her Time," Bernard Malamud in "The Last Mohican," and Philip Roth in "Defender of the Faith," all writers adroit at Jewish introspection and self-exposure, the very qualities Trilling's protagonist disclaims, even as he mercilessly dissects his own behavior.

In some posthumously published notes for a 1971 lecture, Trilling mentions yet another feature of modern writing that shaped his generation, what he calls "the unmasking principle" dear to intellectuals since the French Revolution. Marx and Freud, he says, "taught the intellectual classes that nothing was as it seemed, that the great work of intellect was to strike through the mask." This last phrase, which comes from one of Captain Ahab's fiery speeches, can be applied to what Trilling himself did in "Impediments," and what he largely failed to do in his later fiction. Nothing weakens his fiction more than the paleness of the author's surrogates, such as John Laskell in *The Middle of the Journey*—stiff, dimly embodied figures who are little more than vehicles for the writer's subtle, self-questioning intelligence. Trilling himself had the perpetually concerned look of someone wary of entanglements, who examined everything through a fine moral prism. This vantage point of the sensitive observer, of someone who stands apart, damaged his fiction but gave strength to his criticism. He had remarkable empathy for writers in conflict, writers under pressure like Fitzgerald and Keats and Isaac Babel, but also for writers who developed a stoical mask for surviving such pressure, like Wordsworth and Santayana.

Trilling's 1956 piece on George Santayana is, like so many of his best essays, a sketch for a self-portrait—in this case the portrait of someone (like the narrator of "Impediments") who "was manifestly not a sweet man" but rather "defined himself in the universe by detachment from it." In a typically disarming opening, Trilling writes: "One doesn't have to read very far in Santayana's letters to become aware that it might be very hard to like this man—that, indeed, it might be remarkably easy to dislike him." Partly speaking for himself, Trilling ascribes Santayana's "brilliant youthful reserve" to his "knowledge of the abyss, the awareness of the discontinuity between man and the world." He notes that Santayana lost hope early, but that this did not propel him towards nihilism; it did not cause him to devalue the world or even to abjure friendship, but "its limits were clear to him very early and he never permitted himself to be deceived into thinking that a friend was himself. Nothing could be more striking than Santayana's equal devotion and remoteness in his youthful letters to his friends. He put all his intelligence and all his sympathy at their service, but never himself."

What redeems Santayana for Trilling, what he identifies with strongly, is the unwavering quality of his self-definition. "That he was a good man has been questioned," Trilling concludes, "and the question seems to me a very

reasonable one—there is something deeply disquieting about his temperament. But there can be no doubt of the firmness of his self-definition; there
can be no doubt that he did not peter out." A decade later the same themes
surface darkly in a review of Joyce's letters, where Trilling notes the contrast
between Joyce's ferocious commitment to art and his equally complete
detachment from other people, except for his immediate family. This apart-
ness is modified only superficially as Joyce grows older. "By his middle years
Joyce had developed a talent, if not for friendship, then at least for friendliness; . . . there sounds a note of geniality, often of a whimsical kind, which, as
the reviewers noted, is at variance with what is often reported of his forbid-
ding reserve." Even with its darker shadings, this "reserve" was one of
Trilling's favorite motifs. It was one of many neglected nineteenth-century
qualities that he came to admire. The Joyce essay takes special pleasure in
exploring the Victorian side, the almost archaic temperament, of a great
modern writer.

Trilling's fascination with Joyce's old-fashioned qualities of will, detachment, grandiose ambition, and class consciousness was both temperamental
and cultural. Despite his affinity for Freud, or perhaps because of it, Trilling
hated the modern therapeutic culture of self-exposure, confessional intimacy, and psychological manipulation. Just as the protagonist of "Impediments" prefers people's outsides to their messy insides, the Victorian virtues
were a refuge for Trilling, an alternative to the modern insistence on transparency and authenticity that goes back to Rousseau. For Trilling, Freud
was the last of the great Victorians, and Trilling identified at least as much
with his character as with his ideas; he admired Freud's probity, his work
ethic, his almost Napoleonic determination to impose himself, his clear-
eyed persistence in old age, and finally his stoicism and fortitude in the face
of death. He too did not peter out.

In a less heroic, more Woody Allen–like vein, I can offer an anecdotal
counterpart to these revealing essays. Trilling once interrupted a faculty
meeting to express his concern that a departmental assistant didn't speak to
him and seemed to dislike him. Several colleagues quickly assured him that
the student in question was no doubt awed by him and his reputation.
Trilling seemed greatly relieved. "Oh, it's not rudeness, you think," he said
triumphantly. "It's just manly reserve." I was charmed by this. He had heard
what they said but had translated it into his own terms. In some ways he was
living in another century, and took a certain comic pleasure in being out of
touch.

Between comments like this and writings like "Impediments," or the
essays on Santayana and Joyce, I began to understand why I had never gotten
past the barrier of civility that shielded him. Trilling himself recalled rather

starchily in 1966 that when he was young, "seniority was more of a bar to communication than it has since become." But difference of age or temperament was hardly the whole story. He wrote a brief memoir of his troubled relationship to one of his own teachers, Raymond Weaver, who for years had blown hot and cold toward him. He recalls how Weaver tried to get him fired before becoming his strongest supporter. Trilling fought for his job, and Weaver, who "set great store by anger," eventually relaxed his "characteristic reserve" towards him. Trilling who was exactly my father's age; I must have unconsciously appealed for the kind of paternal approval he found hard to give, especially to me. Like Hettner I no doubt seemed needy and over-eager, effusively intellectual, always at risk of baring my soul. I had grown up in the immigrant cauldron of the Lower East Side; like Hettner I was inescapably Jewish in a style that disturbed him. I could be restrained, even stoical, but no on would have mistaken it for "manly reserve."

The ambivalence that Trilling habitually acted out, and described openly in his fiction and journals, became one of the sources of his vitality as a critic. Its greatest gift to him was his style, with its ironic distance, its mask of civility, and above all its sinuous dialectical turnings as he restlessly tried on one viewpoint after another. There's a palpable vein of Jewish insecurity in Trilling's subtle modulations. He evolved his conversational manner not simply out of the familiar essay of the nineteenth century but from his dialogue with himself, which also turned on conflicts in the larger culture. Like all good writers, he projected his divided feelings into a picture of the world. In the opening essay of *The Liberal Imagination* this became a kind of credo: "A culture is not a flow, nor even a confluence—it is nothing if not a dialectic. And in any culture there are likely to be certain artists who contain a large part of the dialectic within themselves, their meaning and power lying in their contradictions." Instinctively, but also out of a personal necessity, Trilling made this contentious vision of art and culture a model for his critical writing.

The mask that made Trilling so elusive as a person lent exceptional interest to his essays. He was a reactive critic, attuned to each occasion, whose work cohered around shifting polarities rather than a single point of view. His emphasis varied from book to book, from decade to decade. He was ingenious at shaping his collections around themes that arise only obliquely, if at all, in each essay. The "liberal imagination" appears prismatically, not consecutively, in that book, as the "adversary culture" flickers in and out of view in *Beyond Culture*. But Trilling's shifting, open-weaved argument created enigmas that endlessly intrigued viewers, as John Rodden documents vividly in these pages. Trilling's books and essays became conversation pieces, markers of the cultural moment, and he himself became a secular cleric to a generation of postwar intellectuals that looked to literature rather than to politics or religion for guidance.

Weaned on modernism, Trilling's literary generation aimed to strike through the mask, but one of *his* achievements was to construct an absorbing series of masks that gave full play to his opposing selves. He grew uneasy with the far-reaching social visions of modernism, especially its hunger for apocalyptic transformation. Instead, he offered his contemporaries a model of critical refinement and sensibility in place of old utopian hopes and progressive reforms. Thinking against himself, resisting closure, endlessly reweaving and unweaving his own point of view, Trilling crafted essays that were at once tentative and definitive, transparent and inexhaustible. Keeping the world at arm's length, he turned openness into something more than a style. It became a principle of mind, something baffling to encounter in person, inspiriting to observe in practice, but certainly not the worst standard a young critic could find.

# Editor's Acknowledgments

This collection is a selective reception history of the criticism and fiction of Lionel Trilling. To honor such a contemporary critic in this way is an unusual gesture, one that testifies to the significance and impact of his work. Indeed, in Trilling's case, not just the writer's work but the man's life have exerted strong, if fluctuating, influence on several generations of intellectuals. It seems appropriate, therefore, to gather together in a single volume a broad cross section of critical response to Trilling, whose literary reception constitutes a sharply focused lens through which readers can view the main issues of twentieth-century Anglo-American cultural and intellectual history.

*Lionel Trilling and the Critics: Opposing Selves* comprises an assortment of documents: short book reviews, essay-reviews, articles from intellectual quarterlies, obituaries, memoirs, and reassessments. I have selected these items with an eye variously toward their critical quality, historical significance, biographical interest, generational importance, ideological slant, and general representative value.

As a contribution to intellectual history, this collection has a dual aim: to illuminate the unfolding of Trilling's literary reputation and to recapture the lively debates in American cultural politics to which his writings contributed (and continue to stimulate in our own day). In selecting the materials for this volume, I have chosen responses to Trilling by influential intellectual contemporaries and successors in the United States, writers whose work possesses its own intrinsic interest. Moreover, to illustrate Trilling's high standing in the United Kingdom, which reflected and, in turn, elevated his reputation in American intellectual-academic circles, I have included a number of responses to Trilling from influential British intellectuals. Each document included in this book is preceded by a biographical headnote that discusses the author of the selection and, in most instances, highlights the key claims of the item, places it in the context of its author's career, and/or clarifies its author's relationship to Trilling.

My work on Lionel Trilling emerged via my twin, related interests in the

intellectual quarterly *Partisan Review*, for which publication Trilling long
served as advisory editor, and the life and times of George Orwell, about
whose reputation and legacy I wrote a critical study in the 1980s. Originally
I intended to devote a similar book to Trilling and his influence. Although
circumstances have limited me to completing this edited volume, I wish to
acknowledge the many people who have given generously of their time and
knowledge to my work on Trilling; their help has saved me from numerous
errors of fact or interpretation as I edited this collection.

My sincere appreciation goes first to the late Diana Trilling, who corre-
sponded with me and sat for lengthy interviews about her husband on two
occasions, in 1990 and 1994, in her Claremont Avenue apartment near
Columbia University. I am also grateful to acquaintances of Trilling who
variously shared insights about Trilling's oeuvre, alerted me to little-known
biographical facts, or otherwise enriched my understanding of Trilling's
milieu and the world of the New York intellectuals: Richard Howard,
Irving Howe, Alfred Kazin, Richard Kostelanetz, Steven Marcus, William
Phillips, Norman Podhoretz, Gerald Stern, and George Watson.

Still other friends and colleagues assisted me by providing moral support, sharing their thoughts about the vocation and responsibility of the
intellectual, and otherwise honoring my commitment to this project: Jack
Bemporad, John Buettler, Daniel Burke, Paul Cantor, Erica Carson, Thomas
Cushman, Pam Daniel, W. S. Di Piero, Martin Green, Jonathan Imber, John
Keenan, Vincent Kling, Claude Koch, William Lee Miller, George Pani-
chas, Tom Paulin, Jonathan Rose, and Jack Rossi.

I am especially indebted to several friends and colleagues who read the
manuscript, whole or in part, at my earnest request: Morris Dickstein,
Maurice du Quesnay, Steve Longstaff, Neil McLaughlin, Tom Samet, and
Denise Weeks. I am deeply grateful to Rob Dowling, who devoted several
afternoons to tracking down the photographs and illustrations appearing in
this volume. I also thank Mark Krupnick and William E. Cain, who read the
manuscript for the University of Nebraska Press and gave me both detailed
criticism and warm encouragement. Doug Clayton was a model editor, not
just facilitating the book's production but contributing to its intellectual
shape and substance.

My Texas friends and family have helped me in countless ways. Deanna
Matthews and Margaret Surratt responded to my ceaseless requests for logis-
tical help with unceasing good will, and with a refreshing gulf stream of
faith, irony, and plain common sense. Chip Wells read through an early draft
carefully and skeptically, suggesting that I annotate those references in
Trilling's work probably unfamiliar to readers today. Bill Shanahan displayed an analytic exuberance reminiscent of the *Partisan Review* editors in

the magazine's glory days, repeatedly challenging me to air out my own smelly little orthodoxies. Paul Rodden acted as my alter ego, asking subtle questions that made me examine critically my own opposing selves as well as those belonging to Lionel Trilling.

Two Texas friends blessed me with exceptional unselfishness. Cristen Carson read through the entire manuscript closely and handled the permissions with indomitable good cheer, serene confidence, and delightful dispatch. Beth Macom put her repertoire of talents—editorial laser beam, mental reference library, and rapier wit—in the full service of the manuscript, deftly retouching it—and unfailingly rallying my spirits in the process.

Last but not least, I owe a large debt of gratitude to three of my old Virginia colleagues. Each man is an outstanding teacher who, I believe, carries forth Trilling's rich legacy through his distinctive, exhilarating, albeit self-effacing, pursuit of the intellectual vocation: Jim Aune, an engaged critic and historian, whose intellectual integrity and enlightened tact serve as a beacon that has guided many students; Michael Levenson, a worthy successor to Trilling within my generation of scholars of British literature, whose natural grace, verbal elegance, and passionate dedication to the life of the mind have always inspired me; and Walter Sokel, a cultural historian and former Columbia student and colleague of Trilling, whose gracious manner and consummate grasp of the European intellectual tradition make him one of a dying breed of urbane scholar-intellectuals in an American academy increasingly divided between disciplinary specialists and polemical "public" intellectuals.

I dedicate this labor of love to my mother and father, Irish Catholics from County Donegal who are not so different in crucial ways from Trilling's own Russian Jewish immigrant parents. It was my parents' immigrant American dream of a "better," educated life that called their eldest son as a young man drawn—perhaps as Lionel Trilling had felt drawn—to the study of English language and literature and beyond: the call of self-cultivation toward my field of dreams.

## Note on Annotations

Lionel Trilling was a public intellectual whose work was read in its time by a general audience; this volume aspires to make the critical response to his work and life available to the general reader of today. A collection of critical pieces, however, especially one that includes many book reviews, can pose a difficult challenge of appreciation and even understanding to the nonspecialist reader, a challenge only intensified when its contributions date from an era that has passed. Because critics and reviewers frequently write in a shorthand that assumes contemporaries' knowledge of topics and names of immediate circulation and takes for granted that audiences will recognize the writers, book titles, issues, and other matters that the critics address, much criticism is difficult to appreciate outside of its original context.

Because of this critical shorthand, therefore, many readers, even scholars, interested in Lionel Trilling's literary reception may not know the writers and writings familiar to Trilling's contemporaries in the British and American literary public. For this reason, I have, quite selectively, annotated entries in some of the critical pieces that follow. My criteria have been accessibility and impact: I have clarified references to assist the reader to understand or appreciate a critic's claim, analogy, or specific line of argument.

# Chronology

1905   Lionel Mordecai Trilling (LT) is born to David Trilling, an immigrant tailor from Bialystok (Poland), and Fannie Cohen Trilling, a Russian/Polish immigrant from London, in New York City on 4 July.

1905–21  LT grows up in the New York City suburb of Far Rockaway and on the Upper West Side.

1918   LT receives his bar mitzvah at the Jewish Theological Seminary after training with Max Kadushin, author of *The Rabbinical Mind* and a former student of Rabbi Mordecai Kaplan.

1921   LT graduates from DeWitt Clinton High School, New York City, and matriculates to Columbia College at the age of sixteen.

1924   Along with friends Clifton Fadiman and Meyer Schapiro, LT takes John Erskine's honors course in English at Columbia, later called the Colloquium on Important Books. LT publishes his first poem ("Old Legend; New Style," a sonnet) and first essay (on Emily Bronte's poetry) in *Morningside*, Columbia College's literary magazine, in November.

1925   LT publishes his first short story ("Impediments"), which is also his first contribution to *Menorah Journal*, a secular Jewish magazine edited by Elliot Cohen; LT earns a B.A. from Columbia College, Columbia University.

1925–31  LT contributes stories and reviews to the *Menorah Journal*.

1926   LT completes a Master's thesis on Theodore Edward Hook, a minor Romantic poet, and is awarded an M.A. in English literature from Columbia University.

1926–27  LT teaches as instructor in Alexander Meiklejohn's experimental pedagogical program at the University of Wisconsin at Madison.

1927   LT meets Diana Rubin, his future wife.

1928   LT teaches evening courses at Hunter College, New York City.

1929–30  LT is hired as a part-time editorial assistant at *Menorah Journal*.

| | |
|---|---|
| 1929 | LT marries Diana Rubin on 12 June; he addresses the Convention of the Intercollegiate Menorah Association in December. |
| 1930 | LT begins reviewing books for *The New Republic* and *The Nation*; teaches in the Menorah summer school. |
| 1930–32 | LT teaches as part-time instructor at Hunter College. |
| 1932–33 | LT participates in some meetings of the National Committee for the Defense of Political Prisoners, a Communist front organization headed by Elliot Cohen. Diana Trilling volunteers as an administrative assistant to Cohen. |
| 1932–39 | LT teaches as an instructor at Columbia University, at a salary of twenty-four hundred dollars for four courses; also continues to teach in Hunter College's night school. |
| 1934 | LT begins a fruitful, intermittent classroom collaboration with Jacques Barzun of Columbia's French Department. LT and Barzun teach together in the Colloquium on Important Books, an innovative Columbia College course in literature and ideas. |
| 1936 | LT is informed by the Columbia English Department that, because of his slow progress on completing the dissertation, his contract will not be renewed; he protests the decision and gains an extension. |
| 1937 | *Partisan Review* is re-founded as an anti-Stalinist organ. LT contributes to the first issue. |
| 1938 | LT receives a Ph.D. in English from Columbia University. |
| 1939 | *Matthew Arnold*, LT's dissertation, is published by Norton in the United States and by G. Allen & Unwin in the United Kingdom. |
| 1939–45 | LT is assistant professor, Columbia University. Nicholas Murray Butler, president of Columbia, arranges the promotion. LT is the first Jew in the English Department at Columbia to rise to the ranks of the full-time faculty. |
| 1942–63 | LT is advisory editor, *Kenyon Review*. |
| 1943 | *E. M. Forster* is published by New Directions. "Of This Time, Of That Place" is published in *Partisan Review*. |
| 1944 | Hogarth Press publishes *E. M. Forster* in the United Kingdom. |
| 1945 | LT declines Elliot Cohen's invitation to join the advisory board of newly founded *Commentary* magazine, causing a breach between Trilling and *Commentary* that will last until the mid-1950s. "The Other Margaret" is published in *Partisan Review*; "The Lesson and the Secret" is published in *Harper's Bazaar*. |
| 1945–48 | LT is associate professor, Columbia University. |
| 1946 | LT writes the introduction to *The Partisan Reader*, which collects the best work of the first decade of *Partisan Review*. |

1947    *The Middle of the Journey* is published by Viking. LT is awarded a Guggenheim Fellowship.

1948    Secker & Warburg publishes *The Middle of the Journey* in the United Kingdom. LT, John Crowe Ransom, and F. O. Matthiesen found the Kenyon School of Letters, a summer school in literary studies at Kenyon College in Ohio.

1948    LT's son James Lionel is born on July 22.

1948–61    LT is advisory board member, *Partisan Review.*

1948–65    LT is professor, Columbia University.

1949    *Matthew Arnold* is reissued by Columbia University Press. *The Portable Matthew Arnold* is published by Viking. *The Middle of the Journey* appears in Swedish translation.

1950    *The Liberal Imagination* is published by Viking.

1951    Secker & Warburg publishes *The Liberal Imagination* in the United Kingdom. *The Middle of the Journey* appears in French translation. LT edits and writes the introduction to *The Selected Letters of John Keats*, published by Farrar, Straus, and Young. LT is elected to the National Institute of Arts and Letters; he stops teaching graduate classes, limiting himself to undergraduate lecture courses and seminars.

1951–63    LT is member (with W. H. Auden and Jacques Barzun) of the editorial board of the Reader's Subscription, a monthly book club, and contributes essays to its organ, *The Griffin.* When the Reader's Subscription becomes the Mid-Century Book Society in 1959, LT contributes essays to its organ, *The Mid-Century.*

1952    LT is appointed fellow of the American Academy of Arts and Sciences.

1953    LT chairs the Columbia faculty committee assigned to review the Communist affiliations of faculty and staff; based on the committee's report, one junior professor does not win a contract renewal. Delmore Schwartz publishes "The Duchess' Red Shoes" in *Partisan Review*, the first prominent attack on LT's work.

1955    *The Opposing Self* is published by Viking in the United States and Secker & Warburg in the United Kingdom; and in Portuguese translation. LT receives D.Litt., Trinity College, Hartford. LT is first lay speaker invited to deliver the Freud Anniversary Lecture to the New York Psychoanalytical Society, published that year as *Freud and the Crisis of Our Culture* by Beacon Press.

1956    *A Gathering of Fugitives*, a selection of pieces from LT's contributions to *The Griffin*, is published by Beacon Press. *The Liberal Imagination* and *The Opposing Self* appear in Spanish translation.

1957    Secker & Warburg publishes *A Gathering of Fugitives* in the United Kingdom.

1958        *The Middle of the Journey* appears in Spanish translation. *The Liberal Imagination* appears in Japanese translation.

1959        At a party for Robert Frost in honor of the poet's eighty-fifth birthday, LT delivers a controversial speech in which he calls Frost a "terrifying poet." Criticism and reviews of LT's remarks appear in *The New York Times Book Review*, *Newsweek*, and other mass circulation publications.

1960        *The Liberal Imagination* appears in Korean translation.

1961        With Steven Marcus, LT edits *The Life and Works of Sigmund Freud* (abridgment of the three-volume biography by Ernest Jones), published by Basic Books in the United States and Hogarth in the United Kingdom.

1962        LT receives D.Litt., Harvard University.

1963        LT receives L.H.D., Northwestern University.

1964        Revised edition of *E. M. Forster* is published by New Directions. *The Middle of the Journey* appears in Italian translation.

1964–65     LT is George Eastman Visiting Professor, Oxford University.

1965        LT delivers Henry Sidwick Memorial Lecture at Newnham College, Cambridge University, in February. *Beyond Culture* is published by Viking.

1965–70     LT is George Edward Woodberry Professor of Literature and Criticism, Columbia University.

1966        Secker & Warburg publishes *Beyond Culture* in the United Kingdom. LT receives Mark Van Doren Award from the student body of Columbia College.

1967        *The Experience of Literature* is published by Doubleday.

1968        LT sits as a faculty representative on the tripartite commission at Columbia (composed of faculty, administrators, and students) charged with mediating between student protesters' demands and Columbia officials' positions on the Columbia student strike. LT receives D.Litt., Case Western Reserve University, and Creative Arts Award, Brandeis University.

1969        *Beyond Culture* appears in Spanish translation.

1969–70     LT is Charles Eliot Norton Visiting Professor of Poetry, Harvard University.

1970        *Literary Criticism: An Introductory Reader* is published by Holt, Rinehart, and Winston. Trilling is named to the list of the ten "most prestigious American intellectuals" in a poll conducted by sociologist Charles Kadushin.

1970–74     LT is University Professor, one of three at Columbia University.

1972       *Sincerity and Authenticity*, a revised version of LT's Charles Eliot Nor-
           ton Lectures at Harvard during 1969–70, is published by Harvard
           University Press in the United States and Oxford University Press in
           the United Kingdom. LT delivers Thomas Jefferson Lecture in the
           Humanities, Washington DC.

1972–73    LT is visiting fellow, All Souls College, Oxford University.

1973       *Mind in the Modern World*, a written version of LT's 1972 Jefferson
           lecture, is published by Viking. LT is co-editor (with Harold Bloom)
           of *The Oxford Anthology of English Literature*, volumes 4 and 5 (on
           Romantic and Victorian literature) of the six-volume series, pub-
           lished by Oxford University Press. LT receives D.Litt., University of
           Durham, and D.Litt., University of Leicester.

1974       LT retires as University Professor but continues part-time teaching.
           LT receives L.H.D., Brandeis University, and L.H.D., Yale Univer-
           sity.

1975       *The Middle of the Journey* is republished. LT receives Guggenheim
           Fellowship. He dies in New York City on 5 November.

1976       "Why We Read Jane Austen," LT's last publication, appears in the
           *Times Literary Supplement* on 5 March.

1977       *Art, Politics, and Will*, a memorial volume for LT edited by his former
           Columbia colleagues Quentin Anderson, Stephen Donadio, and Ste-
           ven Marcus, appears.

1977–82    *The Uniform Edition of the Works of Lionel Trilling*, edited by Diana
           Trilling and issued in twelve volumes, is published by Harcourt
           Brace Jovanovich in United States during 1977–80 and by Oxford
           University Press in the United Kingdom during 1980–82.

1979       Diana Trilling publishes "A Jew at Columbia," a memoir of LT's
           successful 1936 plea to Columbia's English Department faculty to
           retain his job, in *Commentary* in March.

1980       *Beyond Culture* appears in Italian translation. *Sincerity and Authenticity*
           appears in German translation.

1984/1985/ Excerpts from Trilling's journals are published in *Partisan Review*,
1987       edited by Christopher Zinn, under the title "From the Notebooks of
           Lionel Trilling."

1993       Diana Trilling publishes *The Beginning of the Journey: The Marriage of
           Diana and Lionel Trilling*, a memoir of the couple's life together until
           1950.

Lionel Trilling and the Critics

# Introduction

## Lionel Trilling's Opposing Selves

### The Reputation of Lionel Trilling

For the last quarter century of his life, Lionel Trilling was a reigning presence in the American literary academy. His death at the age of seventy in November 1975 was mourned on both sides of the Atlantic as more than the loss of a major critic: it was memorialized in wistful and even elegiac tones as the passing of an era, eliciting a front-page obituary in the *New York Times* and a poetic flight from Robert Conquest:

> What weaker disciplines shall bind,
> What lesser doctors now protect,
> The sweetness of the intellect,
> The honey of the hive of mind?[1]

The relations among literature, politics, and society were Trilling's main preoccupation, with particular emphasis on problems of character, identity, and tragedy. Trilling was a cultural critic, stationed always near what he called "the dark and bloody crossroads where literature and politics meet,"[2] and he produced the most influential body of American cultural criticism of the early postwar era. Indeed, along with H. L. Mencken, Van Wyck Brooks, Edmund Wilson, Lewis Mumford, Kenneth Burke, T. S. Eliot, F. R. Leavis, Raymond Williams, and Northrop Frye, Trilling stands as one of the most important English-language critics of the twentieth century. His Columbia University colleague Jacques Barzun has gone so far as to call him "one of the great critics" in the tradition of English men of letters, ranking him just behind Hazlitt, in the company of Coleridge, Bagehot, and Arnold.[3]

Six book-length critical studies of Trilling's work have already appeared, and at least three biographies are presently under way.[4] No event signified more clearly Trilling's unique status than the almost immediate posthumous publication of a Uniform Edition of his oeuvre, edited by his widow,

Diana, and printed between 1977 and 1980 in twelve volumes by Harcourt Brace Jovanovich. Trilling is one of a small handful of American academics to receive such an honor.

How could an English professor—one who exhibited little interest in literary theory, never developed a critical "method," established no school or movement, never published a full-length critical work beyond his dissertation on Matthew Arnold, and indeed never even considered himself a "critic"—achieve such eminence?[5] That ironic story is written in the seventy reviews and essays included in this volume. The man who disavowed the name of critic has been exalted by his fellow critics as one of the great American culture critics of the century.

This volume consists primarily of reviews of Trilling's books as the books appeared, presented in chronological order. It focuses especially on reviews of Trilling's major works before 1960, in order to show the emergence and evolution of his reputation. How his fellow critics' reviews and essays contributed to Trilling's status is a main subject of this introduction. Certain themes recur throughout the decades of critical attention: the preoccupation among critics with Trilling's literary personality, the highly political character of his reception, the significance of particular literary models for his development, and the lines of debate about his legacy. Because Trilling was also held in high esteem in British intellectual circles, this selection of contributions includes a balance of American and British reviews.

Two sets of related issues merit extended attention here. This introduction begins by highlighting the background and conditions of Trilling's reputation, a topic that the reviews seldom discuss in depth. Specific institutional, literary-cultural, and personal factors shaped Trilling's reception and have fueled the controversies associated with his bequest. The remainder of this introduction traces the chronological progress of Trilling's critical reception, giving special emphasis to shifting contexts and key episodes in the history of his reputation. The vicissitudes of Trilling's reputation disclose much about the transformation of modern literary criticism and the changes in the politics of the American literary academy during the last half century.

## Conditions, Controversy, Legacy

To comprehend the circumstances of Trilling's career and reputation one must appreciate that New York City was the undisputed intellectual capital of the nation before the postwar expansion of American universities. New York was also the foundation and horizon of Trilling's world. A native New York Jew, Trilling lived in Manhattan nearly all his adult life and spent nearly his entire writing career as a Columbia University student and faculty member (1921–75). This context warrants emphasis, because a main reason for Trilling's once unrivaled prestige in American intellectual life has to do with his geographical-institutional location and professional affiliations. Chief among these was his unique position as a celebrated Columbia professor with close ties to the (anti-Stalinist and primarily Jewish) group of New York intellectuals who wrote for *Partisan Review*, the premier American intellectual magazine of the wartime and early postwar period. Trilling was the first Jew to be tenured in a nationally ranked English department, and his rise to prominence cannot be understood apart from the wider success of the New York intellectuals and the complicated saga of Jewish assimilation in American culture (see no. 66 in this volume, Rodden). Philip Rieff spoke for many intellectuals when he called Trilling "our teacher" and dubbed him a "Jew of Culture."[6]

Several of Trilling's books were reviewed by friends and associates, some of the reviews appearing in publications for which Trilling himself regularly wrote or served as a contributing editor.[7] Indeed, although Trilling neither founded any school nor directly cultivated any disciples, some of his students became well-known poets (Allen Ginsberg, Jack Kerouac, John Hollander, Richard Howard, Gerald Stern, Louis Simpson), academic and/ or intellectual authorities (Steven Marcus, Quentin Anderson, Norman Podhoretz, Morris Dickstein, Charles Peters, Jeffrey Hart, Marshall Berman, Fritz Stern, Charles Kadushin, Dan Wakefield, Joseph Kraft, Philip Lopate), and prominent men in the publishing world (Jason Epstein, Robert Gottlieb, Sol Stein, Gilman Kraft). Their successes raised Trilling's own reputation and facilitated his smooth traversing of academic, intellectual, and publishing circles (e.g., his memberships on the editorial review boards of *Partisan Review* and *Kenyon Review*, his respected status within the American Psychoanalytical Association,[8] and his supervisory roles in the Reader's Subscription and Mid-Century book clubs (the latter of which was managed by Sol Stein and Gilman Kraft). Trilling's prominent positions in these overlapping spheres were mutually reinforcing, transforming him by the mid-1950s into America's first academic celebrity in the humanities.[9] Indeed his feats of professional commuting gave rise to what Mark Krupnick, discussing the cross-influences on Trilling's life in the 1930s, has called "the two Trillings": the genteel professor from the uptown world of academic literary studies and the urbane essayist from the downtown world of *Partisan Review* intellectuals.[10] In the intellectual climate at the turn of the century— given the near-total absorption of intellectual life by the academy in recent decades, the increasing professionalization of literary studies, and the academy's growing emphasis on specialist theoretical vocabularies, it becomes ever harder to imagine the emergence of another Trilling: the very term "man of letters" evokes a form of cultural nostalgia as an intellectual amateur belonging to a bygone era.[11]

To emphasize Trilling's distinctive affiliations, which placed him at the center of American intellectual life, is not to undervalue his literary achievement. His remarkable gifts as an essayist and cultural critic were crucial reasons why he, rather than another New York academic intellectual (e.g., Sidney Hook, Richard Hofstadter), emerged at mid-century as the leading representative of intellectual America. Although Trilling taught English literature at Columbia for four decades, he was not chiefly a scholar writing in professional journals concerned with the academic discipline of literary studies. Rather, Trilling was a man of letters addressing himself in magazine essays to a general literate audience. His national stature and diffidently high self-regard were reflected in his much-remarked habit of casually speaking in the first person plural, whereby he discussed personal concerns as if they were large cultural issues, a practice that eventually grated on some ears (see no. 26, Redman; no. 46, Hough).[12] But during the two decades of his greatest influence, from the late 1940s to the early 1960s, Trilling's rare facility for dramatizing his divided self on paper did indeed make his often idiosyncratic preoccupations seem matters of general consequence. It was also during this period that Trilling's brilliant rhetorical skills were on fullest display. A number of his lapidary formulations ("moral realism," "the liberal imagination," "the conditioned life," "the opposing self," "beyond culture," "the disintegrated consciousness," "the adversary culture," "the shaped self") entered the intellectual lexicon at once, soon becoming shorthand for the postwar *Zeitgeist* and a terminological hub around which New York intellectual debates raged.

Trilling began as an intellectual biographer (of Matthew Arnold) and writer of fiction, but after mid-century he channeled his talents into cultural criticism. Still, the former two roles distinguished him among the New York intellectuals and conditioned his peculiar intellectual temper—and caused some readers discomfort. While acknowledging the originality of Trilling's thinking and his significant role in American intellectual life, not a few observers have commented on a quality of the enigmatic, the elusive, the slightly vexing—even the vaguely suspicious—in Trilling's style and work (see no. 38, Angus Wilson; no. 39, Donoghue; no. 40, Frank; no. 44, Mazzocco; no. 58, Shechner). For Trilling operated by indirection, and his occasionally labyrinthine subtleties bewildered or baffled less nuanced critics, especially in the ideologically polarized climate of postwar New York. As Steven Marcus once summarized the view: "He never says straight out what he means."[13]

The remark exaggerates, but only to make the point that Trilling's aversion to ideology was so strong that he foreswore even the art of the polemic. (Diana Trilling customarily assumed that task).[14] With a novelist's sensitivity to the tremors of the literary scene, Trilling developed into a cultural seismographer, divining the significance of each intellectual quiver and flutter in New York, and guiding his fellow intellectuals toward more secure ground. Trilling's dialectical sensibility rendered him an "opposing self" ever in pursuit of Arnoldian balance and uncannily capable (merely, as it were, by introspection) of discerning the right moment to apply the cultural corrective. This carefully calibrated sensibility rarely seemed to be overtly "for" or "against" any trend or movement for any length of time. But time and again Trilling sounded the charge (albeit always in muted tones and, toward his life's close, in a reverse direction) that led his generation toward new intellectual terrain—whether toward psychoanalysis and the late Freud, a revaluation of realist fiction and bourgeois values, or the problematics of the modern novel. Trilling became, in Alfred Kazin's phrase, an "Emersonian teacher of the Tribe."[15]

Because Trilling himself preferred the "bloody crossroads" rather than explicitly ideological territory, however, he rarely advanced to the political front of Left sectarian warfare along with his more combative New York colleagues. Instead he was content to stay behind, continuing to work as scout and surveyor. That he claimed for himself these special tasks was often not well understood in New York. And so his summons to charge in a new direction was instead interpreted, especially after 1955 by younger critics, as a call of the Sirens to political retreat. And this suspicion of rightward leanings gave rise, in turn, to controversy about the conservative implications of Trilling's cultural analyses, especially in the 1970s and '80s, when the neoconservative movement sometimes claimed him as a forerunner. Still, so finely modulated were Trilling's essays ("ideas in modulation" was another of his verbal icons) that he usually managed, at least until the late 1960s, to seem both one step ahead of his intellectual colleagues and yet forever the voice of moderation.

Fellow intellectuals did not always appreciate fully the ambivalent character and genuinely dialectical movement of Trilling's mind.[16] Like Freud, his great culture hero, Trilling's thinking remained dynamic and self-critical, always moving toward some new yet invariably provisional and revisable synthesis. What for Trilling was always a tentative formulation, however, became for more ideologically minded intellectuals an established doctrine. Frequently, Trilling's dissenting positions became more than just dissents, ultimately prevailing and helping to lay the foundation for a new consensus in New York, first on liberalism, then on psychoanalysis, and finally on the counterculture. Inevitably, critics then sought to fix him at that moment and in that position, pronouncing him a forerunner, ally, turncoat, or traitor.

Indeed his record as a trend-spotter and -setter was uncanny. That record serves as another notable factor in the general perception of Trilling's status as *primes inter pares* among the New York intellectuals. During the war years he anticipated what would become their collective turn toward a conservatized liberalism, achieved via his call for a marriage of politics and art, that is, for the nuanced, complex "literary imagination" of writers like Forster to enrich the doctrinaire "liberal imagination" of Marxism. After the war he taught his colleagues a new respect for old virtues, that is, for middle-class (and Trillingesque) values such as decency and propriety, exemplified by his praise of "old-fashioned" figures such as Howells and Orwell. In the 1950s Trilling introduced fellow intellectuals to the "tragic" side of Freud, drawing their attention to Freud's own stoical character and to the limits on social engineering implied by *Civilization and Its Discontents.* In the 1960s and '70s, Trilling pioneered a new, expanded role for the literary critic as a cultural conscience, the result of his dismay over the abandonment of that role by the decade's avant-garde artists, whose reaction against Establishment rigidities had, he said, turned them into disciples of the orthodox "adversary culture" of intellectual and campus radicals. In Trilling's view, legitimizing within academe the formerly subversive avant garde merely domesticated it. Finally, the passing of the vogue for avant-garde literary theory and the turn back toward cultural criticism in the late 1980s may even be traced, from the standpoint of the century's end, to Trilling's hostility to post-Freudian "revisionary madness" (in the work of Norman O. Brown, R. D. Laing, and their continental counterparts) and to his scattered remarks in defense of the "shaped self" and critical of structuralism and other anti-humanist attempts to subordinate literature to system.[17]

Although attention to Trilling's professional advantages and his oeuvre is certainly justified, some acquaintances retain the conviction that the telling clue to his influence in New York lay beyond his concrete accomplishments as a writer (see no. 57, Howe; no. 60, Podhoretz; no. 61, Barrett). For them, as well as for many of Trilling's students, it had rather to do with something tacit and even ineffable: a quality of human presence. Or to put it differently: Trilling's achievement was less a professional or literary matter than a human one. And such an intuition must bear, if always uncertainly and imprecisely, in any explanation of Trilling's reputation. For reputation emerges not merely from organizational position or literary response but from human interaction. Because the man, and the man within the writings, has played so significant a role in critics' estimates of the work, I have taken the step of including in this volume several memoirs and retrospectives of Trilling.

Trilling as a Columbia Ph.D. student, c. 1935. Courtesy of *The Columbia Spectator.*

Trilling in his English Department office at Columbia, 1973. Courtesy of *The Columbia Spectator.*

Trilling chats in his
Columbia University
office, fall 1973.

Diana Trilling, pictured here with Edward Said (*left*), attended the presentation of
the Trilling/Van Doren Award at Columbia University on 11 April 1994. The
award commemorated the contributions to Columbia by Lionel Trilling and his
English Department colleague and former teacher, the poet-essayist Mark Van
Doren. Photograph by Richard Santiago, courtesy of *The Columbia Spectator*.

The tributes to Trilling's prose style are frequent. And yet, however admiring are acquaintances' comments about Trilling the writer, the feeling persists: the man was more important than the works. Outstanding as it is, the core of his oeuvre—excluding dozens of interesting short reviews and occasional pieces—is small: a handful of short stories and an early novel, a published dissertation and a monograph of biographically oriented literary criticism, four collections of essays, a few published lectures. Moreover, the virtues cited as characteristic of the writer's style have all been claimed as the man's personal qualities: grace, elegance, urbanity, subtlety, sweetness, kindness, wit, modesty, civility, diffidence. And so too have the prose deficiencies been cited as personal attributes: ponderousness, self-consciousness, fastidiousness, evasiveness. Admirers note that even Trilling's physical appearance and personal manner—the long white hair and deep-set eyes, the hesitant delivery, the relaxed formality, the gracious curiosity, the courtly insistence on decorum, the seigneurial aplomb—radiated a sense of quiet importance (see no. 59, Sennett; no. 61, Barrett; no. 62, Dickstein). Less flattering observers have interpreted these same habits as amiable aloofness, mannered cordiality, and aristocratic pretentiousness; marks of a stiff and stuffy self-importance (see no. 54, Sale; no. 64, West).

Whatever the estimates of Trilling's character, the fact remains that, much as Trilling valued Freud more for his heroic life than for his theoretical prowess, many readers of Trilling have esteemed him more for his persona than his ideas, indeed more for the image and voice he projected in his writings than for the writings themselves. Or for how he seemed so perfectly to personify what he wrote, as if he were a walking avatar of the liberal imagination or opposing self, or as though his personality were specially crafted to illustrate his notion of the carefully shaped self (see no. 55, Holloway).[18] These admirers of Trilling acknowledge, between the lines and not without embarrassment, that the literary achievement by itself cannot explain the weight of significance that successive generations have bestowed upon him.

That judgment derives, however, less from shortcomings in the work than from strengths in the man. For Trilling had *style*—"style that seemed to be second nature with the man himself," as William Barrett once put it. Musing on an old photograph of Trilling in the unfamiliar scene of a bowling alley, Barrett added:

> I had never seen him bowl, and did not know that he indulged, but there in this unsuspecting setting the familiar and natural grace of the man seems to overflow the picture. For the public at large, of course, this grace showed itself principally in his writing: he wrote possibly the best critical

prose of his time—supple, flexible, fluent, yet firm. But the inherent gracefulness of the man came out also in a multitude of small ways. In a casual letter or note, for example, there would always be some distinctive touch of style, though never labored—the personal voice of the man without being affected, overassertive, or strident. . . . This gracefulness was, I think, something of a moral quality, or at least allied to the moral character of the man himself.[19]

The natural grace of the man also overflows the writings, whatever the truth of Buffon's *le style est l'homme même*. Even for someone of my university generation of the mid-1970s, the outline of Barrett's portrait of the man is traceable in Trilling's own work. I came to Trilling's books only after his death and outside the New York milieu, and my sole, wispy thread of connection to him is that my dissertation advisor was his student and junior colleague in the 1950s and '60s.[20] And yet, a feeling of intellectual kinship and of having inherited an intellectual trust abides. If Trilling possessed a mind more restricted in range than those critical geniuses with whom he is often compared, the Wilsons and Leavises and Fryes, he nevertheless confronted problems in a deeply personal way.[21] In making them his own, he somehow managed to live them out via his literary persona as well as in his personal relationships. And his work invites an intensely personal response in the reader, as one similarly engaged in the struggle of shaping a self in a skeptical modern (or postmodern) age. Trilling's considerable weaknesses notwithstanding, I find it all the more inspiring that he made so much of his abilities and preoccupations; his arguably coterie stance, his predominant focus on nineteenth-century Britain, his exclusive interest in cultural criticism all issue forth in rich insight, and finally give even the appearance of a rare openness and breadth. Somehow an awareness of his "ordinariness" humanizes him. I think of Trilling's own exhilarating perception of Orwell's severe limitations: "He is not a genius—what a relief! What an encouragement. For he communicates the sense to us that what he has done, anyone of us could do."[22]

That statement too, of course, is an exaggeration, for Orwell and Trilling were surely two of the most intelligent persons of their generation. But the formulation heightens our appreciation of their literary achievement and brings us full circle. In the end, one need pass no verdict on which—the oeuvre or the author—is the greater. What is clear is that the books alone cannot account for Trilling's cultural influence or inspirational power. For Trilling was not just a major critic or an important man of letters. Nor even, as William Chace has noted, "a moralist, an historian of moral consciousness, or a philosopher of culture," but rather "a sensibility who cultivated thinking so that he might subsume it to the rhythms of his search for wisdom."[23] It was this image of Trilling as a wise man that catapulted him to academic-intellectual celebrity. His greatest legacy is not that of a cultural critic, critical humanist, or public intellectual, but of a teacher. His teaching was the pedagogy of the noblesse, and his theme was nothing less than a style of living: the question of how to live the intellectual life. His answer was his own life; he enacted his own modestly heroic style. In doing so he became, to use his own term for the intellectual hero, a "figure," one of those "whose lives are demonstrations of the principles which shaped their writing" and whose roles in their respective cultures are at least as important as their creative achievements.[24]

## Reception and Historiography

The story of Lionel Trilling the writer began in the mid-1920s, with his stories and reviews in the *Menorah Journal*, a Jewish magazine for which he would serve as an assistant editor during 1929–30. Already by the end of the decade, Trilling was known in Jewish literary circles in New York as a promising young intellectual. He started reviewing for *The Nation* and *The New Republic* in the early 1930s, during which time he and his wife, Diana, briefly became involved with a Communist auxiliary organization.[25] In 1939 Trilling joined the full-time faculty at Columbia. These developments extended his reputation into academic and wider, non-Jewish, intellectual circles. But Trilling's public reputation among the critics—which can be divided into five phases—did not emerge until the early 1940s, after the appearance of *Matthew Arnold* (1939) and *E. M. Forster* (1943).

In the first stage of his critical reputation (1939–45), Trilling became known as a biographer and scholar of Victorian and modern British literature. Filiation with Judaism and the *Menorah Journal* had given way to affiliation with English literature and Columbia. With the history of Jewish exclusion from the American literary academy behind him, and with Arnold's ideal of "disinterestedness" and Forster's "liberal imagination" constantly before him, Trilling shifted his energies from literary journalism and an interest in Marxism toward a deeper commitment to academia and a cultural politics of the self. Trilling cherished Arnold for his subtle dialectical intelligence and insistence on balance; he respected Forster's "moral realism," that steadfast critical intelligence that embraced the variousness of life, refused the oversimplifications of ideology, and heeded Montaigne's counsel to cultivate a mind *ondoyant et divers*.

Critics celebrated the critical biography of Arnold for these same virtues. *Matthew Arnold* was a fortunate first book for Trilling in that dark year of

1939, not just because it suited the temper of a chastened Left reeling from the shock of the Nazi-Soviet pact and horrified at the prospect of a European war, but because it so perfectly embodied the themes of ambivalence and critical humanism that would occupy Trilling for the remainder of his life. Moreover, it is sometimes not well understood that writers' debuts often buoy or burden them for years to come. Because critics' first impressions tend to bear heavily in subsequent evaluations of writers, the "moment of entrance" weighs decisively in charting the future course of literary reputations. This has been especially true of Trilling and *Matthew Arnold*, which was received by critics with lavish praise and repeatedly cited in later years as a touchstone of Trilling's criticism.

Reviewers on both sides of the Atlantic acclaimed the biography, registering scarcely a dissenting voice. In hindsight, we can see that Edmund Wilson's flattering notice served as a virtual anointing (no. 3, Wilson). Usually sparing with his kudos, Wilson lauded Trilling for writing "one of the first critical studies of any solidity and scope by an American of his generation." Coming as it did in the pages of *The New Republic*, the leading intellectual weekly of the liberal-Left, Wilson's tribute had the effect of elevating the thirty-four-year-old Trilling to a commanding position among his academic and intellectual peers. William Phillips, co-editor of *Partisan Review* and a friendly acquaintance of Trilling, also touted the Arnold biography as "one of the best works of historical criticism produced in this country" (no. 5, Phillips). This was an early sign that Trilling was a rising star within the New York intellectuals. In England, the biography won even louder applause. John Middleton Murry opened his *Times Literary Supplement* review (no. 4) with a confession of surprised, even humbled, admiration: "Mr. Trilling, who is an American professor, has written the best—the most comprehensive and critical—book on Matthew Arnold that exists. It is a little saddening to us that this particular glory should fall to the United States." Edward Sackville-West told *Spectator* readers that he had "no hesitation in acclaiming it as the most brilliant piece of biographical criticism issued in English during the last ten years" (no. 7, Sackville-West).

Even though *E. M. Forster* was a short book and much more modest in its aims, similar success followed. Largely on the strength of Trilling's monograph, headlines in *The New Republic* and *The Nation* proclaimed a "Forster revival" (no. 11, Zabel; and no. 13, Mayberry). (In his autobiography, Alfred Kazin recalls Forster's own remark on their meeting in the 1950s in New York: "Your countryman Trilling has made me famous!")[26] Morton Dauwen Zabel, a leading academic critic at the University of Chicago, declared in *The Nation* that the publication of *E. M. Forster* was a wartime contribution: "At this particular moment of literary and intellectual crisis, [it] becomes more than a literary occasion: it takes on the force of a public service" (no. 11, Zabel). In *The New Yorker*, Clifton Fadiman, Trilling's old Columbia College classmate, commended Trilling's insight into the distinctive appeal of Forster's deflationary irony, which consists in "a refusal of greatness" (no. 12, Fadiman). Irving Kristol, then a twenty-four-year-old Army soldier in retreat from the Trotskyist politics of his undergraduate years, also commended Trilling's criticism of Stalinism for failing to uphold "the true principles of liberalism" (no. 15, Kristol).[27]

English critics were more divided in their estimates of *E. M. Forster.* Although David Daiches complimented Trilling's analyses in *Accent*, F. R. Leavis in *Scrutiny* criticized Trilling's ignorance of Cambridge academic life and his tendency to take Forster's self-presentations at face value (no. 10, Daiches; no. 17, Leavis). One sign that Trilling was gaining attention outside literary-academic circles, however, was that he was reviewed, at length and quite favorably, in *Time*.[28] It was the first time a national mass-circulation periodical noticed his work.

Trilling's influence in intellectual circles rose steeply after the war, reaching its summit in the early 1950s, after the publication of his most brilliant work, *The Liberal Imagination.* With this book, Trilling became a public intellectual and cold-war liberal known to a wide audience outside New York. Indeed he emerged as the most distinguished critic of the postwar decade that Randall Jarrell would call "The Age of Criticism." The significant works of this fertile second phase of Trilling's critical reputation (1946–55) are his single novel, *The Middle of the Journey* (1947), and his two essay collections, *The Liberal Imagination* (1950) and *The Opposing Self* (1955). The background of these writings was the fierce wartime politicking over Stalinism. Within New York, the editors' choice of Trilling to introduce *The Partisan Reader* (1946) had already announced Trilling's position as the lead-ing voice of the group. Critics' favorable responses to the two essay collections affirmed this judgment to the wider public.

Although Trilling continued to write short stories during the war ("Of This Time, of That Place" [1943], "The Other Margaret" [1945], both published in *Partisan Review*), he devoted chief attention after the war to *The Middle of the Journey*, a novel of ideas about Left intellectual life in the 1930s. The novel received mixed reviews. Robert Warshow, a younger New York critic and associate editor of *Commentary*, delivered the most severe verdict, claiming that it was not just that Trilling was a "minor talent," but rather that "Mr. Trilling has not yet solved the problem of being a novelist at all" (no. 20, Warshow). Warshow's comparisons between Trilling and Forster show how Trilling inadvertently became a prisoner of his earlier success with *E. M. Forster*; some reviewers had already come to see Trilling as not just a critic, but specifically a critic of Forster. Trilling's achievement in his Forster study induced both Warshow and Mark Schorer, writing in the *New York Times Book Review* (no. 18, Schorer), to measure Trilling by the standard of Forster—and to find him wanting. Warshow's review aroused much controversy in New York, and it may be viewed as the first of many challenges to Trilling's growing reputation that would come in the next decade from a younger generation of New York intellectuals (see no. 33, Schwartz; and no. 40, Frank).[29]

But critics united in their admiration for *The Liberal Imagination*. Clifton Fadiman took the opportunity to announce that Trilling as essayist, by virtue of his "moral seriousness," had already earned a place in the "family" tradition of Jonson, Dryden, Dr. Johnson, Hazlitt, Coleridge, Emerson, Arnold, and Eliot (no. 27, Fadiman). The near-universal enthusiasm propelled *The Liberal Imagination* to sales of more than seventy thousand on its second reprint in 1953;[30] it also sold more than one hundred thousand copies in its Doubleday Anchor paperback edition, an imprint introduced by Trilling's former student Jason Epstein.[31]

Trilling's plea in *The Liberal Imagination* was for politics to open itself to the wisdom and sensitivity of literature. The abstract, Popular Front "liberal imagination" of the 1930s suffered precisely from a deficiency of imagination, rendering it coarse and illiberal, argued Trilling. It therefore required an Arnoldian injection of the vivifying "literary imagination" to assist it toward approaching its balanced, healthy, ideal state of "variousness, possibility, complexity, difficulty." Already the Left's salute to *E. M. Forster* had made it clear that, even though overt political criticism of Stalinism during the war years was untimely, such a renovation of the liberal imagination was welcome.

This revisionist climate was all the more evident by February 1950, when Cold War tensions escalated sharply as Joseph McCarthy seized the national stage. *The Liberal Imagination* appeared two months later, just as the Red scare was gaining momentum, and some Left-liberals have suggested, in hindsight, that Trilling's essays attracted postwar liberals because they lent respectability to a rightward "retreat." The essays appealed, Alfred Kazin observed after Trilling's death, to "a generation that didn't want to resolve its contradictions—unwilling to become openly anti-liberal on the one hand but on the other hand eager to shake off with revulsion whatever connection it had with Marxism and all it represented."[32] Whereas fellow New Yorker Sidney Hook, known and feared as a pugnacious, combative polemicist, took what seemed the low road of cold-war liberalism, implied Kazin, Trilling took the high road. The feisty Hook bashed Stalinists openly in one polemic after another; the urbane Trilling furnished just the right tone of culture and class to lend glamor to an aestheticized, conservative liberalism and to make an overtly progressive politics look shabby.[33]

The main sign of Trilling's growing stature within academe at mid-century was the appearance of long essay-reviews of *The Liberal Imagination* by influential academics such as R. P. Blackmur, William van O'Connor, and R. W. B. Lewis. Blackmur, a prominent voice often in alliance with the New Critics, cast Trilling in the *Kenyon Review* as a regal "administrator of the affairs of the mind" (no. 31, Blackmur). In the *Sewanee Review*, O'Connor baptized Trilling "the conscience of the intelligentsia of the Left."[34] Lewis christened Trilling's centrist politics "the new Stoicism" (no. 28, Lewis). Lewis's *Hudson Review* notice also represented the first intimation among critics of Trilling's conservative instincts. Wrote Lewis: "Trilling, who doubts that there is a conservative tradition in America, feels so strongly the need for an enlightened opposition that he is impelled occasionally to enact that role himself."

But the perception on the Left that Trilling was embracing such a role more from desire than duty grew during the next five years, and the publication of *The Opposing Self* witnessed a revisionist turn and the first public sniping at him from within his intellectual circle. Delmore Schwartz's 1953 article in *Partisan Review*, "The Duchess' Red Shoes," had already portended a change of mind (no. 33, Schwartz); Joseph Frank's 1956 essay-review in the *Sewanee Review* gained classic status (no. 40, Frank). Schwartz castigated Trilling's snobbish overattention to manners in Proust, arguing that Trilling's class biases would obviously be regarded as "reprehensible" were they not couched in literary criticism; Frank's respectful revaluation criticized Trilling for judging politics from the perspective of art, charging that the key to Trilling's imagination was his politics of disillusionment, which accepted biological and political givens and thus issued forth in passivity and social quietism. Frank's essay, "Lionel Trilling and the Conservative Imagination," originated the widespread view that Trilling had become a cultural conservative, setting the stage for the neoconservative claims to his mantle in the 1970s.[35]

In *The Opposing Self*, Trilling redirected his attention from textual criticism back to biography, although this time interwoven with an element of hagiography. His work became less political and more explicitly literary-cultural. In *The Opposing Self*, Trilling developed his notion of the "figure" and concentrated on the nonliterary dimension of heroic writers' lives. His leitmotifs were the dynamics of character, identity, and the formation of self. Trilling's models—most of them English men of letters—were those who managed to integrate the drive to self-creation with a mature recognition of tragedy, that is, of the "conditioned" nature of life.[36] Freud and Arnold reign supreme in the Trilling canon, flanked by Forster, Keats, Wordsworth, James, and Austen. Orwell is the sole twentieth-century member of the pantheon (see no. 66, Rodden).

The appearance of Trilling's next essay collection, *A Gathering of Fugitives* (1956), ushered in a third stage of his reputation (1956–65), a decade during which Trilling gradually assumed the lofty twin roles of cultural sage and arbiter of public taste. Although his fame increased, he became less well-regarded in advanced literary-intellectual circles. *A Gathering of Fugitives* represents the main literary outcome of Trilling's attempt during the period 1951–63, when he served on the editorial boards of the Reader's Subscription book club (1951–59) and Mid-Century Book Society (1959–63), to educate a large public and to use cultural institutions to bridge the ever-growing chasm between high culture and "midcult."[37] His effort also presaged the closer associations in the 1960s between many New York intellectuals and middlebrow culture. *A Gathering of Fugitives* consisted mostly of a selection of Trilling's monthly pieces written for the organ of the Reader's Subscription book club, *The Griffin*. Trilling's style in these short essays was informal. He had turned from the "criticism of ideas," in E. B. Greenwood's phrase, toward variations on "the literary chat" (no. 42, Greenwood).

With the ascendency of the counterculture in the mid-1960s, representatives of the Arnoldian tradition became targets of special attack from the critical avant garde—and the biographer of Arnold was also a casualty in the altered cultural climate. Trilling's prestige made him an inviting target.[38] Objections from younger intellectuals to his cultural politics reached a new pitch of fervor with Trilling's fourth essay collection, *Beyond Culture* (1965), in which Trilling affirmed "the tone of the center," maintaining that one must accept that biology lies "beyond culture" and that the late Freud was a conservative yet also liberating figure. *Beyond Culture* triggered the first open generational attack on Trilling. Robert Mazzocco's lengthy review in the newly founded *New York Review of Books*, then just beginning its radical, pro-counterculture and anti-war phase, assaulted Trilling as an outdated conservative and aimed to deflate his reputation (no. 44, Mazzocco). Mazzocco criticized Trilling as "a complex but thoroughly conservative spirit, heavy with humanist and/or Hebraic 'conduct and obedience' out of Arnold and 'night side' exposure out of Freud, both employed in problematic or disingenuous fashion."[39]

Because Trilling had never been an academic or intellectual celebrity outside the United States, no sharp revisionism occurred in Britain to match Mazzocco's attack. Some reviewers of the generation following Trilling's own did voice harsher criticism of his work than had occurred in Britain previously, usually for the same reasons as did younger American critics (see no. 43, Steiner; no. 45, Williams; no. 46, Hough). But neither a strong generational reaction against Trilling nor a wholesale devaluation of his oeuvre ensued. Indeed, writing in the *New Statesman*, D. J. Enright, one of the young Movement poets in the 1950s, even found Trilling's "magisterial manner" "attractive."[40] In the *London Magazine*, Laurence Lerner rated Trilling above Arnold and pronounced him "probably the finest critic we have today."[41]

During the fourth phase of Trilling's critical reputation (1965–75), many senior critics honored him as an elder literary statesman, even as some younger American reviewers dismissed him as a dusty intellectual monument. For the latter, Trilling had become an Establishment icon suffering from "advanced respectability," that figure whom Harold Rosenberg had once mocked as "an Eliotic [read: "sclerotic"] Cleric of Culture" (no. 62, Dickstein). Indeed, during these years Trilling did fully embrace the role of cultural mentor. He edited three readers (*The Experience of Literature* [1967], *Literary Criticism: An Introductory Reader* [1970], and *The Oxford Anthology of English Literature* [1973]), shifting the focus of his role as public educator from the book club to the classroom.[42] Trilling's main critical works of this period were *Sincerity and Authenticity* (1972), a revision of his Charles Eliot Norton lectures delivered at Harvard in 1970, and a slight book, *Mind in the Modern World* (1972), a lecture delivered on his reception of the first Thomas Jefferson Award from the National Endowment for the Humanities.

In this last decade of Trilling's life, generational and Anglo-American estimates of his work widened further. Numerous academic distinctions (a visiting year at All Souls College, honorary degrees from Durham and Leicester) and respectful notices for *Sincerity and Authenticity* from British critics testified to his eminence abroad (see no. 49, Letwin; no. 50, Bayley; no. 55, Holloway). As Philip French noted, Trilling in Britain was "never the controversial, emblematic, or charismatic figure he became—and continues to be—in America."[43] Unlike the case in New York, British intellectuals never saw Trilling as a political, let alone ideological, writer; they simply appreciated him as a thoughtful, serious literary man.

*Sincerity and Authenticity* and *Mind in the Modern World* were reviewed together respectfully on the front page of the *New York Times Book Review* (no. 51, Hartman). Older critics disappointed in Trilling's work during the previous decade treated *Sincerity and Authenticity* as a great comeback, indeed as just what the liberal academy required to put the "student barbarians" in their proper places.[44] But younger American critics sympathetic to the counterculture and to the New Left greeted both of Trilling's works of the 1970s with condescension and even contempt, though there were occasional exceptions (see no. 52, Graff).[45] For many of them, Trilling towered over the intellectual landscape as a literary Cold Warrior.[46] Reviewing *Literary Criti-*

*cism*, Mark Krupnick derided Trilling's "implicit snobbishness," his "mandarin exclusiveness," and his "enervating overrefinement and precocity . . . in which literary criticism is conceived as a kind of connoisseurship, involving acts of assessment no different fundamentally than in the case of Japanese swords or Greek and Chinese urns" (no. 48, Krupnick).[47] Roger Sale, in a widely quoted review of *Sincerity and Authenticity*, charged that Trilling "treats himself like an institution" and that reading his high-flown, abstract prose possessed "certain affinities with eating a meal consisting entirely of Thousand Island dressing" (no. 54, Sale). Sale found Trilling's stylistic throat-clearing to be mere equivocation, his tendency to address issues via large generalities mere pomposity.[48] The reviews by Krupnick and Sale reflected both a younger generation's fascination with Trilling's cultural significance and a denial of his entitlement to such status.[49] Older reviewers, however, even formerly severe critics, discovered amid the cultural swing to the Left something new to admire in Trilling's moderation and Arnoldian sensibility (see no. 47, Donoghue; and no. 53, Howe). Having sought to dismantle the Trilling statue in the 1950s, they now reassembled it, complete with pedestal. England's John Holloway spoke for them when he said that "in our literary-academic world Trilling has to be called a heroic figure: almost the only one" (no. 55, Holloway).

The encomia to Trilling as a culture hero, at least among American literary intellectuals, having become increasingly lavish since his death, as witnessed in the academic reassessments of his career and the polemical Right-Left battles for his mantle and scholarly reassessments of his career. In this fifth, posthumous stage of his reputation (1975– ), neoconservatives and Left-liberals have engaged in surreptitious mantle-snatching, even as most radicals and academic literary theorists have continued to disown him. Because Trilling often seemed to be an unpolitical literary man, perched far above all internecine squabbling, and because he died just before New York ideological lines demarcating neoconservative, liberal, and radical positions shifted and were re-drawn in the mid-1970s, his name has been used and abused by all sides since his death. Neoconservatives have proclaimed Trilling a foe of the Left, an opponent of the adversary culture, and a defender of humanist values and cultural literacy (see no. 60, Podhoretz; no. 69, Himmelfarb); in his autobiography, William Barrett explicitly nominated Trilling as a major forerunner of the neoconservatism of the 1970s and '80s (see no. 61, Barrett).[50] Left-liberals have emphasized Trilling's high critical standards and his Arnoldian aspiration to reinvigorate liberalism, not abandon it (see no. 57, Howe; no. 62, Dickstein).[51] Some academic radicals have scorned Trilling as the "godfather" of neoconservatism, whose work leads to "an intellectual dead end" (no. 64, West).[52] Still other Left critics, however, have paid respect to Trilling, acknowledging that he was a conservator, though not a conservative: a keeper of the literary heritage whose subtle analyses compelled liberals and radicals to acknowledge their own conserving impulses, even as he licensed an attachment to a more chastened, self-conscious liberalism (see no. 58, Shechner; no. 62, Dickstein). The widespread perception of Trilling's conservation should also be balanced by an acknowledgment of the strain of cultural radicalism in his work, which continued until the end of his life.

Meanwhile, scholars, biographical critics, and memoirists have credited Trilling with exhibiting an exemplary way of pursuing the humanist vocation in the contemporary academy (see no. 59, Sennett). Formerly out of favor, Trilling's critical humanism has, increasingly in the last decade, received sympathetic attention from literary academics and intellectuals.

In the 1970s and early 1980s, Trilling's affirmation of the shaped or unified self seemed naïve and unrigorous; post-structuralism, with its conception of fragmented, decentered selves, held sway.[53] But beginning with the new interest in cultural criticism in the late 1980s, exemplified by the rise of movements in literary academe such as cultural materialism and cultural studies, Trilling's own cultural criticism—despite its relative uninterest in problems of race, class, gender, language, and literary form—has become more attractive, as many literary academics have recoiled from neo-Marxist and post-structuralist theoreticism. In the 1990s, numerous literary academics have also expressed admiration for Trilling's humanism and rationalism, citing his reservations about the social alienation and political irresponsibility of the great modernist writers and his dismissal of the Sixties counterculture ("modernism in the streets," in Trilling's widely quoted phrase) as applicable to current campus debates, especially against the perceived irrationalist excesses of American postmodernism and multiculturalism.

Predictably, conservative and neoconservative cultural critics have been especially inclined to approach Trilling in this light. For many readers, Trilling's inattention to the issues that dominate the American literary academy today—most of them having to do with race, class, and gender—makes him little more than a curiosity of literary history, a period piece. As William Cain writes: "He had a certain canon of texts and set of issues in them to which he returned time and again. His work was very significant, but his work is also *dated*."[54]

Trilling's work is less accessible to the generation of readers born since his death—precisely because Trilling was so immersed in the major cultural, political, and social topics of his day. The complex historical contexts in which Trilling wrote—from the Popular Front and fellow-traveling to the Cold War and liberal anti-Communism—are not easy to establish for younger readers. And because the literary academy has turned toward theory and postmodern modes of criticism since the 1980s, college students rarely encounter Trilling in their literature courses. Nevertheless, I believe that Trilling's work remains valuable and relevant today to the ongoing tasks of reinvigorating liberalism, questioning ascending or reigning orthodoxies, resisting the seductions of ideology, and remaining intensely engaged in contemporary cultural politics.

And I would hold that the same is true of his life: it too remains valuable and relevant, now as much as ever, especially as the definition and role of the public intellectual undergo massive change. For Trilling stands as one of the few instances of a figure who connected the academic and public spheres and yet did not succumb to the trivializing aspects of academic "celebrity," but rather remained seriously engaged with the fundamental political and social questions of his time.

In all these respects, Trilling strikes me as not merely a historical subject for scholars, but someone whose work and example are still vital and important.

## Future Directions

But critics may soon subject these judgments to direct, pointed challenge. Indeed, with the long-awaited publication of Diana Trilling's revelatory memoir of the couple's years together up until 1950, titled *The Beginning of the Journey: The Marriage of Diana and Lionel Trilling* (1993), still another revaluation of her husband's work and achievement is beginning, one that will doubtless address the relationship between Trilling's personal life and his intellectual legacy. Sharing her version of the "private" Lionel with the reader, Diana Trilling shows the man in his private life as very different from the "shaped self" projected in Trilling's writings—and that his tense, sometimes anguished emotional life was sharply at odds with his decorous public image.

Although *The Beginning of the Journey* was treated skeptically by reviewers on both the Left (Mark Krupnick) and Right (Midge Decter, Hilton Kramer), it arrived with the force of a shock to many readers. The memoir renders more complex and poignant the widely held admiring images of Trilling that I have discussed here—and that I myself have held. (Some reviewers of the memoir felt, however, that esteem for Trilling would eventually rise again, this time *because* of his achievement—despite the private demons against which he struggled.)

In her memoir, Mrs. Trilling does not dispute her husband's standing as an excellent and caring teacher, but rather what she considers the idealizations of him by his personal acquaintances as well as his readers. She contends that Lionel Trilling deeply regretted becoming a "figure" himself, perceiving that his high status had cut him off from his students and colleagues. She considers the notion of Trilling as a "virtuous man" or cultural "hero" confining, stereotypical, one-dimensional, and misleading.

"All the critics have misunderstood Lionel," Mrs. Trilling told me in our January 1990 interview. She declined to elaborate, stating only that she would discuss "the tragic Trilling" in her forthcoming memoir.

It is now clear what she meant. Her verdict on the sharp discrepancy between the public and private Trilling is severe. Determined to protect his reputation, she maintains, Trilling "conspired" in his acquaintances' idealizations of him and took pains to conceal his weaknesses even from his closest friends. Caught between the hungers for social respectability and for creative identity, he abandoned his dream of becoming a novelist to become a distinguished professor-critic, thereafter both promoting and despising his image of academic gentility. Mrs. Trilling holds that her husband's soul paid the price of his devil's bargain with intellectual fame: "It was to decency that Lionel felt that he had sacrificed his hope of being a writer of fiction. . . . [D]id his friends and colleagues have no hint of how deeply he scorned the very qualities of character—his quiet, his moderation, his gentle reasonableness—for which he was most admired in his lifetime and which have been most celebrated since his death?"[55] Among Mrs. Trilling's most surprising—and unsettling—revelations about her husband are that he suffered from bouts of depression and rage, had a drinking problem, and sometimes engaged in vehement verbal abuse of her. As she maintains, it is hardly consistent with Lionel Trilling's public image that, at least every other month over a period of many years, "this most peaceable of men and most devoted of husbands indulge[d] in annihilating verbal assaults," accusing her of "being the worst person he had ever met in his life."[56]

"The need not to deviate from truth," writes Mrs. Trilling, "drags like an anchor on this book."[57] Indeed, Mrs. Trilling's deflationary memoir turns out to be perhaps the most powerful challenge to her husband's carefully crafted public image: Diana casts herself as the shocking truth-teller, the figure of Authenticity appointed to unmask Lionel's sham life of Sincerity.[58]

"You have no position," Richard Sennett once upbraided Trilling. "You are always in between." "Between," responded Trilling, "is the only honest place to be" (see no. 59, Sennett).

However true Trilling's contention, there indeed he rests. His adamantly intermediate position has not appealed to all readers. But his contested reception across the ideological spectrum does make clear that he remains in death, as he had been in life, "always in between." And so long as this perception of a Trilling betwixt and between all sides endures, the dualities of his work and life will continue to fascinate his readers—and provoke numerous claims and counter-claims to his ambiguous legacy. Two decades after his death, numerous critics remain engaged by the intricate dialectic of the literary and private personality of Lionel Trilling, still an elusive presence lurking at and yet above "the dark and bloody crossroads" of New York literary politics and American intellectual life, ever a quietly controversial figure in all his radiantly opposing selves.

## Notes

1. Quoted in William Chace, "Lionel Trilling: Contraries and Culture," *American Scholar* 38 (winter 1978): 43.

2. "Reality in America," in *The Liberal Imagination: Essays on Literature and Society* (New York: Viking, 1950), 11.

3. Jacques Barzun, quoted in Philip French, *Three Honest Men: Edmund Wilson, F. R. Leavis, Lionel Trilling* (Manchester, U.K.: Carcanet New Press, 1980), 104.

4. Diana Trilling, interview with the author, New York City, 7 January 1990.

5. As a young man Trilling set out to be a novelist, and he never fully abandoned the aspiration or the self-image. In "Some Notes for an Autobiographical Lecture" (1971), he wrote, "I am always surprised when I hear myself referred to as a critic. After some thirty years of having been called by that name, the role and the function it designates seem odd to me. I do not say alien, I only say odd" (in *The Last Decade: Essays and Reviews, 1965–75*, Uniform Edition [New York: Harcourt, Brace, Jovanovich, 1979], 227).

6. Philip Rieff, *Fellow Teachers* (New York: Harper and Row, 1973).

7. Those personal acquaintances who wrote reviews during Trilling's lifetime include *Partisan Review* editor William Phillips (no. 5 in this volume), Columbia classmate Clifton Fadiman (nos. 12 and 27), and former Columbia student Norman Podhoretz (no. 32). Among the publications crucial to the formation of Trilling's reputation were *The New Republic* and *The Nation*, for which he regularly reviewed in the 1930s; and *Partisan Review* and *Kenyon Review*, on whose editorial boards he served for decades.

8. Trilling was the first lay speaker to deliver the Freud Anniversary Lecture at the New York Psychoanalytic Institute (1955), published that year under the title *Freud and the Crisis of Our Culture*. In 1961 Trilling also edited (with Steven Marcus) an abridged version of Ernest Jones' biography of Freud.

9. The decisive role of this complex dynamic—what I have termed "overlapping spheres" of cross-influence that generated and secured Trilling's reputation—cannot be overemphasized. Trilling developed close relationships with various prominent groups of opinion makers—among them scholar-intellectuals, academic critics, social scientists, psychoanalysts, and publishers—and these diverse coalitions interacted in subtle ways to disseminate Trilling's name and ideas. Trilling's prestige was attributable, in no small measure, to this combination of influences and coalitions, i.e., to sociological factors. His high standing in American intellectual life by mid-century, and indeed his special status within the New York intellectuals until his death, is not explainable solely, indeed perhaps even primarily, by his writings or personal character.

This is not to say that Trilling orchestrated the interactions of these overlapping spheres—the size of the task defies such close management. Rather, Trilling was aware of his multiple roles and how they cut across political lines and ideological positions, and both his institutional locations and his carefully crafted persona (of "moderation," reflected both in his writings and personal life) facilitated his position at the center of New York intellectual conversation about psychoanalysis, mass vs. elite culture, the social role of art and literature, and the counterculture. All these factors have also been at work in the posthumous debates about Trilling's views and the rival struggles to claim his political and intellectual legacy.

I have discussed this dynamic of "overlapping spheres" and the distinctive sociological factors that contributed to George Orwell's reputation, including the (partly) socially constructed myth of Orwell as a "great writer," in my *Politics of Literary Reputation: The Making and Claiming of "St. George" Orwell* (New York: Oxford UP, 1989), especially chapters 1 and 2.

10. On the "two Trillings," see Mark Krupnick, *Lionel Trilling and the Fate of Cultural Criticism* (Evanston: Northwestern UP, 1986).

11. Or, at least, it seemed that way until the recent rise of the black public intellectual, exemplified by such critics as Henry Louis Gates and Cornel West, who are both academics and public figures.

In addition to the black public intellectuals, other academic-intellectuals—whose names appear prominently in the pages of magazines such as *The Village Voice*, *The New Republic*, *The American Scholar*, *The Atlantic*, and *The New York Review of Books*—emerged in the 1990s. Perhaps the most notable among them were Camille Paglia and Stanley Fish. Their visibility seemed to belie Russell Jacoby's elegiac book, *The Last Intellectuals: American Culture in the Age of Academe* (New York: Basic Books, 1987), which judged Trilling and several other elder *Partisan Review* writers among the last of America's public intellectuals (see pages 78–85).

On this view, the public intellectual has not passed away, but rather metamorphosed into someone who not only writes serious criticism, but also writes bestsellers, contributes (and even grants interviews) to mass-circulation publications, and appears regularly on television and radio.

12. Although Trilling's elastic "we" brought many charges that he was a coterie writer, Elinor Grumet has suggested that the usage represented his psychological urge to create a "community-by-incantation" that would share and support his views. See "Trilling's Apprenticeship," *Prooftexts* 23 (1975): 43.

13. Steven Marcus, interview with Philip French in *Three Honest Men*, 102.

14. See especially her *Clarement Essays* (New York: Harcourt, Brace, 1964) and *We Must March, My Darlings* (New York: Harcourt Brace Jovanovich, 1977).

15. Alfred Kazin, quoted in Stephen Tanner, *Lionel Trilling* (Boston: Twayne, 1988), 26.

16. Indeed the subtle dialectic of Trilling's mind, as Morris Dickstein has reminded me, moved not simply between liberalism and conservatism (actually a version of Burkean or Arnoldian liberalism), but between

> the Enlightenment and Romanticism, between civility and incremental ra-
> tionality on the one hand and the irrational and apocalyptic on the other. . . . He
> claimed [in *Matthew Arnold*] that he was first drawn to Arnold not by his prose
> but by the brooding sense of personal and cultural crisis in his poetry . . . ; his
> literary interests were anchored in the Romantics and modernists, with their
> profound explorations of the irrational; his major essay on Freud anticipates
> Marcuse and N. O. Brown in its emphasis on Freud's biologism; he introduced
> radical Freudians like [Philip] Rieff and Brown to educational readers through
> his book club sponsorship; Ginsberg and Kerouac were his students; and his
> journals show how much (and how ambivalently) he was drawn to a sense of
> criminality and adventure that he associates with Hemingway, Kerouac, and
> indeed with art in general.
>
> It's also true that he turns against some of these things—like modernism, the
> counterculture, and radical Freudianism (in R. D. Laing)—when he finds them
> unexpectedly carrying the day. But he never turns against them completely, and
> never buys fully into the neoconservatism already in the air when he died. . . .
> Had he lived, the pendulum would no doubt have shifted yet again. (personal
> communication, 7 September 1996)

17. Robert Langbaum recalls a public lecture in which Trilling criticized struc-turalism as "another system antithetical to will and individual freedom," presenting it as a successor movement to the Stalinism against which he fought in the 1930s. "The Importance of the Liberal Imagination," *Salmagundi* 41 (spring 1978): 56–65.

18. Even his name, which Clifton Fadiman called "the most aggressively eupho-nius name of any writer since Edna St. Vincent Millay," seemed crafted for the part (see no. 13, Fadiman).

Philip French also recalls Franklin P. Adam's jocular couplet on the comic name of the British poet Basil Bunting in the late 1920s, which drew the rejoinder: "To admit defeat we are not willing, / We have one called Lionel Trilling." Quoted in French, *Three Honest Men*, 79.

19. William Barrett, *The Truants: Adventures among the Intellectuals* (New York: Doubleday, 1982), 161–62.

20. Trilling was a member of the dissertation committee of Walter H. Sokel, who received his Ph.D. (in German) from Columbia in 1953 and taught there, as an assistant and associate professor, until 1964.

21. Trilling would have been the first to admit that he lacked the sheer intellectual brilliance and philosophical gifts of some of his contemporaries. He himself distinguished between intellectual virtuosity and critical "intelligence," between a facility with abstract concepts and a perceptive concreteness more akin to British common sense. Trilling possessed and valued the latter, and he spoke approvingly of the motto of his old Columbia College teacher, John Erskine: "the moral obligation to be intelligent." Trilling's emphasis on "intelligence" marked him ultimately as more a moralist and judicial critic than a thinker or speculative critic.

22. Lionel Trilling, introduction to *Homage to Catalonia* (New York: Harcourt, Brace, 1952), ix.

23. Chace, "Lionel Trilling: Contraries and Culture," 47.

24. Lionel Trilling, introduction to *Homage to Catalonia*, xi.

25. On Trilling's involvement with the National Committee for the Defense of Political Prisoners (NCDPP), a Communist-front organization in which Trilling was active during 1932–33, see Krupnick, *Lionel Trilling and the Fate of Cultural Criticism*, chapter 2. Krupnick argues that Trilling's phase of communist activism was very brief (perhaps no more than six months), but that his Marxist sympathies continued for another three or four years in the mid-1930s.

26. Alfred Kazin, *New York Jew* (New York: Knopf, 1978), 222.

27. For a harsher, radical critique of Trilling's "private definition" of liberalism, see Granville Hicks' short review in *Common Sense*, 12 (October 1943), 380.

28. *Time*, 9 August 1943, 98–104. The assignment of the *Time* review may have been prompted by the magazine's interest in hiring Trilling. Otherwise it is hard indeed to explain why the editors devoted a six-page review to works about Forster (featuring Trilling's modest study). In 1942, Trilling had received an offer to work as a full-time house reviewer for *Time*, with the special honor of penning signed reviews. The offer came from Whittaker Chambers, then a regular *Time* reviewer. Trilling declined. See Tanner, *Lionel Trilling*, 24.

29. Warshow's review may have affected Trilling more deeply than any other ever written. One wonders, in fact, if Warshow's notice (along with some other lukewarm reviews) did not dissuade Trilling from pursuing fiction writing altogether. As late as the mid-1950s, Trilling was still announcing in press interviews that he was at work on a second novel. It never appeared. Nor, after *The Middle of the Journey*, did Trilling ever publish even another short story.

The final judgment on Trilling the novelist has yet to be made. Warshow's review has been influential. But it is also well-known in New York that Warshow, then associate editor at *Commentary*, felt some personal antagonism toward Trilling for the distance that Trilling had put between himself and the new magazine. (*Commentary* was founded in 1945 as the successor to the *Contemporary Jewish Record*.) Trilling refused to join the editorial board of *Commentary* or to allow his name to be placed on the masthead; even in the wake of the Holocaust, he seldom discussed his Jewishness in print and maintained what was perceived by *Commentary* as a deliberate aloofness from Jewish questions.

Literary New York has long speculated whether Warshow's harsh review of a first novel by a fellow New York writer constituted a punishment for Trilling's unwillingness to lend his prestige to the magazine in its early years—which is not to say, regardless of his motives, that Warshow's catalogue of Trilling's deficiencies as a fiction writer may not have been accurate. For a perceptive discussion of the novel's strengths and weaknesses, see Mark Schechner, "Psychoanalysis and Liberalism: The Case of Lionel Trilling," in *After the Revolution* (Bloomington: Indiana UP, 1987), 75–81. Later critics, reviewing *The Middle of the Journey* upon its republication shortly before Trilling's death, commended it warmly (see Bayley, no. 23; Furbank, no. 25). Its phenomenal sales in 1975–76—fifty thousand copies in the United States alone within the first six months of its reissue—served as yet another obituary tribute. (See Edward Joseph Schoben Jr., *Lionel Trilling: Mind and Character* [New York: Frederick Ungar, 1980], 54.) This kinder treatment of *The Middle of the Journey* on its republication may have been sentimental; certainly it had to do with extra-literary factors, such as the autobiographical background of the book, which Trilling explained in a new introduction. For the first time, Trilling discussed at length his relationship with Whittaker Chambers and his use of Chambers as a model for the character of Gifford Maxim, a repentant Comintern spy and zealous convert to muscular, fundamentalist Christianity and right-wing ideology.

30. Dan O'Hara, *Lionel Trilling: The Work of Liberation* (Madison: U of Wisconsin P, 1988), 129.

31. Krupnick, *Lionel Trilling and the Fate of Cultural Criticism*, 102.

32. Interview with Philip French, *Three Honest Men*, 95.

33. On Trilling's role as head of the 1953 faculty commission that supervised Communists at Columbia, see O'Hara, *Lionel Trilling: The Work of Liberation*, 25. A more explicit example of Trilling's cold war liberalism—and another sign of Trilling's rising status as a public intellectual during the 1950s—was his relationship with the Ford Foundation and the State Department. Trilling wrote for and guest-edited *Perspectives USA*, the journal launched by the Ford Foundation in 1952 as part of an American cold-war cultural offensive to win European respect for American high culture. On at least one occasion, Trilling also participated in a State Department program with similar aims, traveling through Europe as an American cultural ambassador.

34. William van O'Connor, "Lionel Trilling's Critical Realism," *Sewanee Review* 58 (1950): 485.

35. See also Frank's autobiographical afterword (included here as part of no. 40), in which he reaffirms his critique of Trilling's rightward shift, attributing it to the influence of the conservative later Freud, whose cultural criticism (*Civilization and Its Discontents* and *The Future of An Illusion*) Trilling highly respected.

36. The appearance of *The Opposing Self* signified the high-water mark of Trilling's public reputation, and its biographical focus resulted in numerous passages amounting to veiled autobiography. Trilling's themes of character, identity, and self-formation invited attention, through the act of engaging his models, to his own emerging role as a "figure" and a "heroic" presence on the American intellectual scene.

Implicitly acknowledging all this, *The Saturday Review* featured Trilling and *The Opposing Self* as its cover story on 12 February 1955, under the headline "Nine Glimpses of Our Selves." In an interview published as a sidebar to the book review, however, Trilling made clear that he intended to move beyond his chief identity of literary critic. Trilling said that he wished to be identified thenceforth as a novelist and reported that "from now on I plan to give a good deal of time to [writing fiction]. I'm writing a second novel at the moment." He apparently never completed the novel, and no part of it has ever been published. (Viking's dust jacket for *The Opposing Self* had also announced the "good news" that the author of *The Middle of the Journey* was "at work on a new novel.")

37. A 10 May 1959 advertisement, published in *The New York Times Book Review*, reflected Trilling's changing image and interests as it announced the newly founded Mid-Century Book Society. The ad's middlebrow headline—"for people who love books more than automobiles"—makes clear that the book club sought to reach an educated middle-class audience eager to distance itself from lowbrow tastes and instead acquire a highbrow sensibility. "The books will never be offered because of faddish appeal," emphasizes the ad copy, "but solely because they meet an undeviating standard of excellence."

Trilling served as co-editor and judge for the book club's selections, along with his Columbia colleague Jacques Barzun and the poet W. H. Auden, who lived in New York City. Trilling also wrote short, two-thousand-word essays to introduce the editors' selection in *The Mid-Century*, the club's monthly magazine. Managed by Trilling's former student, Sol Stein, the club survived until 1962. It succeeded another book club, the Readers' Subscription, which Trilling, Barzun, and Auden edited from 1952 to 1959.

38. Trilling was the only literary academic among the top ten in Charles Kadushin's list of the seventy "most prestigious contemporary American intellectuals." Based on dozens of interviews in 1970, the list appears in Kadushin's *The American Intellectual Elite* (Boston: Little, Brown, 1974), 30.

39. For two other sharp assaults on Trilling by a younger generation of intellectuals in New York, see Richard Kostelanetz, "Men of the '30s," *Commonweal*, 3 December 1965, 266–69; and Dan Jacobsen, "Beyond Whose Culture?" *Commentary*, March 1966, 87–93.

40. D. J. Enright, *New Statesman* 71 (15 April 1966): 539.

41. Laurence Lerner, *London Magazine*, July 1966, 108–12.

42. Especially after the 1968 Columbia student strike, this new classroom orientation also became discernable locally, in Trilling's campus activity at Columbia. Trilling viewed the particular campus issues that had provoked the 1968 strike as ephemeral and insignificant. He interpreted the strike as a symbolic attempt by students to gain a voice in the American political process, indeed as a coming-of-age youth protest that signified the changing status of the American university as an institution.

One sign of Trilling's effort to address the larger cultural forces that shaped these issues was his public lecture at Columbia on 25 October 1973. Trilling delivered a widely discussed talk on the role of general education in the mission of Columbia College. He argued that U.S. secondary education should be more closely coordinated with the liberal arts curricula of universities, whereby American high schools could assume some of the functions of college humanities programs. Such a change, Trilling contended, would foster better continuity between secondary and higher education.

The substance of Trilling's talks was published, along with three responses from Columbia faculty, under the title "General Education and the American Preparatory System," in Columbia's *Seminar Reports* magazine, 7 December 1973.

43. French, *Three Honest Men*, 75.

44. The appearance of *Sincerity and Authenticity* also marked the first time that the American Right openly welcomed Trilling to join their ranks. As D. K. Mano wrote in *The National Review*: "Trilling, a traditional and now superannuated liberal, is hesitant, polite, but finally defiant of the New Left—how very profoundly the experience of spring '68 at Columbia must have hurt this shy and gentle man. He closes [his book] by repudiating the radical concept that insanity is the only sanity, the only authenticity. I found his ultimate words powerful and moving." D. K. Mano, *National Review*, 22 December 1972, 1417.

45. For another exception, see Richard Ohmann, "Teaching and Studying Literature at the End of Ideology," in *The Politics of Literature: Dissenting Essays in the Teaching of English*, ed. Louis Kampf and Paul Lauter (New York: Vintage Books, 1973), 131–34.

46. Trilling had criticized the student disturbances at Columbia in 1968, especially the strong campus presence of the Weathermen, a terrorist group that grew out of the radical wing of Students for a Democratic Society. Trilling saw the Weathermen as little more than an updated version of 1930s Stalinism.

47. Krupnick became an admirer of Trilling in later years. See chapter 8 in his *Lionel Trilling and the Fate of Cultural Criticism*, where Krupnick discusses his change of mind.

48. These put-downs make clear how much Trilling's American reputation had fallen since the 1950s, especially among students and avant-garde critics. By the 1970s he was no longer regarded by them as a master teacher and cultural sage, the "figure" whose English courses at Columbia had been trumpeted by Viking Press (in the jacket copy for *The Opposing Self*) as "a Mecca for the most inquiring minds among successive student generations."

49. Sometimes the younger generation did not shrink from bare-knuckled criticism. Richard Kostelanetz pronounced Trilling the "chief" of the New York literary "mob" associated with *Partisan Review* and derided him as "an elder statesman before his years." *The End of "Intelligent Writing": Literary Politics in America* (New York: Sheed and Ward, 1973), 51, 53.

50. For a liberal-Left critique of the neoconservative response to Trilling, see Mark Krupnick, "The Neoconservative Imagination," *Salmagundi* 51 (1980): 202–8.

51. See also O'Hara, *Lionel Trilling: The Work of Liberation*; William Phillips, *A Partisan Decade: Five Decades of the Literary Life* (New York: Stein & Day, 1983), 75; and Robert Boyers, *Lionel Trilling: Negative Capability and the Wisdom of Avoidance* (Columbia: U of Missouri P, 1977).

52. Many other radical and left-of-center intellectuals have also aligned Trilling with the neoconservatives. For instance, grouping Trilling with neoconservatives such as Daniel Bell and Philip Rieff, Christopher Lasch identified Trilling as an opponent of New Left thinking in *The Minimal Self: Psychic Survival in Troubled Times* (New York: Norton, 1984), 200–201.

53. Critics debated whether the decline in Trilling's standing was merited. Jacques Barzun lamented his friend's "unwarrantably subdued reputation" during his later years; Jay Martin, however, found "Trilling's [posthumous] reputation immensely greater than his achievement." See Jacques Barzun, "Memoir: Remembering Lionel Trilling," *Encounter*, September 1976, 82–88; and Jay Martin's review of *Lionel Trilling: Mind and Character* by Edward J. Schoben, *South Atlantic Quarterly* 82 (spring 1983): 216–18.

The fall in Trilling's reputation after 1965, and especially after his death, had much to do with the absorption of intellectual life by the literary academy and the growing dominance of European theory among American scholars. Gregory S. Jay argues persuasively that Trilling's reputation suffered because of his relative uninterest in questions of language during the ascendancy of linguistic methods in American literary criticism. Indeed, one could say that time—or literary fashion— passed Trilling by. Whereas in the 1940s and '50s Trilling's non-Marxist cultural criticism had seemed an attractive alternative to the near-total dominance of the New Criticism—whose exegetical approach seemed by contrast narrow, limited, too immersed in textual details and distant from big ideas and cultural politics—Trilling's work seemed impressionistic and unsophisticated by the 1970s and '80s. During those decades, the combined force of the rise of structuralism and post-structuralism, the availability of Marxist and other critical alternatives to Trilling's form of criticism, and the (temporary) near-disappearance of the public intellectual rendered Trilling's work dated and irrelevant. See Gregory S. Jay's review of *Lionel Trilling and the Fate of Cultural Criticism* by Mark Krupnick, *South Atlantic Review* 52 (January 1987): 103–7.

54. William Cain, personal communication, 12 August 1995. Cain is a scholar of American literature at Wellesley College.

55. Diana Trilling, *The Beginning of the Journey: The Marriage of Diana and Lionel Trilling* (San Diego: Harcourt, 1993), 372–73.

56. Diana Trilling, *The Beginning of the Journey*, 380.

57. Diana Trilling, *The Beginning of the Journey*, 50.

58. Mrs. Trilling also does not flinch from challenging one of the most prominent of Lionel's posthumous "opposing selves": his reputation as a forerunner of neoconservatism. She points out that, on two occasions, the Trillings declined opportunities to side with the nascent neoconservatism: in 1965, they declined the request of Irving Kristol, the neoconservative editor of *The Public Interest*, to join the new magazine as its literary editors; and in 1972, they resisted the entreaties of the historian Gertrude Himmelfarb (to whom Kristol is married) to sign a petition supporting Richard Nixon's re-election, even though the Trillings had sharp reservations about McGovern's liberalism.

Nor does Mrs. Trilling cringe from entering the fray on the topic, "If Lionel Were Alive Today." Her response categorically rejects the neoconservative claim to his mantle: "Lionel did not live long enough to witness the rise of the neoconservative movement, but I have little question that if he had been alive and working in the eighties, he would have been highly critical of this swing to the right by our old friends." Mrs. Trilling maintained this view right up to her death, in October 1996, at the age of ninety-one. In his obituary of Diana, Hilton Kramer made clear that he considered Diana's own writings about her husband to constitute a form of political grave-robbing. (Kramer approvingly quoted a mutual acquaintance who remarked that Diana had engaged in a project after her husband's death of "moving Lionel's coffin to the left" to prevent the neoconservatives from snatching it. See Hilton Kramer, "Diana Trilling," *The Independent*, 30 October 1996, 14.)

But Kramer's view of Diana Trilling's leftward leanings elided her sharp reservations toward contemporary radical movements. For instance, Mrs. Trilling assailed multiculturalism and left-wing political correctness as "a continuation of Stalinist culture" and pondered writing a book (what she called her "last political will and testament") that would trace the development of twentieth-century liberalism from the communism of the 1920s and '30s to the rise of political correctness. See

Sally Jacobs, "The Indomitable Diana Trilling Girds for a New Foe: Political Correctness," *Boston Globe*, 20 September 1995.

Mrs. Trilling never wrote that book, but she did complete another memoir before her death, *A Visit to Camelot* (1997), an account of an evening that the Trillings spent as guests at the Kennedy White House. The memoir does not engage issues in contemporary cultural politics. Instead, it strikes me as if Mrs. Trilling were taking a respite, gathering her energies by recalling a brief and shining moment in the 1960s before turning again to "gird" for battle against both old and new political foes. Unfortunately, she died in November, 1996, before she had the opportunity to tell her version of the rest of the journey of Diana and Lionel Trilling.

Matthew Arnold (1939)

## 1

*Robert Morss Lovett*

*"The Mind of Matthew Arnold,"* The Nation

*March 1939*

Robert Morss Lovett (1870–1956), educator, literary critic, and author, was a leading American radical, eventually becoming editor of *The New Republic* (1921–29). Lovett began his career as a professor of English at the University of Chicago. He collaborated with the poet William Vaughn Moody on the massive *History of English Literature* (1902), which was updated over the course of the next three decades and went through several editions. Lovett published a number of books of criticism, including *Edith Wharton* (1925) and several studies of British drama, and he also wrote two novels and a play.

A Christian Socialist, Lovett resided for long periods at Hull House, the settlement house in Chicago founded for the poor and underprivileged by Jane Addams. As a *New Republic* editor and contributor, he wrote sympathetically about the Bolshevik Revolution and the Spanish Loyalists during the civil war; he campaigned vigorously against capital punishment and British colonialism. In 1939, at the time of this book review, Lovett was appointed secretary to the Virgin Islands by Franklin Roosevelt. While he was in office, two congressional committees investigated his alleged Communist associations and recommended that he be discharged from office without pay. Roosevelt bowed to congressional pressure in 1943 and asked for Lovett's resignation; a 1946 Supreme Court decision reversed the congressional decision and awarded Lovett back pay.

A committed socialist critic, Lovett commends Trilling in the review below for highlighting those aspects of Arnold that cast him as a socialist precursor.

It is understood to be in accordance with Matthew Arnold's wish to have no biography of himself written, that his descendants have maintained careful guard over his private papers. Mr. Trilling admits that he had available only published sources of information. It may be said, however, that if family piety could have made terms with the inevitable it could not have found a biographer of greater intelligence and discretion than Mr. Trilling. He has followed with patient study the development of Arnold's thought from the thin sheaf of poems published in 1849 to the "Last Essays on Church and Religion" and the later "Essays in Criticism." He has written, as he says, a biography of Arnold's mind, and if Arnold had contemplated any record of his life this is the one he would have wished.

Among the many virtues of Mr. Trilling's book a thorough study of Arnold's intellectual background is the first. He has gone to Arnold's sources and influences, to Dr. Thomas Arnold, to Spinoza, to Senancour, to Joubert. He has emphasized the contemporary aspect of Arnold's writings—his emergence as poet when the smoldering ashes of the French Revolution were flaming up in 1848, his entrance upon the field of modern controversy in the middle sixties when "The Origin of Species" shook the gates of revealed religion, when the opposition between the schools of Mill and Carlyle was brought to a focus by the trial of Governor Eyre and the rioting over the Second Reform Bill, when Home Rule for Ireland was beginning to shatter the Liberal Party. The proper way to read Arnold's essays is in the magazines in which he appears in the lists with Carlyle and Newman, Gladstone and Mill, with Kingsley for the Broad Church, Mallock for Catholicism, Frederic Harrison for Comtism, Huxley, Clifford, and Leslie Stephen for science. Mr. Trilling supplies the background which is necessary for the comprehension of Arnold as a prose writer in an age of controversy unmatched since the early seventeenth century.

Although amid the dust and confusion of contemporary conflict Arnold strove to hold himself aloof, above the mêlée, he was nevertheless subject to winds of doctrine. Mr. Trilling makes no effort to attenuate the fallacies in Arnold's thinking. His famous apology for the status quo, drawn from Joubert's maxim, "Force until right is ready," is mere sophistry born of his wish to maintain expansion without revolution. His theory of the dominance of a racial strain, "of blood," prominent in his view of Celtic literature, is bad anthropology, discredited today by ignoble use. His doctrine of the state in which classes should rise above their interests to their "best selves" suggests a mythical concept, likewise discredited. As Mr. Trilling remarks: "Class is a category whose very essence is interest—the reason of a class is its interest."

Above all, Mr. Trilling disposes of Arnold's new version of Christianity by quoting F. H. Bradley's devastating comment on the famous definition of religion as "morality touched by emotion." All morality is touched by emotion, and when it is touched by religious emotion it is religious. This religious emotion gathers about some external reference which Arnold calls God, but his definition of God as "a stream of tendency by which all things fulfil the law of their being" makes little appeal to emotion, and is, moreover, as Mr. Trilling points out, a begging of the question—it is no more than to say "things act as they act."

Arnold's crusade in behalf of religion, like his defense of literature, was the expression of what Mr. Trilling recognizes as the cardinal point in his thought, the pursuit of unity, integrity, totality for the individual and for society. In his preface to the poems of 1853 he took occasion to enforce the principle of classic as opposed to romantic art by comparing a tragedy of Sophocles, in its emphasis on the central theme, with Keats's "Isabella," so remarkable for beautiful detail in which the main action is obscured. The lack of a principle of unity to guide the poet was the source of his dissatisfaction with his own art. Wordsworth had found such a principle in his belief in man's relation to nature, but Arnold felt the dichotomy between the inscrutable ways of the cosmos and the values which man's consciousness gives to life. Morality is not found in nature. "Nature is cruel, man is sick of blood," he wrote, and again, with reference to moral striving, "Man must begin where nature ends." This discontent supplied the prevailing emotional color of Arnold's poetry. Harold Nicolson attributes Tennyson's lyrical gift to the emotion of fear—fear of God, fear of death, fear of sex. Mr. Trilling finds the mood which assures Arnold the lyric gift in self-pity. This mood obtains direct expression in many of his poems, such as "The Buried Life" and "Dover Beach," and it is the undertone of others in which the subject is dramatic—"The Scholar Gipsy," "Thyrsis," and "Rugby Chapel." To escape from this melancholy, to bring release from it to the world, Arnold thought was the true aim of poetry. What men want is "something to animate and ennoble them—not merely to add zest to their melancholy or grace to their dreams." It was in deference to this judgment that he suppressed for many years the most pessimistic of his poems, "Empedocles on Etna." It was in obedience to it that he turned from poetry to criticism.

Arnold made the great discovery that criticism of art must necessarily depend on criticism of life. Carlyle had anticipated this position in his comparison of German with English criticism, but Arnold made its announcement in "The Function of Criticism at the Present Time" in such explicit terms that he became for the half-century that preceded the Great War the dominant force in English criticism, which after his example seldom fails to take account of the special and political determination of literature. Criticism of life he declared to be the function of literature, of poetry. In the chief doctrine of his applied criticism he emphasized his objective of totality. Culture, the remedy for present discontents, he defined as the pursuit of one's *total* perfection, by getting to know the best that has been thought and said in the world. It was in recognition of this principle of totality that culture for Arnold became a social doctrine.

The papers which made up "Culture and Anarchy" were written with reference to the social disorders of the late sixties, as was Carlyle's "Past and Present" with reference to those of the forties. But Arnold's social doctrine was the reverse of Carlyle's dependence for salvation on the hero. Already he had written to Clough: "I am more and more convinced that the world tends to become more comfortable for the mass, and more uncomfortable for those of any natural gift or distinction—and it is well perhaps that it should be so—for hitherto the gifted have astonished and delighted the world, but not trained or inspired or in any way changed it." In this acceptance of democracy Arnold perceived the overwhelming importance of ideas, response to which is the only ground for human advance. It was the function of literature to make ideas prevail in a democracy; hence the value which he attributed to literature over science in education. He opposed the individualism of the Liberals no less than that of Carlyle. Freedom, the fetish of the Liberal Party, was to him merely machinery, depending for its value on its results. "It is a very great thing to be able to think as you like, but after all an important question remains: what you think."

With all his assertion of integrity and totality Arnold was far from absolutism of thought. In one of his ironical quotations he cited Frederic Harrison's objection that he lacked "a philosophy with coherent, interdependent, subordinate, and derivative principles."[1] Mr. Trilling finds frequent parallelism between his attitude and that of the pragmatists. His defense of belief in God is on the lines of William James's "The Will to Believe," and like John Dewey he insists that things must be taken for consideration in the complexity of their relations, not in the simplification which logic requires.

The chief of Arnold's contributions to modern thought sprang from the combination of practical sense with reason, a bias toward relativity, a sense of emphasis according to the needs of the age. Thus with his recognition that conduct is three-fourths of life, and that Hebraism is concerned with "strictness of conscience," he asserted the present need of his countrymen for Hellenism, or "spontaneity of consciousness." Again, in his recommendation of the state as an authority he admits that the French have the idea in excess, the English not sufficiently. He anticipated present-day social thought in seeing that private property was the great obstacle to social wealth, but he saw that this obstacle was one erected by law and limited to it. Indeed, in his sympathetic anticipation of social transformation and recognition of tendencies toward it he was almost the only notable Englishman of his class to view the Paris Commune of 1871 with anything short of horror. "Paris does not make me so angry," he wrote, "as it does many people, because I do not think well enough of Thiers and the French upper class generally to think it very important that they should win. What is certain is that all the seriousness, clear-mindedness, and settled purpose is hitherto on the side of the Reds."

Mr. Trilling is sure that Arnold never read Marx, and he does not attempt to work Arnold's ideas into Marxist formulas. What is much more important, he shows, with an art which conceals design (if any), that in his view of history, literature, and politics Arnold is in line with the thought that is replacing the liberalism of the nineteenth century with the socialism through which alone democracy can survive.

## Notes

1. Frederic Harrison (1831–1923), British social and political critic. In July 1867 Arnold published what ultimately formed the opening chapter of *Culture and Anarchy*. That November Harrison wrote a satirical reply in *The Fortnightly Review* in which he assumed the role of an ironic defender of Arnold's conception of culture. Arnold admired the satire and found it most amusing.—Ed.

## 2

*Jacques Barzun*

*"Trilling's Matthew Arnold,"* Columbia University Quarterly

*March 1939*

Jacques Barzun (1907– ), French-born professor emeritus of history at Columbia University, is a distinguished historian, cultural and fine arts critic, and essayist. He is the author of *Darwin, Marx, Wagner: Critique of a Heritage* (1941), *Teacher in America* (1945), *The House of Intellect* (1959), and *A Stroll with William James* (1983), among other books.

Barzun and Trilling were lifelong friends. They met as classmates at Columbia College and, beginning in the 1930s, taught together in Columbia's Colloquium on Important Books. Later the pair also co-taught a famous graduate seminar on nineteenth-century culture. Barzun dedicated *Romanticism and the Modern Ego* (1943) to Trilling. As Columbia's dean of graduate faculties (1955–58) and dean of the faculties and provost (1958–67), Barzun worked with Trilling to revise Columbia's humanities curriculum. The pair also headed the editorial board (along with W. H. Auden) of the Reader's Subscription and Mid-Century book clubs during the 1950s and '60s. After Trilling's death in 1975, Barzun also contributed to the Trilling memorial volume *Art, Politics, and Will* (1977), along with writing two other short memoirs of their relationship and joint teaching.

The following review, which was signed "J. B.," commends Trilling's ability to render Arnold relevant and accessible to the twentieth-century reader.

"The Critic's business is to carp; the scholar's business is to bore." No one, of course, has the courage to honor these maxims in words, but many of us show by our actions that our feelings approve them. We read the biographies of Lytton Strachey's followers because they are "critical" and we shy away from this or that new book because it is *too* scholarly. What we (not as specialists, but as members of the general reading public) stand most in need of to counteract these prejudices is critical scholarly writing that is neither superficially faultfinding nor irretrievably dry-as-dust.

Lionel Trilling's recently published *Matthew Arnold* is the model of such writing. The fruit of some ten years' scholarly labor, it affords the solid intellectual pleasure that one has looked for in vain since Raymond Weaver's *Melville* or Perry's *William James*. There is the same all-seeing competence, the same evocative power of phrase and tone. Mr. Trilling's subject is, moreover, of the utmost contemporaneousness. As Hansen put it in the *World-Telegram*: "Who wants to read a book about Arnold?—Read it and learn all about the 20th century."

The Arnold we are likely to remember is a critic and poet who should have been a professor of pulpit oratory and pastoral care, and who has been relegated by us moderns—including T. S. Eliot—to that circle of Hell reserved for Victorians. The Arnold whom Mr. Trilling has re-created is no less sober but infinitely more possible, and, as a result, profoundly engaging. It is one of the errors perpetuated by the carping critics to suppose that historical figures can hold our interest only if they are—or are made to seem—buffoons. Arnold is not only a real man and a serious one, but he is also, by the profundity and variety of his thought, much more real and far more serious than most of our contemporary critics and prophets. They seem scratchy and finical in comparison with his robustness, angular in comparison with his subtlety. Which is only another way of saying that Lionel Trilling has completely mastered the fullness and intricacy of his subject's thought and has known how to give us in words that we respond to a speaking likeness of a great mind. The book has the order and fidelity we demand from a report and the accent we expect from a living man.

In this double achievement lie the scholarship and the critical spirit of the biographer. The scholarship, for example, pondered and compared Arnold's numerous opinions on government, social classes, individual and group culture; scholarship painstakingly gathered the contemporary allusions and sought to discover what other events, not mentioned by Arnold, might have struck his sensitive and thoughtful nature. These were the raw materials of the great chapter on "The Failure of the Middle Class." The "facts" could have been strung together in an endless sandwich of quotation-paraphrase-comment-authority. It lay with the critical function to make of all this an imaginatively true presentment, which required a knowledge of our own contemporary scene. The ideas of Dewey and Shaw, Marx and Freud, Havelock Ellis and Huxley, the events which are so familiar to us as to be stenographic, if not symbolic, had to be woven by the critic into the texture of the recorded past before the fabric as a whole could show us a meaningful design.

This work of criticism necessarily involved an appraisal of what Arnold said and did. Mr. Trilling is wholly this side of idolatry, but his taking issue with Arnold—on race, for example—is a result of understanding, not of an arrogant *a priori* superiority. How easy it would have been to deride with a show of elegance, to crackle with light innuendoes over the surface of Arnold's life, giving the reader an impression that Arnold was an old fogy and his "critic" a bright young man. Did not Mr. Hugh Kingsmill show in *his* book what great critical sport can be had by calling Arnold "Matt" and thus disqualifying him from having valuable ideas about translating Homer or from falling in love with an interesting and well-born woman?

As we rise from surface details like these to the treatment of expressions like "noble" or "sweetness and light," or of documents like the Marguerite poems, the ordinary biographer's difficulties and temptations increase. Our unconscious opposition to the Victorian era takes on the bitterness that Dostoevsky ascribed to all sons against their fathers. The language of Arnold is, to be sure, near enough to seem fully intelligible, but that is the source of the trouble: it is far enough to be misconceived and not far enough to make us aware of its self-consistent distinctness from ours. Hence the need for Mr. Trilling's constant act of translation, often stressed by him as necessary, but even more subtle and easing to the mind bristling with irritation at Arnold's apparent gaucherie. For such a mind, a great social philosopher is born within the pages of this new biography.

For those, on the other hand, who have long loved Arnold as a poet, this book will offer an explanation of the sterility that struck the pure fount rather early in life, without diminishing the value of what first flowed from it. Those for whom Arnoldism has connoted not, indeed, culture in lace cuffs, but the good life as Montaigne preached it, will discover that their picture, without being unfair, is incomplete. Those who think that religion is one of those problems that the work of Marconi and Edison extinguished will come face to face with questions of disquieting immediacy. Those, lastly, for whom problems of style are organic and no less relevant to philosophy than to politics will be given cause for reflection at a time when the survival of democracy seems so largely to hinge on philosophic choice and preferences of style. And all of these will feel deep gratitude to the critic and scholar who has made it possible for them to greet on terms of respectful intimacy a Victorian who, if he was destined for Hell, has only now come there, like Vergil, to guide and sustain us through its horrors.

# 3

*Edmund Wilson*

*"Uncle Matthew,"* The New Republic

*March 1939*

Edmund Wilson (1895–1972), one of the leading American literary/cultural critics of the twentieth century, was the author of *Axel's Castle: A Study in the Imaginative Literature of 1870–1930* (1931), *To the Finland Station: A Study in the Writing and Acting of History* (1940), *The Wound and the Bow* (1946), and *Patriotic Gore: Studies in the Literature of the American Civil War* (1962), among numerous other critical works. Wilson also published novels, poetry, plays, autobiography, and journals.

Wilson and Trilling were slightly acquainted. Trilling wrote reviews for *The New Republic* during the late 1920s and early 1930s, when Wilson served as literary editor; and Wilson was also acquainted with members of the circle around *Partisan Review*, eventually marrying Mary McCarthy, an associate editor at *Partisan Review* before and during the war. (With sardonic humor and perhaps also with a slight touch of anti-Semitism—even though the majority of its editors were non-Jewish—Wilson referred to the magazine condescendingly as "Partisansky Review.") After the war, Trilling testified for the defense at the obscenity trial of Wilson's controversial story collection, *Memoirs of a Hecate Country* (1946); he also favorably reviewed Wilson's *The Shores of Light: A Literary Chronicle of the Twenties and Thirties* (1952) in *The Griffin* (collected in *A Gathering of Fugitives*). In his posthumous memoir of Trilling, Irving Howe wrote that, "with the exception of Edmund Wilson," Trilling was "the most influential American literary critic of the century." This judgment has been echoed by other intellectuals.

Trilling, who in 1929 moved to a Greenwich Village apartment located just across the street from Wilson, received encouragement in the early 1930s from Wilson about the value of writing a book about Matthew Arnold. The vote of confidence from Wilson, whom Trilling then admired as a model of the radical intellectual whom he sought to become, helped

Trilling complete his Arnold dissertation and reaffirm his commitment to scholarship.

In the following review of *Matthew Arnold*—which is Trilling's dissertation published in book form—Wilson praises Trilling for writing "one of the first critical studies of any solidity and scope by an American of his generation."

This is not a biography of Matthew Arnold; it is a history and criticism of his thought. "Whatever biographical matter I have used," Mr. Trilling explains in his preface, "is incidental to my critical purpose." Yet I believe that it would have contributed to the accomplishment of this purpose to have filled in the biographical background a little more completely than he has done. We do not see Arnold quite clearly enough in his habitat; and it seems to me that there are certain personal values which ought to be solidly planted in the picture. The figure of Clough,[1] for example, which contrasts with the figure of Arnold and throws it into relief—since Clough, with perplexities similar to Arnold's, lacks the principle of life which Arnold always possessed. Mr. Trilling indicates their relationship, but he really does not show us Clough—though he is later at some special pains to recreate the Victorian super-crank, Francis Newman.[2] And what about Matthew Arnold's marriage? Mr. Trilling does not tell us a word about his wife—though he speculates about the unknown "Marguerite" of Arnold's early poems. Mrs. Arnold, also, though he is not known to have mentioned her, must count for something in Arnold's work.

Let us add that the summaries of Arnold's poems and essays become occasionally a little dull (anyone who has ever tried it, however, knows how hard it is to make this kind of thing readable); and that the whole book is probably too long, could perhaps have been cut down fifty pages.

But this said, let us hasten to say that Mr. Trilling's study of Arnold is a valuable and most interesting book. Matthew Arnold has stood up remarkably well; he has managed to sail on into our own time when many ships that seemed once to draw more water have gone down with the Victorian age. He was always uncomfortably conscious of being a "modern man," and the curious thing is that he still seems to be one—which one could never say about Tennyson or Browning, Ruskin or Carlyle. He appeared to be less brilliantly gifted than these; his achievements appeared to be slighter; and yet he was not only more intelligent, in some sense he was also more serious. At a time when the more famous of his contemporaries had taken to drugging themselves with rhetoric of the richest and most stupefying kind, Matthew Arnold saw the realities of his time, stated sharply the problems they presented, and would not desist from worrying about them even though he was never able to produce any solution of which the inadequacy was not absurd and patent. If he always remained a little of an amateur, he was able to escape the destiny of allowing himself to be degraded through his very professional competence into a hollow official spokesman like Tennyson or to intoxicate himself with the optimism of the prosperous merchant class like Browning. Matthew Arnold was never able to bring himself to pretend that things were all right. Some of the poems and some of the essays of Arnold still recur as living thoughts to our minds when so many of the works of his fellows have turned into period pieces:

> He looked on Europe's dying hour
> Of fitful dream and feverish power;
> His eye plung'd down the weltering strife,
> The turmoil of expiring life;
> He said—*The end is everywhere:*
> *Art still has truth, take refuge there.*[3]

The probability, however, with most of us is that the curve of Arnold's development and the general structure of his thought have always remained for us rather indistinct. What we have retained from him are the poetic expression of the emotions of bewilderment and conflict, of the melancholy twilight of faith, and a critical temper of mind which unites in an exceptional way fastidiousness with varied appreciation. Even those famous definitions of his which have become passwords of the higher literary commentary, we might find ourselves at a loss to explain.

Mr. Trilling has here told us the whole story and gone to the bottom of all the uncertainties. He justifies our instinctive faith in Arnold and even makes us respect him more. He lays the indispensable foundation for his edifice in a chapter on Thomas Arnold, which provides a needed corrective for the impression left by Lytton Strachey's caricature.[4] The contrast between the two accounts is a remarkable illustration of the relativity of ideas. Strachey made Arnold odious from the point of view of a cosmopolitan morality and ridiculous from the point of view of a Cambridge sophistication; whereas Trilling reveals Thomas Arnold[5] as he figured to the eyes of his own age, not only as a man of electrical energy and able and positive intellect, but, in spite of some grotesque British prejudices, actually—in religion and education at least—rather impressively enlightened and progressive. Matthew Arnold had had really in his father an example both noble and vital. When the dandyism, the romanticism and the apparent frivolity of Matthew's youth gave way before the repetitive didacticism of the schoolmaster and the preacher, it was not the ordinary schoolmaster or preacher that reasserted himself. Thomas Arnold had been somebody, an original doer and thinker: he had created Rugby School; he had been fighting all his life as a publicist to induce the Church of England to do something to elevate the working class. Matthew Arnold had the fortunate tradition of a father who, by virtue of unusual character as well as of public position, had fortified a base of operations somewhat outside the social groupings and who regarded himself as responsible to society as a whole. Matthew, for all his upper-middle-class snobberies—Pearsall Smith[6] has just been telling us about them—did try to fulfill these responsibilities, just as, for all his sometimes comic British provincialisms—his ideas about French poetry, for example—he did, as the son of a schoolmaster who saw the importance of French and German, try to play out his literary role in terms of the great intellectual world.

Mr. Trilling shows how Arnold was driven by the waning of the authority of the Church to want to transfer this authority to a State which should command an allegiance from all classes; yet how, unable in the long run to bring himself to do away with revealed religion, he attempted to formulate for himself a purely philosophical concept of God at the same time that he left to the masses the ritual and creed of the Church; how he came to tend more and more—and even at the time of the Paris Commune—to sympathize with the working classes as against the bourgeoisie; how he visited the United States in the eighties and was divided between a horror of American uncouthness and a satisfaction in our democratic manners; and how he finally went so far as to declare in a lecture on "Equality" before the Royal Institute that "our present social organization," though it had "been an appointed stage in our growth" and "enabled us to do great things," had come to the end of its usefulness, that though "certainly equality will never of itself alone give us a perfect civilization," yet "with such inequality as ours, a perfect civilization is impossible." Mr. Trilling makes the important point that Arnold always tended to see literature and thought in relation to the society which had produced them and which he believed they ought to be called upon to serve, and that his thinking about social phenomena belonged to the same general Hegelian category as that of Marx and Engels in that he saw that there were "dialectical" reverses which altered the values of the past, so that one age's or society's meat might be another age's or society's poison.

Mr. Trilling has thus, if I am not mistaken, written one of the first critical studies of any solidity and scope by an American of his generation. And he has escaped the great vice of that generation: the addiction to obfuscatory terminology. Dealing in a thoroughgoing fashion with the esthetic, the philosophical and the social-political aspects of his subject, he is almost entirely free from the jargons of any of these fields. I believe he has been influenced by the fashion in a little neglecting the literary aspect of Arnold as well as the biographical. The reaction against the impressionism of a criticism which was dominated by the example of such writers as James Huneker and Arthur Symons has made the critics of the period since the War tend to scorn what used to be called the "appreciation" in favor of the purely technical or philosophical or sociological treatment of literature; and also to forget that a really first-rate critical study ought to be a work of art.

But if Mr. Trilling has followed this fashion, it is evidently not due to lack of competence. His observations on Arnold's style are admirably phrased as well as just: "The Victorians, with Keats and Tennyson in mind, like to watch for the soft intertwinings of vowels and liquid consonants. But what slips off the tongue may slip easily from the mind, and the soft liquidity could not represent the struggle with the world and the self"; "Arnold breaks into melody only occasionally, but through all his verse runs the grave cadence of the *speaking* voice . . . his very colloquialism . . . is one of Arnold's charms; it is the urbanity of the ancient poets . . . which assumes the presence of a hearer and addresses him—with a resultant intimacy and simplicity of manner that is often very moving"; Arnold's prose is "elegant yet sinewy, colloquial yet reserved, cool yet able to glow into warmth, careful never to flare into heat. It was a stlye that kept writer and reader at a sufficient distance from each other to allow room between them for the object of their consideration."

In any case, Mr. Trilling's book is a credit both to his generation and to American criticism in general. Even aside from the interest of its subject, it is stimulating as a study of the past which, largely conceived and diligently carried through, provides us with a new and firmer grip on old intellectual experience by subjecting it to the intelligence of the present.

## Notes

1. Arthur Hugh Clough (1819–61) was a friend of Matthew Arnold who commemorated him in his poem "Thrysis." Clough was a Victorian poet whose work reflects the moral skepticism and religious doubt that characterized the intellectual atmosphere at Oxford University during his days as an Oxford student and fellow (1837–48). In the 1949 edition of *Matthew Arnold*, Trilling regretted that his study devotes little attention to the Arnold-Clough relationship.—Ed.

2. Francis Newman (1805–97), a translator of Homer and brother of John Henry Newman, criticized Arnold's theory of literary style (which Arnold formulated in *On Translating Homer*, 1861). Arnold had criticized Newman's translation of *The Iliad*, which failed to meet Arnold's criteria for a good Homer translation in the "Homeric" or "grand" poetic style: rapidity, plainness, directness, and nobility.

Arnold's attack was met by Newman's *Homeric Theory and Practice: A Reply to Matthew Arnold* (1861). Newman's polemic provoked a rejoinder from Arnold (*On Translating Homer, Last Words*, 1862). In *Matthew Arnold*, Trilling argues that Arnold considered Newman incapable of a sublime Homeric style because Newman himself lacked sublime qualities. Trilling sums up Arnold's attitude: "Faddist, populist, liberal, agnostic, eccentric, this man puts his hand to Homer" (172).—Ed.

3. Matthew Arnold, "Memorial Verses" (1850). Arnold is commemorating Goethe in this passage.—Ed.

4. Portrayed as the ideal English headmaster in such works as Thomas Hughes's novel *Tom Brown's Schooldays* (1957), Thomas Arnold was ripe for Lytton Strachey's demythologizing in *Eminent Victorians* (1918). Strachey's book featured a new, humorous, even cynical, demythologizing biographical method toward the leading, much-idealized figures of the Victorian age. *Eminent Victorians* ushered in a still-thriving literary genre: the popularized reductive biography.—Ed.

5. Thomas Arnold (1795–1842) was a headmaster of Rugby School whose innovations and classical education philosophy made Rugby the prototype of the Victorian school for gentlemen.—Ed.

6. Mrs. Pearsall Smith, a.k.a. Hannah Whitall Smith (1832–1911), a British devotional writer, published such works as *The Christian's Secret of a Happy Life* (1888) and *The Unselfishness of God, and How I Discovered It* (1904).—Ed.

4

*John Middleton Murry*

*Excerpt from "Lionel Trilling's Matthew Arnold," in* Poets,

Critics, Mystics *{originally published as "Matthew Arnold*

*Today,"* Times Literary Supplement*}*

*1970 {March 1939}*

John Middleton Murry (1889–1957) was one of Britain's leading men of letters in the first half of the twentieth century. Although he published three novels, a play, and a volume of verse, Murry was chiefly known as a passionate, controversial literary critic and a skilled editor.

Murry's best-known full-length critical works are *Fyodor Dostoevsky* (1916) and *Keats and Shakespeare* (1925), both of which examine the relation of the authors' spiritual values (as represented in their writings) to their artistic visions. Murry was also a keen champion of modern literature, and his criticism did much to shape the modernist canon. As editor of *The Atheneum* (1919–21) and *The Adelphi* (1923–48), Murry helped establish the reputations of several modern writers (Proust, Joyce, Valery, and Hardy's poetry). Above all, Murry promoted the work of his close friend, D. H. Lawrence (*Son of Woman: The Story of D. H. Lawrence* [1931]), and of his first wife, Katherine Mansfield, who died in 1923 at the age of thirty-four (*Katherine Mansfield, and Other Literary Studies* [1959]). Both Murry's writings and his magazines combined literary analysis with a liberal-Left politics and a religious, indeed mystical (though often preachy), sensibility.

Like Trilling, Murry was a moral critic. Both men were deeply indebted to Arnold, but whereas Trilling owed more to Arnold's cultural and political writings, Murry drew on Arnold's religious orientation, specifically Arnold's relation of literature to religious thought and practice. In the review below, Murry judges Trilling's work to be "the best book" ever written on Arnold. Although Murry criticizes Trilling's excessively secular approach to

Arnold, he expresses strong admiration for Trilling's emphasis on Arnold's politics, especially Arnold's relevance to ideological issues gripping the Western democracies in the 1930s.


Mr. Trilling, who is an American professor, has written the best—the most comprehensive and critical—book on Matthew Arnold that exists. It is a little saddening to us that this particular glory should fall to the United States; but there is no doubt that it has so fallen; and we sincerely congratulate the author. That plain duty done, we turn to wondering whether there may not be a reason why it has happened that, although a thoroughly good book on Arnold has been badly needed for a long while, it has been written by an American and not an Englishman. We believe there is a reason: it is that, although Matthew Arnold is always *d'actualité* for any Anglo-Saxon mind, he is a little more actual for the thoughtful American than for the thoughtful Englishman to-day. . . .

. . . The State was the only conceivable vehicle of what Arnold meant by "culture" when he set before his recalcitrant contemporaries the famous choice between culture and anarchy.

To some extent, in a characteristic half-hearted and grudging fashion, we English have pragmatically accepted the doctrine. We have at least finally and irrevocably abandoned what was once the universal maxim of English politics: that the functions of the State must be reduced to a minimum, and that its positive usefulness was limited to being the strong arm of the Common Law. We are half-way, at least, to the general conviction that the activities of the State may be positive, beneficent and indeed creative. But precisely this is the urgent question in the domestic politics of the United States to-day. . . .

Thus there is a reason why Matthew Arnold should meet with the fullest appreciation from the thoughtful American to-day; and why it has been left for an American critic to grasp, with exemplary clarity, the remarkable unity of Matthew Arnold's thought, and—what is more remarkable still— the unity between his thinking and his life.

## 5

## William Phillips

### Excerpt from "Whitman and Arnold," Partisan Review

### spring 1939

William Phillips (1907– ) has served as editor or co-editor (with Philip Rahv) of *Partisan Review* since the magazine's founding in 1934. He is the author of *A Sense of the Present* (1967) and *A Partisan View: Five Decades of Literary Life* (1984).

Given his editorial position at *Partisan Review*, Phillips was an influential member of the circle of New York intellectuals who wrote for the magazine, among whom the most prominent was Trilling. By the close of the war, Trilling's stories "Of This Time, of That Place" (1943) and "The Other Margaret" (1945) and essays such as "A Sense of the Past" (1942) and "A Note on Art and Neurosis" (1945) had appeared in *Partisan Review*'s pages. In 1946 Phillips and Rahv co-edited *The Partisan Reader, 1934–44*, for which Trilling wrote the introduction.

Although the perception that Trilling was turning conservative is generally dated to essays by Delmore Schwartz and Joseph Frank in the mid-1950s, Phillips writes in his intellectual memoir, *A Partisan View*, that already in 1951 he tried to tell Trilling that "he was being read as a conservative thinker" in New York intellectual circles. Trilling "became agitated and indignant," Phillips recalls, "and in an angry voice . . . insisted that he wrote what he believed and didn't care what people thought." Phillips notes that Trilling, though a liberal, "often appeared to be somewhat conservative because he distinguished himself from the pro-Communist liberals." Phillips adds: "Far from being a forerunner of neoconservatism," as William Barrett and other neoconservatives have claimed, "Trilling stood for moderation and was against fanaticism of any kind."

The following favorable review of *Matthew Arnold* appeared when Phillips was a thirty-two-year-old editor at *Partisan Review*. According to John Peale Bishop, the review appeared after the editors of *Partisan Review* de-

clined to print Bishop's own commissioned review, a rather harsh assessment of Trilling's book. (Bishop's review later appeared in his *Collected Essays
of John Peale Bishop* [1948]. It is reprinted as no. 9 in this volume.)


Arnold, on the other hand, worked within the established tradition of British thought, and if he too was unable to reach a satisfactory resolution, it was
largely because he could not make a sufficient break with the past. Resting
as it did on the contradiction between those two great opposing forces of the
nineteenth century, science and theology, it was inevitable that much of his
work should be made up of incompatible elements. Unlike Arvin's, however, Trilling's "biography of Arnold's mind" does not attempt to recast
Arnold in our own image: on the contrary, Trilling's book is an extremely
intelligent and exhaustive analysis of the organic consistency and logical
inconsistency of Arnold's thought.[1] If one were to quarrel at all with Trilling's method, it would be to point out that it is somewhat diffuse and
overburdened with details and quotations. But it would be captious to stress
these faults when we consider that Trilling's extraordinary fidelity to the
subject makes his book one of the best works of historical criticism produced
in this country.

What is perhaps most remarkable about Arnold's career is that, though
primarily a man of letters, he crossed swords with the most pressing cultural
and social problems. His thought-span, as Trilling tells us, covered the
functions of criticism, the uses of theology, the place of science, methods of
education, the theory of the state, and the political role of the working class.
But however wide may have been the spread of his interests, they all revolve
around a concern for the survival of British civilization. France had already
been shaken up in 1789, and all of Europe in 1848. Class differentiation was
growing, and Arnold feared the anarchy that might result from further up-
heavals. Yet the picture on the side of conservatism was scarcely more attractive, for the aristocracy was dying, the middle class was becoming more
philistine and less stable, and the symbols of religious and governmental authority were being questioned by the findings of science. Arnold's solution,
as Trilling points out, was in the nature of a compromise: hence he was constantly tossed between conservative theories of order and revolutionary theories of freedom. Originally embarking, like most nineteenth century critics
of society, on a criticism of religion, he soon began to retrace his steps, and he
ended with a secular version of religion and a clerical version of society. He
professed sympathy for the social aims of the French Revolution and the
Paris Commune, yet he found their moral values unacceptable. He was committed to the principle of individual conscience and conviction, yet he con-

structed a morality of checks and balances. And Arnold's conception of the strong state as a firm base for Culture, that is, as a central discipline to check the growing anarchy of thought, is a striking example of Arnold's life-long effort to reconcile the principle of reason with the principle of authority.

As Trilling shows, Arnold's literary criticism was bound up with his theories of social reform. He believed, for example, that a heroic society was necessary for a truly noble and tragic literature, and he expected that poetry would take on the function of unifying and refining man's values which had been performed in the past by religion and philosophy. Even his theory of "the grand style" flowed from the serious and dignifying aims he attributed to literature. As a result, much of his own poetry was academic and his criticism had a hygienic tone which is somewhat alien to modern taste. Yet his sensitiveness to the modulations of contemporary thought saved his poetry from the facile optimism of so much Victorian writing. And Arnold's social interests may be said to have led to that awareness of the responsibilities of literature to the general needs of humanity which has had so great an influence on subsequent criticism.

Both biographies seek to define the relevance of Arnold and Whitman to our time. And both suggest that Arnold's "ideal of order, of peace and of unity" and Whitman's democratic enthusiasm might well be rediscovered at a time of social frustration and intellectual panic. Yet the methods of historical analysis employed by Trilling and Arvin have very little in common. Arvin, apparently conceiving the present as but the prolongation of the past, ascribes to Whitman the values of "contemporaneity." Trilling, on the other hand, finds in our consciousness the necessary detachment for a more objective view of the past than it was able to have of itself. Hence Trilling's admiration of Arnold comes not from any suspension of criticism but rather from a recognition that Arnold's "failures in judgment" did not diminish the largeness of his aims.

## Notes

1. Newton Arvin (1900–63) wrote *Whitman* (1938), a critical biography of the poet, which is also under review by Phillips here. Arvin was a critic and biographer of major American literary figures of the nineteenth century, including Longfellow, Hawthorne, and Melville.

6

## Robert Penn Warren

## "Arnold vs. the Nineteenth Century," Kenyon Review

## spring 1939

One of the most prominent American men of letters of the twentieth century, Robert Penn Warren (1905–89) is best known for his novel *All the King's Men* (1946), which earned him the 1947 Pulitzer Prize. Among numerous other awards for both his fiction and poetry, Warren received the Pulitzer Prize for *Promises: Poems, 1954–56* (1957) and *Now and Then: Poems, 1976–78* (1979) as well as the Bollingen Prize for *Selected Poems: New and Old, 1923–66* (1967). Warren was also the first official American poet laureate, appointed for 1986–87.

In addition to his poetry, fiction, and playwriting, Warren was an influential literary critic, one of the most visible members of the New Critics, the leading critical movement in the academy during the 1940s and '50s. Despite Warren's southern roots and his affiliation with the conservative "Agrarian" writers of the 1920s and '30s, which contrasted sharply with Trilling's urban origins and left-wing politics, Warren and Trilling highly respected each other's work. The two men were also personally acquainted via their service on the editorial boards of *Southern Review* (which Warren founded with Cleanth Brooks) and *Kenyon Review* and their teaching in the summer school of the Kenyon School of Letters.

In the following review, Warren commends Trilling for placing Arnold's career in the context of the still-ongoing Science v. Literature and Culture debate, or what Warren refers to as the battle between "the scientific attitude and the poetic sensibility."

This presentation of Matthew Arnold gives us an admirable book, well written, thoughtful, and dispassionate. It is not, properly, a biography, although it does present such facts of Arnold's life as seem to be relevant to the main business of the study, the systematic analysis of Arnold's ideas in their development, and it does undertake to indicate the nature of the relationships existing between his personal history and his ideas. For instance, the youthful Arnold's Disraelian dandyism, "gay, careless, cocky," his attitude toward Clough, and his social and aesthetic philosophy are seen by Mr. Trilling as manifestations of the same central impulse, the attempt to define the terms on which a man could be a poet in the England of the mid-Nineteenth Century, a country and a time dedicated to industrial expansion, scientific rationalism, and the political philosophy of Liberalism. The dandyism, the attacks on Clough, represented efforts to flee the "feverish contact," the strong "infection of our mental strife"; efforts to affirm, in a more personal application, the doctrines of the wholeness of man and the integrity of poetry which became the fundamental concerns of his later criticism. "If we are to understand the relation of Arnold's poetry to his life," Mr. Trilling writes, "we must understand the relation of the cockiness to his philosophy; for when the dandyism was at work, Arnold produced poetry, but when the dandyism failed, poetry failed too." In Hartford, Connecticut, Arnold—not now the Arnold whose unseriousness, years before, had so shocked his friends—met Mark Twain. "But is he *never* serious?" Arnold demanded. The young Arnold, perhaps, would not have asked precisely that question.

Mr. Trilling's book is not only admirable in itself; it fills a positive need. In the first place, it is greatly superior to such general studies as those by Stuart P. Sherman, G. W. E. Russell, Herbert W. Paul, or George Saintsbury, whose book is chiefly memorable, perhaps, because of its contemptuous reference to Tolstoi's "dealings" with that odd compound of crudity and rottenness, the Russian Nature." In the second place, Mr. Trilling's book, by its emphasis on Arnold's fundamental motivation and attitude in criticism rather than on specific pronouncements on literature and affairs, possesses a certain timely therapeutic virtue. "In a world where action presses," Mr. Trilling writes, "and where it is believed that the coexistence of two ideas must keep us from acting on either, it is very easy for Arnold's subtle critical dialectic to be misrepresented." In fact that world where action presses is apt to be less kind than Mr. Trilling surmises; it is not only apt to misrepresent Arnold's dialectic, but is apt to describe his conception of the relation of the ideal of criticism to action in such unflattering terms as infantilism and retreat. For Arnold's ideal of disinterestedness is steadily opposed to the appetite for action as action, the passion which, even when arising from and vindicating itself in fundamental moral principle, may fulfil itself in a dehumanizing fanaticism.

Mr. Trilling wishes, apparently, to emphasize Arnold's ideal and method, but he has endeavored to present in considerable detail the contexts of Arnold's pronouncements and to analyze the motives which prompted Arnold to make particular applications of his ideas. Mr. Trilling has, in fact, gone far toward the preparation of a chapter for that important book on the Nineteenth Century which will, sooner or later, be written—a critical history of the conflict between the scientific attitude and the poetic sensibility, a conflict which our own age yet experiences and has made desperate efforts to resolve. More clearly than anyone else in the century, Arnold stated in his criticism and poetry, and dramatized in his personal situation, the full context of the conflict. "It is precisely the interest which he had in education, politics, and religion," Mr. Garrod has maintained, "which makes his criticism original." But Arnold's resolution of the characteristic conflict of his century in education, politics, literature, and religion has not served for us— Arnold pleased to call himself a Liberal of the future, but we are not that future. "To us," Mr. Eliot comments, "Arnold is rather a friend than a leader. He was a champion of 'ideas' most of whose ideas we no longer take seriously. His Culture is powerless to aid or to harm."

Arnold does not give us solutions. But he gave us his poems, for which we are in his debt. The debt is considerable, because a few of the poems—and there is an unusual unanimity in naming these—are poetry, and because all of them afford a peculiarly instructive occasion for the analysis of the modern poet's problems. His poems represented, he himself prophetically said, "on the whole, the main movement of mind in the last quarter of a century, and thus they will probably have their day as people become conscious to themselves of what that movement of mind is, and interested in the literary productions which reflect it." (Thus Arnold, who was so scornful of the historical approach to literature, appeals to the historical interest of his poems to insure an audience for them.) Mr. Trilling has ably analyzed the poems as documents of that "main movement of mind," describing the poetry, on the one hand, as "a plangent threnody for a lost wholeness and peace," and, on the other hand, as "the exploration of two modern intellectual traditions which have failed him and his peers, the traditions of romanticism and rationalism," and which he attempted to synthesize. But Mr. Trilling, with some exceptions, such as the brilliant study of "Merope," has scarcely undertaken the task—a task which he may have felt to lie beyond the range of the present book—of analyzing very closely the poems as poems and of relating their specific poetic method and quality to the body of Arnold's ideas.

Arnold's criticism tries to affirm the wholeness of man; it is the foe of those forces which were, he thought, shattering the integrity of man, which were making for abstraction. He was the foe of abstraction, but abstraction had its full revenge; its tooth was busily and insidiously gnawing at the roots of every poem before it could be brought to blossom. To the modern reader, perhaps, this appears most obviously, if not fundamentally, in the timidity in the use of imagery. Arnold's poetry is a poetry of idea, always uneasy in the assimilation of the items of perception. On the one hand, it is best remembered for its statements, sometimes almost epigrammatically apposite, and on the other for the passages of mere description, such as the famous ones from "The Scholar Gipsy" and "Thyrsis." When some image is used, as in the poems named or in "Sohrab and Rustum," to resolve a poem, it may not bear very close scrutiny. The instinct prompting the conclusions of these poems, the attempt to focus the total effect in a symbol, is a sound one, but the applications tend to be general rather than susceptible to detailed application. If the poetry, for the most part, suffers from too much dependence on mere logic, these instances of resolving images suffer somewhat from a defect of poetic logic; they do not afford an adequate potential of correspondences. In these instances, Arnold, as a poet, is violating one of his basic doctrines concerning the relation of man to nature: he is, as it were, letting his poems "sink into nature." For it is only the precision and complication of function that could raise these concluding images from the order of nature into the human order of art.

But this failure in the functional assimilation of imagery is intimately related to the mechanical and obvious manner in which Arnold attempted to dramatize, in the larger sense, the themes of his poems "Mycerinus," "Merope," "Balder Dead," "The Strayed Reveler," "Empedocles on Etna"— all of these pieces have something stagey and arbitrary, as does "Sohrab and Rustum" in a lesser degree. Arnold was, it appears, a victim of the misapplication of his theory that the subjects which the poets "need for the exercise of their art are great actions, calculated powerfully and delightfully to affect what is permanent in the human soul," and that the present age "wanting in moral grandeur can with difficulty supply such, and an age of spiritual discomfort with difficulty be powerfully and delightfully affected by them." But in Arnold's shorter pieces in which he did not attempt a purely dramatic frame, something of the same difficulty appears. In "The Future" or "The Buried Life," for instance, the theme is presented in terms of a crude allegorical mechanism which supports the argument.

It may be objected that there is, and in English, fine poetry which is not profuse in imagery and which does not employ an overt dramatic form, that there is a poetry of statement. That is true; but in such poetry the statement is dramatized, is realized directly, in terms of rhythm, syntactical structure, and such technical resources. It is only necessary to analyze such examples as Milton's "On the Late Massacre in Piedmont," some of Donne's devotional sonnets, many passages from Shakespeare and Dryden, or even some of Wordsworth's sonnets to substantiate this point. But Arnold's work, in general, is deficient in these respects. His statements tend to rest their effect upon their paraphrasable content or on the interest of argument. The following lines by Dryden, who in them, as Arnold did, indicts a century, are with the exception of the second line poetry of statement:

> All, all of a piece throughout;
> Thy chase had a beast in view:
> Thy wars brought nothing about;
> Thy lovers were all untrue.
> 'Tis well an old age is out,
> And time to begin a new.[1]

But these lines are not paraphrasable.

Arnold said that his poetry attempted a fusion of the "poetical sentiment" of Tennyson with the "intellectual vigor" of Browning; and Mr. Trilling says that the effort of his poetry was to synthesize the two traditions of rationalism and romanticism. Rarely, and then most precariously, was that fusion achieved; and the achievement, when it did occur, seems now to have been something of a happy accident. The obscure legend of the Oxford scholar, and the career and death of Clough, gave him, as it were, the ready-made and fortunate dramatizations of his theme; otherwise, except for one or two short poems, the theme was dramatized only in his life. He could not assimilate a fluctuating and various world of actualities to his obsessive theme. He thought much about the relation between life and art; but when he was confronted by Tolstoi, who suffered also from Arnold's malady but who could master, in terms of art if not of philosophy, the world of actualities, he wrote:

> The truth is we are not to take *Anna Karenina* as a work of art; we are to take it as a piece of life. . . . The author has not invented, and combined it, he has seen it; it has all happened before his inward eye, and it was in this wise that it happened. . . . and what his novel in this way loses in art it gains in actuality.

The passage reveals a peculiar notion of the psychology of the creative process. What happened before Arnold's inward eye? Little, it may be ventured: the beach at Dover, in the moonlight, with the tide withdrawing across the shingle, the face of the grave Tyrian trader, the prospect from

Cumner Hill, the starlit reaches of the Aral Sea. But when he came to write his criticism, he could not remember what had happened.

### Notes

1. John Dryden, "The Secular Masque" (1700). The poem is an allegorical summary of what literary historians sometimes call "the Age of Dryden": the eras of James I, the civil wars, and the reigns of Charles II and James II, in which Dryden played a large part.—Ed.

7

*Edward Sackville-West*

*"The Modern Dilemma,"* The Spectator

*April 1939*

A fringe member of the Bloomsbury circle (his cousin was Vita Sackville-West), Edward Sackville-West (1901–65) was a novelist, art and music critic, and literary odd-job man. His most widely read novel was *Simpson* (1931); he also translated Rilke and wrote a biography of Thomas De Quincy.

In 1939, at the time of this review of *Matthew Arnold*, Sackville-West had joined the BBC, becoming a radio producer; his program *And So To Bed*, which consisted of readings of poetry and prose, was a wartime favorite with the British public. One of his most notable successes was his 1943 radio play *The Rescue*, a melodrama based on *The Odyssey*, to which Benjamin Britten contributed the musical score.

In the following rave review, Sackville-West praises *Matthew Arnold* as "thrillingly interesting" and "the most brilliant" work of English-language criticism of the 1930s.

This was the moment to remind us of Matthew Arnold, for his problems were, *mutatis mutandis*, ours, and his resolution of them, however partial, a very important step in the integration of Action and Contemplation. Mr. Trilling has seen that to tell Arnold's story usefully must be to concentrate on the very complex evolution of the inner man; this he has done, touching lightly but sufficiently on the exterior events, in a book that deserves to be called wonderful—for its clarity and brilliance, its profundity and scholarship, its fairness and wit. In all its 406 admirably written pages there is not one flat sentence—a considerable feat. Thrillingly interesting, this book is the work of a wise and clever man who has read widely and never failed to connect what he read.

After first sketching out the shape of the young Arnold's problem, Mr. Trilling, in a chapter which could scarcely be better, fills in the background—Dr. Arnold, his character and his England. From this emerges the conclusion that the father's lifelong contest, on the side of Morality *versus* Dogma, was paralleled in the development of the son's political thought. Hereafter, for some time, poetry holds the stage—the poetry of *The Strayed Reveller*, *The New Sirens*, and *Resignation*. The latter was a temporary feature in Arnold's life—a phase whose end is marked by the expostulation with Clough over the latter's defeatist view of life. Arnold's *Weltschmerz* was quite as real as his friend's, but his spiritual toughness prevented him from weakening into an English equivalent—not of his admired Senancour, whose own despair was alike offset by a stoic insight into his true position—but of the woolly Amiel.[1] Melancholy is the most disintegrative of the passions, because it is so negative: abortive hatred turned back upon the self. For a time Arnold seems to have believed in "controlled self-pity"; but he soon found that that way lay invalidism or madness, and ended by finding the true answer in Goethe.

> No one has a stronger and more abiding sense than I have of the "daemonic" element . . . which underlies and encompasses our life; but I think, as Goethe thought, that the right thing is, while conscious of this element, and of all that there is inexplicable round one, to keep pushing on one's posts into the darkness, and to establish no post that is not perfectly in light and firm.

he wrote to his mother in 1865; but years before this he had written the line: "Resolve to be thyself." The slow but steady evolution of the malleable personality into character had begun before Arnold himself was fully aware of it; it shows in his early poems, in *Empedokles*, and in his choice of heroes. He refused any "escape"; for him art is never a self-sufficient activity, as witness the famous definition (which, however, as Mr. Trilling observes, does not define poetry, but only describes what poetry *does*). Those who take this view of art will tend to resume their lives in what they write, and Mr. Trilling squeezes every drop of significance from the poetry.

The transition which so agonised Matthew Arnold is one which everyone must make; but if it is made at the proper (i.e., the body's) time, it does not cause so prolonged an agony, nor trail so much regret. The later the break is made, the more is left behind, so to speak—as an old tooth, when extracted, is apt to tear away pieces of the jaw. A bulwark must then be found—in Arnold's case what he called *Tüchtigkeit* (capability), which took the concrete form of the Chair of Poetry at Oxford and an Inspectorship of Schools. Such things open out on to life—into action, away from contemplation—and the resulting decline of Joy (= poetic wonder) spelt the gradual retirement of the Muse. The two *Obermann* poems are the milestones on this *Via Crucis*, and Mr. Trilling is careful not to underrate the importance of Senancour in Arnold's life. He could in no case have ignored that name and Goethe's; that he has also invoked those of Balzac, Vigny, Gorbineau, Stendhal, Baudelaire and Brandes (to mention but a few), are signs not only of true cleverness on his part, but of the importance of Arnold's position in nineteenth-century history. Every current of thought and feeling met in him, and was inflected. He attacked the problem of life from many angles—literary, political, religious; but Mr. Trilling makes it clear that he never succeeded in his main endeavour, which was to "see the object as it really is."

Arnold's conception of "balance" is primarily an affirmation of the truth of the human soul. The latter may now be defined as that interior regulator which says no to anti-social conduct and prompts the actions of love—a definition which avoids mysticism and a reference to supernatural sanctions. Arnold, I think, perceived this, but the language in which he proclaims it (the passage is quoted by Mr. Trilling on p. 342) dances round the central problem.

> Man must begin, know this, where Nature ends;

he had written, in an early poem. But it is significant that Spinoza provided—as he so often does, for sensitive intellectuals—the alibi which enabled Arnold to eat the cake of Christianity and have it. "Culture" meant "reason experienced as a kind of grace by each citizen, the conscious effort of each man to come to the realisation of his complete manhood." Unfortunately for Arnold, Spinozism squares ill with a church, just because it can do without one. Arnold's definition of religion is on a par with his definition of poetry. "Morality touched by emotion" may have satisfied him, but to us it seems a shuffle, because it balks the fundamental issue of the historical and objective truth of Christianity. "That Christianity is true: that is, after all, the one thing that Arnold cannot really say." The result of this shuffle was an amateur's view of religion. It was to be considered as an expression of Beauty; dogma was to take a back seat and poetry (but not Arnold's) was to come to the fore. The fact is that Arnold clung to Christianity as he felt his poetical inspiration deserting him—hypostatised it out of the poetry he could no longer write.

Yet when it came down to the brass tacks of political conflict in the England of the sixties, Arnold knew that "the way of Spinoza is not enough for most men." And he did not see how it could be made enough; the "possible Socrates in each man's breast" was but another phrase; and his political speculation foundered on the rock that has proved too much for many a sensitive spirit. As Mr. Trilling drily puts it:

> Out of the belief that the best self, Hero or State, is in touch with the order of the universe . . . may flow chauvinism, imperialism, Governor Eyre, the white man's burden—all the things which make us turn to Mill and scepticism, well-nigh willing to rest in "anarchy."

But the "crude issue of power" is a stumbling-block only to those who found their system of thought on Hegel, who—as can now be seen—threw the largest monkey-wrench of all into the delicate motor of human progress, driving (to change the metaphor) a wedge between word and meaning, and confusing *à tout jamais* the fundamental issues of epistemology. Neither Arnold nor those who came after him were able to see that the Best Self, the General Will (Rousseau), the Collective Man, the State, are all posterior to the question of the individual psyche and its development from childhood into adulthood.

To the last Matthew Arnold saw the object, not as it really is, but at one remove. This was the burden of Walt Whitman's criticism, and it was justified. It was a temperamental, as much as an intellectual, failure. Everything, with Arnold, tended to turn into something else, as he looked at it, because the contemplation was unaccompanied by action. His contacts were always mediate, and nothing is more fatal. Even in the affairs of his heart, he seems to have been remarkably—even pathetically—inadequate. Mr. Trilling sensibly refuses to play the traditional game of Spillikins with the story of Marguerite,[2] but he puts his finger on the spot by adroitly enlisting the testimony of Baudelaire. "It is simplicity which saves. . . . Love should be love." Arnold relinquished the girl, whoever she was, because he knew that his love for her was *not* love, as she, a simpler nature, conceived it.

Here once again the poems fill the gap: *Dover Beach* is there to console us for the inadequacies of its author's thought. When poetically inspired, Arnold no longer shuffles; here the object is seen as it is; love really *is* love. As a poet he kept to the last that grave fluency, rendered poignant by single lines of memorable loveliness, which makes his poetry the opposite of Swinburne's, for example; so that one prizes it more, not less, as one grows older. He is the perfect poet of middle age, when vague hopes have given place to energetic resignation.

Such are some of the reflections induced by a book of which it would, I think, be hard to overestimate the value. I personally have no hesitation in acclaiming it as the most brilliant piece of biographical criticism issued in English during the last ten years.

## Notes

1. Etienne Pivert de Senancourt (1770–1846) is remembered as the author of *Oberman* (1804), an epistolary romance about an ascetical stoic seeking redemption via retreat from the world. Henri Frederic Amiel (1821–80) was the author of *Journal Intim*, to which Arnold devoted attention in his *Essays in Criticism* (second series).

2. Spillikins, an English nursery game developed in the eighteenth century, is played with small rods of bone or with wood splinters. The object of the game is to pluck each one without disturbing (or "spilling") the rest. "Spillikins" is sometimes also a synonym for "splitting hairs." Marguerite is addressed in Arnold's love poems "Switzerland" and "Faded Leaves," among others. It is suspected that she was a Frenchwoman with whom Arnold had a love affair, but the facts remain uncertain.—Ed.

# 8

*T. Sturge Moore*

*Review of* Matthew Arnold, English

*summer 1939*

T. Sturge Moore (1870–1944) was a poet, dramatist, art critic, and illustrator. Best known for his verse, Moore is well-represented by *The Poems of T. Sturge Moore: Collected Edition* (1931–33), *Selected Poems* (1934), and *The Unknown Known and a Dozen Odd Poems* (1939). Moore was a friend of Yeats, who admired Moore's illustrations and invited him to illustrate several of Yeats's own volumes; a few critics, most notably Yvor Winters, have held the eccentric view that Moore was also a greater poet than Yeats.

Moore was a Romantic Arnoldian, and hence—despite his sharp criticism of Arnold as a poet—he was fully engaged with the argument of Trilling's *Matthew Arnold*. A Romantic deeply influenced by the Pre-Raphaelites, Moore also admired Arnold intensely, especially Arnold's allegiance to the classical tradition and rational mind.

This book supplies far more background for Arnold's thought than has been attempted before; and thus is valuable, although Mr. Trilling makes the usual mistakes as to what those thoughts were, because he ignores the fact that Arnold made a point of not addressing everybody in general nor yet himself alone. There were enough writers talking eternally to both these audiences; he selected definite groups whose difficulties he could appreciate, not to argue with them but to try to persuade them to experiment practically. Like F. H. Bradley and T. S. Eliot, Mr. Trilling supposes that Arnold can be answered by logic,[1] yet he started with an assumption which he knew could not be proved but which he felt sure those whom he could help would grant. He repeats *ad nauseam* that he is not talking to philosophers or to metaphysicians. He appreciates Spinoza, not for a true and comprehensive sequence of thoughts, but for being in the 'grand style' and evoking a noble temper. So with Plato and Marcus Aurelius they 'get you nowhere', but they call your finest nature into play. Mr. Trilling tries to make him appear to address everybody, or else confess himself publicly, against both of which self-indulgences Arnold maintained a constant struggle. The history of the positions taken up in this life-long battle with himself is valuable, though they had often been tacitly assumed before Mr. Trilling becomes aware of them. Arnold believed that what lay behind appearances was divine. He held that the intellect neither with dogma nor with logic could assure us of this, about which we agree together because being human we are of one mind and love the same incomprehensible object, however wildly we fail to find appropriate words. Still, he only spoke to those who already felt they could say little or nothing. The glib and the cocksure he left alone, and tried to free the modest from their snares.

Mr. Trilling's criticism of the poet and literary critic is less useful than his account of the politician and theologian, where it is chockful of persons and quotations now little known or quite forgotten. He follows modern fashions in aesthetics, so cannot appreciate Arnold's difficulties, who resisted those of his day till he transformed them. Rabelais, Molière, and Voltaire are for Mr. Trilling on the same plane as Homer, Shakespeare, and the Book of Job; nothing in the temper of these last is more profoundly human than in the first three. To laugh is as human as to wonder. All moods are equal for science; they exist or not, they will fit into an hypothetical psychology or will not, and there is no more to it. Poetry envisages joy as more essential than mirth. Science merely describes what is, but for good men and lovers of beauty there are vast scales of value which cannot be described. Applying would-be science where I hold it out of court Mr. Trilling decides that the closing passage of *Sohrab and Rustum* in which the Oxus finds the Aral Sea reflects Arnold's self-pity.[2] He uses a process by which I think anything can be made of anything, one that is to say entirely idle and futile. He argues also to distinguish *serious* from *awe-inspiring*; but l'Avare, enslaved by dehumanizing passion, is awful to contemplate and yet is not on a level with *King Lear.* Psychology cannot directly help the critic of poetry, it can only deal with the defined. Poetical language is 'fluid' and only uses definition to create illusion. No, as a critic of poetry Mr. Trilling is decidedly out of his element, whereas Arnold was *in his*, as his felicity of quotation proves: however one may discard his elucidations for his *then* readers and I myself reject most of them; yet the way he puts them forward convinces me that in reserve he holds something more cogent—taste. It is the same with religion. I have tried to counter Bradley's and Eliot's theological incomprehension in the essay already referred to. Arnold was convinced that neither dogma, nor logic could get near the object, only poetry could do that, and even then not explicitly. Morality can be formulated, but must be transfigured, not only in language but in life, to become religion, though, avoiding every appearance of a wish to bamboozle, he usually said 'touched with emotion'. Of course there is an emotional appeal to man's common nature in all morality, only monsters can escape. Arnold does not argue, he takes for granted what unprejudiced humanity allows, that there are three values, truth, kindness, and beauty, though science only knows of one. Still, in spite of prolixity, this book is interesting, sometimes almost fascinating.

## Notes

1. See "Matthew Arnold" in *Essays and Studies*, 1938. Edited by Laurence Binyon, 7–27.

2. The tragedy of *Sohrab and Rustum* (1853), which Arnold based on the *Shahname*, the Persian national epic by Abu'l Qasem Ferdowsi, chronicles the fate of Sohrab, a warrior for the Tartars. Not realizing that Rustum, the rival Persian chieftain, is his father, Sohrab challenges him in combat. Rustum wounds Sohrab mortally, only to discover then that the warrior is his son. The epic poem, written in blank verse, laments the tragedy of lost youth. It has also often been read autobiographically as a reflection of Arnold's own inner struggles or desire to reinvent himself via a classical, heroic persona. Arnold's poem ends with a famous passage in which the Oxus River, which flows from east to west through Afghanistan and central Asia, then reaches the Aral Sea, a large lake in central Asia.—Ed.

## 9

## John Peale Bishop

## *"Matthew Arnold Again," in* Collected Essays of

## John Peale Bishop

## *1948*

John Peale Bishop (1892–1944) was a poet, fiction writer, and essayist. His most significant works are his story collection *Many Thousands Gone* (1931), his novel *Act of Darkness* (1935), and his *Selected Poems* (1941). Posthumous acclaim came with the publication of *The Collected Poems of John Peale Bishop* (1948) and *The Collected Essays of John Peale Bishop* (1948), edited by Allen Tate and Edmund Wilson, respectively.

A classmate of Wilson and F. Scott Fitzgerald at Princeton (where their teacher Christian Gauss considered Bishop the most talented writer among his peers), a member of the Paris colony of post–World War I American expatriates that included Ezra Pound and Ernest Hemingway, and a friend of the Nashville Agrarians who produced the 1920s magazine *The Fugitive* and the literary manifesto *I'll Take My Stand* (1930), Bishop is probably best known today for his illustrious literary associations, which also included close friendships with Archibald MacLeish and Allen Tate.

In the negative review below, which was not published until 1948, Bishop bemoans that *Matthew Arnold* constitutes "an example of contemporary scholastic criticism": "Of quotations there is no end. . . . Mr. Trilling seems to prefer any opinion to his own." In a note, Bishop adds that the review was written in 1939, commissioned by *Partisan Review*, "but the editors declined to print it." (William Phillips, editor of *Partisan Review*, eventually wrote a positive review of the book for the magazine. It appears as no. 5 in this volume.)

On the dust-cover of Lionel Trilling's book on Matthew Arnold is reproduced the head only from a photograph of the poet.[1] The eyes are cast down and we cannot see what it is that draws them. But as we look at the scarred face, tortured more, it would seem, by certainty than doubt, we cannot but conjecture that the object of its stare is one more occasion for that long contemplation which has left its agony on Arnold's countenance. I became, as I read Mr. Trilling's book, so fascinated by that face, constantly turning back to it, that presently I started a line drawing of it. The hair is curled—"that perpetual miracle of my hair," as Arnold called it—I saw it rising from the sides of the head like the peaks of little horns. I set down the twisted eyebrows, the great virile nose, the strong and sensual mouth. When I had traced the lines that accentuate the coarse cheekbones, I found that what I had drawn so far was the face of a satyr. But the chin was still to come. And the chin was massive and firm. To add the chin was to destroy the effect of all I had done. No, what I had drawn was not a satyr; it was a man

> Never by passion quite possess'd
> And never quite benumb'd by the world's sway.

It was the son of Dr. Arnold of Rugby.

The face on the dust-cover is only a fragment of a photograph which is shown as the frontispiece of the book. When we turn to it, we find that what Arnold is looking at is a dachshund—perhaps that very Geist whose death he recorded in an elegy. The whole thing has been carefully posed to bring out Arnold's love of animals. And the dog very oddly dominates the portrait, so that his master appears almost like a kindly Mr. Murdstone. If ever there was a satyr, he has disappeared under folds of heavy broadcloth.

Now, the difference between these two photographs—which are really the same photograph—may be made to stand for the difference between the Arnold who was critic and poet and the Arnold who was to become so acceptable to the academic and the timid mind, the Arnold of "culture," of "the best that is thought and known in the world," the Arnold of "sweetness and light." And yet "sweetness and light" was a phrase that Arnold adopted from that most savage and bitter man, Jonathan Swift. He used it to mean something. Indeed, there is none of the celebrated phrases of Arnold which does not, as he uses it, mean something, and what it means is usually quite clear from the context. It is only when taken away from all that qualifies and reinforces them, that they lose precision. Arnold himself was the first to detach them, Mr. Trilling says, because he thought of them as having an almost magical power. That may be true. But it is also true that Matthew Arnold, for all the clarity with which he wrote, did what he could to make himself an equivocal figure to his contemporaries.

His sister, who was accustomed to sitting with the young Matthew,

across from him at the breakfast table, was surprised by *The Strayed Reveller*.[2]
She had never supposed that her brother had any such thoughts as his poems
revealed. This was the time of the gay waistcoats and of the hair unclipped
by English scissors. The secretary of Lord Lansdowne passed for a dandy.
Now, the point of the dandy, if he happens also to be a poet, is not in the
immaculate attire, but in the imperturbable countenance. That we know
from Charles Baudelaire, who could write *Mon Coeur Mis à Nu*, but whose
appearances among his contemporaries were celebrated for their dandiacal
sobriety.[3] He would show, as he moved among the tables of literary cafés, the
simplicity of the English gentleman and above it a head impassively prepared for the guillotine. The middle classes were in power, and the poets,
distrusted, had to disguise themselves. They had the choice either by their
negligence to show their contempt for middle-class conventions or by their
elegance to surpass them. They could pretend to be bohemians, or they
could, like the young poet of *The Strayed Reveller*, deliberately stand out as a
dandy. Matthew Arnold's friends remarked the constant play of humor over
his conversation. His poems were something else again. But there was another alternative, beyond those I have mentioned, for the poet's conduct, one
by which Baudelaire was for a moment tempted and to which, it seems to
me, Arnold after his father's death succumbed. And that was consciously to
accept a middle-class condition. At least it was possible to take on the
middle-class conception of what was proper work for a man to do. And
Arnold, married, bound himself to a tasked morality. What was hidden
seemed abandoned. Of poetry there was little. Last was the Arnold who
came to America; he was past sixty and stiff beyond the touch of kindness,
the poet concealed and congealed. He disturbed those who came to see
him as much by the coarseness of his features as by the British eyeglass and
the trousers whose rumpled folds had the momentary approval of Bond
Street.

   To undertake a life of Matthew Arnold could not but be an ungrateful
task. He wanted none written and he took care as he went along to destroy
all papers—even those of a purely literary nature. The best he had thought
and known was in his books and it was in his books that he would descend to
posterity. For the rest, he had learned to prepare a face to meet the faces that
he met. Yet he was no Prufrock; he was not timid, and there is no doubt that
when he heard the sirens singing, it was not each to each, but directly to
him. He sought to silence them and put a stop in the sensual ear.

   Mr. Trilling's *Matthew Arnold* is not a biography, but rather an effort to
discuss critically the published record of the poet's mind and to relate his
thought to the historical and intellectual events of his time. It is the work of

a professional scholar and to me, who am none, it seems that Mr. Trilling has consulted all the material available in print that is relevant to his purpose. The amount of his reading is immense; his way of reading seems to me something less than admirable. His book might well be taken as an example of contemporary scholastic criticism in America. We have, there is no doubt about it, a great number of critics in this country, all more or less scholarly, who write very well. But the number of people, scholars or not, who know how to read seems to be constantly diminishing. Mr. Trilling quotes Goethe with apparent approval: "What is really deeply and fundamentally effective—what is truly educative and inspiring, is what remains of a poet when he is translated into prose." Now, it is true that many of Arnold's compositions can readily be translated into prose, for the simple reason that they have never got very far beyond prose. If we contrast *Haworth Churchyard* with a poem of Yeats rather similar both in subject and vocabulary, *In Memory of Eva Gore-Booth* and *Con Markiewicz*, it is easy to see, though not to explain, how in the case of the Irish poet all the words have been transformed into poetry, whereas in Arnold's recollection of Harriet Martineau and the Brontës, for all the emotion that the words convey, that transformation has not taken place. And yet Arnold was a poet and at his best can only be read as a poet. Mr. Trilling avoids the best. He is timid with poetry whose sense is implicit, even when, as in *Sohrab and Rustum*, he has divined that sense. He is not happy until he has brought back the poetic idea into the realm of abstract ideas. He must, for instance, by a quotation, connect the last stanza of *Morality* with Hegel, though, as he admits, it is probable that Arnold never read the German philosopher. Now, that is no way to read poetry. Unless we are prepared to grant that the poet's criticism of life—to use Arnold's phrase—is important in its own right, we had much better leave him alone.

Of quotations there is no end. There are indeed so many that I can only conclude that Mr. Trilling's scholarship must provide him with a very restful sort of activity. He writes a book the way Tom Sawyer white-washed the fence. Whenever he can find somebody else to do his work for him, he lets him do it. He seems to prefer any opinion to his own.

In place of the conventional Arnold, he gives us one that is vastly more complicated. But his Matthew Arnold to the last is dim. Having assembled the material for an important study, he has completed it in a way which will, I suppose, win the approval of professional scholars. He has known the long range and the industrious search of the Swiftian bees, but, unlike them, he has produced neither honey nor wax. He has failed to furnish us with "the two noblest of things, which are sweetness and light."

## Notes

1. This review was written for *Partisan Review*, but the editors declined to print it.

2. Jane Arnold, Matthew's elder and favorite sister, also known as "K," was an outspoken liberal and married William Forster, a Liberal member of Parliament who supported Arnold's proposals for educational reform.—Ed.

3. Baudelaire's *Mon coeur mis à nu* (1866) is a collection of maxims on the consolations and joys of love.

E. M. Forster (1943)

# 10

*David Daiches*

*Review in* Accent

*spring 1943*

David Daiches (1912– ), a British-born critic and travelogue writer, taught mainly at Cornell University, Cambridge University, and the University of Sussex. He is the author of *The Novel and the Modern World* (1939) and *A Study of Literature for Readers and Critics* (1948), among many other books, including numerous works of literary criticism on British and American authors.

With the publication of *The Novel and the Modern World* in 1939, the twenty-seven-year-old Daiches had established himself as a prominent critic in Britain and America. In the following review, Daiches criticizes Trilling for attending to Forster's ideas or "message," rather than engaging in a literary criticism chiefly concerned with verbal art.

A literary critic has at least two primary tasks. He must *demonstrate* the work under discussion, so that when we look at it again we see more clearly not only what it is but where we must stand if we are to observe it as it is; and he must also provide for the work a context that makes possible fruitful and suggestive comparison. Proper analysis and proper comparison are both necessary: if I had to choose between them (and I hope I never shall) I would choose the latter, provided it were really well done. Nothing, of course, is less easy to do, or more easy to do sloppily and conventionally. But at its most profound, critical comparison can lift the scales from our eyes (and what else is the critic trying to do?) more effectively than any other kind of commentary. If one were given twenty pages in which to try to make clear the essential reality and significance of *Hamlet* and were told to restrict oneself either to "pure" analysis or to "pure" comparison, the latter, if perfectly done, would be more likely to include the former than the other way round. If the critic were able to put *Hamlet* besides *The Brothers Karamazov*, *Oedipus Rex*, *Le Rouge et le Noir* and *Phèdre* and explore all the possibilities of that frightening juxtaposition, he could achieve more than if he stuck only to the text, however intelligently.

For literature, like life, is a series of successes and failures, and of many mixtures of both; it is a series of struggles to achieve significance, each of which can only be properly assessed and interpreted if we see it beside others. The good critic is known by his choice of comparisons. One of the most fundamental questions the critic can ask himself is: Beside what other works will this work be seen most clearly for what it is?

Some such thoughts as these were in my mind as, having re-read *The Longest Journey*, I tried to justify to myself my preoccupation with the fact that it stands today as a brilliant exposé of the superficiality of *Crome Yellow* and the crudity of *The Way of All Flesh*.[1] This thought, to be sure, gives Forster a neat historical niche: but does it represent a critical insight? Does it help us to understand Forster's novel to see its hero, Rickie, as a subtler Ernest Pontifex and a more serious Dennis (I cannot remember the name of Huxley's poor character)? I was grateful to Mr. Trilling, whose book I fortunately read right after reading *The Longest Journey*, that his remarks added point and new meaning to my impression.

This may seem a curiously egotistical way of setting about a review of Mr. Trilling's book; but the fact is that if one is to write a criticism of a book which is itself a criticism of other books, the only way to bring the discussion down to earth, and to prevent it from becoming querulous or gushing or simply unreal, is to anchor the discussion in some point which both critic and critic's critic have independently faced.

This comparison was one of the points I chose. I was struck by the fact that Forster constructed his novels largely in terms of insights which represented a transition between the militant revolt of the nineteenth-century liberals and the cynical revolt of the prematurely disillusioned generation of the 1920s. Could Mr. Trilling—I asked myself before I opened his book— give a critical meaning to that historical insight (if it was an insight)?

I will reassure the anxious reader at once: Mr. Trilling did give a critical meaning to my historical observation—at least he succeeded in giving an account of Forster's literary intentions and insights which put that observation in its proper place. Mr. Trilling is distinguished among contemporary critics for his admirable sense of European culture. He can make a pertinent observation about the Greeks or the eighteenth-century English without any trace of exhibitionism; and that is more than can be said of nine out of ten American critics. Modern critics, from Pound and Eliot on, have been far too prone to the exhibitionist use of cultural illustration, and modern readers have in turn been far too prone to encourage this vice. It is, indeed, the great vice of our time—one might go so far as to say that it is the ultimate, unforgivable Sin against the Holy Ghost of literary criticism—and has bid fair to turn one of the most important of intellectual activities into a game of musical chairs distinguished from the normal playing of that game by the fact that every odd man out finds himself a new chair of his own and sits on it pompously. Literary criticism as an honest desire to get to the guts of a problem—to face up squarely and thoughtfully to the facts and values presented by works of literature—has declined sadly since Arnold's day. Modern critics are often much cleverer than Arnold, but far less intelligent.

Mr. Trilling, perhaps on account of his own careful work on Arnold, has something of Arnold's decent respect for intelligence and for the truth. There is not a trace of showmanship in his work. The only reason that I can think of why the reviewers have been so kind to his book on Forster is that they were misled by the opening chapter into expecting hosts of really snappy generalizations and then didn't read any further. It is a reasoned, thoughtful, well mannered book.

It is, however, limited, as a book of this kind is bound to be. Mr. Trilling tends to avoid the final critical issue, taking refuge in explanations. It is the most difficult thing in the world to distinguish between defects in your author's imagination and defects in your author's works: yet one is a personal judgment, the other a literary. The line of literary criticism winds continually between description and evaluation, between history and judgment. Mr. Trilling's line winds a little too much. In the last analysis what are we to say of *Howard's End* and *A Passage to India*? I do not mean one must give each book so many marks; but there is, after all, the final literary judgment to make and to substantiate. The trouble with Mr. Trilling's judgments is that too often he detects in the novels evidences of defects in the author's insight, but does not proceed to make quite clear how, why, and to what extent those personal defects are bound up with literary defects. He is too often content with extracting, explaining and criticizing the "message" of the novels, and letting the result stand as a literary judgment. But is it a literary judgment? It is a question few of us can answer clearly.

It seems to me that there are two outstanding aspects of Forster as a novelist: the first, an historical aspect, is that fact that his hero stands midway between Butler's Ernest and Huxley's Dennis; the second, a literary aspect, is that he has a constant tendency to confuse myth and symbol. As I use the terms, myth in literature is the use of some external (but accessible) pattern in the light of which the pattern of the literary work takes on its full meaning; whereas symbol is what character and event become in the light of the parts they play and the positions they take up in the plot. Now this confusion between myth and symbol—which is responsible for Forster's peculiar charm as well as for his failure to achieve "greatness"—may be causally connected with the first aspect of his work; it may have something to do with the psychological problems peculiar to a sensitive writer of Forster's time and place. Any number of comparisons suggest themselves. One thinks of Yeats's alternation between symbolism and mythology, of Eliot's search for a storehouse of symbols, of Huxley's bewilderment when the old symbols lost meaning—in other words, I am suggesting that Forster's limitation can be linked to one of the main problems confronting modern intelligence. But the explanation that makes that link clear is historical, whereas the demonstration of the qualities themselves is critical. The final end of critical discussion is to enable the valuative to emerge and stand apart from the descriptive. But in Mr. Trilling's book they remain embedded in each other.

This is rigorous criticism—perhaps unfair criticism, for I am not sure that the ideal I am desiderating could ever be wholly achieved. But in the presence of Mr. Trilling's work it is proper to be exacting, to hold up the ideal ruthlessly. Mr. Trilling uses comparisons excellently, and he is capable of shrewd analysis. His talents demand that we insist on the most adequate synthesis of insights of which he is capable. Of such a critic we demand more than first-rate diagnosis: we demand the ultimate transition from diagnostic to critical statements, in which the latter are nevertheless so closely related to the former that the unwary reader can never see at what point the transition takes place.

## Notes

1. *Crome Yellow* (1921), Aldous Huxley's first book, is a comic novel that satirized the intellectual pretensions of the educated classes in post–World War I Britain. *The Way of All Flesh* (1903), a posthumously published novel by Samuel Butler, is a harsh critique of the patriarchal conservatism of Victorian home life and Butler's own veiled spiritual autobiography.—Ed.

## 11

*Morton Dauwen Zabel*

*"A Forster Revival,"* The Nation

*August 1943*

Morton Dauwen Zabel (1901–64), who taught English at Loyola University in Chicago and the University of Chicago, was a distinguished literary critic. He also published four volumes of poetry and was an editor of *Poetry.*

Best known for his literary criticism, Zabel was the editor of *Literary Opinion in America: Essays Illustrating the Status, Methods, and Problems of Criticism in the United States* (1937), which went through several editions. (Trilling contributed two essays to Zabel's 1951 edition: revised versions of his 1940 *Partisan Review* piece on Vernon Parrington and of his 1940 *Kenyon Review* essay on Freud.) Zabel also wrote *Craft and Character: Texts, Method, and Vocation in Modern Fiction* (1957), an essay collection that includes his flattering review of *The Middle of the Journey.* Chiefly a scholar of modern fiction, Zabel edited volumes on Dickens, Conrad, James, and Melville.

The least expected literary event of the season is one of its happiest and most inspiriting—a revival of the fiction of E. M. Forster. Alfred A. Knopf reissues "Where Angels Fear to Tread" and "Howard's End" ($2.50 each); New Directions reprints "The Longest Journey" and "A Room with a View" ($1 each); with "A Passage to India" already in the Modern Library, all five of Forster's novels are thus restored to circulation. To accompany them comes the best full study of Forster's work and ideas yet written, by Lionel Trilling. The event, at this *particular* moment of literary and intellectual crisis, becomes more than a literary occasion: it takes on the force of a public service.

One would like to argue that a general enthusiasm for these brilliant but still neglected novels requires no critical instruction. They are among the wittiest, most original, most acutely stimulating and entertaining books of our time. They adhere to an established tradition of English comedy and criticism of manners and social conflict. The "condition of interest" is fully present, and old Forsterians will envy the uninitiated their impending shock of discovery and delight. But the possibility also exists of being deceived by Forster's superficial charms or vexed by his nettling reproof to passive attention and assent. He presents, as Mr. Trilling observed earlier, "a paradox which reverses the familiar one of the hard-boiled writer: his work looks soft but inside is hard as nails." The time has passed when the exactions of his critical insight and justice, his unflagging exercise of a moral realism very nearly unequaled in our time, can be left to accidental notice. Today it is not only the doldrums of fiction that his reappearance may relieve. It is also the greater atrophy or abdication of human and moral values—or the simplifying rigor of militant action on their behalf in which Forster has, for forty years, seen a danger fully as great as that of selfish apathy or liberal tolerance.

Forster has his limitations, his decided curtailment of creative temperament and action. They exist not only in his sometimes skittish mannerism and elusive decision of sympathy, in his condescension to adroit idiosyncrasy and "demurely bloodless gaiety" in his essays and shorter stories, in the refusals of recognition that shrink his critical perception (his judgments on James and Joyce sink to a pettiness which no creative prejudice can excuse), in his abrupt check to the demands of political commitment and responsibility. They appear more decisively in the fact that, "having twice mastered his art, he has twice abandoned it." Our feeling about him fluctuates, as Mr. Trilling says, "between disapproval of a dereliction from duty and a sense of relief that a fine artist has not seen art as a grim imperative." He seems to push his suspicion of action to passivity, and of beliefs to something close to a defeatism of will. His latest critic denies him the titles of great novelist, great critic, great thinker. But all this is the result of measuring by Forster's own standards the wholeness of his moral vision and his absolutely honest pursuit of the means by which that vision may be realized and applied to the life of muddle, evasion, compromise, and fear, of masked or stupefied purpose, at which his contemporaries have arrived. He is the historian of the fatal estrangements that underlie the defeats and humiliations of his age. He has offered it no easy palliatives. To its ethic of righteousness he has applied the Primal Curse, "the knowledge of good-and-evil"; to its morality of force and competition he has opposed the complex riddle of human relations; to its compulsive addiction to action and aggression he replies that it is the Inner Life that "pays"; to its tragic divisions of prose and passion, intellect and will, generous vitality and the protective hostilities of modern society, he poses his most passionate conviction—"Only connect." Lowes Dickinson once said that Forster's "kind of double vision squints."[1] So it may—but we should compare what a microscope or the more ruthless lens of art exacts of our eyesight with what has been produced in this age of the fish by the smug eye of sanctimony, the glazed stare of obsession, or the lidless gaze of idiot fatuity before we credit that squint to myopia or a tic of nerves.

What plays everywhere in Forster's work is what plays in another form—to my mind in a lesser ethical and imaginative strength if in subtler directions—in the only other contemporary writing with which it closely compares, Gide's.[2] It is a restless disquiet of moral sensibility, an uncompromising empiricism of sympathy and sincerity, the impulse, *ondoyant et divers*, of the skepticism of Socrates and Montaigne which takes as its duty the quickening to consciousness of human values and necessities that are eternally betrayed to the intolerance and brutality of social prejudice and force. This sensibility Forster has applied to a wide range of phenomena: to English cant and inhibition in conflict with the "vital mess" of Italy; to the rival claims of business and intelligence, ideals and actualities; to liberal tolerance at odds with the demands of emotion and of privation; finally to the baffling and dangerous hostility of races, worlds, and cultures in the enigma of India. Gide's ideal of the novel is also his: "a crossroads—a meeting place of problems," and so is another article of the Frenchman's faith: "Whatever your station or country, you should believe only what is true, and what you would be disposed to believe if you were of another country, another station, another religion." The dialectic intelligence of his art escapes casuistry by rooting itself in the facts of politics, of economy, and of passion. He has been, for forty years, one of the most privileged ushers down "the sinister corridor of our age" who have put their gifts at the disposal of statesmen, moralists, and educators. The fate of those gifts in these hands is a tragedy, but the tragedy is not literature's.

All this, and much more, is presented with superb tact and enviable understanding in Mr. Trilling's admirable study. He has written more than a book on Forster. It is an examination of the conscience of contemporary literature and thinking. His chapters on the five novels are brilliant successes in making summary and analysis count for critical results; his quotations are copious but always controlled; he has traced Forster's sources, problems, and thought without misrepresenting their variety and complex conditions; he has treated with the finest justice Forster's "refusal of greatness" and the compensations that dignify it. I question some of his points: I doubt that "Howards End," with its excessive schematization, is Forster's masterpiece; for me it compares with the imperfect but more profoundly suggestive and inclusive power of "The Longest Journey" or "A Passage to India" as "The Ambassadors" compares with "The Wings of the Dove" in the work of James. I differ with some of his censures of detail and method in the novels, and with some of his indulgence of Forster's methods as a critic. But this is only to say that he has written an alive and stimulating book as well as a sound and just one—one which will stand, beyond Rose Macaulay's effusive tribute or the shorter studies of Richards, Woolf, Leavis, Austin Warren, Shanks, and Peter Burra, as the classic estimate of its subject.[3] When he says that Forster is "for me the only living novelist who can be read again and again and who, after each reading, gives me what few writers can give us after our first days of novelreading, the sensation of having learned something," I would qualify his "only living" with *English*, but the caution would not be wholly convinced. It is twenty-five years this summer since I read my first Forster novel; I have read some or all of his work every year since then and have not yet finished. When Mr. Trilling adds that "a consideration of Forster's work is, I think, useful in time of war," he says what his book fully verifies and what, with luck, this revival of the novels may succeed in proving. And when he concludes by saying that Forster "is one of those who raise the shield of Achilles, which is the moral intelligence of art, against the panic and emptiness which makes their onset when the will is tired of its own excess," he arrives at a tribute which few living artists, of any kind, as honestly inspire or deserve.

### Notes

1. G. Lowes Dickinson (1862–1932), British liberal political philosopher and essayist, wrote such works on democracy and political institutions as *Justice and Liberty: A Political Dialogue* (1908). Trilling reviewed Forster's 1934 biography of Dickinson favorably in *The Nation* (4 July 1934; reprinted in *Speaking of Literature and Society*).

2. Andre Gide (1869–1951), the 1947 Nobel Prize winner, was a relentlessly self-questioning writer and rebel who, in novels such as *The Immoralist* (1902) and *The Counterfeiters* (1925), explored the passions, the soul, and the price and value of individual freedom. Along with his fiction, Gide's plays and journals mark him as one of the leading French literary figures of the twentieth century. A man of action as well as a thinker, Gide was an early sympathizer with Soviet Communism, though he turned outspokenly anti-Stalinist in the 1930s.

3. Trilling reviewed Rose Macauley's *The Writings of E. M. Forster* (1938) for *The New Republic* (5 October 1938). Austin Warren (1899– ), American literary critic, wrote (with Rene Wellek) *The Theory of Literature* (1948), the single best-known statement of the principles of New Criticism. Edward Shanks (1892–1953), British poet and critic, was the author of studies on Shaw and Kipling, among other writers.—Ed.

# 12

*Clifton Fadiman*

*"E. M. Forster,"* The New Yorker

*August 1943*

Clifton Fadiman (1904– ), a writer and critic, has written numerous nonfiction books, including *Party of One* (1955), *The Lifetime Reading Plan* (1960), and *Enter, Conversing* (1962), in addition to writing juvenile fiction and editing more than two dozen books.

A classmate of Trilling at Columbia College and a fellow student in John Erskine's famous General Honors course, Fadiman remained a lifelong friend of Trilling. While still in their twenties, both men began contributing to the *Menorah Journal*, a Jewish cultural magazine edited by Elliot Cohen, and to other New York literary organs.

Like Trilling, Fadiman was devoted to general education and participated in "middlebrow" cultural institutions committed to art and cultural appreciation (e.g., Fadiman was an editorial board member of the Book-of-the-Month Club and *Encyclopaedia Britannica*, a host of educational radio and TV programs such as *Information, Please!* and *Quiz Kids*, and a member of the board of directors of the Council for Basic Education).

Fadiman was working as the book editor of *The New Yorker* and had been friends with Trilling for two decades when he wrote the following review of *E. M. Forster.*

He has been saved by his own journalistic obtuseness; he has never known how to write about what interested the public at the moment. His attention has always been directed to what goes on inside, rather than around, people. Thus, though his books hardly ever reflect current events, they are still perfectly current. Mr. Trilling opens his critique, which he has simply called "E. M. Forster," by remarking that the author of "Howards End" is for him "the only living novelist who can be read again and again and who, after each reading, gives me what few writers can give us after our first days of novel-reading, the sensation of having learned something."

I have spent much of the past week rereading Forster and admiring the justness, the penetration, the delicate gravity of Mr. Trilling's insight into his work. In a way the experience has been unsettling to me as a reviewer. Forster makes most other novelists seem like children, bright, earnest, passionate children. Even writers as glittering as Steinbeck and Hemingway appear brash and blundering beside Forster. The very vigor and masculinity in which they so clearly excel him appear to have the ludicrous aspect of muscle-flexing. By comparison, they are insufficiently serious though incomparably more solemn.

Yet there is something unsatisfying about Forster, too. His literary influence has been pervasive rather than decisive. He is, as Mr. Trilling says, "sometimes irritating in his refusal to be great." His books ask large questions and give large moral issues their proper names, but they do not make memorable pronouncements. Greatness in literature, to quote Mr. Trilling once more, "seems to have some affinity with greatness in government and war, suggesting power, a certain sternness, a touch of the imperial and imperious." This touch Forster lacks entirely. He does not believe that the secrets of the human heart can be forced; they must be surprised by what he calls the "relaxed will." What makes it difficult to apply the word "great" or "genius" to Forster is this atmosphere of relaxation in which even the most melodramatic of his novels are bathed, this undulation of the comic spirit on which they float.

The central theme of his work—particularly marked in his masterpiece, "Howards End," but dominating "A Passage to India" and even the lesser novels ("A Room with a View," "Where Angels Fear to Tread," and that extraordinary story, "The Longest Journey")—is, as Mr. Trilling points out, "the theme of the undeveloped heart." Forster recognizes neither heroes nor villains, but he shakes his head most sorrowfully over those who ruin themselves and others through their inability to feel, to "connect." His whole attack, the subtlest in modern literature, on the British middle class, proceeds out of his perception that it glorifies unawareness. Yet this attack is never whole-hog. His most insensitive Englishmen have curious redeeming qualities and his counterweight pagan Italians and emotional Indians are often represented as cruel, greedy, or sycophantic. He does not believe that there are absolutes in human character. He has, as Mr. Trilling neatly puts it, "nothing of the taste for the unconditioned."

Whether or not you know Forster's novels, I commend to you Mr. Trilling's brief monograph. It says not only many wise things about Forster but also many wise things about literature in general, about the novel, and about

England. It is a model of the kind of criticism not too easily discoverable among us today—restrained, balanced, unashamed of its roots in a long intellectual tradition, academic in the finest sense. It is an admirable introduction to and summation of a novelist whose work, still largely unappreciated in America, quietly refuses to die.

13

George Mayberry

"*The Forster Revival*," The New Republic

*September 1943*

George Mayberry (1901–78) was an editor and author. He co-authored (with Daniel Boorstin and John Rackliffe) the pamphlet *Anti-Semitism: A Threat to Democracy* (1939) and edited *Toward Stendhal* (1945) and *A Concise Dictionary of Abbreviations* (1961). His major work was his editing of *A Little Treasury of American Prose: The Major Writers from Colonial Times to the Present Day* (1949).

Mayberry was an editor at *The New Republic* (1943–48) and a contributor to *The Nation* and other magazines. The following mixed review was written during Mayberry's brief tenure as literary editor of *The New Republic* (1943–44); Mayberry gave *E. M. Forster* a favorable review in the pages of *The New Republic* in 1943.

It will amuse the author of "My Own Centenary" to know that he has become the subject of a revival on this side of the Atlantic. I was under the impression, with the deaths of Joyce and Virginia Woolf that, for whatever little it was worth, E. M. Forster had been quietly recognized by literate Americans as the most important surviving English novelist. It appears, however, that the devoted readers of Daphne du Maurier and J. B. Priestley have continued to confuse him with E. M. Delafield, Norman Foerster and S. Foster Damon. We must therefore be grateful to the trumpetings of the reviewers of *The New Yorker*, *Time*, *The Nation* and *The New York Times Book Review* for calling to our attention Lionel Trilling's critical study of Forster and the reprints of his four early novels.

Mr. Trilling's book—one of the Makers of Modern Literature Series, so brilliantly inaugurated by Harry Levin's "James Joyce"—is an excellent introduction to Forster, if it completely disarms the reader by admitting nearly everything that can be said against Forster in the course of setting him down as "the only living novelist who can be read again and again and who, after each reading, gives me what few writers can give us after our first days of novel-reading, the sensation of having learned something." In place of the rambling appreciation of Rose Macaulay's "The Writings of E. M. Forster," an earlier book-length study of the writer, Mr. Trilling focuses upon Forster as a deliberate artist and conscious moralist. An introductory chapter—"Forster and the Liberal Imagination"—is a provocative study of a thinker who shares the doctrines of liberalism, but who is "at war with the liberal imagination." In subsequent chapters the significance of Forster's education and early travels is revealed and his short stories neatly brought together and explored for the themes that are to dominate his longer fiction. A chapter is devoted to each of the novels, and a final chapter surveys his literary criticism and doubling back on the introductory remarks emerges with a master.

Forster's shorter fiction and his critical and miscellaneous writings suffer heavily from outmoded fantasy, archness and an appalling lack of rigor for a serious writer. Faced with his undoubted peers—the great Russians, say—he is frequently very good indeed, but in commenting on his immediate superiors—James and Joyce, for example—he is often merely peevish. Mr. Trilling sees this, and it is vastly to his credit that he does not let his beloved author get away with his petty and slighting remarks on his betters. I wish that Mr. Trilling had been as severe with Forster's style, which has been overpraised too often. Magnificent as it is at times—he is one of the world's few epigrammatists who do not constantly annoy the reader, and there are descriptive passages in the English novels and in "A Passage to India" that have never been equaled by an English novelist—his prose is too often platitudinously allusive, the metaphors strained and literary, the manner as overblown as that of Lytton Strachey. Witness, for example, these not unrepresentative sentences from "Howards End":

> The letter that she wrote Mrs. Wilcox glowed with the native hue of resolution. The pale cast of thought was with her a breath rather than a tarnish, a breath that leaves the colors all the more vivid when it has been wiped away.

At least one of Mr. Trilling's crucial judgments I would question sharply: is, as he holds, "Howards End" Forster's masterpiece? I think not, although I am less certain after reading Mr. Trilling's cogent effort to endow it with a larger symbolic and social significance than anyone else has seen in it. From his analysis it emerges as one of the great fictional commentaries on the class struggle and a deeper and truer "Heartbreak House" of modern life. But I remain persuaded that "A Passage to India" is his best novel and "The Longest Journey"—his single ambitious failure—the book that Forsterians will most eagerly return to. For in them there are long moments in which Forster suspends his "refusal of greatness" and writes with the passionate understanding which for me at any rate is largely verbal in most of the rest of his work.

On the whole I think that Professor Trilling, along with the reviewers referred to earlier, has taken Forster too seriously. I say this with the instruction and delight that Forster so frequently offers fully in mind, but it must be said of the writer who justifies the claim of England's most important living novelist, or we put too high a value upon him and upon the modern English novel. As Harry Levin has reminded us,[1] English fiction has been pretty thin fare for a long time, enriched most generously by the Pole, Conrad, the American, Henry James, and the Irish-European, James Joyce. Set beside them Galsworthy, Bennett, Wells, Virginia Woolf and more recently Aldous Huxley, Elizabeth Bowen, Graham Greene and Christopher Isherwood (I list only those writers I can read with pleasure) are much smaller figures.

The greater English novelists of the recent past are dead. Among the living are the middle-aged writers like Huxley who have left unfulfilled the promise of their early work and younger writers like Isherwood and Henry Green who may in their own good time extend the great traditions of the English novel. And there is Forster, preëminent among the survivors. By all means let us cry up his virtues to the unbelieving, but let's not go around like Clifton Fadiman using him as a club with which to beat the bloody head of D. H. Lawrence.

## Notes

1. Harry Levin (1912–94) was an American literary critic who helped establish the academic field of comparative literature.—Ed.

# 14

*Alan Pryce-Jones*

*Review in* The New Statesman and Nation

*November 1943*

Alan Pryce-Jones (1908– ) was editor of the *Times Literary Supplement* in the 1940s and '50s and book critic for *The New York Herald Tribune* during 1963–66. He is also the author of a volume of poems, an opera, and a musical; his books include *The Spring Journey* (1931), *Private Opinion* (1936), *Prose Literature: 1945–50* (1951), and his autobiography, *The Bonus of Laughter* (1987), among other works.

While noting that Trilling fails to understand some nuances of the Cambridge scene, Pryce-Jones lauds *E. M. Forster* as a "concise critical handbook."

E. M. Forster has talked—instinctively one avoids "written"—without affection of "the naked worm of time." He has used another metaphor too. Any novelist, he suggests, ought to dislike the clock. One thing has to follow another; the life in time has to begin with bread and butter before saying yes to cake; the evocative scarlet bus has to go somewhere, has even at times, for the sake of the passengers, to stop; appointments are made and kept, cheques are signed and then cashed. And yet what, he murmurs, has this to do with the life by values? How can the double allegiance be kept? The worm of time is a tape-worm, arbitrary and interminable; the clock swings up the half-hours and down again with imbecile rectitude. How can the life by values match its uneven glow against the unfaltering sequences of day following day?

These are the anxieties of a novelist writing about the novel; and with what heightened sensibility when the novelist is Mr. Forster. For his working life, at least viewed from outside, has been an undecided conflict with the life in time. It is the obvious fact about him. Twenty-five years of preparation, six years of victory, thirty-three years of abstention—not total, it is true, for *A Passage to India* was completed and from year to year the clock has struck up a pamphlet or an essay; but an abstention all the more mysterious when its values are weighed against those of the rich years which closed in 1910. When we consider that Mr. Forster is not yet an old man, that his war against the clock was abandoned, saving one battle, and on the full tide of victory, nearly a decade before the death of Henry James, it is hard to explain why the vitality of his art seems still so inevitable. The long silence ought to suggest a false start or at least the atrophy of a promising middle age; in fact, however, the echoes of that earlier voice are still rolling, and the life by values has achieved, perhaps, thereby one of its signal triumphs.

The most typical example of Mr. Forster's technique is the apparently narrow margin by which it avoids the commonplace. In fact, within this margin lies his whole art. Anyone in search of a nice book can pull one of his novels out of Boot's Library and try a chapter or two without suspecting anything amiss. Like the city of Chandrapore, it will present nothing extraordinary. But, like the city of Chandrapore, it can be viewed from the high lands with quite unexpected delight. Mr. Forster will fill the middle distance with a landscape as unforced as the branches and beckoning leaves of the little civil station where Mrs. Moore learned her lesson. The little civil station will always be there. With faithful cruelty, the conversation in the club-house will float over the afternoon. The air is fulll of conversation. An anonymous world and its palpable citizens greet one another in the hesitant approaches and withdrawals, the occasional smart raps, of conversation. But there is always the middle distance casting its generous shade over the bazaar and the bungalows. That shade is Mr. Forster's contribution to the novel, reflected now in an overtone, now in a momentary silence apprehended, experienced, by one listener while the others are thinking of their talk.

Perhaps it is a pity he does not assert himself more. Mr. Trilling says pertinently that he is "sometimes irritating in his refusal to be great." But greatness implies a taking of sides, and the one constant quality in Mr. Forster's books is the avoidance of affirmation except as a conversational counter. His *Aspects of the Novel* shows exactly where he stands. "Yes—oh dear yes—the novel tells a story." So much for the life in time. "It is a pity, it is a pity that we should be equipped like this." So much for the life by values. And it may be only logical that an attitude so worldly-wise, so tender and so fastidious, should end by preferring comment to creation. The mood of Heraclitus is not adapted to the novel, which demands an attitude—a tribute, as Mr. Forster himself has said, to the illusion of perspicacity and of power bestowed upon the reader. The elaborate offhandedness of Mr. Forster's manner is only an attempt to escape from his own creations. There are the opening words of *Howard's End*, for example: "One may as well begin with Helen's letters to her sister." This is one of the supreme bluffs of fiction. On the back of a postcard, as it were, the author is going to scratch down a few notes of some kind—something about Helen, and about her sister too no doubt. And though the bluff is not maintained, though the postcard is expanded to three hundred pages, Mr. Forster all through his masterpiece asserts his refusal to be great. Mrs. Wilcox is never uneasy in Boot's Library as would be, say, Mrs. Newsome, let alone Mrs. Marion Bloom or Madame Verdurin.[1] The ordinary Boot's subscriber need never notice the subtleties to which Mr. Trilling calls attention. He need never consider *Howard's End* as a novel about the fate of England, never remember that Margaret and Helen are the heroines of the two parts of *Faust*, incarnations of the practical and the ideal. But that the story of the Schlegel sisters can carry a symbolic superstructure without collapsing is at least the proof of an unusual intention. Mr. Trilling may have read the symbols wrong. The author may have had no precise symbolic intention at all. He has passed his own test, however. "Not completion. Not rounding off but opening out."

Mr. Trilling is already well known in England for an excellent book on Matthew Arnold. His present study, more modest in intention, is a concise critical guide-book. It sets out to anatomise the novels with that affectionate acumen which his previous work entitled us to expect. To do this without an intimate knowledge of the Cambridge standards by which all Mr. Forster's values are measured cannot have been easy. To enjoy Mr. Forster a bowing acquaintance with Cambridge is all that is necessary, but the lack of a Cambridge background is at once perceived when it comes to explaining him. He is not one of the majestic writers whose work can be strapped down in the theatre and dissected to exemplify the rules of literary anatomy. So Mr. Trilling, writing from Columbia University, inevitably misses some of the finer points. The bones are accurately exhibited, but subtleties of nerve and complexion and bearing are sometimes to seek. A prefatory chapter on "Forster and the Liberal Imagination" and a few concluding pages on "Forster's Literary Criticism" reach out to more general conclusions. And at this point an odd contradiction becomes apparent, a contradiction which seems always to grow out of any consideration of Mr. Forster's work. Mr. Trilling begins his book by stating that "E. M. Forster is for me the only living novelist who can be read again and again," and then goes on to show that each of the novels is rather less good than it ought to be. Similarly, Virginia Woolf, whose essay on Mr. Forster in *The Death of the Moth* remains the best that has been written about him, exalts the whole at the expense of the parts. He is too whimsical, the critics say. He is too arbitrary, or too lyric, or too prim. His liberalism is too guarded, his sense of outrage is too easily evoked.

The novels, taken singly, lack the calm, the instinctive control, of the highest art. Nevertheless, the critics add with conviction, this man who produced a few imperfect works of art twenty and thirty and forty years ago is himself a master. We think of him as we think of Hardy and Meredith and Conrad, even though the five novels in themselves offer nothing so unmannerly as a challenge to *Jude* and *The Egoist* and *Nostromo*. They do not underline their convictions by bursting out of their frame. There is no Willoughly Patterne among Forster's heroes; no fashioning of an epic structure at the expense of taste and probability; no preoccupation with magnificence or excitement—compare the overripeness of Conrad's Sulaco[2] with the elegant suffocation of Chandrapore. It may even be that Mr. Forster's reticence has added to his reputation. After the peremptory voices of the most voluble of centuries had subsided, it was at first extraordinarily refreshing to greet the age of inhibition. Housman, trying not to say too much, Valéry and Rilke struggling to say anything at all, Proust and Joyce binding the whole material of daily life into the aqueduct of a narrow stream; these are approximately Mr. Forster's contemporaries. A few little books on the shelf: their collected works amount to no more. And beside the long lines of the preceding generation they suggest abstinence, devotion, exactitude.

These virtues are Mr. Forster's too. And finally, to his credit must be added the gift of approachability. Abstinent, devoted, exact, yes; but also entirely human. We are back again in Boot's Library here, watching, over the reader's shoulder, the narrow margin of genius which the reader may never analyse for himself. It does not contain Mr. Forster's admirable technique—good as it is, this is not especially his own (for example, the wasp symbol which Mr. Trilling notices in *A Passage to India* can be traced back to *la petite phrase* of Vinteuil's sonata). His margin of genius is more than anything else an attitude of mind, and its expression in the most limpid, unforced prose. "That dull glow of the mind of which intelligence is the bright advancing edge"; so Mr. Forster, in a limited context, speaks of the reader's memory. Precisely, however, this is the response which his novels evoke. Where other novelists assert or reject, Mr. Forster beautifully sheers off; but with a warm humanity he pours out the evidence which allows us to divine his intention. We can even swallow the absurdities: "To me the best chance for future society lies through apathy, uninventiveness and inertia"; "Curiosity is one of the lowest of the human faculties." As if his novels did not reveal, like every good novel, a teeming curiosity, and his reactions to society, future or present, the most ingenious liveliness! It would hardly be too much to say that the ultimate Forster is a tone of voice, solitary, passionate, politely ironical, paradoxically fluent considering how seldom it speaks. And so we can account for the fact that he never falls out of fashion. For the tone of voice has been communicated to so many others. Its echoes are revived so constantly wherever people write or talk about human relationships, the personal life, the knowledge of good and evil. The battle between Sawston and Italy is, after all, for those who are aware that a fight is on, the main theatre of life. Mr. Trilling defines the contestants as the undeveloped heart on the one hand, passion and truth on the other. There is never any doubt as to Mr. Forster's position; and we have already used the image of a battle to illustrate his approach to the novel. Sawston, stupidity, the unvarying clock: all are faces of the same enemy. It would appear that Mr. Forster, since *A Passage to India*, has been fighting the enemy in another and subtler way. Neither Mr. Trilling nor anybody else can do more at present than indulge one of the lowest of the human faculties, curiosity.

## Notes

1. The Boots Company was the first modern chain store. Founded by Sir Jesse Boot (1850–1931) in the 1870s, it became a household name in Britain by the early decades of the twentieth century. Its national significance and popularity among British book buyers are reflected in Sir John Betjeman's lines from "In Westminster Abbey" (1940): "Think of what our Nation stands for / Books from Boots and country lanes." In Henry James's *The Ambassadors* (1903), Mrs. Newsome, the betrothed of Lambert Strether, dispatches him to Paris in order to bring her son back to Massachusetts to run the family business. Madame Verdurin is a vulgar bourgeois woman in Proust's *Remembrance of Things Past* who eventually marries into the old aristocracy after her first husband's death.

2. Sulaco is a province in Conrad's *Nostromo* (1904) that secedes from Cartagena. These fictional South American settings resemble Colombia, which Conrad visited, and are also described in terms of the Polish city of Cracow, where Conrad resided as a young man.—Ed.

# 15

*Irving Kristol*

*"The Moral Critic,"* Enquiry

*April 1944*

Irving Kristol (1920– ) is the author of *Two Cheers for Capitalism* (1978), *Reflections of a Neoconservative: Looking Back, Looking Ahead* (1983), and *Neo-conservatism: Autobiography of an Idea* (1995), among other books. Frequently regarded as the intellectual leader (or "godfather") of the neoconservative movement that arose in the United States in the 1970s, Kristol was a Trotskyist during his college days and a member of the famous Alcove No. 1 (the cafeteria meeting place of his political student group) at City College of New York, from which he graduated in 1940. In 1943 Kristol became (under the name "William Ferry," his Trotskyist party name) a contributing editor to *Enquiry*, a little magazine of the sect of Trotskyists headed by Max Schachtman, and he later became acting editor under his own name.

Kristol abandoned Trotskyism and dropped his commitment to socialism toward the close of his World War II service in the army. After the war, he began writing for little magazines and literary quarterlies, and he became well known in American and British intellectual circles as an essay-ist/polemicist, an editor, and a provocative thinker and merchant of ideas.

Kristol became acquainted with the *Partisan Review* circle of intellectuals during his tenure as managing editor of *Commentary* (1947–52). (Kristol's 1980 essay, "The Adversary Culture of Intellectuals," interprets Trilling's concept from a neoconservative perspective.) Moving to London, Kristol founded and edited (with Stephen Spender) *Encounter* (1953–59), then returned to the United States and worked as editor at the liberal biweekly *The Reporter* (1959–60) and as executive vice president of Basic Books (1960–69).

Perhaps the organ most associated with Kristol and the public policy orientation of neoconservatism is *The Public Interest*, which Kristol founded (with Nathan Glazer) in 1965 and still edits. In its pages, and in several other books that he has edited, Kristol has argued for welfare-state capitalism, vigilant maintenance of the national interest, a strong military, and the social value of religious belief.

Kristol has often expressed admiration for Trilling; along with Norman Podhoretz, Kristol is the intellectual most responsible for the widespread view of Trilling as a neoconservative forebear. In *Neoconservatism*, Kristol calls Trilling one of the "two thinkers who had the greatest subsequent impact on my thinking" in the early postwar era (along with Leo Strauss); later Kristol adds that Trilling was one of the "two intellectual godfathers of my neo-ism" (along with Reinhold Niebuhr). Placing Trilling in the context of the ideological debates of the mid-1990s, Kristol writes in *Neoconservatism*: "The one certain thing about Lionel Trilling was that he was not a politically correct 'progressive'—not in politics, not in education, not in cultural matters, not in manners and morals."

The review below, which Kristol wrote at the age of twenty-four, reflects his growing distaste for Marxist politics of all stripes. The title of the review—"The Moral Critic"—is Kristol's characterization of the "Forster-Trilling perspective" of "moral realism," which Kristol (following Trilling) contrasts with traditional liberalism and with Stalinism.

It was in the *Partisan Review* of September-October, 1940, that Mr. Trilling publicly announced his strategy. Discussing T. S. Eliot's *Idea of a Christian Society* in the light of Matthew Arnold's dictum that criticism "must be apt to study and praise elements that for the fulness of spiritual perfection are wanted," he subjected the liberal-socialist ideology to a vigorous and pointed chiding. His subsequent writings might be viewed as a search for those "elements which are wanted," a brilliant and sustained, if sometimes impatient, exploration of the complexities of moral perfection and of the paths thereto.

In fact, and this is our special interest, in that very same article Mr. Trilling incorporated two distinct chidings. He was angry with the Left for having surrendered its traditional moral vision, and at the same time accused it of allowing this vision to blind it to the true principles of humanism. It was all done with such noble vehemence as to blur any hint of incompatibility. (It is certain that Mr. Trilling felt none.) Yet, the two tendencies are interesting and important in themselves, and have a larger reference which makes them worthy of attention.

The distinguishing feature of modern radical thought, wrote Mr. Trilling, "is that a consideration of means has taken priority over the consideration of ends—. . . . immediate ends have become more important than ultimate ends. . . ." The noteworthy quality of Eliot, contrasted to Trotsky, is his belief in morality as an end, not simply as a means, as an ever present shaping ideal, not a set of prescribed tactics. Moral, rather than historical, criteria are seen as the measure of action: ". . . politics is to be judged by what it does for the moral perfection rather than the physical easement of man." The sense of immanent moral revolution—so profoundly developed in the eighteenth century,—the concern with the potentialities of the individual and the race, have lost their vitality. Instead of asking "What shall man become," socialists have concentrated exclusively upon maneuvering for temporary advantages in the contest for influence and power.

"Lenin," wrote Mr. Trilling, "gave us the cue when, at the end of *The State and Revolution*, he told us that we might well postpone the problem of what man is to become until such time as he might become anything he chose. One understands how such a thing gets said; but one understands too that saying it does not make a suspension of choice: it is a choice already made and the making of it was what gave certain people the right to wonder whether the ethics and culture of communism were anything else than the extension of the ethics and culture of the bourgeois business world. For many years the hero of our moral myth was that Worker-and-Peasant who smiled from the covers of *Soviet Russia Today*, simple, industrious, literate— and grateful. Whether or not people like him actually existed is hard to say; one suspects not and hopes not; but he was what his leaders and the radical intellectuals were glad to propagate as a moral ideal; that probably factitious Worker was the moral maximum which the preoccupation with immediate ends could accommodate."

This critique of radicalism partakes of the normal religio-ethical tone so consistently set forth by men like Maritain, Niebuhr, Dawson.[1] It breaks with secularized politics, with politics, as one writer has called it, as an "independent art in an imperfect world," and insists that politics is but a branch of that broad science of ethics which derives from and is orientated towards the Good. In a sweep of revulsion from the interminably sordid conflict of interests it cries for social action whose goals are dictated by the fixed ethical imagination, not the fluid criteria of expediency; whose motivation is disinterested devotion, not interested gain; whose present status reflects, however crookedly, that image which is ideal. Such an appeal cannot help but be effective in these days when an ideal is at best a momentary, individual vision, and the raw stuff of politics is so pervasive and unyielding. It offers a way of penance and justification, all the more attractive for having so few definite programmatic implications; it stimulates the more pragmatic minded to review their deeds in relation to their ends, and revise the one to suit the other. It encourages frank self-analysis and excites the moral faculties—two very good things.

Yet there appears in the same essay another strain of thought, destined to dominate the later writings, which, while not detracting from the fierce probity of the moralist, leads in a direction more agreeable to the work-a-day world. It is seen in the disparagement of radical philosophers who imply that "man, in his quality, in his kind, will be wholly changed by socialism in fine ways that we cannot predict: man will be good, not as some men have been good, but good in new and unspecified fashions. At the bottom of at least popular Marxism there has always been a kind of disgust with humanity as it is and a perfect faith in humanity as it is to be." It is this simplistic faith in perfectability which cultivates the domineering arrogance of the self-righteous reformer, and which forgives in advance inhumanity disguised as humanistic zeal. The present is only a transitional (almost illusory) epoch, and living men possess value in a potential and inferential sense, never in their own right and by virtue of their present human qualities. "The *ultimate man* has become the end for which all temporal men *are* the means."

The incongruity between the two tendencies is incipient and veiled. Presented in such an eloquent and original fashion, they tend to coerce unified assent through the many truths they both contain. Radical politics has been morally barren, has sacrificed men to means. We do feel disgust with the human quality of any given moment, and carelessly sanction the sacrifice of men to Man. It is only in some of the later reviews and especially in the book on Forster that the divergence and its pertinence to the larger issues becomes evident. And it is the latter of these attitudes which permeates the literary and philosophic judgment.

Mr. Trilling's taste in style will serve as an *entrée*; his 'official' taste, one might add. He is impatient with the modern schools of the novel and points approvingly to the tradition of Dickens and Fielding. (The fact that the modern on whom he wreaks his wrath are always second-stringers, never including a Joyce, Kafka, or Malraux, indicates the grounds for emphasizing the formal nature of these verdicts.) The nineteenth century novel was a form of civilized social intercourse, with a relation between author and reader that was frank and friendly. The casual camaraderie, the good-humored witticism, the clear comic contrivance—all breathed the spirit of tolerant worldliness, "a kind of healthy contentment with human nature;" even satire, with its open avowal of anger, worked within this mood. The novel of modernity, however, reveals quite a different temper. Evil and ugliness are not frontally attacked through the intent of the writer; they are seen as the inevitable product of the characters' transgressions, for which the author disclaims all responsibility. Indeed, the author is no longer human at all, but simply the Eye and Hand which traces the natural logic of character and situation.

This attitude—designated as increasingly sterile—Mr. Trilling sees derived from "liberalism." The liberal state of mind is reformist and humanitarian; a state of mind whose basis is snobbery, self-satisfaction, unimaginativeness. (The religious mind is an aversion to liberalism yet partakes of the same spirit, substituting theological credo for social principle.)

The liberal flatters himself upon his intentions, "and prefers not to know that the good will generates its own problems, that the love of humanity has its own vices and the love of truth its own insensibilities." He is paternal and pedagogic, smug in the knowledge of his righteousness, and sure of the adequacy of his program. He revels in the abstract goodness of the masses and in the abstract badness of Reaction; his art merely dramatizes these axiomatic convictions. Human beings are denigrated into terms for his syllogisms which are then dressed up in fictional form. An insidious cruelty is at work, in which all men are expendable in order to make a point.

In contrast to this facile moralism, E. M. Forster's "moral realism" is extolled, for "he is one of the thinking people who were never led by thought to suppose they could be more than human and who, in bad times, will not become less." Moral realism is aware of the paradoxical quirks of morality; it knows that good-and-evil are more often to be found than good vs. evil. Though dissatisfied, of course, with the ways of men, it foresees no new virtues, but, at best, a healthier distribution of the old. It is non-eschatological, skeptical of proposed revisions of man's nature, interested in human beings as it finds them, content with the possibilities and limitations that are always with us. Dodging the sentimentality of both cynicism and utopianism, it is worldly, even sophisticated. It is partial to the comic manner, which dashes cold water on extremities of sentiment, and yet pursues doggedly its own modest goals. Forster's novels are in a personal, lucid style, omitting the glamorous facades of the tragic-romantic; he is always in the novel, skillfully at work, never hidden behind the screens manipulating invisible pulleys. Preoccupied with moral questions, he is neither overbearing nor sententious. Too sensible and ironic to be "great," he can afford to do his subject-matter justice.

If, as some think, ours is an "interregnum" period, then the Forster-Trilling perspective would seem natural and appropriate. It is a restrictive and somewhat alien focus, unwarmed by the expansive enthusiasm we have been accustomed to expending on matters of salvation. Summing up his political credo, Forster wrote: "So two cheers for Democracy; one because it admits variety, and two because it permits criticism. Two cheers are quite enough; there is no reason to give three. Only Love the Beloved Republic deserves that." (Which moved one left-wing critic to remark: "Two cheers for Forster.") And so it is with politics, reform, revolution, war, social planning: what were once unquestioned goods now call forth two well-modulated cheers. It may not always be so. Perhaps one bright morning nothing but three throaty yells will be able to express a new feeling of assured destiny; or perhaps, and this is more likely, we shall become sated with moderation, insist upon all or nothing at all, and then give three cheers for the hell of it. But, for the present, two will probably suffice.

All of which has some implication for radical political thinking, having to do with the scope of politics, its choice of goals, the sphere of its competence. Aldous Huxley has written that "political action is necessary and at the same time incapable of satisfying the needs which called it into existence." The socialist movement, allied with the recent sweep of collegiate psychology, contends that political action should satisfy these spiritual and psychological needs of the individual; more and more is the libertarian goal identified with a single ideal of personality divested of frustration and complexes. The development of a democratic-cooperative, rational, and sort of well-rounded person is assumed to reveal the purpose of the political struggle. "Moral realism" would incline toward Huxley here: the aim of political action is to change men's status, not their nature; though the two necessarily interact they do so outside of the objective intent of politics, and under the supervision of other forces. A reasonably ordered society can provide the most fertile testing ground for conflicting ideals of personality, since it will have eliminated irrelevant and distracting problems (such as the economic). But these worthwhile activities will spring from their mutual sources—the imaginative arts—not from commissarial decree. Certainly politics has a moral basis, but what does not—science, art, religion? Its *distinctive* feature is its subject matter, problems of statecraft, of the organization of existing forces and specified objectives into an effective union. In so doing, it must see people as they are, which, according to Messrs. Forster and Trilling, would not be at all in the nature of a calamity.

## Notes

1. Jacques Maritain (1882–1973) was a French Catholic theologian, and Reinhold Niebuhr (1892–1971) was an American Protestant theologian. Christopher Dawson (1899–1970) was a British historian of religion and culture, author of works such as *The Making of Europe: An Introduction to the History of European Unity* (1932) and *Religion and the Rise of Western Culture* (1950).—Ed.

## 16

*Kate O'Brien*

*"Refusal of Greatness,"* The Spectator

*December 1944*

Kate O'Brien (1897–1974) was an Irish-born novelist and playwright who lived most of her adult life in England. Best known for her fiction, which largely explored the anxieties and aspirations of the cultured Irish middle class, O'Brien's major novels included *Without My Cloak* (1931), *The Land of Spices* (1941), and *That Lady* (1947), which was a hit on the American and British stage and was adapted into a successful 1955 film (titled *For One Sweet Grape*) starring Olivia DeHavilland.

Students of the novels of Mr. E. M. Forster will read this critical study of him by an American scholar with sustained attention enjoying a frequent sense of agreement with Mr. Trilling, and some moments of enlightenment; appreciative of the fine temper and perceptiveness of his writing, and of the just combination of firmness and sympathy with which he probes for the truth of his subject. But, if hitherto E. M. Forster has seemed to them puzzling and difficult to determine, I do not think that when they close this later book about him they will see him clearer, or understand at last why a writer so magnificently sure and endowed—in intention, in sensitiveness, in control—can swerve so frequently into sheer feebleness; why passion and irony—and each alike true and relentless in his work at his best—are sometimes "changlinged," for a line, a scene, a chapter, into perversity, mischief, or sheer sentimental falseness. Nor can Mr. Trilling explain why a natural-born novelist with great themes implicit in many of his utterances, and with, apparently, every writer's advantage, has written only five novels in thirty-nine years.

"We admire his novels so fully," says this new commentator, "that we want to say that he is a great novelist; somehow he slips from under the adjective and by innumerable gestures—of which the actual abandonment of the novel is not least—signals to us that he is not a great novelist. . . . His refusal of greatness is a refusal of will and that is bad. . . ." True; but perhaps not *exactly* true. Do we admire his novels *fully*? Is "fully" the word? And of his very distinguishing and idiosyncratic "refusal" of greatness, can we really say that it is bad, seeing how peculiarly good, how peculiarly *strong*, is the character it gives to his work? Moreover, is greatness "refused" in *A Passage to India*? Its theme, at least, is audaciously great; and if its people are small and for the most part undignified surely that is by sheer compulsion of the great and painful theme? In any case, that we are undignified and "cursed with the Primal Curse, which is not the knowledge of good and evil, but the knowledge of "good-and-evil," is Forster's ground-conviction, from which springs all his mercy, as well as his impatience and sentimentality.

"The moments of any man's apparent grace are few," says Mr. Trilling, interpreting his writer. "Any man can have them and their effects are not easily to be calculated. It is on a helter-skelter distribution of grace that Forster pins what hopes he has." Since all the novels prove this, one wonders whether one is completely at fault and missing the point in disliking certain moments and passages in some of them—judging them weak and even hysterical? Does the author's despair go deeper and is it more sly and cruel than we have suspected? The Schlegel girls, for instance: do they betray themselves or their creator in that fussy, strange scene they make when a very unhappy young man has walked all through a night, and seen the sunrise? Helen Schlegel is indeed an embarrassing character, but I wish one knew if her author *means* us to be embarrassed by such observations as "Remember you are greater than Jeffries." (Everyone will recall the context.) And Margaret Schlegel, who is not embarrassing, is disappointing, and seems to manage a shade too well in marriage with "the undeveloped heart." Yet these two do, we must believe, stand for those moments of apparent grace in us which E. M. Forster trusts to. But he cannot take the risk of being completely serious even in them, completely simple. Indeed, he sometimes insults simplicity—simplicity of idea, I mean—as when he says that "the very poor are unthinkable, and only to be approached by the statistician or the poet." The second part of that sentence is broadly true, but the first is just a sort of emotional kick.

"Do not allow yourself to be mastered by irony," said Rilke. "If you feel that you are too familiar with it . . . then turn to great and solemn objects, before which it becomes small and helpless." It is debatable advice, and at least not to be offered too blithely to the peculiarly English genius. And it is of the character of E. M. Forster that he would have difficulty in deciding what were and what were not "solemn objects." Nevertheless, irony is not so useful a servant of the novelist as is seriousness; and to be serious in art it is necessary to be simple, to seek simplicity. Effects of simplicity captured repeatedly by delicate artifice throughout the Forster novels may distract us from the author's love of complexity, concealed or half-concealed; and it may be his unwillingness to simplify what he sees as complex—the novelist's task—which leaves us uncertain sometimes, however much and gratefully we may admire. The refusal of greatness, which is great in itself, or gives to Forster's books their characteristic greatness, may screen some vanity of over-subtlety; may be injured a little, and paradoxically, by a refusal of simplicity.

# 17

F. R. Leavis

*"Meet Mr. Forster,"* Scrutiny

*winter 1944*

F. R. Leavis (1895–1978) was the most influential British literary critic-historian of the twentieth century, especially in his shaping of critical opinion about the British novel. In critical works such as *The Great Tradition* (1948)—which Trilling favorably reviewed for *The New Yorker*—Leavis relentlessly championed his own idiosyncratic canon of novelists, which comprised a select group: Jane Austen, George Eliot, Henry James, Joseph Conrad, and D. H. Lawrence. In part, this selectivity had to do with Leavis's commitment to moral as well as aesthetic criteria: Leavis was especially concerned with the "moral element" in literature, which accounted for his generally low opinion of avant-garde modern literature.

Leavis taught at Cambridge University for most of his career. Co-founder (with his wife, Q. D.) of the literary journal *Scrutiny*, Leavis advocated a critical formalism characterized by close textual readings more similar to the New Critics' exegetical methods than to the impressionistic, essayistic criticism of Trilling and the New York intellectuals. Although Leavis regarded Trilling's nuanced cultural criticism as unrigorous and tepid, the two men did share a concern with the moral dimension of literature in general and Matthew Arnold's work in particular.

Among Leavis's most significant books are *Mass Civilization and Minority Culture* (1930), *Revaluation: Tradition and Development in English Poetry* (1936), and *Education and the University* (1943). He also engaged in a much-publicized dispute during 1959–61 with C. P. Snow on the superiority of science vs. literature (the "Two Cultures" debate); Trilling commented on the controversy in a 1962 *Commentary* essay (collected in *Beyond Culture*) that occasioned sharp responses from both Leavis and Snow.

This book doesn't, as one might have hoped it would, exhibit the presumable advantages to be enjoyed by a critic who sees England, and the particular milieu to which Mr. Forster as a writer belongs, well from the outside. Its interest for the English reader is quite other: it lies in the light it seems to throw on the American academic world, to which, I believe, Mr. Trilling belongs. Can it be that for certain elements there the Cambridge of *The Longest Journey* represents something like an ideal—an ideal of the kind of centre of sweetness and light (*hinc lucem et pocula sacra*) a university should be? At any rate, Mr. Trilling appears to be as uncritical as Mr. Forster himself, in that novel, of the Cambridge that emancipated and formed him—the Cambridge he presents there as emancipating and formative (whereas those of us who, closer at hand, see what the King's Hellenism and liberalism of those days [produced] have come to find it hard, perhaps, to be fair to them).

And if Forster's public school presented him with his dominant theme, his university taught him to deal with it.

But surely, what a critic who takes Forster seriously must be very largely concerned with nowadays is how that university didn't equip him to deal with the milieu into which it sent him—the milieu, so closely connected with Cambridge, that became Bloomsbury? There, at any rate, it seems to me, you have a major critical topic where Forster is concerned. How can so sensitive, decent and generous a mind have allowed itself to be so much *of* a milieu so inferior?—so provincially complacent and petty?

But Mr. Trilling seems to take Bloomsbury at its own valuation (and one has an unhappy suspicion that he is a not unrepresentative American intellectual in this). He guilelessly quotes (p. 32):

> Mr. Connolly finds Forster the innovator of the diction used by Virginia Woolf, Katherine Mansfield, David Garnett and Elizabeth Bowen, a statement which is not at variance with his previous remark that one of the reasons why Forster's work still remains fresh is that "his style has not been imitated".

Mr. Trilling has clearly no suspicion that the reasons for such a collocation of names may not be primarily critical, and that (to use a fashionable word) a little sociology might, for an American public, have been enlightening here. But even *The New Republic* seems to show the same innocence, and to contact British culture exclusively and trustfully through that Axis which, owing so much of its cohesive strength to the benefactions of the royal saint, controls our currency of reputations from the metropolitan centre.

Mr. Trilling's own dealings with Forster's prose are not adequately critical. He doesn't seem to see the disconcerting nature of the inequalities which should have been enough to avert him against taking the palpable intention for achievement, the thing too vaguely aimed at for the thing grasped, so that he can pronounce *Howards End* 'undoubtedly Forster's masterpiece'. Actually it seems to me the most patently *manqué*, as it is the most ambitious of the 'pre-war' novels. To be able not to mind the almost adolescent poeticality into which the book lapses in the interests of Significance does seem to me strange. It is not, perhaps, so strange that an American should have been less disconcerted than an Englishman by the unreality of Leonard Bast, the clerk.

But the weakness represented by the following is not specifically American: 'It was a good time for intelligence. . . . If we look at some of the great books published between 1902 and 1906—Butler's *The Way of All Flesh*, Bradley's *Shakespearean Tragedy*, William James's *The Varieties of Religious Experience*, Henry James's *The Wings of the Dove*, *The Ambassadors* and *The Golden Bowl*, Shaw's *Man and Superman*, Hardy's *The Dynasts*—we find that great intelligence is common to them all. . . .'.

# 18

*Michael Levenson*

*"Ernest Ironies: Trilling's Forster," unpublished essay*

*October 1997*

Michael Levenson attended Harvard College as an undergraduate (1969–73) and received his Ph.D. from Stanford University (1980). He accepted an academic appointment at the University of Virginia in 1979, where he is now professor of English.

He is the author of *A Genealogy of Modernism* (Cambridge University Press, 1984) and *Modernism and the Fate of Individuality* (Cambridge University Press, 1991). With Karen Chase he has recently completed *The Spectacle of Intimacy: Family Life on the Public Stage* (forthcoming), and he has just finished editing the *Cambridge Companion to Modernism*.

Levenson has published essays in a wide variety of scholarly journals and in *The New Republic* and *The New York Times Book Review* and has given public lectures at, among others, Harvard, Yale, the University of Chicago, the University of Warwick, and Concordia University. In 1995 he led a National Endowment for the Humanities (NEH) seminar for college teachers. Currently he is serving on the Modern Language Association (MLA) division of late-nineteenth- and early-twentieth-century English literature.

Levenson's current interests pace in the shadow of Lionel Trilling. He works in nineteenth- and twentieth-century intellectual and cultural history, pursuing subjects on both sides of the Atlantic. The culture of London, the American sixties, and the theory of fantasy are among his recent intellectual emphases.

It was an old intention, Trilling's resolve to write a book on Forster, which finally realized itself at an uncanny moment. Composed in wartime and published during the most bitter period of hostilities, *E. M. Forster: A Critical Study* only looks like a standard monograph. Beneath the placidity

and decorum of the surface, within the fine writing and the shrewd discriminations, the book reels with strain and uncertainty: what Trilling writes of
*Howards End* is richly true of his own work: "the war is latent but actual"
(101). Although references to the conflict are few, they carry radiant meanings, lit by the possibility that to admire this author in wartime may be to
risk outraging the grave face of public life. The point is enforced late in the
book when Trilling quotes Forster's own taboo delight in reading Huysmans' *A Rebours* the last time the world was at war. "Oh, the relief of a world
which lived for its sensations and ignored the will—the world of des Es-
seintes! Was it decadent? Yes, and thank God. Yes; here again was a human
being who had time to feel and experiment with feelings, to taste and
arrange books and fabricate flowers, and be selfish and himself (146)."

Forster is not Huysmans. Nor does Trilling cast his devotion in the name
of a decadence and a selfishness. All the same he allows himself to think that
to write such a book at such a time may seem an insolent refusal of what
passes for moral importance. To write in the early 1940s that Forster's comic
manner "stands on the barricade and casts doubt on both sides" (7) is to
choose the most brazen of metaphors. "A world at war is necessarily a world
of will"—what can it mean then to celebrate an author who "reminds us of a
world where the will is not everything" (158), who would betray his country
before betraying his friend, and who dares to express such "weariness with
the intellectual traditions of Europe" (148)? There is no sign that Trilling
ever suffered for his defense of Forster. Who would notice during the inva-
sion of Normandy? But what gives a shudder to the book is the clear sense
that its author is prepared to suffer for dallying with comedy, prepared to
be scolded for untimely meditations on the weak will and the virtues of
passivity.

The war is one bald social fact, closely tied to which is a longstanding
American refusal to appreciate the achievement of Forster. The national
blindness rouses Trilling to his defense, and this because the terms of refusal
depend on such dangerously cramped notions of imaginative vision. Twenty
years later, in a preface to the second edition, he will speak of the "special
energies" excited by his "polemical purposes": "I had a quarrel with American literature as at that time it was established, and against what seemed to
me its dullness and its pious social simplicities I enlisted Mr. Forster's
vivacity, complexity, and irony." (7, 2d ed.) If by the 1960s the polemic
has been absorbed in the mood of retrospection, in the forties it drove the
critic into quiet passion. A brooding solemnity was how Trilling understood the American ideal of seriousness, which yielded excessive admiration
for O'Neill, Dreiser, Anderson, and Steinbeck; which swooned for the false
charm of the "lugubrious"; and which went to war all too well. In this heavy

climate Forster can seem a diverting sprite, given as he is to improbability and exaggeration, and to the airy refusal of "our increasingly grim realistic prejudice" (11). He is wayward, he is playful, protests the lugubrious American, doesn't he understand the seriousness of life and the gravity of art?

Trilling is at his suavely polemical best in trouncing these assumptions. Yes, Forster "teases his medium and plays with his genre"; no, he is not awed by "the sacred doctrine of point of view" (11). But only a trivial habit of thought will fail to see the seriousness of comedy. Many of the early stories, it is true, succumb to the lure of "the quaint, the facetious, and the chatty" (10), but the five novels (Trilling couldn't have known of *Maurice*) are unharmed by these temptations. In a sustained exercise of readerly devotion, he closely follows the course of the early fiction, rehearsing the plots with care, reading with the grain, often pleased just to be able to reenact the satisfactions he has received. Trilling approves of the artifice of Forster's commentary and the willingness to be wise about the characters; at times it's difficult to know where Forster's wisdom leaves off and Trilling's begins. This is an act of symapthy verging on identification.

From such sympathy grows an almost lawyerly advocacy, a continuous argumentative pressure demanding that the reader look past shallow ideals of seriousness and look beyond the viewless room of war. Do you find *Where Angels Fear to Tread* merely a comedy of manners? Then you have failed to see how the farcical collision of England and Italy transforms to "fierceness and melodrama and ends in an enlightened despair" (52). And do you assume that the romantic career of George and Lucy in *A Room with a View* is all light and air? But surely you must see that its sense of evil is "more frightening in its gratuitousness and in its restraint" (86). Will you dare undervalue *The Longest Journey*, which records Rickie Elliot's fall into the knowledge, not of good and evil, but of good-and-evil, and which is "perhaps the most brilliant, the most dramatic, and the most passionate of his works" (67)? In the face of some sharp critical disdain, Trilling builds a staunch and complex defense of these books, and more than half a century later it will still be a cold reader who is unmoved by the appreciation.

Something remarkable then occurs. In making a transition from the three early novels, Trilling launches into an excursus on the impossibility of delivering pure judgments of literary works, pure in the sense of a full concentration on an individual act of imagination set free from all its "accidental" contexts. It can never be done, because knowledge of context will always crowd in upon the isolated work, and in the case of Forster what will always be known is that he is the author of *Howards End*. The supremacy of this work, Trilling argues, will cast a shadow over the others. Certainly, within his critical study, its shadow is sudden and dark. Once the grand fourth novel comes into consideration, the early work finds its luster fading. From the new retrospective advantage of an author's ripeness, the novels whose virtues had been vigorously recovered now look callow and unripe. Their assumptions are now said to be "too easy," they rely too heavily on mythical solutions to their problems, they grow wearying in their suspicion of all authority. After Trilling's magnificent acts of levitation—Rise, early novels, rise into the realm of passion and dignity that will win you admiring readers!—he curtly withdraws his sanction, going so far as to write that in the first three novels, Forster "has not fully done his job as a novelist" (101). The admiring reader of *E. M. Forster: A Critical Study* can only blink and stammer.

Yet, we are meant to be immediately heartened, properly inspired: where the early fiction surrenders to youth, *Howards End* nobly stands up for adulthood, for a "more mature sense of responsibility" (99). In its meditation on the fate of England, the agony of the class struggle, the predicament of the intellectual, and the limits of culture, the novel engages the wide amplitude of liberal conviction and liberal doubt. The Schlegel sisters are the inheritors of the disenchanted tradition of free thought. When they move in their separate ways, one toward the world of business and practicality and one toward the realm of poverty and resignation, they reveal the "sad but comic" confusion of intellectual hope and social failure. What more could one ask of serious fiction in the comic manner?

*Howards End* appears here as the fulfillment of a vocation. If the previous books falter before the highest bar, here at least, here at last, is the meeting and mingling of all that a strong modern talent has to offer: irony and earnestness, politics and personality, vision and skepticism. So strong is the investment in this single gesture of mastery that when Trilling passes beyond it to *A Passage to India*, his generosity seems spent; having given himself to the one masterwork, he now becomes impatient, almost truculent. Forster's last novel is the one that has succeeded best in America, and for Trilling to notice this is already to condemn the novel to simplicity. Fit for American taste, *A Passage to India* strikes him as the most conventional, most public, least capricious and least surprising of the books. Its critique of imperialism is all too clear; it surrenders subtlety of tone in favor of public advocacy; its attack on the coarse repression of British officialdom returns to the pious simplicities of good and evil.

By almost any measure, the reproaches of *A Passage to India* must be seen as overwrought and overdone, but set within the context of the wartime book of criticism, they have a compelling logic of their own. What drives Trilling is a deep problem in the life of taste, desire, and judgment. Where can we find a foundation for our imaginative life? Where can we find a book that, when doubts are creeping everywhere, we can still say, there at least is what I need, there is what I long for? In the midst of a worry that no work is strong enough, full enough, subtle enough, to meet our intense desires, still we long to confirm literary power and imaginative glory. This is what *Howards End* does for Trilling. It stands as one of life's anchors and as the luminous justification, not only of Forster's career, but of the liberal imagination in a century of crisis. If such a work exists, if it is able to inspire the yearning reader, then even an agitated modern culture has at least one sure object of faith.

What makes this critical study moving where it might have been merely intelligent is that even the chastened hope—the discovery of one incontestable success within a long career—begins to waver almost as soon as it is expressed. Within the loving, doting chapter on *Howards End* Trilling already sees weakness inside the strength: Henry Wilcox, the hard voice of practicality is "too thoroughly gelded," and the final scene of reconciliation is "contrived" (116). As he approaches the end of the study, the "greatness" of Forster's novel seems to be forgotten: "We admire his novels so fully that we want to say that he is a great novelist: somehow he slips from under the adjective and by innumerable gestures . . . signals to us that he is not a great novelist" (155). In the book's nervous last chapter, where Forster's criticism stirs up reflection on the meaning of his whole career, Trilling moves from words of sharp disappointment, calling Forster's "casual anarchism" an "affront to the Western mind," to a resurgent defense that sees the intellectual insouciance as a deliberate challenge to the liberal tradition. But again he swerves, naming the retreat from "the strictness of order and law" as "defeatist" and "passive." Then finally in a last refinement of his nervously refining position Trilling asks us to see even the passivity of defeatism as a "strange virtue." It puts in question the very pursuit of literary greatness, which is itself bound up in the muscle-bound exercise of the will, whether it be a question of the liberal will to goodness, the artistic will to mastery, or the military will to conquest.

Forster invites us to relax the will, to accept the weariness of an aging modern consciousness, to give up the heavy theatricality of greatness. He never ceases to care about our moral fate, but he cares from a comic distance that always risks transforming concern into self-defeating absurdity and moral struggle into futility. For Trilling, too, the twin muses of strangeness and weariness are alluring, but drawn as he is to them, he will not let himself give way. The virtues of maturity and responsibility, the imperatives of liberalism and morality, these cannot be laughed aside. Forster is the canny guide to the vulnerabilities of these dignified purposes, and while his admiring professorial critic eagerly follows these skeptical probings, he wants to place them within the context of positive ambitions and remains ever agile in finding ways to turn Forster's refusals to positive account. But it is also a form of Trilling's own earnestness to put limits to the ample generosity, and by the time this tight, dense work is done, the reader must be nearly as struck by its plot as by the plots it subtly interprets. For in its quietest but most affecting movement, the book reveals the chafing away of the close identification between critic and novelist. The late moment of recognition comes with Forster's comment that, unable to "believe in Belief," he will content himself with "tolerance, good temper and sympathy" (147). For Trilling this is an unacceptable abdication, a soft indulgence, patently un-justified as a general principle of ethical conduct, and yet even here he admits a breach only to work to heal it. Sharply conscious of being a critic, a professor, a humanist, an American, a believer in Belief, he recovers even Forster's most unrepentant abstentions as the bracing challenge of a subver-sive ally.

The rapidly shifting attitudes toward Forster's accomplishment display Trilling's deep uncertainty and deeper honesty. The problem of how to judge these novels is at one with the problem of how to conduct a good life, and just because "a world at war is necessarily a world of will," now is the time to put culture to its harshest tests. Can one care for the cause of justice without surrendering to "acrid nationalism"? Is it possible to be fully seri-ous without being lugubrious? ironic without being merely facetious? dis-arming but not quaint? When does a saving detachment grow into chilly indifference? Or where does the healthy respect for bad taste become coarse and unworthy, or the love of the subtle become a taste for the "too subtle"? No program or doctrine or theory can solve these questions. Just when you think you grasp them, they dissolve in your hand. Forster laughs seriously at these difficulties; Trilling weighs, considers, and earnestly defends the rights of laughter. Between them stretches a frayed cord. They hang on it all through this war-shrouded book, close then distant, in tandem then askew, often revising their convictions, sometimes exchanging their roles, but always trundling along together like an allegory of humanism and skepticism.

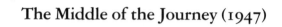

The Middle of the Journey (1947)

# 19

*Mark Schorer*

*"The Vexing Problem of Orientation,"* The New York Times

Book Review

*October 1947*

A novelist and literary critic, Mark Schorer (1908–77) is best remembered for his literary biography, *Sinclair Lewis: An American Life* (1961).

A professor of English at the University of California at Berkeley for two decades (1945–65), Schorer also published several novels and wrote or edited critical works on several nineteenth- and twentieth-century British authors, including Ford Madox Ford, D. H. Lawrence, George Eliot, Charlotte Bronte, and Jane Austen. His *Criticism: The Foundations of Modern Literary Judgment* was first published in 1948. A sweeping collection of fifty-five original selections ranging from the criticism of Plato to E. M. Forster, it constituted one of the first English-language anthologies of the history of literary criticism. Schorer was the lead editor for the volume, whose searching exploration of the functions and ultimate object of criticism raised the postwar generation's estimate of the importance of criticism. Trilling contributed "Freud and Literature" to the original edition (an essay that first appeared in *The Kenyon Review* in 1940).

Schorer and Trilling were literary academics of the same generation who came to national prominence in the early postwar era. They admired each other's work, were personally acquainted from their summer school stints as visiting faculty at the Kenyon School of Letters, and shared similar interests in modern literature and similar aspirations to be public intellectuals. In the flattering review below, published shortly before Schorer established himself as a major critic with the publication of *William Blake: The Politics of Vision* (1946), Schorer commends Trilling's delicate balance of moral and dramatic elements in forming his characters in *The Middle of the Journey.* Already in 1946, in his review of *The Partisan Reader* (which Trilling introduced), Schorer had also lauded Trilling's cultural criticism, especially Trilling's work on Forster.

Trilling expressed his esteem for Schorer more privately. In a postwar notebook entry (first published in *Partisan Review* in 1984), Trilling confided that Schorer was one of two contemporaries (along with Leslie Fiedler) whose praise he most highly valued.

What one admires first about "The Middle of the Journey," a first novel by the teacher and critic, Lionel Trilling, is its assurance—its confidence in its own best qualities, literacy and intelligence, and the lucidity which is the consequence of these, and the rare grace with which it does precisely what it wishes to do. And next, one admires the result of all these qualities—the ease with which Mr. Trilling dramatizes the largest modern subject in what he persuades us are its inevitable human embodiments.

Mr. Trilling's subject is the problem of personal orientation in a non-personal society:

> Laskell wanted to say something . . . that would refer to his own large feelings and yet suit those still larger social considerations which he had often discussed with Maxim, the nature of modern society, the individual and his relation to the social whole, the breaking of the communal bonds. But any remark that would reflect his own isolation would be lacking in tact to this man who was really so much more alone.

The novel takes up these two characters, Laskell and Maxim, at a moment in their lives when their previous orientations have been totally shattered, and we see them—Laskell, the narrator, very intimately, Maxim more fleetingly—through a few summer weeks in about 1940, as they seek out new destinies.

Their search is focused in the character of Laskell's friends, Arthur and Nancy Croom, whom he visits in the country; and through them, Mr. Trilling channels his large theme into the more special one of the quality of modern liberalism. The Crooms are militant liberals, and since they are also among the most intellectually reprehensible couples ever to have appeared in literature, one might at least suggest that they are a triumph of the vindictive imagination.

We see the Crooms as Laskell sees them. He has come to the country after an illness which has left him as completely without enchantment as a new-born child, but charged with un-Wordsworthian reminiscences of suffering and night and the imminence of death; he assumes, of course, that old friends are still old friends, and that the Crooms will be what they have always seemed to be—intelligent, responsible, involved with life, and always right. Then gradually their true quality breaks over him—their dogmatic stupidities, their smug stubbornness, their blindness to human values, their wicked innocence of responsibility, their denial of sin and death, and finally, the cold passion of their wills, which is to say, their immorality.

At the beginning of the novel, Laskell helps the shattered Maxim, an ex-Communist in flight from the murderous vengeance of the party, to the protection of a wealthy friend (editor of a foolish "progressive" periodical called *The New Era*). When Maxim reappears at the end, he has found a new attachment, another authoritarian orthodoxy in a drastic theology. The Crooms loathe him for his defection from the "cause," but in the most brilliant chapters of this considerably brilliant book, we are shown the identity of interest between Maxim and the Crooms, and the polarity of Laskell, who is striving to be "the human being in maturity, at once responsible and conditioned."

I do not wish to emphasize what must now seem to be a certain over-schematization in this novel. Some of Mr. Trilling's readers may not agree (and it should be said that the novel seems to be directed toward a special and notoriously thinskinned audience) that these characters are of interest first as individual portraits, not as typical representations or caricatures. "The Middle of the Journey" is not a *tendenz* novel; yet it defines the tendency of our lives, and it can be most easily discussed in its moral rather than its dramatic terms.

This temptation is to be resisted, for the dramatic terms are always in the fore, and sometimes almost as brightly as in a comedy of manners. Certainly it is a book of great wit, and it is difficult to think of any recent novels which are at all like it. From older writers, one detects, perhaps predictably, the influence of E. M. Forster, especially in the effective combination of wit and gravity, and in the somewhat frosty detachment of style.

In one way Mr. Trilling's style does not serve him quite as faithfully as Mr. Forster's serves him. When Mr. Trilling writes of the Crooms, an odd lack of equivalence appears between the quality of style and the reported emotions of the narrator, and the feeling which the book itself generates. Laskell, discovering their weaknesses, does not hate or even despise the Crooms, but is only rather weary of them; yet one soon becomes aware of the author's much stronger feeling, a profound revulsion, and this feeling finds no dramatic objectification in the novel. There are depths of loathing here which are never plumbed by the novel, and so exist outside its structure, yet are attached to it. The work is not entirely self-contained: a major element in the material as the author has experienced it goes unregistered by his technique. And so that fine lucidity which is so much a part of the book as a whole is sometimes blurred, and one is troubled then by what one cannot see, yet should surely know.

# 20

*Robert Warshow*

*Excerpt from "The Legacy of the Thirties," in* The Immediate

Experience *{originally published in* Commentary*}*

*1962 {December 1947}*

Robert Warshow (1913–55), managing editor of *Commentary* from 1947
until his death from a heart attack eight years later at the age of forty-one,
was a critic of film and the popular arts. An innovative and influential
commentator about Hollywood film in the early postwar era, Warshow's
most important essays dealt with social questions in film: "The Gangster as
Tragic Hero" and "The Westerner."

   *The Immediate Experience: Movies, Comics, Theatre, and Other Aspects of Popu-
lar Culture* (1962) is a collection of Warshow's popular art essays, to which
Trilling contributed an introduction. As Trilling recounts in his introduction (originally published in *Commentary* in 1961), he declined an invitation
to join the advisory board of *Commentary* in 1945, which created tensions
between him and Warshow. The relationship was further strained by Warshow's negative review of *The Middle of the Journey* in *Commentary*.

   Titled "The Legacy of the Thirties," that review of Trilling's novel argues
that the burdensome inheritance of the 1930s for intellectuals such as Trilling was a disabling preoccupation with Stalinism, which left him "unable
to realize and respond to his experience." Warshow contrasted *The Middle of
the Journey* with the work of Forster and, briefly, Edmund Wilson, judging
Trilling inferior. Some intellectuals in New York have speculated that Warshow's review damaged Trilling's confidence in his capacities as a fiction
writer, indeed that it may have so deeply wounded him that he stopped
writing fiction altogether. (Trilling never completed a projected second
novel.)

   Although Warshow never publicly withdrew his harsh judgment of *The
Middle of the Journey*, the rift partly healed in subsequent years; shortly before

his death, Warshow even defended Trilling (in a 1954 *Partisan Review* letter) against Irving Howe's criticism of him in his *Partisan Review* essay, "This Age of Conformity."

In the following review, Warshow contrasts *The Middle of the Journey* unfavorably with E. M. Forster's fiction and with Edmund Wilson's *Memoirs of Hecate County* (1946). *Memoirs*, a short story collection, occasioned comparison with *The Middle of the Journey* because Wilson's protagonist throughout the stories is a lonely intellectual with radical pretensions. But Wilson's stories do not possess the reserve of Trilling's novel. In particular, "The Princess with the Golden Hair," whose length occupies more than half the collection, contains several amorous episodes that are frankly erotic. Indeed, the descriptions of lovemaking are so explicit that *Memoirs* encountered censorship problems and was the subject of an obscenity trial in 1946 in which Trilling testified in defense of Wilson. (*Memoirs* was not banned.)

Lionel Trilling's novel, *The Middle of the Journey*, is in some ways a more explicit attempt to deal with the problem of Stalinism: the hero, John Laskell, an intellectual fellow traveler of the Communists, undergoes an experience that forces him to re-examine the ideological and cultural foundations of his life; in the end, after a series of personal encounters has made the choices clear to him, he rejects the Communist movement and the whole intellectual atmosphere that surrounds it, and seeks a new philosophy more adequate to the needs of experience.

Mr. Trilling's novel is less successful as literature than Wilson's, but—in part for that very reason—it constitutes a particularly clear example of how it is possible for a serious writer to find himself ultimately helpless in the face of mass culture.

Mr. Trilling has shown a profound awareness of the problem of the American intellectual; he has seen also that the center of that problem lies in the Communist-liberal tradition of the 30s. Moreover, his own position, if not unassailable, is at least more solid than most: he partakes of all the serious intellectual currents of our time, but he has not so alienated himself from the general life of American society as to be unable to understand it and sympathize with it. (This is of course an "adjustment," and it produces certain ambiguities of feeling and attitude. But nobody really escapes; in the long run, it is probably better that the ambiguities be near the surface.) Mr. Trilling has intelligence and honesty; more than honesty, he has a clear sense of all the possibilities of dishonesty—this is his greatest protection. Finally, he is a talented writer: there are parts of this novel that are written with beauty, imagination, and intensity.

As a number of critics have pointed out, Mr. Trilling is greatly indebted to E. M. Forster. His method, like Forster's, is to confront his characters with situations for which their moral preconceptions have left them unprepared; the tensions and readjustments that result from these confrontations make up the novel. And, again like Forster, Mr. Trilling is not embarrassed by the necessary artificiality of fiction: he accepts the novel form as a structure of contrivances consciously manipulated to a conscious end. He is thus willing to devote much of his book to the description of serious conversation and thinking, without suffering from the compulsion to be indirect. And he is willing to make use of melodramatic incidents as a convenient means of making his points and establishing the situations in which he is interested; he does not even attempt to disguise the close mechanical resemblance between the climactic incident of his novel and the climactic incident of Forster's *Howards End.* This common-sense approach gives the book a quality of bareness that amounts almost to poverty—a bareness not characteristic of Forster himself, who has a complex sense of character and a richness of wit that Mr. Trilling lacks. In a lesser novelist than Forster, the bareness is a virtue: it is honest poverty, so to speak, as if Mr. Trilling had resolved to make no appeal except to the intelligence, or to the emotions only in the degree that they remain subject to intelligence. But it is a virtue on the private level—or, at any rate, on the level of opinion. It permits Mr. Trilling to deal with experience without compromising himself intellectually; it endears him to the reader for the qualities of his mind—one feels that we should really be better off if more people were like him. But he is removed from experience *as* experience; the problem of feeling—and thus the problem of art—is not faced.

This evasion becomes particularly clear when one considers how much there was in the experience of Stalinism which Mr. Trilling has simply omitted. For a writer with a strong intellectual awareness of psychological complexities, he shows surprisingly little interest in the deeper layers of motivation: in his emphasis on the idea of responsibility, he makes it appear as if the surrender to Stalinism or its rejection was mainly a matter of philosophical decision. Even in his treatment of the character of Gifford Maxim, whose guilt-ridden conversion from Stalinism to religion is plainly the result of deep psychological drives, Mr. Trilling prefers to leave the actual, experiential roots of his behavior unspecified: we never know whether Maxim's guilt is real or delusionary or metaphysical. Such vagueness is of course quite deliberate; it is part of Mr. Trilling's conception of Maxim's character that his motivations should remain unclear, and it is one of the underlying implications of the book's thesis that motivations do not really "count." But the point is that such a thesis and such an approach to character rest ultimately on the assumption that the most fruitful way of dealing with experience is to pass judgment on it—and this is not the assumption of a novelist.

For the same reason, Mr. Trilling does not deal adequately with the fact that Stalinism as he describes it was specifically an experience of the middle class: he is, indeed, constantly aware of the class origins of his characters, and of how their ways of living and thinking are determined by their class, but class, too, does not finally "count," and he does not show how Stalinism offered a way out of the particular psychological difficulties of the middle class as such. More than this, he ignores the fact that the middle class which experiences Stalinism was in large part a Jewish middle class, driven by the special insecurities of Jews in addition to the insecurities of the middle class in general. (This suppression is made all the more obvious by the inclusion of one minor Jewish character in a stock role.) Thus the characters exist in a kind of academic void of moral abstractions, without a history—but Stalinism was in the fullest sense a historical experience, a particular response to particular historical pressures; the people who involved themselves in it were not simply carrying on personal relations within a settled moral order. Here, again, Mr. Trilling is doubtless conscious of what he is doing: he seeks to universalize the Stalinist experience in order to make clear its "essential" significance. But the novel as an art form rests on particularity: the particular becomes universal without losing its particularity—that is the wonder. Mr. Trilling might have come closer to the "essence" of the experience he describes if he had been more willing to see it as the experience of particular human beings in a specific situation; perhaps this means: if he had been more willing to face his own relation to it.

When he does try to create an adequate emotional and moral correlative for his material, it is only to fail in another direction. In Forster's novels, melodrama is always a contrivance of plot or a device to emphasize the deeper content. But Mr. Trilling sometimes invests the deeper content itself with a melodramatic tone. This is especially noticeable in the opening pages, which are like the beginning of a sophisticated spy story, and in the presentation of the character Duck Caldwell, the irresponsible and vicious representative of the lower classes, who is burdened with a weight of moral significance that almost deprives him of all reality (though he is particularly well drawn on the realistic level). Indeed, the excitement that surrounds Duck Caldwell seems a little naive, as if Mr. Trilling were announcing the discovery of evil; if it was a sentimental error to credit the working class with a virtue and an innocence that it never possessed, it is only another kind of sentimentality to make too much of correcting the error.

Yet this tendency to place upon the material a greater weight of meaning than it can bear is almost an unavoidable failing, one more sign of how the problem of creative writing is becoming too difficult for the ordinary talent. When the writer must invent all the meanings of experience, it is not surprising that he should sometimes fail to keep them in proportion.

Most of all, Mr. Trilling lacks Forster's detachment—that almost Olympian disinterestedness (not neutrality) which enables Forster to encompass all the complexities and impurities of experience without strain or shock. Forster is almost never taken in—as little by Margaret Schlegel as by Leonard Bast, not even by Mrs. Wilcox, and least of all by himself. But Mr. Trilling is taken in very often indeed. I have already mentioned Duck Caldwell and Gifford Maxim, whom Mr. Trilling takes at face value whenever, by doing so, he can make them more formidable. There is also Emily Caldwell, who is intended to constitute a kind of positive pole in the book, embodying the "real" world from which the mass culture of Stalinist liberalism has estranged us, but who turns out to be only another creation of that very culture. The brief sexual episode between Emily Caldwell and John Laskell is almost a paradigm of the liberal middle-class dream of sex; it is honest, straightforward, "adult"; it involves affection but no unmanageable passion; it creates no "complications"—which is to say, no responsibilities; it takes place in daylight in the open air, and—immediately after Emily has bathed.

Finally, there is John Laskell himself, the puzzled man of conscience and good will who comes to see the error of Stalinist liberalism and formulates the "conclusions" of the book. (It is worth noting that not even in the simplest of Forster's novels is it safe to take any character as the author's mouthpiece, but Mr. Trilling's identification with Laskell is unmistakable.) Precisely in this formulation one sees how completely Mr. Trilling has failed to detach himself from the cultural atmosphere he seeks to transcend, for he reduces the whole problem of modern experience to a question of right and wrong opinion. There are two opposing orthodoxies: the orthodoxy of Stalinist liberalism, which holds that man is the creature of his environment and thus free of moral responsibility, and the orthodoxy of religion, which holds that man is the child of God and bears an infinite responsibility—that is, an infinite guilt. Laskell rejects both: "An absolute freedom from responsibility—that much of a child none of us can be. An absolute responsibility—that much of a divine or metaphysical essence none of us is." Laskell stands for the free intelligence, for the "idea in modulation." That is what was lost and must be found again. Not to acquiesce is "the only thing that matters."

Mr. Trilling is here finally reduced to the level of his subject; like the Stalinists themselves, he can respond to the complexity of experience only with a revision of doctrine. His doctrine may be sound (though the *via media*, too, can be a form of cant), but the point is that it is irrelevant: the novelist's function is not to argue with his characters—or at least not to try too hard to win the argument.

One might think, perhaps, that the virtue of detachment belongs to the intelligence, and thus has nothing to do with the problem of feeling. But the detachment of a creative writer rests precisely on his ability to create what seems (at least to him) an adequate emotional and moral response to experience, a response that is "objectively" valid in the sense that it seems to inhere in the experience itself and to come into being automatically, so to speak, with the re-creation of the experience. Mr. Trilling, lacking an aesthetically effective relationship to experience, is forced to translate experience into ideas, embodying these ideas in his characters and giving his plot the form of an intellectual discussion reinforced by events. He thus becomes personally involved with his characters in a way that the true novelist never is, for some of the ideas are his own and some are ideas he disagrees with, and he must therefore convince his reader that some characters are "right" and others "wrong" (though "rightness" and "wrongness" are qualities not of human beings but only of ideas); whereas the true novelist tries only to make his characters and their behavior "convincing," which is something entirely different. There are a great many intellectual discussions in Forster's novels; and very often both Forster and his reader know who is "right"; but to have right or wrong ideas is part of experience—it is not an issue.

I have dwelt so much on Forster because it is apparent that Mr. Trilling has tried to model himself most of all on Forster (though to some degree on James) and on the moral and intellectual quality that Forster embodies, and because the great gap that remains between the two writers is more than a disparity of talent. The point is not that Mr. Trilling is not a great novelist; a healthy culture has room for the minor talent. What is significant is that Mr. Trilling has not yet solved the problem of being a novelist at all. And this failure is not his alone: in his failure, he comes in a way to represent us all— as perhaps he would not represent us if he had succeeded. The problem remains: How shall we regain the use of our experience in the world of mass culture?

## 21

*Wylie Sypher*

*"The Political Imagination,"* Partisan Review

*January 1948*

Wylie Sypher (1905–90) taught English and served as an administrator at Simmons College in Boston for five decades. He was the author of *Enlightened England* (1947), *Four Stages of Renaissance Style* (1955), *Comedy: An Essay on Comedy* (1956), *Rococo to Cubism in Art and Literature* (1960), *Loss of the Self* (1962), and *Literature and Technology: The Alien Vision* (1968), among other books.

A contemporary of Trilling, Sypher also frequently addressed the topic of the relations among literature, society, and identity, and he wrote as a public intellectual, publishing his books with major commercial houses and contributing to a wide range of literary periodicals.

In the following review, Sypher commends Trilling as a moralist and liberal critic of postwar liberalism in the Arnoldian spirit.

Gide once noted that, if skepticism is sometimes the beginning of wisdom, it is often the end of art. Mr. Trilling's wisdom as well as his art is the consequence of his skepticism—his disenchantment with the liberal ideologies of the thirties and his exploration of the dark and uncertain business of the ego that eventually expresses itself in opinions, positions held, in all our devotions to abstract systems. Laskell in this novel, like Strether in the Jamesian fiction, is one of the persons upon whom none of our present malaise is lost as he returns to life from the great white peace of his sickness, and, during his summer in Connecticut, emancipates himself turn by purgatorial turn from the unexamined attitudes of those about him: the liberal optimism of his host Arthur Croom, the hard social idealism of Nancy Croom, the possessive benevolence of Kermit Simpson, the fierce revolutionary program of Maxim and his equally fierce defection to religion. The pain and confusion of the world—Laskell's abortive attraction to Emily Caldwell, the death of her daughter, the eruption of Maxim into the quaint liberal order established among the Crooms, the evidences of a coming struggle for power—are the intellectual history of the thirties interpreted through Laskell's sensibility of skepticism. Conflicts of opinion are profound fissures within the modern condition, a dim and slow disintegration of the outward and inward world. To desert a cause is to upset the moral equilibrium.

Trilling had already argued that the question of power has been forced upon us, and that the romantic revolutionism of the bourgeoisie, their excited humanitarianism, their surrender to programs, abstractions, utopian visions—all, in fact, that the Crooms represent—is either a projection of the will or an evasion. The dramatic contradiction between the liberal intention to make a conscious, intelligent choice and the calamitous "badness and stupidity" of liberal action he can explain only as a failure in both mind and imagination—for politics require both.

If Trilling's direction has been political, his vision as an artist has been psychological. With an intense impressionability he has looked at the social commitments of the individual through the deep, unknown motives operating within the self. Somehow they must be brought, as he says, into relation with the known. His criticism has been a function of the imagination, and his most inward exploration of the deeper self has been "The Other Margaret," his story in which the child discovers through her response to the *other* Margaret "the insupportable fact of her own moral life."

The texture of his novel remains psychological, though not so uniformly as in his short stories. Trilling's awareness of unadmitted motives is everywhere—the impulses of Laskell and Maxim to show the snapshots of the dead Elizabeth, Laskell's offering thirty dollars to Maxim, his quoting the sonnet to Nancy, his twisting his ankle while Emily bathes, his pursuit of Duck, his devotion to the rose, his nameless terror. The dimensions of these passages are wonderfully verbal, as they are in James; in both writers the psychological elaboration is wrought by a verbal elaboration and abstraction until the ambiguity between literature and analysis is heightened and the imagery expands indeterminately into the symbolism of the great mural figures of suffering and power about Maxim, or the brown wind rushing at Laskell in the afternoon sunlight.

The most daring feats of the novel occur precisely when the psychological texture is broken, for example in the violence of Susan's death at the hand of her father Duck, and at the church social where Maxim portentously challenges the minister. In these scenes Trilling has presumed—doubtless in the strength of his academic breeding—to project his fiction backward to a plane of Victorian narrative. Is there another "serious" modern novelist who would risk the grotesque confrontation of Maxim, the revolutionary monster, with the harmless, pastoral Reverend Gurney? Or of bland Kermit with the terrible patronage of Miss Walker? Or consider the peril to narrative texture in the melodramatic death of Susan—without contrivance, indirection, or evasion!

If the texture is not uniform, the intelligence of the critique is completely sustained. Laskell has undertaken to dispel the mythological views of the thirties. His Purgatory is a succession of disenchantments—disillusion about the *relation* of Maxim to his ideas; the administrative good will of Arthur Croom; the furtive callousness of Nancy with her disingenuous wish for a life of danger and morality; the enlightenment of Kermit, who buys his humanity from the workers he treats well; the nihilism of Duck, the inadequate man-in-the-street; the hollow independence of the Folgers; the devouring guilt of the converted Maxim. Only Emily maintains herself against disenchantment; she, and Susan, for Trilling shares James's resignation to the innocence of the child, irresponsible and uninvolved in the power and suffering of the world. Laskell's final skepticism, marking his political maturity, is his surrender of middle-class hope for the future. He will not throw his expectations before him as a manufactured and fictitious life. He will live here and now, in a present that is temporal in an almost Bergsonian way.[1] Neither Arthur, the man of the near future, nor Maxim, the bloody apocalyptic man of the far future, is eligible to live with Laskell's new sense of immediacy and responsibility.

In surrendering the future, Laskell also renounces the carefully masked will of every intellectual to impose his program upon the world. In his last encounter with Maxim the struggle for power is defined in its naked alternatives. Maxim offers him a choice between competing systems—the secular law of rights for the masses, or the Augustinian law of duty for the leaders. In this collision of forces Laskell, the "Renaissance" man who is responsible and intelligent, appears doomed. But he does not admit the necessity of this inhuman dialectic: "I do not acquiesce." He will not, like Maxim, vanish as a person. And he is hated by the Crooms and Maxim, whose absolute systems codify their will to power; neither can tolerate Laskell's skepticism, or any "appearance of an idea in modulation."

Maxim virtually admits that his apocalyptic will cannot survive any modulation of an idea. He can enslave Laskell if Laskell defends himself with ferocity; for then Laskell is a fanatic, a victim of the dialectic. But he cannot enslave the tenacious flexible critical intelligence, the skeptical sensibility.

Thus Trilling pays his greatest debt not to the Renaissance as Burckhardt conceived it, but to Matthew Arnold, who was approximately in his own position, a liberal attempting a moral critique of liberalism. The bane of the middle class, Arnold said, is its hard unintelligence, its lack of responsible individualism. Against evasions, codes, partial views, and the hatreds of Jacobinism,[2] Arnold appealed to the saving remnant who could modulate their intelligence into a political instrument. There was, for Arnold, no one law of human development: "The human spirit is wider than the most priceless of the forces which bear it onward." The flexibility of the critical mind, its toleration, its distrust of abstraction, its imagination and immediacy dispel mythological expectations and moderate the will to power. Trilling moves, like Arnold, between two worlds, and his faculty of criticism and disinterestedness assumes the proportions of culture, a political activity. In Gide, too, the protestant intelligence is a means of living immediately. "Everything in life," writes Gide, "must be intentional, and the will constantly taut like a muscle." But Gide's intentions are often released in the gratuitous action, the non-critical behavior of the immoralist. The intentions of Arnold and Trilling are expressed in neither the gratuitous act nor the concealed struggle for power, but in a strenuousness of choice from moment to moment that removes apocalyptic visions and programs into the distance of irrelevancy. The political man survives so long as the critical imagination remains as tenacious and discriminating as it is in Laskell.

Trilling lately complained that the liberal ideology has failed to produce any of the real emotions of literature, that liberals have written mere works of piety. His remark must now be qualified. His own novel has carried the liberal mind deep within the imagination.

## Notes

1. Opposing Darwin's and Herbert Spencer's mechanistic theories of time, French philosopher Henri Bergson (1859–1941) set forth a view of temporality as duration (*durée*)—as a dynamic, experiential process of flux—in such works as *Matter and Memory* (1896) and *An Introduction to Metaphysics* (1903).—Ed.

2. Jacobinism, a term that arose during the French Revolution, is identified with extreme radicalism, ardent patriotism, secular republicanism, and the adoption of a ruthless minority government during times of emergency. Active chiefly from 1789 to 1794, the Jacobins were members of a radical club of revolutionaries that promoted the Reign of Terror and other extreme anti-royalist measures. The Jacobins derived their name from the former Dominican, or Jacobin, monastery where they originally convened their meetings.—Ed.

*22*

*Leslie Fiedler*

*Review of* The Middle of the Journey, Kenyon Review

*spring 1948*

One of America's most stimulating and provocative literary critics, Leslie Fiedler (1917– ) is the author of *An End to Innocence: Essays on Culture and Politics* (1955), *The Jew in the American Novel* (1959), *Waiting for the End* (1964), and his essay collection *Fiedler on the Roof* (1991), among other nonfiction books. His major work of criticism is *Love and Death in the American Novel* (1960; revised 1966), a provocative commentary on sexuality in American fiction that Trilling favorably reviewed in *Mid-Century*. Fiedler has also published three novels and three collections of short stories, along with editing volumes on Whitman, Bernard Malamud, and other American writers.

Fiedler is professor emeritus of English at the State University of New York at Buffalo. He writes often on Jewish issues. During the 1940s and '50s, he was an occasional contributor to *Partisan Review* and identified closely with the circle of New York writers affiliated with the magazine. ("I stand somehow for PR and PR for me," Fiedler wrote in a 1956 essay in *Perspectives USA* about the magazine.) Unlike most of *Partisan Review* writers, however, Fiedler became a vocal supporter of the New Left in the late 1960s.

Fiedler and Trilling admired each other from a distance: Fiedler commented in the same 1956 essay on Trilling's "remarkable aura of respectability not granted to any of his colleagues"; Trilling envied Fiedler's anti-Establishment brashness and confided in an early postwar notebook entry (published in *Partisan Review* in 1984) that Fiedler was one of two contemporaries (along with Mark Schorer) whose praise he most coveted.

Lionel Trilling's extraordinary story, "The Other Margaret," had achieved already a moving and credible embodiment of a view of culpability, and his novel had to encounter perhaps exaggerated expectancies. *The Middle of the*

*Journey*—the Dantesque title, unless we allow for a small irony, promises too much, too. And one is easily misled by the announced subject: Communism and the Intellectual. There is only one Communist in the book, and he is shown at the moment of apostasy, out of the context of Party and Comrades, in the sick-room, in Westchester (not one of the essential characters is, incredibly, a Jew—though much of the flavor of the Communist experience in America is their flavor), known only as he declares himself. Maxim is the least authentic character in the book because he has obviously never been really believed-in; an act of empathy with him is a danger the writer dare not risk; as Communist, as Catholic, his proto-Dostoievskyan dynamism is inscrutable to the protagonist, Laskell—and to Mr. Trilling.

The middle-class people, the Crooms, Laskell himself, the rich liberal publisher, the whole group that are vicariously moved by Maxim's experience of the dark heresy of Communism, are not here as they are in *fact* improbable; but the party functionary, the reality of our lives, will not come alive to illumine their second-class reality.

There are excellent things in the book—the fellow-travelling Crooms chiefly, I think, and the slow revelation to Laskell that their stubbornly youthful charm, their social conscientiousness are aspects of cowardice: an unwillingness to accept *personal* responsibility, and more ultimately a refusal to face the reality of death. But Laskell cannot hold our sympathy as he does that of the writer; he disengages from full hatred, from full love, he dissolves into his ideas. "An absolute freedom from responsibility—that much of a child none of us can be. An absolute responsibility—that much of a divine or metaphysical essence none of us is." It is the noblest version of the liberal position and surely it could support a successful novel, pre-eminently a liberal form; but there is no felt passion at the crux of ideas. The climax of feeling comes oddly enough with precisely the same encounter that stands at the center of *Raintree County*: the passionate chance encounter with a naked blonde woman bathing in a river.[1] In the hysterical liberal and the relaxed one the same image recurs: reality secretly spied at.

Technically, the book dissolves into its ideas, too; it is a schedule not a unity of those things from which a novel is compounded: death, love, suffering, "comedy of manners," a concept of freedom—but there is something, over-relaxation of the will, over-emphasis on the critical, too great self-consciousness, that makes the result not an accomplishment, but a prescription.

### Notes

1. *Raintree County* (1948), is a novel by Ross Lockridge (1914–48).

## 23

*John Bayley*

*Excerpt from "Middle-Class Futures,"* Times Literary

Supplement

*April 1975*

John Bayley (1925– ), professor of English at St. Catherine's College, Oxford University, is best known as a literary critic of British and Russian authors, most especially for *The Romantic Survival: A Study in Poetic Evolution* (1957) and *Tolstoy and the Novel* (1966), which draws on Trilling's critique of Sherwood Anderson's novelistic sensibility. Bayley's *The Uses of Division: Unity and Disharmony in Literature* (1976) also reflects Trilling's influence, particularly in the opening chapter, which includes thoughtful reflections on *Sincerity and Authenticity*. Bayley has also written book-length criticisms on Shakespeare, Hardy, Housman, D. J. Enright, and the short story, along with publishing a novel and a poetry collection.

In the following laudatory review, occasioned by the 1975 reissue of *The Middle of the Journey*, Bayley judges the novel a "masterpiece," "one of the most original humanist novels of its generation." In *Lionel Trilling and the Fate of Cultural Criticism*, Mark Krupnick judges Bayley's review to be "the most intelligent appreciation Trilling's novel has received."

The novel seemed something of a masterpiece to many people when it first came out, and the lapse of almost thirty years appears to me to have confirmed—indeed emphasized—this status: I found myself reading it with even more interest and with more of a particular kind of pleasure than I did originally. To define this pleasure is quite difficult, and yet the effort to do so has itself something pleasurable about it. The novel does not have the quality of a cult book though it became one at the time, when a certain class of reader—a not diminutive but conspicuously fastidious class—entered into its intimacy and perceived its point. It was a class of persons who liked their relation to ideas to be presented in a calm and full aesthetic tableau, grouped like the figures in a Gainsborough portrait. . . .

. . . The manner is not original, is indeed mannered, achieving almost too consciously at times an Anglican or Episcopalian fragrance, an aroma of Matthew Arnold and T. S. Eliot seasoned with E. M. Forster. . . .

The extreme aesthetic pleasure of the book resides in the contrast it achieves between its matter and its manner, between the "solid state" it achieves and the turmoil of ideas, guilts, intellectual anxieties and vulnerabilities encapsulated there like dust and flies in a polished block of amber. Such artistic indirectness is as unfashionable today as is the quietly intelligent dependence on earlier novelists and stylists which it reveals.

# 24

David Caute

*"Summer People,"* The New Statesman

*April 1975*

An unusual example of both a public intellectual and man of letters, David Caute (1936– ) is a British novelist, playwright, critic, literary journalist, and intellectual historian centrally concerned with the fate of the Left and the vicissitudes of socialism. Caute is a committed leftist, and his dozen novels and plays all center on leftist politics, often outside England (and especially in Africa), sometimes addressing historical events specifically (e.g., his 1961 play *Songs for an Autumn Rifle*, which explores the 1956 Hungarian revolt).

Three of Caute's major works of nonfiction, *Communism and the French Intellectuals, 1914–60* (1964), *The Fellow Travelers: Intellectual Friends of Communism* (1973), and *The Great Fear: The Anti-Communist Purge under Truman and Eisenhower* (1978), deal with the same themes that preoccupied Trilling throughout his long career, and especially in *The Middle of the Journey*: the relations among intellectual integrity and group orthodoxy, left-wing politics, the modern state, and self-censorship. In *The Great Fear*, which chiefly portrays how McCarthyism compromised American cultural life and educational policies, Caute discusses—critically if briefly—Trilling's participation (as chairman) in the 1953 deliberations of the Columbia committee in charge of political screenings of faculty and staff.

We are in the mid-Thirties. Through a long, idle, meandering summer, the New Deal liberals while away their generous vacations, rearing their children, painting their small clapboard houses in the Connecticut woodlands, doing a bit of gardening, barbecueing spare ribs, fishing, talking, despising critics of the Soviet Union. These are the American summer people of 40 years ago, the optimists of virtue and rationality and progress and planning, middle-class WASP intellectuals and technocrats who are too fastidious to join the Party yet despise others who quit its ranks.

Serious to the point of smugness, feigning the simple life in the context of an obvious affluence, crassly ignorant of the moral dilemmas they discuss, magnetised by picture-poster causes like SPAIN, the summer people of Trilling's novel turn with insensate fury against their old friend Gifford Maxim, who, after years of militancy in the clandestine lower depths of the Party, has now not only renounced the vision but proclaimed his own life to be in danger. And the nastiest person of all—one of the most repellent progressives in modern fiction—is Nancy Croom, the smug fellow traveller blessed by total immersion in right-thinking values.

Trilling draws attention to Nancy's basic naïveté by emphasising her romantic veneration for the feckless idler and drunkard, Duck Caldwell, whom she regards with Rousseauesque romanticism as the epitome of simple, pre-capitalist libertarianism, just as the right-thinking people in E. M. Forster's *The Longest Journey* (for which Trilling expresses admiration) made extravagant and subconsciously supercilious allowances for the erratic moral behaviour of the young shepherd. In one of his essays collected in *The Liberal Imagination*, Trilling refers to this congenital ailment of the right-thinking people as: 'the replacement by abstraction of natural, decent human feeling'. It is not by accident that Trilling has understood Forster so well.

*The Middle of the Journey*, Trilling's first and last novel, was originally published in 1947, making (he tells us in a new introduction) little impact at the time, but gathering something of a reputation as it became more widely read and known. Judged from a literary point of view now that it has been re-issued, one can admire its quiet, mature style, its sudden flashes of intense feeling, its professional capability in stimulating interest while not pretending that anything more dramatic than dawning awareness is likely to happen. For my taste, Trilling is too direct a writer, almost as if he had not quite achieved the leap from the discursive, explicit language of criticism to the world of inferences, the language of the unspoken, which we associate with the novel. Any thought, feeling or motive which affects a character, particularly the hero, John Laskell, is immediately set down on the page:

> Laskell had not thought of the alternatives before, but he considered them now. 'He might be mistaken,' he said slowly. 'Or he might be deliberately lying.' And then, merely in the way of the next step in a series of possibilities, 'Or he might be right,' he said.
>
> 'You think he might be right?' Nancy said. 'My God, John!'

And Arthur said very gravely, even a little sternly, 'Do you really, John?'

It was, of course, a very important question . . .

In the course of a fine essay, 'Manners, Morals and the Novel,' Trilling once remarked that in novels, whether they be those of Homer, Dickens, or Proust, it is manners that make men. He offered this thrust out of an argument advanced by Henry James that what American novels and novelists lacked by comparison with English ones was what America lacked by comparison with England—a 'thick social texture' of palaces, churches, manor houses, thatched cottages, sporting classes, precise social codes, strong formal conventions. Henry James realised, wrote Trilling, 'that to scale the moral-aesthetic heights in the novel one had to use the ladder of social observation'. But Trilling only spasmodically achieves that 'thick social texture' in *The Middle of the Journey*, so that one is frequently aware of his characters as embodiments of certain attitudes, as pieces in a complex game where the aim is to marry ideological attitudes to their correct emotional affinities.

One explanation for this may be that *The Middle of the Journey* is—or became in the course of writing, as Trilling explains in his new introduction—partly a *roman à clef*, in which the character Gifford Maxim represented that Dostoievskyan ex-communist and professional apostate, Whittaker Chambers, the man who denounced Alger Hiss, the man who, in the words of another ex-radical, John Dos Passos, was 'morally lynched' by the 'right-thinking people'. Trilling had known Chambers off and on, never very intimately, since college days at Columbia, and he had been aware of Chambers's phase as an underground communist engaged in some kind of intelligence gathering during the mid-Thirties. Yet when Trilling wrote and published his novel, Chambers, at that time an apocalyptic scribe for *Time* and *Life*, had not yet sprung to national fame or brought the name of Hiss to the attention of the nation and Trilling.

On reflection, Trilling reaffirms his judgment of Chambers as a 'man of honor', a man of 'magnanimous intention', embarrassing though it is that Chambers should have kept such disreputable company during the time of his redemption—notably a young Congressman from California whom his children affectionately welcomed back to the farm as 'Nixie'. Anyway, that's another story, Hiss versus Chambers, and the reader will find no clue to it in *The Middle of the Journey*, not even in the character of Gifford Maxim. Trilling's brooding ex-communist at least steered clear of *Time* and *Life*.

# 25

*P. N. Furbank*

*Excerpt from "The Gravities of Grown-Upness,"* Times Literary

Supplement

*August 1981*

P. N. Furbank (1920– ), professor emeritus at the Open University in London, is a well-known literary critic and biographer, whose work includes volumes on Samuel Butler, Italo Svevo, Daniel Defoe, and Denis Diderot.

Furbank shared with Trilling a special interest in modern British fiction. His masterwork is his two-volume biography, *E. M. Forster: A Life* (1978). Furbank knew Forster well during his years as a student and fellow at Cambridge University, where Forster resided for many years. Furbank also co-edited a two-volume edition of Forster's letters, published as *Selected Letters of E. M. Forster* (1984–85).

The review below was occasioned by the Uniform Edition republication of Trilling's short fiction in *Of This Time, of That Place, and Other Stories* (1979). Titled "The Gravities of Grown-Upness," the review also devotes close attention to *The Middle of the Journey* and argues that "growing up" is the "central preoccupation" of both Trilling's fiction and nonfiction.

The novel, though, full of brilliant things as it is, strikes me as a failure, for reasons that have to do with maturity versus the childish. Where it fatally goes wrong is in the climactic fifth-act exchange between Laskell and Gifford Maxim, the Whittaker Chambers-like defector from the Party. We are to suppose that Maxim is determined at all costs, for reasons deep in his own guilt-stained political past, to destroy Laskell's new-found maturity and freedom of mind. And we are to suppose, too, that so formidable a man is Maxim and so grandiose is the duel fought between him and Laskell ("Laskell wondered if any man had ever made an attempt on another man such as

Maxim was making upon him"), he comes near to succeeding. Now, this is intellectual melodrama or opera; it is self-indulgent and not really worthy of Trilling. After all, as he himself would have held, to choose to be a liberal intellectual must entail a certain renunciation. It means you are not going to re-unite the Papacy or split the Liberal Party over Home Rule or ever cut such a figure under the heavens as do saints or men of action. Nobody is going to care *that* much about your opinions. . . . There is a great place for intellectual debate in novels and plays, but not, I think—except for purposes of irony—in realistic ones. The carefree Shavian or Chestertonian method, of making the debate the important thing and staging it Lord knows where— under a mid-Western gallows or on the dome of St Paul's—seems much wiser.

The Liberal Imagination (1950)

## 26

Ben Ray Redman

*"Reality in Life and Literature,"* Saturday Review

of Literature

*April 1950*

Ben Ray Redman (1896–1961) was an editor, journalist, translator, corporate executive, and poet. He served as literary editor of *The Spur* (1922–29) and managing editor of *Travel* (1923); he also did editorial work at G. P. Putnam (1924–26) and wrote a column for *The New York Herald Tribune* in the 1920s and '30s, during which time he also translated several French and Italian literary works into English and worked as a vice president in charge of production at Universal Pictures. Redman wrote *The Modern English Novel* (1925), *Edward Arlington Robinson* (1926), and *The Oxford University Press, 1896–1946* (1946). He also edited volumes on Voltaire and Thomas Love Peacock.

   As the regular book reviewer for *The Saturday Review of Literature* (1944–55), Redman reviewed several works by the New York intellectuals (including *The Partisan Reader* [1946], which Trilling introduced, and the 1949 reissue of *Matthew Arnold*). A well-known cultural conservative during the early postwar era, Redman admired Trilling's liberal anti-Communism, though he criticized what he considered to be Trilling's misconception, attributable to the "parochialism" of his New York circle, that conservatism at mid-century did not represent a serious intellectual force in America.

Mr. Trilling's attractive title serves as label for a collection of essays written during the past ten years that range from pure literary criticism to a consideration of the significance and shortcomings of the Kinsey Report. In the course of them he has many interesting and some debatable things to say about "reality" in life and literature; Sherwood Anderson's arrested development; the debts owed by Freud to literature and by literature to Freud; the background, themes, characters, and "moral realism" of "The Princess Casamassima"; the correct interpretation of Wordsworth's "Intimations of Immortality"; Kipling's deficiencies and involvement with the ideals of nationalism; "Huckleberry Finn"; the relevance of Tacitus to mid-twentieth-century readers; Scott Fitzgerald's literary character and stature; the New Criticism's revolt against the historical method; the relation, if any, between neurosis and artistic power; the failure of liberal ideology to produce, "for several decades, a single writer who commands our real literary admiration"; the function of the little magazine at a time when "there exists a great gulf between our educated class and the best of our literature"; the comparative failure of the American novel because of the lack of nourishment to be found in the American social field; "the question of whether or not the novel is still a living form"; the comparative lack of emotional and intellectual power in contemporary American prose literature; and the subjective deviations from objectivity in the notorious statistics regarding sexual behavior in the human male.

In his preface Mr. Trilling claims for these essays "a certain unity," derived "from an abiding interest in the ideas of what we loosely call liberalism, especially the relation of these ideas to literature." They have, of course, the unity which is due to their being products of a single mind that is well furnished with a stock of examined beliefs, ideas, and ideals; but, having read them with steady interest, and I hope with understanding, I am not sure that I know just what Mr. Trilling means by "the liberal imagination," unless he means no more than the liberal way of looking at life and letters, of which he, as a liberal in good standing, is an accredited spokesman. But even then we are left with the question: what, precisely, does he mean by liberal? And at this point the author declines to be specific.

> In its political feeling our educated class is predominantly liberal [he writes]. Attempts to define liberalism are not likely to meet with success—I mean only that our educated class has a ready if mild suspiciousness of the profit motive, a belief in progress, science, social legislation, planning, and international cooperation, perhaps especially where Russia is concerned.

So far, so good. But we are still far short of a usable definition. And if anyone says that, after all, everyone knows perfectly well what is meant by liberal and liberalism, I can only dissent, insist that there are "liberals" of many stripes and colors, with many objectives, and quote with approval Delmore Schwartz's recent reference to the "good intentions of that kind of well-meaning liberalism which cannot tell the difference between a Socialist and a Stalinist, or between a genuine defense of civil liberties and a conspiratorial exploitation of democratic rights."

Mr. Trilling, I hasten to say, suffers from no such mental confusion. Within his frames of knowledge and conviction his thinking is active, straightforward, and seldom clouded. Best of all, perhaps, he does not despise common sense as an instrument too common for an intellectual's use. He does not employ jargon. He recognizes "the dangers which lie in our most generous wishes." Following Wordsworth's lead, he does not dodge the fact that thoughts are rooted in emotions. He has no more respect for liberal than for other clichés, and he is well aware of the failings of most liberal criticism in its differing treatment of the "reality" of Dreiser and James. Nor does he, despite his insistence upon the intimate connection of literature and politics, cut himself off in doctrinaire fashion from good writing by authors with whom he is not in political agreement. It is true that he speaks of his rejection of Kipling as a "literary-political decision." But he does not reject Yeats, Proust, Joyce, Lawrence, Gide, and Eliot, although he believes them to be "indifferent to, or even hostile to, the tradition of democratic liberalism as we know it." So we are entitled to suspect that his rejection of Kipling is really a literary decision which happens to chime with his political inclination.

My respect for Mr. Trilling is so great that I can take no pleasure in hunting out his possible faults, but he exhibits, to my mind, one defect that should not be ignored—parochialism. He is parochial, I think, when he declares that "it is the plain fact that nowadays there are no conservative or reactionary ideas in general circulation"; that "the conservative impulse and the reactionary impulse do not, with some isolated and some ecclesiastical exceptions, express themselves in ideas but only in action or in irritable mental gestures which seek to resemble ideas." What he is really saying here is that he cannot believe in the genuineness of any political ideas save those to which he can himself subscribe. He is parochial, I think, when he says that "the idea of the nation has become doubtful and debilitated all over the world." This in a period when millions upon millions of human beings are tasting the fiery grog of nationalism for the first time! And he is retrospectively parochial, I am sure, when he looks back to "a time when our educated class, in its guilt and confusion, was inclined to accept in serious good faith the cultural leadership of the [Communist] Party." There never was a time when "our educated class," in any substantial meaning of the phrase, did any such thing. As often as he writes in this way Mr. Trilling speaks not for a class but for a small group within a class.

However, as I have noted, his political bias does not corrupt his literary judgments. He distinguishes between "intellectual assent in literature" and "agreement," pointing out that "we can take pleasure in literature where we do not agree. . . . we can take our pleasure from an intellect's *cogency*, without making a final judgment on the correctness or adaptability of what it says." This is a distinction that some other critics would do well to understand, and one that can serve us when we are reading Mr. Trilling himself.

## 27

*Clifton Fadiman*

*"Lionel Trilling and the Party of the Imagination,"*

The New Yorker

*April 1950*

(See no. 12 for biographical information about Fadiman.)

Lionel Trilling bears, doubtless with fortitude, the most aggressively euphonious name of any writer since Edna St. Vincent Millay. He also, it seems to me, owns and operates one of the most adequately equipped critical intelligences in the country. Many readers, trailing his essays through the magazines during the last ten years, must have suspected that this might be so. Now that sixteen of his best pieces are united in "The Liberal Imagination" (Viking), we can be surer of it. This is a pleasant thing to be sure of. We have a plethora of learned critics, a crowd of perceptive critics, and a few entertaining critics. Perhaps not since the days before Mr. Mencken mellowed have we had, however, one who could talk to the generality of educated rather than merely literary Americans. Mr. Trilling may just conceivably turn out to be our man, once he has learned to raise his voice a few decibels (he puts too much energy into undercharging his prose) and to give looser rein to the wit, fancy, and playfulness he conscientiously rations.

Though a professor of English literature at General Eisenhower's university,[1] he does not write as if his cloister were the world. Nor is he imprisoned within that narrowest of cells, the contemporary. He is neither specialist nor popularizer, having too great an affection for ideas to be the first and too great a respect for people to be the second. Rather, he seems linked to that gleaming chain of English and American critics that starts in glory with Ben Jonson and connects, through Dryden, Dr. Johnson, Hazlitt, Coleridge, Emerson, and Matthew Arnold, with T. S. Eliot in our own day. I do not mean that he is on their level; I mean only that he is of their family. He has the family trait—moral seriousness without moral self-appreciation. (I must qualify this ringing phrase by noting that Mr. Eliot's modish version of "The Passing of the Third Floor Back" does occasionally demonstrate an awareness of Mr. Eliot's own—and not here questioned—moral superiority.) Mr. Trilling is also like these critics, and like all the European big guns from Lessing to Valéry, in that he has no subject matter but only a good mind. He is on easy terms with both Tacitus and Dr. Kinsey; he writes of literature as one interested in politics, of politics as one interested in psychology; he has no stake in any doctrine and is a cardholder only in the party of the imagination. He applies to a dozen specialties the tools of a few powerful, nondogmatic ideas—which is as much as to say that the root of the matter, philosophy, is in him.

In many of the essays in "The Liberal Imagination"—those, for example, on Freud, on Henry James's "The Princess Casamassima," on F. Scott Fitzgerald, on Tacitus, and on Wordsworth's Immortality Ode—Mr. Trilling speaks of a useful tension in the mind, of that delicate balance of forces from which issues creative intensity. He quotes with approval Fitzgerald's statement "The test of a first-rate intelligence is the ability to hold two opposed ideas in the mind, at the same time, and still retain the ability to function." His ear is ever on the *qui vive* for the benign sound of the dialectical clash. "In any culture," he remarks, "there are likely to be certain artists who contain a large part of the dialectic within themselves, their meaning and power lying in their contradictions; they contain within themselves . . . the very essence of the culture, and the sign of this is that they do not submit to serve the ends of any one ideological group or tendency."

I would suggest that Mr. Trilling is himself akin to these artists, his mind holding in suspension two opposed commitments. The first is a general commitment to what we vaguely call liberalism. This Mr. Trilling thinks of as "a large tendency rather than a concise body of doctrine" and (a somewhat questionable thesis) as the sole viable intellectual tradition of our day and nation. It points toward egalitarianism, anti-totalitarianism (including anti-Communism), economic security, and a loose neo-Benthamite doctrine of universal happiness, never precisely defined. Mr. Trilling's second commitment is to a more rigorous, more passionate, more complex, and more aristocratic tradition than liberalism so far has found itself in need of—the tradition of the "natural enemies of democracy." Mr. Trilling makes this point in the course of his brilliant dissection of V. L. Parrington. Parrington, for example, takes Hawthorne to task for "forever dealing with shadows." But Mr. Trilling takes Parrington to task for forgetting that "shadows are also part of reality and one would not want a world without shadows, it would not even be a 'real' world."

Thus, Mr. Trilling defends Henry James and F. Scott Fitzgerald and Freud and Faulkner, and assails, always with a courtesy and gentleness rare in current criticism, Dreiser and Wolfe and Karen Horney and Sherwood Anderson. He defends the first group because they have, he thinks, a lively sense of "that interplay between free will and imagination upon which all literature depends." He finds the second group wanting because "it has neither imagination nor mind." In the same spirit, though he praises the Kinsey Report for its liberating effect, he perceives its defect of imagination, "its insistence on drawing sexuality apart from the general human context."

Mr. Trilling's examination of the liberalism he believes in and that most of us believe in is the sole truly helpful kind. It is helpful because it presses liberalism where it is weakest—on its philosophical and emotional front. It suggests that liberalism's defective notion of reality not only is responsible for the barrenness of the literature it produces but may indeed be self-defeating in the political sense. For an unimaginative conception of reality—so curiously linked are metaphysics and the emotions—can wither the power to love, without which society becomes a heap of stones, and of men like stones. "Some paradox of our natures leads us, when once we have made our fellowmen the objects of our enlightened interest, to go on to make them the objects of our pity, then of our wisdom, ultimately of our coercion."

The central value of this book is that, without fanfare or vulgar sloganeering, it indicates the supreme necessity of using the buttresses of intellect and imagination to shore up the trembling pillars of our frangible era. Reactionary politics, whether expressed in Stalinism or Fascism, has already gleefully undermined these buttresses. There is a sorrowful possibility that liberalism, however unconsciously, may engage in the same work of destruction. Perhaps, in fact, in our time there are only two parties—the party of the Party, whatever its political orientation, and the party of the Imagination. What Mr. Trilling wishes to do is to detach as many men as can be detached from the first party and enlist them in the second. "Unless we insist"—so runs his salutary warning—"that politics is imagination and mind, we will learn that imagination and mind are politics, and of a kind that we will not like."

This warning would have little practical effect were it not that Mr. Trilling has the power to write so that, at his best and clearest, his ideas reach the secret places of our hearts and minds. However well qualified in other respects many of our critics may be, few can do us any *good*, for few speak with any moral urgency (jeremiads are not necessarily moral), few are devoid of the impure passion to justify themselves or their school, few are perfect in generosity. ("Our culture," says Mr. Trilling, "peculiarly honors the act of blaming, which it takes as a sign of virtue and intellect.")

I hesitate to use such a banality, but I am forced to it—Mr. Trilling is a constructive critic. He is constructive in his quiet, but not furtive, re-employment, in their correct senses, of the Big Words that Hemingway's generation thought it had choked to death: Love, Imagination, Mind, Morality, the Will. He is constructive because he has so high a view, the highest view that can be attained, of the job of literature—"the human activity that takes the fullest and most precise account of variousness, possibility, complexity, and difficulty." He is constructive because he shares Freud's opinion that artistic thought is not something eccentric or neurotic or "escapist," not a by-product or a luxury, but a natural mode of experiencing life. He is constructive because he helps to exorcise that "political fear of the intellect which Tocqueville observed in us more than a century ago." Finally, he treats you and me not as if we were children to whom ideas had to be patiently explained, or privileged members of some secret order of littérateurs, but as grown men who know that though they cannot increase their stature, they can perhaps save themselves from the waste land by taking thought.

**Notes**

1. Dwight D. Eisenhower served as president of Columbia University during 1948–50.—Ed.

# 28

*R. W. B. Lewis*

*"Lionel Trilling and the New Stoicism,"* Hudson Review

*spring 1950*

R. W. B. Lewis (1917– ), professor emeritus of English at Yale University, is chiefly a historian of ideas and a critic of American literature. Lewis is the author of *The American Adam: Innocence, Tragedy, and Tradition in the Nineteenth Century* (1955) and *The Picaresque Saint: Representative Figures in Contemporary Fiction* (1959), among other books. His greatest success came with *Edith Wharton: A Biography* (1976), which received the Pulitzer Prize, the National Book Critics Circle Award, and the Bancroft Prize. Lewis also wrote or edited books on Hart Crane, Herman Melville, Walt Whitman, Andre Malraux, and Graham Greene.

In the following laudatory review, Lewis considers Trilling's criticism to be a dialectics without transcendence, a centrist "doctrine of sustained tensions" amounting to a "new Stoicism."

The words we encounter most frequently in the essays of Lionel Trilling are: flexibility, variety, difficulty, possibility, modulation. They are the marks of Mr. Trilling's mind, which is capable at once of more range and more exactness than almost any other critic in America today; they are also, one may say, the burden of his song. For variety and complexity are Mr. Trilling's defining terms for a liberal society in good political health, and the sense of them is an earnest of the liberal imagination in good working order. In his disciplined inspection of literature, old and new, we find Mr. Trilling irresistibly drawn toward any writing in which tensions serve to expand the world. He admires those minds ( James, for example, and Mark Twain) who have "contained both the yes and the no of their culture"; he prizes the ability, which Scott Fitzgerald found in himself, "to hold two opposed ideas in the mind at the same time"; he believes the most valuable insights of our time to have been made by men who, like Freud, have offered "a view which does not narrow and simplify the human world for the artist, but on the contrary opens and complicates it." These are the judgments, drawn at random from this volume, of a man working with industry and much patient skill in the main tradition of humanism: a word very nearly synonymous with "the liberal imagination"; and we are not surprised to find him pursing his lips a little over T. S. Eliot and his incorrigible employment of the "spirited phrase" (i.e., the unmodulated opinion). Mr. Trilling, whose style is rarely over-spirited, gravitates more willingly toward an earlier writer like Montaigne, who genially upset an entire system of thought by his rambling insistence upon the "dissemblable," and who was pleased by the man from Delphos because he could even tell one egg from another.

But it is not, primarily, the scholastic proponents of eggness, of the one, the simple and the same, whom Mr. Trilling studies to correct. In his adverse reports, he is concerned rather with the contemporary poets and novelists, psychologists and critics and social statisticians who have looked at our experience and have seen too little of it: who have managed to reduce experience, to make it thinner and narrower than it is or needs to be—who have impoverished it, in their account. Oversimplification is the theme of a number of essays. The sin of reduction is charged with some regret against those stories of Sherwood Anderson in which there is virtually "no social experience at all."[1] The quite different enterprise of the authors of the Kinsey Report is, in a quiet but devastating review, found lacking in the awareness of "any idea that is in the least complex." Even Freud nods, Mr. Trilling maintains, when he restricts the effect of a play like *Hamlet* to a single source and mode: an unnecessary, schematic contraction of the mystery of dramatic experience. And in the literary history of Vernon Parrington and the novels of Theodore Dreiser, Mr. Trilling detects an inadequacy of perception, of a sort unhappily common with the liberal mind—an assumption about "reality" which delimits the real by excluding from it the mental, the moral, the shadowy, the ambiguous.[2]

A right perception of reality is a major aim of these essays, and no doubt the unifying terms I have mentioned help define both the quality of perception and the nature of the thing perceived. I am not sure I can say anything very enlightening about Mr. Trilling's own idea of reality, he conceals it so gracefully. It evidently touches mind as well as matter, morality as well as economy; it is seemingly large, it contains multitudes, it contradicts itself. It resists formulation. But if the content of the real is richly obscure (and I seriously suspect that this is almost a doctrinaire richness, and that the tendency to hide is in the nature of the idea and is involved with its definitive refusal to be defined), still, the locus or habitat can be uncovered. Reality, whatever its character, has to do with society; it is to be looked for amidst the actions and interactions of men, and there only; it must be talked about, if at all, in terms of the felt motion of social organizations toward certain ends. The social, properly understood, *is* the real; and to the real, consequently, the ambiguous and the conceptual must be admitted, for they are undeniable factors in the motivation of men. In saying so, I do not imagine that I am doing anything more than repeating that Mr. Trilling is a humanist; for what identifies the humanist in any age is the habit of sub-suming metaphysics under politics—of translating questions about reality into the study of moral and political tendencies. Mr. Trilling is almost conventionally humanistic, as well, in his feeling for history ("Tacitus," "The Sense of the Past") and in his affection for rhetoric and his suspicion of logic: for rhetoric can move men to worthy actions, while logic works dryly and inhumanly with the essences and attributes of things.

It is misleading and perhaps unfair to fix Mr. Trilling's critical position in terms of this kind, especially when he is so ready to avoid fixity himself and to remind us constantly of variety and possibility. But the identification may be useful, as I follow Mr. Trilling along one of the lines of argument dictated by the humanist conviction. His idea of reality leads him to pose the critical question most often at the point of intersection between literature and society. He urges critic and poet alike to center their attention there. "I should instruct the creative artist to look long at the pattern of life and customs, and thence to draw living expressions." I am borrowing the phrase from Horace, but it is suitable enough, for Mr. Trilling is a good deal like Roman Horace (and unlike Greek Aristotle) in his method—a method which, needless to say, involves him with the novel, the narrative portrait of society, rather than the lyric. Looking long at the pattern of life and customs in our time, Mr. Trilling wonders, with V. S. Pritchett,[3] whether it continues to provide the novelist with adequate material; life, he suspects, is deficient in custom and therefore, possibly, lacking in pattern. The case, which is very cogently argued in two essays, "Manners, Morals and the Novel" and "Art and Fortune," cannot be fully rehearsed here; Mr. Trilling is nothing if not complex. But it turns on two propositions: first, that the disappearance of recognizable classes in society has effected a diminution of those "manners" which the novelist must depend upon; second, and more fundamental, that a general failure of will before the convulsive spectacle of human depravity has robbed the novelist of subject—which is nothing less than the will in act—and even of power to cope with such subject as remains. A part of this contention, at any rate, is a pretty old story in America, as Mr.

Trilling knows: it was made by Cooper, E. T. Channing,[4] and others even before Hawthorne and James, and the great novels of the mid-century may have confirmed rather than refuted it, in their motion away from "actual" society toward an earlier or a more fantastic dramatic setting.

But Mr. Trilling, who is a novelist himself, concludes with what looks like a paradox. For if the age has let the novelist down, the novelist is nonetheless one of our major hopes, and is enjoined to "do something in the work of reconstituting and renovating the will." It should be said at once that Mr. Trilling does not make the writer solely responsible for our redemption; the task is to be shared by the statesman and the man of social conscience, and the writer will be happier, Mr. Trilling indicates, as soon as he can be relieved of duty. But for the duration, he had better address himself to the business of strengthening the ideas of liberal democracy (variety, flexibility, etc.)—to invest his writing with them, and so to help give them renewed vitality in the society which his writing reflects. There is a trace of Philip Sidney[5] here; there is more than a trace of Matthew Arnold, about whom Mr. Trilling has written an extended study and an editorial introduction. Mr. Trilling shares the "humanistic valuation," which he has attributed to Arnold, "of discourse and letters." Like Arnold (and unlike the more limited and professorial humanists of the twenties), Mr. Trilling appears to cherish a very lofty opinion of the power of literature in the regeneration of society; against, perhaps, the pretensions of science. Clearly, at least, he dissociates himself from yet another familiar suggestion:

> Since liberal democracy inevitably generates a body of ideas, it must necessarily occur to us to ask why it is that these particular ideas have not infused with force and cogency the literature that embodies them. This question is the most important, the most fully challenging in culture that at the moment we can ask.
>
> The answer to it cannot of course even be begun here. . . . But there are one or two things that may be said about the answer, about the direction we must take to reach it in its proper form. We will not find it if we come to facile conclusions about the absence from our culture of the impressive ideas of traditional religion. I have myself referred to the historical fact that religion has been an effective means of transmitting or of generating ideas of a sort which I feel are necessary for the literary qualities we want, and to some this will no doubt mean that I believe religion to be a necessary condition of great literature. I do not believe that; and what is more, I consider it from many points of view an impropriety to try to guarantee literature by religious belief.

The passage deserves a very careful gloss: something which could study in detail the decline from the sharpness and luminosity of the question as stated in the first paragraph to the plethora of modifications, undercuttings, and protective adjectives of the second; which might end by listing the fascinating ambiguities in the operative word, "impropriety" in the final sentence. It may at least be noted that the pressure of words and phrases like "absence from our culture," "impressive," "traditional," "historical fact," "effective means of transmitting," "feel are necessary for the literary qualities"—that this pressure is such as to reverse proper relationships and identify opposites. But I rather think that what the passage reveals in particular is a characteristic contemporary restlessness before, as they are distressingly called, "absolute values." Both the language and the texture of the thought indicate the way in which affirmation or rejection inevitably appears to anyone who sincerely wishes to contain simultaneously in his mind the yes and the no of his culture.

This unease is a part of what has sometimes been called "the new liberalism": which is a commitment, as a colleague of Mr. Trilling has said, "to the tensions and harmonies within extremes," rather than to the extremes themselves. We will have trouble with titles here, since just about the same commitment has recently taken on the name of "the new conservatism," as right and left, retreatingly warily, back into each other at the center. It is interesting to observe that Lionel Trilling, who doubts that there is a conservative tradition in America, feels so strongly the need for an enlightened opposition that he is impelled occasionally to enact that role himself. He is short with Rudyard Kipling for being a bumbling, rather than an effective conservative. I hope it is not thought that I take lightly either the issue or the resolution of it by men as gifted as Mr. Trilling, when I suggest, as a more useful description of the centrist position, that it be called a new Stoicism.

Humanism always takes on the guise appropriate to the time: Cicero, John of Salisbury, Montaigne, and John Stuart Mill are differently clothed. But contrary to the usual definition, humanism is not exclusively, I doubt that it is regularly, optimistic and affirmative by nature. It is often characterized by a note of noble sadness, as its peculiar angle of vision picks up the apparently hopeless contrariety of human life. Finding it impossible to justify either assertion or denial, the humanist has frequently withdrawn to a doctrine of sustained tensions; and the courage, sometimes called the duty, to endure, in the midst of interminable and irresolvable polarities, tends to become the chief human virtue. This is a hint of what I mean by Stoicism. And in a period when political and social tensions, literally cosmic in stature, are simply the inescapable facts of life, the Stoic way of meeting experience can become almost irresistibly compelling.

It is not to belittle the contemporary attitude of the new liberals and conservatives to say that they are Stoics. Mr. Trilling's intellectual heroes, Arnold and Mill, both regarded the poet of Stoicism, Marcus Aurelius, as one of the sublime figures in history; and rightly so. But at the same time, I think it fair to say this much: that contemporary Stoicism, in its various forms, is not a program for creative action, but a device for shoring up defenses. It is a plan for holding one's own. It cannot conclude in what Mr. Trilling looks for, the renovation of the will for the benefit of art and life, though it may succeed in piling up enough sandbags for the will to endure a little longer. Stoicism is dedicated largely to containing the enemy, in the cold war it believes to be always with us.

Mr. Lionel Trilling is not the only, but he may be the most eloquent spokesman for the doctrine of sustained tensions. Kenneth Burke comes to something of the same position when he advocates, as in *Attitudes to History*, a "comic vocabulary" which transcends acceptance or rejection. The attitude to history I am trying to describe is in fact the one which has attracted the most distinguished support in our generation. It is neither blind nor narrow nor lacking in many varieties of courage. But the impulse behind it has managed to bisect the field of conflict and agreement—which results both in distortion and discouragement. I suspect that what we lack in our society is not so much classes and manners as a ritual investment of daily and critical behavior whereby we announce our awareness of the relationship between the human and the more than human: the theme of the greatest literature at all times. And I suspect that what we are apt to get from the Stoic reinforcement of the will is a heightening of tragic pity, the sense of identity with the human sufferer; but a lowering of tragic terror, the acknowledgment of the secret cause.

### Notes

1. Sherwood Anderson (1876–1941) rendered sensitive portrayals of small-town Midwesterners in such works as his story collection *Winesburg, Ohio* (1919).—Ed.

2. Vernon L. Parrington (1871–1929) celebrated populism and Jeffersonian democracy in his three-volume history of American literature, *Main Currents in American Thought* (1927–30). Novelist Theodore Dreiser (1871–1945) sympathetically depicted the lives of common Americans in such books as *Sister Carrie* (1900) and *An American Tragedy* (1925).

3. V. S. Pritchett (1900– ) is a British short-story writer.—Ed.

4. James Fenimore Cooper (1789–1851) was an American fiction writer and author of the Natty Bumpo series of adventure novels. Edward Tyrrel Channing (1790–1856) was an American literary-social critic and Harvard professor.—Ed.

5. In works such as *An Apologie for Poetrie* (1579–81), the first English essay of literary criticism, Philip Sidney (1554–86) argued that literature provides the highest form of human learning because it moves readers toward wisdom.—Ed.

## 29

*Irving Howe*

*"Liberalism, History, and Mr. Trilling,"* The Nation

*May 1950*

Irving Howe (1920–93) was a distinguished literary critic and a vocal democratic socialist and radical humanist. Howe wrote or edited works of literary criticism on Sherwood Anderson, William Faulkner, Thomas Hardy, Edith Wharton, George Gissing, George Orwell, and numerous other British and American authors; his most influential critical work was *Politics and the Novel* (1957). Howe's most widely read works of nonfiction were *World of Our Fathers: The Journey of the Eastern European Jews to America and the Life They Found and Made* (1976), which became a national bestseller and received the National Book Award, and his intellectual autobiography, *A Margin of Hope* (1983).

Although Howe taught in the English departments of Brandeis University, Stanford University, and Hunter College of the City University of New York for four decades, he considered himself not an academic but an intellectual and man of letters (which included his editing of *Dissent*, a quarterly devoted to democratic socialism that he co-founded in 1954). A frequent contributor to *Partisan Review* and a key member of the generation of New York intellectuals that followed Trilling, Howe was, despite political disagreements that caused a rift in their relationship during the 1950s and '60s, a friendly acquaintance of Trilling and a lifelong admirer of his work. The rift was occasioned by Howe's sharp criticism in *Partisan Review* of Trilling's conservative liberalism ("This Age of Conformity," 1954) and Howe's outspoken, dissenting radicalism during the 1950s and early '60s. Before and after this rift, the two men engaged each other's work in public as well as privately: Trilling reviewed Howe's *Sherwood Anderson* (1951); Howe reviewed several of Trilling's books. Howe also contributed an essay on Kipling's *Kim* to the Trilling memorial volume, *Art, Politics, and Will: Essays in Honor of Lionel Trilling* (1977).

The following review was written not long after Howe's definitive break with sectarian Trotskyist activism in 1947. In the 1930s and early 1940s, Howe had belonged to a Trotskyist sect led by Max Schachtman. In this review, Howe criticizes Trilling for mistaking liberalism's doctrinaire weaknesses at mid-century as fundamental to it rather than to its degeneracy and "shabbiness" in its modern, Stalinist form.

Lionel Trilling's new book of essays, "The Liberal Imagination" (Viking, $3.50), has as its central purpose a criticism of the liberal mind "as it drifts toward a denial of the emotions and the imagination." Trilling's indictment charges this mind with an emotional shallowness that often reduces life to a problem in ameliorative legislation, a drab rationalism indifferent to the possible varieties of experience, an unevaluative obsession with measurements and "quantification" that passes as science, a feeling that poetry, while possibly laudable, is ultimately frivolous and that such writers as Dreiser apprehend a basic "reality" that is unavailable to, say, Henry James.

Trilling relates this liberal shallowness to an excessive dependence on the "moral passions" that accompany ideology. He warns that "moral passions" can be even more wilful and restrictive than the "self-seeking passions," and that while it is right to act against social injustice, such action does not settle all moral problems but raises difficult new ones. Though I cavil at Trilling's pejorative use of the term "ideology," I must, as a writer more deeply involved in ideology than he, assent to his warning; his essays, I have found, do help prevent intellectual calcification. But I would also suggest that perhaps the time has come to stand his warning on its head, to urge that while a concern with moral problems is right in itself, it is no adequate substitute for an *active* moral passion against social injustice. Has, in fact, the past decade of American intellectual life been conspicuous for "moral passion"? My impression is that recent American liberalism has been tainted by opportunist self-compromise, which a writer inclined to harshness might even connect with the "self-seeking passions," and that much of the imaginative barrenness Trilling rightly finds in liberalism has been due less to intransigent commitment than to the shabbiness of what that commitment has become.

Yet my quarrel is not with Trilling's description of the liberal mind, which seems to me very keen, but with what I think is his failure adequately to place that description in history. What has liberalism meant to the Western world? First, a code of intellectual tolerance and freedom. Second, the Enlightenment—the life of reason, secularism, confidence in man's power to shape his fate. Third, a political doctrine that, with whatever ameliorative qualifications, has meant the support of capitalism. Now in the first sense we all presumably wish to be liberal; in the second we all should; but when we reach the third at least a few of us get off the train.

Once, however, we recognize this specific political component of liberalism, which Trilling does not quite do in his essays, we must also grant that its fate is intimately related to the condition of society. Liberalism, Trilling writes, "has not been able to produce a literature which can strongly engage our emotions." This is true—*but it has not always been true.* Stendhal, Dickens, Turgenev, Byron, Wordsworth in by no means his worst days— these are writers who do engage our emotions and, in various ways, were animated by liberalism. When political liberalism seemed a creative force, as indeed it once was, it could "produce" a rich literature. Of course even at its height liberalism aroused anxiety among these writers, largely because they could already see the contradiction between its larger claims and immediate usages. Had liberalism been more successful in solving the problems of society, poets would have been less prone to find it lacking in tragic depth.

Trilling, however, does not believe the separation between liberalism and literature to be caused by the weakness of liberal ideas in themselves. He finds the cause in the liberal's habit of conceiving "ideas to be pellets of intellection . . . precise and completed, and defined by their coherence and their procedural recommendations." An active literature, he suggests, will again be possible only when ideas are treated as "living things, inescapably connected with our will and desires," and recognized as susceptible to change and corruption. I must confess that after his powerful indictment of the liberal mind Trilling's corrective seems to me weak. Except for the word "completed" there is nothing in the first attitude toward ideas that is undesirable or incompatible with the second one, for surely to define ideas precisely is not to impede a recognition that they may also become corrupted. And I would question whether liberalism at its creative apogee treated ideas any less in the manner Trilling deplores than in the one he approves.

That the decline of the liberal imagination must be seen as closely related to parallel declines of political liberalism and capitalist society seems to me the essence of the problem. Liberalism is today unable to face social reality with that desperate and bold vision the facts require; it concerns itself with trifles pantingly accumulated because it fails to acknowledge the collapse of its entire structure; and such a world view is not likely to attract imaginative writers who, whatever their limitations as systematic thinkers, can recognize a ruin when they see one. Trilling's attempt to reinvigorate the liberal imagination from within the liberal orbit therefore seems to me without historical basis or urgency and excessively dependent on that mere will whose dangers he has so often observed.

A secondary difficulty in his approach to liberalism is that in his criticism he sometimes substitutes for a total literary judgment an overvaluation of those moral *aperçus* that might reconcile liberalism with the imagination. In essays on Dreiser and Anderson he accurately points to the stupidity of the one and the sentimentality of the other but out of impatience with their minds neglects their specifically literary achievements. With some asperity he remarks that the defenders of Dreiser always praise his power but fail to specify its kind. The answer is easily available: Dreiser's power is in dramatic representation, in rendering concretely Drouet's flirtation with Sister Carrie and Hurstwood's disintegration, and that power exists despite the frequent callowness of his own mind.

I have given so much of my space to Trilling as ideologue because in that capacity he so engages one's attention, but it would be a rank injustice not to say a few words about his literary essays, well known though they are. Remarkably diversified in subject matter, they are yet bound together by the fact that all derive from an active and lambent mind. Two of the essays seem to me perfect of their kind. A short essay on "Huck Finn" completely evokes the meaning and spirit of the book, is itself a beautiful piece of prose, and moves to the highest level available to criticism—that state of cultivated rapport between critic and reader which transcends a mere exchange of opinion because it is something better, a sharing of tastes. And the long essay on "The Princess Casamassima" is a remarkable piece of virtuosity in which several critical "approaches" are effortlessly employed but all subsumed under Trilling's individual voice. One here feels that criticism comes not from a metaphor-chopping machine but from a deeply concerned human mind.

The two essays on Freud and Literature and Art and Neurosis are compelling statements, though the latter seems to me marred by Trilling's failure to acknowledge the role of social "alienation" in shaping the artist's psychic condition. And in the book's last three essays, generalized discussions of the modern novel, it is highly pleasing to find Trilling insisting that ideas, far from being unassimilable in the novel, are often essential to it; that there is no large gap between elemental emotion and sophisticated thought but that on the contrary power of thought is usually a condition for depth of feeling; and that the most fruitful possibility for the novel in the coming years will be in the sort of minute examination of conflicts between ideological groups that it once made of the conflicts between social classes.

Unlike a good many critics of our day Trilling writes with a high regard for the possibilities of the English language, for the dramatic gesture an essay may become, and for the sheer pleasure discussion of literature can bring. At one point he remarks that intellectual assent is not the same as agreement, and that we can respond "to the power or grace of a mind without admitting the rightness of its intention or conclusion." There are many places in Trilling's book where one finds the pleasure of agreement, but I take it as the particular value of his essays that the pleasure is no less when one's response is assent.

# 30

*Stephen Spender*

*"Beyond Liberalism,"* Commentary

*August 1950*

One of Britain's prominent men of letters in the twentieth century, Stephen Spender (1909–95) was a poet, playwright, critic-essayist, editor, and translator. Often associated with the circle around W. H. Auden, Spender gained fame as a poet in the early 1930s, when he experienced his poetical and political comings-of-age, embraced communism, and began writing committed left-wing poetry such as the collection *Poems* (1933). By the time of *Ruins and Visions: Poems, 1934–42* (1942), Spender had distanced himself from communism, a move that evolved into a complete break and issued forth in Spender's contribution to Richard Crossman's famous collection of anti-communist testimony from former communists, *The God That Failed* (1950). Spender's poetic achievement is best represented by his *Collected Poems, 1928–85* (1985).

   As the following review suggests, the arc of Spender's relationship to the liberal imagination thus resembled, even if the trajectory were indeed longer and more extreme and burdened, that of Trilling on the topics of communism, ideology, and collectivist panaceas. Spender and Trilling were personally acquainted as a result of their active participation in London–New York intellectual circles and their contributions to magazines such as *Commentary*, *Partisan Review* (on which Spender served as a consulting editor), and *Encounter* (which Spender co-edited for several years). In this review, written at the time of Spender's own reconsideration of his political evolution in *The God That Failed*, Spender faults Trilling for failing to go "beyond" his liberal *Partisan Review* circle and fully appreciate the conservative critique of liberalism.

This is a difficult book to review. The difficulty is that Mr. Trilling has a single theme—a critical examination of the influence of liberal ideas on contemporary literature—but this theme is too often not at the center of his book. Indeed, at moments one almost suspects that he discovered his theme after he had finished it. *The Liberal Imagination* consists of writings suited to occasions; lectures delivered, papers read, essays, prefaces, and so on. All these are certainly worth collecting into a volume. But the book falls rather between two stools of being a miscellaneous collection and being a series of connected essays to illustrate one thesis.

In an earlier review which I have destroyed, I allowed myself to be too easily distracted by trailing several of Mr. Trilling's opinions which—important as they are—remain outside his main argument. For example, his view—extravagant to my mind—that *The Princess Casamassima* can be grouped with the great realist novels of the 19th century: *Le Rouge et le Noir*, *Le Père Goriot*, *Great Expectations*, and *L'Education Sentimentale*. But—I protested—is it conceivable that if Balzac or Flaubert had been writing in English a novel of London low political life, he would have called his hero "Hyacinth"? All Mr. Trilling's demonstrations that the kind of fantastic plotting in which James involves his characters is feasible because such things did happen at the time in St. Petersburg, Dublin, and Paris, do not convince me that *The Princess Casamassima* is a Londonish novel: and that is what has to be proved.

The foregoing remarks will illustrate how easy it is to be led away from the subject of Mr. Trilling's book into a discussion of his critical views. So now I shall resolutely direct my attention to the main subject, which gives the title to this book: *The Liberal Imagination.*

Mr. Trilling thinks the liberal imagination defective, and it is scarcely too much to say that his book might well be entitled "The Liberal Lack of Imagination." What it amounts to is that liberals are inclined to—or do—live within a spiritual orthodoxy of belief in progress and support of humanitarian causes, which is based on their having a generalized view of humanity as a whole and neglecting to examine closely the nature of the individual human heart. Thus the situation arises that the liberal creative writers, with their diffused social vision, have not had the profoundest things to say about people, and are in fact not the best writers: despite the generally accepted liberalism of our educated society, the best writers are men with illiberal views.

It is necessary here to quote rather extensively from Mr. Trilling's analysis of the situation, in order to discuss it without the risk of distortion. One reason for quoting is that Mr. Trilling makes assertions about liberalism in the United States which could not possibly be made about it in Europe; and as a European it is necessary for me to keep this distinction before me; it is very evident in the following:

"In the United States at this time liberalism is not only the dominant but even the sole intellectual tradition. For it is the plain fact that nowadays there are no conservative or reactionary ideas in general circulation. This does not mean, of course, that there is no impulse to conservatism or to reaction. Such impulses are certainly very strong, perhaps even stronger than most of us know. But the conservative impulse and the reactionary impulse do not, with some isolated and some ecclesiastical exceptions, express themselves in ideas but only in action or in irritable mental gestures which seek to resemble ideas."

The above paragraph is very puzzling to a European like myself, firstly because, from three thousand miles away, America often appears the most conservative country in the world. However, it is quite possible that America could be conservative and all the writers liberals—though I am left wondering whether Allen Tate, William Faulkner, and a few others can be described as such, and if they are not, whether their conservatism can be dismissed as a gesture. But my second reason for being amazed is that European intellectual life without "conservative or reactionary ideas" seems almost unthinkable. For instance, a great part of the genius of modern French literature is profoundly conservative and even reactionary. And in England, a conservative movement, led by the ex-American T. S. Eliot, and certainly including writers like Evelyn Waugh and Graham Greene, has a wide influence.

In fact, I can only consider a liberal orthodoxy in relation to a conservative one. To me, liberalism is the belief in the improvability, if not the perfectibility, of man: conservatism (from a literary point of view at all events—politicians we need not discuss, because they have long ceased to know what political principles are about) is the belief that individual man cannot be improved, therefore he must be disciplined and must exist in a hierarchy which owes much to a tradition based on an understanding of the unchanging qualities of human nature; though the order of the hierarchy and the conditions it imposes may be adjusted in order to alleviate man's circumstances.

So, fundamentally, the conservative-liberal controversy is a debate about the nature of man. And curiously enough this kind of political thinking exists far more deeply today in our intellectual life than in politics itself, where divisions of interest have more and more superseded divisions of philosophy.

The difficulty of Mr. Trilling's position—which appears to be that, being an American intellectual, he simply cannot believe that a conservative intellectual life exists—is that he still has to explain why the best writers in our time are not ideologically liberals, and why the liberal critics are so sentimental as to regard Theodore Dreiser as a realist and the world of Henry James as quite unreal. The great and enormous virtue of Mr. Trilling is that he is extremely honest and he sees all the liberal failings very clearly. Faced, though, by the illiberalism of the best modern writers, he simply shrugs off their conservatism as though it were accidental, and uses their creative achievement as a critical weapon against the liberals:

"If . . . we name those writers who . . . are to be thought of as the monumental figures of our time, we see that to these writers the liberal ideology has at best been a matter of indifference. Proust, Joyce, Lawrence, Eliot, Yeats, Mann (in his creative work), Kafka, Rilke, Gide [why Gide?—S.S.]—all have their own love of justice and the good life, but in not one of them does it take the form of a love of the ideas which liberal democracy, as known by our educated class, has declared respectable. So that we can say that no connection exists between our liberal educated class and the best of the literary minds of our time. [But it is fallacious to argue that because the best writers are not liberals therefore the liberals have no connection with their work.—S.S.] The same fatal separation is to be seen in the tendency of our educated liberal class to reject the tough, complex psychology of Freud for the easy, rationalistic optimism of Horney and Fromm." [But surely if ever there was a liberal it was Freud himself, and by the argument which Mr. Trilling himself has just used, this would seem to show that there is a connection between the liberals and the liberal Freud.—S.S.]

My inserted remarks demonstrate how difficult it is to review Mr. Trilling without being led astray by the red herrings of his generalizations. Generalization, of course, is not necessarily wrong, or "fatal" as Mr. Trilling would probably call it. It is a method of argument, but a peculiarly disconcerting one if misused: and I think that Mr. Trilling's generalizations (like the one about there being no American conservative intellectual life—which I really am beginning to doubt at this stage of my review) make his main argument into a kind of obstacle race in which one is continually being tripped up by some extremely dubious statement.

However, I agree with the general drift of the paragraph I have quoted, even though the drift is far too general. Mr. Trilling defends the writers he has cited for their seriousness, and accepts their position as critics of a too easygoing liberalism. But he does not inquire what that orthodoxy is which all these writers share, and which is absent from the liberal intellectuals. I suggest that it is belief in original sin. Leaving Gide out of it (I don't know why Mr. Trilling ever put him in), what Proust, Joyce, Kafka, Rilke, Eliot, Yeats, and perhaps even Lawrence have in common, is an underlying conviction that man has fallen, and that each individual human being has inherited a burden of guilt which extends far beyond himself and for which nevertheless he must in some way atone in order that he may be redeemed.

I do not have to inquire into the theological implications of such a view in order to pose what I think is the central question of a debate between the liberal and the "traditionalist conservative" views. It is: does the view that man is fallen and innately sinful give us a deeper insight into the individual human heart than the one that he is a creature whose bad qualities are entirely the result of his environment, so that individual man improves in a ratio proportionate to the improvement of social conditions?

Now the opposition of these points of view confronts us with the discomforting paradox which explains, among other things, the defection of many writers, during the past century, from a youthful liberalism to a middle-aged conservativism. The paradox is that the views which politically are most useful to humanity may give us a too optimistic picture of individual man: whereas those which tell us the most important truth about the human heart—that it is indeed black—encourages reactionary and even tyrannical politics. Writers shift from liberalism to conservatism because it is more important to them in their work to have an exact picture of the nature of individuals than to have vaguely beneficial views about the whole of society.

Both conservative and liberal views if they are developed in isolation from one another are false, and, if pushed to extremes, reveal their falsity. Contemporary politics does push things to extremes, and we get the extreme of one aspect of the liberal view in Communism; and the extreme of cynicism about human nature in fascism. The Communist argument (economic liberty under political dictatorship) is that given good conditions, human nature will improve, therefore the men who are committed to introducing good conditions (i.e., the members of the Party) can use whatever methods an abstract necessity dictates. This leaves out of account the fact that the men who direct the Communist society are bad and fallen like all men, and are motivated not just by objective history, but by self-interest, vanity, and lust for power. The fascists start from the opposite point of view that all men are bad and therefore must be dictated to by a reactionary traditionalist elite.

What democracy really requires is a synthesis of that which is true in conservatism and that which is true in liberalism. Liberalism should be tested by the capacity of liberals to combine their programs for improvement with a realistic view of the qualities of human individuals; conservatism should be tested by the determination of those who believe in original sin to improve man's environment nonetheless. In effect, the conservative-liberal opposition should wither away in a living democracy and be superseded by a kind of revolutionary traditionalism; that is to say, a determination to improve conditions, inseparably fused with a determination that the most valuable characteristics of tradition should be reborn within the future.

This brings me back to *The Liberal Imagination.* Mr. Trilling has stated two or three of the positions which most need stating in this book. He has analyzed with great authority the relationship of literature to the deepest political currents of a country and an age. He puts his finger on the weaknesses of the liberal orthodoxy, and he has indicated the self-criticism of which the progressive thinkers stand in need: "A criticism which has at heart the interests of liberalism might find its most useful work not in confirming liberalism in its general sense of rightness but rather in putting under some degree of pressure the liberal ideas and assumptions of the present time. If liberalism is, as I believe it to be, a large tendency rather than a concise body of doctrine, then, as that large tendency makes itself explicit, certain of its particular expressions are bound to be relatively weaker than others, and some even useless and mistaken."

He might be criticized for analyzing the symptoms of liberal weaknesses rather than searching for the root of the disease. He accepts perhaps too easily the Goethean view that "there is no such thing as a liberal idea, only liberal sentiments." The test of sentiments today lies in action: and action seems to be above all what is required of American liberals. For liberals, action may mean giving up a great deal, if not all, in order to save the soul of the world: and it is this kind of action which the vague liberal benevolence seems disinclined to undertake. But perhaps to have considered this would have led Mr. Trilling too far into politics. What seems the most serious defect in his book is his quite remarkable unawareness of any points of view which seriously challenge liberalism. The kind of discussion which is to be found in the remarkable correspondence between the socialist-minded J. B. Yeats and his son, the poet W. B. Yeats, does not exist here. Yet surely there are not just liberal writers and those who are not liberal through some kind of deficiency which nevertheless enables them to write better than the liberals? There is a serious anti-liberal ideology which has produced the best literature of our time, and this is the real challenge to liberal intellectuals. It is a pity that Mr. Trilling can find nothing to take seriously in the conservatism of W. H. Auden, Ezra Pound, T. S. Eliot, Allen Tate, Robert Lowell,

Peter Viereck,[1] and others—considered, that is, as conservatism, and not just as lack of liberal ideology.

## Notes

1. Peter Viereck (1916– ), an American poet and conservative critic, is author of *Conservatism Revisited: The Revolt against Revolt, 1815–1949* (1950) and *Shame and Glory of the Intellectuals: Babbitt Jr. vs. the Rediscovery of Values* (1953).—Ed.

## 31

*R. P. Blackmur*

*"The Politics of Human Power," in* The Lion and the

Honeycomb *{originally published in* Kenyon Review*}*

*1955 {autumn 1950}*

R. P. Blackmur (1904–65) was a poet-critic and essayist. He wrote three books of lyrical poetry and thought of himself chiefly as a poet, but he was also a brilliant textual critic and influential literary theorist. Among his main works of criticism are *Double Agent: Essays in Craft and Elucidation* (1935), *The Expense of Greatness* (1940), and *The Lion and the Honeycomb: Essays in Solicitude and Critique* (1955), which includes the essay below.

A member of the English department at Princeton University for a quarter century, Blackmur was known as one of the prominent members of the New Critics, though by the time of the review of *The Liberal Imagination* in 1950, he had distanced himself from the movement and indeed from practical criticism altogether, turning instead toward literary theory and aesthetics (though he continued to write criticism about the novel).

Blackmur and Trilling were personally acquainted and taught as visiting faculty members in the summer school of the Kenyon School of Letters. In the positive review below, Blackmur praises Trilling for "cultivat[ing] a mind not entirely his own," that is, for his self-questioning and dialectical sensibility, his resistance to ossified ideological "thought," and his commitment to flexible "thinking" and to "experience." Trilling's subject is the condition of the public mind and "the politics of human power," and his critical humanist "platform" is the independent, non-doctrinaire liberal imagination, insofar as it "survives in him and us."

Part of the pleasure of seeing Mr. Trilling's essays brought together surely consists in finding what he has been up to all along. As they came out in periodicals, or as one heard them from platforms, it always seemed that their author wrote from a solid, though developing, point of view, from some vantage, not precisely that of the audience, but which the audience was under the natural expectation to share, like the weather, or even like the momentum of society. The words seemed to have a source and a purpose, an origin and a destination. It was rather like Reinhold Niebuhr's iteration that in Christianity, and in Christianity alone, history is meaningful[1]—but the meaning is not yet. Now reading the essays all together, although we see that the meaning is still not revealed, we see better by what means, and against what difficulties, the author goes about the business of cultivating his long hope.

We see that he cultivates a mind never entirely his own, a mind always deliberately to some extent what he understands to be the mind of society, and also a mind always deliberately to some extent the mind of the old European society taken as corrective and as prophecy. He is always aware, to use one of his phrases, of the *cost* of civilization. He knows the price of glory and the price of equity; that the price of one may be the expense of the other; that the two are incompatible; and that both prices must be paid. He knows; or at any rate he knows that he does not know. I suppose that if he accepted this language at all, he would allow that this knowledge represents the Human price; and he might go on that this is why he has cut down on tykish impulses and wild insights, why he insists on using a mind never entirely his own.

He has always wanted a pattern, whether a set or a current, a pattern of relevant ideas as a vantage from which to take care of his occasional commitments. When he can find the current he will swim in it, when he cannot he will accept the set; in either case they will be the ideas which seem to be the furniture of the American liberal imagination; and in either case he tries to make these ideas the tools of positive reaction and response. He does not ask the question in so many words, but his book asks it: What on earth else is the American mind to do in the effort to control the understanding of that new thing in history, the mass urban society? What else can be done in a society committed to universal education which yet at every level distrusts the intellect?

One of the alternatives is to call Mr. Trilling's habit of mind, as R. W. B. Lewis has done, the New Stoicism, and that is the alternative I would rather expect to be popular among the heirs to nineteenth-century humanism whether in its liberal form or not. Stoicism is a confession of failure and in our society the confession of failure is a howling success. But Mr. Trilling does not confess failure; it is one of the freakish qualities of his mind that he does not make any confessions at all. More formally, I do not believe that Mr. Trilling makes virtue the highest good in any practicable sense; nor does he concentrate on ethics and the control of passions; nor is he indifferent to pleasure and pain; nor does he blot himself out in favor of self-control. He wants only to control what is there; he finds special forms of reality in the quarrel of pleasure and pain; he finds passion a source of thought and the overestimation of virtue a tragic impulse. These are very different matters, and whatever they may be called they ought not to be called stoicism. Nor does he grin and bear it in the Boy Scout adulteration of stoicism. His fortitude, which he shares with the stoic, and most other forms of surviving life, is of a very different order; his fortitude may cut his gains along with his losses out of obstinacy in particulars or weakness in sensibility, but so does any fortitude that rests on choice. He has the fortitude, in his essays, to act by choice as a public (res publica) mind. It is his business to take a position, to react and to respond, between incommensurable forces. He is an administrator of the affairs of the mind. He is everywhere against the passive as he is against escape into the long view or aggression into the moral view. (He quotes approvingly Niebuhr on Kant that the Radical Evil is "man's inclination to corrupt the imperatives of morality so that they may become a screen for the expression of self-love.") There is a world of difference between the kind of acceptance which is a surrender of the insurrectionary and initiatory powers of mind and the kind of acceptance which is an insistance (even when it does not share them) on the conditions of effort and which derives from that insistence the necessity for insurrection and initiative. It is the difference between saying that the job cannot be done and saying that the job must be done over again at the cost of any insurrection and any initiative. It may be that to hold such notions and be without the power of anything but critical action is to be a stoic in fact. To Mr. Trilling it is an aspect of what he calls moral realism; it is a very different thing from the stoicism which Henry Adams used to call moral suicide. Put another way, Mr. Trilling requires the development not the attrition of values in the conflict between morals and experience; and his chief complaint is against the attrition of value after value, often mistaken for the hardening, and sometimes for the prophecy, of value in the contemporary American mind.

It is true that he makes these distinctions chiefly in discussing novelists, but I do not see any radical distinction between the novelist's mind and other minds. He gives us Faulkner and Hemingway as exceptions to the very stoicism which Mr. Lewis fastens upon him; he presents them as writers in whom ideas flourish and the mind has power. The mind in question would seem to be the mind of primitive terror and childhood piety, almost a nightmare piety, and it would seem to me Mr. Trilling gives this mind more credit than it deserves, for it reaches full action in the "moral realism" of the reader, not its own.

But let us take an example of what Mr. Trilling actually does in an essay which raises these questions in a substantively remote form, though it no doubt reached Mr. Trilling as a piece of occasional writing, that is, as a book review. This is the short essay on a new printing of the Annals of Tacitus. The commitment of course was to find a living value in a classic, a classic which perhaps Mr. Trilling had never previously read. A living value is what the liberal imagination is supposed to find in a classic, especially in one newly read or re-read. Well, Tacitus is an historian, and the relevant pattern of ideas with which to think about an historian has to do with the special relation of the individual to history, to *historismus* as it trespasses into literature, and to the philosophy of history as it corrects the other two relations. In the Annals, there is the staring fact that the Rome Tacitus described is such a sink of human degradation that it ought not to have survived but did survive. Tacitus left out all the history which to most modern historians has to do with survival; he contented himself or exacerbated himself by giving a close account of what did actually survive. Tacitus had nothing of that long view of the modern historians of the Empire which abstracts the survival from those who lived. His own "long view" was republican and ancestral and his ancestors were dead: alive only as standards of perception and indications for judgment; and under those standards he made a work of art. It is one of the possibilities of history, taken as an art, to remind us in images of permanent horror and permanent glory, that although we live because of the long view, because of some leap or at least some overlap of minds, the conditions of life are anterior and posterior to any long view whatsoever. Seeing that, Froissart and Bede are better historians than we think when we do not see that.[2] The conditions of life are immitigable; its significance always to be created, again.

This is of course not Trilling's language, and he might take affront at these mutilations of his ideas. Yet something of this sort of translation of what he actually wrote is the only way I know to make a response to it; my part of the general mind is not exactly his; and to translate his remarks on Tacitus, surely the most occasional piece in the volume, seemed on reflection to give the best illumination of the general working of his mind. Think of Tacitus, think of literature, think of society in between. It is because in his thinking none of these terms can be ignored that Mr. Trilling is primarily a literary critic, and neither an historical critic nor a social critic except secondarily; and it is because all three terms are continuously present (no one can be used to get rid of either of the others) that he is, in intention, finally the critic plain, without distinction. It is only in his excesses, or lapses, that he teeters into the social or the historical; the balance for that would be a teeter into either the purely literary or the purely speculative, the wild or the tykish; but that balance his decorum does not contain. His is a public mind.

No doubt his special form of public mind—more valuable than anything except a special form of the individual mind—is the result of his modification and development, his *correction*, of his two masters, Arnold and Freud. If, remembering this, the remarks on Tacitus are re-examined, we see at once that Mr. Trilling is providing us with a double example of the rational mind at work to control the irrational mind in the name of wholeness, virtue, and humanity. There is the example of Tacitus and the example of Mr. Trilling himself. Because of Freud, the contingency of incentive and dread is clearer than in Arnold; because of Arnold, the intellectuality and sanity of art are clearer than in Freud. For Mr. Trilling—who says that it is elementary "that whenever we put two emotions into juxtaposition we have what we can properly call an idea"—for Mr. Trilling, Freud and Arnold are two emotions which, in the concert of conflict, generate the dominant ideas of his criticism; and it is thinking of this conflict and this concert that we see that Mr. Trilling is praising his own hopes when he says of the novelist: "His inconsistency of intellectual judgment is biological wisdom." Neither Arnold nor Freud would have said exactly this. It is precisely what of Arnold and Freud remain in conflict in one mind, that gives Mr. Trilling a sense of incentive in this characterization of the novelist. As he is primarily a literary critic, Mr. Trilling is also fundamentally a novelist; and for the same reason that he is in intention finally the critic plain, so, finally, as a novelist, he would deal "in his co-existent hatred and love" not with the individual as a literary, or historical, or social object, but with the individual *in* literature, *in* history, *in* society, the individual, where as Eliot says he can alone exist, *in* a community. In short, let us say that Mr. Trilling takes for himself the vantage of the humanist who is also the critic and the novelist. It is not the only role appropriate to the writer, but it is in any society a dignified and necessary role.

The reader will perhaps come nearer to accepting this short view of Mr. Trilling's vantage as accurate if he will run lightly through the essays in *The Liberal Imagination*, and count as he runs how often the word *human* turns up, how often what is human is found or is disastrously missing in the novel, and how often the human is linked with three powers of mind: the power of story (as for Thomas Mann, the focus of the novel is in the anecdote, and Mann, too, is a liberal humanist in hard straits, a creature of Goethe and Freud); the power of meaningfully presenting the conditions of daily life; and the power, the generalizing, abstracting power, of the systematic intellect. The repetition is sometimes harsh, sometimes forced, and has sometimes the strident tone that goes with things never let alone: quite as if the discourse had the urgency of scholarship, or religion, or politics. Indeed, for Mr. Trilling, his discourse has this urgency. His subtitle is *Essays on Literature and Society*. There is a sense in which his subject is the politics of human power, with his platform that of the independent liberal imagination so far as it survives in him and us.

The essay on Tacitus is perhaps not the best example of this aspect of Mr. Trilling's mind. The essay on the Kinsey Report, with an emphasis on the indignation with which he wrote it, will at least serve. If anger, as Aristotle thought and Dante agreed, is the emotion most kin to reason, then the liberal imagination, as Mr. Trilling observes, finds its natural relief in moral indignation. Though the indignation may falsify, it is better than a half truth, and is often the only admirable response a mind can make. If you see your great subject as the politics of human power and are confronted by a world which sees its subject as power simply, a world which is fearful of politics and distrustful of the human, you have your maximum right to moral indignation. And if you see your colleagues in the liberal imagination going along with that world, you will say, as Mr. Trilling says, that the loss amounts to the loss of the prevailing sense of human politics, the loss of piety, of history, and purpose. It is precisely like the absence of Alma Venus in the Kinsey Report: the loss is unnoticed because it is total. In dealing with Dr. Kinsey, Mr. Trilling reaches his peak of indignation: his sense of the enormous indignity of a work on sexual behavior which pays no tribute to the goddess of love and no attention to love either as a personal or as a social relation. There used to be a question which troubled Henry Adams, whether the force of sex had not degenerated in America into a sentiment. The Kinsey Report, as Mr. Trilling sees it, suggests the question whether the sentiment has not become a kind of idiosyncratic appetite, satisfied at evacuation: a mere unimplicated puny act of individual power, of which, as Mr. Trilling says the Report concludes, the "more the merrier." And he ends: "In short, the Report by its primitive conception of the nature of fact quite negates the importance and even the existence of sexuality as a social fact. That is why, although it is possible to say of the Report that it brings light, it is necessary to say of it that it spreads confusion." No novel could be written on the experience handled in the Report; it is behavior without its politics and without its humanity, but with a kind of power conceived to be in charge which in any other field would be called brutal, murderous, and arbitrary, without memory, purpose, or horror. Mr. Trilling would have said this better; and I wish he could have added his version to his present concluding sentence, for it would have raised, at a very apt point, the whole question of the politics of human power. However, he does not; his book goes on into the next essay, on Scott Fitzgerald, with a remark of Racine's Orestes: "So be it! I die content and my destiny is fulfilled." Mr. Trilling is quoting from Gide on the glory of the exemplary role as envisaged by Racine and rehearsed by Goethe; he then proceeds to praise Fitzgerald by affixing to his intention, if not to his achievement, the sense of this role. I should myself say that Fitzgerald was more representative than exemplary; but I am in the minority of those who do not feel the greatness of Fitzgerald; to me even the horror of his career is of the accidental kind which lurks in any corner. But, assuming that Mr. Trilling is right in the sense that we have no better exemplar available of the role of greatness, is not that, too, in a way other and deeper than that represented by the Kinsey Report, an example of the failure of the politics of human power? In asking that, I am not certain whether it is American culture or Mr. Trilling who has failed along with the politics. I would myself say that Mr. Trilling's essay gives an excellent account of a man who had fallen into Kant's Radical Evil: Fitzgerald made of his morality a screen for his self-love. If the novelist in Mr. Trilling had only got the upper hand, I must believe that on the basis of his own facts he would have seen this for himself. It would not have made Fitzgerald less readable, but it would have made more certain what was read, which is a human and political gain.

But this is only a disagreement in judgment, the one part of an argument least likely to stand. I would say that Fitzgerald would do very well to represent, not the calling of greatness, but what had happened to the idea of greatness in the America of the 'twenties and 'thirties. Mr. Trilling took the long view; if he had taken the direct view, with only the standard of perception in mind of some longer view, he would have altered only the tone of what he said about Fitzgerald. With that alteration it would have been in consonance with the tone of what he says about Wolfe and Anderson and O'Neill; not the same thing but in consonance with the tone. Then the essay would have stood appropriately between those on Henry James and Mark Twain. What a correction of Gatsby would be involved by the pressure, on either side of him, of Hyacinth and Huck! As Mr. Trilling notes that Huck said, the conscience is bigger than the self—which is I suppose why one's conscience is better than one's morals, which are so much smaller than most selves. This is what Mark Twain and Henry James understood, and what, like the nostalgia for the unknown, merely tortured Fitzgerald.

The question raised by the Fitzgerald essay, the one I mention and others which I do not, make a very good and not at all excessive road to Mr. Trilling's own final questions: those he asks about the failure of the liberal imagination (a phrase which the more I repeat it the less am I willing to use on my own account) to provide an even relatively great literature. Mr. Trilling ties his questions in—it is a matter of counting his frequencies of reference again, just as if we were Kinseys—to the terms which have to do with intellectual power *and* emotion or feeling or passion or sensibility. To him great literature has to do with great ideas, and ideas have to do, not with "thought," which is a subject for history, but with thinking, which is a matter of experience, and which is to be apprehended as emotion. Here are two passages from "The Meaning of a Literary Idea" which express his conviction most sharply. Say what we will, he says, "we as readers know that we demand of our literature some of the virtues which define a successful work of systematic thought. We want it to have—at least when it is appropriate for it to have, which is by no means infrequently—the authority, the cogency, the completeness, the brilliance, the *hardness* of systematic thought." That is one; here is the other. "Those poets of our time who make the greatest impress upon us are those who are most aware of rhetoric, which is to say, of the intellectual content of their work. Nor is the intellectual content of their work simply the inevitable effect produced by good intelligence turned to poetry; many of these poets—Yeats and Eliot himself come most immediately to mind—have been at great pains to develop consistent intellectual positions along with, and consonant with, their work in poetry."

I cannot imagine a society, I cannot imagine any form of public mind, though I know and do not have to imagine many individuals of our own time, to whom these texts would not seem either the expression of an ideal or a noble lie for the sake of an ideal not yet revealed. But I do not know of a time when a body of such literature flourished, or when a body of literature animated, as it thought, by such an ideal, was great literature. There is the Athenian literature, which Plato attacked; and there is the literature of the Enlightenment, to which we are still in reaction. There is also Dante, but Dante is singular. It is with these reservations, and only when I am exercising the public part of my mind in the public interest, that I would assent to Mr. Trilling's use of language in the passages quoted. I like the intention, but I deplore the record of those who wrote or wanted others to write on a similar declared intention. In short, the intention is only good if kept at an impassable remove from the practical work of the mind. For my own evangelism, I much prefer the intellectual inconsistency which is biological wisdom, the "holy stupidity" of the novelist, and the "negative capability" of the poet, all of which Mr. Trilling praises on one page of the essay called "Art and Fortune." I prefer them because they seem in better support than the texts quoted of the very power of the mind, its *hardness*, brilliance, system, and all, which Mr. Trilling wants; and not only that but also better suited to promote the restoration, in the broadest possible sense, of the politics of human power, which has a *harder* seriousness than any system.

In saying all this, I believe I am on Mr. Trilling's side, only further over into the tory anarchy which is just the other side of liberalism, but I say it not to express an irritating sort of agreement but in order to explain my repudiation of his question of why it is, of the ideas which have been generated by liberal democracy, that they "have not infused with force and cogency the literature that embodies them." I don't mind the question so much as I do the attributes he gives it. "This question is the most important, the most fully challenging question in culture that at this moment we can ask."

This is the trouble with a feeling for systems; it makes such questions possible and makes them seem legitimate. The law I know says that liberal democracy, like Stalin's communism, the despotism of the seventeenth century, or the omnicompetent state of Dante's Italy, is an incentive to literature only in the sense that it is a barrier to it. The politics of existing states is always too simple for literature; it is good only to *aggravate* literature. The politics of the state is the politics of what Lord Acton meant by power, and it is only when it is "out of power" that it can construe life, as literature needs, in terms of the politics of human power.

That is half the objection to Mr. Trilling's question; and the second half is like this first. The true business of literature, as of all intellect, critical or creative, is to remind the powers that be, simple and corrupt as they are, of the turbulence they have to control. There is a disorder vital to the individual which is fatal to society. And the other way round is also true. The reader who thinks Mr. Trilling does not know this when he is not thinking about it has only to consult the remarks about Kipling and Nationalism. The trouble is that his masters, Arnold and Freud, both extremists in thought, occasionally overpower him: they make him think too much. The remedy is Tacitus, the enemy Kinsey; for all of us. But as Mr. Trilling says, thinking of the great image of the politics of human power, "We are all ill."

## Notes

1. Niebuhr argued along these lines in such books as *The Nature and Destiny of Man* (1941).

2. Jean Froissart (1338–1410) wrote *The Prison of Love*, among other works, in which he vividly and often playfully chronicled his knightly adventures in England, France, and Spain between the reigns of Edward II and Henry IV during the Hundred Years' War. The Venerable Bede (672–735), theologian and writer, is best known for his *Ecclesiastical History of the English People*, a powerful narrative that assisted missionaries in converting the Anglo-Saxon tribes to Christianity. Bede was a pioneering historian who originated the method of dating events from the time of Christ's birth—i.e., A.D.—a practice that came into general use after his death due to the presence of his historical works in the libraries of European monasteries.

$$32$$

*Norman Podhoretz*

*"The Arnoldian Function in American Criticism,"* Scrutiny

*June 1951*

Norman Podhoretz (1930– ), former editor-in-chief of *Commentary* (1960–95), is the author of *Doings and Undoings: The Fifties and After in American Writing* (1964) and the autobiographical volumes *Making It* (1967) and *Breaking Ranks: A Political Memoir* (1979), among other books. An undergraduate student of Trilling, Podhoretz earned his B.A. in 1950 from Columbia. The title of his essay collection, *The Bloody Crossroads* (1986), alludes to a widely quoted line from Trilling ("the dark and bloody crossroads where literature and politics meet," which appeared in the context of a discussion of Theodore Dreiser and Henry James in "Reality in America" [1940], an essay collected in *The Liberal Imagination*).

Podhoretz has acknowledged Trilling as his "intellectual father," and he has been both an admiring and a severely critical son. More polemical than Trilling—and more interested in current political questions and issues of national policy—Podhoretz moved rightward during the early 1970s and spearheaded the growth of the right-of-center intellectual movement known as "neoconservatism." As a leading figure in this movement, Podhoretz has sometimes (in an obvious nod to Trilling) been called—both by opponents and supporters—the tribune of "the neoconservative imagination."

The following review was written when Podhoretz, then a twenty-one-year-old Columbia graduate and Kellett Fellow at Cambridge University, was admitted to F. R. Leavis's weekly discussion circle and invited to contribute to *Scrutiny*. Podhoretz describes the circumstances of Leavis's assignment to him to review *The Liberal Imagination* and Leavis's response to the review in *Making It*.

Only one of the essays collected in *The Liberal Imagination* has appeared previously in this country, but all of them were published in America during the last decade, the period, that is, which followed directly upon the first edition of Mr. Trilling's authoritative biography of Matthew Arnold. These facts immediately suggest that the influence of Arnold was bound to be strong in Mr. Trilling's future essays in criticism, and so it turned out. Of those essays, Mr. Trilling has chosen sixteen to be included in this book, and they cover a very wide area under the headings 'writers and writing', 'art and psychology', and 'politics and culture' (this last group, as is proper, might have been incorporated into the first). Now that they have been collected, however, it has become remarkably apparent that Arnold exerted the most fertilizing kind of influence on his biographer, the kind that results in what can best be called a kinship, a deep affinity. And the fact that the depth of Arnold's impress only now becomes clear is a measure of how fully and creatively Mr. Trilling has responded to the mind of his great predecessor. For the thing to remember about Arnold is that his real importance lay in the large purpose which coursed through the whole of his work, expressing itself in terms of a committed responsiveness to the problems of his age. So that a properly Arnoldian critic is one who places himself in a certain relation to his immediate cultural environment and maintains his position of vigilance through the years. This relation I want to define and estimate, for *it* is what defines and estimates the worth of Mr. Trilling's book.

*The Liberal Imagination*, because of its title and still more because of the preface which asserts Mr. Trilling's intention of supplying American liberals with a critique from the inside, invites discussion as a political dissertation in disguise. Some reviewers, particularly in America, have indeed treated it as such. It is therefore unfortunately necessary to point out that this is not a book on liberalism;[1] it is a collection of critical essays. Part of the function of criticism is of course to clear the air. Musty evaluations have their source in false notions and thin attitudes which begin by preventing intelligent reading and—as Mr. Trilling all too desperately knows and as Arnold knew before him—end by fashioning a whole civilization in their own meagre image. If Mr. Trilling is right when he says that 'in the United States at this time liberalism is not only the dominant but even the sole intellectual tradition' (p. ix), then we can take it for granted that his unifying interest in the ideas of that tradition, especially as they relate to the making and the reading of literature, means very simply an informing concern with American culture. This concern is what finally gives to the book its enormous pertinence to the major problems of contemporary America, and precisely for that reason, we owe it to Mr. Trilling not to misunderstand its place in his work. His critique of the liberal imagination is not systematic; it does not have even the sketchy systematization of Mr. Eliot's attack in *The Idea of a Christian Society.* Mr. Eliot believes that the doctrines of liberalism amount to no more than a set of negatives; Mr. Trilling believes—and this is central—that liberalism has a native 'primal' strength to maintain it. Not the doctrines of liberalism, then, but the attitudes of liberals are under fire here. For Mr. Trilling's critique grows out of an awareness that the tradition is less in danger of turning into a name for an elaborate series of negatives than of becoming the cloak and defence of vicious positives inimical to its own interest. And to save itself, liberalism must first of all grow conscious of its deeper meanings; it needs, in short, to become critical. So that the much-quoted preface to these essays cannot be said to state their theme, but rather to set the stage.

Because Mr. Trilling has constant reference to the particularities of the scene, we think of him as Arnoldian. But it is because his sense of the details is so penetrating, and his methods of dealing with them directly through the discussion of literature so subtle, that he commands attention as the most significant American critic now writing. There is, incidentally, some point in calling Mr. Trilling's book significant; one would hardly be tempted to use the word of most contemporary American criticism. Textual analysis and the 'elucidation of complex structure' have by now routed the old literary historians out of the academy; the New Criticism is all but enshrined as a New Academicism with a sterility that begins to make Dryasdust look in retrospect rather like an oasis. Mr. Trilling has been pretty much alone among American critics in reminding us that a return to the text must be followed by a fresh departure from the text if criticism is to come alive. And we all know where the departure leads—into society, and politics, and history. That the poet has the power to modify the cultural climate and to be effective in the solution of problems was an idea which the socially-conscious 'thirties contributed to American criticism. As a general proposition this is forceful enough, but its worth, after all, depends on further definition, and here the early Marxists fell into the usual traps of the dogmatic thinker. They did great damage to their case for the social bearings of literature by resting with an entirely inadequate notion of what constitutes a problem and an even faultier understanding of what the effectiveness of art is likely to consist in. Mr. Trilling's essays do much to clarify these difficulties, and they go a long way toward deepening the possibilities of historical method in criticism. He brings together scholarship commensurate with that of the old literary historians, an analytic subtlety comparable to Brooks';[2] and a sense of the all-important interplay between literature and society that successfully counters the stigmatized Marxist approach. It will perhaps be seen a bit more clearly, then, why he has so solid a claim to the Arnoldian title in the American context.

Observe, for example, how the two essays on Freud ('Freud and Literature' and 'Art and Neurosis') together suggest that the misunderstanding by literary critics of a system of thought does not remain in monographs, but spreads its tentacles into many departments of life. 'Freud and Literature' gives us a masterly summation of the limitations of Freud with respect to literature, and goes on to show in the first place that the usefulness of Freudian psychology is not to be found in such confining literal applications as the Ernest Jones study of *Hamlet*, nor even in such modest attempts as Franz Alexander's interpretation of *Henry IV*.[3] Instead, what must be pondered is the philosopher whose sense of the human mind was of an organism to which the making of poetry was a *natural* activity, and whose principles 'are so clearly in the line of the classic tragic realism' (p. 57). This is a Freud whose views do not 'narrow and simplify the human world for the artist but on the contrary open and complicate it' (p. 57). In other words, this is a Freud who creates the climate for great literature. The other Freud, the one who has been invoked to support the belief that neurosis is the cause of genius, is imaginary, and Mr. Trilling in 'Art and Neurosis' supplies us with a most cogent refutation of that alarmingly current view, as well as a much more congenial representation of what Freud actually had to say on the matter. In itself the essay is a demonstration of the right kind of use to which Freud can be put by a literary critic. Mr. Trilling's characteristic method can also be seen at work in one of the largely theoretical pieces in the book, the one called 'The Meaning of a Literary Idea'. 'Since liberal democracy inevitably generates a body of ideas, it must necessarily occur to us to ask why it is that these particular ideas have not infused with force and cogency the literature that embodies them' (p. 301). The answer to this question is not to be found 'in the weakness of the liberal democratic ideas in themselves'. We must look for it, says Mr. Trilling, 'in the kind of relationship which we, or the writers who represent us, maintain toward the ideas we claim as ours, and in our habit of conceiving the nature of ideas in general' (p. 302). And in the essay, which beautifully puts its finger on the weakness of Wolfe, O'Neill, and Dos Passos as a radical failure of mind, Mr. Trilling gives ample evidence that the shallow attitude he is exposing is by no means confined to the philistine population, but has permeated the academic atmosphere as well.

But the method is in action perhaps to clearest advantage in the piece dealing with Parrington and Dreiser ('Reality in America'). Dreiser was celebrated while James and Hawthorne were being rejected, this in the name of 'liberal' assumptions—in the name of that tradition of 'realism' which found its major defence in Parrington's *Main Currents in American*

*Thought.* The disposal of Parrington was long overdue, and Mr. Trilling does an effective job mainly by a demonstration that Parrington's ideas are derived from the more debilitating notions latent in liberal thinking. As for Dreiser, who was caught up completely by the tradition and owed fame and power to his almost symbolic status as exponent and representative of what was best in American culture—Mr. Trilling carries out a devastating analysis of his work in the latter part of the essay. Dreiser's stupidity and his stylistic clumsiness are exposed for what they are—not reflections of the hard, jagged world of 'reality' but incompetence and lack of intelligence; and the celebration of him as a novelist is exposed for what *it* represents— not liberal and democratic sentiment, but a total misconception as to what liberal and democratic sentiment really mean. All of which leaves us with the renewed perception that to relax the critical sense leads to matters much more dangerous than wrong judgments of novelists; it leads pretty directly to the misvaluation of the very stuff of politics and culture.

Along with this intense understanding of what America is goes a parallel concern for what its possibilities are. Mr. Trilling knows his country, but he knows 'the mind of Europe' too, and he is like nothing so much as a latter-day Henry James of criticism who sees that the future of our world depends upon the infusion of something European into the American pattern. For James the 'something' amounted to what can loosely be called sensibility or 'civilization', and the American pattern meant innocence combined with great material strength. Well, both cultures have changed somewhat since James' day, and if the marriage is still to take place, it will have to base itself on slightly altered mutual attractions. Whatever the precise nature of the changes which have taken place may be, the fact is that the situation in America has grown in complexity at highly strategic points, while the position of England with respect to America has itself shifted considerably in the last thirty-five years. There are many new problems to be dealt with, and the old ones have taken on deeper colourings and added difficulties. In short what America needs is no longer the simple consciousness of the life of the spirit, and it seems to me that Mr. Trilling tells us, by dramatic enactment and explicit suggestion, something about the new terms of the marriage James envisaged.

At the very beginning, in the piece on 'Reality in America', we come across a basic formulation which crops up again and again in Mr. Trilling's thinking—that there is a metaphysics behind the assertions of 'liberal' criticism. It is an Idea of reality, and Mr. Trilling is quick to point out that there exists an opposition in Parrington's scheme of things—as, indeed, in the traditional American feelings on the subject—between the 'reality' he admires and ideas or mind (Hawthorne, for example, dealt with 'shadows' according to Parrington, and Melville was 'idealist' or unconcerned with the solid realities of life: pp. 9–10). No doubt this is the metaphysic of industrialism, but that is beside the point. For Mr. Trilling's purposes, the important point to make is that this assumption about the nature of reality has its repercussions. We see it at work in the American view of such things as the relation of ideas to literature, the importance of class and manners to the novelist, the meaning of 'social significance', and a host of other matters which lie at 'the bloody crossroads where politics and literature meet'. How obfuscating such attitudes are becomes especially noticeable when we recall that the diversity and variety which naturally result from a rigid class structure and which provide the novelist with a thick vein of ore, are and always have been lacking in America.[4] Consequently, the disgust of 'a vulgar and facile progressivism' at, say, class-thinking prevents the recognition of how fertile a field there is for the novel in the new groupings and divisions which America seems to have developed since James' day—a system based on conflicting ideologies.[5] This is a system analogous to class in its possibilities for literary exploitation, and yet withal indigenously American. Mr. Trilling, largely in order to make these recognitions possible, wants, quite frankly, to clear away the hostility to class-thinking in the American consciousness, and, to expedite matters further, he wants to banish the suspiciousness of the presence of ideas themselves in a work of art.[6] There are hints here, it will be seen, at a new form of influence which England can have on American culture.

I think these considerations will explain what to many British readers may perhaps seem strange and exaggerated overtures to the class basis of the English novel (in 'Manners, Morals, and the Novel' and 'Art and Fortune'). And it certainly explains Mr. Trilling's somewhat disproportionate interest in F. Scott Fitzgerald, the writer who pre-eminently saw the line which the American novel, in Mr. Trilling's view, will have to take. Fitzgerald caught up something fundamental in the American spirit, and in his awed remark that 'the really rich are different from us', Mr. Trilling hears a note of the kind of perception no native American novelist has been able to make live in the practice of his art. Furthermore, Fitzgerald was in the tradition of 'moral realism' (a concept Mr. Trilling is fond of pitting against the Parrington sense of realism), and his failure to achieve anything finally significant is all the more disconcerting because he was a step in the right direction, that direction which leads away, far away, from Theodore Dreiser. He was, then, searching for the sort of variety, within the American framework, which was easily available to the nineteenth century British novelist. A precise sense of the area in which the potential analogies lay was not given to him. Mr.

Trilling's suggestions that they are to be found, for example, in the ideological divisions of American life are not as fully developed as we might have hoped, but they have the unique merit of offering a new approach to the Jamesian problem.

I hope I haven't done Mr. Trilling the disservice of making it sound as if he had a roundly formulated Programme For Our Time, or that his book has a more pressing unity than he wishes it to have. Space does not permit extended discussion of some of the other interesting essays in the book, but those on 'The Kinsey Report' (probably the most remarkable review of a statistical report ever written), 'Huckleberry Finn', and 'The Sense of the Past' (a piece which says some very penetrating things about the study of literature and the cultivation of the historical sense), should at least be singled out for praise. His essay on Kipling, also, is a distinguished performance, and seems to me, by virtue of a lively awareness of how difficult it is to separate Kipling the straw-man of liberalism from the Kipling who is still interesting, the most valuable of the recent estimates we have had from both sides of the Atlantic. It says what has to be said about Kipling, with no embarrassed bows, and with a poise and reasonableness which are remarkable for an American critic. We are not accustomed to the kind of prose from American critics that British readers usually think of as 'civilized'; Americans have a reputation—no doubt justly—for a tone of ruggedness and fierceness and loud assertiveness. Perhaps for this reason the reviews in this country have been quick to acclaim Mr. Trilling for his 'goodness' and his 'generosity', not to mention his 'sweetness' and his 'gentleness' (the suggestion of gentility is of course suspiciously at work in that word). Mr. Trilling's judgments, however, are anything but gentle: the paragraphs on Parrington, Dreiser, Wolfe, O'Neill (like the Kipling essay as a whole) are no more or less gentle than the quick slash of a scalpel.

T. S. Eliot has remarked that if Arnold were alive to-day, he would have to do all his work over again. Of *The Liberal Imagination* and of its author, it is possible to feel that they are doing for America, at least, the work Arnold himself might have done.

### Notes

1. It is perhaps in place to remind the British reader that American liberalism has little in common with the political sentiments professed by Lord Samuel. Mr. Trilling means the loose confederacy of ideas which descend largely from Mill. But in his use of the term it has no strict reference to any political party, though it would be untrue to say that the New Deal, for example, was not more consciously liberal and progressive than the Old Guard Republicans. One of Mr. Trilling's main points is that there is no living conservative tradition of ideas in America, and that the

wide attitudes of liberalism, particularly those which embody its vicious potentialities, have so permeated American culture that they crop up even in the most
unlikely quarters. This contention—that liberalism is the sole intellectual tradition
in the United States—aroused a great deal of discussion among the American
reviewers, but the British reader will not be so easily misled by it if he keeps the
above points in mind.

2. Cleanth Brooks (1906–94) helped formulate the New Criticism.—Ed.

3. Ernest Jones (1879–1958), psychoanalyst and biographer of Sigmund Freud,
wrote *Hamlet and Oedipus* (1949). Franz Alexander (1891–1964), a Viennese colleague of Freud, wrote various psychoanalytic essays on Shakespeare's plays.—Ed.

4. Mr. Trilling (p. 212 *f.*) aptly quotes the famous passage from James' life of
Hawthorne 'in which James enumerates the things which are lacking to give the
American novel the thick social texture of the English novel'. The catalogue includes court, aristocracy, palaces, parsonages, thatched cottages, cathedrals, and
public schools.

5. The distinction between ideas and ideologies which Mr. Trilling makes should
be kept in mind at this point. 'Ideology is not acquired by thought but by breathing
the haunted air. The life in ideology, from which none of us can wholly escape, is a
strange submerged life of habit and semi-habit in which to ideas we attach strong
passions but no very clear awareness of the concrete reality of their consequences'
(pp. 275–6).

6. I have been tying several essays ('Reality in America', 'Art and Fortune', 'Manners, Morals and the Novel', 'The Princess Casamassima', most notably) together
for reasons which should become clear below. It must be repeated that I am not at all
trying to give the impression that Mr. Trilling has a 'system', But several of his ideas
flow together in what seems to me a highly suggestive way.

## Delmore Schwartz

### Excerpt from "The Duchess' Red Shoes," Partisan Review

## January–February 1953

Delmore Schwartz (1913–66) was a poet and short-story writer. His celebrated short story, "In Dreams Begin Responsibilities," was the featured
work of fiction in the opening issue of the refounded *Partisan Review* in 1937.
Schwartz also published two well-received books, the story collection *The
World Is a Wedding* (1948) and *Summer Knowledge* (1960), a poetry collection
that won the Bollingen Prize.

An associate editor of *Partisan Review* during 1943–47, Schwartz was also
a personal acquaintance of Trilling. In his memoir, *The Truants: Adventures
among the Intellectuals* (1982), William Barrett suggests that the essay below
on Trilling—one of the first negative criticisms of Trilling from within the
*Partisan* circle—reflects Schwartz's anger toward Trilling for allegedly scut-
tling Schwartz's chance to gain an appointment in the English Department
at Columbia. The essay criticizes Trilling's attention to manners in literary
fiction as a veiled, elitist defense of the manners of the middle class.

Mr. Trilling writes with much care, lucidity and solicitude for all sides of
every question. His style is one of extreme tact and judiciousness. But
beneath the surface of Mr. Trilling's style, a powerful point of view asserts
itself.

In "Manners, Morals and the Novel," as elsewhere, Mr. Trilling pleads for
moral realism. It is mere carping to observe that no one in his right mind
will admit that he is against moral realism and in favor of moral unrealism.
For by moral realism Mr. Trilling means a view of life which is critical of
moral idealism, and its twin, social idealism. Of course no moral idealist and
no social idealist will admit for a split second that he is not also a moral
realist: he would claim of course that he is morally more realistic than most.

Nevertheless I think Mr. Trilling's basic point is that we have too much moral and social idealism or have been too uncritical, particularly as social idealists and liberals, so that moral realism is now necessary to right the balance.

The novel, Mr. Trilling says, is one of the best ways in which we can achieve moral realism, for "the characteristic work of the novel is to record the illusion that snobbery generates and to try to penetrate to the truth which, as the novel assumes, lies hidden behind all false appearances. . . ." But to get the truth beneath false appearances, one must concentrate upon or possess a knowledge of false appearances, and here the novel excells and the observation of manners becomes very important: "The novel then, is a perpetual quest for reality, the field of its research being always the social world, the material of its analysis being always manners as an indication of man's soul." This eloquent formulation is marred by the double use of "always" and by the extremely ambiguous reference, given the context, to manners. For Mr. Trilling began his essay by saying that what he meant by manners was virtually indefinable. He continued by making a series of assertions which were intended to substitute a kind of circumscription for a definition: he did not mean "the rules of personal intercourse in our culture; and yet such rules were by no means irrelevant" nor did he mean "manners in the sense of *mores*, customs," although that meaning was also relevant. "What I understand by manners, then, is a culture's hum and buzz of implication . . . that part of culture which is made up of half-uttered or unuttered or unutterable expressions of value . . . the things that for good or bad draw the people of a culture together." This is Mr. Trilling's broad definition of manners. Throughout his essay, however, he sometimes uses a limited and very different definition of manners, namely, the manners of particular social classes and groups in a given social hierarchy. It is by moving back and forth between his broad (and tentative) definition and his limited (and unexpressed) definition that Mr. Trilling is able to hold forth *Don Quixote* as a true novel (here the broad definition works) while *The Scarlet Letter* (here it is the limited definition) suffers "from a lack of social texture" and is, like almost all American novels, not concerned with society at all.[1] How can one say, in terms of Mr. Trilling's broad definition, that *The Scarlet Letter*, *Moby Dick*[2] and *Huckleberry Finn* lack social texture? The equivalent would be to say that *Walden* is not about society because it deals with a solitary individual. In the same way, again, it is only by using his limited definition and ignoring his broad one that Mr. Trilling can quote and agree with James Fenimore Cooper and Henry James on "the thick social texture of English life and the English novel" in the nineteenth century as opposed to the thinness of American life and the American novel: for in terms of his broad definition there was just as much social texture in America as in England; it was a different social texture as it was a different society and it was not the kind of social texture that James was interested in; but it had just as much of "a culture's hum and buzz of implication," etc., which Mr. Trilling says he means by manners.

There was an adequate subject matter for some kinds of fiction in Hawthorne's and James's America, as we can see when we read the great historians, or a history of American politics, or the poems of Whitman and Emily Dickinson, or the biographies of Poe, Hawthorne, Melville, Aaron Burr, John Randolph of Roanoke,[3] Daniel Webster, Henry Clay, Stephen Douglas, Abraham Lincoln, Mark Twain, Henry Adams, and others. It is true that Hawthorne and James did not know how to get into any full relationship with this rich subject matter. The reasons for their estrangement are complicated and have to do with personal disabilities as well as the literary and intellectual traditions which nurtured them. To say, however, that the thinness of American life caused the thinness of American fiction is an extreme oversimplification. It is not far from criticizing the Civil War as a war and as a subject for epic poetry because no major American poet has written an epic about it! And in this labyrinthine question, Mr. Trilling's intuition and insight are superior to James's, although he quotes James with approval. For Mr. Trilling sees, as James did not, that there is often something wrong in the relationship of the sensibility of the American writer to American society. It is Mr. Trilling's description of what is wrong which is extremely questionable: he says that Americans have the wrong idea of reality, but his conception of the right idea of reality, so far as I understand it, merely substitutes a new overemphasis and a new one-sidedness for an old one. If we are asked to choose between Jane Austen's and Henry James's idea of reality, on the one hand, and John Steinbeck's or Theodore Dreiser's on the other hand (Dreiser is Mr. Trilling's example), what can we answer but that we choose both and neither?

To continue, however, with Mr. Trilling's positive recommendations: "Now the novel as I have described it has never really established itself in America. Not that we have not had great novels, but that the novel in America diverges from its classic intention which, as I have said, is the investigation of reality beginning in the social field. The fact is that American writers of genius have not turned their minds to society." The latter sentence makes sense only if Mr. Trilling gives a very limited meaning to the word society. This becomes clear when Mr. Trilling explains why American writers have turned away from "society": "Americans have a kind of resistance to looking closely at society. They appear to believe that to touch upon a matter of class is somehow to demean ourselves." Which is to say that unless one is concerned with class and snobbery one is not really concerned with "society." One has turned one's mind away from "society" unless one is at least in part concerned with "high society" where, it is commonly believed, most snobbery begins or resides. And thus, since class, snobbery, and high society must be involved, the manners in question may after all be the good manners of so-called "polite society."

Recent American novelists have been concerned, Mr. Trilling says, with society in still another sense of the word, the sociological and political one. They have been concerned with social problems and social ideals, social conditions and broad human sympathies which educated Americans tend to think more important than the observation of manners. Hence "we have no books that raise questions in our minds not only about conditions, but about ourselves, that lead us to refine our motives and ask what might lie behind our impulses." The novel which is truly concerned with the social world and "society" has been "the literary form to which the motives of understanding and forgiveness were indigenous." Moreover, "so creative is the novelist's awareness of manners that we may say that it is a function of his love," and in neglecting the observation of manners, "we have lost something of our power of love."

What, it may well be asked, can be the reasonable objection to a critical doctrine which calls for moral realism, the observation of manners, the pursuit of reality, and the penetration of snobbery for the sake of understanding, forgiveness and love? Who can possibly be against understanding, forgiveness and love? Clearly we can never have too much of these qualities; we often have too little; and a vision of the novel which will increase our portion of charity certainly deserves the most passionate assent and allegiance.

It is also difficult to see how there can have been great American novels, as Mr. Trilling says there have been, if the novel as he has described it "never really established itself in America." Here Mr. Trilling is operating again with several ambiguous definitions at the same time; the novel in its classic form which begins with the observation of manners and of the "social" world; the great American novels which are somehow great, although unconcerned with manners, lacking in social texture, and turned away from society; and lastly, some unformulated but all-reconciling conception of the novel which permits novels of classic intention and American novels to be, in the same sense, novels, and, in the same sense, great novels. The truth, I would guess, is that Mr. Trilling likes novels about society, and about the social world, better than other kinds of novels; and he makes it clear that he wants novelists to write about manners and the social world, presenting a thick social texture. There is no reason to question this as a personal preference; but it is erected by Mr. Trilling into a standard of judgment and a program for the novelist, and it leads Mr. Trilling to suggest, indeed almost to insist, that novels about society and the social world are the *best* vehicles of understanding, forgiveness and love, while other novels are inferior vehicles, if indeed they are capable of supporting these qualities at all. But is it, after all, true that *The Scarlet Letter*, *Moby Dick* and *Huckleberry Finn* possess less understanding, forgiveness and love than the novels of Jane Austen (which are certainly concentrated on manners), or the novels of Dickens, Thackeray and Meredith (which are presumably part of what Mr. Trilling has in mind when he praises the nineteenth-century English novel as superior to the nineteenth-century American novel)?

*The Brothers Karamazov* is the best novel I ever read about understanding, forgiveness and love. It is not, to reiterate, in any literal sense about manners, society and the social world; nor, for that matter, are *The Idiot* or *Crime and Punishment*, which are almost as good, and which are of permanent interest to all human beings not because they present the observation of the manners of a given society (or make essential use of such observation), but because they are about the innermost depths of all human beings.

Mr. Trilling is often difficult to understand because he is so sensitive to all points of view, so conscious of others and of opposition, so active and ingenious at formulating his own view in such a way that it does not seem to disturb but rather to accommodate and assimilate itself to other points of views. And his critical method and style are an admirable expression of this sensitive attitude. Mr. Trilling is not using literature as a springboard toward sentiments and ideas about society. He is not using ideas about society in order to illuminate literature. Fundamentally (at least so far as I can make out), Mr. Trilling is interested in the ideas and attitudes and interests of the educated class, such as it is and such as it may become: it is of this class that he is, at heart, the guardian and the critic. Hence he cannot be criticized without bearing this intention in mind.

But given this intention, his use of the medium of literary criticism is misleading. He advocates literary opinions which would be immediately repugnant if he did not introduce them and connect them with a critique of social tendencies. And he entertains social views (and social misgivings) which would be intolerable if they were presented nakedly, as social criticism or a political program, instead of being united with literary considerations.

The best example of this process of mind, and one directly relevant to his essay on "Manners, Morals and the Novel," is the critique of liberalism throughout *The Liberal Imagination*, which he makes as one who is a professed liberal and a professional literary critic. He uses literary standards and values to establish the weaknesses and limitations of liberalism when he writes: "The modern European literature to which we can have an active, reciprocal relationship, which is the right relationship to have, has been written by men who are indifferent to, or even hostile to, the tradition of democratic liberalism. Yeats and Eliot, Proust and Joyce, Lawrence and Gide—these men do not seem to confirm us in the social and political ideals which we hold."

This is an inaccurate formulation and a false emphasis for a number of reasons. First, the great authors whom Mr. Trilling cites do not confirm any social and political group whatever in their social and political ideals: what group, political or social, has found in Joyce, Gide or Proust a genuine confirmation of their ideals? Second, there is the apparent fact, to which I will return, that Mr. Trilling does not admire these authors very much or with a great deal of conviction. And lastly, although these great authors are not democratic liberals, there is one important and essential element in their creative work which does literally support democratic liberalism, if indeed one has to ask whether democratic liberalism is being supported by any work of contemporary literature: Yeats was inspired by Irish nationalism, by folk poetry, and by the speech of the people; Eliot, on the surface the least sympathetic to liberalism, not only draws upon cockney speech and the music hall, but he presents a vision of modern life and modern human beings which, despite his avowed social allegiances, lends itself to a doctrine of social change and not to a doctrine of social conservatism, if again, the question must be raised; Proust's extensive and crucial use of the Dreyfus case is identical with democratic liberalism and would have been impossible without it; Lawrence's sexual heroes are lower class: they are game-keepers, and the like, and possess an emotional vitality lacking in the middle class and the aristocracy who are impotent or somewhat crippled sexually by their social station and by the tyranny of industrial capitalism; Joyce's sympathy for and concentration upon the common man (who is a Jew and a target of anti-Semitism), upon daily life, and upon the speech of the people, is the center of his work, and he is certainly neither indifferent nor hostile to the tradition of democratic liberalism; and finally Gide's justification and celebration of individualism, like his concern with social injustice, is one essential part of his work and genuinely "confirms" the tradition of democratic liberalism.

It is true that very often only *one* essential element in these authors supports the democratic liberal; other elements move in other directions; and all elements move in the direction of something which transcends all social and political ideals and is relevant to all of them, since the books in question are works of the imagination. And if we distinguish between the creative works of these authors, and their critical prose (in which, in an erratic and fey way, they sometimes praise a landed aristocracy as one might praise Shangri-La and Utopia), we cannot assert that their creative work is unequivocally indifferent to or hostile to democratic liberalism unless a merciless condemnation of French society in terms of the Dreyfus case can be interpreted as hostility and indifference to liberalism.

But though Mr. Trilling cites the greatness of these great authors, whenever he deals directly with literary values he is much more drawn to Forster, James, Howells and Keats, than to Joyce and Eliot; and he has the most serious misgivings about the extremism, the bias and the methods of all modernist authors.

But my emphasis upon Mr. Trilling's literary opinions also verges on exaggeration and falsehood. Mr. Trilling is neither a social liberal nor a social reactionary, neither a literary modernist nor a literary philistine. His literary allegiances depend upon the relationship of any author's work to Mr. Trilling's essential concern and anxiety, which is, to repeat, the welfare of the educated class: he is a guardian of its interests and a critic of its ideas. As the prestige and the problems of that class change, Mr. Trilling's literary opinions and social views also tend to change, and quite rightly, given his essential purpose.

To mention but one such change: In "Manners, Morals and Fiction" (1947), Mr. Trilling writes: "Howells never fulfilled himself because, although he saw the social subject clearly, he would never take it with full seriousness." In "The Roots of Modern Taste" (*Partisan Review*, Sept.–Oct. 1951), he praises Howells while virtually disregarding any failue to take the social subject with full seriousness. Among Howells' other virtues, "For Howells the center of reality was the family life of the middle class."

## Notes

1. It is important to note, in passing, that unlike Yvor Winters, Mr. Trilling believes that James knew very well that to write novels, one had "to use the ladder of social observation." Hawthorne did say, as Mr. Trilling points out, that his books were "romances," and not "novels." But Hawthorne meant by a romance precisely such a book as *Don Quixote*.

2. As Irving Howe has observed, *Moby Dick* is, among other things, a celebration of the manners of a free, open, democratic society in which candor, friendship and equality are always desirable and necessary.

3. Sir John Randolph of Roanoke (1773–1833), a fiery orator and champion of state's rights, served in the U.S. Senate (1825–27) and in the House of Representatives for almost three decades.—Ed.

$$34$$

*Quentin Anderson*

*"Reconsideration: Lionel Trilling,"* The New Republic

*April* 1977

Quentin Anderson (1912– ), professor emeritus of English at Columbia University since 1981, is the author of *The American Henry James* (1957), *The Imperial Self: An Essay in American Literary and Cultural History* (1971), and *Making Americans: An Essay on Individualism and Money* (1992).

    Like Trilling, Anderson spent almost his entire career at Columbia University. He knew Trilling not just as an English Department colleague but as an undergraduate and graduate student, receiving his own B.A. in 1937 and receiving his Ph.D. in 1953 after attaining his M.A. at Harvard. Such writings as *The Imperial Self*, which obliquely attacked the counterculture and the excesses of radicalism and individualism, draw on Trilling's work and bear close affinity with Trilling's conservatism and indirect manner in *Sincerity and Authenticity.*

    Indeed, *The Imperial Self* also exerted a major influence on the shape and direction of American literary studies. Along with the work of another Columbia colleague, Richard Chase, especially *The American Novel and Its Tradition* (1957), Anderson's work greatly expanded upon Trilling's views of the American literary tradition, particularly via analysis of our tradition of apocalyptic novels and outsized, vainglorious heroes. For instance, Anderson and Chase drew heavily on Trilling's contrast posing the balanced, narrative vision of life and adjustment to reality represented in the English novel against the artistic disorder and unreconciled contradictions characterized by the classics of the American house of fiction, especially Hawthorne's *Scarlet Letter* and Melville's *Moby Dick.*

    Anderson co-edited (with his Columbia colleagues) and contributed an essay (on *The Middle of the Journey*) to a memorial volume on Trilling, *Art, Politics, and Will: Essays in Honor of Lionel Trilling* (1977). The following review appeared on the occasion of the posthumous reissue of *The Liberal Imagination*.

*The Liberal Imagination*, the best known of the late Lionel Trilling's collections of essays, published in 1950 and now reissued, makes in its title the demand that Trilling made on us in all his work: that we look at the imaginative consequences of our politics, and the political consequences of our uses of the imagination. "Unless we insist," he puts it, "that politics is imagination and mind, we will learn that imagination and mind are politics, and of a kind we will not like." The immediate political service of art was to put before us the complication and variety of the human situation which had clearly been lost to view among those middle-class Americans whose greed for apocalypse blinded them to Stalinist terror. Art could render this service only to those who conceived of themselves as having a consciousness without internal membranes which walled off politics from art or art from moral values; who were aware that the complexities and splendors of art were the consequences of perceptions, creative energies, wills and ideas akin to their own. A part of such an awareness was a sense of the whole inward drama and the unavoidable conflicts of being a self, and a sense of individual possibilities fuller and more generous toward other human existences and their distinctiveness than that of the "liberals" of the 1950s. Freud could help, since "the Freudian man is . . . a creature of far more dignity and far more interest than the man which any other modern system has been able to conceive." It was this high estimation of our inward variousness, engaging unexpectedness, and worth which freed Trilling to employ the idea of class. He did not fear that individuals would be destroyed by an admission that we were all visibly conditioned by social circumstances. His contemporaries usually did have this fear; whether they were Marxists or not they wrote as if people who were inwardly qualified by membership in this or that group were automatically excluded from a nascent Emersonian or Stalinist utopia.

The 16 essays in this volume include the masterful pair ("Freud and Literature," "Art and Neurosis") in which Trilling sorted out the relations between art and psychoanalysis, disposing of many confusions, including those loosed by Edmund Wilson in *The Wound and the Bow*, and showed that although we might all be called ill, art issued from strength rather than from psychic strategies to secure gratification for a wounded psyche. There are essays of cultural commentary, among them that on the early years of *Partisan Review* and its place in the culture; another which deals with the

Kinsey report and its reduction of our sexuality to statistics which have covert cultural meanings. Two great essays on the novel and social reality appear here: "Manners, Morals and the Novel," and "Art and Fortune"—a third which deals with a single novel, Henry James's *The Princess Casamassima*—is of special importance to Trilling's admirers. James's social vision of the 1880s, supplemented by Trilling's extrapolation of its significance, becomes a shrewd and suggestive forecast of subsequent Western politics. The appetite for a novel of the sort Trilling sees in *The Princess* had already been satisfied, for me at least, by Trilling's own novel, *The Middle of the Journey* (1947) which articulates political ideas and the actualities of class with personal passions as no other American novel has—although some of its intentions are foreshadowed in Howells's neglected book, *The Vacation of the Kelwyns.*[1] *The Liberal Imagination* also includes essays on Dreiser and Parrington, on Sherwood Anderson, and on Twain. Other essays deal with Tacitus, Wordsworth's *Immortality Ode*, the relation of ideas to literature, and the relation of literature to history. With the exception of the essay on Dreiser and Parrington and that on Anderson, which are tied to their period in a somewhat limiting way, the whole of this collection of essays opens out toward the issues of literature and society as freshly as ever. Everything Trilling touches seems to ring with its own note; he had the secret of welcoming a larger and more variously peopled world than other critics of a generation ago. The chief mark of the criticism of the time—it was one in which reappropriation, revaluation was the watchword—was a kind of breathlessness of discovery, as in R. P. Blackmur, who seemed illicitly imbrued in the very creative process he was examining. The light and the pleasure Trilling got from books did not involve using them to affirm his own existence, or attempts, such as those of Robert Penn Warren's fiction, to patch our impaired sense of social reality with esthetic constructs. Trilling stood on the social ground implied by his recognition of the full existence of others. His tone created a social space in which the work or issue at hand was being considered by the critic in the presence of an expected reader. Both the reader and he had been conditioned by the culture—hence Trilling's use of the first person plural—both now stood apart to look afresh at the question at hand. The reader was challenged to occupy the space Trilling reserved for him.

Many of Trilling's original readers responded with a lively gratitude, but there is reason to suspect that not a few had a residual discomfort. They had been given exhilarating glimpses of their chances for a fully developed power of judgment—an esthetic experience which came from their encounter with the movement of the prose of Trilling's essays, which suggested the very cadences of thought. The prose voice staged a drama of perception and implication, set the scene for the turn—or the transformation—which was to follow, and had the capacity to bring disparate things together and make them resonate with a fresh significance. That voice was enlivening proof that mind and sensibility could hold a stressed and fractured world in view without being overset. But the residual doubt, which might be paraphrased, "Can I possibly be this much at home with my powers in a world that must be wholly changed?" persisted for some readers, and I suggest that it arose from the culturally determined flaws in the modern self which Trilling exposes.

In 1950 liberalism was strongly tinged with Stalinism, which worked to mask the individual's will from himself, making use of ostensibly impersonal political ideas to satisfy the psychic needs of the "well-loved child of the middle classes," as Trilling had made clear in *The Middle of the Journey*. Another doctrinal strain in the consciousness of the readers of the 1950s made for difficulty in the reception of the gift of full selfhood Trilling offered his reader. The idea of literature and of the imagination was suffused by acceptance of I. A. Richards on Coleridge, and of T. S. Eliot on the purely literary character of the literary tradition. These influences worked to disjoin the imagination and its products from practical and political existence; it came to be believed by those disenchanted with Stalinism that art could only be saved from turning into propaganda if the power that produced it was quite separately conceived. The artist's alienation was not simply painful isolation in a degraded society; it had the positive meaning of the need for a fierce and principled detachment. In the work of Philip Rahv, William Phillips, Alfred Kazin or Irving Howe these divisions persist; we find the critic functioning with these internal and external disjunctions in mind. Political ends must be pursued apart from the creation and appraisal of art. Of course the separation is not total; cross-references are admissible, but it remains true that the critic stands guard over divided powers and discriminable activities which have to be kept apart in himself and others. Trilling's response to all this was massively simple; he did not assent to the notion that human beings were inwardly split in this way. In *The Liberal Imagination* and the books that followed he had the boldness to try to recreate a sense of our humanity out of what had been implicitly fractured, by these influences and by the whole course of western culture since the time of Rousseau.

I can only suggest how he made an image of man for us: the human creature was a dreamer, and therefore natively a poetry-making animal; he was a fatally single desiring, willing, judging self, and a home, not simply for the turbulent ghosts of his immediate ancestors, but for the culture in which he was found, and the residence as well of indefinable powers which required celebration and licensed hope—and of human cussedness which called for irony. These traits of ours are felt as much in the texture of the critic's prose as in overt statement, and they are evidence of a power of love which is truly extraordinary because it is not reductive and goes out to all things in their quiddity. Trilling remarks of Tolstoy that what we call his "objectivity" is simply his wide-ranging capacity to cherish the variety of existence, and the remark applies to Trilling as well, suggesting that it was not science, nor institutions nor explicit morality that made it possible to conceive of the 19th century as a scene of human possibility, but a more widespread capacity to give affectionate credence to the separate existence of other people than we now have.

This remarkably inclusive sense of humanity did not comprise a method, but it was the ground on which Trilling employed his characteristic strategy: bringing to bear conceptions of self from the 19th and earlier centuries, and of their grand object, society, in his consideration of modern writers, our culture, and our society. Given the amplitude and reach of such juxtapositions as these Trilling could do things others no longer dared to attempt. He could use the names of the virtues, he could speak with authority to tragedy, he could invoke the great stubborn persons of the 19th century—Hegel, Stendhal, Nietzsche, Freud, and especially Wordsworth and Keats. They had shouldered the burden of being a self in a world in which the loss of faith had enforced upon the self the necessity of a creation which would complement it and be its inclusive other: society. Our present inability to bring society into focus as an object of thought is a consequence of the incapacity to imagine individuals who have such ample faith in the existence of human community. These persons of the past had—with the help of Rousseau and others—worried 'society' into being, made fictional representations of it, condemned it, tried to correct it—yet it now seems that they did most for us by simply believing in it, and being unmistakable officers of hope, the hope that human affairs were in some measure ours to understand and command.

As these progenitors of the modern slip out of mind, their grand object, society, slips away; we appear to be implicated in an industrial, technological, informational web whose forms and ends are incommensurate with individual human agency. Literary criticism lately has become an enthusiastic recruit in this process of depersonalization. What was in Northrop Frye an interesting departure, the exploration of the "iconography of the imagination" and of Western artistic forms as rituals endemic in the species, has hardened into the much more impersonal system of structuralism or the practice of "deconstruction," all equally impermeable to the intrusion of individual agency or of history, unless history be monolithically conceived as it is in Foucault. There are instances of comic extremity: a literary scholar writing about the *bildungsroman*, which Trilling had treated in "Art and

Fortune" as the exemplary case of the attempt on the part of an individual to come to terms with the great world, speaks of the need to "dispense with ego values" if we are to understand the patterns which inform such works! The human will is to be extirpated as idea and as cause.

To say these things, even in this impressionistic way, explains why some critics wish to consign Trilling to the shades now gathering about the psychoanalyst and the historian who are committed to the attempt to tell true stories about persons and events. What is left of our humanity in current criticism is a shadow, such as the "performing self," a self invented not to complement the human world but as the bare abstract responsible for the products of the imagination. It has no ancestors and no expectation of issue save in esthetic structures; it fears death, but has no concern with 'history' or 'society' which are competing esthetic constructs lacking the absolute and enduring forms of art.

Trilling commented on such efforts at the reduction and depersonalization of man in writing about the 1960s. But he never conceded that the current dispositions of culture amounted to an absolute which wholly contained us, as his title, *The Opposing Self*, indicates. The immediate actuality of the time had to be confronted in order to find its relation to Trilling's stubborn biological faith in human possibility. The larger contention he had with us resides in his great dialectic confrontation of our century with its immediate predecessors. It was this that caught us, and did so for the best of reasons: it lends dignity, force and clarity to our own effort to marry individual perception to individual act. Wordsworth, Jane Austen, Keats and Dickens are of course antecedent, but they remain exemplary for us; what is finally required of us is that we should recognize and greet achieved human powers when they appear. Trilling says of Wordsworth, "It is an attractive thing about Wordsworth, and it should be a reassuring thing, that his acute sense of the being of others derives from and serves to affirm and heighten, his acute sense of his own being." This reassurance is what Trilling himself offers us, and it is a gift we refuse at the risk of diminishing our sense of our own being.

## Notes

1. *Vacation of the Kelwyns* (1920), by William Dean Howells (1837–1920).—Ed.

The Opposing Self (1955)

## 35

## Harry Levin

## *"An Urgent Awareness,"* The New York Times Book Review

## *February 1955*

Harry Levin (1912–94) taught English and comparative literature at Harvard University from 1939 until his retirement in 1983. He was the author of *James Joyce: A Critical Introduction* (1941), *Contexts of Criticism* (1957), and *Why Literary Criticism Is Not an Exact Science* (1968), among his dozen books of literary criticism on British, American, French, and classical authors.

Trilling and Levin were sometimes paired, given that they were the first Jews to receive tenure in major university English departments. By the time of Levin's review of *The Opposing Self* in 1955, Levin and Trilling were generally regarded, along with M. H. Abrams at Cornell, as the leading Jewish literary academics in the United States.

A scholarly genius fluent in the major European languages and a brilliant, erudite interpreter of specific literary texts, Levin introduced the work of Joyce to the American academy. Not only was Levin the moving force behind the development of Harvard's comparative literature program, he played a central role in the development of comparative literature as an academic discipline. Like Trilling, Levin was an early champion of literary modernism whose writing and teaching helped institutionalize a modernist canon in postwar American literary studies.

Trilling and Levin were personally acquainted. But their relationship was not warm, partly due to a sense of rivalry between them. Their relationship cooled even further after Steven Marcus wrote a severe critique of Levin's work in *Partisan Review*, in an essay titled "Three Obsessed Critics" (1959). Levin and several Harvard colleagues believed that Trilling was behind the attack, since Marcus was his student and protégé.

Most of these essays were written and first published during the past five years, as critical introductions to new editions of other books. It is good to have them together in this volume, where they amply justify the claim of unity that is now put forward by their collective title. Nearly all of them deal with writers of prose: even Keats is viewed through his letters, and Words-worth through analogues in rabbinical thought. The subject-matter consists primarily of Anglo-American fiction (Jane Austen, Dickens, James, How-ells) and, rather more marginally, continental (Flaubert, Tolstoy). Most sig-nificantly, as these names will indicate, the purview of the book is the nineteenth century. The single exception among its subjects, George Or-well, proves the rule; for, as is aptly demonstrated here, his virtues were notably old-fashioned.

Now the author, Lionel Trilling, is not only an accomplished interpreter of the nineteenth century; he is, in his own right, a thoughtful mind of the mid-twentieth. The distance between this position and the mentality of the early twentieth century may be gauged by the very breadth of sympathy with which Mr. Trilling, Professor of English at Columbia, treats the com-mitments and sanctions of mid-Victorianism.

Not that his mood is nostalgia for the past; rather it is a pathos of the present, an urgent awareness of "our modern fate" well calculated to impress contemporary readers. "We have lost the *mystique* of the self." A lost *mystique* cannot easily be recovered, but something can be gained by revaluation—which, in these cases, means higher evaluation—of writers whose sense of individuality struggled against the encroachments of conformity.

Thus culture, which Mr. Trilling now conceives in anthropological terms rather than in the terms of Matthew Arnold, stands in opposition to self, which is subjective by definition. And the various selves, the literary person-alities that confront us, bear a closer kinship to each other because of the self—the critic—through whom they are related to us. "What constitutes 'us' " is a question which Mr. Trilling raises in his opening paragraph and re-phrases on every succeeding page. He pauses at one point to wonder whether Howells was using the editorial "we" or speaking for the people of America. I confess I sometimes feel the same curiosity about Mr. Trilling. However, his characteristic use of the pronoun is simply an aspect of his persuasive-ness; and, whoever we may be, we are fortunate in having so lucid and sensible a spokesman.

Self-consciousness to such an intensive degree, "the concern with being and its problems," also characterizes the literature of survival in Europe today. Mr. Trilling has no occasion to speak of Existentialism, and his specu-lative adherences are never doctrinaire but freely eclectic; yet latterly he tends to be more concerned with values than motives. Now and then he seems to achieve his intimacy with the reader by moving away from the writer under discussion.

His interpretation of "Bouvard and Pécuchet" attempts to reverse Flaubert's explicit intentions. It is indeed a fascinating paradox that this notorious team of stupid hacks, through whom Flaubert meant to satirize all the foibles of his day, should look comparatively admirable when judged by the canons of twentieth-century intellectuals.

Mr. Trilling's mental agility permits him to utilize a large frame of reference and to suggest many happy juxtapositions. His comparison between Little Dorrit and Beatrice sheds a new light on Dickens if not on Dante.[1] His common sense, insisting that a man in search of an apartment is not necessarily the hero of a symbolic quest, might well be emulated by other contributors to literary quarterlies. Only rarely is he swept away by the largeness of his generalizations, as when he explains Henry James's "The Bostonians" by a dualism so transcendent that it might be invoked to explain the cosmos. At the other extreme, he oversimplifies by generalizing too quickly when he declares that Tolstoy lacked "the imagination of disaster." But, after all, Mr. Trilling was asked to introduce "Anna Karenina" rather than "War and Peace."

Tolstoy's lifelikeness carries Mr. Trilling to the limits of criticism beyond which, he says, "the literary critic can do nothing more than point." Yet he is much too articulate to abide by the self-imposed limitation, and always ready to cross into the bordering domain of human conduct: to discuss Keats as a hero or Orwell as a virtuous man. Other critics may push esthetic perception or historical scholarship somewhat further, but their writing often seems dry and technical; whereas Mr. Trilling's is increasingly and deservedly popular because he has the courage to be a moralist.

## Notes
1. Trilling's essay "Little Dorrit," written for the 1953 Oxford edition of Dickens's *Little Dorrit*, is collected in *The Opposing Self.*—Ed.

## 36

*Paul Pickrel*

*"The Voice beyond Ideology,"* Commentary

*April 1955*

Paul Pickrel (1917– ) taught English at Lafayette College, Yale University, and then Smith College, where he taught for more than two decades and has been professor emeritus since 1987. During 1949–66 he worked full time as managing editor and book review editor of the *Yale Review*, while also serving during the mid-1950s as the chief book reviewer at *Harper's*.

Like Trilling, Pickrel was especially interested in nineteenth-century British literature and also wrote one novel (*The Moving Stairs*, 1949).

The vigor of Lionel Trilling's criticism arises from the fact that he has been forced to work out an intellectual position that goes against the grain of his own mind. He is the most metropolitan of our critics—only a great city like New York could have produced him—yet the direction of his thought becomes increasingly anti-metropolitan. He has brilliant powers of analysis, yet more and more the object of his analysis is the vindication of the image-making faculty of the human mind against the analytical faculty. He is a true son of the age of ideology, feeling fully the appeal of the intellectual aggression we call ideology, the determination to make reality conform to the mind's reading of reality; yet the essence of what he has to say is that the universe speaks in a voice beyond ideology, and that man can realize the fullness of his being only by listening to that voice.

Trilling's criticism appeals to his contemporaries (his earlier book of essays, *The Liberal Imagination*, is said to have sold 70,000 copies in the inexpensive reprint) because he faces, with learning and intelligence, the problem every intellectual is up against in one form or another. Since, for the last century and a half, ideology has been the chief content of intellectual life, the failure of ideology leaves the contemporary intellectual sunk in guilt. Ideology, he feels, ought to have worked; perhaps it would have worked if only he had tried the right brand, or had read the directions more carefully before application. And if our problems fail of solution before the mind's aggression, he asks, is not the commitment that forms the very basis of the intellectual life, the commitment to mind, rendered suspect or void? Personal pride is involved: if the intellectual ends up voting for the same political party his old aunts vote for, and for very much the same reasons what availed the whole intellectual ordeal? National safety is involved: how can a nation survive which has to put its programs in a handful of embarrassingly flimsy slogans when it is faced by an empire crashing through history in the heavy armor of ideology? Finally to listen to the voice beyond ideology—isn't that anti-intellectualism, the intellectual's sin against the Holy Ghost?

Trilling can speak to the ideologist *manqué* in the contemporary intellectual because there is so much of the ideologist *manqué* in himself. He carries weight because in abandoning ideology he has not abandoned his commitment to intellect. And if at times all his travail ends in something like platitude, the very reluctance with which he reaches that result gives it a moral tension and an intellectual excitement that revitalize it.

The hero of *The Opposing Self*, the subject of its first and longest essay, is John Keats. In him Trilling finds the last triumphant expression of his own image of how the life of the mind ought to be lived. For John Keats lived with ideas lovingly without in any way becoming their victim; he was able to realize himself as an intellectual being without becoming encased in ideology. Keats gave his admiration to the man capable "of being in uncertainties, mysteries, doubts, without any irritable reaching after fact and reason"; at the same time he said of himself, "I find that I can find no enjoyment in the world but a continual drinking of knowledge." "He boldly put pleasure, even contentment, at the center of his theory of poetry"; yet, "the only salvation that Keats found it possible to conceive" was "the tragic salvation, the soul accepting the fate that defines it." He trusted the imagination, the sense of the wholeness of life, because he was himself whole.

Of the many endowments that went into such a life Trilling singles out one for special scrutiny: Keats's profound sense of "condition." This will hardly come as a surprise to readers of Trilling's earlier work, since the concept of condition is the rock on which his thought is built. Even the plot of his novel, *The Middle of the Journey*, is a brilliantly elaborated pun on the word condition. But in *The Opposing Self* the concept has deepened and broadened beyond its earlier use. By condition Trilling means everything that makes it impossible for us to think whatever we please about ourselves and the world we live in. He means all the ways the universe modifies and qualifies and limits our spirits, all the recalcitrance and perverseness and abrasiveness the universe exhibits when we try to deal with it as ideologists. It is the law that springs into being whenever spirit touches matter. It is the voice beyond ideology.

The sternness of this concept is not new in Trilling's work; it was already apparent in the discussion of *Billy Budd* in *The Middle of the Journey*. Nor is the idea that condition is the source of value new, though perhaps it has not before been put so strongly as in *The Opposing Self*, when Trilling says of Jane Austen that she recognized the fact "that spirit is not free, that it is conditioned, that it is limited by circumstances," and it is only on this account that spirit has "virtue and meaning." But Trilling's favorite quotation from E. M. Forster has long been "Death destroys a man but the idea of death saves him"—that is, the inevitability of death is the condition under which we lead our lives and the source of the value we attach to life.

What is new in the concept of condition in *The Opposing Self* is the notion that condition is not only the iron law of the universe and the source of value, but that it is also a kind of benediction, a blessing, a principle of reconciliation, a source of joy and pleasure. No other of Trilling's books has been concerned with joy and pleasure to anything like the extent *The Opposing Self* is; no other speaks in such a spirit of reconciliation, of "calm submission to the law of things." The reason is that condition has now become something like a religious principle in Trilling's thought: the way God manifests Himself in His creation. It comes close to fitting Trilling's own description of the Torah of the Rabbis and Wordsworth's Nature: something "which is from God and might be said to represent Him as a sort of surrogate, a divine object to which one can be in an intimate, passionate relationship . . . which one can, as it were, handle, and in a sense create, drawing from it inexhaustible meaning by desire, intuition, and attention."

Now it must be confessed that a good deal of *The Opposing Self* leaves the impression that it deals with what Trilling thinks he ought to feel rather than with what he feels. The discussion of pleasure, for instance, may convince both writer and reader that they ought to feel more pleasure in their lives than they do but it will hardly increase the amount of pleasure either feels. The concept of condition often remains just a concept, with a speculative, postulated quality about it; it is necessary to Trilling's position and so it must be there, but it has little reality except as an intellectual construct. It is like the rural setting of *The Middle of the Journey*—as landscape it is a stage set, as action it is melodrama: the book remains a story of New Yorkers on vacation, and the best part of it is the conflict of ideas they bring with them out of the ideological metropolis they have left.

But if Trilling is the intellectual equivalent of the New Yorker who is convinced that the country is the true seat of all virtue yet would not think of living anywhere but in New York, that is one of the chief reasons for the respect with which we read him: he acknowledges the paradox which is ourselves. If he arrives at his position against the grain, if it requires powers with which he is only moderately endowed and makes less call on powers he has in abundance, that constitutes a part of his claim to intellectual leadership in this post-ideological age.

With the exception of George Orwell, the writers discussed in *The Opposing Self* all belong more or less to the 19th century, and with the exception of Howells they are more or less the writers to be expected. The acknowledgments make clear that most of the essays were written to meet requests for commemorative addresses, introductions to editions of texts, and the like. As a result, the essays are not always suited to the purposes of the book. It is unfortunate, for instance, that the essay on Tolstoy concerns *Anna Karenina*—a choice that makes Tolstoy appear irrelevant to the argument, whereas in fact there was probably no other 19th-century writer whose career as a whole so dramatized the problem under discussion. It is easy to think of writers not touched on who would have been fascinating subjects for essays in this context—D. H. Lawrence and G. B. Shaw, to name two. And a critic has a responsibility to living writers.

More important than what subjects have been left out or put in the book is the suspicion that, however innocently, Trilling somewhat misrepresents his own work in his preface, his title, and some of the essays. He calls his subject the opposition of the self to culture, and it may be idle to dispute his choice of words, especially since the word culture means in his usage just about anything or everything, as it does among many contemporary intellectuals. But the whole drift of Trilling's book makes clear that what he is really talking about is the resistance Being puts up to ideology. Self and Being may be for his purposes interchangeable, but ideology and culture are not; they differ as a blueprint differs from a building. The grand discovery which is the central fact the book deals with is the discovery that a blueprint (say—to borrow Trilling's own figure—a blueprint for a society without Bastilles) can be more imprisoning, can crucify Being more, than a building (even a Bastille) because a building is conditioned and a blueprint is not.

*The Opposing Self* is an impressive example of why literary criticism is at present a central mode of intellectual discourse. Actually Trilling is as concerned for society, as concerned for the life of the mind in general, as he is for literature; and the Arnoldian breadth of his concern is a source of strength to his criticism. But he makes works of the imagination the vehicle of his thought because such works are the images of wholeness most available to us. Of all the mind's artifacts they are least violable by ideology; being of condition all compact, they have to speak with the voice beyond ideology.

# 37

*Roy Fuller*

*Excerpt from a review in* London Magazine

*November 1955*

Roy Fuller (1912–91) was a British poet, novelist, and solicitor. Among his twenty volumes of highly descriptive, sometimes didactic poems are *The Middle of a War* (1942), *A Lost Season* (1944), *Brutus's Orchard* (1957), *Selected Poems 1936–61* (1962), and *Buff* (1965); his dozen realistic novels—most of them mystery, crime, and suspense stories—include *With My Little Eye* (1948) and *Second Curtain* (1953).

The great interest of Trilling's book (apart from its numerous purely literary generalizations and *aperçus*) is in the ideas which interconnect all the essays—the ideas of the opposition of the modern writer's self to his society and of his ideal aim nevertheless to project the experience of art 'into the actuality and totality of life as the ideal form of the moral life'. Thus Trilling finds even in the writers most violently opposed to their 'culture' the measure of their greatness in what, and what amount, they are able to accept of life. Bouvard and Pecuchet, he says, exist beyond culture, but still alive, still human. The stiff moral sanctions of *Mansfield Park* are those of 'our secret inexpressible hopes'. Keats's requirement of beauty and the telling of 'heart-easing things' in poetry really embraces a knowledge and acceptance of life's cruelty and evil. Wordsworth's creation of humble people is intended 'to suggest that life is justified in its elemental biological simplicity'. And so on.

One does injustice to the subtlety and paradox of Trilling's arguments and examples by trying to present them in this fashion. Through his constant sense of the predicament of the modern Western intellectual during his examination of these nine writers (from Keats to Orwell), he brings out in a strong, though scarcely compressible form, the sense of the possibilities of greatness, of life, of affirmation, from artists surrounded by cultures however inimical to those possibilities. Considered as literary criticism *simpliciter* this book, as some critics have found, may seem to make too much *use* of the material it examines; to bend, by rigorous selection and daring comparison, that material too much to its philosophical aim. But this seems to me to miss the point of *The Opposing Self.* When, for instance, in the essay on *Anna Karenina* Trilling refuses to analyse the method of its success, it is only after he has explained that Tolstoy's 'lifelikeness' is the result of his pervasive, constant, equitable love, so that in the novel everything exists 'as everything in Nature, without exception, exists in time, space and atmosphere'. And this is sufficient for the lesson he wishes to draw from Tolstoy. Again, it is the long digressions on modern taste in the essay on Howells which are important, and not the criticism of the man who triggered them— who, indeed, exists for Trilling less as a literary figure than a symbol which he can oppose to our own age's dangerous appetite for literary cynicism, evil and violence.

## 38

*Angus Wilson*

*"To Know and Yet Not to Fear Reality,"* Encounter

*1955*

Angus Wilson (1913–91), distinguished British man of letters, was a novelist, short-story writer, playwright, literary critic, and biographer. One of the major fiction writers of his generation, Wilson's most important novels were *Anglo-Saxon Attitudes* (1956) and *The Middle Age of Mrs. Eliot* (1958). Wilson's chief work of nonfiction was his critical biography, *The World of Charles Dickens* (1970). Wilson also wrote or edited books on Kipling, Maugham, and other nineteenth- and twentieth-century authors.

Trilling reviewed Wilson's *Emile Zola* (1952) sympathetically in *The Griffin*; the article was collected in *A Gathering of Fugitives*.

Most of these essays were written as introductions to books, and all of them were written for occasions which were not of my own devising. The occasions were quite discrete from one another, the subjects are in some ways diverse, and I wrote the essays with no thought of achieving an interconnection among them. In each case my intention was only to serve the given subject, to say what made a particular book or author interesting and valuable to us. Yet inevitably an interconnection among the essays does exist—apart, I mean, from whatever coherence is to be found in their writer's notions of what constitutes the interesting and valuable, of what constitutes "us." The essays deal with episodes of the literature of the last century and a half, and they all, in one way or another, take account of the idea that preoccupies this literature and is central to it, and makes its principle and unity—the idea of the self.

I have quoted in full the first paragraph of Professor Trilling's introduction to his new volume of eight essays [*The Opposing Self*], not only because it describes the contents of the book, but also because it speaks so excellently both in defence and in condemnation of the essays that follow it. The essays, in fact, have little unity, and such as they have derives from the author's own general standpoint towards life and literature. That attitude is only partially and imperfectly represented by the "idea of self" as the dominant concept of post-18th century literature, which he develops in the rest of the introduction. The thesis by which he attempts to unify these unrelated pieces is characteristically wide and abstract. "The modern self," he says, and by this he means the self that has emerged from the late 18th century onwards, "is characterised by certain powers of indignant perception which, turned upon the unconscious portion of culture, have made it accessible to conscious thought." And in language hardly less difficult, he explains that this is a description of the writers' hostility which has extended beyond society in its purely institutional and formal aspect to embrace unconscious assumptions, unformulated valuations, habits, manners, and superstitions. This is clearly true. There is and has been for the last 150 years a growing and deepening criticism of the very texture and style of our civilisation. Literary expression of this criticism has inevitably made more explicit the nature of this texture and style, which Professor Trilling more conveniently than aptly has called society's "culture."

In stating that from 1780 or thereabouts writers have been more deeply preoccupied with the antagonism of the self to the unformulated penumbra of society which he calls "culture," Professor Trilling is not perhaps guilty of expounding a truism; the analysis has not perhaps been so exactly made before; yet it is hardly a surprising one. Above all, it is a very wide and abstract thesis which extends far beyond the position of the writer. To apply it to individual authors, and more still to individual books, would hardly seem likely to illuminate more than a very general outline. So, in fact, in these eight essays, it proves to be. This need not, however, detain us; for the thesis, clearly an afterthought when the essays were brought together, plays only a very minor role.

It is, nevertheless, interesting that Professor Trilling, in searching for an unity, should have devised so wide, so abstract an argument, for it is these qualities which above all mark, and, I think, mar his literary criticism. On first thought, it would seem likely that introductions to individual books would suffer in reprinting from their too particular nature, their too close relation to the text which they were intended to introduce. Such a presumption might apply to many literary critics, but not to Professor Trilling. His abstracting tendency can be relied upon to speak above and beyond any text. No one would wish to dispute the great depth which has been given to literary criticism by harnessing to its services other branches of learning. Semantics, metaphysics, theology, psychology, moral philosophy, all have done service to rescue the discussion of literature from the aimless ambling of belle lettrism, the profitless track of historical descent, the wild flights of biographical hunches; the danger is now that the new and more powerful steeds will run away with literature all together.

The reaction from the old methods came with the demand for more close relation to the text. At the same time, it is the peculiar glory of the modern school of critics that they should have asserted so firmly the integral connection between literature and life, the deadness of literary criticism that does not take account of other branches of human thought and activity. It is also peculiar and perhaps peculiarly unfortunate that this same school should be so largely drawn from the Universities. Professor Trilling's humanity speaks loudly for itself; it speaks with a stentorious voice above that of many of the leaders of the New Criticism; even so, the most vital of critics needs constant injections of humanity. Paradoxically, I think that these injections will come best from an almost pedantic attachment to text, for the text gives us the writer and it is from the writer's humanity that the critics must be fed. It is sad, then, in these essays to find how seldom the author—so penetrating a student of literature, even, on occasion, so exciting a discoverer—draws upon text for his vitality, how often he dilutes his humanity with draughts of philosophy, of psychology, of any other widely abstracting discipline of mind that may swell the original seed of his literary penetration into a shapeless, unappetising fruit.

The full flavour of this fruit may be found in Professor Trilling's style and it is very unpalatable. The opening passage of his introduction, which I have quoted, may once again serve as an example. It labours after philosophical exactitude; it eschews ornament; yet it demands abstraction where none is needed—"of what constitutes *the interesting* and the *valuable*, of what constitutes *'us'* "—and it abounds in repetition: "preoccupies this literature, and is central to it, and makes its principle and unity." It has like most serious modern American criticism a touch of the rhetorical, a ring of the sermon, but rhetoric that is carefully dessicated, a sermon that is self-consciously dry as dust. His style has not so much of the philosophical jargon, the Germanic compounds and syntax that make most of the American New Criticism so distasteful, though it is not utterly without them; but it is needlessly difficult, at once dry and verbose. Though ornament or figure are forbidden, yet there is on occasion a distastefully affected ring in the choice of words—"the strengthening of these bonds by the acts and *attitudes* of Charity is a great and *charming* duty." It is, in short, a style of writing that never assists and often seriously hinders the reading of these excellent essays.

For excellent and illuminating they are, despite all that has to be said in general criticism of them; and, above all, stimulating—both to contradiction and to further exploration along the same exciting tracks. Like most occasional pieces, they are of unequal merit; but, above all, the most successful are those whose themes lie closest to the author's own view of life. The formulation, the elucidation of his own philosophy always preoccupies Professor Trilling. When his theme lies within the orbit of this preoccupation, he feels free to explore at will, to go along with his subject—with Keats or Wordsworth, with James's hero Basil Ransom, or with Flaubert's saintly copy clerks—to an exposition which is complete and wonderfully illuminating. It is then that the subordination of the latter to philosophical exploration seems least damaging, seems indeed hardly to damage at all. On occasion, however, his contact with his theme is only partial or tangential and then, too often, a good essay, a promising line of thought is damaged by being cramped into the mould. So it is, I think, with the essays on *Little Dorrit* and *Mansfield Park.* Finally, there are those themes which seem hardly to touch his preoccupations at all and then he is often content with conclusions that are hardly more than banal. Such, I think, is the essay on *Anna Karenina.*

It may perhaps be best cursorily to examine some aspects of this failure before attempting to outline what seems to me to be Professor Trilling's view of life as illustrated in the best of these essays.

In the essay on *Anna Karenina,* he seems almost content to tell us that Tolstoy's greatness lies in "the trueness to life" of his work. No reader of *Anna Karenina* can have failed to feel this. It is here surely that an analysis of the *mise en scène* of the novel, of the juxtaposition of events, of the suddenness by which the reader's expectations are deceived and he is led on to accept a new expectation as inevitable, of such technical brilliance, would have been enlightening. For it is by these means that, in part at any rate, Tolstoy convinces us. Professor Trilling warns us that Tolstoy's truth is not necessarily "truer" than Dostoevsky's; but he says nothing of the strange contrast in which each diminishes and elevates man's soul in entirely different aspects. Tolstoy's truth, in fact, hardly touches the author's, and so he has little to say about him.

The essay on *Little Dorrit* is more illuminating. He sees clearly Dickens' complex treatment of self-pity and injured gentility—the self-mutilation that the social will imposes upon such characters as Fanny Dorrit and Harry Gowan, on Miss Wade and Mrs. Clennam. He rightly regards *Little Dorrit* herself as the holy child, the negation of the social will by which alone we are freed from the prison house that dominates the novel. To make *Little Dorrit* only a story of negation of the social will, however, leads him to reduce Mr. Dorrit to a minor role, mitigate the vileness of Mr. Merdle, and elevate the importance of Blandois. A single reading of the novel will show that this is absurd—the author's preoccupation has forced a living work of art into a convenient box.

Something of the same sort occurs in the essay on *Mansfield Park*. His analysis of this novel up to a point is quite masterly, though I believe that much of what he argues about Fanny Price would have been unnecessary had he compared her with Ann Eliot and not with Elizabeth Bennet. However, he sees almost to the core of Jane Austen's moral æsthetic, to the contrast between Fanny's commitment to duty and Mary Crawford's commitment to impersonation, to insincerity. One of his preoccupations, however, is a defence of passive, vegetable virtue—it is the theme he so brilliantly expounds in the Wordsworth essay—and so he is led away from the penetrating study of the significance of the house in Mansfield Park for Fanny, into an elaborate attempt to exalt Lady Bertram as a half-ironic exposition of the virtues of vegetable existence. Once again, no reading of the novel, of Edmund's decent observance of his mother's position—decent but no more—can possibly admit such an absurdity.

What, then, are the aspects of life which so strongly predispose Professor Trilling that they can so make or mar his literary criticism? He stands, it seems, with the heroes of the modern literary critical world—with Yeats and Lawrence and Eliot—up to a point. His agreement with them is well expressed in a remark of Basil Ransom, the hero of James's *The Bostonians*. "The whole generation is womanised," says Ransom, "the masculine tone is passing out of the world, it's a feminine, a nervous, chattering, canting age, an age of hollow phrases and false delicacy and exaggerated solicitudes and coddled sensibilities, which, if we don't soon look out, will usher in the reign of mediocrity, of the feeblest and flattest and the most pretentious that has even been. The masculine character, the ability to dare and endure, to know and yet not to fear reality, to look the world in the face and take it for what it is—a very queer and partly very base mixture—this is what I want to preserve, or rather, as I may say, recover."

It is this theme that Trilling so admires in *The Bostonians* and the essay, as a result, is quite brilliant. He finds this same manly courage and acceptance in Keats's letters, and with it another quality which he demands of life, Keats's famous "Negative Capability," the refusal to shut out life by going out for dogmatic truth. It is here that he parts company with his Anglo-

Catholic allies. Indeed, it is somewhat in the teeth of Mr. Eliot that he further pursues this Negative Capability aspect of virtue in the vegetable, almost mineral existence of Wordsworth's old men, in the goodness, the acceptance of life of the Idiot Boy—the virtue of simply being. In a brilliant side hit at Mr. Eliot, he shows how little it is possible for the author of the *Cocktail Party* to conceive a *living* virtue that is not violent and extreme, how dead is the virtue of those who must accept the simple round in this play. Finally in "Bouvard and Pécuchet," he pursues another sort of sanctity, the sanctity of these active-minded, simple, *loving* men, the sanctity of Leopold Bloom.

These four essays, then, are a recompense and more for all the faults of the book. They are quite brilliant in themselves, but they have a courage rare in these days to accept the reaction against liberal sloppiness, to demand a manly, courageous acceptance of a "partly very base" reality, and yet to refuse the violence, the sin obsession, the dogmatism, and the aristocratic arrogance that usually accompany this reaction and insist on the virtues of passivity, acceptance, negative capability, and love.

## 39

*Denis Donoghue*

*"The Critic in Reaction,"* Twentieth Century

*October 1955*

Denis Donoghue (1928– ), professor of English at New York University and at Trinity College in Dublin, was born and educated in Ireland. Donoghue is the author of *The Third Voice* (1959), *Ferocious Alphabets* (1981), *The Arts Without Mystery* (1984), and *We Irish* (1990), among more than fifteen other works of literary criticism. His autobiographical memoir, *Warrenpoint* (1990), discusses his youth as an Irish nationalist and traditional Roman Catholic in Protestant Ulster.

A high modernist who is conservative in his aesthetic tastes and sharply skeptical of literary theory, Donoghue is a prolific, sensitive literary essayist and reviewer, a working critic who writes for American and British publications on a wide range of literary figures and topics.

In the following review, the twenty-seven-year-old Donoghue chides Trilling for his "pet sociological tangents" in *The Opposing Self*, claiming that Trilling is more a sociologist than a literary critic. Trilling is happiest "when roaming about the large triangle whose sides are Sociology, Politics, and Literature (in that order)."

If one had the time and the energy to examine the British reviews of two recent American books (R. P. Blackmur's *Language as Gesture* and Randall Jarrell's *Poetry and the Age*) one would find a remarkable amount of agreement on the kind of literary criticism currently in favour. In general, the British critics have rushed to show their impatience with any criticism that smells even faintly of formalism; we are encouraged to regard wit and enthusiasm as infinitely more important than analytical skill; the New Criticism, for instance, is to be used only as a swear-word. These notions were very largely responsible for the welcome which Mr Jarrell's book received in this country, just as they combined to freeze Mr Blackmur. Similar assumptions have now gathered to acclaim Mr Lionel Trilling on the strength of his new book, *The Opposing Self* (Secker and Warburg, 15*s*.) Sir Harold Nicolson, for instance, started off with a flourish by describing Mr Trilling as 'the most important of modern critics': just like that.[1]

This simple judgement puzzles me. Not that there can be any doubt about Mr Trilling's importance; when you add this new book to *The Liberal Imagination*, the study of Forster, the book on Matthew Arnold, and the brilliant novel *The Middle of the Journey*, you have an impressive total. But none of these books (leaving the novel aside) seems to me to move on the level of critical achievement represented by, say, John Crowe Ransom's *The World's Body*, Yvor Winters's *Maule's Curse* or F. R. Leavis's *The Great Tradition*.

The title of Mr Trilling's new book refers to the affirmative self which opposes the reality of hostile circumstance, and which thereby gains definition and identity. These terms come to the surface in the first essay, on Keats, and they are implied throughout the book. When Mr Trilling speaks of 'the modern imagination of autonomy and delight, of surprise and elevation, of selves conceived in opposition to the general culture,' he touches the unifying principle of his studies:

> This imagination makes, I believe, a new idea in the world. It is an idea in the world, not in literature alone. If these essays have a unity, it is because they take notice of this idea, and of its vicissitudes, modulations and negations.

This idea has special interest for us to-day because the rhetoric of the contemporary novel, as of modern drama, so insistently presents the self as beaten and passive. Albert Guerard has recently examined this situation as it is reflected in such novels as Dino Buzzati's *The Tartar Steppe*, John Hawkes's *The Cannibal*, Orwell's *1984*, Camus' *The Plague*, and Ennio Flaiano's *The Short Cut*, and his conclusion is worth bearing in mind:

> So one is forced to agree with J. Donald Adams and others that the modern novel does indeed see man as almost wholly bereft of freedom of choice; and one is forced to agree that some of these novels are depressing. And so? I should like to think of them also as 'demoralizing' in the best sense. It is only when we come to recognize how completely we *have* lost our freedom, how monstrously we *are* the victims of political abstraction and inhuman historical process, how thoroughly we *have* been bemused by words—only then will we perhaps begin to feel . . . our almost extinguished longing for freedom.

According to Professor Trilling, Keats's 'massive importance' is in relation to precisely this situation:

> He stands as the last image of health at the very moment when the sickness of Europe began to be apparent—he with his intense naturalism that took so passionate an account of the mystery of man's nature, reckoning as boldly with pleasure as with pain, giving so generous a credence to growth, development, and possibility; he with his pride that so modestly, so warmly and delightedly, responded to the idea of community. The spiritual and moral health of which he seems the image we cannot now attain by wishing for it. But we cannot attain it without wishing for it, and clearly imagining it.

*The Opposing Self* and *The Liberal Imagination* are, of course, all of a piece; to read both books is to see Mr Trilling emerging more clearly than ever before as the guardian of the intellectual class. He himself has described what 'intellectual' means in this context:

> The name implies, as I understand its use, a certain intensity of commitment, the belief that the existence and the conduct of the intellectual class are momentous in and essential to the life of society, the acceptance of intellectual activity as a mandate, a status, a personal fate.

As a distinguished member of this class, Mr Trilling in *The Liberal Imagination* was dismayed to find that the best of modern European literature has been written by men who are indifferent or even hostile to the tradition of democratic liberalism: Yeats, Eliot, Proust, Joyce, Lawrence, and Gide 'do not seem to confirm us in the social and political ideals which we hold.' Largely as a result of this fact Mr Trilling has become a divided and reactionary man; he realizes that if one is to concern oneself with modern literature at all one must do so by way of these six writers, but his own heart is not in the work. For the truth is that Mr Trilling does not really *like* the Big Six; he speaks of them respectfully but with no conviction; he is much more at home with Forster, James, and Howells.

The nine essays in *The Opposing Self* deal with Keats's *Letters*, *Little Dorrit*, *Anna Karenina*, Howells, *The Bostonians*, Wordsworth, Orwell, *Bouvard and Pecuchet*, and *Mansfield Park*. The last is by far the best, the one on Orwell the weakest, but, weak or strong, each shows the same virtues and defects. It has often been suggested that in Mr Trilling criticism has become a *whole* activity, that his work uses the best of the skills which have been developed by the formalist, sociological and historical critics. A typical statement on behalf of Mr Trilling is that together with such writers as F. O. Matthiessen, Edmund Wilson, and Kenneth Burke he has been known for his belief that critical theory must account for the social and even the political elements in literature without in any way abandoning the rigour that has marked the earlier, more purely linguistic or textual criticism.

I am afraid this lofty ideal has not been achieved by Mr Trilling; indeed, after reading his new book I am more than ever convinced that his central interest is not in literature at all but in ideas; which are not, need it be said, quite the same thing. One searches in vain in *The Opposing Self* or in *The Liberal Imagination* for that passionate devotion to the work of art in all its concreteness and particularity which the best of the New Critics have continually shown. I suspect that Mr Trilling is drawn to the novel rather than to the poem because in dealing with the novel he can more plausibly move out along his pet sociological tangents. Indeed, on the rare occasions on which he discusses a poem he reveals no great interest in it as a *thing*; the lecture he gave at Cornell University in 1950 on the occasion of the Wordsworth Centenary, for instance, concerned itself mainly with Wordsworth's Christianity and with his affinity to the Judaic *Aboth*, ignoring the central literary questions to which, characteristically, John Crowe Ransom addressed himself. Even in discussing the novel Mr Trilling's characteristic procedure is to work on a paraphrase and to ignore the words. In the last analysis he is not really interested in the fact that the words of an individual poem or novel are *these* words and not some others, in *this* order and not another; inevitably, this indifference puts out of his reach the critical success represented by Morton Zabel's essay on Conrad or Allen Tate's brief study of Poe. Mr Trilling is astonishingly slow to quote from the author he is discussing (witness his essay on Scott Fitzgerald). He doesn't need to; the most important things he has to say are about 'manners', and they do not emerge from any particular passage nor do they find their justification in any particular text. He likes the wide open spaces; or rather, he is happiest when roaming about the large triangle whose sides are Sociology, Politics, and Literature (in that order). Indeed, it is not at all surprising that his best essays have titles like *Art and Neurosis*, *Art and Fortune*, or *The Kinsey Report*.

I am not denying the power and range of Mr Trilling's mind; on the contrary. His strong grasp of the ideological organization of our society, for instance, is a virtue of tremendous importance, not least for the literary critic. But, given all this and more, the problem remains: Why are so few of Mr Trilling's comments *literary*? Is he afraid of the Word? Take, for instance, the essay on Howells, one of the most characteristic pieces in the book. Mr Trilling does not examine a single line of Howells's writing, not even *Criti-*

*cism and Fiction*, but he uses Howells as an excuse to muse at large on the idea of the family in literature, on the sense of evil, on 'what has happened to the humanistic idea in the modern world'. The passage which I value most in the essay reads:

> Disintegration itself fascinates us because it is a power. Evil has always fascinated men, not only because it is opposed to good but also because it is, in its own right, a power.

This is splendid, whatever it is; it makes one think and it gives one the excitement of a new idea. The best parts of *The Opposing Self* are of this kind: I offer two examples, the first from the essay on Wordsworth, the second from the *Anna Karenina* piece:

> Nor do we need to go beyond our own daily lives to become aware, if we dare to, of how we have conspired, in our very virtues, to bring about the devaluation of whatever is bold and assertive and free, replacing it by the bland, the covert, the manipulative. If we wish to understand the violence, the impulse toward charismatic power, of so much of our literature, we have but to consider that we must endure not only the threat to being which comes from within but also the seduction to non-being which establishes itself within. We need, in Coleridge's words, something to 'startle this dull pain, and make it move and live'. Violence is a means of self-definition; the bad conscience, Nietzsche says, assures us of our existence.
>
> Nowadays the sense of evil comes easily to all of us. We all share what Henry James called the 'imagination of disaster', and with reason enough, the world being what it is. And it is with reason enough that we respond most directly to those writers in whom the imagination of disaster is highly developed, even extremely developed. To many of us the world to-day has the look and feel of a Dostoevski novel, every moment of it crisis, every detail of it the projection of exacerbated sensibility and blind, wounded will. It is comprehensible that, when the spell of Tolstoi is not immediately upon us, we might feel that he gives us, after all, not reality itself but a sort of idyl of reality.

I am sure that to read these passages and think about them will make one a better reader of literature, but surely no one will claim that writing of this kind is the proper *central* activity of literary criticism. It may well be that we need something more than the New Criticism and that there is room in literary study for many different kinds of inquiry; but will anyone seriously maintain that *The Liberal Imagination* or *The Opposing Self* is more central, more authentic literary criticism than, say, *The Well-Wrought Urn*?[2] It is perhaps worth mentioning that the particular kind of pleasure which I have derived from reading *The Opposing Self* is closely akin to that provided by the sociological studies such as David Riesman's *The Lonely Crowd.*

Mr Trilling has no interest in language as such: the enemies of the New Criticism have often alleged that Mr Blackmur is interested in nothing else. As I see it, Mr Blackmur's characteristic fault is that, even outside the poem, he is prone to be obsessed with the precise implications of simple words like 'perform': when he starts fussing over things like this he becomes painful and unprofitable reading. But Mr Trilling's characteristic defect is another kind of fuss; as, for instance, his intellectual dance with the various meanings of the word 'genial' and his platitudinous discussion of the ingestive appetite in Keats. Exhausted by this kind of activity he very often freewheels for pages through commonplaces such as this:

> It is when the novelist really loves his characters that he can show them in their completeness and contradiction, in their failures as well as in their great moments, in their triviality as well as in their charm.

And this gem, from *The Liberal Imagination*:

> Wordsworth's *Immortality Ode* is acceptable to us only when it is understood to have been written at a certain past moment; if it had appeared much later than it did, if it were offered to us now as a contemporary work, we would not admire it.

A fair example of Mr Trilling's work is provided by his essay on *Anna Karenina.* There is the general description of Tolstoi as 'the most central of novelists', a reference to 'the unique illusion of reality that Tolstoi creates', and a comment on the 'energy of animal intelligence' that marks him. Much of this sounds familiar and there is very little in Mr Trilling's essay that has not been provided already by Mr Philip Rahv in his *Partisan Review* essay of 1946; in particular, there are strong and acknowledged echoes of Mr Rahv's phrases, 'artist of the normal' and 'unity of art and life'. If one reads both essays one finds that neither Mr Rahv nor Mr Trilling finds much to say about Tolstoi as a literary artist; but Mr Rahv at least makes an effort in that direction and achieves something with his comments on Tolstoi's use of generalization and of parallelism of construction.

In fairness, one must emphasize the essay on 'divine Jane' and quote characteristic fragments. This, for instance:

> In *Emma* the heroine is made to stand at bay to our adverse judgement through virtually the whole novel, but we are never permitted to close in for the kill—some unnamed quality in the girl, some trait of vivacity or

will, erects itself into a moral principle, or at least a vital principle, and frustrates our moral blood-lust.

Hugh Kenner often writes with control and perception of this kind but the gift is rare.[3] It is at work again in this passage from the same essay:

> Much of the nineteenth-century preoccupation with duty was not a love of law for its own sake, but rather a concern with the hygiene of the self.

The most constructive part of this essay is an interpretation and an elucidation of the dispute about the amateur theatricals in *Mansfield Park*; this and the comments on Mary Crawford make the essay a delight to read:

> In Mary Crawford we have the first brilliant example of a distinctively modern type, the person who cultivates the *style* of sensitivity, virtue, and intelligence.

Mr Trilling appears to owe something to Mr Marvin Mudrick's *Jane Austen, Irony as Defense and Discovery* (1952) but several of the most penetrating insights in this essay are, in an important sense, new.

I am acutely conscious that I represent a minority view on Mr Trilling's criticism and, since reading *The Opposing Self*, I have worked out, at least to my own satisfaction, the main reason for his acceptance as the Whole Critic. In many ways the most important factor is that his prose shows no trace of modern critical jargon; he never talks about tensions, ambiguities, density, irony, tenor, symbolic action, the heresy of paraphrase or the affective fallacy. And, of course, everybody scorns the use of such expressions, although most of them have been recruited to deal with poetic *things* for which no simpler words are available. Mr Trilling does not discuss these difficult things and therefore finds no need of an appropriate language to cope with them. Secondly, Mr Trilling's criticism has the comfortable feeling of *copia*, but it is a *copia* quite unlike Mr Blackmur's (which is technical and literary); Mr Trilling's is the *copia* of ideas, over and above their literary context. When Mr Blackmur discusses social or religious ideas (as he often does) he is interested in them only as they function or fail to function within the poem; even though, as Mr Ransom says, 'they may be ideas from which, at the very moment, out in the world of action, the issues of life and death are hung.' When Mr Trilling finds himself in that position he simply leaves the poem to look after itself and goes out into this world of action; and many people admire him for doing so. So do I, and I am deeply interested in what he has to say about that world, but I insist that at the point at which he moves out into the world of action he moves away from the central preoccupation of literary criticism. Is that agreed or do we fight about it? Finally, Mr Trilling's special acceptance is probably related to the feeling that here is a critic who derives from the tradition of genteel discourse, by comparison with which the direction of Mr Blackmur's muscular prose is regarded as somehow vicious and retrograde. Mr Trilling himself has reproached the New Critics on the grounds that 'they make the elucidation of poetic ambiguity or irony a kind of intellectual calisthenic ritual', and there is a widespread feeling that such labours consort but poorly with scholarship and a classical education. Mr Trilling is on the safe side in all this, and for that reason he is likely to remain the Intelligent Man's Guide to Literature.

Yet there are larger achievements, and over against Sir Harold Nicolson's judgement I would offer such a work as Francis Fergusson's *The Idea of a Theater*, the particular distinction of which is that its continuous involvement with 'ideas' entails no injustice to the literary and dramatic values which are its central concern.

There remains, of course, the question of whether any of the criticism written in the past thirty or forty years will live for, say, a century. Richard Eberhart's[4] opinion has a considerable amount of weight behind it:

> The best poetry of our time will be read a century from now. Life will shine out of it. The best criticism will have only an academic interest, a period value.

And that includes, according to Mr Eberhart's account, the work of Messrs Tate, Blackmur, Eliot, Ransom, Richards and Empson; he does not mention Mr Trilling. And here in turn I would suggest that in a hundred years' time Mr Trilling will be remembered, not as a critic but as a novelist and as the author of a splendid story called *The Other Margaret*; perhaps there is a moral here somewhere.

## Notes

1. Sir Harold Nicolson reviewed *The Liberal Imagination* favorably in *The Observer* (25 March 1951).—Ed.

2. *The Well-Wrought Urn* (1947), by Cleanth Brooks, was one of the landmark books that established the New Criticism.—Ed.

3. Hugh Kenner (1923– ), American critic specializing in modern British literature, is author of works on Joyce, Pound, T. S. Eliot, and Wyndham Lewis.—Ed.

4. Poet Richard Eberhart (1904– ) is best known for his *Collected Poems, 1930–60* (1960) and *Ways of Light: Poems 1972–1980* (1980).—Ed.

# 40

*Joseph Frank*

*"Lionel Trilling and the Conservative Imagination," in* The Widening Gyre *{originally published in* Sewanee Review*}* 1963 *{spring* 1956*}*

Joseph Frank (1918– ), professor emeritus of comparative literature at Princeton University and currently a professor at Stanford University, is the author of *The Widening Gyre: Crisis and Mastery in Modern Literature* (1963) and *The Idea of Spatial Form* (1991), among other books. His masterwork has been his definitive biography of Dostoevsky, of which four volumes have thus far appeared. Frank received the National Book Critics Circle Award in 1984 for the second volume of the biography, *F. M. Dostoyevsky: The Years of Ordeal* (1850–59). In the early postwar era, Frank wrote occasionally for *Partisan Review*, *Commentary*, and other journals to which the New York intellectuals frequently contributed.

Frank's influential 1956 essay-review, "Lionel Trilling and the Conservative Imagination," was republished in 1978 with an appendix. The essay posits that *The Opposing Self* represents Trilling's step away in the mid-1950s from the "liberal" imagination toward "the conservative imagination." In *The Opposing Self*, argues Frank, Trilling "reject[s] the political imagination" by "endow[ing] social passivity and quietism *as such* with the halo of aesthetic transcendence."

The career and reputation of Lionel Trilling as a literary critic pose something of an anomaly. Not, we should hasten to add, that Mr. Trilling does not deserve all the encomiums that have been lavished on him or the considerable influence he enjoys as a spiritual guide and mentor. But Mr. Trilling is by no means the kind of critic who has dominated the American literary scene since the end of the Second World War. His concern with literature has always been broadly moral and historical—like that of his master Matthew Arnold—rather than more strictly aesthetic or formal—like the group of New Critics who sprang into prominence exactly at the time Mr. Trilling's own star was on the rise. The anomaly posed by his career is that of explaining his reputation, when the whole drift of American literary opinion seemed to be moving in the direction opposite to the one he chose to take.

Part of the answer may be found in an observation of Mr. Trilling himself about such men as John Crowe Ransom, Allen Tate, and R. P. Blackmur. It is an illusion, he writes in *The Liberal Imagination*, to believe that these critics are as free from ideology as they pretend; in reality their so-called aesthetic judgments are profoundly steeped in concealed cultural preferences and moral assumptions. This remark is perfectly just. In defending the autonomy and integrity of the work of art, the New Critics were repulsing the claims of the liberals and radicals to appropriate it for social or political ends; their influence was part of the wave of disillusionment with politics that marked the generation of the fifties. And, though Lionel Trilling approached art with overt moral and historical assumptions, the substance of what he had to say was by no means dissimilar to what the New Critics were advocating in their own way. For the pervasive disillusionment with politics was given its most sensitive, subtle, and judiciously circumspect expression in the criticism of Lionel Trilling—and this is the real answer to the anomaly of his success.

Mr. Trilling's strategy was far more elaborate than that of the New Critics and was deployed with far more finesse. Instead of pretending to immure himself in a confining aestheticism, he showed himself open to all the currents of the political and social life; but in his famous attack on "the liberal imagination" he criticized liberalism for attempting to measure the complexities of reality exclusively by a sociopolitical yardstick. Only literature, he argued, could truly cope with the intricacies of the moral life; and he recommended that politics appropriate for itself some of the suppleness of literature.

"Unless we insist that politics is imagination and mind," he declared in *The Liberal Imagination*, "we will learn that imagination and mind are politics, and of a kind we will not like." It was never made clear just how politics was supposed to metamorphose into "imagination and mind"; but phrases of this kind, turned with Mr. Trilling's consummate skill, show how perfectly he was able both to crystallize the temper of the moment and to appear to escape its limitations at the same time. For while he rejects the crudities of politics in one breath, in the very next he holds out the hope of a new politics that will incorporate all the discriminations of literature.

It is hardly necessary to say that no such latter politics has ever existed—or ever will exist. As R. P. Blackmur remarked in an acute review of *The*

*Liberal Imagination*: "The politics of existing states is always too simple for literature; it is good only to *aggravate* literature."[1] No political ideology of any kind can compete with literature in the delicacy of its reaction to human experience. Even Mr. Trilling would agree that his favorite Edmund Burke, whom he so often quotes with approval, hardly rivals Wordsworth in the range of his responses to the French Revolution. In other words, Mr. Trilling's criticism of the liberal imagination revealed nothing that was not equally true of any politics that set itself up as a total view of human reality; and he actually criticizes politics from the point of view of art—a point of view happily free from the limiting conditions of all political action. Yet by confining his criticism to the *liberal* imagination, and not extending it to politics in general, Mr. Trilling implied that his views had immediate practical and political relevance. He thus, as it were, filled the intellectual vacuum left by the New Critics. For Mr. Trilling's readers among the erstwhile liberal and radical intelligentsia could continue to feel that they were actively engaged in the political life, while in fact they were tacitly rejecting it from the standpoint of art that the New Critics defended with less tact and more belligerency.

## II

The delicate poise of *The Liberal Imagination* was thus based on an unresolved tension in Mr. Trilling's thinking between art and politics. This tension has since been resolved in his succeeding volume, *The Opposing Self.* For this latter volume of essays is a development of those aspects of Mr. Trilling's thought—aspects that were already present even in his books on Matthew Arnold and E. M. Forster—which come closest to constituting a rejection of the political imagination as a whole.

The best way to approach *The Opposing Self* is to turn to one of the key essays in *The Liberal Imagination*, the essay entitled "Art and Fortune." Here Mr. Trilling speaks of the modern will dying of its own excess; and he suggests that literature, particularly the novel, might be of great service in renovating and restoring the will to health. How can this be done? "The novel has had a long dream of virtue," Mr. Trilling answers, "in which the will, while never abating its strength and activity, comes to refuse to exercise itself upon the unworthy objects with which the social world tempts it, and either conceives its own right objects or becomes content with its own sense of its own potential force." The way for the modern will to renovate itself, according to Mr. Trilling, is to abnegate its action on the unworthy objects of the social world and attain a state of pure contemplative being; and the chosen agent for this renovation is literature.

Mr. Trilling's antipathy to the will, as we can see, is thus of long standing; and there are moments when, for all his candor, alertness, and receptivity to the historical moment, we seem to feel the "inner check" of Babbitt and More—not to mention the Nirvana of Schopenhauer—lurking ominously in the background. But in any case Mr. Trilling's essays in *The Opposing Self* are all devoted to exploring this theme of the abnegation of the will which he had broached in *The Liberal Imagination*. Indeed, he now argues that this abnegation of the will, this substitution of contemplation for an active grappling with social reality, is an important key to modern culture.

The modern self, he writes in the preface to *The Opposing Self*, has an intense and adverse imagination of the culture in which it exists. But this opposition of the modern self to culture takes a very special form. "What virtually every writer of the modern period conceives," he states, is "the experience of art projected into the activity and totality of life as the ideal form of the moral life." Dissatisfied with its habitual life in culture, the modern "opposing self" seeks to transcend culture's moral burdens in the free play of imagination and desire; and this, Mr. Trilling adds, "makes, I believe, a new idea in the world."

One may doubt whether all this is as new as Mr. Trilling would like to think. The Hellenistic self of the Alexandrian era and the Christian self of the first centuries after Christ were also, one suspects, "opposing selves" by Mr. Trilling's standard. But he insists, nonetheless, that the modern self has given birth to a new cultural mutation; and to prove the point he invokes the formidable authority of Hegel. Hegel, he writes, "understood in a re- markable way what he believed to be a new phenomenon of culture."

> This is the bringing into play in the moral life of a new category of judgment, the category of quality. Not merely the deed itself, he said, is now submitted to judgment, but also the personal quality of the doer of the deed. . . . For Hegel, art is the activity of man in which spirit expresses itself not only as utility, not only according to law, but as grace, as transcendence, as manner and style. He brought together the moral and aesthetic judgment. He did this not in the old way of making morality the criterion of the aesthetic: on the contrary, he made the aesthetic the criterion of the moral.

It is unfortunate that Mr. Trilling decided to venture into such deep philosophical waters because, strictly speaking, the ideas he so generously attributes to Hegel are entirely of his own devising.[2] Hegel, it may flatly be asserted, never made the aesthetic the criterion of the moral; and if Mr. Trilling thinks he did, then he should read Hegel's criticism of Friedrich Schlegel and Romantic irony in the lectures on aesthetics.[3] From the reference to style and grace as providing a standard from which law and utility may be judged, it is possible to infer that Mr. Trilling is here confusing Hegel with a recollection of Schiller's *Letters on the Aesthetic Education of Mankind*; but these questions of attribution and accuracy are of course picayune. What is important is to see that Mr. Trilling *himself* now wishes to make "the aesthetic the criterion of the moral," just as previously, in *The Liberal Imagination*, he had made the aesthetic the criterion of the political. This is the point, however, at which it is necessary to tread very cautiously— at least as cautiously as Kant, for instance, who (in *The Critique of Judgment*) also viewed art as a projection into nature of the ideal form of the moral life, but who hastened to add that this ideal was realized *only* in the state of aesthetic apprehension, or, more completely, in that of aesthetic creation.

For it is one thing to make the experience of art—the experience of pleasure and beauty, of harmony and reconciliation—the *ideal* form of moral life. It is quite another to attribute the virtues of this aesthetic ideal to concrete social behavior which, quite independently of any relationship with art, merely exhibits an abeyance or absence of the will. In other words, it is of the utmost importance not to confuse the boundaries of the ideal and the real, the aesthetic and the social; not to endow social passivity and quietism *as such* with the halo of aesthetic transcendence. Mr. Trilling regrettably does not always keep this boundary well defined, and he tends occasionally to identify all forms of being in which the will is absent or quiescent with the ideal values of the aesthetic attitude. As we shall see, this leads him, by a devious path, to end up in justifying a good many of the degrading objects of the social world which the will had once been required to shun and to despise.

## III

The best essay in *The Opposing Self*, as might be expected, is the one in which Mr. Trilling portrays the true transcendence of the artist at its highest peak of aspiration and achievement. This is done in his admirable study of Keats's letters, which ranks with the essay on *The Princess Casamassima* among the finest performances of contemporary criticism. The central purpose of Mr. Trilling's article is to show how Keats's self, while accepting the immitigable reality of evil, was yet capable of affirming a faith in life through aesthetic transcendence. The point is very forcefully made in Mr. Trilling's gloss on the famous conclusion to *The Ode on a Grecian Urn*.

When Keats wrote that "Beauty is truth, truth beauty" he was not evading issues but confronting them. What he meant, according to Mr. Trilling, "is that a great poet (e.g., Shakespeare) looks at human life, sees the terrible truth of its evil, but sees it so intensely that it becomes an element of the beauty which is created by his act of perception. . . . Keats's statement is an accurate description of the response to evil or ugliness which tragedy makes: the matter of tragedy is ugly or painful truth seen as beauty." By transcending the reality of evil in this fashion, Keats affirmed "the creativity of the self that opposes circumstance, the self that is imagination and desire, that, like Adam, assigns names and values to things, and can realize what it envisions." (This last, presumably, means to "realize" artistically.)

What Mr. Trilling so rightly admires in Keats is the courage and resilience of the self, the gallantry of the spirit accepting the challenge of circumstance and the world's evil and asserting its heroic resolution nonetheless. This spirit, according to Mr. Trilling, is no longer of our time. "We have lost the *mystique* of the self." This mystique does not consist in the struggle of the will against fate, but rather in the transcendence of the will by a self that feels capable of rising superior to any onslaught. "Shakespeare suggested the only salvation that Keats found it possible to conceive, the tragic salvation, the soul accepting the fate that defines it." Certainly when man is faced with the problem of ultimate evil, the Keatsian heroism of acceptance may be seen as the finest flower of the cultivation of the self. But not every evil is ultimate, not every acceptance is heroic; and while there is no need to stress this point for Mr. Trilling, with his acute sense of moral nuance, the fact remains that he does not always keep it in mind in developing his arguments.

As an example we may take the wide-ranging essay on "Wordsworth and the Rabbis." This title is a pretty *jeu d'esprit* that Mr. Trilling works out with graceful ingenuity; and there is no reason to take it more seriously than he does himself. Wordsworth has as much (or as little) to do with the rabbis as with the lamas, the fakirs, the gurus, or the bonzes. What Mr. Trilling wishes to bring out by this comparison is the "sentiment of being" in Wordsworth's poetry, a sentiment very close to the natural piety shared by disciples of all the great spiritual religions.

This sentiment of being is perfectly expressed in the lines from *Tintern Abbey* (though Mr. Trilling does not use this passage himself), where Wordsworth speaks of

> that serene and blessed mood,
> In which the affections gently lead us on,—
> Until, the breath of this corporeal frame
> And even the motion of our human blood
> Almost suspended, we are laid asleep
> In body, and become a living soul:

While with an eye made quiet by the power
Of Harmony, and the deep power of joy,
We see into the life of things.

Mr. Trilling believes that Wordsworth's loss of contemporary reputation, his relegation to the status of a school classic, is caused by the preference of our time for the apocalyptic and the charismatic, our inability to experience the sense of being illustrated by these lines as anything but alien and repugnant. "The predilection for the powerful, the fierce, the assertive, the personally militant is very strong in our culture," he writes. Wordsworth's sentiment of being is thus foreign to our sensibility.

To prove this point Mr. Trilling refers to T. S. Eliot's *The Cocktail Party*—specifically, to the scene in which Eliot depicts the way of life of the "common routine" as contrasted with that of the saint or the martyr. Many critics have objected that Eliot's picture of the common routine is far from appealing—that it is, in fact, perhaps even more terrifying than the way of martyrdom. There is no reason, of course, for a Christian like Eliot to glorify ordinary earthly existence. But in the context of his evident desire to make the resolution of the common routine a plausible one, his failure to brighten up its colors a bit more is unquestionably an aesthetic defect. Mr. Trilling attributes this weakness in the play to our modern insensitivity to the values of the nonassertive, which he now associates both with Wordsworth's "sentiment of being" and with "the common routine" to which Eliot had failed to do justice. He argues that even the way of martyrdom is made factitious by Eliot's inability to portray the simple joys of the common routine. And Mr. Trilling castigates this "system of feeling which sets very little store by—which, indeed, denies the possibility of—the 'beatitude' which Wordsworth thought was the birthright of every human soul."

Here Mr. Trilling's covert passage between two very different levels of experience becomes apparent. Whatever one may say about the feelings depicted in the lines from *Tintern Abbey*, it is obvious that they have little to do with the routine trivialities of modern middle-class life. Wordsworth himself, as Mr. Trilling is surely aware, felt his sentiment of being in opposition to the life of the common routine, or at least to the routine of the urban middle class of his time (and we can be sure he would have felt the same about our time). He turns to images of nature that revive his sentiment of being "'mid the din of towns and cities" and "In darkness and amid the many shapes / Of joyless daylight; when the fretful stir / Unprofitable and the fever of the world / Have hung upon the beatings of my heart."

In other words, by lumping Wordsworth's "beatitude" with Eliot's "the common routine," Mr. Trilling is being false to the spirit of Wordsworth;

but even more, he is trying to make us believe that a passive acceptance of social convention is on the same level of spiritual dignity as the quasi-mystic experience of Wordsworth. The only element the two have in common is that of passivity, the suspension of the will. And while the sentiment of being of Wordsworth or Keats may truly be called a projection of the experience of art as the ideal form of the moral life, it is difficult to see how the same may be said of a simple acquiescence in the common urban routine.

The same type of illegitimate identification between two quite different kinds of being—to use Mr. Trilling's own criterion—comes out even more sharply at the conclusion of the Wordsworth essay. At this point Mr. Trilling is maintaining that "again and again in our literature, at its most apocalyptic and intense, we find the impulse to create figures who are intended to suggest that life is justified in its elemental biological simplicity." And he then goes on to give a list of such creations—D. H. Lawrence's primitives, Dreiser's Jennie Gerhardt and Mrs. Griffiths, Hemingway's waiters, Faulkner's Negroes and idiot boys. According to Mr. Trilling, all these figures show the tendency of our literature to "depict the will seeking its own negation—or, rather, seeking its own affirmation by its rejection of the aims which the world sets before it and by turning its energies upon itself in self-realization."

But what, one cannot help asking, has the biological *justification* of life to do with the will seeking its own negation? And what have these examples to do with anything that can remotely be called self-realization? The transcendence of the will by the artist (or by the ascetic and the saint) is self-realization; but this idea carries with it the implication of conscious purpose, self-dedication, discipline, struggle—it implies, in short, having a will to surrender. From Mr. Trilling's examples it is clear that he makes no distinction between such self-realization and a blind and dumb submission to destiny—a condition of being that never reaches a level on which the will may properly be spoken of. Here, too, Mr. Trilling is assigning the ideal values of the aesthetic attitude to a condition of being with which it has in common only an absence of will.

This tendency of Mr. Trilling's thought, working with another set of categories, may also be observed in his provocative essay on "William Dean Howells and the Roots of Modern Taste." The announced intention of this piece is the laudable one of removing Howells from the history of American culture and giving him a place in literature. All too many writers belong in the first category, and Mr. Trilling thinks that Howells deserves a better fate. No modern critic excels Mr. Trilling in giving fresh and perceptive readings of novels; and one would have expected him to do for Howells what he did for *The Princess Casamassima* and the novels of E. M. Forster. But, instead of concerning himself at length with Howells's creations, Mr. Trilling adopts the same oblique tactic as in his Wordsworth essay. He argues that our modern apocalyptic and charismatic culture, addicted to power-worship and the deification of evil, is incapable of justly evaluating the sunlit merits of Howells.[4] And Mr. Trilling goes on to talk not about Howells but about the roots of modern taste, using some remarks made by Henry James as indices to what disqualifies us from appreciating Howells.

Modern taste is dominated by an antipathy to what Mr. Trilling calls "the conditioned" and favors what he calls "pure spirit" (whose agent and instrument is the will). The conditions to which we moderns respond, he says, "are the ones which we ourselves make, or over which we have control, which is to say conditions as they are virtually spirit, as they deny the idea of the conditioned. Somewhere in our mental constitution is the demand for life as pure spirit." Now Mr. Trilling contends, roughly, that our longing for pure spirit has made us blind to such aspects of the conditioned as the family and our class status, and has caused us to deprecate such necessary matters as those which Howells listed among possible subjects for a novelist—"the family budget, nagging wives, daughters who want to marry fools, and the difficulties of deciding whom to invite to dinner."

Our dislike of the conditioned also accounts for our passion for form and artifice in literature, since the triumph of form is primarily that of spirit imposing its own conditions. And then, after having identified the conditioned in Howells with the most commonplace concerns of civil life ("for Howells the center of reality was the family life of the middle class"), Mr. Trilling clinches his argument in the following startling fashion: "The knowledge of the antagonism between spirit and the conditioned—it is Donne's, it is Pascal's, it is Tolstoi's—may in literature be a cause of great delight because it is so rare and difficult; beside it the knowledge of pure spirit is comparatively easy."

In the light of what Mr. Trilling has told us about Howells's sense of "the conditioned," this invocation of Donne, Pascal, and Tolstoy is unexpected to say the least. What has Howells to do with Donne's conflict between a skeptical sensuality and a passionate religiosity? With Pascal's conflict between the impasses of reason and the eternal silence of the infinite spaces? With Tolstoy's titanic search for the meaning of history, and his anguished struggle to reconcile the abundance of life with the gnawing awareness of physical death?

It is Mr. Trilling himself who has called our attention to the importance of qualities of being; and his own attempt to wipe out the differences between the social trivia of Howells and the tragic sense of the conditioned in Donne, Pascal, and Tolstoy is thus all the more disturbing and disconcerting. Once again Mr. Trilling's antagonism to the will has led him to assign the same spiritual significance to totally diverse levels on which "the conditioned" may enter into a relationship with "pure spirit." And the result is that the will, instead of transcending the social world and its particular aims, now finds itself enjoined to treat the most casual conventions of the family life of the middle class as the sacrosanct conditions of life itself.

## IV

The remaining essays in *The Opposing Self* are dominated either by the idea of transcendence and negation of the will in a quasi-religious sense (Dickens, Flaubert), or by the dialectic of pure spirit and the conditioned turning up in an explicit or implicit form (James, Tolstoy, Orwell, Jane Austen). Mr. Trilling shows remarkable skill in working these diverse subjects around to conform to his ideas. And while one may feel that he too often and too readily finds what he is looking for, with the aid of the convenient ambiguities of such words as "culture" and "self," all these studies are nonetheless valuable and suggestive contributions. Taken as a whole, however, the total impression they create serves to reinforce Mr. Trilling's preference for stability and stasis over the restless agitations of pure spirit. In his brilliant interpretation of *Mansfield Park*, which one does not have to agree with to admire, Mr. Trilling speaks of the antivital element in the novel, the self-mockery of spirit, the choice of the sanctions of principle over the exigencies of consciousness. And it is this facet of the novel, lovingly caricatured in the somnolent and almost inanimate figure of Lady Bertram, that he says "speaks to our secret inexpressible hopes." It speaks, at any rate, to the hopes of Mr. Trilling; and in a language considerably different from the one we had heard in *The Liberal Imagination*.

In his earlier book Mr. Trilling had attacked the tyranny of the will in wishing to impose its aims on other modes of apprehending reality. Naturally, in the course of doing so, Mr. Trilling stressed art's tragic sense of the conditioned nature of life and of the ultimate insolubility of most human dilemmas. But this was still done in the name of freedom—in the name of the artist's freedom to transcend the concerns of the will and in the name of what Mr. Trilling called "the lively sense of contingency and possibility, and of those exceptions to the rule which may be the beginning of the end of the rule." On the literary level this concern for freedom appeared also in Mr. Trilling's defense of plot, fable, and form in the novel against the realistic prejudices of liberal critics. Authorial minds playing with reality, Mr. Trilling wrote, were for him "the great and strangely effective symbols of liberty operating in a world of necessity."

Mr. Trilling, however, is no longer concerned to defend this authorial freedom from the hampering clogs of realism; he now feels that his urgent task is to defend not freedom but the virtues of acknowledging necessity. For he seems to have acquired an uneasy sense that the spirit of man is ready to fly off at any moment to some distant goal "pinnacled dim in the intense inane"; and for man's own protection Mr. Trilling keeps recalling him to his earthbound condition. Writing of Howells's preference for the "smiling aspects of life," Mr. Trilling concedes that these latter may not be very exciting; but at least, he adds, they will serve "to bind us to the earth, to prevent our being seduced by the godhead of disintegration."

No doubt this anxiety about disintegration is linked to Mr. Trilling's puzzling inability to conceive of the will (pure spirit) except in terms of an apocalypse. Even in *The Liberal Imagination* he had already defined the modern idea of "progress" as being in reality the extinction of history; and in his intellectual world no alternative now seems left but total acceptance or total disintegration. It is one of the paradoxes of his position that his aversion to the apocalyptic and charismatic, instead of causing him to reprobate extremism in any form, should simply have driven him to adopt the alternative extreme himself.

From a critic of the liberal imagination, then, Mr. Trilling has evolved into one of the least belligerent and most persuasive spokesmen of the conservative imagination. For, on the plane of the imagination, the distinction between liberal and conservative—as Karl Mannheim has explained in his *Ideology and Utopia*—pivots precisely on this feeling for the conditioned. "The deepest driving force of the liberal ideas of the Enlightenment," Mannheim writes, "lay in the fact that it appealed to the free will and kept alive the feeling of being indeterminate and unconditioned. . . . And if one wishes to formulate the central achievement of conservatism in a single sentence, it could be said that in conscious contrast to the liberal outlook, it gave positive emphasis to the notion of the determinateness of our outlook and behavior."[5] However he may have misread Hegel, Mr. Trilling's flair did not betray him when he thought to find sustenance in Hegel's work. For Hegel is the philosopher who, to quote Mannheim again, "set up against the liberal idea a conservative counterpart"; in Hegel, "reality, the 'here and now,' is no longer experienced as an 'evil' reality but as the embodiment of the highest value and meanings."[6]

Some light on this evolution, which hardly seems to have been noticed, may perhaps be cast by a quick look at Mr. Trilling's brochure on *Freud and the Crisis of Our Culture.* Freud has generally been considered a radical and

234    *The Opposing Self*

disintegrating influence, but it is striking to see how Mr. Trilling singles out for special praise one of the few Freudian ideas which have been called "reactionary." Man, Freud contended, is biologically determined; he is not simply a creature of cultural conditioning; and Mr. Trilling praises this notion because, if we refuse to accept it, then "there is no revision of the nature of man that we cannot hope to bring about." Far from being reactionary, Mr. Trilling considers Freud's position "liberating" because "it suggests that there is a residue of human quality beyond the reach of cultural control, and that this residue of human quality, elemental as it may be, serves to bring culture itself under criticism and keeps it from being absolute."

One can sympathize with Mr. Trilling's revulsion against the idea of man as infinitely malleable and helplessly exposed to the "conditioning" imposed by the brave new world of 1984; but this is no reason to locate the ideas of freedom and liberation in stasis, immutability, and barely conscious biological existence. For the problem still remains of understanding how immutable biological determination can be a root of *freedom*, and how purely biological attributes can "criticize" culture and exhibit "human quality" without the intervention of some more positively human spiritual force. The curious concatenation of stasis and freedom in Mr. Trilling's thought thus very probably has a Freudian source; and one suspects that Freud's sympathy for socialism, his battle against sexual obscurantism, and his general aura of radicalism, may well have enabled Mr. Trilling to adopt an essentially conservative position under Freud's aegis without feeling it as self-betrayal.

The weakness of the liberal imagination, as Mr. Trilling shows in his book of that title, is that it views the realm of the ultimate, the eternal, and the immitigable in the perspective of the will. But we may now retort that the weakness of the conservative imagination lies in imposing its sense of the ultimate conditioned nature of life on areas where the will may fruitfully intervene. One of the great merits of *The Liberal Imagination* was that it criticized the illegitimate ravages of the will without openly impugning its efficacy or necessity in its proper realm; but in adopting the positive standpoint of the conservative imagination, Mr. Trilling has taken over its weakness as well as its strength. And it is to bring out this weakness that we have emphasized so strongly those passages in which Mr. Trilling seems to have yielded too easily to this congenital conservative temptation. For it would be a great pity indeed if Mr. Trilling were to use his scrupulous sensitivity, his lucid and ingratiating style, and his considerable moral authority to encourage the all-too-prevalent failing of the conservative imagination. And one cannot help but feel that, if he continues to do so, he will unwittingly promote what he himself characterizes, in the Howells essay, as "a debilitation of the American psychic tone, the diminution of moral tension."

Howells had already noticed, at the end of the nineteenth century, "the displacement of doctrine and moral strenuousness by a concern with 'social adjustment' and the amelioration of boredom"; and Mr. Trilling refers to David Riesman's *The Lonely Crowd* as proof that this process has by no means slackened in our own time. The society of *The Lonely Crowd*, however, is hardly threatened by the godhead of disintegration—at any rate, not so far as that godhead takes the form of pure, free, and independent spirit striving to impose its own conditions on life. The real danger to such a society surely does not arise from an excess of pure spirit; it is far more likely to stem from a submissive acceptance of the conditioned in the form of social pressure and convention.

When Mr. Trilling defended art and the tragic sense of the conditioned in *The Liberal Imagination*, he performed a distinct service to American culture. These values always need defenders against the overwhelming predominance in American life of a shortsighted optimism and utilitarianism. But in defending the conditioned on the level of middle-class values, and in endowing the torpid acceptance of these values with the dignity of aesthetic transcendence, Mr. Trilling is merely augmenting the already frightening momentum making for conformism and the debilitation of moral tension. The presence of spirit and will has always carried with it the danger of disintegration; but the absence of these qualities inevitably carries with it the far more immediate danger of moral and cultural stultification.

Indeed, if we are to judge from a little essay on Edith Wharton called "The Morality of Inertia," which appears in Mr. Trilling's most recent volume, *A Gathering of Fugitives*, it may well be that he is becoming uneasily aware of this danger in his position. It would be wrong to say that such a morality of inertia was explicitly advocated all through *The Opposing Self*—or at least, if such an assertion were not literally mistaken, it would yet be unforgivably heavyhanded. Still, Lady Bertram comes uncomfortably close to symbolizing such a morality; and Mr. Trilling, as we have tried to show, did not pay sufficient attention to the moral and qualitative difference between inertia and tragic acceptance. It is thus only fair to cite what he now has to say.

"The morality of inertia," he writes, "of the dull, unthinking round of duties, may, and often does, yield the immorality of inertia; the example that will most readily occur is that of the good simple people, so true to their family responsibilities, who gave no thought to the concentration camps in whose shadow they lived. No: the morality of inertia is not to be praised, but it must be recognized." To which one can only say "Amen!"—with the reminder that more than biological determination has always been needed for the immorality of inertia to be conquered and surpassed.

## Notes

1. R. P. Blackmur, *The Lion and the Honeycomb* (New York: Harcourt, Brace, 1955), p. 41.

2. Mr. Trilling cites no evidence for his contention about Hegel except a reference to a passage in the fourth part of the *Philosophy of History*. This passage turns out to deal with the German barbarians who invaded the Roman Empire and to whom Hegel attributes a quality that he calls *Gemüth*. This latter is a common German word meaning, roughly, the emotional temper of a man or a group. Hegel, however, gives it a special definition. "Character is a particular form of the will," he writes, "and of the interests that manifest themselves through the will. *Gemüthlichkeit*, however, has no particular aims, such as riches, honors, and the like; in fact, it does not concern itself with any worldly conditions of wealth, prestige, etc., but with the entire condition of the soul—a general sense of enjoyment."

Mr. Trilling is quite captivated with this idea of *Gemüth*—no doubt because it seemed to furnish a term for expressing the condition of the will that he had tried to define in "Art and Fortune." But this should not have led him to pretend that Hegel's remarks about the German barbarians refer to the relation of the modern self to culture since the French Revolution.

Hegel clearly is not talking about the "modern self" in Mr. Trilling's sense—unless we assume that nothing significant happened to culture between the *Völkerwanderung* and the French Revolution. Moreover, even if we overlook this anachronism, Hegel's text does not bear out Mr. Trilling's interpretation. "*Gemüth*," Hegel also writes, in a passage that Mr. Trilling fails to cite, "in the abstract is stupidity, and so we see in the original condition of the Germans a barbaric stupidity, confusion and indeterminacy." Far from making *Gemüth* the basis of a new category of cultural judgment, Hegel regards it as an empty form of infantile self-enjoyment and self-preoccupation. In his view, it only became valuable after having assimilated the objective content of Greco-Roman culture preserved by the Catholic Church. G. W. F. Hegel, *Werke*, Jubilaumsausgabe, ed. by H. Glockner (Stuttgart, 1927–1930), Vol. II, pp. 447–449.

3. Ibid., Vol. XII, pp. 100–105.

4. In this connection, it may be apposite to cite a critic writing in the halcyon days of 1912, and by no means unfriendly to Howells.

"Instead of demonstrating that life was interesting," John Macy says, "that the commonplace is uncommonly interesting if you get under it and understand it, *A Modern Instance* demonstrates with fine precision that life is not interesting to the people that live it and that the commonplace is just as commonplace as the romantic had always supposed it to be." John Macy, *The Spirit of American Literature* (New York: Modern Library, n.d.), p. 284.

It would seem that times have not changed as much as Mr. Trilling would have us believe!

5. Karl Mannheim, *Ideology and Utopia* (New York: Harvest, Harcourt, Brace, n.d.), p. 229.

6. Ibid., p. 232.

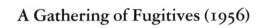

# A Gathering of Fugitives (1956)

# 41

David Daiches

*"The Mind of Lionel Trilling: An Appraisal,"* Commentary

*July 1957*

(See no. 10 for biographical information about Daiches.)

Daiches' *Two Worlds: An Edinburgh Jewish Childhood* (1956), published shortly before the appearance of the following review, echoes the experience of the Jewish members of the New York intellectuals. Son of an orthodox rabbi who was the accepted head of Scottish Jewry, Daiches traveled between the world of his orthodox family and that of the secular world of Edinburgh and modern British culture. In a sense, he was the assimilated British intellectual that some part of the Anglophile Trilling yearned to become.

Daiches was acquainted with the New York intellectuals in the 1940s and '50s as an occasional contributor to *Commentary* and participant in its symposia. In the review below, Daiches sees Trilling as "the perfect New York intellectual"—"intelligent, curious, humane, well-read, interested in ideas, fascinated by other times and places, immensely knowledgeable about European culture"—yet strangely uninformed about American life outside his circle.

Lionel Trilling is in many respects my idea of the perfect New York intellectual. Intelligent, curious, humane, well read, interested in ideas, fascinated by other times and places, and immensely knowledgeable about European culture, he is at the same time metropolitan (with the provincialism that goes with true metropolitanism), self-conscious and professional in the practice of literary criticism, very much the *observer* of the great stream of American life that goes on around him, the sophisticated urban observer who is proud of the fact that his observation is undoctrinaire and untainted with snobbism. He castigates his fellow intellectuals for their complacent sense of superiority to the masses. "His [the intellectual's] sense of an inert mass resistant to ideas, entirely unenlightened, and hating enlightenment, is part of the pathos of liberalism in the Twenties and Thirties, which is sedulously maintained despite the fact that the liberal ideas of the Twenties and Thirties are . . . strong and established, truly powerful." Mr. Trilling is being fair; he is in the tradition of anti-Stalinist modern American liberalism which increasingly distrusts the old attacks on babbitry and feels that the once popular intellectual game of jeering at America's anti-intellectualism is to be deplored. But it is all acted out in the mind. I don't want to pursue an *ad hominem* argument, but I would suggest that if Mr. Trilling had taught freshman English at a Midwestern state university (I have just been looking at some themes from one), or spent some time with the staff and pupils of, say, Western Kansas State Teachers' College, or even spent more time than I suspect that he has ever done talking with junior colleagues from minor colleges and universities at annual meetings of the Modern Language Association, the terms in which he discusses the relation between the American intellectual and the American mass would be significantly different.

Trilling's metropolitan intellectualism gives him knowledge, understanding, sympathy, often wisdom—and that, in all conscience, is an impressive list of qualities—but it constricts him in odd ways. "To the literary intellectual any profession other than that of literature condemns itself by the mere fact of its being a profession." This is a remark he makes in passsing, in the course of an article on "The Situation of the American Intellectual at the Present Time" originally contributed to a *Partisan Review* symposium. Now where can he have picked up such a notion? It simply isn't true, outside perhaps of New York literary cocktail parties. In an essay on David Riesman (and how welcome Riesman's investigations and conclusions are to Trilling, extending as they do the range of his own concerned observation) he makes the same point again, that the literary intellectual "seems to find more and more difficulty in believing that there is a significant reality to be found in anything except literature itself . . . or in believing that any profession save that of literature is interesting and deserves credence." This is the remark of a metropolitan intellectual; I think he would find few to agree with him in, say, Paul Engle's creative writing classes at Iowa or among young people trying their hands at poems and short stories on the Pacific Coast or in the Midwest or the South. My own knowledge of America is of course not that of a native, though it has extended intermittently for almost twenty years now; but I see Trilling as a man who looks out on the civilization of his country with a perspective a little like that of the famous New Yorker's map of the United States which appeared many years ago in the *New Yorker* magazine.

Of course, his perspective is not really like that. No man with such a perspective could have written as brilliantly as Trilling has on Mark Twain, for example. He knows what there is to be known about both American and European history, and knows it with his own kind of intellectual inwardness. He can be sometimes almost startlingly luminous in breaking out a string of analogies that joins different points in European culture. "The analogues with Zola's work are not to be found in science but in the work of such fantasts as Breughel and Bosch, or Ben Jonson, Baudelaire, and James Joyce—which is not surprising, for the line between a truly passionate naturalism and an extravagant fantasy is always a thin one." This is admirable; it stems both from clearly realized knowledge and clearly apprehended ideas. But when talking of E. M. Forster's biography of his great-aunt and the house in which she lived, Battersea Rise, he remarks: "Battersea Rise stood on Clapham Common. Clapham, of course, proposes the Clapham Sect."[1] This is too bookish for anything. Clapham proposes the sights and sounds of a district in London; the sect of that name is far from the first thing that springs to mind when Clapham is mentioned—except, perhaps, to a New York intellectual. It is like saying that Boston proposes the Boston Tea Party—but the analogy is not a very good one, for the Boston Tea Party is more universally known than the Clapham sect ever was.

In the essay on the American intellectual to which I have already referred, Trilling asks rhetorically: "Who amongst us has any adequate idea about the quality of the teaching staffs of the schools? What is the literary curriculum of our high schools? What is taught in 'Social Studies'? What actually happens in a 'progressive' school—I mean apart from what everybody jokes about? What happens in colleges?" The assumption is that the intellectual doesn't know the answer to these questions. We must beware, the argument runs (and "we" are the intellectuals) of behaving in a superior fashion toward the American school systems or of adversely criticizing progressive education, and so on, because, as intellectuals living in a world of our own, we really know nothing about these things. This is an odd way to rehabilitate American education. But, apart from the logic of the method, the facts are surely disputable. The metropolitan intellectual may be as aloof from the facts of life as Trilling indicates; my own experience suggests that elsewhere in America he is far less aloof. Certainly, here at Indiana University, where I am at the moment Visiting Professor, I have found few of my colleagues who do not know, and who are not actively concerned about, what is being taught and how it is being taught in the high schools and teachers' colleges of the state. I could have a good shot myself at telling Mr. Trilling what is taught in "Social Studies," what actually happens in a "progressive" school, and what is the literary curriculum of at least some high schools. Has he never cross-examined his students on what and how they learned before they came to college?

And yet how wise, how discerning, how knowledgeable, how aware of cultural contexts, Mr. Trilling can be when he allows his well-stocked mind to contemplate its contents! "Mr. [Robert] Graves as a prose writer is a first-rate secondary figure in our literature. Such figures are a British phenomenon—we don't breed them in America, and we don't know how to respond to them. An intelligent American who has a lively or a professional interest in literature wants only the Very Best, the *oeuvre* that is certified by whatever literary Consumers' Union he subscribes to as having a top rating for spirituality, apocalypticality, and permanence. One might spend one's life pleasantly and very profitably with the secondary writers of the English 19th century, the writers whom no one would think to call 'great,' the odd, quirky spirits from George Borrow to Mark Rutherford,[2] the travelers, the autobiographers, the essayists, the men who had a particular, perhaps eccentric, thing to say, and said it fully and well, with delight in what they were doing and no worry about greatness." There is a genial perceptiveness here, a confident and relaxed drawing on both knowledge and awareness, that modern American criticism too often lacks.

Every now and again, in reading his new collection of essays [*A Gathering of Fugitives*], one is struck by a felicitous remark, a genuine *aperçu*, a pointing to a *relationship*; for Mr. Trilling is at his best and most characteristic when making connections—between the aesthetic and the moral, between literature and life, between culture and environment. "Whenever the characters of a story suffer, they do so at the behest of their author—the author is responsible for their suffering and must justify his cruelty by the seriousness of his moral intention." This is a comment on *Ethan Frome*, but it would serve admirably as an introduction to a symposium on the nature of tragedy. Having diagnosed "the morality of inertia" in *Ethan Frome*, Trilling proceeds to enlarge the context, in a characteristic movement which takes us from Edith Wharton to Wordsworth. The passage is worth quoting at some length; it is an admirable example of the kind of critical insight Trilling can communicate:

> Literature, of course, is not wholly indifferent to what I have called the morality of habit and biology, the morality of inertia. But literature, when it deals with this morality, is tempted to qualify its dullness by endowing it with a certain high grace. There is never any real moral choice for the Félicité of Flaubert's story "A Simple Heart." She is all pious habit of virtue, and of blind, unthinking, unquestioning love.

There are, of course, actually such people as Félicité, simple, good, loving—quite stupid in their love, not choosing where to bestow it. We meet such people frequently in literature, in the pages of Balzac, Dickens, Dostoievski, Joyce, Faulkner, Hemingway. They are of a quite different order of being from those who try the world with their passion and their reason; they are by way of being saints, of the less complicated kind. They do not really exemplify what I mean by the morality of inertia. Literature is uncomfortable in the representation of the morality of inertia or of biology, and overcomes its discomfort by representing it with the added grace of that extravagance which we denominate saintliness.

But the morality of inertia is to be found in very precise exemplification in one of Wordsworth's poems. Wordsworth is pre-eminent among the writers who experimented in the representation of new kinds and bases of moral action—he has a genius for imputing moral existence to people who, according to the classical morality, should have no moral life at all. And he has the courage to make this imputation without at the same time imputing the special grace and interest of saintliness. The poem I have in mind is ostensibly about a flower, but the transition from the symbol to the human fact is clearly, if awkwardly, made. . . .

And Trilling goes on to discuss Wordsworth's poem on the lesser celandine, returning in the end (via the Book of Job and *The Brothers Karamazov*) to his earlier point. This is the sensitive and well-stocked mind at work, and it is a delight, as well as an education, to watch.

The well-stocked mind: everything that the mind can observe from books, contemplation, the free exercise of intellectual curiosity, Trilling has, within a large area of American and European culture, observed. How sound and balanced and utterly *right* is his careful estimate of the achievement and the limitation of F. R. Leavis as a critic. He knows the English critical scene (though he visited it physically for the first time only very briefly a short while ago) in which Leavis is embattled, he understands so clearly the springs of Leavis's loves and hates, he discriminates between liberating and constricting uses of social ideas in criticism, and, while firmly praising Leavis for his great positive achievements, he can remark with calm justice: "In Dr. Leavis's own critical practice, the failure to be explicit about even the disproportionately small social issue of Bloomsbury has led to his assimilating a social antagonism into his general critical sensibility, where it works to distort his perception of an important aspect of literature." No English critic of Leavis has been able to put such an unerring finger on both his greatness and on his weaknesses.

This Trilling can do from his metropolitan isolation, because the data have all been written about. He knows more about the intellectual atmosphere of Cambridge, England, than of Bloomington, Indiana: the former has been written about. Trilling's mind will play luminously with what he knows, and what he knows is what has a *literature*. It seems hardly an exaggeration to say that it was the writings of David Riesman which led him to see American society as a *subject*.[3] He knows London and Paris and New England and the American Frontier as they have been rendered, interpreted, discussed, projected, evoked, in innumerable books. He is at home in the world of Western culture in a positively enviable way. And yet in a sense that world of Western culture exists only in the mind of a few highly cultivated American intellectuals. In fact, it is more fragmentary, more impure, more confused, and perhaps even sometimes more exciting than the civilized and sensitive American metropolitan mind conceives it to be. Perhaps it can be said that men like Trilling (and there are all too few of them) have created Western culture, for only in their minds it lies as an ordered whole. But at least in looking on it as an ordered whole he is not looking *back* on it in Alexandrian fashion to classify and entomb: it all lives for him, vibrant with both moral and aesthetic reality; it is part of a present, or perhaps of a timeless, order, an order that is always relevant, however much one needs a sense of the past to understand it. It is this conviction of the present reality of all literature that makes Trilling such a lively and compelling critic.

## Notes

1. The Clapham Sect, a group of evangelicals in the Church of England during the late eighteenth and early nineteenth century, played a leading role in the movement to abolish slavery in the British colonies.—Ed.

2. George Borrow (1803–81), British adventurer and author, wrote *Gypsies in Spain* (1942) and *Ballads of All Nations* (1950). Mark Rutherford (pen name of William Hale White) (1831–1913), British critic and autobiographer, was a champion of Wordsworth and Coleridge.—Ed.

3. David Riesman (1909– ) is the author of *The Lonely Crowd: A Study of the Changing American Character* (1950). Riesman made the celebrated distinction among "tradition-directed," "inner-directed," and "other-directed" societies: the first type uses tradition, the second employs the person's internal values, and the third utilizes other people's expectations to form its citizenry. Trilling reviewed Riesman's *Individual Reconsidered* (1954) in *The Griffin* (May 1954); the article was collected in *A Gathering of Fugitives*.—Ed.

42

## E. B. Greenwood

## *"The Literary Criticism of Lionel Trilling,"* Twentieth Century

## *January 1958*

E. B. Greenwood (1933– ) read for his undergraduate degree at Oxford University, where he wrote a thesis on Matthew Arnold. Following his graduation in 1954, he taught in New Zealand, at the University of Glasgow. He is presently a professor at the University of Kent. Greenwood is a contributor to numerous British literary magazines and the author of *Tolstoy: The Comprehensive Vision* (1975) and *F. R. Leavis* (1978), the latter of whom Greenwood pronounces in his monograph "the greatest critic of the twentieth century."

The appearance of Professor Trilling's *A Gathering of Fugitives* is a sufficient occasion for trying to get his critical work as a whole into some kind of perspective. He is obviously a critic who has his roots in the nineteenth century. The very form of his books, that of a loose collection of essays which have previously appeared at various times and in various places, is that of Matthew Arnold's or Ernest Renan's.[1] It was indeed the critical biography of Arnold which he wrote in the 1930s that gave him his orientation in criticism and ever since that time he has been at pains to emphasize the continuity between nineteenth- and twentieth-century literature. He reaffirms that continuity in his latest book:

> to read Kafka's life and works under the aspect of the parental relations of, say, *Dombey and Son*, of *David Copperfield* and of *Little Dorrit* (this last especially pertinent with its overshadowing prisons and its Circumlocution Office in which no official may ever give an answer) is to understand the perfect continuity of the twentieth century with the nineteenth.

Both the strength and weakness of Professor Trilling's first two collections of essays lay in his overriding concern with ideas, with the drama of dialectic. That concern is, as we shall see, less to the fore in his third book, which calls for a somewhat different approach than the other two. *The Liberal Imagination* and *The Opposing Self* showed him abstracting the cultural conflict embodied in various and very different works of art and then, with an intelligent and loving care, making this abstraction the core of his own exploration of the nature of things. In some ways one felt a novelist *manqué* was at work, and the fact that he had attempted the genre seemed to bear out, rather than contradict, the feeling. Did not his composite culture heroes, the young man from the provinces, the man whose sense of self is in reciprocation with his sense of evil and the man whose culture secularizes his own spirituality, take on a kind of independent life in his pages, possess a kind of give and take imparted, that is, by Professor Trilling himself rather than by the authors from whose pages he had made the abstractions? It is true that every critic must abstract, but the greatest critics are those whose abstractions subsume the largest number of specific impressions, or, if that seems too quantitative a way of putting things, those whose abstractions are continually tested by recurrence to the concrete; for the obvious danger of abstraction is that it will become too disengaged from the specific. Professor Trilling did not altogether escape this danger. He was not a critic who gave us a rich feeling of the specific quality of Stendhal or Dostoevsky or Proust. He gave us instead a drama of dialectic in which the counters were ideas he had found common to many authors rather than peculiar to one.

To say this is, of course, to isolate the main tendency in those books, it is not to maintain that Professor Trilling never gave us a sense of specific quality, the essays on *The Princess Casamassima*, *Anna Karenina* and *Little Dorrit* would effectively disprove such an assertion. Even here, however, it may be noted that he dealt with *Little Dorrit* so well because the symbolism of that book afforded him a schematic pattern which he could discuss in terms of his interest in the conflict between the will and society, while his remarks about *Anna Karenina*, interesting as they were, were confined, as he admitted, to pointing, because he had no method capable of penetrating beneath the surface of that most undialectical and unsymbolical of novelists, Tolstoy. Similarly, the reason why Professor Trilling's study of E. M. Forster was so disappointing was that he never really dealt with his subject from the standpoint of literary criticism. He remained a critic of ideas throughout, and thus the crucial problem in any discussion of Forster as a novelist, the continual gap between the author's evident intentions and his available artistic means, was never touched on at all.

Though the main tendency of Professor Trilling's criticism had its disquieting aspect this does not invalidate the fact that it was, in the main, a healthy and profitable tendency. We shall always need the criticism of ideas, and Professor Trilling at his best gave us some of the finest examples of work in that genre. Indeed, in his essays 'Art and Fortune' and 'The Meaning of a Literary Idea' he followed Spinoza and Arnold in defining ideas in such a way as to provide a valid justification for his own critical method. There seems some point in considering here, however, why Professor Trilling has never come up to that first collection, *The Liberal Imagination*. The reason is not far to seek. Even a volume which professes to be no more than a collection of essays makes a deeper impression when it has a certain unity of impact (whether this is provided by the critical method or theme or both), and *The Liberal Imagination* had such a unity, as Professor Trilling himself indicated in the preface. Much of that book dealt with a single main theme, the ambiguities latent in the word 'real'. As is the case with Matthew Arnold's best work, moreover, it was critical in the more common sense of the word critical; that is to say, it corrected certain mistaken views by showing their inadequacy to the facts, to 'things as, in themselves, they really are'. Professor Trilling has never written anything better than the essay 'Reality in America', and the theme of that essay, the criticism of Liberalism's tendency to take a reductive view of the meaning of the word 'reality' and the demonstration of the paradoxes that that tendency leads to, is a theme which is continued in the essays on *The Princess Casamassima*, 'Manners, Morals and the Novel' and 'The Kinsey Report.'

Professor Trilling's second collection, *The Opposing Self*, showed that move towards looseness which his latest volume has continued still further. The insistent dialectic was still present, but it seemed weaker because it stemmed less from the process of criticizing the inadequate views of others than from an attempt to establish certain views of his own about the self and its relation to society and culture. As a result of this, Professor Trilling's tendency towards abstraction was less restrained by the offices of criticism. This volume contained perhaps his most unsatisfactory essay, 'Wordsworth and the Rabbis', and most of the book, while interesting, lacked the sense of urgency, of an immediate preoccupation with the problems discussed, which made *The Liberal Imagination* so much more stimulating.

*A Gathering of Fugitives* continues the move away from unity. There is an additional evolution too; it is an evolution away from the criticism of ideas and towards the literary chat, the *causerie* fathered ultimately by Sainte-Beuve[2] rather than Matthew Arnold. Indeed many of the essays in it are quasi biographical: 'The Great Aunt of Mr Forster', 'The Dickens of Our Day', 'Edmund Wilson: A Backward Glance' and 'Profession: Man of the World'. The latter essay does for Richard Monckton Milnes the sort of thing E. M. Forster did for Hannah More in *Abinger Harvest*,[3] and it will be recalled that Professor Trilling himself drew a contrast between the criticism of T. S.

Eliot and E. M. Forster when he suggested that the dialectic of the former stimulates while the impressionism of the latter invites us to relax. No better way could be found of epitomizing the difference between *The Liberal Imagination* and *A Gathering of Fugitives*. The essay on Milnes, for example, strikes one as the sort of thing anybody who has read a certain number of Victorian memoirs could do, where 'Reality in America' required Professor Trilling's peculiar gifts.

This collection of essays is then the least unified and the most mellow of the three; in some ways, therefore, it is the most directly enjoyable. Indeed, Professor Trilling tends in it to insinuate that we are not enjoying ourselves as much as we might. In a for the most part admirable note on 'Dr Leavis and the Moral Tradition' he takes occasion to rebuke that critic for discounting the element of sheer performance in works of art and invites us to partake of an 'intentional relaxation of moral awareness'. Quite what we are being invited to do we don't, except in the most general way, know, and it appears that the invitation serves mainly to show that Professor Trilling has the sterling virtues of uncommittedness and catholicity. We may remember with regret, however, that it was the virtue of committedness, of continual moral awareness, which gave *The Liberal Imagination* its impact. Again, in both 'Criticism and Aesthetics' and 'On Not Talking', he appears to be pleading with us to emerge from our preoccupation with nothing but literature and to broaden our minds by sampling the more immediately aesthetic pleasures of the visual arts. Once more the advice is admirable, but did it need a man with Professor Trilling's critical gifts to take it upon himself to proffer it?

On such a wide but important theme as 'The American Intellectual at the Present Time' Professor Trilling's new uncommittedness leads to a certain vagueness in comparison with the essays on abstract themes in *The Liberal Imagination*. It is perhaps regrettable that the main impression his essay leaves is that the American literary intellectual, despite any appearances to the contrary, is pretty ignorant not only of most things about American social life, but also about the 'more transcendent matters' with which the intellectual is supposed to be concerned. Professor Trilling is himself a most distinguished American intellectual, and he ought at least to have provided us with some notion in his essay of why the American intellectual is so out of touch with the facts of American social life, and let us know whether he personally is aware not simply of 'the questions which the intellectuals have been content to leave to the education editor of the *New York Times*', but of the answers to some of them as well.

The last essay in the book, a review of Santayana's letters, is in some ways the most interesting one, for here Professor Trilling, whom we have characterized as essentially a critic of ideas, is dealing with perhaps the greatest modern critic of ideas. It is probably the best essay too, although Professor Trilling seems, at the outset, to overestimate the influence of the aestheticism of the late nineteenth century on Santayana's thought. He obviously admires Santayana, but he no less obviously does so with reluctance and discomfort. Is this because he himself has been unable to achieve in his work that very firmness of self-definition which, as he so rightly says, characterizes Santayana? *The Liberal Imagination* was a book to place on the same shelf as *Character and Opinion in the United States.* Professor Trilling's last collection, however, has moved away from the astringency which characterized his first volume to an amiable catholicity which soothes rather than stimulates.

## Notes

1. Ernest Renan (1823–92), French scholar and essayist.—Ed.

2. Charles Augustin Sainte-Beuve (1804–69), was the preeminent French literary critic of the nineteenth century. His *Monday Chats* (1851–62), which consists of both essays and public lectures, have heavily influenced world criticism.—Ed.

3. Trilling took seriously the work of Baron Richard Monckton Milnes (1809–85), British poet and literary critic, just as Forster's *Abinger Harvest* (1936) treated with respect and made widely known the works of British devotional writer Hannah More (1745–1833), such as *Search After Happiness: A Pastoral Drama* (1774) and *Sacred Dramas, Chiefly Intended for Young Persons* (1796). Milnes was regarded condescendingly by his contemporaries and dismissed as a pollyannaish sensibility and a mediocre thinker.—Ed.

Beyond Culture (1965)

$$43$$

*George Steiner*

*"An Overture to Silence,"* Book Week

*October 1965*

One of the most erudite intellectuals of his generation, George Steiner (1929– ) is regarded on both sides of the Atlantic as a major cultural critic and essayist. Fully conversant with all schools of contemporary cultural theory and centrally preoccupied with inquiry into the potential and limitations of communication via language, Steiner writes cultural criticism in French, German, and English; he reads and has addressed himself to literature written in every major European language. A professor of English and comparative literature at the University of Geneva and a fellow of Churchill College at Cambridge University, he is the author of *Language and Silence: Essays on Language, Literature, and the Inhuman* (1967), *In Bluebeard's Castle: Some Notes toward the Redefinition of Culture* (1971), *After Babel: Aspects of Language and Translation*, and *On Difficulty and Other Essays* (1978), among other books.

By the mid-1960s, when he wrote the following review as the regular book reviewer for *The New Yorker*, Steiner was already a well-known critic in New York intellectual circles.

For my generation, Lionel Trilling was part of growing up. As they appeared individually and were then collected in *The Liberal Imagination* (1950), Trilling's critical essays were more than just that. They showed, as had Edmund Wilson in the preceding decades, that a man could write about writers and in that way define or enact some of the primary gestures of contemporary politics and intelligence. The sum of the voice was greater than the individual parts. Though they ranged from Tacitus to Kipling, the essays came from a vital center, from an implicit base of vision. And that center was a subtle, necessary thing: a belief in the tremendous importance to a mass society of "variousness, possibility, complexity, and difficulty." In these essays the very act of dubiety, the refusal to cut corners, had a liberating force. In them, Trilling exhibited that energy of the uncertain which is characteristic of so much modern literature and which provides, I imagine, our equivalent to what the 17th century called wit.

Moreover, the critical judgments had behind them the qualifications and authority of art. American literature is not notable for adult political fiction, but in the short list which would include Henry Adams and Robert Penn Warren, Trilling's *The Middle of the Journey* (1947) would rank high. It seems to me the best novel to come of the political stress of the late Forties. Add a powerful short story addressed to a similar theme, and one had the feeling that Trilling was working both as observer and actor toward a goal of informed consciousness. One waited for the next essay or fiction as one waits for an echo.

When it came, with the publication of *The Opposing Self* in 1955, the sound was not very bracing. The individual essays, particularly that on Keats, showed the same fineness of perception, the same delight in complexity as before, but little new had been added. I remember feeling confident at the time that Trilling was clearing the deck, that a major statement was in hand, some urgently needed provocation to the cliché conventions of the Eisenhower era. It was exciting to wait because one knew that the mind at work, and presumably gathering impetus, was one of the richest, most discriminating in modern letters.

Instead, there came a long silence, interrupted by a handful of essays and lectures. It is these which have now been assembled and reprinted under the title *Beyond Culture.* Noting the long break, the publisher's blurb rightly speaks of "an event," of an event that is "momentous indeed." But in what way?

The eight essays in this book were written and/or published between May, 1955, and February, 1965, a time of history which would, one would have thought, instigate certain radical queries and reappraisals. They are, in the proper and traditional sense, occasional. The essays on Jane Austen and Isaac Babel are prefaces, of the kind incessantly solicited by publishers to brighten a classic or quicken a neglected work. The paper on Freud is the Anniversary Lecture delivered to the New York Psychoanalytical Society. "The Two Environments" is the Henry Sidgwick Memorial Lecture delivered at Newnham College, Cambridge. "Hawthorne in Our Time" was occasioned by the *Hawthorne Centenary Essays.* "A Comment on the Leavis-Snow Controversy" is precisely that; and the two remaining papers were, I believe, first delivered in an academic context. We find here, in neat proportion, the range of official critical and didactic media: the preface, the conference paper, the festive lecture, the piece of high journalism.

Which is perfectly in order; and one is grateful to acquire between hard covers (though by no means at a bargain price) what one has been saving as a magazine article or pamphlet. But what of the claim, advanced with necessary crudity in the blurb, but very much present as well in Trilling's preface, that these occasional pieces cohere, that they have a common design deliberately unfolded? What of the title, whose dual Freudian resonance—*Beyond the Pleasure Principle* and *Culture and Its Discontents*—is itself a portentous assertion?

It is the preface one focuses on, not only because it is the one strictly new thing in the book, but rather because it is the most elusive. In it, Trilling looks once again at the notion which is central to his whole enterprise: that of *culture*, and the meanings and potentialities of that notion in the contemporary moral, literary, social and academic climate. As before, Trilling defines the modern period as that which had "its beginning in the latter part of the eighteenth century and its apogee in the first quarter of the twentieth century. We continue the direction it took. . . . the conscious commitment to it is definitive of the artistic and intellectual culture of our time." Crucial to that direction is "the adversary program," the deliberate attempt of the modern writer to detach the reader from the habits of thought and feeling that the larger, normative culture imposes.

But there has been a very important change. "Between the end of the first quarter of this century and the present time there has grown up a populous group whose members take for granted the idea of the adversary culture." Trilling is examining the impact of this development on the teaching of literature in the university, on the control of taste in the art market, on the very function of criticism (here as elsewhere, Matthew Arnold's attempt to define the function of criticism for *his* society, is the point of departure and assumed reference).

Around the "adversary culture" there has formed a class. As it becomes itself an establishment it produces its own preconceptions, its own defense mechanisms, its own unanimities of nervous or intellectual response. It comes to resemble that which it set out to challenge and subvert. The core of spontaneous experience on which the "adversary culture" founds its claims to relevant heresy may itself degenerate into unexamined abstraction. Hence certain characteristic ambiguities of relationship between the "adversary culture" and the general cultural ensemble. It is with these the essays are meant to deal.

I think this is a fair summary of Trilling's preface. But I am not altogether certain. The preface is written in a peculiarly gray, evasive style. This is, of course, the most disturbing aspect. Jamesian turns are frequent: Trilling notes that "it isn't possible to be wholly grave" about this or that; he feels himself impelled toward a view "which will seem disastrous to many readers and which, indeed, rather surprises me." These are the "we may say" gestures of an Edwardian essayist. I am not trying to carp; but I can't escape the worry that there is something wrong about a prose so mannered, so self-consciously soft-spoken. What had been in the 1940s a toughly argued subtlety, a refusal to simplify, has become a somewhat saddened academic preciousness. And whether or not I have rightly understood this hushed, sybilline prologue, one thing is clear: the essays that follow, and whose weight and *raison d'être* are so manifestly diverse, do not constitute a unified case.

They do not, in fact, argue out the new conventionalities of dissent or demonstrate, except by occasional, oblique appraisal, Trilling's most important supposition: "that art does not always tell the truth or the best kind of truth and does not always point out the right way, that it can even generate falsehood and habituate us to it." This is a matter of tremendous consequence. I have tried to argue over these last years that we must re-think our entire concept of humanism, that our starting point as writers and teachers must be the fact that a man can read Goethe or Rilke in the evening and do his job as a torturer in a concentration camp the next morning, that neither Bach nor Mozart preclude Belsen[1] or do very much to refine a society against barbarism.

My hunch is that we must go even further: an education founded decisively on the *written word*, on the training of the mind toward imaginary realizations, may gradually enfeeble our awareness of the real, our ability to respond to the rawness and disorder of actual human need. We train ourselves and our students to a condition in which the cry in the novel sounds louder, more *real* and demanding of full psychological and moral response than the cry in the street. It would be invaluable to know that Trilling is now hammering out this grave paradox, that his fine, patient revaluation of literary studies will clarify our precarious situation. Perhaps the preface is a hint. But the essays that follow do not bear out the sudden perception of a great darkness.

This does not, of course, mean that they are without interest. Everything Trilling says about literature and the life of feeling has a persuasive elegance. The study of Jane Austen, of the ideal of a "community of 'intelligent love'" in her fiction, is beautifully observant. Trilling remains one of our foremost connoisseurs of an England now very much altered. (Has he, one wonders, come to realize the extent and character of the changes which have taken place in the society of Arnold and E. M. Forster?) The introduction to Babel's *Collected Stories* is a moving study of the intellectual in extremity, of the special temptations which violence holds out to the introspective temper.

"Hawthorne in Our Time" is perhaps the best essay in the collection, fully comparable to Trilling's earlier treatments of Mark Twain, Henry James or Sherwood Anderson. The analysis of the differences between James' reading of Hawthorne and our own, the refusal to regard our own as wholly superior, lead to an acute portrayal of Hawthorne's talent. The ensuing comparison with Kafka is already a part of our general critical equipment.

The Leavis-Snow essay, on the other hand, strikes me as being as unsatisfactory as when it first appeared. It is, perhaps quite unconsciously, patronizing. In his urbane judgment of the excesses committed on both sides of the debate, Trilling seems to miss the crucial point. At stake for both Leavis and Snow is not the general dilemma of culture or some abstract paradigm of didactic and social efficacy, but the actual shape and tenor of England, the kind of place it will be for their children to grow up in. Hence the ferocity and wide resonance of the clash.

This is a distinguished, thoughtful set of literary essays and addresses. It is not a statement of what lies "beyond culture" (whatever that phrase may really signify) or of the uncertain nature of the humanistic ideal in a society that has wrought and witnessed the utmost of inhumanity. Trilling's silence, and the failure of this book to do more than it does, are of themselves a challenge. They may tell us something about the special genius and limitations of that New York intellectual circle to which Trilling himself often refers. They may point to the conditions of stress in the two decades which have brought McCarthyism and Eisenhower, the death of Kennedy and the tragic exactions of Viet Nam. But Lionel Trilling cannot, must not, be thought of as a "case," however exemplary. He is too much needed for that; he has too much yet to give.

## Notes
1. Belsen (in full: Bergen-Belsen), a German village in Lower Saxony that was the site of a concentration camp during the Third Reich.—Ed.

## 44

*Robert Mazzocco*

*"Beyond Criticism,"* The New York Review of Books

*December 1965*

Robert Mazzocco (1933– ) is a poet and reviewer. He has published *Trader: Poems* (1979). Mazzocco became well known in literary New York during the 1960s and early 1970s for his pungent essay-reviews in the pages of *The New York Review of Books*, for which he began reviewing in 1965.

The following harsh review of *Beyond Culture* was one of Mazzocco's first contributions to *The New York Review of Books*. The review provoked two sharply worded letters in defense of Trilling from senior members of the *Partisan Review* circle of intellectuals. Fred Dupee, who was also an English department colleague of Trilling at Columbia, criticized Mazzocco's review as a "monstrous injustice" to Trilling; Martin Greenberg, a former *Commentary* editor, condemned Mazzocco for "the brutality of his callousness."

*Beyond Culture* is Lionel Trilling's first collection of essays in ten years. Three of these essays were published in the mid or the late 1950s, the remaining five date from the present period. A number have appeared in *Partisan Review* and the concluding one, "The Two Environments," recently printed in *Encounter*, created something of a stir. All are carefully composed, or overcomposed, depending on how you view Professor Trilling's later prose style. I view it, unhappily, as a good deal more attenuated than what one found in *The Liberal Imagination* or *The Opposing Self.* Aside from an acute and amiable assessment of Babel's short stories, the usual impression is that of trudging uphill, scanning hazy vistas martyred with abstractions, pestered by fuddy-duddy phrases: "for such it can be called," "if we consent to call it that," "in the degree that," and so on.

Plain speech, of course, has never been one of Professor Trilling's numerous virtues, though Wordsworth has always been one of his interests, not to mention Lawrence. And possibly, given both the friskiness of American journalism and the tight brilliance of much little magazine writing, Professor Trilling's liturgical modulations once held considerable charm, seeming, perhaps, formidably "English"; Bloomsbury Square on Morningside Heights, to put it crudely. But the tone now is wearily genteel. And that is unfortunate. Trilling is an academic and literary figure of tremendous distinction, and I assume he again has something of importance to say.

> Several of the essays touch on the especial difficulty of making oneself aware of the assumptions and preconceptions of the adversary culture by reasons of the dominant part that is played in it by art. My sense of this difficulty leads me to approach a view which will seem disastrous to many readers and which, indeed, rather surprises me. This is the view that art does not always tell the truth or the best kind of truth and does not always point out the right way, that it can even generate falsehood and habituate us to it, and that, on frequent occasions, it might well be subject, in the interests of autonomy, to the scrutiny of the rational intellect. The history of this faculty scarcely assures us that it is exempt from the influences of the cultures in which it has sought its development, but at the present juncture its informing purpose of standing beyond any culture, even an adversary one, may be of use.

I confess that only after a second reading of that spun-glass passage did something shine through, and then only in a verbal sense. For if one wishes to know what art or artist is or has been lying, if one wants a definition of "the best kind of truth," or if one is curious about the exact maneuvers involved in standing beyond *any* culture, one will have a hard time finding answers either in the Preface from which the passage is taken, or anywhere else.

The trouble is not with Trilling's overall message; stripped of its finery, it is simple enough, or familiar enough. Trilling contends that the intent of modern literature has always been subversive, and being subversive it has acted in opposition to the dominant culture, thereby creating the adversary culture he mentions. But now that very culture is working its way into the dominant culture, with the latter's more or less willing assistance, and thus it is losing, or has lost, its bite. The animal is domesticated, the beast in the jungle is a matter of aesthetics or chit-chat, "as witness the present ideational or ideological status of sex, violence, madness, and art itself." But though Trilling makes a number of remote overtures towards the political arena, that is not his province; it is culture, and culture of a perplexing sort, at once pedagogically circumscribed and spacious.

The fact is that the student today is at liberty to choose between two cultural environments. One of them can no doubt be described in terms not unlike those that Sidgwick[1] and Arnold used of the class-bound England of a century ago—it is perhaps less proud and less self-praising, but we can take it to be Philistine and dull, satisfied with its unexamined, unpromising beliefs. The other environment defines itself by its difference from and its antagonism to the first, by its commitment to the "sources of life," by its adherence to the imagination of fullness, freedom, and potency . . . and to what goes with this imagination, the concern with moralized taste and with the styles which indicate that one has successfully gained control of the sources of life or which are themselves a means of gaining that control.

The phrase in quotes comes from Yeats, and two of the illustrations Trilling presents are odd, if memorable. It was D. H. Lawrence who said that not until men once again got themselves up in tight red hose and short jerkins that showed the buttocks would they come into a right relation with the sources of life." Nor is the sentence which follows more illuminating. "It was Yeats who asserted the peculiar moral authenticity of gray Connemara cloth."

Now Professor Trilling's argument, as it appears and disappears, like knitting needles within these essays, is ultimately concerned with the question of morals and manners—to my mind, a stuffy subject, but one which he has in the past invested with vigor, and which he here now and again brightens with a favorite word. For Trilling, the darkness of modern thought is always "liberating," if only because it can renew our reverence for the light. Thus while *Beyond the Pleasure Principle* ends in a vast gloom, and thus while much in our literature is unduly morbid, "let us recall that although Freud did indeed say that 'the aim of all life is death,' the course of his argument leads him to the statement that 'the organism wishes to die only in its own fashion,' only through the complex fullness of its appropriate life."

The equanimity observed here concludes an extraordinary examination of "The Fate of Pleasure," in which Trilling describes, with his customary erudition, the erosion of Wordsworth's Edenic ideal of "the naked and native dignity of man," first in the person of Keats, who unwittingly produced "an erotic fulfillment which implies castration," and then, and most devastatingly, through the dark, demeaning utterances of the Underground Man, Dostoevsky's anti-hero who scorns "the sublime and the beautiful," whether as mouthed by the bourgeois world or by the socialist brotherhood. Trilling then links the "spiritual freedom" exemplified by Dostoevsky's *nouvelle*, one based on "unpleasure," and obscurely directed "toward self-definition and self-affirmation," with Freud's ego instincts, which he reminds us are synonymous with the death instincts, and seemingly suggests that the psychic energies these represent (whether expressed or suppressed, I'm not sure which) may very well have to be "taken into eventual account by a rational and positive politics." But why any such account should be made (given Dostoevsky's denunciation of rationalism), or how (given Freud's ambivalent summary of civilization), or toward what political ends (given Professor Trilling's own idea of "gratification" as "not within the purview of ordinary democratic progressivism")—well, there, as with so much else in *Beyond Culture*, your guess is as good as mine. Professor Trilling is an adventurous voyager; only he always drops anchor in the middle of the journey. And adventures of that kind, I regret to say, are depressingly evident throughout.

In his fine, Solomon-like disquisition on "The Leavis-Snow Controversy," both gentlemen come off a little soiled. Sir Charles is rapped for his scientific bias and his blunder concerning the Victorian writers; Dr. Leavis is chastised for fumbling the literary advantage and for speaking with undue emphasis. Later, however, they are redeemed, or held up, as cautionary figures "who have jointly demonstrated how far the cultural mode of thought can go in excess and distortion." What the cultural mode of thought constitutes is, or has something to do with, the very fabric of society and though that fabric may present its seamy side, there are "the passions which attend it," as well as a certain puritanical strain. "An instance of mediocrity or failure in art or thought is not only what it is but also a sin, deserving to be treated as such." In "The Fate of Pleasure," there's a similar stringency: "Now and then it must occur to us that the life of competition for spiritual status is not without its own peculiar sordidness and absurdity." In any case, out of the trinity of modernism—Marx, Freud, and existentialism—a lesson triumphantly emerges: "we learn and the one thing that can be disputed, and that is worth disputing, is preference or taste." That may sound flat, but it has, according to Trilling, interesting implications. For what is taste but a life-style, and what does a life-style presuppose but the organization of classes, and how are classes set in motion today, as, distinct from the materialist vulgarity of the past, except along aesthetic lines: "even when we judge moralities, the criterion by which we choose between two moralities of, say equal strictness or equal laxness is likely to be an aesthetic one." In our post-Victorian age, however, aesthetics can degenerate into Madison Avenue, and here Professor Trilling pauses for a characteristic reflection:

> In our more depressed moments we might be led to ask whether there is a real difference between being the Person Who defines himself by his

commitment to one or another idea of morality, politics, literature, or city-planning and being the Person Who defines himself by wearing trousers without pleats.

Professor Trilling has other worries, equally weighty. In "On the Teaching of Modern Literature," he recalls, with much grace, how after singular deliberation he introduced his students to "the official version of terror," by which he means the writings of, among others, Diderot and Conrad, Nietzsche and Mann. Now these men, disparate as personalities and distant from one another in time, were all nevertheless involved not merely with freedom from the middle class, "but freedom from society itself," even "to the point of self-destruction," or to the point of pathology, for as *The Genealogy of Morals* troublingly insists, "only by his sickness does man become interesting." Professor Trilling offered these insights not without concern. At Columbia College, alas, his students "looked into the Abyss," as he says, and far from being desolated, merely found it a suitable subject for a term paper. Curiously enough, as presented here, the gap existing between generations is a gap not without an element of self-congratulation, for it confronts "those of us who do teach modern literature with the striking actuality of our enterprise." Or as Trilling puts it more endearingly in his essay on Freud: "it is worth noting that, for perhaps the first time in history, the pedagogue is believed to have a sense of reality."

Trilling's Freud Anniversary Lecture was delivered before the New York Psychoanalytical Society and the New York Psychoanalytical Institute. It too has a liberating cadenza. "We reflect that somewhere in the child, somewhere in the adult, there is a hard, irreducible, stubborn core of biological urgency, and biological necessity, and biological *reason*, that culture cannot reach, and that reserves the right, which sooner or later it will exercise, to judge the culture and resist and revise it." It is liberating because when "we think of the growing power of culture to control us by seduction or coercion, we must be glad and not sorry that some part of our fate comes from outside the culture."

Here I am at a loss to understand what is meant. Historically or psychologically, man has always possessed such drives, and if they have not prevented tyranny in the past, why should it be assumed they will do so in the future? Leaving aside that disputed business of the unconscious and one's awareness of it, what is to stop these drives from being sociologically or bureaucratically shaped like everything else? Certainly, one can say, to take two obvious examples, that the behaviorists seek to control (and apparently with success) subliminal responses, and that propaganda, whether in the East or West, is used, in some compelling sense to exploit passive or aggressive impulses, or sado-masochistic drives. More important, what *is* "biological *reason*"? Is that, paradoxically, Professor Trilling's euphemism for infantile sexuality, for that great prairie of childhood called the "polymorphous-perverse"?

Now the idea of a sexual revolution one could easily credit, if only because sex is so readily adaptable to fantasy, but no such revolution is either mentioned or implied. What Professor Trilling considers consequential is that Freud "conceived of the self as being not wholly continuous with culture, as being not wholly created by culture, as maintaining a standing quarrel with its great benefactor," and he honors Freud for placing so radical a conception "at the very center of his thought."

The conception may be radical, but how radical is Professor Trilling's appreciation? Trilling duly deplores our loss of "instinctual" power, and at the same time he deplores us for deploring it. In one breath he is attracted, in the next repelled, by what he calls the "furthest reaches," the primitive depths—a ticklish state he regards as one emotionally shared by all intellectuals today. True or not, what particular import does the implication have? In "The Two Environments," we are told that culture is not construed "rather as if it were a work of art," and we judge ourselves and others "in the feel of the chosen cloth, in the fashion of the house inhabited." Such judgments are "rather cruel, really, but fascinating," and constitute the new critical mode. The image apparently conveyed is that those of us who are, so to speak, à la mode are now equipped with a personal radar with which we can detect the latent epic in the most modest or effete event. On the other hand, modern literature, Trilling acknowledges, is one of doctrine; damnation and salvation are its subject; but it is a doctrine upon which the "moralizing attitude" of the intelligentsia has fastened uncritically, full of pieties about alienation, and fatted with a spoils system of its own.

One must, he exhorts, grapple ethically with the phenomenon. And he approvingly cites Saul Bellow's National Book Award address, in which the author admonished that unless our novelists begin to *think* and make "a clear estimate" of things, what they produce will be "truly irrelevant."[2] But one could as well say the opposite: that the trouble with the modern novel, with the essay-novel (and perhaps even with *Herzog*), is that it exudes too much "thought," and precious little life-blood. And one might contend that the fundamental question is why our society, with all its rather fascinating judgments, offers an increasing depletion of the senses, leaving less and less *to do*, less and less to react with. (The other society of the newspaper headline, it goes without saying, is notably absent from the discussion.) Moreover, if generalizations are to be made about the contemporary novel, why limit them to Bellow? Or if one does, why not present Bellow where his position has some strength, namely in his "Recent American Fiction" essay, published in *Encounter* two years ago? Is it because Professor Trilling would then not be able to say, as he is able to say here, that Bellow's so-called controversial speech entered "that great new transcendent gossip of the second environment" or "the *mythos* of that environment"? And how piddling, anyway, is all such talk of two environments, and how suspect that use of "gossip." It seems to me, over and over, that at the heart of these essays is a complex but thoroughly conservative spirit, heavy with humanist and/or Hebraic "conduct and obedience" out of Arnold and "night side" exposure out of Freud, both employed in problematic or disingenuous fashion. Thus, it is hardly surprising that in Professor Trilling's comments on Jane Austen, the novelist assumes legendary size precisely because she represents "the possibility of controlling the personal life . . . of creating a community of 'intelligent love'," which is an "extraordinary promise" and a "rare hope." Rare indeed. But what does it mean? As read within the context of Trilling's essay, "intelligent love" amounts to nothing more than the blossoming of one human being under the tender and beneficent guidance of another. That is surely "idyllic" (not to say trite), but it does appear more appropriate to horticulture than to the modern condition, or to the modern quest for personal autonomy, a quest, incidentally, which Trilling puzzlingly assents to and dissents from.

A related dichotomy seems to be at work in "Hawthorne in Our Time." Here Professor Trilling goes to extreme, and often truly ingenious, lengths to both identify and later disinfect our new understanding of Hawthorne—that is the Hawthorne of "Dionysian darkness," of "My Kinsman, Major Molineux." For Trilling, ultimately, Hawthorne's "ambivalence and ambiguity" do not bring him close to Kafka; "through them, rather, he approaches to Montaigne's '*Que sais-je?*' . . . the question which conscious or calculated modesty asks, out of which all questions come. And so, if as readers we now wish to be left alone to look into the dangerous aspects of Hawthorne in our own way, then "our judgment of Hawthorne may have to be that he is not for us today, and perhaps not even tomorrow. He is, in Nietzsche's phrase, one of the spirits of yesterday—and the day after tomorrow." While I hesitate to press the point, it is possible that some of us, instead of floating harmoniously between ports, might very well wish to touch land.

Professor Trilling concludes "The Two Environments," which closes the book, with a valiant thrust presumably intended to clarify the preceding two hundred-odd pages:

There is a passage in Keats' letters which, when it is read by anyone who has anything to do with literature, should make the earth shake, although it does not; which should momently haunt our minds, although it does not. It is the passage in which Keats, having previously said that poetry is not so fine a thing as philosophy, ends with the phrase, ". . . an eagle is not so fine a thing as truth." Considering the man who wrote it, it is an awesome utterance. . . .

But why, I wonder, should Professor Trilling portentously render it an "awesome utterance," even given the facts of Keats's life? After all, anything can be called "a truth," as the history of philosophy, for example, monotonously demonstrates. And if one is interested in Keats's letters, one could quote the contrary: "The only thing that can ever affect me personally for more than one short passing day, is any doubt about my powers for poetry—I seldom have any, and I look forward to the nighing time when I shall have none." One can also quote Yeats: "The abstract is not life and everywhere draws out its contradictions. You can refute Hegel, but not the Saint or the Song of Sixpence."

What these lines express, perhaps best, of course, is the *irrational* temper, the modern *mystique*, the exultation in some sort of vatic force, and about that Professor Trilling has always had doubts. Fifteen years ago, in his essay on Wordsworth, another eagle dropped out of the sky:

> . . . that eagle which André Gide's Prometheus says is necessary for the successful spiritual and poetic life: "*Il faut avoir un aigle.*" This fierce but validating bird, this bird *comme il faut*, suggests the status of the feral and the violent in our literature. Nothing is better established in our literary life than the knowledge that the tigers of wrath are better than the horses of instruction. . . . We do not, to be sure, live in the fashion of the beasts we admire in our literary lives—the discrepancy is much to the point. . . .

It is; and at bottom, I believe, such a discrepancy is what Professor Trilling is indicting; and such an indictment of our literary "bad faith" might well have been salutary. But I do think, if one wishes to strike through the mask, one should not be masked oneself. I think if one desires to prepare an indictment, one should name names, define terms, delineate issues. Evasive effusions, however learned, however humane, are not enough. Looking back, whether these essays represent, by and large, an interminable muddle, or a subtlety "refined beyond the point of civilization," I do not know; though I imagine the latter estimate is the truer. Whatever the case, in the end, I'm afraid, Professor Trilling's book is really beyond criticism and, in that sense, I suppose, "beyond culture" as well.

## Notes

1. Henry Sidgwick (1838–1900) was an English philosopher and exponent of utilitarianism as a moral theory. Sidgwick argued in *The Methods of Ethics* (1874) that right and wrong actions are determined by their relation to the general welfare.—Ed.

2. Saul Bellow (1915– ), the 1976 Nobel Prize winner for fiction, received the National Book Award in 1965 for *Herzog.*—Ed.

# 45

## Raymond Williams

## "Beyond Liberalism," The Manchester Guardian

## April 1966

Raymond Williams (1921–88) was the leading Marxist literary and cultural critic-theorist in Britain of his generation. An important innovator in the socialist intellectual tradition, Williams was one of the first British critics to scrutinize television and other forms of popular art, approaching them as artifacts of "cultural materialism," whereby Williams examined them in the context of their social production and reception.

Williams's major works of nonfiction included *Culture and Society, 1780–1950* (1958), *The Long Revolution* (1966), *The Country and the City* (1974), and *Marxism and Literature* (1977). A lecturer in English and later a professor of drama at Cambridge University for more than two decades, Williams also wrote seven novels, the best known of which is his trilogy of Welsh border novels, *Border Country* (1961), *Second Generation* (1964), and *The Fight for Manod* (1979).

Although Williams and Trilling were both cultural critics of the first order, Williams's view of criticism was much more systematic and politically committed. Beginning in the mid-1960s, Williams lamented Trilling's impressionistic approach to literature and allegiance to the allegedly bourgeois liberal imagination. Before this time, Trilling and Williams had had a warm relationship, viewing each other with esteem as a senior and junior man of letters, respectively. Indeed, Trilling played a crucial role in persuading Columbia University Press to bring out *Culture and Society* and *The Long Revolution* in the United States, Williams's first book-length American publications.

In the following review, Williams argues that Trilling's criticism of the "adversary culture" of the 1960s from a liberal standpoint is insufficiently radical.

The essays collected in this book do not compose an argument, but most of them indicate a mood. This is in itself ironic, since its tendency is to reject what is called the idea of culture—an intimation of value through manner and style—in favour of something else called the idea of mind—the establishment of truth through rational discourse. But the irony is not only that none of the arguments is sustained: in detail, indeed, they are careful and scrupulous, and we can perhaps be asked to cast a restrospective benison on the fact that they are all short by the shared reminder that they are all occasional—lectures here, introductions there, contributions to magazines. Yet what has to be said, beyond the possibility of irony, is that in this form, and with these credentials, the suggestions of a new position must be radically discounted, the more firmly because in their mannered way they seem exactly adapted for instant repetition.

I make this latter point for a reason which only became clear to me in reading the first essay: a sad and uncomfortable retrospect on the teaching of modern literature. I had been puzzled for many years to know the source of a particular North Atlantic definition and structure of "the modern." I had met it repeatedly, at my end of the large-scale commuter traffic of literary academics. Just who, I continually asked, had so curiously selected and so powerfully cemented that particular genealogy: a tradition already, but with the hard confident buzz of modernity about it—a modernity, however, that seemed curiously dated and fixed. Frazer's "The Golden Bough." Nietzsche's "The Birth of Tragedy" and "The Genealogy of Morals," Freud's "Civilisation and Its Discontents," and then arranged through and around them Conrad's "Heart of Darkness," Mann's "Death in Venice," Dostoevsky's "Notes From Underground," Tolstoy's "Death of Ivan Ilyich." I had been fighting that structure for many years: the structure, with its built-in connections and its built-in implacable conclusions, but by no means necessarily the particular works, which could lead in many directions, especially if other works, as indisputably modern, were put into evidence beside them. It was then something of a relief but also, in view of his eminence and his friendliness, something disturbing, to discover from this essay that for all those years I had been fighting Professor Trilling and his course in modern literature at Columbia College, New York.

Is it all to happen again? Shall we all be told, with that hard and weary certainty that comes straight off the plane, that the cultural mode has much in common with the procedures of advertising; defining being by style? Told that, on that wind? Perhaps not. Behind this new structure—and it is the best thing about it—is an audible sadness, that is almost a craving for silence; a regret and a protest, almost physically communicated, as the old structure begins to break down. What Trilling once saw as an "adversary culture," in the ideas and literature he so persuasively arranged and communicated, has been domesticated, conventionalised, fed back to him in conformist essays. To his great credit, he cannot stand it, and is looking for other directions.

On the evidence of this book, though, he is looking the wrong way. It amazes me—it is what for years I was fighting—that anyone could ever have seen that selection of culture as "adversary." What it taught, and was arranged to teach, is what we can best call post-liberalism; the desperate adherence to a liberal idea of the self at the point where the liberal idea of civil society had broken down. It was never truly an adversary, but a variation, within a society based on individualism. And when that society failed, because by definition it was open to an infinite extension, of other peoples and classes, who then threatened the learned image of the self, there was a darkening and a retreat, self and society were only the first enemies; the next, and most desperate were self and self. As I read this latest argument, the terms "culture" and "mind" seem to be counters for a more radical distinction; "culture" is the inevitable and hated social process; "mind" is the individual, scrutinizing and separate. There can be no such separation, between mind and culture, except in fantasy; but this fantasy is needed to preserve a threatened identity.

"What was once a mode of experience of a few has now become an ideal of experience of many." This observation incidentally on the rejection of the pleasure principle can be extended, I believe, to much else that Professor Trilling is writing about. Well, it was taught, and like other teaching got its disciples, except that this teaching, by its innermost logic of the rare adversary individual, cannot stand disciples, and must fight them off in the very process of attracting them.

The decline of liberal criticism, since Arnold, has brought many such agonising moments, but every attempt to rationalise them, to alter the superficial terms, only prolongs the illusion. And if a book is to be made out of them, it will have to be different in substance from this one; not the grave occasional retrospect, but either the full humanity of the novel, or the rational discourse of sustained argument, in which with the whole mind we can seek to examine our whole and changing culture.

## 46

## Graham Hough

## " 'We' and Lionel Trilling," The Listener

## May 1966

Graham Hough (1908–90) was a literary and cultural critic, a reviewer and essayist, and a poet. He wrote *Image and Experience: Studies in a Literary Revolution* (1960), *The Dream and the Task: Literature and Morals in the Culture of Today* (1963), and *An Essay on Criticism* (1966), among numerous other books. Among his chief literary interests were Spenser, Meredith, Coleridge, Wilde, and Yeats, on whom he wrote or edited books. Hough began teaching at Cambridge University in 1955 and was affiliated with the university as a fellow and professor for thirty-five years.

In the influential, mixed review below, Hough voiced objections—which would be heard louder and more frequently in the next decade in America— to Trilling's expansive use of the pronoun "we" and to Trilling's "monotonously apocalyptic" assessment of radical cultural trends (Trilling's "adversary culture").

Hough's review was the first sharp assessment of Trilling's work by a British critic in almost two decades. Unlike the case in the United States, however, the review did not portend a general British devaluation of Trilling's work. Still, it registered the sea change in Trilling's reputation during the mid-1960s: just three years earlier, Hough himself (in *The Dream and the Task*) had pronounced Trilling, with no qualifications, "the finest untechnical critic of our day" and "a general cultural mentor to modern America."

*Beyond Culture*: the title of Lionel Trilling's new book means two things. One, that men sometimes need to stand outside their own culture, to free themselves, if only temporarily, from the society to which they belong. Secondly, taking culture in a more exclusively aesthetic sense, it means that culture is not enough, that men need other values beyond those provided by literature and the arts. This is a book of miscellaneous essays on subjects as various as modern literature, Jane Austen, Freud, Isaac Babel, and Nathaniel Hawthorne; so I cannot say that it develops these two themes at all systematically—but at any rate it has a set of linked preoccupations which are somehow related to them.

## Modern America's *Matthew Arnold*

It has long been apparent that Professor Trilling is something very like the Matthew Arnold of modern America. He invokes the same respect, in some breasts the same irritation, and he assumes the same responsibilities. With less of what Arnold used to call 'vivacity', but with a quite Arnoldian dignity and feeling, he has campaigned on the frontiers of literature and society, and has made it his mission to present the educated American public with a just and liberal picture of its own condition. He has always been at his best when his material has been most concrete—an individual literary work, a specific social phenomenon. So I cannot regard it as an unmixed blessing that in this new book his role seems to have become extended, that he now seems to have assumed the same kind of responsibility for the whole modern literate Western world.

To those whom we value and respect we owe the compliment of speaking plainly. So I shall say at the outset that, though the literary insights are as good as ever, and some of the social observations, I do not find Mr. Trilling entirely convincing in his new role. With admirable clarity and candour he puts the awkward question about this book at the beginning. He starts his preface by saying that he has been reproved for his use of the word 'we'. A writer in *The Times Literary Supplement* has said that when Mr. Trilling speaks, as he often does, of what 'we' think or feel, it is confusing because sometimes it means 'just the people of our time; more often still Americans in general; most often of all a very narrow class consisting of New York intellectuals as judged by his brighter students in Columbia'.

Mr. Trilling patiently acknowledges these ambiguous possibilities but then proceeds gently to reassert the unity of modern culture, in spite of local variations; and by implication to reassert the justice of his own view of it. In short, he affirms his right to use the word 'we' to include thinking men the world over.

I do not know who the *Times Literary Supplement* writer was, but I feel as he does. I feel impelled to challenge Mr. Trilling's universal 'we'; and I think in justice to him this ought to be done, for the ecumenical claims do not distinguish the real nature of his enterprise.

When Mr. Trilling says, as he does, that there is pretty sure to be a natural understanding between New York intellectuals and an analogous class in Nigeria, he evidently believes it. He sincerely feels that the view of the world from Morningside Heights is the real view, and that to an honest observer in Bloomsbury, the Boulevard St. Germain, or the Ringstrasse, things are bound to look pretty much the same. This seems odd to me; and since I cannot hope to examine the situation by a survey of world culture, I shall do it by the simpler method of producing a contrary instance. There is, I believe, a large class of persons, to which I myself belong, not illiterate, not wholly ill-informed, not quite unaware of the world they live in, who signally refuse to be included in Mr. Trilling's 'we'. I do not know how to define this class; a rough description would be that it consists of nonreaders of *Partisan Review.* I speak of (I hope I speak for) a class that finds the particular kind of American literary and social culture that Lionel Trilling represents always a matter of interest, often of admiration, but not something in which they share, not something to which they belong. I shall now try to pick out some of the points that give me this clear sense of non-inclusion in Mr. Trilling's 'we.'

### Overpowering Pedagogical Tone

First there is the overpowering pedagogical tone of his discourse. The opening essay in the book is now called 'On the Teaching of Modern Literature'. When it originally appeared in *Partisan Review* it was called 'On the Modern Element in Modern Literature'; and it is in fact an inquiry into the essence, the specialty, of the literature of our time. I do not think it would occur to anyone on this side of the Atlantic to organize such an inquiry by asking how modern literature should be taught to a class of undergraduates and what the effect on them is likely to be.

But to Professor Trilling it seems a matter of course that the natural home of the arts is inside the university. There is a passage in the preface on this. We are referred to Dr. Clark Kerr's 'vision of the super-university he expects to come into being'. Mr. Trilling goes on:

> His prophecy stipulates that this intellectual imperium . . . shall provide a commodious place for what Dr. Kerr calls 'pure creative effort', that is to say, the arts. There will perhaps be some people who regard this prospect with dismay. . . . Their fears are surely anachronistic. No one who knows how things really stand is afraid of the university. Dr. Kerr's prophecy is but a reasonable projection into the future of a condition already established and regarded with satisfaction by those who might be thought to be most jealous for the freedom of art and thought.

I teach in a university and I have a proper respect for these institutions. I know something of how they are administered and I think I have as good an idea of how things really stand as the next man. But I cannot share Mr. Trilling's satisfaction. The whole problematic situation of modern literature does not seem to me a matter to be fought out in classrooms and regulated by the selection of set books. It is to be settled in the forum of grown-up public discussion—eventually, as Dr. Johnson said it would be, 'by the common sense of readers uncorrupted by literary prejudice'. To replace this by the professional anxieties of dons would seem to me disastrous. Fortunately with us it is most unlikely to happen. The encapsulating of the arts within the university sphere may be the American condition; but it is not the European one.

## Monotonously Apocalyptic

My second point is that the American style in discussing these matters is too monotonously apocalyptic. One of Mr. Trilling's key books is Dostoevsky's *Notes from the Underground.* He says of its hero: 'He hates all men of purposeful life, and reasonable men, and action, and what he refers to as "the sublime and beautiful" and pleasure', and Mr. Trilling goes on to maintain that these painful and scornful conclusions 'have established themselves not only as part of our moral culture but as its essence, at least so far as that culture expresses itself in literature'. This seems to me to be considerably overstated.

Let us take a writer whose disgust—violent disgust—with almost all existing social values is notorious. I think of D. H. Lawrence. Yet Lawrence described himself as a man whose societal impulses were frustrated. His revulsions and rejections were all part of a lifelong quest for some form of society in which he and others could live freely and happily. If the hero of Dostoevsky's *Notes from the Underground* is to be presented to us as the guiding spirit of modern literature I think we should also recall Yeats's admiration for order and the dignity of life; the sanity and humanism of Auden; Camus's almost over-insistent reassertion of solidarity and social duty; that part of Sartre's work which affirms man's power of making purposeful choices, which are also choices for all other men; Gide's insistence on precisely that pleasure which Trilling says modern culture has denied.

Of course we know what Mr. Trilling is talking about—the revolt against bourgeois values, the appetite for an impossible transcendence, the disgust and the occasional revelling in disgust. But these things do not stand alone. To see them alone is to reduce the whole of modern culture to the viewpoint of one huge unhappy city. But the world is not yet one huge unhappy city.

God knows too much of it is, and probably more of it will be. But this is not the only theme of modern letters, and as far as that is its theme I can only quote a writer who is modern within Mr. Trilling's chronological limits, but whom he does not mention—Hardy: 'If way to the better there be, it exacts a full look at the worst'. The nihilism, the smash-up sentiment, is the dung-heap out of which it is nevertheless hoped that something may grow.

All this, it may be said, is the legitimate moral to be drawn from Lionel Trilling's title; it is in these respects that men need to stand outside their culture, and that the values provided by literature and the arts are not enough. But here I find myself at a loss before the manifold ambiguities of his own attitude. He has immersed himself in the destructive element of modern literature; he seems to identify himself with its passions. Yet for an exponent of these predominantly Nietzschean ideas his personal style is curiously muted. We cannot doubt that there is an edge to his mind, but he likes to wrap it in many layers of flannel. When he wants to disagree he says: 'My sense of the matter is quite otherwise'. At one point he wonders whether Henry James was not touched with the Philistinism of his time; and then adds a footnote—a *footnote*—to explain that the phrase is intended to be ironic, that he does not really think Henry James is a Philistine. Nobody belonging to my 'we' has to explain away his irony in footnotes.

In the discussion on the teaching of modern literature he describes himself as entertaining the notion at one point that modern literature ought not to be taught at all. He then says: 'This line of argument I have called eccentric, and maybe it ought to be called obscurantist and reactionary. Whatever it is called, it is not likely to impress a Committee on the Curriculum'. But here we are in the domain of practical reason. Here Professor Trilling is doing his professional job. Surely it is his duty to make up his mind whether his point of view is eccentric, obscurantist, and reactionary, or whether it is right; and if it is right, to stop shaking his sad, wise old head and to set about impressing it on the curriculum committee. To indulge so consistently in these hesitations, dissociations, and withdrawals is not, it seems to me, to stand beyond one's culture, but simply to occupy a very indeterminate position within it.

### Pre-Marxian Illusion

This I think describes the real situation. It is an Arnoldian, a pre-Marxian, illusion to suppose that the intellectual can stand outside his culture; but the academic literary intellectual occupies a very ambiguous position within it. It is his business to know of other cultures; as a reader, a writer, and a teacher he must in imagination identify himself with other cultures. Literature cannot be studied 'objectively'; one who lives by literature has lived in many worlds, and when he comes back to the present one in which he really lives he is more likely than most men to feel himself a stranger and a pilgrim.

This feeling is stronger in America than elsewhere, for all the obvious reasons—the modern world is more pressing, more insistent, and more flourishing.

For other reasons less obvious too. I am not a sociologist, and one's private and accidental observations have little evidential value. But surely in America the intellectual is more isolated, more cut off from the main feeling of national life, than he is in England or France. Not that he is rejected. That is a misconception. Professor Trilling is an intellectual leader in a sense that no one in this country manages to be. He has a huge audience ready to listen to his words. But it is an academic audience, and it listens to him within an academic context. And—I say this with hesitation—it seems to me that the academic and literary intelligentsia in America has rejected, at least in an academic and literary way, the society to which it belongs far more markedly than the comparable class in Europe has done.

An article I read in *The New York Review of Books* last summer dealt with two travel books, picture books by non-Americans, about New York City. It treated them amiably enough, but with a kind of knowledgeable contempt. These surveys by intelligent outsiders, it suggested, are not revealing the truth; they cannot know what the place is really like. And the review concluded, with every evidence of heart-felt sincerity: 'For we know that we are living in hell'. That is a way of standing outside one's culture; but it is not a way of which Trilling could approve. His aim, steadily held before him throughout the various essays in this book, is to accept this desperation as a literary attitude and yet to find some means of going beyond it. But the quality of the desperation and the means of transcendence are both, I believe, of a peculiarly American kind.

### Despair in Manhattan

'We know that we are living in hell'. This springs from a conviction that the distresses of megalopolitan industrial society are getting worse, not better. This conviction has not reached Europe. We may sometimes say that London is hell, but we do not mean it, as the New Yorker writer gave every evidence of doing; for we know perfectly well that it was far worse hell twenty-five or fifty or a hundred years ago. So what we meet here among those who find much to hate in the quality of our present living is anger, frustration—but not on the whole despair. In America it tends to be despair.

And that is why the catastrophic, apocalyptic, and nihilist elements of modern literature are the only ones distinctly visible from Manhattan. It is these qualities that express the real sensibility of large parts of the American intellectual world.

But Trilling's purpose is to find a way out. And if we go on a little farther the climate seems to change. We begin to wonder how much weight we should really have attached to these apocalyptic imaginative attitudes. For the way out seems remarkably easy—if indeed it is a way out at all. I spoke of the attempt to transcend desperation, and I used the word advisedly; for there is something of the Emersonian transcendentalist in Trilling's writing: a sort of fixed hopefulness for which no grounds whatever are given; the positing of an ideal which is flatly contradicted by all actual tendencies and circumstances; the blank unawareness of political causation and political solutions. It is notable that Dr. Clark Kerr, whose vision of the super-university evokes Mr. Trilling's approbation, is President of Berkeley—Berkeley, whose students last year demonstrated in view of the whole world how far they were from sharing this complacency. But the super-university is an ideal; the fact that a number of its potential inmates had to be given prison sentences in order to keep them quiet somehow seems to be irrelevant.

The book ends by quoting Keats: poetry is not so fine a thing as philosophy 'for the same reason that an eagle is not so fine a thing as a truth'. But what kind of truth are we concerned with in this book? The truth that the America whose culture is being discussed is involved in a tragic and savage war, and a still unsolved problem of racial strife? The truth that the whole world is involved in a prolonged political and social revolution that may yet transform culture as we have known it out of all recognition? They are not so much as hinted at in these pages. In the long list of preliminary reading for that famous course in modern literature we find Frazer and Freud, Nietzsche and Dostoevsky; but something seems to have slipped out. I cannot help wondering what has happened to *The Communist Manifesto.*

### No Political Dimension

The disorders of sensibility that loom so large in this discussion, if they can be corrected at all can only be corrected politically. In Europe we can hardly think otherwise. For Mr. Trilling the political dimension is wholly absent. It is replaced by a sort of American universalism, an unquestioned assumption that the anxieties experienced in the Hudson valley are pretty much the same as those experienced by the Yangtze or the Niger. But of these matters I have no claim to speak. Let me take a very small example that comes within my own sphere. There is an essay here on Hawthorne; and the American estimate of Hawthorne in recent years has seemed to non-Americans a patriotic idiosyncrasy with which outsiders cannot agree, but which they need not quarrel with too seriously. Here we find Mr. Trilling seriously comparing this mild fabulist with Kafka. At this point I begin to wonder what meaning I am to attach to any of the judgments, any of the values, expressed in these pages. Clearly the whole scale is strange, for all its reassuring appearance.

This is very much as it should be. The justification for national culture is diversity—that each should utter its distinct note. I should be sorry to think that we in England, or the French, or the Germans—or the Nigerians for that matter, since their witness has been invoked—should go to New York intellectuals for the analysis of their condition. But it is of great importance for us to know how a New York intellectual, how a cultivated and serious American, looks at the world. We all have an interest in how the United States looks at the world, since for good or ill the United States is the greatest material power within it. But if the status of an intellectual has any value in helping us to stand against surrounding pressures, it is here that it should operate; it should enable us to refuse the universal cultural 'we' that emanates, blandly and insistently, from centres of world power. Mr. Trilling's 'we' is something for us to study, with interest, with respect, and with care—not least in order that our own 'we' may continue to maintain its difference.

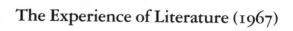

The Experience of Literature (1967)

# 47

*Denis Donoghue*

*"A Literary Gathering,"* Commentary

*April 1968*

(See no. 39 for biographical information about Donoghue.)

*The Experience of Literature* (1967) was a thirteen-hundred-page introductory anthology of poetry, drama, and short fiction, published by Doubleday, which included substantial commentaries on fifty-two of the selections. It reflected Trilling's own tastes and interests, and it was largely restricted to British and American literature. Unlike the New Critics, whose anthologies (e.g., Cleanth Brooks and Robert Penn Warren's *Understanding Poetry* and *Understanding Fiction*) emphasize formal questions of interpretation, Trilling stresses, as his title suggests, the general reader's "experience of literature."

In the review below, Donoghue lauds Trilling's social orientation, pronouncing *The Experience of Literature* "a significant document in contemporary American culture," an "attempt to assemble . . . a Sacred Book of the Arts."

In Lionel Trilling's short story, "Of This Time, Of That Place," a college instructor, Dr. Howe, is teaching a composition class, English IA, at Dwight College. The text for the course is Jarman's *Modern Plays*, revised edition. Two members of the class are particularly engaging; Theodore Blackburn, because his stupidity is invincible and sinister; Ferdinand R. Tertan, because he is mad. Their colleagues are predictable; DeWitt is a straight A, no problem; Johnson a B; Arthur J. Casebeer is a B-minus or a C-plus; Stettenhover was born to get a C-minus. I forget what grade Hibbard got; he sounds C to me. But the chief interest of the story is in Tertan. Mad, yes, but it cannot be said of him, as Polonius said of Hamlet, that he is "nothing else but mad." The story implies that he is the most significant member of the class, and it urges us to question the scheme of things by which he is deemed mad and Blackburn sane. Mr. Trilling has remarked:

> If the story has any power at all, it surely lies in its ability to generate resistance to the certitude that Tertan is deranged. The impulse to resist the undeniable fact comes, I suppose, from the common apprehension, conscious or unconscious, that the fabric of our reason is very delicate and always in danger. This impulse is reinforced by our modern anxiety at confronting a painful fate which cannot be accounted for in moral terms and which cannot be said to result from some fault of society.

The same argument is explored in the story itself when the class-discussion takes up Ibsen's *Ghosts.*

It is my impression that *The Experience of Literature* was compiled for the general purposes of English IA, but particularly with Dr. Howe's class in mind. "This is an anthology," Mr. Trilling writes, "designed to be used in college courses that undertake the study of literature in general, often with a view to 'introducing' the student to an art that he perhaps thinks of as remote from his interest." This is accurate as well as urbane, but Mr. Trilling's book, no ordinary anthology, is more ambitious than the statement implies. It is, in fact, an extremely important book; useful, of course, and excellent for its official purpose, but it is also a significant document in contemporary American culture. I believe that Mr. Trilling has tried to assemble a great book, a Sacred Book of the Arts; DeWitt will enjoy every word of it, Johnson may be inspired to get an A-minus, Casebeer, Hibbard, and Stettenhover will find enough to keep them enrolled. Blackburn will flunk the course. Tertan will pick out a few items which are chosen with great care and affection for him alone.

The big book is divided into four parts. The first part is all drama; complete texts of *Oedipus Rex*, *King Lear*, *The Wild Duck*, *The Three Sisters*, *The Doctor's Dilemma*, *Six Characters in Search of an Author*, *Purgatory*, and *Galileo.* I would have voted for *Heartbreak House* rather than *The Doctor's Dilemma*, but otherwise the list is excellent. The second part is all fiction; short stories, rather, by Hawthorne, Melville, Tolstoy, Maupassant, Chekhov, James, Conrad, Joyce, Kafka, Forster, Lawrence, Mann, Babel, Isak Dinesen, Hemingway, Faulkner, O'Hara, Trilling, Camus, and Malamud. There is also "The Grand Inquisitor" from *The Brothers Karamazov.* The stories are splendidly chosen except for the inclusion of Maugham's "The Treasure": Mr. Trilling makes a case here, but I would use the space for something better. The third part is Poetry, crucial poems from a 15th-century ballad to Robert Lowell's "For the Union Dead." In these three parts every item is followed by a commentary, a short essay by Mr. Trilling somewhat on the lines of the essays in *A Gathering of Fugitives*. But we have still nearly four hundred pages for a fourth part, "Poetry for Further Reading," a more ample selection from the poetry of the same period, the early ballads, then Skelton, Wyatt, Spenser, and so forth until we reach Berryman, Lowell, Dickey, and two of my favorite lines from Ginsberg:

> the war in Spain has ended long ago
>   Aunt Rose

These poems are given without comment.

It is an extraordinarily rich book, reminding us that if literary education is defective the fault is not in our literature but in ourselves, that we are indolent. Think of the books that Mr. Trilling has praised: in no particular sequence, *Rameau's Nephew, Notes from Underground, Heart of Darkness, The Golden Bough, The Birth of Tragedy, The Death of Ivan Ilyich, Little Dorrit, Our Mutual Friend, Emma, Howards End, Culture and Anarchy, The Bostonians, The Princess Casamassima, Rural Rides, Mansfield Park, Homage to Catalonia, Character and Opinion in the United States, Pot-Bouille*; to keep to prose. There is room for little of this great work in the anthology, but we feel its presence even when shorter works by the same authors have been chosen. Instead of *Heart of Darkness* we have "The Secret Sharer"; instead of *Howards End*, "The Road from Colonus." There is space for "My Kinsman, Major Molineux" and Babel's "Di Grasso," both already praised in *Beyond Culture*. At every turn, there is the same impression of care, the sense of public and private relevance informing the choice. If "Bartleby" is included, we know that Mr. Trilling is proposing the story not merely because, in its kind, it is a masterpiece, but because that kind is especially relevant, in the best sense instructive. So it is not an exaggeration to say that the anthology is an imortant part of a critical process which has already produced *The Liberal Imagination*, as well as studies of Matthew Arnold and E. M. Forster, *The Opposing Self*, *A Gathering of Fugitives*, and *Beyond Culture*.

The care is evident in the commentaries as in the selection of items. Mr. Trilling's particular gift has always been an astonishingly graceful sense of the relation between literature and society. Or, to put it more accurately, a sense of the pressure of a particular book, say a novel, upon the society which receives it. When we admire his relevance, this is the grace we have in mind; that he can read an author whose books, to the conventional eye, seem irrelevant beyond redemption, and he sees at once where one force meets another. The essay on Howells is an outstanding example in *The Opposing Self*, or the essay on Keats's letters in the same volume. In the anthology the essays must be short, in the nature of the case, but they are unfailingly vivid;

and tactful, never too much, never too little, just enough to stimulate the reader's mind, his values, his conscience. Perhaps the commentary on *The Three Sisters* is a little odd; Mr. Trilling writes of Chekhov in terms which make him sound like Tolstoy or Lawrence—celebration of life, reverence for life. I find it hard to see the play in that way; Mr. Trilling is so persuasive that I promise to try. The commentaries on Kafka, Babel, and Hawthorne are particularly good, but it is unnecessary to choose; the quality is very high throughout.

Of course an anthology may be used in many different ways. It is clear that Mr. Trilling favors one way, in particular; where the story, the play, or the poem sets off a lively discussion of the morality it proposes. The discussion of *Ghosts* in "Of This Time, Of That Place" is not remarkable, but it is the kind of engagement which Mr. Trilling approves. "The question was, At whose door must the tragedy be laid?" Casebeer blames heredity, Johnson blames Pastor Manders, DeWitt blames Society. I am not sure that I would always want the discussion to move along those lines; at some point the teacher should remind the class that there is a difference between *Ghosts* and, say, any other topic that invites moral discussion; Vietnam, the ethics of war, the Great Society; the difference being that *Ghosts* is drama, art, literature, and the other topics are not. On the chosen ground, however, Mr. Trilling's discussions are bound to be lively, perhaps because of his own ambiguities. He is a moral critic in the sense that he never willingly loses sight of the relation between books and life. When he refers to the order of the book, we know that he is not thinking of a self-enclosed order, closed on all sides. Indeed, a crucial question in his later criticism is the question of chaos. How much disorder should a feasible order embrace? How much irrationality should a rational society be capable of receiving?

Mr. Trilling is devoted to order, and he is alive to chaos; so his mind is constantly engaged with the double problem proposed by these terms. In other words, Mr. Trilling's inescapable terms, as a critic, are morality and politics. But he knows that one of the most fundamental tests of morality and politics is the test enforced by great literature. This is, for him, the perennial interest of literature. When it comes to the question of imagination, there are as many possibilities as those represented by Dr. Howe's class. Surely Tertan would speak, if he were to speak at all, in behalf of an autonomous imagination; the "imagination of catastrophe" going about its proper apocalyptic business. Kafka would be his master, "the autonomy of spirit" his gospel. It is not clear who, in Dr. Howe's class, would speak for the kind of imagination which is offered, all differences being allowed, in Tolstoy,

Lawrence, Keats, and Wordsworth; the imagination which glories in the finite world, with all its crimes.

The first imagination is, to use Mr. Trilling's word in *Beyond Culture*, "peremptory"; it lives by insistence. At its own extreme point, it regards the actual world as "the creation of some inferior imagination"; the dream of the self is freedom. Now Mr. Trilling is so alive to this imagination in literature, so deeply aware of its rights, that he gives it, if anything, more than its due. I have sometimes thought that one of the most compelling visions in modern criticism is the sight of Mr. Trilling falling over backwards to be fair to intransigence. I am a Tory in these matters. Or at least I take particular delight in that imagination which, to use Yeats's phrase, holds reality and justice in a single thought; which, to revert to Mr. Trilling's idiom, consents to the power of the imagination being controlled by the power of the world. The victories of the autonomous spirit are, however desperate, too easy; apart from genius, they require nothing but isolation. There is a sense in which Tertan, mad or not, has been given the easiest part in the play; "experience without alloy," as he says, meaning intransigence without responsibility. The sight of Tertan has made Mr. Trilling so guilty that he is prepared to make the world all over again in his favor.

This is not the whole story. It is hardly even a beginning. I mention it only to say that these ambiguities, which have already animated Mr. Trilling's critical books, are now active again in this remarkable anthology. If you put "The Grand Inquisitor" beside "The Death of Ivan Ilyitch" you are, as we say, "making a point," you are not merely filling up an anthology. If you put Kafka's "The Hunter Gracchus" beside Lawrence's "Tickets, Please," you are making another implication. Mr. Trilling has done these things.

Literary Criticism: An Introductory Reader (1970)

## 48

*Mark Krupnick*

*Excerpt from "Lionel Trilling: Criticism and Illusion,"*

Modern Occasions

*winter 1971*

Mark Krupnick (1939– ), professor of literature and religious studies at the University of Chicago, is the editor of *Displacement: Derrida and After* (1983) and the author of *Lionel Trilling and the Fate of Cultural Criticism* (1986). Krupnick grew up near New York City, became acquainted with the world of the New York intellectuals, met Trilling on a couple of occasions, and was friendly with several New York intellectuals who knew Trilling well. During 1970–72, Krupnick was an associate editor of Philip Rahv's short-lived journal, *Modern Occasions.* Chiefly a literary-cultural critic in the tradition of Trilling, Krupnick writes mainly about Jewish fiction writers such as Saul Bellow and Bernard Malamud.

An admirer of Trilling as an undergraduate, Krupnick turned sharply critical of Trilling in the late 1960s and early '70s. Since the 1980s he has rediscovered Trilling and discerned new and enduring qualities in him worthy of admiration. In his excellent *Lionel Trilling and the Fate of Cultural Criticism*, Krupnick presents Trilling's self-critical sensibility, his brand of accessible criticism, and his career as a public intellectual as a model for contemporary academic and literary critics.

Krupnick's evolving response to Trilling mirrors Trilling's own rigorous self-questioning and evolution beyond youthful radicalism, and it typifies the changing views of a younger generation of New Left critics toward Trilling. In a personal communication, Krupnick writes: "I was an admirer of Trilling for all but ten years of my [adult] life from the mid-60s to the mid-70s."

In the following essay, titled "Lionel Trilling: Criticism and Illusion," which was written for *Modern Occasions* during Krupnick's anti-Trilling phase, Krupnick criticizes Trilling for his opposition to radical literature, traceable to his politics of "premature resignation, social passivity, and relentless privatism."

*Literary Criticism* represents a further development, according to Krupnick, of Trilling's critical stance toward radical politics and modernist art—that is, his preference for a "royalism of the imagination"—as exemplified by his 1951 essay on Howells ("William Dean Howells and the Roots of Modern Taste," reprinted in *The Opposing Self*) and his 1964 essay on Hawthorne ("Our Hawthorne," reprinted in *Beyond Culture*).

These same ideological tendencies—or How I Learned to Hate the Revolution—inform the present anthology [*Literary Criticism*], which like the previous one is intended primarily for beginning students in the subject. The editor himself participates in the post-Arnoldian identification of the moral with the aesthetic, but he has included no specifically aesthetic criticism of the type students are most used to. There are no elaborate explications of individual texts; indeed very few of the selections concentrate on individual authors. The concern throughout is with the nature and uses of literature generally. Theoretical statements have been culled from the work of such critics as Pater, Pound, Eliot, Wilson, Tate, Sartre, Leavis, and most recently Borges, Robbe-Grillet, and Susan Sontag ("Against Interpretation"). At its best this collection, with its implicit valuation of criticism as a central activity of culture, is a useful introduction to the last 200 years of Western thought. Trilling's choices have the admirable virtue of calling us back to first principles. In a time of general confusion about standards this is where beginning students ought to be beginning. The problem is that first questions usually are susceptible to more than one answer, and Trilling's anthology does not always imply such a possibility.

At its worst the present anthology is terribly exclusive, exalting the aesthetic aim of literature over its connections with the rest of life. In his later period Trilling appears more and more to regard literature, in Harry Levin's phrase, "as an institution," housed, it would appear, in a palace of art (of the Tennysonian rather than the Soviet variety), and antithetical to social reality. This is, finally, an *étatiste* view of literature, as exemplified in Hazlitt's essay on *Coriolanus*, in which the poetic imagination is defined as an "aristocratical" faculty. Far from being a medium of liberation, the imagination, writes Hazlitt, is "right-royal, putting the one above the infinite many, might before right."

Trilling might have included a section of Tolstoi's *What Is Art?* to counter Hazlitt's royalism of the imagination. But this anthology is anything but dialectical. Trilling has even managed to find a part of Sartre's *What Is Literature?* that makes the French proponent of *littérature engagée* sound like Stephen Dedalus in *Portrait of the Artist*. And F. R. Leavis is represented by an unimpressive lecture given at the London School of Economics which appears to have been included solely because it attacks Marxist theories of culture. "There is a certain measure of spiritual autonomy in human affairs," Leavis announces portentously, as if the best Marxist critics were too benighted to know that.

In general the present anthology defines the essential morality of literature as "aesthetic joy," a condition of freedom supposedly denied by literary realism and the naturalistic philosophies (Freudianism as well as Marxism) which underlie it. Most important this freedom is a condition of being unavailable, in Trilling's view, outside of art and especially not on that darkling plain where rhetoric and anarchy (called politics) prevail. This splendid isolation of art goes along in Trilling's recent writing with an increasingly priggish distaste for less elevated conditions of being. An enervating overrefinement and preciosity are not lacking in his long introduction to the present anthology, in which literary criticism is conceived as a kind of connoisseurship, involving acts of assessment no different fundamentally than in the case of Japanese swords or Greek and Chinese urns. This comparison implies, of course, a social distinction, and in its implicit snobbishness a spirit entirely opposed to the democratic simplicity of a Whitman or Tolstoi, or the Wordsworth of the revolutionary years.

Trilling's mandarin exclusiveness reminds one less of Matthew Arnold at this point than of Nabokov in his afterword to *Lolita*, where he writes: "For me a work of fiction exists only insofar as it affords me what I shall bluntly call aesthetic bliss, that is a sense of being somehow, somewhere, connected with other states of being where art (curiosity, tenderness, kindness, ecstasy) is the norm." Now it is one thing for a romancer to propel us out of space and time to some imaginary kingdom by the sea. It is a very different matter for a critic to leave history behind whose real strength has been his acute intuition of writing in its sociological and cultural context. In Trilling's writing as the historical sense has faded it has been replaced by abstraction and dogmatism. Witness his cavalier dismissal of Marxist criticism as "simplistic moralizing. . . . The demonstration of how . . . social turpitude manifests itself in the corruption of artistic consciousness."

"Conservative" is finally no more appropriate than "liberal" to define

Trilling's present stance. Other writers who have glorified art's transcendence of time, like Nabokov himself, have called themselves liberals. What is more important is to see that Trilling's aestheticism is a function of revulsion against American culture and estrangement from it, reflected in his long silence on contemporary writing.

Sincerity and Authenticity (1972)

## 49

## Shirley Robin Letwin

## *"On the Birth and Death of the Individual,"* The Spectator

## *October 1972*

Born of Russian Jewish immigrant parents and educated in the United States, Shirley Robin Letwin (1924–93) moved to Great Britain in 1963 after completing a Ph.D. thesis at the University of Chicago on British political philosophy from Hume to Beatrice Webb. The dissertation was eventually published as *The Pursuit of Certainty* (1965); Letwin subsequently became a philosophy lecturer at the London School of Economics and member of the Centre for Policy Studies, a conservative think-tank.

Well-known in British intellectual circles as a Tory philosopher, a conservative economist devoted to monetarism and privatization, and a strong admirer of Margaret Thatcher, Letwin also published *The Anatomy of Thatcherism* (1992), which celebrated "Thatcherism" as a heroic attempt to restore "the vigorous virtues" (thrift, providence, self-reliance, individualism) that she ascribed to Britain's glorious past.

Letwin was also interested in literature and the history of ideas. One understands her admiration for *Sincerity and Authenticity* by looking at her study *The Gentlemen in Trollope: Individuality and Moral Conduct* (1982), in which she examined Trollope's novels to explain the moral strength of nineteenth-century England (such as the code of The English Gentleman), an approach broadly similar to (if rather more doctrinaire than) Trilling's novel criticism. Like Trilling, though with a sharp right-wing ideological edge and far less sensitivity to questions of literary aesthetics, Letwin took an internal, textual approach to fiction, assumed it to be a text representative of its time, and excavated it for large generalizations about history and ideas.

If we wish to be 'authentic,' must we rebel against all social authority? Professor Trilling's answer is, No, and he supports his answer with a rich account of how we have come to take for granted "that the prescriptions of society pervert human existence and destroy its authenticity." The terms in which Trilling couches his argument ought to make him persuasive among the heathen. Those already converted should welcome his direct attack on insidious enemies of civilisation. But they may wish that he had made his case in another manner.

The story begins, as Trilling sees it, with "something like a mutation in human nature." The mutation was connected with urbanisation and social mobility, perhaps also with the advent of the looking glass. As a result, "men became individuals." Once the 'individual' arrived, people began to reflect on an entity called 'society,' not for the purpose of understanding it but in order to change it. To establish their disinterestedness, critics laid claim to a new virtue—sincerity, and Rousseau's *Confessions*, disclosing the worst about himself, set the pattern for such exhibitions of sincerity. 'Society' too was required to be sincere, by making the conduct of social life correspond to the principles declared to govern it. Moreover the quality of a society was thought to depend on whether it fostered or corrupted an identity between the public and private selves of its members.

The fact that social mobility was seen to be possible but was not easily available brought a new recognition of the benefits of dissimulation. The theatre therefore flourished and novels along with the stage became peopled with villains—Iago, Tartuffe, Blifil, la cousine Bette, Uriah Heep[1]—illustrating how those who attempt to leave their given place in society lose or surrender their sense of identification between their private and public selves and so become insincere. The villain of eighteenth- and nineteenth-century plays and novels is, Trilling says, "characteristically a person who seeks to rise above the station to which he was born. He is not what he is . . . because by his intention he denies and violates his social identity and because he can achieve his unnatural purpose only by covert acts, considered independently of his excursions into history. The first writer to make authenticity an ideal according to Trilling, was Rousseau. He has taught us that "society" destroys authenticity by making "our sentiment of being" dependent upon the opinions of others. But his "natural man" seems "merely not inauthentic." For a model of authenticity, we must look to the hero of Wordsworth's poem, *Michael*, who is "hard, dense, weighty, perdurable," in whom there is no "within and without" because "he and his grief are one." His distinctive strength can be accounted for only by "a more strenuous moral experience than 'sincerity' . . . a less acceptant and genial view of the social circumstances of life."

Trilling is at his best when he goes on to show how this new perception about moral experience became distorted until it turned into an exaltation of madness. As the drive toward authenticity affirmed "the unconditioned nature of the self," he tells us, individualism too was renounced. The self became identified with what Nietzsche called the Dionysian spirit that destroyed all "limits and distinctions" and sought "ecstasy and the extinction of the individuated self." What used to be considered "the fabric of culture" was dispatched into the realm of "mere fantasy or ritual or downright falsification," and disorder, violence, and unreason were singled out for praise. The "moral certitude" of Jane Austen became redundant.

"Liberation" in the arts has been just as destructive. Professor Trilling makes a perceptive and telling criticism of writers who denounce conventional art for being pedagogic and for trying to seduce the audience by pleasing it. Nathalie Sarraute, he points out, is at least as pedagogic as the host of writers she condemns, indeed she can be "relentlessly censorious."[2] Both in her novels and her criticism "she is concerned to teach her readers how they are not to be if they really wish to *be*." And in doing so she illustrates what Nietzsche meant by "the terrible phrase, 'culture-Philistine,' " which describes the "use of art and thought of high culture . . . for purposes of moral accredition."

For all the shouting of 'authentic' artists about their indifference to pleasing the audience, Trilling says, no artists ever had a more uncritical audience. It has been seduced not by pleasure but by intellectual cant. The sad truth is, Trilling concludes, that the "concerted effort of a culture . . . to achieve authenticity generates its own conventions, its generalities, its commonplaces, its maxims, what Sartre . . . calls 'the gabble.' To the gabble, Sartre has himself by now made his contribution. As has Mme Sarraute, as did Gide; as did Lawrence. . . ."

Most recently, the cult of authenticity has apotheosised madness. Freud has been replaced by the British psychiatrist, R. D. Laing, Trilling believes, because Laing promises liberation from the "duress" of all moral authority. He and his disciples tell us that madness is health and propagate "the appalling belief that human existence is made authentic by the possession of a power, or the persuasion of its possession, which is not to be qualified or restricted by the co-ordinate existence of any fellow man." Every man can be God without danger of crucifixion. But those who assure us that madness is health have no intention of going mad. In giving their assent to the apotheosis of madness without seriousness, they demonstrate their own inauthenticity. Nor are they capable of being authentic, Trilling argues, because they cannot accept the necessity of suffering.

That is why they have rejected Freud. *Civilisation and Its Discontents* stands "like a lion in the path of all hopes of achieving happiness through the radical revision of social life . . . it undertakes to lead us beyond the idea with which we are familiar and comfortable—that society is the direct and 'sufficient' cause of most frustrations." The brutal truth told by Freud is that the human mind "has so contrived its own nature that it directs against itself an unremitting and largely gratuitous harshness." And this irrational suffering is essential to civilisation which develops only as "external coercion gradually becomes internalised." The character of this development is "given of biology, definitive of man's nature, and its consequences are not to be reversed."

In this fashion, Trilling believes, Freud has rescued the possibility of genuine authenticity which the loss of religion destroyed. Freud has given us a reason beyond doubt or qualification for the "hardness, intractability, and irrationality" of life. He tells us in a manner suitable to a scientific age that human life is a "fabric of contradictions," that it is ultimately "recalcitrant to preference, to will, to reason," and cannot be "lightly manipulated." We are thus saved from the fate that Nietzsche dreaded—"the weightlessness of all things" resulting from the death of God.

That human life cannot be 'lightly manipulated' certainly needs restating in this day of utopias. But by grounding this truth on Freudian doctrine Trilling accepts an assumption that bedevils those against whom he is arguing. They believe that a conclusion is rational only if it is demonstrably and necessarily true. Faced by a dearth of such truths, they have surrendered themselves to irrationality. Professor Trilling attempts to avoid their fate not by renouncing their basic misconception, but by discovering a new ground for certainty. He tells us that we no longer share the Victorians' need to discover "in the order of the universe" some "validation of such personal coherence and purposiveness as we claim for ourselves." Yet what he finds in Freud satisfies this need by calling on biological necessity, a common temptation for atheists. By suggesting a biological substitute for God, Trilling fails to resuce an understanding of men as rational creatures.

Professor Trilling does not accomplish his worthy mission because he never questions the dichotomy between 'society' and the 'self' that has given rise to all the nonsense about authenticity, and other matters. As he rightly points out, Rousseau started this line of thinking by distinguishing between 'natural man' and 'social man' and thus setting the individual against 'society.' This dichotomy remains the basis of Freud's effort to find a justification for an addiction to suffering, such as Rousseau's, outside the realm of ideas. That suffering is "the authenticating imperative" of human life may be the most reasonable conclusion in line with such a premise. But we would do better to question the premise than to insist on the conclusion.

Another quite different and less dramatic understanding of human life permeates the English literature from which Trilling draws many illustrations. It is an understanding, as old as Western civilisation, that sees the distinctiveness of human beings in a capacity to imagine alternatives and to make choices. On this view there is no 'natural' man who is not social and no 'I' at war with 'society' but only persons trying to reconcile constantly revised wants and constraints.

The finer intricacies of this understanding as it affects the moral conduct of ordinary men is what interests the English novelists that Trilling cites. Certainly they are concerned with sincerity, but only a reader schooled to dwell on references to social class would see in this a preoccupation with 'social mobility.' Blifil, in *Tom Jones*, is a dissembler, but Tom, rather than Blifil, is out to make his fortune. Professor Trilling's own interesting comments on Jane Austen do not support his general thesis, which requires her to be displaying moral certitude. They are more in keeping with the view that she is exploring the subtle ways in which moral beliefs and dispositions are manifested, connected, enforced, confused, betrayed, modified. Emma's plans for Harriet ignore distinctions of class, but their place in the novel is to show that although Emma supposes herself to be inspired by benevolence, she is really, as Knightley tells her, amusing herself by playing with other people's lives. Trollope is at least as insistent as Jane Austen on the value of sincerity. Yet he shows us characters—Mary Thorne, Mme Max Goesler, Frank Traeger—who are distinguished for sincerity while moving up sharply in social status.

Neither Jane Austen nor Trollope thinks of human life as a struggle between individuals and 'society.' Their characters are shaping their lives out of wants that they could neither have conceived of nor satisfied apart from social life. The constraints they feel in satisfying these wants are neither imposed by nor independent of their life with other people. What interests Austen and Trollope is how differently people can make themselves in the same social context.

They are preoccupied with sincerity because they see in dissimulation the best weapon available to an ordinary man for compelling others to do what he wants. They believe that anyone who regularly deceives others is denying them respect and using them as instruments. The possibility of such exploitation by lying was known even to the ancients, as the wiles of Odysseus show, and remains plausible still because it is inseparable from rationality, whatever the social arrangements. One can only envy Professor Trilling's good fortune when he tells us that because social advancement is easy now, it is incredible that anyone might "systematically misrepresent himself in order to practise upon the good faith of another."

If Victorian novelists and their predecessors admired sincerity, they knew that civilisation is an artefact before Oscar Wilde, whom Trilling commends for his praise of 'masks.' For they understood men not as creatures divided between nature and falsehood, nor as kernels of purity hidden beneath social husks, but as makers of images. Neither did they assume that everything could or should be made explicit. Gibbon and Swift used irony to make their points sharper and more subtle by indirectness even though they did not believe that the universe was a scene of confusion, which Trilling takes to be the source of irony. And no one supposed that 'culture,' or what used to be called tradition, imposes a burden because its intricacies cannot be laid bare.

The grievous problems that torment the apostles of authenticity vanish if one understands the character of contingent existence and sees rationality as an infinitely rich source of alternatives. Then there is nothing startling about the contradictions and ambiguities in human behaviour and thought. But at the same time it remains possible to recognise that men can bring order into their lives. The discipline required for being civilised can be seen to be necessary without recourse to the "authenticating imperative" of suffering.

This does not mean that we can avoid pain. The picture is something like this: Living involves accommodating to other people because without them a human life is inconceivable. Learning to live with others is not a process of repression or a struggle for authenticity but an activity of composing a harmonious arrangement out of disparate materials. Recognising the circumstances within which one has to live one's life is not a matter of conforming to or rebelling against social pressures, or playing a role or wearing a mask, but of exercising prudence. This is the capacity to make good practical judgments, knowing that they cannot be either certainly right or wrong. Not only may our choices be wrong or go wrong or seem undesirable from the outset. Death may come at any moment. One cannot then expect to get through life without discomfort and unhappiness. But the need to endure pain must not be made an occasion for embracing suffering. What matters is that the disappointments, conflicts, misery to which our imagination makes us prey can, thanks to the same power, be transcended—leaving us with a more strenuous, and inspiring, imperative than suffering.

Professor Trilling's book provokes disagreement. This is, however, a testimony to the interest of the questions he raises and the breadth and seriousness with which he makes his argument.

## Notes

1. Tartuffe is the religious impostor in Moliere's comic drama *Tartuffe* (1669). Blifil is the odious rival of Tom Jones, the founding hero in Henry Fielding's 1749 novel of that title, for the hand of Sophia. Bette is the heroine of Balzac's *Cousin Bette*. Uriah Heep is the unctuous villain in Dickens's *David Copperfield* (1849–50).—Ed.

2. Nathalie Sarraute (1902– ), an opponent of the traditional social novel and a leading exponent of the French *nouveau roman*, has experimented with narratives built via tropes and metaphors, all of which is meant to convey how the amorphous, evanescent sensations and impressions of individuals determine their words and gestures.—Ed.

## 50

*John Bayley*

*"The Last Honest Souls,"* The Listener

*October 1972*

(See no. 23 for biographical information about Bayley.)

These lectures, given when their author was Professor of Poetry at Harvard, constitute a kind of *summa* of his long-standing inquiry into the history of the creative self-consciousness. They make a superb book, and a persuasive one. Luminously, without a trace of tendentiousness and not altogether gravely, Professor Trilling probes his conflated topic. 'When I chose as my subject the cognate ideals of sincerity and authenticity historically considered, I could not fail to be aware that no six lectures could conceivably encompass it. This encouraged me in the undertaking'.

Sincerity—'to thine own self be true'—is an ideal only tenable by social man, pre-Hegelian man, who takes for granted his organic relation to society and the goal of that society itself. Authenticity is the criterion of post-Hegelian alienated man, 'the spirit in self-estrangement'. To be authentic is to recognise a total personal autonomy: all the rest, as Sartre would say, being *mauvaise foi.*

Sincerity in a work of literature may be discerned by the extent to which it embodies and reveals a social dynamism. The writer is giving a voice to what society accepts or would wish to accept; presenting the sincere man as completed by the society his virtues accredit; usually saying 'what oft was thought but ne'er so well expressed'. Authenticity is in a sense much harder to achieve—reflecting as it does the Hegelian *Geist*'s struggle towards full self-awareness, for it must add to the sum of existing reality a new and independent consciousness, a portent which, whatever its relation to the past, is recognisably and strikingly different, and expressing this difference by a contempt, implicit or explicit, for values and ideas taken for granted.

Two key works which Trilling chooses to show sincerity at grips, as it were, with authenticity are Diderot's *Le Neveu de Rameau*, written somewhere about 1770, and *The Sorrows of Werther*, a work of the same decade. Himself committed to the ideal of sincerity and the *honnête homme*, Diderot records the clowning self-display of the great musician's nephew, for whom utter shamelessness seemed the only index of the individual's integrity. This buffoon without a self to be true to was gleefully seized on by Hegel as the representative of 'spirit moving to its next stage of development'. Emergent *Geist* is here revealed as comic to itself and others: but in Goethe's *Werther* it becomes tragic. Werther can really see a sincere and idyllic world personified in Charlotte, but then he realises that neither she nor it can be for him. Albert, to whom Charlotte is betrothed, is the sublime of an honest consciousness, which for Werther, who is spirit seeking its freedom, is an impossibility. He wills what the dialectic forbids him to be; his world disintegrates; death is the only way out.

The fantastic success of *Werther* shows that the consciousness of the time in a sense understood it and returned its echo, though the Victorian 'honest soul', personified by Thackeray, sought later to exorcise it with defensive derision. Jane Austen, too, could apprehend that the sub-Werther cult threatened the authority of the novel as much as that of honest society, and for the same reasons. A vital, though unstated aspect of Trilling's thesis indicates how the novel, to use the appropriately Hegelian metaphor, took its majestic flight like Athene's bird, when darkness was already falling. In its heyday the novel of society was already an anachronism, the mode of nostalgia, of definitive retrospection, plain in Scott and Balzac as well as in George Eliot and Hardy, for the headlong march of *Geist* had passed it by, and the sincerity which defined the ideal individual relation to society was already situated in the past.

That ideal relation is symbolised in *Mansfield Park*, another of Trilling's examples and one which he rightly calls pedagogical. Notwithstanding the superb humour and seriousness with which Jane Austen can still bring the Mansfield ideal home to us, our resistance to those emphatically-presented honest souls, Fanny and Edmund, reveals, it may be, our sense of their archaism. Such archaism can wear, of course, a revolutionary guise: and with an effect as suggestive as it is unexpected Trilling offers us the names of Robespierre and Jane Austen as twin incorruptibles—champions of social ideals incongruent but destined alike to succumb to the anarchic *Geist* of Napoleonism and Byronism.

To be 'authentic', therefore, the novelist must abandon the authority of narrative as well as the claim to social authority—must abandon, indeed, psychologising self, for a 'story' and a 'character' are alike aspects of a vanished social organisation and persona. Trilling is not enthusiastic about the *nouveau roman*, whose logic embraces and endeavours to exploit the situation, but he is even more doleful (c.f.ing Philip Roth and Saul Bellow) about those novels of today which try to preserve or resurrect the old appearances. They bore us, he implies, because they can have no sincerity in the old sense, no real confidence in their attempt to be 'humane'. (He does not mention, however, that fiction's embarrassment has proved to be poetry's opportunity: the most striking artistic phenomenon of recent years is the capacity of traditional poetic form to authenticate and apotheosise in such works as Lowell's and Berryman's[1] new manifestations of Hegelian self-determination.)

There are of course dangers in using works of art to propound a thesis and illustrate a schema, and Trilling necessarily ignores the power of genius to embrace by fathomless equivocation, a power about which his two terms can tell us little. We see this power at the end of *War and Peace*, celebrating a mode of life which commands our total and fascinated response, our 'worship and enthusiasm', even though—or perhaps because—it rests on the support of hypocrites and fools. Jane Austen may believe in her ideal as deeply as Robespierre in his, but it does not make her a prig and comic monster. Pedagogue she may be in *Mansfield Park*, but at the great climax when Sir Thomas returns to find the play in progress she is the vessel both of serene authority and of joyful anarchy: in the exercise of her art she is both Rameau and Diderot, honest soul and wilful *Geist*. But Trilling knows this very well: his awareness of the solidity and 'this-ness' of a work of art is as great as his capacity to render it transparent for us in the prism of history and of conscious idea. It is worth emphasizing, however, since he does not, that some works are more transparent than others. *Mansfield Park* or *War and Peace* will never yield up their souls to the historian of ideas as *Rameau* or *Werther* can be made to do. And our objection to most 'meaningful' novels today is that they have been rendered transparent by the author himself.

## Notes

1. Robert Lowell (1917–77) and John Berryman (1914–72) were friends and notable American poets of their generation in the middle decades of the twentieth century. Whereas Lowell addressed the importance of private interests over social and religious traditions, which reflected his conviction that individuals not become depersonalized by war and the pressure of Society, Berryman engaged in more experiments in form and relentlessly explored poetic traditions.—Ed.

## 51

*Geoffrey H. Hartman*

*Excerpt from review of* Sincerity and Authenticity *and* Mind

in the Modern World, The New York Times Book Review

*February 1973*

Geoffrey H. Hartman (1929– ), Karl Young Professor of English and Comparative Literature at Yale University, is the author of *The Fate of Reading* (1975), *Criticism in the Wilderness* (1980), *Saving the Text: Literature/Derrida/Philosophy* (1981), and *Minor Prophecies: The Literary Essay in the Culture Wars* (1991), among other books.

A leading American exponent of phenomenological criticism and, during a brief period in the 1970s and 1980s, deconstruction, Hartman began his career in literary criticism as a specialist in English Romanticism, an interest that he and Trilling share. And like Trilling in his later work, Hartman has frequently been criticized for his opaque style and mandarin assumptions.

In the following front-page *New York Times Book Review* notice (later collected in *The Fate of Reading*), Hartman criticizes Trilling's "unremitting solemnity" and his theoretical inadequacies (his lack of "grand philosophy") as a historian of ideas.

Trilling's aim has been to acknowledge the discontents or psychic difficulties of modern life yet to prevent their becoming a blind—that is, a politically reckless—ideology. . . .

Trilling is especially wary of ideological criticism (be it religious, feminist, Marxist or whatever) and its willful bending of works of art to its own purpose. His urbane and crafted essays—so casual yet so woven, digressive yet powerfully recursive—have a decided touch of Arnoldian "sweetness" or of that flexibility, that "belief in the relaxed will" he once attributed to E. M. Forster. . . .

A deliberately relaxed style has its problems, of course. One often yearns for that more forceful and trenchant kind of comment found in Trilling's contemporaries, Philip Rahv and Irving Howe. "Sincerity and Authenticity" can read like a Commonplace Book, where thoughts remain *pensées*—though by one of the truly cultured scholars of our time. . . .

Yet Trilling knows that our scrutiny of the human will, either masked (as in art) or naked (as in politics), should remain subject to the oldest question: Is it good or is it evil? It is precisely the difficulty of this question in the modern period (though Trilling conceives of modern widely, as including many figures of the 18th and 19th century) that leads to the writing of "Sincerity and Authenticity." A powerful diagram of the moral life from Shakespeare to the present, it shows the force as well as fallibility of two substitute questions: Is it sincere, and is it authentic?

## 52

*Gerald Graff*

*"On Culture and Society,"* Dissent

*spring 1973*

Gerald Graff (1937– ), professor of English at the University of Chicago, is the author of *Poetic Statement and Critical Dogma* (1970), *Literature against Itself: Literary Ideas in Modern Society* (1979), and *Professing Literature: An Institutional History* (1988), among other books.

An innovative academic literary historian and critic, Graff has evolved from a sharp critic to a critical supporter of post-structuralist and other avant-garde modes of literary criticism and theory—a conversion that places Graff in implicit opposition to the traditional cultural values that Trilling championed.

The following review was written during Graff's early period, when—unlike many left-oriented critics of his generation such as Mark Krupnick and Roger Sale—Graff found Trilling's traditionalist stance and "anachronistic" sensibility valuable for a contemporary critic.

The comedian Lenny Bruce occasionally used to open nightclub performances by stating his intention to piss on the audience. "I'm going to piss on you," he would announce. This being greeted by much laughter and applause, Bruce would then say:

> Always so much *acceptance*, you see that? I can't take the bit out. . . . I just started it as a gag once, you know? And they just said, hooray, hooray, hooray! But just let me do a few *talk* bits. No! Piss on us first, then you'll do the rest of it.

What Lenny Bruce caught in his unique idiom has become the object of increased analysis in the last decade or so—the assimilation, or at least benign toleration, by a large segment of the middle class, of cultural attitudes originally designed to affront it. In *Beyond Culture*, Lionel Trilling termed this phenomenon "the legitimization of the subversive," specifically referring to the postwar social and academic respectability of the literature of the avant-garde "adversary culture." Trilling's important new book returns to this topic in the course of a critical assessment of the history and fate of the concept of *authenticity* in modern culture.

Trilling believes that since the collapse of the traditional social order and its unified world view around the close of the 18th century, *sincerity* has progressively given way to *authenticity* as the dominant ideal of moral consciousness. The earlier ideal of sincerity, which arose in the Renaissance as a result of an unprecedented awareness of the deviousness of public life, did not entail a repudiation of public and social experience as such. Rousseau's "honest soul," which was counterposed against the corruption and hypocrisy of established society, presupposed its own social ideal; moreover this sincerity harmonized with certain simple, unified moral norms acknowledged by the generality of mankind. The new "authentic" social type, by contrast, is "characterized by its departure from singleness and simplicity, by the negation of self through role-playing, by commitment to an artistic culture and what this entails of alienation from the traditional ethos." Authenticity presents itself as prior to or "beyond" the fixed good and evil that underwrite the ethics of sincerity, viewing these norms as deceitful abstractions superimposed upon the contingency and open-endedness of experience. Trilling cites Diderot's Rameau's nephew, of whom Diderot as a "sincere" moralist explicitly disapproves, as an early example of an authentic character type. Appropriately, it is the nephew's character upon which Hegel draws in the *Phenomenology of Mind* in order to illustrate his notion of the "distintegrated consciousness." For Hegel, this multiple consciousness represents a progressive advance of Spirit in its evolution toward ever greater consciousness of itself.

In this, Hegel anticipated the strategy of numerous modernist writers (Wilde, Yeats, Gide, Sartre) of assuming successive "masks" in quest of an authenticity superior to that of the predefined and predetermined self-conceptions of bourgeois society. At the same time, the recognition of the ubiquity of masks in human experience has generated a literature of "unmasking" which undertakes profound explorations into the "heart of darkness" concealed by moral and social convention. There are a number of paradoxes here. The modernist concern with authenticity is highly ambivalent, for the discovery of the fragility and "weightlessness" of the self is both liberating and terrifying. Indeed, the inner logic of the doctrine of authenticity seems to foreclose the possibility of actually arriving at an authentic state of being, since any state of arrival would be static and thus by definition inauthentic.

Trilling suggests that the awareness of the protean nature of consciousness, entertained with ambivalence by the earlier modernist writers, has today reached an extreme phase, expressing itself in an unqualified negation of all "limiting conditions" on the self. One consequence of this is seen in the crafts of fiction and historical writing, where the theory of the radical open-endedness of experience has diminished the prestige of narrative form and storytelling. Another is found in the psychological and social theories of Norman O. Brown, Herbert Marcuse, R. D. Laing, and David Cooper, where the dissolution of the strongly individuated ego is often equated with personal and social liberation.[1] Certain passages in the writings of Laing and Cooper go so far as to endow schizophrenia and madness with the authority of visionary revelation. Despite the revolutionary aspirations that have accompanied the drive to free the self from all boundaries and limits, Trilling finds a kind of despair beneath it all, a feeling that life is not "susceptible of comprehension and management." The utopian fantasy of transcending the reality principle betrays an inability to come to terms with any possible reality.

Trilling's distinction between authentic and sincere character models might be further illuminated by aligning it with Jacob Brackman's distinction, in his book, *The Put-On*, between the "put-on" and the old-fashioned practice of "kidding."[2]

> The object of kidding, . . . [Brackman writes] is always manifest: to *pass off* untruth as truth just for the fun of it. . . . At first, the victim believes the false to be true, whereas the kidder knows the truth. Then, the gulling accomplished, the kidder lets the victim know he's been taken for a ride.

The put-on, by contrast, "is an *open-end* form. That is to say, it is rarely climaxed by having the 'truth' set straight—when a truth, indeed, exists." With the put-on the distinction between truth and untruth is obscured, and the "real" identity and intention of the perpetrator remain ambiguous, even to the perpetrator himself. Like innumerable contemporary artists, the adept of the put-on disclaims responsibility for or interest in the interpretation of his meaning.

Though Trilling does not mention this one specifically, fads like the put-on might be adduced as evidence of his contention that the once-subversive tradition of authenticity has been domesticated and trivialized by its recent popularity. "The concerted effort of a culture or of a segment of a culture to achieve authenticity," he writes, "generates its own conventions, its generalities, its commonplaces, its maxims, what Sartre, taking the word from Heidegger, calls the 'gabble.' " What began in an effort to subvert gabble has become gabble in its turn. This rigidification, Trilling suggests, is an aspect of "developments in the ecology of art" such as "the unprecedented proliferation of art, the ease with which formerly esoteric or repellent art forms are accepted, the fascinating conjunction of popular and commercial art with what used to be called advanced art." These developments have lessened the artist's "adversary relation to the dominant culture," with a corresponding lessening of intellectual individuality.

Against the dizziness of the new authenticity, Trilling counterposes a rival concept of authenticity, best exemplified for him by the Freud of *Civilization and Its Discontents*. A commitment to Freud's "classic tragic realism," as Trilling once called it, has served him before as a point of moral reference for measuring some of the more self-indulgent tendencies of the age. In an essay first published in 1941 (and reprinted in *The Liberal Imagination*, 1950), Trilling asserts that "the Freudian man is, I venture to think, a creature of far more dignity and interest than the man which any other modern system has been able to conceive." In *Beyond Culture* (1968), Trilling interprets Freud's "emphasis on biology" as a "liberating idea" because of its implication that "there is a residue of human quality beyond the reach of cultural control." Like Paul Goodman,[3] Trilling has fought a continuous battle against the assumption of liberal, technological society that, as Goodman phrased it, "the essence of 'human nature' is to be pretty infinitely malleable" and thus subject to unlimited manipulation and control.

Trilling's endorsement of the Freudian view against the new vogue of the protean self thus parallels the strategy of his earlier critiques of liberalism:

> The fabric of contradictions that Freud conceives human existence to be is recalcitrant to preference, to will, to reason; it is not to be lightly manipulated. His imagination of the human condition preserves something—much—of the stratum of hardness that runs through the Jewish and Christian traditions as they respond to the hardness of human destiny.

Trilling here sees Freud as reinstating "the tragic element of Judaism and Christianity" in an age which has lost the objective moral authority which gave solidity to those systems. In "the fabric of contradictions" that he saw as limiting the human fate Freud, according to Trilling, located a kind of substitute for this authority, an "authenticating imperative," that is, something to be authentic in relation *to*. This imperative anchors and affirms "the authenticity of him to whom the fate is assigned." Though somber in its implications, Freud's view attributes to life a certain stability which lends scope to human operations. Precisely by understanding the limits of man's ability to transform himself, this view delimits an area in which intelligent direction can be effective.

Furthermore, the fact that man is incurably divided against himself and his culture provides a context of *resistance* which makes individual self-definition possible. It is just this resistance, "the hardness of human destiny," which is eroded—or concealed—by a bureaucratic, technological society that has become "affluent, permissive, and pleasure-oriented" and thus able to create the illusion that all the ancient obstacles to human happiness are about to be overcome. A line of American critics from the early Van Wyck Brooks to Richard Chase, John W. Aldridge, and Alfred Kazin,[4] has shared Trilling's conviction that sharply individuated character type needs a dialectic within which to operate, that it tends to disappear in a fluid, incoherent, and faceless society. Such a dialectical perspective is found in much of the social criticism of the 1950s expressing the reaction against "other-directedness" and conformity. Trilling's effective restatement of this line of criticism demonstrates that it is far from obsolete.

Yet, Trilling speaks almost as if he considers himself the last survivor of this tradition, rarely missing an opportunity to describe his own views as "archaic" or "anachronistic." This despairing and apologetic self-dramatization makes a greater concession than seems necessary to the naive apocalypticism which he attacks. After all, if there *are* permanent human imperatives, as Trilling thinks, then something in the spirit must eventually rebel when these imperatives are repeatedly denied.

And I think something in the spirit must indeed rebel at writing like the following, which comes conveniently to hand from the November issue of the *Saturday Review of the Arts.* In an essay entitled "New Heaven and Earth," Joyce Carol Oates writes:

> We have come to the end of, we are satiated with, the "objective," value-less philosophies that have always worked to preserve a status quo, however archaic. We are tired of the old dichotomies: Sane/Insane, Normal/Sick, Black/White, Man/Nature, Victor/Vanquished, and—above all this Cartesian dualism, I/It. . . . They are no longer useful or pragmatic, They are no longer *true.*

That is to say, they are no longer authentic. Note here the implication that what "we are tired of" need not count as true or real, that the criterion of the truth of a proposition is now to be its capacity to interest or give pleasure. This is the new voice of authority: the Western purposive ego is dead;[5] distinctions between subject and object, reality and illusion, etc., have been abolished, the "self" is now (or is shortly to be) a fluid and unconditioned fiction that is free to improvise infinite avatars of itself and its mythoplastic "reality," and both the self and reality are no more than a kind of undifferentiated oatmeal that can be kneaded and manipulated into the shape desired at each transitory moment. Here the ideas of open-endedness and authenticity have merged with the slogans of affluent-society optimism.

Insofar as the contemporary avant-garde has persisted in this kind of thinking, it has tended to lose its adversary thrust, a development that Trilling, as we have seen, ascribes to changes in "the ecology of art." But what brought about these changes? With respect to this question Trilling forces us to make what we can out of a few suggestive hints, hints that unfortunately are not developed into any general hypothesis. Although the book aims to be suggestive rather than definitive, this failure to treat the causes of the tendencies it attacks is its most serious limitation. As an approach to such a diagnosis, I would suggest the following.

There has taken place in the present century a cultural transformation of the bourgeoisie itself, which has deprived the adversary culture of the resistance that once stimulated its creative self-definition. The bourgeois "establishment," cut off from its 19th-century traditions, has ceased to hold firm religious, moral, and intellectual convictions; therefore, nothing much prevents it from co-opting "radical" cultural styles for the uses of the media and the marketplace (especially since such cultural permissiveness requires no redress of material and social inequalities). Furthermore, as capitalist, technological society becomes more meaningless and impersonal and outlets for social boredom become more necessary, there arises an increased taste for psychological experimentalism—e.g., "immediate experience," "exploration of inner space," encounter-group psychology, etc. This psychological experimentalism, which the adversary culture had initiated as a form of discipline, becomes mediated and trivialized by the machinery of consumerism and publicity. Open-endedness loses its radical, liberating force in a social context that not only is itself bewilderingly open-ended and without fixed reference-points but which turns such metaphors into media clichés.

As bourgeois opposition has softened, the pressure of the adversary culture's resistance to co-optation has simultaneously lowered. This culture's inveterate suspicion of theory and programmatic principles—a corollary of the doctrine of authenticity—has been the source of its traditional immunity to exploitation by ideological interests. Yet its very elasticity and resistance to static formulations makes the adversary culture not only highly unstable as a force of opposition but vulnerable to another type of exploitation—subservience to a dynamic but incoherent and superficial mass society.

The history of such movements as Futurism suggests the area of latent agreement which has always existed between certain avant-gardes and technological society—e.g., the taste for perpetual innovation, the exaltation of technique over ends, the hostility to tradition—and such agreement enhances the likelihood of co-optation. Last, the logic of perpetual transcendence tends to subvert the very concept of an *adversary* culture, requiring the liquidation of "reactionary" or "élitist" dualisms which oppose intellectuals to society.

As a result of these developments we have a rapprochement today between avant-garde intellectuals and mass society that promises to reestablish in the cultural sphere a complacency comparable to what was witnessed in the American '50s. Paradoxically, this new complacency comes about through what profess to be radical auspices. The new accommodation between high and mass culture is alleged to represent a cultural revolution of liberating proportions, "the end of alienation." But what is being claimed as the end of alienation might more accurately be described as its democratization. The condition in which large numbers of people are forced to relieve a diminishing sense of selfhood by experimenting with the psyche is not a matter to be derided; but it will scarcely be improved by pretending it is a sign of vitality. The pretense that mass alienation is liberation, like the pretense that schizophrenia is health, testifies to the depth of the longing in our day to construe the symptoms of cultural pathos as the signs of a cultural revolution. As Trilling observes, it is "significant of our circumstance that many among us find it gratifying to entertain the thought that alienation is to be overcome only by the completeness of alienation, and that alienation completed is not a deprivation or deficiency but a potency."

Such statements will appear retrograde to some intellectuals, who interpret a lack of sympathy with the outlook of the New Sensibility as a symptom of a "new cultural conservatism," which presumably carries over into politics. But "conservatism" has become an almost meaningless term in the arts today when constant innovation for its own sake and total rejection of the past have become routinely expected norms of "advanced art," and when the mere belief that a work of art should have some meaning is sufficient in many quarters to convict one of being "conservative." Furthermore, the alleged connection between conservatism in the arts and conservatism in politics is an unexamined assumption—as is the notion that the destruction of the reality principle and the spread of undifferentiated forms of consciousness represent steps in the direction of social equality and freedom. On the contrary, the abandonment of critical thinking to a politics of ecstatic consciousness clears the way for further acquiescence to existing forms of social control.[6] As Trilling says, à propos of certain contradictions in Marcuse's writing, the "political implications of reduced individuality" are far from promising. Marcuse defines revolutionary consciousness in terms of the polymorphous self. But he cannot help recognizing that such an unfocused self is likely to be more easily manipulated—the final irony of the revolt he encourages against "limiting conditions"—and "that moral intransigence and political activism are brought into being by renunciation and sublimation," i.e., that radicalism depends on the survival of critical intelligence. The abolition of distinctions between reality and myth, sanity and insanity, would appear to be coming at just the right moment for governments whose policies depend upon keeping citizens from making such distinctions.

## Notes

1. Norman O. Brown (1913– ) is an American scholar and author of *Life Against Death: The Psychoanalytical Meaning of History* (1959) and *Love's Body* (1966). R. D. Laing (1927–89) was a Scottish scholar and author of *The Divided Self* (1960), in which he challenged conventional conceptions of mental illness and argued, for example, that schizophrenia is a survival strategy invented by persons in order to cope with excruciating situations. David Cooper (1941– ) is an American psychotherapist and author of *Philosophy and the Nature of Language* (1973), *The Manson Murders: A Philosophical Inquiry* (1974), and *Existentialism: A Reconstruction*, among other books.—Ed.

2. *The Put-On: Modern Fooling and Modern Mistrust* (1971), by Jacob Brackman, deals with deception, popular errors, and the role of impostors and imposture in promoting them.—Ed.

3. Paul Goodman (1911–72) was a poet, fiction writer, essayist, and literary critic. A contemporary of Trilling's and fellow member of the New York intellectuals, Goodman's major nonfiction books include *Growing Up Absurd: Problems of Youth in the Organized Society* (1960) and *Utopian Essays and Practical Proposals* (1962).—Ed.

4. Van Wyck Brooks (1886–1963), Richard Chase (1914–62), John W. Aldridge, and Alfred Kazin (1915–97) are prominent American critics of American literature.

5. George Orwell's remarks on the "proletarian cant" of the '30s are pertinent once more: "Everyone knows, or ought to know by this time, how it runs: the bourgeoisie are 'dead' (a favorite word of abuse nowadays and very effective because meaningless), bourgeois culture is bankrupt, bourgeois 'values' are despicable, and so on and so forth. . . ." [*The Road to Wigan Pier*, 1937]. It seems that at one time intellectuals tried to discredit an opponent by demonstrating he was *wrong*. Now one simply dismisses him as *dead*—a gesture that requires less effort, is unanswerable, and tends to suggest that one is oneself vibrantly and excitingly alive.

6. The May 1972 issue of *Psychology Today* features an article by Kenneth J. Gergen

entitled "Multiple Identity." Its thesis is that "the healthy, happy human being wears many masks . . . multiple identity is real, right and good." A complex, rapidly changing society, says the author, renders the traditional, unified self obsolete. "We are made of soft plastic," he says, "and molded by social circumstances." No clearer illustration could be found of the compatibility of the "radical" psychology of protean man with the requirements of social "adjustment."

## 53

*Irving Howe*

*"Lionel Trilling: Sincerity and Authenticity," in* Celebrations

and Attacks *{originally published as "Reading Lionel Trilling"*

*in* Commentary*}*

*1979 {August 1973}*

(See no. 29 for biographical information about Howe.)

The following selection, which is a warm appreciation of *Sincerity and Authenticity*, reflects the reconciliation that occurred between Howe and Trilling in the early 1970s. Putting political differences aside, the two men began to meet for lunch and to find common ground in each other's aesthetic judgments and fundamentally liberal, anti-Movement convictions. The review also marks one of the last times in which Howe appeared in the pages of *Commentary*, which had become, since the mid-1960s, increasingly conservative. Howe and *Commentary* had agreed during the late 1960s on the need to fight the New Left and the excesses of the counterculture; by the early 1970s, the need had passed. Evidence of Howe's gradually widening distance from *Commentary* and its emergent neoconservative direction became clear with the 1974 publication of *The New Conservatives* (which Howe co-edited with Lewis Coser).

The Italian novelist Ignazio Silone once remarked that most writers keep telling the same story over and over again: it is the story that releases their controlling sense of existence, their springs of anxiety and dilemma. Critics may seem to enjoy greater possibilities for dispersing or disguising their deepest interests, but that is probably a mere illusion. Those who are truly engaged with the movements of their own minds also keep telling the same "story," returning to a single question or group of questions.

For several decades now Lionel Trilling has written on a wide range of topics, yet in most of his criticism there keeps breaking out a dispute of his inner mind, so that in reading his essays one becomes witness to a drama of self-recognition. An essay of perhaps a decade ago, "On the Teaching of Modern Literature," brought this dispute to a sharpness unusual for a critic who generally prefers the canny pleasures of the tangent. In that essay Trilling exposed a dualism of response that many other literary people feel but few care to state. There is the Trilling who teaches, writes about, and defines himself culturally through the modernist masters, writers of the oblique, perverse, complex, problematic. This Trilling responds to the violence, the moral chaos proudly thrust forward, the refusal of simple virtues or verities, the negation of worn or indeed any certainties, all of which we know to be the glory of our literature.

But another Trilling makes himself heard, a little weary with the suave virtuosities of the first one, more and more ironic toward the performance of ironies that has become the set-piece of the "advanced" critic, falling back with some didactic bravado on the moral assurances of the 19th-century writers. This second Trilling seems to wonder—he cannot suppress the heresy, and then finds relief in venting it, since that defines *his* authenticity—whether the whole modernist enterprise will turn out to have been a brilliant detour of Western culture from which, at great cost, we may have to find a path of return.

Whereupon the first Trilling has his answers, for he knows how conclusive have been the historical imperatives behind modernism and he will not brook a retreat into limp traditions that we can still name but do not really possess. He is a resourceful man, this first Trilling, and he finds himself suspicious of his "archaic" alter ego.

From our quarrels with others we make rhetoric, said Yeats, and from our quarrels with ourselves, poetry. He might have added, criticism too, first-rate criticism, from our quarrels with ourselves. Lionel Trilling's *Sincerity and Authenticity*, is deceptively modest in scale, though tremendously ambitious in reach. It leaps, without pretense of transition, from one crucial moment to another in the history of Western culture; it offers no explicit conclusions or theses in the course of sketching the turn from sincerity to authenticity as guiding cultural norms—a method bound to trouble minds like my own, captive to at least the illusion of historical continuity and thematic connection. But *Sincerity and Authenticity* is a wonderful book, precisely in its tentativeness, the way it perches at a given historical moment to dramatize through variations a deep, abiding theme.

Novelists and poets, familiar in the Trilling cast, are brought in to testify; so too philosophers like Hegel and Diderot; ideologues like Rousseau, Marx, and Sartre; and, of course, Freud. One can read the book for its recurrent pleasures of local insight: a clever section on Oscar Wilde's defense of the truth of masks as against the self-deceits of sincerity; a moving passage in which Trilling asks himself whether the enormous moral credence, tantamount to a religious yielding, which some of us have placed in literature may not prove to be undone by a "proliferation of art" transforming it into a trivial commodity; and an uncharacteristically fierce polemic against Sartre and Sarraute for the haughtiness with which in the name of authenticity they attack figures, indeed people, like Emma Bovary.

Trilling begins by remarking that there are moments in history when the assumptions of moral life suddenly become subject to intense scrutiny and radical transformation. One such moment, crucial to the whole subsequent experience of Western civilization, occurs as the post-Renaissance concern with the value of sincerity, "the avoidance of being false to one's own self." The "congruence between avowal and actual feeling" becomes in Europe a passion, even a craze, toward the end of the 18th century, by no means confined to the intelligentsia. Yet this has certainly not always been a crucial or even recognizable norm of conduct. As Trilling puts it:

> We cannot say of the patriarch Abraham that he was a sincere man. That statement must seem only comical. The sincerity of Achilles or Beowulf cannot be discussed: they neither have nor lack sincerity. But if we ask whether the young Werther is really as sincere as he intends to be, or which of the two Dashwood sisters, Elinor or Marianne, is thought by Jane Austen [in *Sense and Sensibility*] to be the more truly sincere, we can confidently expect a serious response in the form of opinions on both sides of the question.

In time, however, the cult of sincerity, with its program for harmony within the self and *thereby* without, gives way (I would think with the rise of modernist literature) to a celebration of the inharmonious state of authenticity. Indeed, authenticity is usually regarded as possible only to those who have discarded the delusion of wholeness, and in whom the relation between me and myself is not harmonious. This relation must also be, for the program of authenticity, close to self-contained, so that the inner, fragmented struggle for definition or recreation is uncontaminated by social constraints. A similar expectation operates in regard to the work of literature:

> [It] is itself authentic by reason of its entire self-definition: it is understood to exist wholly by the laws of its own being, which include the right to embody painful, ignoble, or socially inacceptable subject-matters.

Similarly the artist seeks his personal authenticity in his entire autono-mousness—his goal is to be as self-defining as the art-object he creates....
When, in Sartre's *La Nausée*, the protagonist Roquentin . . . permits himself to entertain a single hope, it is that he may write a story which will be "beautiful and hard as steel and make people ashamed of their existence."

Now, all this may seem abstract and unanchored, as in summary form it must, but Trilling takes pains to show the interweaving and diverging paths of his two categories as they are embodied in the movement of Western culture—or at least, he shows some crucial points along the graph of their development. Perhaps the clearest exposition appears in a chapter called "The Honest Soul and the Disintegrated Consciousness," devoted mainly to Hegel and Diderot. Starting with a text that has long fascinated him, Dide-rot's *Rameau's Nephew*, Trilling contrasts the *Moi* of that great dialogue, Diderot himself, the "honest soul" who lives for the moderate virtues of sincerity, with young Rameau, the *Lui*, scoundrel and scapegrace who boasts of his crimes in order—quite as if he were our contemporary—to solicit admiration for the candor, the shining authenticity, with which he confesses them. Hegel, entranced by Diderot's book, uses the epithet "honest" in its

old condescending sense, implying a limitation both of mind and power. The "honesty" of Diderot-*Moi*, which evokes Hegel's impatient scorn, consists in his wholeness of self, in the directness and consistency of his relation to things, and in his submission to a traditional morality. Dide-rot-*Moi* does not exemplify the urge of Spirit to escape from the condi-tions which circumscribe it and to enter into an existence which will be determined by itself alone.

And again:

I have remarked the obvious connection between sincerity and the inten-sified sense of personal identity that developed along with the growth of the idea of society. Sincerity was taken to be an element of personal autonomy; as such, it was felt to be what we might call a progressive virtue. But considered in the light of Hegel's historical anthropology, it must be regarded in the opposite way, as regressive and retrospective, standing between the self and the disintegration which is essential if it is to develop its true, its entire, freedom.

For Hegel, anticipating many writers of our own moment, feels that only by cracking the facade of coherence, integrity, and sincerity of "the honest soul" can the reality of fragments (as we might call it) be reached.

The opposition so beautifully dramatized by Diderot appears, in somewhat different variants, as the two sides of Rousseau, who speak both for "honest consciousness" and "disintegrated consciousness," with particular reference, as Trilling is quick to underscore, to the problem of the moral value of art. In another chapter called "The Heroic, the Beautiful, the Authentic" Trilling is at his most brilliant, but incomplete and difficult, as he contrasts the pedagogic intent of narrative with the heroic gesture of tragedy, the traditional view that beauty inheres in the design of art with that "settled antagonism to beauty" which authenticity, as a tacit polemic against historical continuity, brings to bear upon art.

In his concluding essay, "The Authentic Unconscious," Trilling touches on the contemporary implications of his study. There is a discussion of Freud, which I find deeply absorbing but finally recalcitrant—when we reach the point where a segment of the ego is said to overlap the unconscious, it becomes hard to share Trilling's patient readiness to follow step by step the journey of the master. More accessible by far is an amiable, even touching polemic against Herbert Marcuse, with whom Trilling nevertheless finds some ground for kinship, since it turns out that Marcuse, though prophesying in his more utopian writings "the virtual end of necessity, discovers in it a perverse beneficence—upon its harsh imperatives depends the authenticity of the individual and his experience." Marcuse, as Trilling notices with a sly friendliness, "*likes* people to have 'character,' cost what it may in frustration. He holds fast to the belief that the right quality of human life, its intensity, its creativity, its felt actuality, its weightiness, requires the stimulus of exigence." Anyone who has ever had an encounter with the author of *Eros and Civilization* can testify to the keenness of this description.

With R. D. Laing, Trilling is harsher, and rightly so, since Laing has a much simpler mind than Marcuse. Laing is ready, at least in his writings, to go all the way into the chaos of the "disintegrated consciousness," and it is with regard to Laing's frivolous evocation of madness that Trilling reaches the conclusion of his book:

> Perhaps exactly because the thought [that "alienation is to be overcome only by the completeness of alienation"] is assented to so facilely, so without what used to be called seriousness, it might seem that no expression of disaffection from social existence was ever so desperate as this eagerness to say that authenticity of personal being is achieved through an ultimate isolateness. . . . The falsities of an alienated social reality are rejected in favor of an upward psychopathic mobility to the point of divinity, each one of us a Christ—but with none of the inconveniences of

undertaking to intercede, of being a sacrifice, of reasoning with rabbis, of making sermons, of having disciples, of going to weddings and to funerals, of beginning something and at a certain point remarking that it is finished.

*Sincerity and Authenticity* is essentially beyond summary, because its value consists largely in detailed nuance and variation. Let me try, instead, to push the distinction between sincerity and authenticity to a point of high focus, perhaps overfocus, in ways that Trilling might not always approve, and with the end of bringing into the glare of the explicit some of the implications I gather from his book.

Sincerity involves aspiration, an effort to live by a moral norm; authenticity directs us to a putative truth about ourselves that depends on our "essential" being, "beneath" and perhaps in disregard of moral norms— though it demands that we drive toward that "essential" being with an imperiousness that is very much akin to traditional moralism. Sincerity implies a living up to, authenticity a getting down into. Sincerity is a social virtue, a compact between me, myself, and you; authenticity is an assertion, a defiance, a claim to cut away the falsities of culture. It takes two to be sincere, only one to be authentic. Sincerity speaks for a conduct of *should*; authenticity for a potential of *is*. Sincerity is a virtue of public consciousness, authenticity a repudiation of its bad faith. Sincerity implies a recognition of our limits, authenticity asserts the self as absolute. We are to be persuaded toward sincerity, but stripped, shocked, and shamed into authenticity. And—though Trilling avoids these linkings—sincerity strikes me largely as an attribute of Romanticism, authenticity as a straining of modernism.

Now, in truth, there are no such sharp distinctions between the two, nor is it mere carelessness that allows us in ordinary speech to use them, at times, interchangeably. For as Trilling shows, historically there has been a slide from one to the other, and the compartments of discourse are not always respected in the development of actuality. What the passion for sincerity and the search for authenticity share, and what makes them first cousins within the family of modern sensibility, is their common if tacit dismissal of the premise of objective truth. To be true to oneself replaces being true to the truth. Authenticity is a brilliant if often destructive bastard offspring of sincerity, and sincerity a token of that "psychology of exposure" through which the 19th century unmasked itself, or thought it was unmasking itself. The triumph of literary modernism is signalled by a shift from impersonal truth to personal sincerity, from belief in objective law to search for unimpeded response. The first of these involves an effort to apprehend the nature of the universe; the second an effort to apprehend the nature of our inner being. Sincerity becomes a defense for men losing religious belief, authenticity the term for destroying absolutes, systems, moral claims. Nor is it an accident that the quest for the reality about our selves should eventually lead to a nagging, violent attack upon the self—just as the desire of the "honest soul" to be faithful to the commonplace virtues has led, through the cunning of history, to a modernist contempt for ordinary consciousness, ordinary life, ordinary people, all dismissed as "inauthentic" (or "two-dimensional"). One of Trilling's most forceful passages is a comment on Nathalie Sarraute's dismissal of Emma Bovary:

> . . . this poor, doomed Emma, although inauthenticity certainly does touch her, is not a being of no actuality or worth whatever. . . . She has a degree of courage, although of an imprudent sort, an attractive presence, a sexuality which is urgent when once it is aroused, an imagination which kindles to the idea of experience . . . and a will to overcome the nullity of her existence. . . . Mme. Sarraute [cannot] give the forlorn creature even a wry compassion. A similar harshness of judgment informs Mme. Sarraute's fiction, beginning with her first book, *Tropismes*, a work which induces us to wonder why this gifted and imperious author should choose as the objects of her fierce discernment such *little* and, so to speak, merely incidental persons as she depicts. . . . Why does she descend from the height of her privileged state of being to make explicit her disgust at the nothingness of these persons who, as the title of the work proposes, are not persons at all?

Apart from the issues it raises, *Sincerity and Authenticity* is a deeply interesting book by reason of making clear the controlling concerns of a writer who has been one of the two or three most influential American critics during the past thirty years. Trilling refers at one point to Nietzsche's injunction that we "look below the surface of rational formulation to discover the *will* that is hidden beneath, and expressed through, its elaborations." If we make this effort in regard to Trilling himself, two observations come to mind.

First, his deepest interest in literature is not the critical act narrowly conceived, the description or analysis of a work and judgment of its merits—though he has often performed this act with force and delicacy. His deepest interest is in searching for the animating biases, the all-but-unspoken modulations of sentiment and value which give shape to a moment in cultural history. In an earlier time he might have been called a philosopher or historian of "moral consciousness," when that term did not carry the aura of faint depreciation it now does and when "moral" would have been assumed to include a range of experiences for which we have since found other names.

Perhaps my description of Trilling's central concerns may be clarified if I mention the school of critics who take a no-nonsense delight in ascribing recurrent turns of action and qualities of feeling in literary works to the shaping presence of "conventions." It is a "convention" that heroes behave as they do in epics, that sonnets often deal with romantic love, that Gothic novels are set in haunted castles. But to say this, while useful, is only a beginning. For the "convention" is a patterned, sometimes calcified record of historical turmoil and cultural innovation: the conduct of romantic heroes in 19th-century writing often follows a convention set in Goethe's *The Sorrows of Young Werther*, but for that fixing of premise and style to be possible there had first or concurrently to take place a revolution in sensibility. Now, what fascinates Trilling and comprises, I think, the main burden of this work is the way a major work of art "comes out of" (I use quotation marks because we do not really know how that happens) the seedbed of a culture and then how the major work helps to define the very terms of the influence exerted upon it. How or why does a given moment of historical consciousness find it so hard to yield to the attractions of physical pleasure? How or why does another moment turn away from the quest for transcendence and accept the small change, if small change it be, of quotidian contentment?

In his role as historian of moral consciousness Trilling is far from systematic. He relies very heavily on the premise, shared with F. R. Leavis, that the major text is a decisive instance, and his work is steadily open to the criticism of compacting the history of "consciousness" into a realm too self-contained and insufficiently complicated by mere events.

Second, we see in *Sincerity and Authenticity* the guiding norm, the goal, the working of *will*, to recur to Nietzsche's phrase, that inspires Trilling's work. It is a sense of life which makes Freud deeply congenial to him, and many recent cultural prophets uncongenial. Freud's "imagination of the human condition preserves something—much—of the stratum of hardness that runs through the Jewish and Christian traditions as they respond to the hardness of human destiny. Like the Book of Job it propounds and accepts the mystery and the naturalness—the natural mystery, the mysterious naturalness—of suffering." In advancing this austere vision Freud "had the intention of sustaining the authenticity of human existence that formerly had been ratified by God." Nietzsche too had wished for some such sustenance, as he "dreaded the 'weightlessness of all things,' the inauthenticity of experience, which he foresaw would be the consequence of the death of God." It is a wonderful if all-but unglossable phrase, that "weightlessness of things" dreaded by Nietzsche quite as if he had foreseen California. And as Trilling invokes it in behalf of his own sense of authenticity, he gains one's assent—

yes, we know what he is trying to suggest here, we share his underlying uneasiness and urge to historical salvage. Until another question comes to mind: is not the very category of authenticity too coarsened in tone, too abrasive and lacerating in its effects, too inextricably associated with impulses toward dismissal and contempt? Might there not be some point in easing that self-assault, at one time liberating and later a mere complacent mimicry, which has been one of the less happy directives of modern culture? If *Emma Bovary, c'est moi*, and if she merits the compassion, even the sliver of respect, that Trilling would give her, might there not be some benefit in a similar indulgence for the rest of us? In short, would there not be some value if human beings, especially those who pride themselves on their cultivation, were to learn to like themselves a little once again—and authenticity be damned?

# 54

*Roger Sale*

*"Lionel Trilling," in* On Not Being Good Enough *{originally published in* Hudson Review*}*

*1979 {spring 1973}*

Roger Sale (1932– ), professor of English at the University of Washington, is the author of *On Writing* (1970), *On Not Being Good Enough: Writings of a Working Critic* (1979), *Literary Inheritance* (1984), and *Closer to Home: Writers and Places in England, 1780–1830* (1986), among other books.

Sales's areas of specialization in literary studies have been Renaissance literature, modern British fiction, and literary-cultural criticism. The following impassioned review reflected a turn in the late 1960s and early '70s—chiefly among a younger generation of literary academics—toward a harsher assessment of Trilling.

Lionel Trilling is probably as famous now as he was twenty years ago, but unless I am much mistaken, his reputation is nowhere near as high as it was in the fifties, the years of *The Liberal Imagination* and *The Opposing Self*, and the little essays for the Reader's Subscription. Back then, if this country had a leading literary critic, or, more precisely, a leading literary spokesman, it was Trilling. He was at the center of a number of concentric circles important to the literary intellectual life of the country. He was a famous and respected teacher at Columbia. He was widely known in American universities, and perhaps was the only critic frequently read by historians, philosophers, social and natural scientists. He was one of the best-known "New York intellectuals," by which was usually meant "Columbia" or "the *Partisan Review* crowd," a group sufficiently coherent in its cultural and political centrality that its enemies, especially the younger ones, always knew who to attack when they wanted to strike their father dead.

Those days are long ago. Liberalism no longer has a near monopoly on intelligence; the *Parisan Review* is just another journal; the categories "Jewish intellectual" and "young Jewish novelist" no longer are rallying terms of hate, respect, and envy; teaching by means of the formal lecture is much less prevalent and is considered much less desirable, and courses that assume the centrality of Western Culture no longer dominate the curriculum. All these facts serve in varying degrees to deny Trilling the place he once had. His is not a voice that one could expect to adapt itself easily to the sixties, and now that the sixties are almost as dead as the fifties, no one seems to be rediscovering him, finding out that he was right all along, or doing much more than vaguely wondering if he is still alive. A dozen years ago I gave a group of undergraduates some passages from Trilling's *Matthew Arnold* for comment. There was, I remember, a shuffling of voices and feet. Well, yes, Trilling didn't do very much, and Arnold seemed mostly a hatrack on which Trilling was neatly piling the sombreros of all the best-known names in the West. But no one could say that straight out, or even directly agree with it, and under my prodding the students got sullen with me rather than articulate about Trilling. Last year I gave a group of graduate students—people temperamentally much more cautious and respectful—the same passages, and they just hooted, not with the glee that one associates with the discovery that the emperor is not wearing clothes, but with the more casual derision that accompanies the question, "Who does this guy think he is, anyway?"

Well, admittedly *Matthew Arnold* is not the best Trilling. After that book he never again attempted to sustain a long consecutive argument, and he discovered that perhaps his most congenial form is the lecture. The voice of *The Liberal Imagination, The Opposing Self,* and *Beyond Culture* speaks from a lectern: here is a subject, a problem, a matter for an hour's serious thought, let us see what we can say about it. His latest book, *Sincerity and Authenticity,* is an attempt to carry on a single argument through a series of lectures given at Harvard a couple of years ago. The voice is still strong, sure of its centrality despite the events of the last twenty years, and if reading Trilling in bulk does bear certain affinities with eating a meal consisting entirely of Thousand Island dressing, it cannot be said that the years have really taken much toll. Trilling is calm, measured, judicious, generous, as always, and he continues precisely to make the kinds of distinctions he was always most interested in making. One need feel no embarrassment—such as one feels reading the later Eliot, Leavis, or C. S. Lewis—while reading *Sincerity and Authenticity*; whatever he was good for, Lionel Trilling is good for still. That last sentence implies a question I must try to answer later; but first, a look at these lectures.

Anyone who teaches the literature of the last few centuries has had to talk to students about the question of "sincerity." Is Cleopatra "sincere" when she offers her hand to Caesar's messenger to be kissed? Is Marvell *ever* "sincere"? When Clarissa says she wants only to submit to the reasonable will of her father, does she mean it? Etc. Trilling's opening answer is good:

> We cannot say of the patriarch Abraham that he was a sincere man. That statement must seem only comical. The sincerity of Achilles or Beowulf cannot be discussed: they neither have nor lack sincerity. But if we ask whether the young Werther is really as sincere as he intends to be, or which of the two Dashwood sisters, Elinor or Marianne, is thought by Jane Austen to be the more truly sincere, we can confidently expect a serious response in the form of opinions on both sides of the question.

The rest of the opening lecture is good too. When "society" was invented, when Machiavels traipsed stages of theatres and countries, when villainy became associated with duplicity, when plain speaking became possible and plain speakers could be applauded or laughed at, the question of "sincerity" became a real issue. The more some people simulated selves, and others dissimulated "sincere" selves, the more threats there were both to the society and to the individual attempting rightly to perceive the world around him.

One ideal that such an age will foster is that to be found in Shakespeare's late plays:

> The hope that animates this normative vision of the plays is the almost shockingly elementary one which Ferdinand utters in *The Tempest*—the hope of "quiet days, fair issue, and long life." It is reiterated by Juno in Prospero's pageant: "Honour, riches, marriage blessing, / Long continuance and increasing." It has to do with good harvests and full barns and the qualities of affluent decorum that Ben Jonson celebrated in Penshurst and Marvell in Appleton House. . . .[1]

But as society became less whole and real, that ideal tended to become the lynchpin of a reactionary, hypocritical, "insincere" aristocracy, and the ideal that replaced it became more fragmented and confused, given to multiple and complicated tones in order "sincerely" to respond to society. In the second lecture Trilling is at his best. True, he consistently uses his familiar lineup of Big Names—Rousseau, Diderot, Hegel, Goethe—but Trilling knows these figures well, and he is very convincing at outlining the shifts they show us in moral consciousness. Empson, writing about the history of the word "honest" in the same period, is perhaps better than Trilling at this kind of thing, because he can catch more odd and partial tones, but Trilling is always assured and accurate when he retells the history of High Culture, and if such a history can show us the modern consciousness becoming born, Trilling can do the showing.

But at this point Trilling relaxes just when he should have been most cautious and vigilant. When he comes to the nineteenth century he conveniently shifts the focus from the "sincere" to the "authentic," and this allows him to go skating over ponds where the ice is never thin. He carries on from his earlier essay on *Emma* as pastoral idyll, he gives us Emerson on the English authentic virtues, and Conrad's Marlow on the authentic cruelty of Kurtz. We have all been here before, and a good deal of the time Trilling himself has been our guide. What the opening lectures beautifully set us up for is something much more interesting and difficult: the fate of "sincerity" from the time when Jane Austen could tell us who is the more "sincere" Dashwood sister down to the time in this century when "it all depends on your point of view." The most serious writers of the nineteenth century wrestled with the problem as if their lives depended on it. If the Machiavel survives in a figure like Morris Townsend in *Washington Square*, the hard questions about sincerity do not concern him but Dr. Sloper. We sit and stare at the narrations of Esther Summerson and Nelly Dean, and their very innocence and lack of self-consciousness leads us to wonder at their "sincerity."[2] Perhaps most interesting is Thackeray and Becky Sharp. Trilling puts Becky at the end of a list of duplicitous characters, wolves in sheep's clothing, like Tartuffe and Blifil. But Becky, plotter and schemer though she is, at the crisis of her life claims she is guiltless of Rawdon's charge that she has been unfaithful with Lord Steyne, and Thackeray knows he does not know what to answer.[3] "What *had* happened?" he asks, "Was she guilty or not?" The questions are not coy; Becky is living on Lord Steyne's money, or, more properly, living well on nothing a year; the morality that can label her "whore" (and therefore duplicitous and insincere) cannot easily operate when transactions are a matter of credit rather than cash. There is sufficiently little difference between Becky's relations with Rawdon and with Steyne that Thackeray cannot say, and knows he cannot say, with whom she is "wife," with whom she is "mistress," to whom she is false or true.

The pity is that the questions I have just raised are right up Trilling's alley, precisely the sort of historical, moral, and literary problems he enjoys most. But instead of asking these questions Trilling sets up the deeply sincere but fundamentally inauthentic command of George Eliot to do one's duty and plays it against the really authentic command of Oscar Wilde to be as artificial as possible, and he does this, presumably, because he knows how to do so, has done so before. But the argument is familiar, to say nothing of doing injustice to George Eliot. This lapse into the familiar, furthermore, continues right through the lectures on the twentieth century: Marinetti's attacks on Ruskin—which, by the way, may be characteristic of early modern attitudes, but are not in themselves worth serious consideration—and a long discussion of Freud that is only slightly different from earlier ones in *The Liberal Imagination* and *Beyond Culture*, ending with predictable, if salutary, slaps at Marcuse and Laing.

At the very end, though, Trilling speaks out with full resonance, and we can perhaps use his closing sentences as a means of locating what is best and most limited in Trilling's liberal faith. He is responding to Laing's invitation to all of us to go mad, and Trilling calls this mere cant:

And when we have given due weight to the likelihood that those who respond positively to the doctrine don't have it in mind to go mad, let alone insane—it is characteristic of the intellectual life of our culture that it fosters a form of assent which does not involve actual credence—we must yet take it to be significant of our circumstance that many among us find it gratifying to entertain the thought that alienation is to be overcome only by the completeness of alienation, and that alienation completed is not a deprivation or deficiency but a potency. Perhaps exactly because the thought is assented to so facilely, so without what used to be called seriousness, it might seem that no expression of disaffection from social existence was ever so desperate as this eagerness to say that authenticity of personal being is achieved through an ultimate isolateness and through the power that this is presumed to bring. The falsities of an alienated social reality are rejected in favour of an upward psychopathic mobility to the point of divinity, each one of us a Christ—but with none of the inconveniences of undertaking to intercede, of being a sacrifice, of reasoning with rabbis, of making sermons, of having disciples, of going to weddings, and to funerals, of beginning something and at a certain point remarking that it is finished.

There is much that can be said of this passage, but the most obvious is its conviction, its sincerity and authenticity; the voice that intercedes, that reasons with rabbis, that here comes to an end, knows that for whatever else the mantle of reasonable discourse is to be discarded, it will not be for the chicness of a sentimental madness. And I for one find the patriarchal quality of that list at the end quite moving.

But the passage also reveals the way Trilling's prose is his own worst enemy. In the first sentence it gains nothing to redefine "don't have it in mind to go mad" as "assent which does not involve actual credence," because all it yields is the repetition of "the intellectual life of our culture" as "our circumstance," and to a repetition of Laing's doctrine at the close of the sentence. Having thus wrapped himself in his own thick phrasing, Trilling can only go on saying where he quite obviously already is, and the second sentence, full sixty words, adds absolutely nothing, leading neatly, in the final sentence, to still another repetition of Laing. The man, it must be admitted, just loves the sound of his own orotundity. Nor is my example unfair; the heaviness, the repetitiveness, is everywhere in Trilling's prose, and has been there from the beginning. When one says Trilling's writing can be flexible, one does not mean that it is not ponderous.

What the prose shows in every gesture, of course, it reveals about the mind. Trilling treats himself as an institution, and so he can never speak with anything less than full assurance. It never occurs to him that we may not want to know what is on his mind, or that we might entertain an idea of Western culture different from his, or that we might approach it in different ways. Trilling does not think the history of the last five centuries is fully recoverable, but he unfailingly does think he can recover enough to make it relevant for any question that happens to be pressing; all you do is make patterns, continuities, trends, emphases. That way you seldom have to go one-on-one with an author, or to wish you knew more, or, occasionally, less. He never gives the impression of having read anything for the first time, of being surprised, confused, delighted, enraged, or captivated by anything he has read. That the past can rebuke the present is clear enough to him, though he never takes this idea seriously enough to think that perhaps now is not the best time to say something.

The impulse is to be masterful, to make sermons, to have disciples, and anyone who has ever taught or written knows it well. But since it is an impulse that easily can blind us to what we have not said, it is one which anyone of conscience and intelligence must guard against. The easiest and best way to keep the guard up is to quote, to quote a lot, to quote at length, because, unless one does this in the spirit of a copyist, one is forced to face the fact that the subject is another mind, one is forced to try to make one's prose responsive to the words of another, even if the response is scorn or laughter. Trilling quotes, but almost always in a summary way, so that what he is quoting can easily be folded into Trilling's argument and Trilling's demeanor need never alter. The point is not that Trilling is René Wellek or A. O. Lovejoy or George Steiner[4] or someone else whose impulse to mastery leads to mongering the humorless, the absolute, or the fashionable. The point is, rather, that for all his serious and generous intelligence, he shares with these and similar writers the quality of seeming much better in the reading than in the memory. The way he seeks to gain himself, to be the master, is a way that tends to mean that he loses us because he never fully lets his subject live separately from him.

One suspects that for the average reader Trilling will be most admired for his utility in speaking to and perhaps even settling issues where literature is only part of the subject: "Reality in America," the essays on Freud,

"The Meaning of a Literary Idea," "On the Teaching of Modern Literature," "The Two Environments," etc. The advantage Trilling enjoys is that he is a thinker, he is generous, but he is no theoretician, and as a result these essays have and probably will continue to find their way into anthologies; they are useful, if one admits their subjects to be anything like as interesting or crucial as Trilling takes them to be. But for me these essays reread very badly, and for two reasons: the subjects themselves tend to date, and the whole idea of being plumply judicious about subjects of concern is one which has seen better days. There is no better way to see this than to look at the references to individual authors and works in the essays where the subject is a general one. The Dostoevsky, the Proust, and most devastating, for me at least, the D. H. Lawrence that Trilling speaks of when he is not thinking directly and carefully about those writers are all caricatures, and worse, caricatures that appeal to the most fully received clichés about them. If the occasion to respond to the Leavis-Snow affair[5] or new fashions in psychoanalysis is going to lead someone as learned and thoughtful as Trilling into these caricatures, then the occasions themselves perhaps had better be avoided.

Trilling is better than this, I think, when forced to address himself to a particular writer or work. This focus is no guarantee of success, but then it never is, and when quotation is what is called for and Trilling won't quote, the results can be damaging, as in his failure to note how flaccid Wordsworth is in the first half of the *Intimations Ode*, or to see how very good is Vernon Parrington's description of Hawthorne, even though his estimate of Hawthorne is much lower than Trilling thinks it should be. But even here Trilling is really interesting; if he cannot settle subjects, be truly decisive with individual works, he can almost always be counted on to ask good questions, to open something up: the essays on *Emma* and *Mansfield Park*, the appreciation of Keats's letters, the piece on *The Bostonians*, the sections on Diderot and Hegel in the present volume—give Trilling a subject where his penchant for generalizing is called for, and he is a careful and fine critic. One wonders why he has never done more than allude to the late Augustan writers—Fielding, Johnson, Gibbon, Burke—for surely here, if anywhere, is his real métier, the sober, the wise, the ironic, the heroically reasonable and learned. Trilling needs centrality of concern to be himself central; he cannot respond well to quirkiness and eccentricity, to slippery surface texture, to unargued assertion, to prejudice or mere opinion. He might feel he can twit Leavis about Leavis's apparently insistent moral tone, but he could never have written with Leavis's delicacy about Jonson, Carew,[6] and Pope.

If Trilling's moment of highest fame and respect has passed, it is not likely to return, because he just does not write well enough, care enough for words, to outlive the world he received and in which he flourished. If we are to maintain our link with the European past we will have to do so more fugitively and eagerly than Trilling has done, and with a more urgent sense that we are liable to lose it if we fail to speak in our own voice, our ignorant voice, our American voice. Trilling wanted to be Matthew Arnold, and there was a time when that was taken as a wonderful thing to try to be. Trilling filled the role well. One might complain that he chose the wrong model, that Mill, or Ruskin, or George Eliot are more worth the effort. Perhaps the better complaint is that we had best be done with models, that we can keep the past alive not by imitating or emulating it but by reading its words aloud and by answering them in whatever authentic voice we have, wildly, loudly, or in hushed tones.

## Notes

1. Juno and Prospero are characters in Shakespeare's *The Tempest* (1611). "To Penshurst" is Ben Jonson's (1572–1637) tribute to the house of Sidney. As a young man in his twenties, Jonson worked as a tutor for the Sidneys. "Upon Appleton House" is by Andrew Marvell (1621–78), English poet and Puritan member of Parliament.—Ed.

2. Townsend is a character in *Washington Square* (1881), a novel of manners by Henry James. Sloper is a character in Mary Renault's *The Coils of War.* Esther Summerson is a main character in Dickens's *Bleak House* (1850). Nelly Dean is the housekeeper in Emily Bronte's *Wuthering Heights* (1847).

3. Beckey Sharp, Rawdon, and Lord Steyne are all characters in Thackeray's *Vanity Fair* (1847–48).—Ed.

4. Rene Wellek (1903–95), educator and literary critic, was a founder of comparative literature as a discipline. Arthur O. Lovejoy (1873–1962) was a historian of ideas who integrated philosophy and literature into intellectual-cultural history. George Steiner (1929– ) is a cosmopolitan literary and cultural critic especially concerned with English, French, and German literature.—Ed.

5. A Cambridge University lecture by Charles Percy Snow (Lord Snow), "The Two Cultures and the Scientific Revolution" (1959), inaugurated a famous controversy with the Cambridge literary critic F. R. Leavis about the modern gulf between the sciences and humanities as two mutually incomprehensible "polar cultures."—Ed.

6. Thomas Carew (1595–1640) was a friend of Ben Jonson and one of the first English Cavalier poets.—Ed.

55

*John Holloway*

*"Sincerely, Lionel Trilling,"* Encounter

*September 1973*


John Holloway (1920– ), professor emeritus of English at Queen's College, Cambridge University, has written more than a dozen volumes of poetry and is the author of *The Victorian Sage* (1953), among numerous other books.

Often called an "intellectual" poet for his subtle, traditional verse written in colloquial language and a meditative tone, Holloway exemplifies the Arnoldian sensibility that Trilling admired. Personally acquainted with Trilling, Holloway saw him occasionally during Trilling's year at All Soul's College, Oxford University in 1972–73.

In the review below, Holloway praises what other critics have perceived as the Arnoldian quality of Trilling's keenly dialectical temperament, which Holloway calls his capacity to "enter into everything but never lose his balance one iota."


*Sincerity and Authenticity* consists of the Charles Eliot Norton lectures Lionel Trilling gave at Harvard in 1970. At one point in these lectures, Trilling found himself linking the names of Robespierre and Jane Austen. He paused to say it must be the first time those two names had ever been linked like that. Maybe: and it indicates what at this stage I am going to call merely the flexibility of mind of the book, that they were. Thinking these lectures over, I found I wanted to link two names that also don't often come together: Gerard Manley Hopkins, whom Trilling doesn't mention, and the other, whom he says a good deal of, Hegel.

In the *Phenomenology*, Hegel has an opaque yet inexhaustibly illuminating section called "Spirit in Self-Estrangement—the Discipline of Culture." It offers much in respect of Trilling's position. Hegel seems to start with the conception of the individual self in a primitive, primal relation to the so-called "kingdom of consciousness", the social world which lies outside itself. The self's primary relation to this is undifferentiated activty: the exercise may be of power, may be of benevolence. But it is an unstable relation. As soon as the self begins to look at what it is doing, it in effect puts itself across into the opposite camp. It makes itself into an object of attention. So, it now stands among other objects. They too are objects of attention, so they're no longer just the polarity to the self's undifferentiating activity. Everything is now singled out, so it loses its primal reality; and so does the self along with it.

Yet, even as this happens, something opposite to it happens too. The self in its primal simplicity was scarcely a self at all. It comes to be a self as it departs from this primal simplicity. "The estrangement on the part of spirit from its natural existence is here the individual's true and original nature, his very substance", says Hegel. Suppose we try to say, "the individual wakes up to his position in society"—that's no good. What has not yet woken up is not an individual. Put this now in a given social context—that, say, of the individual who is simply the unquestioning servant of the power of society collectively, of the state. Suppose that this individual comes to have reservations about what he is doing. In one sense, his singleness of purpose and of being are destroyed. But what results is an individual who may be said to know where he stands: know that he must play a role, even if that role is one of unspoken doubt and self-doubt, of conscious submission to something outside him. In Hegel's historical context, that something takes the form of a monarch who can now be served only through dissimulation and flattery. Such a role will actually be a heightening and intensifying of the self. Hegel says: "The heroism of dumb service passes into the heroism of flattery . . . flattery raises the individual singleness." It now does so, in a complex social mesh of accepting an understood place in an understood scheme of things— of striking out a position which is at the same time a disintegration of position, a place which is at the same time a non-place, in a *culture*, Trilling's favourite word.

I have tried to paraphrase Hegel because he has expressed, in general terms, exactly the predicament underlying this book, and Trilling's work over twenty years. And Hopkins? Hegel was perhaps over-terse about that position of primal and integral activity from which his train of thought started. He drew it out of an enigmatical darkness. But at one stage in his life, Hopkins understood it perfectly and expressed it luminously. So much so, that the absolutely right word coined itself for him as he wrote. You'll hear that coinage in the middle of these lines from "As Kingfishers Catch Fire":

As kingfishers catch fire, dragonflies draw flame;
As tumbled over rim in roundy wells
Stones ring; like each tucked string tells, each hung bell's
Bow swung finds tongue to fling out broad its name;
Each mortal thing does one thing and the same:
Deals out that being indoors each one dwells;
Selves—goes itself; *myself* it speaks and spells,
Crying *What I do is me; for that I came.*

I say more: the just man justices;
Keeps grace: that keeps all his goings graces;
Acts in God's eye what in God's eye he is—

*Selves.* If ever the philosopher's mode of apprehension, and the literary mode, stood over against each other, they do so here.

Hopkins uses the word again—or rather, its opposite—in one poem where he notices (as he was almost the first English poet directly to notice) what Trilling calls "the deterioration of the organic environment." I am thinking of "Binsey Poplars." "Strokes of havoc *unselve* / The sweet especial scene." Hopkins often touched on how development and modernity, especially the modern world of commerce and productivity, were invading and disrupting the primal thisness of things, their capacity to *selve*, and our own capacity along with them.

This (and all about modernity that is implied by it) has long been among Trilling's major preoccupations. "The simple humanitarian optimism which, for two decades, has been so pervasive . . . has been politically and philosophically inadequate"—that's what he said back in 1940. In his new book, the starting-point is "the extent to which a society fosters, or corrupts, the sincerity of its citizens." Previously, in one major essay after another— "Manners, Morals and the Novel" of 1942, "The Situation of the American Intellectual at the Present Time" of 1952, "The Two Environments" of 1965—Trilling has addressed himself to engagement with literature in a context of diagnosing what modern civilisation is like, and in particular what pressures it imposes on the individual. So of couse have many others; though not quite with his breadth, perspicacity and control. But the others have usually told us about literature and society, or literature and morality, mainly by way of diagnosing what Hegel called "the external element": what demands for conformity an externalised world of moral order makes on the individual. Trilling has never forgotten that literature is in the first place less a *pillar* of society than a *questioner* of society and a champion of something else. In 1955 he wrote: "In its essence literature is concerned with the self; and the particular concern of the literature of the last two centuries has been with the self in its standing quarrel with culture."

Those words epitomise the two main themes of the present book. There is the great primal fact of the self's urge towards authenticity of being, and without authenticity it cannot risk sincerity; and the corresponding literary reality is that literature's perennial message has been (as Trilling puts it in respect of Conrad's *Heart of Darkness*) a "strange and terrible message of ambivalence towards the life of civilisation." No one has seen that strangeness and terror in literature with more concern than Trilling.

There is a certain amount in this book, of a quite straightforward kind, about what sincerity is; or about what authenticity is. But surprisingly little. At one point the author speaks of "such effort at definition" (of authenticity, that is) "as I shall later make": yet there isn't much later, and some aspects of both sincerity and authenticity hardly get touched on at all. For instance: I find myself not agreeing that sincerity in a person means either just "telling the truth about oneself *to* oneself and others" (the French meaning, Trilling says); or, "singleminded commitment, without deceit, to a dutiful enterprise" (the English pattern: though by Jane Austen's time the two patterns seem to have merged). For example: can one really say something like: "He was quite sincere, he told me he meant to seek only his own advantage"? Or can one say: "his sincerity shows at least in his unfailing selfishness"? I don't think so: or only in some stretched, sarcastic fashion.

Sincerity in the full sense seems to mean something about openness before others, as *means*; as means to something beyond that openness, some direct concern for others and for their selfhoods. Sometimes it has no regard to being open about oneself. At the end of George Eliot's *Middlemarch*, Dorothea Brooke thinks she has seen the man she's in love with, more or less in Rosamund Vincy's arms. She's stricken to the heart, but next day she goes to Rosamund, who's married, and tries—disinterestedly—to warn her against the destructiveness of what she seems to be doing. It's a moment of breathtaking sincerity in Dorothea, in some sense: but that, actually because she's at pains to try not to speak of her personal involvement—of course, it would only have confused the issue. I don't see how Trilling could accommodate Dorothea.

Again, it's uncommon to say that an individual is "authentic" though certainly one can say it. Yet there's some rather strange difference between using "authentic" of people and of things. We could say a man was authentic, "the real thing", as a monk, maybe, or a soldier, and we shouldn't in the least be put off by knowing that he'd modelled himself on the pattern of someone else—was in a sense a copy. "The sentiment of being", which for Trilling is the key to authenticity, is, he says, "the sense of being strong. Which is not to say powerful." If I understand the sentiment of being at all, it's something more primitive.

Trilling doesn't take such points far, because he's not trying to make a general psychological map of the territory of sincerity and authenticity. He cares about how the individual's sincerity and authenticity relate to society: whether society is the enemy of these things, or their ally, and more particularly, how literature, over the past two hundred years, has charted the relations and tensions between the two.

Of course! What else would Trilling be doing, what else would seem to stand like a culmination of his work? One thinks back, over the years, to his essays on Jane Austen, on "Wordsworth and the Rabbis," and the rest, and these are the problems he has recurrently tackled. And it is here, in this field of how and where literature bears on the tension between society and the individual, that the joy of this splendid book resides.

For it is a splendid book. Trilling once wrote an essay called "The Fate of Pleasure", and it would appear from this, and from a good deal else, that he is not over-drawn to writing as a source of pleasure: rightly, no doubt, he thinks its dividends more substantial. All the same, how much pleasure this book will give its readers!—the richness and adroitness of the style; but at the same time, plenty of crispness that never becomes abrasiveness:—"a comedy of principle, perfidy and blood"; "this suggestion Rousseau repels with rational indignation." Above all, there's our sense of the writer himself. Not how well Trilling brings other works to a focus, writing as if from a really perfected familiarity with them; not his powers of interconnection; not even his patrician considerateness towards the reader. These are graces— though Hopkins's poem had a place for graces even at this modest level—or at most they are substantial matters of the second rank. The great thing is that with Trilling we have a writer who is approaching an academic task, a task of study and criticism, in a spirit of total largeness, lucidity and directness with regard to the deepest questions of man, life and the world. Trilling does not (as Arnold put it) "strive or cry." He has no opposing self, nothing to denounce. In an earlier volume, written on Tacitus, he was able to call up Portia's words about the "good deed in a naughty world", and add: ". . . a naughty world, literally a world of naught, a moral vacancy so great and black that in it the beam of a candle seems a flash of lightning." Trilling can bring the darkest issues of our own time into academic discussion with a kind of sad but dauntless clarity. "Dauntless" . . . I use the word, strange to our ears, deliberately; because, of all things, in our literary-academic world

Trilling has to be called a heroic figure: almost the only one. This book includes one character-sketch. Here's how it reads: ". . . uncompromising commitment to duty . . . continuous concentration of the personal energies upon some impersonal end, the subordination of life to some general good . . . *singleness of mind and openness of soul.*" Whoever is this? Trilling thinks it's a sketch of the ideal of the naval officer. Trilling's books make it sound like Trilling.

Not that I find myself always agreeing with the accounts of individual books or passages. He makes a good deal of how Rousseau said that listening to novels read aloud to him in his childhood gave him "the unbroken sentiment of being." But Trilling quotes this in English, and I ask myself if he has turned up the French, which is far less resonant and anyway seems to mean something rather different. When he discusses the famous *Letter to d'Alembert* in which Rousseau denounces the idea of opening a theatre at Geneva, Trilling doesn't do enough to separate out the interesting strand in the argument from the others (all actresses immoral, etc., etc.) and show how closely Rousseau tried to formulate this argument in terms of a quite special Genevan society, and so how what he says here is opposite to what he says elsewhere. Trilling gives a brilliant rendering of the almost demented versatility, tumultuous prescience, fantastic sincerity-in-insincerity of Diderot's extraordinary character, Rameau's Nephew: and then—there is something he cannot do. Suddenly his power over words has gone. He says the nephew is "reduced to a bare subsistence", "hardly manages to maintain himself." Phrases like these don't speak with Trilling's full voice. They miss the streak—an early Romantic streak—of grotesque pathos and squalor in Rameau's Nephew, his nearness to what was brutal in his time, his nasty daily battle with the 18th-century commonplace of simple starvation. And if it comes to that, when Trilling describes Conrad's Kurtz, in his "kingdom" in *Heart of Darkness*, with the curious words, "his reign being remarkable for its cruelty", there is the same current failing again. Why?

Isolated moments of weakness, but do they point somewhere? Suppose we are rather crass, and simply ask, straight out, whether the individual should seek sincerity and authenticity within the social bond, or outside and against it; or suppose we ask whether our, as he calls it, "most esteemed certitude" personal autonomy, is really fostered by art, or whether art is "one of the agents of conformity." In his heart of hearts, Trilling has answers, for sure; and they peep out. When he writes of how Hegel endorses the in a sense gallantly anti-social feelings of Rameau's Nephew, he does so, yes, with eloquence and sympathy. But when he writes of the "archaic noble life" of the "great and beautiful houses with the ever-remembered names" in Jane

Austen, where the sentiment of being is one with the sentiment of society, in the highest sense, the note is altogether more inward and devoted. When he writes of the disreputable modern cult of madness as true selfhood in the "coercive inauthenticity" of modern society, his pain and contempt are apparent. Yet what does he say? Only that it represents "the intellectual mode which once went under the name of cant."

We can see all these as symptoms, inconspicuous maybe, of how Trilling strives to enter into everything but never loses his balance one iota. An impossible task maybe, and the result is a rather pervasive inconclusiveness as regards ultimates. There is a great interplay and intermesh of irony in this book, which is another way of describing the "flexibility" I mentioned before. But Trilling himself once wrote: "not more than a little irony is appropriate." Perhaps some readers will sense that interplay as settling down in the end to sharp edges everywhere, but I can't quite do that.

The key seems to lie in the very nature of the liberal imagination. Trilling is a rather conservative liberal—his warmth over Jane Austen, reverence for the traditional in Wordsworth, instant allegiance to the Apollonian side of Freud, all suggest that. But he is also what James would have called "an immense sensibility." Wherever there is a challenge to the patrician rationality which is Trilling's first love, he pursues it, not indeed with fascination, but with "singleness of mind and openness of soul." The wild men, and the wilder, darker side, of Diderot, of Hegel, of Freud, and elsewhere than in the present book of writers like Conrad or Isaac Babel, he explores with eager, dedicated, or hopeless resolve. He feels what he himself once called "the excitement of suddenly being liberated from Aristotle" and Aristotle's logicality. The "immense sensibility" wants to enter into everything, giving it not just an academic kind of justice, but a robust and pregnant felt life; and to fill itself, and us, with awareness that times have been changing, that the academic apprehension is not enough, that we must stretch every way, see a hundred modes of authenticity, and somehow draw on them all in striving to create one for ourselves.

A hundred modes of authenticity . . . I can understand it if Trilling forgot that poem of Hopkins. That primal authenticity, open to a stone or a string, is far from his kind. If I had to diagnose his kind, I should venture to do it an odd way. Trilling seems to me the opposite *moment*, in a Hegelian sense, from Rameau's Nephew. Not the plain, polar opposite: a stone is that, or maybe Wordsworth. But if you think of an equal to the Nephew in brilliance, charm and versatility, yet at the same time a man with sympathy, instead of cynicism, to go out in every direction; and with "a personal character that is grave, dense and persistent"—exuberance of responsibility and self-dedication, not parasitism; and yet at the same time someone who finds his own sincerity and authenticity exactly in that activity of endless and ubiquitous self-departure—if you try to imagine such a character, in all its complexity, all its great but troubling winningness—it's Lionel Trilling.

Appreciations, Influences,

Controversies, Reconsiderations

## 56

*Steven Marcus*

*Excerpt from "Lionel Trilling, 1905–75," in* Art, Politics, and

Will *{originally published in* The New York Times*}*

*1976 {November 1975}*

Steven Marcus (1928– ), professor of English at Columbia University, is the author of *Dickens from Pickwick to Dombey* (1965), *The Other Victorians* (1966), *Engels, Manchester, and the Working Class* (1974), and *Freud and the Culture of Psychoanalysis* (1984), among other books.

Both an undergraduate and graduate student of Trilling, Marcus earned his B.A. in 1948 and his Ph.D. in 1961 from Columbia. He co-edited with Trilling an abridged one-volume edition of Ernest Jones's authorized biography, *The Life and Work of Sigmund Freud* (1961), and also co-edited (with Columbia colleagues) the Trilling memorial volume *Art, Politics, and Will: Essays in Honor of Lionel Trilling* (1977). In addition, Marcus has served on the *Partisan Review* editorial board since 1960.

In the memoir below, which originally appeared on the front page of the *New York Times*, Marcus memorializes Trilling as "our historian of the moral life of modernity, our philosopher of culture," and "our teacher."

. . . To my mind Trilling's spiritual heroism was in large part bound up with his exigency and his minimalism—his ability to affirm, without illusion, qualities and virtues that his own group, his own culture, his own audience had largely given up on as being at once excessive in their demands upon us and insufficient in the gratifications they return.

During the political and cultural storms of the sixties Trilling continued to sustain himself in these attitudes. As he considered some of the more bizarre lunacies of the New Left or wilder manifestations of the counter-culture, he thought he saw in these rapidly fluctuating formations genuine threats to the cultural order that he affirmed, albeit minimally and with a cold, skeptical eye. He tended on the whole to see tragedy in such developments, while others tended to see farce. . . .

He was our teacher, and I believe that future generations of readers will continue to learn from him as well. They will read his writings and discover that they too have become better acquainted with themselves. The faculty of rational intellect, the idea of mind, that he had once described as a poor gray thing was not so gray after all. In some of the writers whom he most admired—in Hazlitt, Arnold, Tocqueville, Mill, and George Orwell, to name but a few—that faculty, rigorously and pertinaciously exercised, had led to its own self-transcendence and to its transformation into literature.

## 57

*Irving Howe*

*"On Lionel Trilling: 'Continuous Magical Confrontation,' "*

The New Republic

*March 1976*

(See no. 29 for biographical information about Howe.)

This selection, which focuses on Trilling's influence upon postwar American culture and also reflects Trilling's personal influence on his colleagues
and acquaintances, constitutes Howe's final statement about Trilling. His
praise is lavish: "With the exception of Edmund Wilson," writes Howe,
"Lionel Trilling was the most influential literary critic in America these past
few decades." Howe's review appeared as he himself was about to experience
the height of his own influence in American intellectual-cultural circles
with the publication of *World of Our Fathers* (1976), his story of the history of
the East European immigrant Jews to America, which reached the bestseller lists and earned him the National Book Award for 1977.

It would be foolhardy in a few paragraphs to try for an inclusive portrait of
Lionel Trilling's career as critic and writer; and now that we have the admirable summary description by Steven Marcus in the *Times* of a few weeks ago,
it would be superfluous. I propose here to write about a single aspect of
Trilling's work, but the aspect that seems to me crucial for a grasp of his
extraordinary prestige in our culture.

With the exception of Edmund Wilson, Lionel Trilling was the most
influential literary critic in America these past few decades. By "influential"
I mean something simple: that a critic's essays be read by a public extending
beyond the limits of the academy. Some literary people might argue, though
they would have trouble persuading me, that we have had better critics than

Wilson and Trilling, but I doubt that anyone would dispute my estimate of their influence.

Once Wilson turned away from radical politics, he came to be admired as a virtuoso reader, a brilliant writer, a public critic forever eager to tell us about still more books, still more writers. But Trilling, while often performing superbly as an interpreter of texts, was not read primarily for literary guidance. His influence had to do with that shaded area between literature and social opinion, literature and morality; he kept returning to "our" cultural values, "our" premises of conduct, for he was intent upon a subtle campaign to transform the dominant liberalism of the American cultivated classes into something richer, more quizzical and troubled than it had become during the years after World War II. One way of saying this may be that he sought to melt ideological posture into personal sensibility.

Trilling's intellectual adversaries—among whom, in earlier years, I was one—felt that his work had come to serve as a veiled justification for increasingly conservative moods among American intellectuals. We felt this especially during the '50s when his most influential book, *The Liberal Imagination*, came out. As it seems to me now, the matter is terribly complicated and I still can't pretend to have sorted it out. If we believe that liberalism as a politics cannot avoid a reductionist and smug militancy, or if we hold, as Trilling charged some liberals with holding, that "all" human problems can be solved merely through social action, then there was force to Trilling's criticism. But why must the premise attacked by Trilling be accepted by liberals (a term, as Trilling and others have used it, that seems also to include non-Communist radicals)? Why was it not possible to bring together the dialectical reflectiveness and subtlety of response that Trilling's criticism encouraged with a readiness to do public combat for liberal or radical ends?

In principle there was no reason whatever; in practice—and especially in America—it was hard. Perhaps there always has to be some disharmony between the life of the mind and the life of politics; perhaps there is something about liberalism which does make for simplification and righteousness; and perhaps it was also true, as some of us felt at the time, that Trilling was providing, not a rationale for a new conservatism, but an inducement for a conservatized liberalism. Nor did he always make it easy for those of us attracted by his wonderful essays to acquiesce readily in the values they advanced. His grave elegance of style, his disinclination toward polemic, his use of uncomfortable terms like "will," "spirit," "sentiment of being"—all these were disturbing in one or another way, making us uneasy in our admiration.

Yet, as I now think back to the years in which Trilling did his major work, I cannot really believe that his conservatism, real or alleged, was the major reason for his influence. What drew serious readers to his work was something else which, at the risk of seeming perverse, I want to call a "radical" approach to culture.

In an age which had yielded to a host of determinisms and virtually took it for granted that literature constitutes some sort of "reflection" of a fixed and given external reality, Trilling believed passionately—and taught a whole generation also to believe—in the power of literature, its power to transform, elevate and damage. The work of literature, he wrote in his essay on Freud, is "a being no less alive and contradictory than the man who created it." Not many critics, certainly not many in our own time, have really believed, as Trilling wrote in *The Opposing Self*, that art "expresses itself not only as utility, not only according to law, but as grace, as transcendence, as manner and style."

The contrast could hardly be stronger than between this belief in the autonomy and originating power of the literary imagination and tendency of some modern critics to see "the text" as inert material to be worked upon or, still more alarming, worked up. Like other human beings, Trilling had his weaknesses, mostly for mannerism, but he never succumbed to mere methodology. When his mind began to work, when his engagement with a novel or poem was spontaneous and strong, there occurred for many readers an experience of opening and enlargement, what T. S. Eliot has called "the full surprise and elevation of a new experience of poetry." Trilling would circle a work with his fond, nervous wariness, as if in the presence of some force, some living energy, which could not always be kept under proper control—indeed, as if he were approaching an elemental power. The work came alive and therefore was changeable, alive and therefore was never quite knowable, alive and therefore could even threaten the very desires and values that first made us approach it.

As he grew older, Trilling felt freer to express a growing uneasiness with literary modernism. There were critics, comfortable by now with the worn familiarities of the new, who mocked him for writing about modernism as if it were . . . well, a beast in our jungle which might rear up and strike us a blow. But they failed to see that Trilling was actually paying this beast a kind of tribute, acknowledging its powers of beneficence and maleficence, whereas for the run of modernist critics Joyce and Mann and Mayakovsky had been mauled into docility.

Circling that living presence we call a novel or poem, never forgetting that it was a shadowed embodiment of a man or a woman's imagination, Trilling would try to connect with it through the strategems of reason. What other strategems does a critic have? Yet what he also responded to most deeply was the possibility of surprise, even of the demonic. Utterly civilized, he kept looking beneath civilization. In his essay on Keats, perhaps the greatest he ever wrote, there is a passage about the poet's attitude toward life which I take as a tacit indication of what Trilling wanted criticism to be:

> Keats believed that life was given for him to find the right use of it, that it was a kind of *continuous magical confrontation* requiring to be met with the right answer. He believed that this answer was to be derived from intuition, courage, and the accumulation of experience. It was not, of course, to be a formula of any kind, not a piece of rationality, but rather a way of being and of acting. And yet it could in part be derived from taking thought, and it could be put, if not into a formula, then at least into many formulations. Keats was nothing if not a man of ideas. [Emphasis added.—I.H.]

In the Keats essay the "continuous magical confrontation" took the form of celebrating the heroism of energy, the abundance and delight of youth, but in essays Trilling wrote on Jane Austen's novels he saw the power of imagination not as thrust and striving but as a yielding to idyll and calm. All states of being, from the erect to the crouched, from the assertive to the passive, interested him, and he wrote best about those writers, like Dickens, who were drawn to the sheer plenitude of existence or to those, like Babel,[1] who embodied the tensions following from a struggle between conflicting desires.

Trilling's deep absorption with Freud must have had its source in similar feelings: the sense that Freud recognized, as almost no one else in our time has, the power of imagination to go beyond the routines of mimesis, to startle and terrify us with all that it might *bring up.* Just as Freud saw the role of the analyst as that of a mediator in the battle between what we have made of ourselves and what we have made it from, so Trilling would turn toward a work of literature, attentive to its modes of order and strategies of control but also on the lookout for the unexpected. Freud was probably the single greatest influence on Trilling's work, not through anything so tiresome as "the psychoanalytic approach" to literature, but through a world-view that was inherently dramatic, fluid and tragic, a world-view that saw consciousness itself as a kind of poetry.

Precisely this alertness to the upswell of imagination, even the fury of its primitive elements, in the most highly wrought structures of literature, allowed Trilling to release that yearning for pleasure which he felt had been sacrificed, perhaps unavoidably, in the triumph of literary modernism. Pleasure came from an equilibrium, maintained no doubt for only a moment or two, between rage and poise, energy and constraint, heroism and surrender.

And pleasure inhered in the organic unfolding of a story, that mirror to our fate, that fundamental unit of the disciplined imagination.

It was the sense, then, that Trilling spoke for the imperilled autonomy of our life—for the large possibilities of our private selves and the dangers and betrayals which the modern obsession with self has brought—it was this, I think, that explains the hold he had upon his readers. There remains, of course, another kind of influence, that which he exerted upon colleagues, students, friends. And here we come to the mystery of quietness, the power that a reflective calm may have in the passage of our life.

## Notes

1. Isaak Babel (1894–41) was a Russian-Jewish short-story writer.—Ed.

## 58

*Mark Shechner*

*"The Elusive Trilling,"* The Nation

*September* 1977

Mark Shechner (1941– ), professor of English at the State University of New York at Buffalo, is the author of *Joyce in Nighttown: A Psychoanalytic Inquiry into Ulysses* (1974), *After the Revolution: Studies in the Contemporary Jewish American Imagination* (1987) and *The Conversion of the Jews and Other Essays* (1990). Most interested in postwar Jewish fiction and American intellectual life, Shechner has written on Saul Bellow, Norman Mailer, Allen Ginsberg, and Philip Roth, among other authors. He has also edited *Preserving the Hunger: An Isaac Rosenfeld Reader* (1988).

Shechner is one of Trilling's most perceptive critics. The following wide-ranging essay discusses Trilling's inveterate "preference for defining himself by negatives" and constitutes an illuminating analysis of Trilling's main ideas in the context of his New York intellectual scene.

A review of some of the commentary on Trilling by his contemporaries leads one to conclude that Trilling's mind was one of those to which it is difficult to give assent without bouts of irritation and distrust. Yet from the tone of the eulogies that have followed his death it would be hard to know that his ideas encountered much opposition in his lifetime—and not just from New Critics, unrepentant Stalinists and unredeemed liberals—and that his voice was one of the more tormented, ambiguous and elusive of the postwar period. Recent efforts by Steven Marcus [*New York Times Book Review*, February 8, 1976] and Quentin Anderson [*The New Republic*, April 23, 1977] to press the claim for Trilling's moral heroism give the impression that his greatest achievement was to embody a kind of clearsighted resistance—to be a leading stoic, a spokesman for "moral realism" and the conditioned life, and an expert in admonition who was instrumental in setting a wayward literary culture to rights in the 1940s and 1950s. "To my mind," says Marcus, "Trilling's spiritual heroism was in large part bound up with his exigency and his minimalism—his ability to affirm, without illusions, qualities and virtues that his own group, his own culture, his own audience, had largely given up on as being at once excessive in their demands upon us and insufficient in the gratifications they return."

It does appear that Trilling is at present best remembered among the New York intellectuals largely for his resistances, his antagonism to the articles of progressive faith held dear by his own literary culture: Stalinism, liberalism, the emphasis placed upon "authenticity" by the counterculture of the 1960s. If there is meaning beyond the obvious to the witticism that cosmopolitanism is the Jewish parochialism, the remark has particular application to Trilling, whose brand of cosmopolitanism was resolutely parochial after its own fashion, not only in its exaggerated regard for Bloomsbury manners but in Trilling's general preference for defining himself by negatives. He set himself against the grain of avant-garde ideas, casting out those areas of modern thought of which he could not approve. Here was a cosmopolitanism with a stringent sense of limits and a habit of being old-fashioned in the name of the higher Hegelian syntheses.

If Edmund Wilson is the model of the cosmopolitan intellectual for our time, it is plain how much broader was Wilson's range than Trilling's, and how much more vigorous and adept his grasp. To consider modernism, one of the few areas in which their overlap is significant, is to think of Wilson's pioneering *Axel's Castle* and Trilling's essay, "On the Teaching of Modern Literature," and to observe the difference between a catholic imagination and a scrupulous one, an imagination of enthusiasm and one of measure and concern. To place this penchant for disapproval in its best light, we might say that Trilling was a master of negation whose contribution to discourse in America was a brilliantly dialectical style of setting "the self" against the *Zeitgeist*, even while taking full advantage of its influence.

But, as Trilling was at pains to point out in his studies of writers divided against themselves, such oppositionism arises out of an inner need and reflects a mind in contest with itself. And it is as such interior quarrels that his own stands against the spirit of the age come most clearly into view. There is no outstanding virture let alone moral heroism to devil's advocacy where nothing is risked or where the positions set forth are not attempts to resolve internal tensions by giving them over to formal expression. Trilling's case against the liberal imagination, which sustained him ideologically through three books: *E. M. Forster*, *The Middle of the Journey* and *The Liberal Imagination*, was nothing if not the fallout of his efforts to unburden himself of the vestiges of his own beleaguered liberalism and to justify to himself his waning interest in the ruling passion of his generation: social justice. For if the organizational and ideological facets of liberalism could be quickly dispensed with in the 1940s, the lingering claims of conscience, such as they were, could not, and it was largely for reasons of self-exhortation that Trilling's accounts of the 1930s portrayed it as so brutal, rigid, and soul-deadening an age.

Trilling held the liberal era to be not only the birthplace of the intellectual class, as we now understand it, but also the scene of its original sin. Indeed, the liberal era in Trilling's view was a time of profound moral failure, and he adverted to it in his introduction to Tess Slesinger's *The Unpossessed*[1] with a peculiar loathing, remembering above all "the dryness and deadness that lay at the heart of [the liberals'] drama and that they had brought to the fore a peculiarly American dessication of temperament." Such views not only lacked any hint of fondness for the moral conflicts of his own youth but repressed all memories of such social realities as the depression, unemployment, the vicious labor battles, the advances of fascism in Europe, and the pervasive belief in the exhaustion of American, and indeed, Western, institutions. What remained was a movie of the 1930s starring the self-deceived and self-destroying intellectuals themselves and consequently dominated by its ideas of itself rather than the circumstances that made those ideas, at least to some, seem important.

I think Marcus and Anderson mistaken in viewing Trilling's efforts at redeeming liberalism by the infusion of tragic views, stoic ethics and complicating ironies as fundamentally the expression of his running feud with Stalinism, since it is Trilling's feuds with himself that gave his arguments their intellectual vitality and account, I believe, for their continuing influence. Such popularity as *The Liberal Imagination* retains depends less upon the positions for which it is now difficult to muster any enthusiasm as it does upon the show of competing ideas in a mind that was learning how to draw strength from its own ambivalence and from a style of thought that successfully subordinated its tensions to an overarching grace of intellect. The book's initial importance in the 1950s, I think, was similarly based.

As to Anderson's belief that *The Liberal Imagination* was a salutary corrective to a liberalism that, in 1950, was strongly tinged with Stalinism, the fact was that American Stalinism had already been gutted politically and its organized ranks so thoroughly infiltrated by the FBI that it had ceased to be very interesting to anyone save those who were condemned to rehearse the old battles and the gathering ranks of professional anti-Communists who were tuning up the crusade for loyalty that was to mark the decade. As a force to be dealt with in American politics, liberalism had performed so miserably behind Henry Wallace[2] in 1948 that it was hardly on the map except as a dim remembrance of things past. It is difficult to imagine how, in such an atmosphere, *The Liberal Imagination* could have become doctrinal to a generation of literary intellectuals, as it did, were there not something more to contend with than just the feeble remnants of Stalinism in politics and Socialist Realism in art.

In fact, the book's importance did not lie in its demonstration of how the last nail could be driven into the coffin of progressive ideas—others would do that with less torment and greater efficiency—but in how intellectual and political energies that could no longer be released through social thought or action could be sublimated into higher planes of sensibility.

What made *The Liberal Imagination*'s call for the transcendence of socially defined versions of reality attractive was the palpable urgency of the conflicts that smoldered beneath the repose of style and coolness of doctrine, the shadow of powerful emotions being held in check and turned magically into limpid phrases and fine ideas. It was the emotional alchemy that was gripping, the transmutation of the lead of inner contradiction into the gold of literary intelligence. The retreat from the boldness of social rhetoric toward "ideas in modulation" would scarcely have qualified as a serious appeal to Left intellectuals were not the compensations of interpretive boldness offered in exchange, and did not Trilling's obvious vigor of mind seem to surpass that of those stymied intellectuals after whom Slesinger's *The Unpossessed* was named. It was they who seized upon *The Liberal Imagination* as a handbook of intellectual survival and took lessons on how to give ground on the political front while pretending to upgrade the terms of political discourse. Such a turn to politics in the larger sense announced, as it always does, that politics in the narrower had been defeated. The establishment of taste and sensibility in the place formerly held by justice and progress, coupled with a renewed interest in psychoanalysis as a key to art and a view of the novel as an elixir for weary emotions were new directions for liberal energies, and constituted a program of interior revitalization that was supposed to enrich liberalism through infusions of complexity and depth.

The intellectual strength of such a plan for renovating "the modern will" was also its political weakness, since the effort to rejoin politics and the imagination was made at the expense of politics. As Morris Dickstein now points out, "Somehow Trilling's . . . insistence that the political and literary minds had much to teach each other turned into the notion that they were fundamentally inimical, perhaps because most of the lessons flowed in one direction." By finessing all talk of issues, power and institutions except at the highest levels of abstraction, Trilling could attack the shallowness of liberalism without having to confront the world in which such shallowness seemed, to some at least, to have merit. As a critic of contemporary ideas, Trilling departed from the example of his mentors—Mill, Arnold and Coleridge—in proffering no social ideas of his own, only social sentiments and tastes which did not and could not add up to an alternative liberalism, or, for that matter, an alternative conservatism. His revitalized version of the liberal imagination could never be put to any political tests but only aesthetic ones, in which their validation was assured.

Such an improved liberalism was the elevation of an hypostasized *mind* over circumstances and a thrusting forward of *ideas* against the liberal, and American, conception of reality which is, as he put it, always material reality, "hard, resistant, unformed, impenetrable, and unpleasant." By renovation of the will, Trilling meant something like transcendence or grace, qualities of mind more spiritual than engaged, and standing quite apart from ordinary political categories. Dickstein's observation that Trilling was a "Tory radical" is useful if we understand the radical element to have been largely a genius for manipulating ideas and imagining ever more subtle essences rather than a program of uncovering roots. If radical thought in its customary modern forms is the paring away of "superstructures" in order to lay bare the brute facts of biological need or infantile experience or class interest behind an idea or ideology, then Trilling's brand of radicalism was just the opposite, an upward distillation of the vapors of thought into their rarest and most abstract expressions.

And yet, ever at odds with his own insistent spirituality, Trilling would enter frequent pleas for the conditioned nature of experience and even for biological determinism, especially in the essays that make up *The Opposing Self* (1955) and *A Gathering of Fugitives* (1956). By the mid-1950s, as music master in his own fast game of musical chairs, he was taking the liberals to task for too rare a spirituality, for failing to see "that spirit is not free, that it is conditioned, that it is limited by circumstance." However disorienting this may be to a neophyte in dialectical thought or the tactics of legal reasoning or ordinary ambivalence, it was a characteristic ploy of Trilling's to disavow liberalism in order to adopt and regenerate its categories: the reality principle, the durability of the world, the inexorability of conditions.

Having put aside the vulgar Marxist rhetoric of social determinism which dominated the aesthetic realism of the 1930s, he was prepared, as a Freudian, to assume spokesmanship for the reality principle, conceived of modestly as "the familial commonplace . . . the materiality and concreteness by which it exists, the hardness of the cash and the hardness of getting it, the inelegance and intractability of family things." And though such views would seemingly have brought him into alliance with liberals in acknowledging the harshness of circumstances, he continued to cast a cold eye upon simple theories of environmental conditioning and the blueprints for social engineering to which they gave rise, and indeed upon all organized hopes for social melioration. Here was a Hebraism with a passion for righteousness but little of the accompanying faith in social machinery. Bolstered by Freud's dubious conception of a biological death instinct as a fundamental property of life itself, the tragic view that was first expressed in *The Middle of the Journey* and *The Liberal Imagination*, seemingly in response to the war and the Holocaust, was refined into a metaphysic, taken out of history and made an autonomous property of the modern spirit.

But to go any further into this strange fondness for the conditioned and the circumstantial as it was wedded to a thoroughgoing idealism would take us far afield and get us into the perplexities of the later thought, including a surprising turn against art, which can't be talked about in brief. Trilling's growing impulse to take refuge in reified abstractions, like *mind, thought, the self* and *the modern will*, which were often locutions for himself, and his continuing efforts to transcend culture while recommending those novels in which it was most diligently recorded, and his fondness for a Hegel who promised to lend order to such ambiguities, exfoliated into a vast and airy labyrinth of thought in which his positions became more elusive as the dialectics grew more hermetic and the abstractions more rarefied. *Beyond Culture* (1968) and *Sincerity and Authenticity* (1972) are troubled and troubling books whose difficulties reflect the perplexities of Trilling's own thought and the ambiguities of his own increasingly obscure system of metaphysics and masks. The very title of his last publication in book form, the monograph, *Mind in the Modern World* (1972), bespoke the evanescent mentalism and sense of embattlement that in later years came to dominate his self-conception.

These later books do not appear to have exerted any influence comparable to that of *The Liberal Imagination*, though their prestige may grow at some future time when their exquisite ironies and superb balances can be better appreciated. Though they are brilliant exercises in dialectical reasoning, their brilliance is abstract and cold, and their pose of cultural oppositionism seemingly assumed more from force of habit and a resolute will to be disengaged than from a reasoned assessment of conditions. Unfortunately, certain centers of reaction among the New York intellectuals, notably *Commentary* in its post–Elliot Cohen incarnation, have seized upon Trilling's case against modern culture and in particular against the episode of cultural insurgency in the 1960s that he called "modernism in the streets" to cast a glow of high seriousness upon what is otherwise a strident and rear-guard cultural politics.

To observe Trilling's influence in *Commentary*, where it just now seems most heavily concentrated, is to note how easily his efforts at transcending vulgarity have lent themselves to a *haute vulgarisation* of their own when interpreted without his generosity of spirit. For what can be heard of his ideas when they have been pitched to the level of a cultural cold war betrays little of his modulation, finesse, irony and self-doubt, and rather too much of his anti-Stalinism, his love of the grand formulation, his fretfulness over the manners and morals of the educated middle class and his cultural conservatism. But Trilling's legacy is really another issue entirely, and one that can't be taken up in brief just here.

Indeed, the factor that complicates any assessment of Trilling's legacy is that it is not localized in New York or at Columbia but diffused through academia where it has accompanied his students and been passed on to their students in turn. It may even be thought that Trilling's career was the signal for that dispersal of Jewish energy into the literary profession which precipitated the decline of the New York intellectuals as focal points of intellectual influence, and saw the rise of the English departments and university presses as independent centers of thought after the war. But the radically altered demography of postwar "English" and Trilling's role in it is another subject for another essay, and will have to await in any case a fuller evaluation of his ideas and their cultural meaning in the 1940s and 1950s.

## Notes

1. *The Unpossessed* (1934), a novel by Tess Slesinger (1905–45), a fringe member of the New York intellectuals and a contemporary of Trilling, who wrote the afterword to the 1966 edition.—Ed.

2. Henry A. Wallace (1888–1965), American vice president (1941–45), was fired in 1945 as secretary of commerce for his criticism of the hard-line Cold War policy toward the USSR adopted by President Harry Truman. Wallace ran an unsuccessful campaign for the presidency in 1948 on the Progressive Party ticket, advocating extensive social reform and friendship with the USSR.

## 59

*Richard Sennett*

*"On Lionel Trilling,"* The New Yorker

*November 1979*

Richard Sennett (1943– ), professor of sociology at New York University, is the author of *The Uses of Disorder* (1970) and *The Fall of Public Man* (1977), among other books. He is also the co-author (with Jonathan Cobb) of *The Hidden Injuries of Class* (1972), which was nominated for the National Book Award in 1973.

A personal acquaintance of Trilling during the 1960s and '70s, Sennett shared Trilling's interest in modernity, society, and culture. Like Trilling, Sennett has defended modernist culture and the Enlightenment tradition and expressed strong reservations about postmodernism.

The following memoir was occasioned by the publication of Trilling's Uniform Edition, which included the reprinting of *Sincerity and Authenticity*, regarded by Sennett as Trilling's "greatest, and least appreciated, book."

Lionel Trilling belonged to a generation of Americans who, in the nineteen-thirties, grew up believing that the answer to the horrors of the Depression and of Fascism lay in some kind of revolutionary Socialism. This generation had a difficult time with a deeply held American conviction. In a fine book called "The Imperial Self," Quentin Anderson has described that conviction as the faith that we are open to all experience and all experience is open to us. We have little sense of limits, Anderson says. If our jobs, communities, marriages constrain us, we move out. Resignation is a quality foreign to the American character. The radicals of the thirties felt the sense of limitlessness of which Anderson writes: the revolution was at hand; the evils of history were about to disappear; the whole character of life could be transformed. Trotsky once called the American radicals "wonderfully naïve." But history would not let them remain so.

By the late nineteen-thirties, many radical intellectuals had begun to recognize that the revolutionary language of Russian Socialism had become a language of slavery. The process of facing the facts was painful, and became very personal in its terms—a matter of mutual accusations and expressions of betrayal. Confronting the limits that history put on one's faith immobilized many writers of that generation. They became locked in the past. Trilling, however, grew and prospered intellectually, because he understood what Anderson believes Americans are anxious to avoid: faith and desire must inevitably be compromised. Not to recognize this truth, Trilling thought, was morally dangerous; the most destructive acts are committed by decent people who have no doubts.

In 1975, the year of his death, Trilling wrote, "At this distance in time the mentality of the Communist-oriented intelligentsia of the Thirties and Forties must strain the comprehension even of those who, having observed it at first hand, now look back upon it . . . That mentality was presided over by an impassioned longing to believe." In reaction to that "impassioned longing," Trilling was led to a much larger effort. He undertook to discover through literature how modern culture came to be so victimized by credulity, and by its mirror opposite, despair. That he chose to do this through literature was old-fashioned. Matthew Arnold, about whom Trilling wrote a doctoral dissertation, thought of literature as a criticism of life, as did many other Victorians. At its worst, this view was sugary: a bad Victorian critic would read Miss Austen to find out how a proper young lady ought to behave. But, at its best, this view made literature more than a text, and the writer more than a craftsman. Writing—more broadly, aesthetic imagination—provides insights into moral problems in politics, psychology, and manners which can be gained in no other way. Trilling observed that the philosopher Hegel "made the aesthetic the criterion of the moral," and this tradition of criticism Trilling continued in a world far more vicious than the one the Victorians knew.

The range of Trilling's interests was broad. He wrote on English and American literature, psychoanalysis, politics, the Kinsey report, social and political theory, Jewish theology in the early Christian era. He also wrote a novel, "The Middle of the Journey," and short stories. It will soon be possible to see this work in full, thanks to a twelve-volume "Uniform Edition of the Works of Lionel Trilling," which Harcourt Brace Jovanovich is publishing. The Uniform Edition is a model of its kind. The books are handsomely printed, sturdily bound hardcovers. They are meant for the library of a home. Eight volumes have so far appeared: a biography of Matthew Arnold, a book of short stories, and six collections of essays, including Trilling's most famous work, "The Liberal Imagination," and a volume of previously uncollected essays, "The Last Decade." The remaining volumes—a study of E. M. Forster, Trilling's novel, a collection of reviews, and his last work, "Sincerity and Authenticity"—will be published next year.

I came to know Trilling, in a way characteristic of him. He called me early one morning in 1973 to ask me to lunch that day. He had read a book of mine, disagreed with parts of it, and wondered if I'd be willing to talk with him. I was flattered, of course, but also apprehensive. After we had talked for five minutes—in a large, noisy Szechuan restaurant on upper Broadway which he seemed to love—I saw that my fears were misplaced. Trilling spoke as if there were no barriers of age or history between us. Our talk, however, was no heart-to-heart. He was relaxed, curious, and formal. These qualities of the man are the qualities of his prose. His words are always simple, he never uses academic jargon, but his sentences are often convoluted. They have a kind of eighteenth-century gravity:

> It is charged against Freud by his opponents that he devaluates human life, that he does not sufficiently respect culture, or art, or love, or women, or the shape of human progress. Yet of those who make the accusation none has yet equaled Freud in actual respect for mankind by equaling him in the full estimation of human suffering or of the forces that cause it.

This simple, formal prose is the perfect foil for Trilling's moral passion. He is determined to understand the moral value of any subject he addresses, but he is equally determined to speak about morality without the least trace of moralizing. There is in Trilling's writing none of the corrosive irony that diminishes whatever it touches in order to keep dangerous, embarrassing, or distasteful matters at a distance. He took the world around him too seriously to be ironic about it; this seriousness constitutes his dignity as a writer.

Trilling struggled to chart the history of the moral imagination, using three concerns of his own: his Jewishness; his belief in psychoanalysis; and his fascination with how a work of literature can cohere as ordinary life cannot. I use the word "struggled" because these three concerns did not rest easily with each other until the end of Trilling's life, in his greatest, and least appreciated book, "Sincerity and Authenticity." I could never tell from talking with Trilling if he was devout, but he had been steeped in the Jewish classics as a youth, and in old age these texts were still vivid in his mind. In his writing, Judaic morality is presented so that it calls moral heroism in question. One of Trilling's essays in "The Opposing Self" compares the poetry of Wordsworth to the "Pirke Pooth" (the thoughts of the Fathers, collected in the second century A.D.). Neither Wordsworth nor those ancient writers were conscious of heroism. Trilling writes:

Of the men whose words are cited in the *Aboth*, many met martyrdom for their religion, and the martyrology records their calm and fortitude in torture and death; of Akiba it records his heroic joy. And yet in their maxims they never speak of courage. There is not a word to suggest that the life of virtue and religious devotion requires the heroic quality.

As much as anything else in my boyhood experience of the *Aboth* it was this that fascinated me. It also repelled me. It has this double effect because it went clearly against the militancy of spirit which in our culture is normally assumed.

The hero is a poor teacher of human limits. He may easily seduce people into giving him unrestrained, tyrannical powers. He is a man who thirsts for recognition through his exploits; he wants the world's praise but is indifferent to its needs. "The predilection for the powerful, the fierce, the assertive, the personally militant, is very strong in our culture," Trilling writes. He believes that the union of heroic violence with religious faith is characteristic of Christianity—a union he finds not only out in the open in a writer such as Dostoevski but also in more covert forms in Yeats and D. H. Lawrence. This is how Trilling's own moral imagination was Jewish: he wanted to divorce heroism from fortitude.

But what, then, does human strength consist in? To answer this question, Trilling turned to psychoanalysis. His interest in the subject was lifelong. (In addition to writing on Freud, he condensed, with the collaboration of Steven Marcus, the three-volume biography of Freud by Ernest Jones into a concise one-volume edition.) What Trilling saw in Freud was, I think, an explanation of two kinds of human strength. One is the strength to act according to the dictates of "reality" as opposed to the dictates of pleasure. The other is the strength to resist the culture in which we live. Freud tells us how these both develop; he is a psychological historian. Trilling is concerned less to evaluate whether or not Freud was a good historian than to make sense of the morality of the tale. The notion that we would destroy other people if we acted solely according to our pleasure is an ancient one; it appears in Plato, Dante, and Hobbes. Freud began with a more complex notion—that the desires of each person are internally at war. His genius was to see the consequences of this inner warfare. If loving and destroying, nurturing and aggressing, are at odds with one another, they cancel one another out. A person given over wholly to pleasure would be an immobilized human being—literally trapped into inaction by the contrary play of his desires. Trilling drew from Freud's psychology a moral about modern culture. The problem with our culture, he believed, is that we all lack will. We have idealized the pursuit of pleasure as a substitute for a politically revolutionary ideal. We do not realize that by idealizing pleasure we are sapping our ability to make choices, to act purposefully, to rise above the stalemated warfare of our lives.

Trilling was the first to see in Freud the problem that has become ever more pressing: Is morality at odds with biology? Certainly many of Freud's current critics, from biologically minded psychiatrists to writers in the gay and women's movements, think Freud would have to say yes: we cannot escape our bodies, and they are our enemies. Trilling thought that the answer would be more complicated. In an essay on Freud in "Beyond Culture," he writes:

> Now Freud may be right or he may be wrong in the place he gives to biology in human fate, but I think we must stop to consider whether this emphasis on biology, correct or incorrect, is not so far from being a reactionary idea that it is actually a liberating idea. It proposes thus that culture is not all-powerful. It suggests that there is a residue of human reality beyond the reach of cultural control, and that this residue of human quality, elemental as it may be, serves to bring culture itself under criticism and stops it from being absolute.

In Trilling's mind, both culture and biology are sources of possible human misery. But culture can never wholly nurture human life. Even at the hands of the worst tyranny, people have a natural source of resistance, which lies, however vague the terms, in the integrity of the human body and its desires. Once, I pressed Trilling about this. "You have no position, you are always in between," I said. "Between," he replied, "is the only honest place to be." In the last few years, I've come to see how anti-liberal this seemingly liberal comment is. Trilling's morality was one of self-acceptance. What human beings have to accept is a dangerous uncertainty. A body that can immobilize itself through the search for gratification; a nature that can, like the Stalinist reactionaries of Trilling's youth, immobilize its citizens in the name of freedom—these are the antinomies of his morality. It is harder to see clearly than to idealize. But aren't we then condemned to a life without form?

For the aesthetes of the eighteen-nineties, pure art was always the victor over impure everyday life. In Trilling's youth, he was surrounded by people who thought that literature was the servant of politics—form should be sacrified to realistic description. Neither of these views appealed to Trilling. In Trilling's view, it is precisely because the novelist controls the world he creates that he has the power to criticize everyday life, which those of us plunged in its messiness lack. But Trilling was no aesthete; a poet or a novelist who sought to avoid the mess seemed to him a bad artist. In one part of "The Liberal Imagination," he writes that "the novel was better off when it was more humbly conceived than it is now." He goes on to say:

> The novel was luckier when it had to compete with the sermon, with works of history, with philosophy and poetry and with the ancient classics . . . Whatever high intentions it may have had, it was permitted to stay close to its own primitive elements from which it drew power. Believing this, I do not wish to join in the concerted effort of contemporary criticism to increase the superego of the novel. . . .

Elsewhere in "The Liberal Imagination," the artist is charged with telling the truth no one else can, or will, tell. This is perhaps the most famous sentence from the book:

> Life presses us so hard, time is so short, the suffering of the world is so huge, simple, unendurable—anything that complicates our moral fervor in dealing with reality as we immediately see it and wish to drive headlong upon it must be regarded with some impatience.

Yet the artist has to warn others of the dangers of feeling fervent. To prevent the good from doing evil—a corruption that is "the most ironic and tragic that man knows"—"we stand in need of the moral realism which is the product of the free play of the moral imagination."

Here was the tension in Trilling's thinking. I do not mean a flaw or an error. It was something more serious: a dilemma. There are pleasures in art unlike the pleasures of love or of being a parent. An artist can succeed in making a coherent world. Complicated as the process of creating it is, a well-made story or poem gives pleasure that is straightforward. But the artist who can create this pleasure also has an obligation to introduce doubt, to chasten fervor, to create ambivalence. If this obligation is discharged, won't the artist sap the will of the reader? And shouldn't the genuine pleasures of art be enough in and of themselves in a harsh world? Art may lose its integrity if it is forced to carry too large a moral burden.

Throughout the nineteen-fifties and sixties, Trilling returned again and again to the conflict between the pleasure and the morality of art. In one of the essays in "The Last Decade," the conflict appears as art governed by the will versus art free of the will. Here Trilling was on the side of the will. But in his notes for "an autobiographical lecture," published in the same volume, he was on the other side: will is power, and power is the enemy of art. In "Sincerity and Authenticity," he created a work that changed the terms of the problem without explaining it away. In this book, he also fashioned a concrete, evocative language to describe the history of the moral imagination. "Sincerity and Authenticity" is based on the Charles Eliot Norton lectures that Trilling gave at Harvard in 1970. He notes that no one would think to call the Hebrew Prophets or King Oedipus "sincere"—it is an irrelevant sort of judgment. About four hundred years ago, in the English Renaissance, sincerity became important to the way in which people judged others and themselves. Hamlet is the first great imaginative character who thinks of being sincere as a quality apart from telling the truth. For three hundred years, the concept of sincerity haunts the moral imagination of writers. In our century, a new term appears, and the concept of sincerity becomes less important. This new term is authenticity.

A beautifully simple theme, one might think, until one asks what kind of person worries about being sincere and what kind of person worries about being authentic. Sincerity is a social condition; it is showing to others what you have come to know about yourself. Authenticity is a more isolated condition; it is the attempt to know only yourself. The demands that other people make on you seem like interference. If only you could escape, be alone, then you would know yourself. By tracing the evolution of sincerity and authenticity, Trilling has a deft, economical way of tracing the evolving concepts of the self from the Renaissance to the modern day. But this is not enough for him. Imagination is implicated in different ways in sincerity and authenticity. From the Renaissance to eighteenth-century Paris, Trilling says, people used their imaginative, and particularly their dramatic, powers to display to others what they knew about themselves. Sincerity involves not only knowing oneself but convincing others about that knowledge; the arts of ritual and courtesy were ways of convincing others that what one knew about oneself was something for the common good, something sociable. In the eighteenth century, this idea began to break down. In a series of brilliant passages on "Rameau's Nephew," by Diderot, Trilling shows how men began to doubt whether the truest things in the self were things that relate one person to others: what no one else could understand might be what each person truly was.

The result of this doubt was that the tissues of culture—manners, courtesies, rituals—began to seem shams. In modern times, the self has come to use its imaginative powers to envision anti-social "disorder, violence, unreason." The savagery and depression that we see in certain films of Ingmar Bergman are the imaginative world of the authentic self that Trilling has in mind. Trilling recalls the Greek derivation of the word "authentic"— "Authenteo: to have full power over; also, to commit a murder. *Authentes*: not only a master and a doer, but also a perpetrator, a murderer, even a self-murderer, a suicide." And this insight leads him back to Freud: "The informing doctrine of 'Civilization and Its Discontents' is that the human mind, in the course of instituting civilization, has so contrived its own nature that it directs against itself an unremitting and largely gratuitous harshness." The evolution of modern culture has ended in a Hebraic punishment rather than in a Christian apocalypse. The moral vision of the modern person is to imagine that one's authentic self is somewhere else, like a missing key, and that in searching for this authentic self one must live in a world empty of other people and full of depression and pain.

In none of Trilling's books does his relaxed and formal style of writing better serve him than in this last, darkest one. His style conveys the sense of a man who has not been captured by his own foreboding, and so, by implication, conveys that the reader need not be, either. The book ends with Trilling's criticism of R. D. Laing for glorifying "an upward psychopathic mobility to the point of divinity, each one of us a Christ—but with none of the inconveniences of undertaking to intercede, of being a sacrifice, of reasoning with rabbis, of making sermons, of having disciples, of going to weddings and to funerals, of beginning something and at a certin point remarking that it is finished." In this book, at the end of his life, Trilling had not put to rest the dilemma of the pleasures of art as opposed to its moral mission. But he had finally clarified that dilemma. Imagination has a timeless power. Because of it, we know Greeks and Elizabethans in the most coherent way in which they knew themselves—through their works of art. Imagination is also time-bound. The bonds of time on the modern imagination appear in the change from a sociable world of selves to the harsher, isolated world of the self—a world in which the truth is never imagined in terms of living, being disappointed, making some mistakes and doing some things right, and then dying. "Sincerity and Authenticity" is Lionel Trilling's final statement on the moral problem of his youth, and, as he came to show us, of modern culture as a whole: the necessity—indeed, the humanity—of knowing oneself as a limited human being.

# 60

Norman Podhoretz

*Excerpt from* Breaking Ranks

*1979*

(See no. 32 for biographical information about Podhoretz.)

Although in *Making It* (1967) Norman Podhoretz had characterized Trilling as "the single most influential" member of the *Partisan Review* writers during the 1950s—an intellectual "exactly in tune with the temper" of the decade—the two men fell out after Podhoretz's radical turn upon assuming the editorship of *Commentary* in 1960. When Podhoretz adopted a neoconservative politics in the early 1970s, he and Trilling—who held, however ambivalently, to his liberal anti-Communist stance throughout the postwar era—argued again over their political differences, now from opposite positions on the ideological spectrum.

The following selection, excerpted from Podhoretz's *Breaking Ranks*, criticizes Trilling's "failure of nerve" for refusing to join Podhoretz's neoconservative campaign against the New Left, which Podhoretz regarded as the ideological equivalent of the Stalinism that Trilling had criticized in *Partisan Review*'s pages in the 1930s.

Trilling had been through the antiradical wars as a young man in the thirties, and though (in contrast to many of his contemporaries) he was not in the least inclined to repent of his political past by switching sides in the latest outbreak of hostilities, neither did he have the stomach to enter the lists again. It was too hard—even harder than the last time. Then there had only been the Communists and their fellow travelers to fight, whereas now the whole phenomenon was so much more diffuse and elusive. Describing the group of intellectuals with whom he had been associated in the thirties (the group led by Elliot Cohen), Trilling once wrote that any member of it "would have been able to explain his disillusionment" with "radical politics" by "a precise enumeration of the errors and failures of the [Communist] party, both at home and abroad." But now radical politics offered no such precise target. Now "subjects and problems got presented in a way that made one's spirits fail."

In addition to being more difficult intellectually, the new struggle was also more dangerous than the first one had been. In the thirties, a young writer fighting the Stalinists could expect a good deal of punishment in the form of vilification (and despite the nursery rhyme, "names" can harm at least as much as "sticks and stones" and many people are with good cause more afraid of the former than the latter). Yet even though, as Trilling himself once put it, "Stalinism was established as sacrosanct among a large and influential part of the intellectual class" in the thirties, the part in question was not nearly so large or so influential as was the case with the radicalism of the sixties. In the thirties one risked being wounded; in the sixties—to borrow from an old joke about a soldier's explanation for refusing to leave his foxhole—one could get killed out there, or anyway (as Trilling predicted would happpen to me) incapacitated for the duration.

Finally, there was the problem of his own implication in the spread of the adversary culture as a critic and a teacher of literature—and especially of modern literature, which had played "a dominant part" in the formation of the adversary culture's "assumptions and preconceptions." Although he had been something of a Stalinist for a very short time in his early thirties, in subsequently joining the fight against Stalinism he had never felt personally responsible for having once contributed to its "sacrosanct" status within the intellectual class. By contrast, for all that Philip Rahv and others accused him of having been a conservative all along, he could not easily dissociate himself from the radicalism of the sixties. Allen Ginsberg had been a student of his, even as I had been; and Ginsberg continued throughout the sixties to treat him with high regard and to acknowledge a debt of influence. Nor did Trilling deny this or attempt to disown Ginsberg. Still less did he attempt to disown the many younger students of his who became academic fellow travelers and apologists of the counterculture. Then, when Columbia erupted, not only did he say that, contrary to his first expectations, he had "great respect" for "the relatively moderate but still militant students" and that their "demands" made sense to him, he also said privately that he could not simply oppose them because they were, after all, his own students.

Nevertheless, he *was* opposed to the new radicalism, and he tried to express this opposition in his writings of the late sixties and early seventies. To the extent that Communism as such was still, or had once again become, an issue, he could be as clear and tough—and simple—as ever without losing his hold on the complexities that were the essence of his mind and style.

Thus in his introduction to a reissue of Tess Slesinger's novel of the thirties, *The Unpossessed* (it is from that introduction that the passage quoted earlier about the sacrosanct status of Stalinism comes), or in his introduction to a new edition of his own novel, *The Middle of the Journey*, where he defended the much-vilified Whittaker Chambers as "a man of honor," or in his brief contribution to the *Commentary* symposium on "Liberal Anti-Communism Revisited," where he testily and unequivocally reaffirmed his commitment to anti-Communism, he sounded like the Trilling of *The Liberal Imagination*. The prose of those pieces was a little fussier and more self-regarding, per-haps, than the prose of his best early essays, but the complexities and nu-ances and qualifications were still mainly there for the sake of precision, to sharpen and refine and enrich the point being made and to add plausibility and credibility to the stand being taken.

In criticizing the cultural radicalism of the sixties and its historical sources, on the other hand, Trilling increasingly seemed to use both the idea of complication and the prose embodying it not so much to clarify and deepen his own point of view as to disguise and hide it. Reading the series of lectures he gave at Harvard in 1970 and then gathered together in *Sincerity and Authenticity*, for example, one got the impression of a writer no longer trying "to see the object as in itself it really is" but trying instead to conceal as much as to reveal, to say something and to deny at the same time that he was really saying it, to take part in a battle while at the same time pretend-ing to be above it.

To be sure, there had always been a touch of this tendency in Trilling. More than most writers, he hated being labeled, or even characterized; he thought—or rather he felt, since in theory he understood as well as anyone than universality can only be achieved through particularity—that it lim-ited him intolerably. But this standing temptation to deny his own particu-larity was aroused more irresistibly by the effort to pin certain labels on him than others. Most of the time, for example, he did not object to being called a liberal and in his younger days he even used the term of himself. But almost always he fought against being called a conservative.

The first time I ever got a real sense of how strongly he felt on this point was at a party at the home of Richard Chase in the late fifties. Chase, a younger colleague of Trilling's at Columbia who had also been a devoted disciple, was then in the process of developing a new theory of American literature that implicitly involved a break with Trilling's general perspec-tive. As everyone present that evening knew, and as anyone who did not know would have understood from the tension between Chase and Trilling, this apparently academic dispute was not in reality academic at all. Chase's work of that period—a book on American culture called *The Democratic Vista*

and a study of the American novel and its tradition—was one of the first
harbingers of the new radicalism, and like some of my own pieces of the late
fifties, the case it made inevitably depended on a repudiation of certain basic
assumptions behind the prevalent liberal temper of the day—and where
literary criticism was concerned that meant Lionel Trilling. That Trilling
should have resented and resisted what smacked to him of personal betrayal
by a disciple was to be expected. But what astonished me was his refusal to
admit that his work had any wider implications whatsoever: all he ever did,
he kept insisting (as though he were a particularly disingenuous New Critic)
was interpret texts.

For Trilling this was only the beginning of what would be a difficult
time. For about ten years, from the late forties to the late fifties, his name
had rarely been mentioned in print without admiration or at least great
respect, but now he was often sniped at and sometimes subjected to full-
scale attack. "I love being attacked," he once told me, "it gets my blood up."
But in truth he no more loved being attacked than anyone else, and he
responded with a testy defensiveness and with an irritability that often crept
into his once perfectly poised prose.

Unlike many liberal academics, who knew how to handle criticism from
the Right but were simply shattered by the eruption of thunder on the Left,
Trilling was a specialist in how to deal with radical assaults on the liberal
position. But underlying and exacerbating the difficulties I have already
mentioned in trying to explain why he was inhibited in practicing this
specialty, there was a great impatience in him, which grew greater as he
grew older, to achieve what might be called a position of venerability.

If he had been English he would, like his friend Isaiah Berlin, have by
now become Professor Sir Lionel Trilling, resting on his intellectual laurels,
admired by all, and already in his own lifetime seeming to be not for the age
but for the ages. The trouble was that there was also a side of Trilling—the
New York or Jewish side—that did not wish to be above the battle; and as
the example of Sidney Hook so vividly demonstrated, not even a record of
distinguished work was enough to make an aging American intellectual
venerable if he remained on the field of political and ideological combat. In
sharp contrast to Isaiah Berlin, who kept his diplomatic distance from the
fray, a benevolent friend to both sides (though a touch more benevolent to
the radicals who, after all, were the dominant power in his world), Hook
went on fighting the New Left and its liberal fellow travelers as vigorously as
he had fought the Stalinists and their fellow travelers in the thirties and
forties and fifties, giving no quarter and getting none. For Trilling, Hook
was the cautionary figure of his own generation—the one who had gone too
far in the rebellion against radicalism—just as Irving Kristol was of the

generation below him and as I myself, ten years younger than Kristol, was rapidly becoming for the generation below that. Trilling's fear of the fate of Sidney Hook was not nearly so great as that of William Phillips, who would have done almost anything to avoid it. But Trilling did, I believe, grow fearful enough in the late sixties to shy away from too close an identification with the antiradical position.

Torn, then, between the exemplary roles of Isaiah Berlin and Sidney Hook, unable to become the one and afraid of becoming the other, Trilling exhausted himself in the last years of his life. It showed in most of the writing he did in those years, but never more than when he was chosen in 1972 to deliver the first of a series of Jefferson Lectures sponsored by the National Endowment for the Humanities. This was a moment that any novelist would have relished for the richness of its revelations. That Trilling should have been chosen meant that he had not altogether failed in his ambition for venerability; Hook would have been too controversial for such an honor. At the same time he decided to touch on the very theme—the mounting assault on the idea of "professional excellence" in the universities and the concomitant institutionalization of quota systems in hiring practices—that Hook himself was just then actively engaged in discussing on every possible occasion, and to take much the same position as Hook had been taking against this "liberal" outgrowth of the Movement's belief in the inability of the American system of equal opportunity to promote progress among blacks. Yet so long did he spend in getting to the point, and so heavily did he load it with academic baggage, that its power to impress—and to offend—was almost entirely dissipated.

## 61

*William Barrett*

*"Beginnings of Conservative Thought," in* The Truants:

Adventures among the Intellectuals *{originally published as*

*"The Authentic Lionel Trilling," Commentary}*

*1982 {February 1982}*

William Barrett (1913–92), who taught at New York University and Pace University, was a philosopher and associate editor of *Partisan Review* (1945–53). Conversant with European intellectual life and continental philosophy and blessed with a lucid style, Barrett helped introduce existentialism to America in the early postwar era, through both his translations (of writers such as Hannah Arendt) and his book *Irrational Man: A Study in Existential Philosophy* (1958). An agnostic until the 1960s, Barrett eventually returned to his Irish Catholicism; his subsequent work reflected, directly or indirectly, his philosophical quest for religious faith. Barrett also published *Time of Need: Forms of Imagination in the Twentieth Century* (1972), *The Illusion of Technique: A Search for Meaning in a Technological Civilization* (1978), and *The Death of the Soul: From Descartes to the Computer* (1986).

Along with Barrett's return to the church came a turn away from the radicalism of his early years. Barrett espoused Trotskyism during his student days at the City College of New York in the 1930s and was a liberal anti-Communist during his years at *Partisan Review*. By the 1970s he had embraced neoconservatism and generally supported a politics close to that voiced by *Commentary*. In his autobiographical memoir of his *Partisan Review* years, *The Truants: Adventures among the Intellectuals* (1982), Barrett not only casts a sharp eye on his own political past and that of the New York intellectuals but also draws lessons from their misadventures and defends his neoconservative swerve.

The following selection, excerpted from *The Truants*, is Barrett's much-disputed chapter on Trilling, in which Barrett argues that Trilling—by his appreciation of the "value of class distinctions for the writer," his sympathy for the middle class, and his esteem for "conventional novelists like E. M. Forster and Jane Austen"—challenged *Parisan Review*'s commitment to "Marxism and modernism," thereby preparing the way for the rise of neoconservatism in the late 1970s and '80s. Barrett's chapter is titled "Beginnings of Conservative Thought." (In its original appearance in *Commentary*, the article was called "The Authentic Lionel Trilling.") Yet Barrett stops short of claiming Trilling as an erstwhile neoconservative. Although Trilling's conservative shift was "ahead of his time," he remained "a thoroughgoing liberal to the end."

If he could be called doctrinaire about anything, it is in his adherence to Freudianism. Freud is the one fixed pillar of conviction to which he personally held. He had had a "successful" psychoanalysis, which seemed to have come at a crucial period, and evidently remained one of the central and transforming experiences of his life. While in such happy cases a transference usually occurs between patient and doctor, here it had reached beyond the particular analyst to invest with a compelling glow the primal father-figure of psychoanalysis, Freud himself. When Freud's name is invoked by Trilling, it is nearly always bathed in something of a numinous glow.

Trilling's Freud, therefore, is a very selective and idealized Freud: a heroic figure, in his way a great poet who brings myth once again to the attention of modern readers and who urges upon the enlightened liberal mind the unpleasant reminder that it too is bound within the confines of our instinctive life. No doubt, there is a heroic side to Freud in the courage and stubbornness with which he fought to bring his ideas before the world; but admiration for the man should not lead us to overlook the persistently negative and reductive aspects of those ideas. Trilling has written about a threat now stalking our culture in words that are frequently quoted:

> A specter haunts our culture—it is that people will eventually be unable to say, "They fell in love and married," let alone understand the language of *Romeo and Juliet*, but will as a matter of course say, "Their libidinal impulses being reciprocal, they activated their individual erotic drives and integrated them within the same frame of reference."

without perceiving, apparently, that these words could very well apply to Freud himself. To be sure, Freud is a stylist and would not put matters quite so crassly, but the deflating and reductive aspects of his systematic thought come to the same thing. But this was a side of Freud that Trilling chose not to see, and when he says:

> The pleasure I have in responding to Freud I find very difficult to distinguish from the pleasure which is involved in responding to a satisfactory work of art.

we are puzzled by what seems an extraordinary confusion of genres until we realize that Trilling is reading another Freud, a poem that he himself has created.

Time has passed, and the situation of Freud and psychoanalysis looks different to us today than in 1950. Trilling belonged to the generation for whom D. H. Lawrence and Freud were a challenge and a revelation. Since then, familiarity has rubbed away the sharp edge of shock. So many people have been through therapy, are under therapy, or are clamoring for therapy that we have to wonder what it is in this civilization that produces such a crying need. The needs seem clearly to lie beyond the purview of the original theory. The psychotherapist, even when he considers himself a Freudian, is usually operating in a domain of human problems quite beyond the confines of his theory. Freud's psychology, we now perceive, with its emphasis upon libido or sexuality as motive force, was tied too closely to the Victorian primness that surrounded the question of sex at the turn of the century. We have had the Sexual Revolution since, and it has brought some very different problems in its wake. Sexual Liberation has turned into the Sexual Nihilism of Venice Beach, California, which in this respect is merely a concentration of attitudes that are dispersed throughout American life. The patient in treatment now is no longer your Victorian aunt who came to the doctor plagued by some nervous tic from the excessive repressiveness of her life; she is more likely to have gone through all the adventures of sex in an atmosphere of "anything goes," and is now confused about the sense of it all. What is it all about? What does it mean? In short, the questions of Nihilism again.

And for such perplexities Freud does not offer a philosophy of life nor even an adequate theory of the human Self. His tripartite map of the soul—ego, id, and superego—is an arid and artificial construction. The ego is so obviously the ego of Utilitarianism calculating pleasures and pains. The id, the unconscious, is a morass of desires, to be drained away like the Zuyder Zee (one of Freud's most famous metaphors); it has little connection with the creative and revelatory unconscious of the Romantics, as Trilling tries to suggest. And the superego is the repressive voice of the parents, never the call of conscience that is able to stir our latent and unconscious energies. In short, a picture of Bourgeois Man according to the model of classical economic theory, but now in disarray and going to ruin, stirred by unruly desires, and his touted morality experienced only as an irksome restraint. What is lacking to the theory is any adequate conception of the unity of the Self.

Trilling was, in my view, the most intelligent man of his generation—or at least the most intelligent I knew. The reader will therefore understand, I hope, why we are trying to follow the workings of that intelligence here in some detail. It was also a very subtle and complex intelligence, far more than the lucid and engaging surface of his prose would lead one to believe on first reading. Delmore Schwartz, in his hostility, found it devious; we could at least agree that it was sometimes labyrinthine. And nowhere is it more labyrinthine than when he is touching on a topic in any way religious, as in his well-known essay on Wordsworth's ode, "Intimations of Immortality." It is only on repeated reading that one becomes aware how uncompromisingly naturalistic and Freudian Trilling's outlook is, and how unwilling he is to entertain any kind of religious experience or belief in its own terms.

The essay also seems to me the only one of Trilling's where I find him deliberately at odds with his subject. When one disagrees with him elsewhere, it is usually a matter of tone, emphasis, fine shading, or for not pushing his point far enough, but never for being at variance with the plain sense of the text he is to expound. He begins, for example, by telling us that Wordsworth's ode is not about immortality at all. This would be news to poor Wordsworth unless he was altogether woolgathering when he gave the poem its title. But if not about immortality, then what is the poem "really" about? It really deals, says Trilling, with "optical" phenomena—the ways in which we look at nature. (The introduction of optics here is a touch of pseudotechnical contrivance in which literary critics so often indulge but from which Trilling himself is usually beautifully free.) True enough, the poem is about the ways in which we see nature; but our vision of nature, for Wordsworth, is different as it is or is not accompanied by the sense of some encompassing Presence within which we and our lives unfold. But this is the kind of idea into which Trilling cannot enter on its own terms; he must somehow incorporate his own aesthetic enjoyment of Wordsworth's poem into some more naturalistic position of his own. Thus Wordsworth's mysticism is to be understood in Freudian fashion as an extension of our infantile narcissism. Our adult sense of oneness with nature—what is usually called the mystical experience—is a carryover from the stage of early life when the infant cannot distinguish the stimuli of his own body from those of the external environment. When one thinks of the long history of mysticism, and the variety of cultures and human types in which it has been expressed, from Lao-tse to T. S. Eliot and Wittgenstein, this is a vast body of human culture and reflection to drop into the lap, or should we say crib, of infantile narcissism. It is surely a strange civilization we live in where such a view can become intellectually fashionable.

It happens also to be a reductive view which deflates not only Wordsworth's experience but the poetry he made out of it. If you keep the Freudian interpretation in the forefront of your mind, the sense and force of the poetry disappear. Even if you hold the Freudian view on other grounds, it is only when you forget it that you can have any satisfactory enjoyment of the poetry. Wordsworth himself would have preferred the interpretation of Kant, which he probably heard from Coleridge: that in our experience of the sublime and beautiful in nature the unknown depths of the Self seem to respond to some unknown and supersensible depths of nature itself, and to be at one with the latter. In the modern parlance: this is one experience in which at last alienation is overcome. But this may be an experience which the modern intellectual, preferring his alienation, has chosen to abandon.

# 62

*Morris Dickstein*

*"The Critics Who Made Us: Lionel Trilling and* The Liberal

Imagination,*"* Sewanee Review

*spring 1986*

Morris Dickstein (1940– ), professor of English at Queen's College of the City University of New York, is widely known as the author of *Keats and His Poetry* (1971) and *Gates of Eden: American Culture in the Sixties* (1977), which was nominated for the National Book Critics Circle Award.

Dickstein, who received his B.A. from Columbia in 1961 and taught in its English department during 1966–71, was acquainted with Trilling as a student and junior faculty member and has also served as a contributing editor to *Partisan Review.* A member of the younger generation of New York intellectuals, Dickstein has been hailed by Mark Krupnick for his "attempt [in *Gates of Eden*] to revive the old New York intellectual style in criticism."

Although Dickstein's sympathy for the cultural radicalism of the '60s contrasts with Trilling's ambivalence toward it, *Gates of Eden* does indeed bear the imprint of Trilling's sensibility and interest in cultural politics. Dickstein both criticizes Trilling's defense of "bourgeois values" and acknowledges his debt to Trilling in *Gates of Eden*, noting that "when the new consciousness" of the 1960s emerged, "Trilling's work helped me to receive it."

Still, as Dickstein rightly observes in the following essay, Trilling did not cultivate disciples, for he was "a sorcerer who took no apprentices." The essay was part of the *Sewanee* series entitled *The Critics Who Made Us*, and it was also included in Dickstein's book *Double Agent: The Critic and Society* (1992).

When it was first published in April 1950, *The Liberal Imagination* constituted far more than a collection of Lionel Trilling's best literary essays of the previous decade. It was one of the subtlest attempts to find a new political and cultural position for the generation that had passed through Marxism and then disillusionment in the 1930s. In many ways the book is a belated obituary for a set of attitudes we associate with that period—Trilling seems at times to be beating a dead horse. But the book also became an intellectual credo for the 1950s in ways Trilling himself may not have expected. Rereading *The Liberal Imagination* twenty-five years after I first encountered it, I was most surprised by the insistent argumentative thread that draws nearly all the essays together. Yet paradoxically the collection also gives an impression of abundance, elusiveness, variety. In a late essay in 1973 Trilling himself chose to underline the book's "polemical purpose" and its "reference to a particular political-cultural situation," though such overt polemics generally do not characterize his work. His animus was directed, he tells us, against "the commitment that a large segment of the intelligentsia of the West gave to a degraded version of Marxism known as Stalinism." In *The Liberal Imagination* this word *Stalinism* never appears, for Trilling was determined to avoid the sectarian debates that betrayed the very cast of mind he meant to bring into disrepute.

Trilling's "liberalism" is a code word for *Stalinism* that relocates the debate on higher ground and indicts a whole set of assumptions about progress, rationality, and political commitment. This has been a source of confusion for many readers, for "liberalism," as he uses it, has very little in common with the usual economic, administrative, and electoral meanings. Yet the vagueness of Trilling's terms enabled many readers, myself among them, to nod with approval at arguments that would have seemed more dubious in baldly political terms. Besides, by the time I read the book as a sophomore at Columbia in 1959, Trilling's positions—at least on Morningside Heights, and among New York intellectuals in general—had been canonical so long that they seemed self-evident, and one could attend without distraction to the superb play of mind by which he exemplified his call for "variousness, possibility, complexity, and difficulty." Though Trilling held out some hope for a politics that could also be subtle and discriminating, he appeared to be saying that only art and imagination, abetted by the critical mind, could truly do justice to the fullness of experience. This cultural hope, almost a civilizing mission, involved part of what made Trilling's own writing so attractive. To be a literary critic in this sinuous and elegant mode, to combine aesthetic sensibility with a sense of social urgency, to fuse intellectual analysis with so much moral awareness—this seemed a worthy professional calling. When I first read Trilling as a green undergraduate, I was astonished that criticism, which I took to be a secondary enterprise, could be pursued with such grace, immediacy, and moral seriousness. Trilling wrote about books the way the best writers write about life itself—as a vivid and pressing actuality, a personal challenge.

To Trilling all genuine criticism is a form of autobiography, a straining after self-knowledge. He conceives of an essay as an interior dialogue, the oscillations of a mind in motion working through its own ambivalence. According to his recently published journals (*Partisan Review*, no. 4, 1984) he once considered writing an essay about the "ambivalent moments" we have as readers, "when we neither hate nor love what the author is saying but hate and love together: when our mind is poised over a recognition of a truth which attacks other truths, or when the author has brilliantly caught half the truth, and denies the other half. These are the most fertile moments. They are the moments of the critic." Trilling's ambivalence, like his emphasis on tragic realism, became one of the essential notes in the cultural register of the 1950s—the sense that the genuinely discriminating mind, unlike the political or ideological mind, does not understand itself too quickly, and doesn't move easily from reflection to action.

This had been one of the main themes of Trilling's mentor Matthew Arnold, whose credo for critics had put a similar stress on poise and balance. "To handle these matters properly," Arnold had written in response to Francis Newman's attack on his Homer lectures, "there is needed a poise so perfect that the least overweight in any direction tends to destroy the balance."[1] In the most neglected essay in *The Liberal Imagination*, the one that comes closest to a self-portrait, Trilling applied virtually the same words to Tacitus: "Some essential poise of his mind allowed him to see events with both passion and objectivity." Trilling attributes this attitude in part to "the bitter division which his mind had to endure"—that is, his hopeless and tragic feeling for the vanished republic, the burial ground of all his political ideals.

It is hard not to associate this portrait with the elegiac quality of some of Trilling's own writings,[2] and his loss of utopian hopes in the 1930s. The self-identification becomes even clearer when Trilling adds that "the poise and energy of Tacitus's mind manifests itself in his language." Trilling's style as much as anything else charmed and won me in 1959. A wonderfully supple and flexible instrument, a speaking voice at once formal and colloquial, it modulates easily from abstract ideas to anecdotes and epigrammatic asides. More playful than genteel, it answers to Arnold's demand that the critic "should have the finest tact, the nicest moderation, the most free, flexible, and elastic spirit imaginable."

In person Trilling seemed to exemplify the same values. He had an aloof but gracious amiability that did not make him particularly accessible, but Harold Rosenberg[3] once described him as an Eliotic Cleric of Culture and mocked his formal demeanor, hedged with irony, as a case of advanced respectability. A longtime friend, William Phillips, speculates a little invidiously that he "was able to preserve his working self by dissociating himself from the draining and time-consuming entanglements of human relations," but no doubt he was more guarded with some people than with others. When I got to know him as a student in 1960, he appeared to stagger under the burden of his eminence, as if it were a solemn trust that had descended upon him. Despite his courtly Anglophile manner he showed anxieties and strengths that were distinctly Jewish. He weighed his words as though he were an institution, as if one thoughtless remark could make the edifice crumble; and he repelled would-be disciples on the Groucho Marx principle of not joining any club that would have him for a member. A deep streak of humility colored his self-importance, and a twinkling humor, perhaps defensive in origin, usually kept him from becoming too pompous. By the same token he had an ingrained and enviable habit of thinking against himself: he avoided taking hard-and-fast positions that would limit his freedom, and he would puckishly refuse to say whatever was most expected of him, to the consternation of his neoconservative admirers.[4]

Since Trilling's cast of mind was balanced, judicious, and highly mobile, the unremitting asperity of his critique of liberalism comes as a shock today. We can hardly be surprised by his hostility to the rigid ideological posturings of American communism, with its subservience to Moscow and its bizarre turns of policy. But his antagonism in *The Liberal Imagination* is directed at the political mind in general, not simply at its progressive variant. Apparently he also inveighs against the whole mentality that puts its faith in enlightened planning and melioristic reform—not simply against totalitarianism, social engineering, or apocalyptic revolutionism. Trilling attacks the liberal impulse "to organize the elements of life in a rational way," noting that "organization means delegation, and agencies, and bureaus, and technicians," which will inevitably incline to "ideas of a certain kind and of a certain simplicity." On the cultural side Trilling's attacks on old Marxist critics like Granville Hicks and Edwin Berry Burgum[5] are also puzzling, for by 1950 the cultural policies of the Popular Front had long since been discredited. But here too Trilling is reaching for wider implications. When he attacks social realist writers like Dreiser for "naive moralizing" and a blind worship of "brute" reality, when he criticizes "the simple humanitarian optimism which, for two decades, has been so pervasive," he is subsuming the Popular Front in a long-standing American tradition of middlebrow boosterism, cultural nationalism, and a pragmatic faith in technology and democracy. In Trilling's view George Babbitt had become a Marxist by 1935, writing book reviews for the *New Masses*, attending the

Writers' Congress, and helping to organize the fellow-traveling League of American Writers.[6] By the late forties he had grown completely respectable, writing a chatty column for the *Saturday Review*, doing occasional pieces for *Harper's* and the *Atlantic*, and reviewing frequently for the *Times Book Review*. You can easily guess which American authors were his favorites. I can assure you that Babbitt didn't think much of the gloomy ideas of the "advanced" intellectuals.

*The Liberal Imagination* is Trilling's only book that deals principally with American writers. Trilling's critical mission is to clear the cluttered scene of the Dreisers and Steinbecks and Sherwood Andersons to make room for a cosmopolitan European tradition that descends from Flaubert, James, and Conrad through the great modernists of the early twentieth century to Hemingway and Faulkner. This is an aesthetically intransigent line of writers strenuously hostile or indifferent to our own liberal pieties. The European modernists remain off stage in *The Liberal Imagination*, implied but only occasionally invoked; but Hemingway and Faulkner make a momentous appearance in the closing pages, where they are compared favorably with Dos Passos, O'Neill, and Thomas Wolfe, who were then among the reigning middlebrow favorites. Trilling finds that he can no longer "live in an active reciprocal relation" with most modern American writers—they present themselves to him only as passive objects of his attention—and in effect he trades them in for the European modernists, as he was soon to do in his teaching at Columbia.

Purely as literary judgments Trilling's have held up very well, despite the qualms he later developed about the modernists. But those judgments were not strictly literary: they were also social—as Trilling himself observed of Leavis's *The Great Tradition*—and they encouraged a generation of students and critics to neglect the strong native tradition of American naturalism. While insisting that the European social novel had never taken hold in America—a belief shared by observers of our fiction from Hawthorne and James to D. H. Lawrence to Richard Chase and Leslie Fiedler—Trilling managed to ignore or belittle our principal social fiction. The injustice was most flagrant in the case of Dreiser. Trilling's sweeping polemic against Dreiser in "Reality in America" was so persuasive that it kept me from reading Dreiser for several years. Trilling's watchwords of "variousness, possibility, complexity, and difficulty"—as embodied in writers like Henry James—became so canonical for the high culture of the 1950s that seminal figures like Dreiser and Richard Wright were relegated to the shabby ghetto of propaganda rather than art. When I first read *Sister Carrie*, a novel not mentioned in Trilling's assault on Dreiser, I was surprised at how Jamesian it seemed, how subtle in its psychological insight as well as in its social notation. Far from being an American primitive, Dreiser is if anything too analytical in this book, as James himself sometimes was.

To attribute Trilling's animus against Dreiser solely to political differences would be foolish, for Dreiser's weaker novels do have many of the faults Trilling ascribed to them. Trilling's purpose is broader, more admonitory. By coupling his critique of Dreiser's naturalism with a dissection of Parrington's liberal historiography, Trilling seems bent on undermining a whole range of cultural attitudes. His constant emphasis on mind and ideas serves to rebut the antiintellectualism of the populist tradition. He has little use for the progressivism of the 1920s avant-garde, with its muckraking reformism, its attacks on middle-class gentility, its bouts of primitivism, and its simplistic invocation of Freud and Lawrence as liberators of the instinctual life. These same attitudes, in his view, fed into the coarse and sentimental proletarianism of the literary culture of the depression. Trilling's ploy, like that of Marx, Engels, and Lukács before him, is to rest his case on the deeper social and psychological awareness of more conservative writers like Balzac and James, as well as a Freud whose outlook is essentially stoical and tragic. Trilling mobilizes Freud to counter the "simple humanitarian optimism" of the progressive mind, a Freud who understands man not "by any simple formula (such as sex)" but rather as "an inextricable tangle of culture and biology," social demand and individual need. Freud's "tragic realism" does not "narrow and simplify the human world," as democratic liberalism tends to do, "but on the contrary opens and complicates it," as the best art does.

Yet Trilling remains ambivalent about the application of Freud's ideas to art, and this helps make "Freud and Literature" far superior to his one-sided account of Parrington and Dreiser. Trilling's cautious application of Freud to works of art paradoxically contributes to making him one of the best of all psychoanalytically oriented critics, the one most alert to the dangers of reductive and mechanical interpretation. Trilling sharply attacks the rigid determinism of most Freudian criticism, insisting on the inadequacy of even Freud's own positivist conceptions of the nature of art. Anticipating the skeptical outlook of later deconstructionists, as well as their emphasis on the operations of language itself, Trilling argues that it is impossible to pin down any work to a single meaning. But he demonstrates the profound compatibility between the formal operations of poetry and the mental processes described by Freud, especially in his psychology of dreams. In one particularly resonant passage, Trilling tells us that Freud discovered "how, in a scientific age, we still think in figurative formations" and therefore created "what psychoanalysis is, a science of tropes, of metaphor and its variants, synecdoche and metonymy. . . . Freud discovered in the very organization of the mind those mechanisms by which art makes its effects." Trilling's ambivalence toward Freud makes his final appreciation fresh and discriminating. As in the fine Kipling essay—where politics and class preju- dice are the issue, rather than art and psychology, and where the critic's own early affinities complicate his judgment—Trilling's criticism works best when he is of two minds about a subject. This accords well with his belief that the best writers are those richest in contradictions, who contain within themselves a large part of the dialectic of their culture and their age.

Trilling's criticism is far less successful with works like *The Princess Casa- massima*, which are too feeble to bear the weight of significance Trilling attaches to them. This lengthy and much-celebrated essay contains virtually none of the quotation that a critic like Leavis would bring to bear to justify his high evaluation. Instead Trilling slips away repeatedly from the book itself into wonderful divagations on themes like "the Young Man from the Provinces," or else allegorizes the characters of the novel into vehicles of his own defense of art and imagination against radical politics. The essay is Trilling's sermon on a text from James; with perversely misdirected bril- liance it opens up a whole vein of nineteenth-century fiction to which James contributed only modestly. Fiction plays a key role in the moral economy of Trilling's book: he sees it as the genre which best embodies the variousness and possibility that run counter to the narrow idealism of the political mind. But this judgment is truer of the novels James disliked—the "loose baggy monsters" and "fluid puddings" of Tolstoy and Dostoevsky, for exam- ple—than of the ones James wrote.

Trilling's case for James as a political novelist and for Hyacinth Robinson as his aptly named protagonist is unconvincing, as Trilling must sense, for when he writes about Hyacinth he drifts unconsciously toward autobiogra- phy and apologetics. When Hyacinth discovers that the glories of art have been erected on centuries of injustice, Trilling turns him into a spokesman for the deradicalization of his own generation: "He finds that he is ready to fight for art—and what art suggests of glorious life—against the low and even hostile estimate which his revolutionary friends have made of it, and this involves of course some reconciliation with established coercive power." Thus James's credo becomes Trilling's own, with poor Hyacinth pumped up into its spokesman. The character of the princess, on the other hand, calls forth Trilling's most fierce indictment of the liberal mind, "the modern will which masks itself in virtue, . . . that despises the variety and modulations of the human story and longs for an absolute humanity." To Trilling she is the very type of the ideologue, symbolizing "the political awareness that is not aware, the social consciousness which hates full consciousness, the moral earnestness which is moral luxury."

This essay exemplifies one of the limitations of Trilling: his relative indifference to form as opposed to theme, and his rapid translation of literary elements into ideas.[7] This essay's dithyrambic conclusion is typical of several pieces in the book which, in their last few pages, leave their immediate subjects behind and rise to a prophetic intensity that irresistibly recalls Trilling's Victorian forebears. They too wrote secular sermons on literary texts and freely enmeshed literary commentary with social criticism and cultural diagnosis. Norman Podhoretz has praised Trilling's "highly developed sense of context," but of course one man's context can be another's pretext, as Podhoretz's own coarsening of Trilling's themes has repeatedly demonstrated. Podhoretz argues that Trilling's work was "drenched in politics," regardless of his own hesitations; but "drenched" is just the kind of hyperbolic word Trilling himself would have avoided, for he was acutely aware of the general loss of precision that would follow if the case against ideology itself turned ideological.

Nevertheless a passage like the concluding description of the princess shows us why Trilling's collection became one of the important documents of the 1950s, influential for its subtle and ingenious attack on ideology, its arguments for the saving power and complexity of art, and its Niebuhrian emphasis on tragic realism as opposed to utopian idealism. Trilling's own sensibility was strongly antiutopian, but he felt an undeniable attraction to the extreme, the romantic, and the apocalyptic that he never ignored: that attraction gave his work its dialectical poise, and kept his mind from taking its ease in any comfortable certainties. It is instructive to watch his stories and essays for the moment when the Anglophile mask turns upon itself and brings into question its own carefully cultivated pose. (His first story, "Impediments," ends with a twist that indicts the aloofness and snobbery of its protagonist.) These pendular shifts were not simply personal in origin: Trilling had a remarkable nose for cultural change, and as a critic he understood acutely how contexts alter texts.

This sense imbues his essays with one of their most appealing qualities: their highly nuanced strategies for bringing virtually any subject ancient or modern into a tense dialectical relation with contemporary concerns. His historicism was based on a sense of the present as much as a sense of the past. The idea of "relevance" was no creation of sixties radicals: it was practiced instinctively by Trilling and his nineteenth-century predecessors; to a student in the fifties it made them far more attractive models than their academic rivals, with their dull, fussy, antiquarian interests, or the New Critics, who sacrificed context to texture and achieved virtuosity as close readers. Trilling's work had a long tradition behind it, but it was hard to imitate, for it was eccentrically rooted in his own sensibility. At best his followers learned that the intricate filiations between literature and culture resisted easy formulations; at worst they aped the surface mannerisms of his style. In general he held himself apart, offering encouragement to many, approval to few. He was a sorcerer who took on no apprentices.

If Trilling's manner suggested the Victorian man of letters or the more relaxed essayists of the *Edinburgh Review*, his central theme—the conflict between the political mind and the literary imagination, between a faith in progress and a tragic awareness of man's limitations—had an even longer lineage that Trilling revitalized in contemporary terms. Behind Trilling's argument one hears the undersong of Burke's attack on the "sophisters, oeconomists, and calculators" behind the French Revolution, of Hazlitt's great discussion, apropos of *Coriolanus*, of why the bent of great art tends to be antidemocratic and why "the language of poetry naturally falls in with the language of power," of Blake's dialectic of reason and energy and Keats's antithesis of poetry and truth, of Coleridge, Carlyle, and the running Victorian critique of the practical, reforming spirit of Benthamite utilitarianism, and especially of the many ways Arnold found to contrast Hellenism and Hebraism, being and doing, culture and conscience. This nineteenth-century tradition of cultural criticism, which F. R. Leavis revived and Raymond Williams studied, shows itself most plainly in Trilling's witty demolition of the crude social and psychological assumptions that underlie the first Kinsey Report, with its quantitative mechanical standard of sexual health.

Whatever else in the fifties Trilling's work links up with, sexual repression is certainly no part of it. He was one of the first to praise Marcuse's neglected *Eros and Civilization*, and he virtually sponsored Norman O. Brown's *Life Against Death* when it was published to no fanfare by a small university press. He anticipated their radical reinterpretation of Freud in *Freud and the Crisis of Our Culture* (1955). Yet he recognized that Brown was "nothing if not Utopian" and therefore a problem for his own "thoroughly anti-Utopian mind." To understand Trilling correctly means you should not pin him down to this or that position but grasp the dialectical quality of his temperament, his attraction to minds drastically different from his own, and his impulse to right the balance upset by the prevailing cultural mood. When the romantic poets—or a later romantic writer like F. Scott Fitzgerald—were being dismissed as immature, antirational, or technically faulty, Trilling offered different readings that portrayed them as writers growing up, learning from politics and experience, and developing a tragic sense of the complexities of life. Even an essay as culturally detached as the one on the Immortality Ode fed directly into the mood of the fifties, with its premium on maturity and a chastened adult sobriety. Bypassing the strict formal concerns and stern emotional hygiene of the New Critics, with their distaste for romantic sentiment, Trilling helped create an image of Wordsworth, Keats, Fitzgerald, Dickens, and other romantic writers that a new literary generation could readily accept.

Trilling was such an engaging and seductive writer, with such a shrewd sense of the cultural moment, that many of his dissenting positions not only prevailed among intellectuals but turned into a new consensus. Some of them were already being established by the time *The Liberal Imagination* appeared. Trilling's arguments against radicalism and liberalism gave way to a thorough depoliticization, a premature celebration of the "end of ideology." In literature his favorite romantics and modernists eventually triumphed completely over the native middle-brows and muckracking naturalists. Anticommunism became the official creed of a Cold War society and its most influential intellectuals. Thus by the end of the gray fifties Trilling was drawn to extreme and apocalyptic figures like Norman O. Brown and R. D. Laing (when few others had heard of them), only to turn against them in the next decade, when their sensibility became, in his view, a new and dangerous orthodoxy. (Similar oscillations can be observed from decade to decade in Matthew Arnold's work between the 1840s and the 1880s.) If the ideological critic is always promoting a fixed set of values, and the academic critic has turned literature (in Trilling's terms) into an "object of knowledge" rather than a source of power, then the Arnoldian critic—the historical critic, the critic of sensibility—offers his own inner dialogue to amplify the cultural contradictions of the moment.

As R. P. Blackmur noted in reviewing *The Liberal Imagination*, Trilling's mind, his famous "we," was always at least partly a mind not his own, the "public mind" that he highlighted as a way of thinking against himself. His way of paying tribute to writers or dramatizing social tendencies was to call them into question, or at least to bring them into high relief, by finding their antitype. His attempt to rehabilitate the reputation of William Dean Howells in 1951 was an extreme example. When this essay first appeared in *Partisan Review*, it caused something of a scandal, for it was understandably taken as apostasy to the creed of modernism that had nurtured the magazine since its inception. Trilling had portrayed a Howells entirely devoted to the quotidian and the commonplace, for whom "the center of reality was the family of the middle class." But Trilling's feelings about Howells and the middle class were no more clear-cut than his feelings about modernism.

Before most of modern art, Trilling wrote in an unfinished memoir shortly before his death, "I stood puzzled, abashed, and a little queasy. . . . I took the view, pious and dull enough, that the advanced art of one's own age cannot possibly be irrelevant to one's own experience, and that one is under the virtually moral obligation to keep one's consciousness open to it." However, ells does not nullify modernism, but his values put it in question, for Trilling's image of Howells is not arbitrary or accidental: it is fashioned precisely as a dialectical foil to the modern temperament. When Trilling writes of the Victorians or earlier writers, he half makes them more modern than we ever dreamed they were, and half makes them proleptically critical of everything modern that haunts and fascinates him.

Writers who have labeled Trilling a conservative go astray here, as do others like Podhoretz and William Barrett who are disappointed that he proved, to them at least, insufficiently firm and militant in the war against the political and cultural Left. Trilling's distinctive style is rarely noticed by commentators who try to give his work a strongly ideological character. When they cut through his rhetoric to the Archimedean point of his belief or commitment, they are cutting away nearly everything we are likely to value about him—not his certitudes, which were few, but his way of arriving at them, not his ideology but the undulations of mind that ran counter to the fixities of ideology. This genuinely dialectical movement of mind was Trilling's deepest contribution as a critic, more than any fixed positions he was ever tempted to take. The campaign against Stalinism, the founding experience of the whole *Partisan Review* circle, was the last good war; but by 1950 Trilling saw that that war was essentially over and that nothing could ever be quite so simple again.

Feeling "the virtually moral obligation"—the solemn yet playful duty— "to keep one's consciousness open," Trilling wielded irony as a way of both exploring his inner uncertainties and playing on the expectations of the audience. "Jane Austen's irony," he once wrote, "is only secondarily a matter of tone. Primarily it is a method of comprehension. It perceives the world through an awareness of its contradictions, paradoxes, and anomalies. It is by no means detached." Trilling's irony was frequently misunderstood, especially in his most pervasively ambivalent book *Beyond Culture*, in which one poignant footnote announces that "it will perhaps save trouble if I explain that the sentence is ironic." Unfortunately this did nothing to protect other sentences, so that, in a new preface added to the paperback edition, he observed that "the ironic mode has lately become riskier than it formerly was"—an opening sentence that is itself ironic. In his later work Trilling possibly lost control of the ironic mode and became the victim rather than the master of his own method. But perhaps Trilling's more simpleminded readers violated his intentions, even betrayed his spirit, when they turned his subtle doubts about the "adversary culture" into a full-scale onslaught on modernism, the counterculture, and the "new class."

Readers of a book like *Beyond Culture* rarely understand Trilling's way of building up polarities such as self and culture as a magnetic field hospitable to the play of mind, or as an almost musical play of categories and antitheses. To write this kind of fluid criticism must have been nerve-racking; surely it was a difficult role for any intellectual to sustain. No one was ever comfortable being Hamlet, of two minds about everything; once positions are taken in print, they can turn into a rampart that cries out to be defended. Yet such a role was particularly congenial in the fifties, a contemplative rather than an activist period. But Trilling's work may have suffered from the complete rout of his radical adversaries. An aura of stoical quiescence, even depression, hangs over several of the essays of *The Opposing Self* (1955), an abeyance of the will and an emphasis on "the conditioned life" that bespeak a crisis of middle age. It was perhaps then—and during the *Kulturkampf* that followed— that Trilling in his chosen style and role risked seeming ineffectual.

   *The Liberal Imagination* concludes with a eulogy of Keats's idea of negative capability, the power to remain open to mysteries, uncertainties, and doubts. Once Trilling had used fiction to dramatize his own inner dialectic, his buried feelings of attraction and repulsion toward characters outwardly different from himself, like Hettner, the "scrubby little Jew" in "Impediments," Tertan, the mad and brilliant young student in "Of This Time, Of That Place," and the charismatic Gifford Maxim, the Whittaker Chambers figure in *The Middle of the Journey.* But Trilling's modest fictional gifts, like Matthew Arnold's poetic powers, were gradually sublimated into the drama of his critical voice, and he published no more fiction after the success of *The Liberal Imagination.* Trilling's constitutional ambivalence is related to his ordeal of being a Jew in a gentile world, of teaching English literature in a gentile university. This problem of identity was a theme in Trilling's early stories, but he turned away from it in his mature fiction, with fateful results.

   Behind a mask of civilized irony his essays thrived but his fiction grew discursive and vague. Darker personal feelings he confined to his journals: the recently published excerpts are frequently touched by self-doubt and self-loathing as well as self-affirmation. These ruminations take a literary turn when Trilling is visited by his former student Allen Ginsberg, now convalescing at a psychiatric institute (the year is probably 1949): "We spoke of Kerouac's book. I predicted that it would not be good & insisted. But later I saw with what bitterness I had made the prediction—not wanting K's book to be good because if the book of an accessory to a murder is good, how can one of mine be?—The continuing sense that wickedness—or is it my notion of courage—is essential for creation." A great deal of Trilling coalesces in this passage. On the surface he belongs entirely—defensively— to the party of gentility, the camp of the superego. But an equally strong personal pressure drives him toward self-criticism—and to an association of art with criminality and moral adventure. I hope I have not overstressed Trilling's ambivalence and irony, the angular movements of his mind. He turned self-questioning from a personal habit into a principle of criticism. The form of the journal suited him as well as the form of the essay, of which it is a more intimate crystallization. In complicated remarks such as this passage about Ginsberg and Kerouac, Lionel Trilling's life and work merge in a lacerating gesture of introspection that is also a source of an impersonal strength.

## Notes

1. Francis Newman (1805–97), a translator of Homer and brother of John Henry Newman, criticized Arnold's theory of literary style (which Arnold formulated in *On Translating Homer* [1861]). Arnold had criticized Newman's translation of *The Iliad*, which failed to meet Arnold's criteria for a good Homer translation in the grand style: rapidity, plainness, directness, and nobility. Arnold's attack was met by Newman's *Homeric Theory and Practice: A Reply to Matthew Arnold* (1861). Newman's polemic provoked a rejoinder from Arnold (*On Translating Homer, Last Words* [1862]).—Ed.

2. See, for example, in "Manners, Morals, and the Novel," his description of the stillness of the past as we experience it in the present: "Some of the charm of the past consists of the quiet—the great distracting buzz of implication has stopped and we are left only with what has been fully phrased and precisely articulated. And part of the melancholy of the past comes from our knowledge that the huge, unrecorded hum of implication was once there and left no trace—we feel that because it is evanescent it is especially human."

3. Harold Rosenberg (1906–78) was a member of the New York intellectuals and one of the major art critics of early postwar abstract expressionism.—Ed.

4. See his deft undercutting of Norman Podhoretz and Hilton Kramer when they try to maneuver him into their own ideological camp in a round-table discussion of "Culture and the Present Moment" (*Commentary*, December 1974). After Trilling's death Podhoretz would accuse him of a failure of nerve for not joining *Commentary*'s no-holds-barred campaign against the remnants of sixties radicalism. Podhoretz is not one to allow any honor to his less militant friends, let alone to his adversaries.

5. Granville Hicks (1901–82), American radical critic, was author of *The Great Tradition* (1935), a revisionist Marxist study of American literary history. Edwin Berry Burgum (1894– ), American literary critic, is author of *The New Critics* (1930) and *The Novel and the World's Dilemma* (1947).—Ed.

6. George Babbitt is the hero of Sinclair Lewis's novel *Babbitt* (1922). Created to combat the twin dangers of war and fascism, the League of American Writers was a literary-political association founded at the first American Writers Congress in

April 1935 in New York City. It was organized and funded by left-wing groups, chiefly the Communist Party, and was headed by several leading American writers, including Van Wyck Brooks, Joseph Freeman, Newton Arvin, Malcolm Cowley, and Granville Hicks.—Ed.

7. Compare Leavis's "E. M. Forster" (1938), reprinted in *The Common Pursuit*, with Trilling's short book-length study (1944). The Leavis is aggressively evaluative and judgmental, while Trilling's work is a generous, finely wrought series of thematic appreciations, which Forster himself very much welcomed. The difference may remind us of John Stuart Mill's powerful comparison of Bentham and Coleridge: "By Bentham, beyond all others, men have been led to ask themselves, in regard to any recent or received opinion, Is it true? and by Coleridge, What is the meaning of it?"

## 63

*Mark Krupnick*

*"The Neoconservatives," in* Lionel Trilling and the Fate of

Cultural Criticism

*1986*

(See no. 48 for biographical information about Krupnick.)

Trilling's critique of the adversary culture was adapted for their own purposes and popularized by a number of New York intellectuals who had
previously been associated with the political left but who, from the late
sixties on, formed the nucleus of a new neoconservatism. These writers—
above all Daniel Bell, Irving Kristol, Hilton Kramer, and Norman Podhoretz—have been zealous in trying to liquidate the residues of the sixties.
But, indifferent to "the imagination of complication" that was Trilling's
ideal, they have often simplified his antiradicalism nearly as much as the
student radicals of the sixties had simplified his earlier advocacy of the
adversary impulse of modernism.

Right-wing simplification has usually taken the form of politicizing
concepts originally intended to be more specifically cultural in their reference. Thus, for example, Kristol and Podhoretz expanded Trilling's idea of
"the new class" far beyond anything that Trilling himself had intended.
There is nothing in fact in Trilling's own writing to indicate that he shared
the neoconservative belief in the existence of a newly dominant class that
functions as a kind of radical fifth column within the government, media,
and academe to mold society according to its own "anti-American," anti-
capitalist views.

Although Trilling's major themes, like that of the adversary culture, were
easily appropriated for neoconservative ends, he never assented to the politi-

cal program of the neoconservatives. On cultural issues he was clearly conservative, but politically he remained an old-fashioned liberal, closer in sensibility, say, to nineteenth-century English liberals like Arnold than to contemporaries like Irving Howe. It is true that Trilling's 1972 Jefferson Lecture, "Mind in the Modern World," argues, as do the neoconservatives, against affirmative action quotas in the universities. But liberals have traditionally supported the principle of meritocracy, and such a commitment by itself does not place Trilling on the political right.

Some neoconservatives have oscillated between claiming Trilling as a distinguished forerunner and being irritated that he never conferred his blessing on their movement. Podhoretz in particular has made explicit the group's frustration with Trilling. In his "political memoir" *Breaking Ranks* (1979), Podhoretz says that Trilling "retreated in the face of the radicalism of the late sixties." Podhoretz says that, far from having joined the neoconservative campaign against the adversary culture, Trilling displayed a "failure of nerve." In a roundtable discussion of contemporary culture sponsored by *Commentary* in 1974, Podhoretz nearly confronted Trilling directly in proposing to the conferees that the aversion of some New York intellectuals from fighting more aggressively against the new radicalism of the late sixties had been owing to "an epidemic of cowardice." Trilling gave this response:

> There is a reason to say cowardice in individual cases, but as a general explanation of the situation Norman Podhoretz refers to I think the word *cowardice* might lead us astray. One has to conceive of it in terms of fatigue.... Subjects and problems got presented in a way that made one's spirits fail. It wasn't that one was afraid to go into it, or afraid of being in opposition—I suppose I am speaking personally—but rather that in looking at the matter one's reaction was likely to be a despairing shrug.

Trilling's repeated "one," instead of "I," suggests the awkwardness, the "despairing shrug," to which he alludes. But embarrassed as this statement may be, it has the ring of sincerity. There is no evidence that this was not the way Trilling actually experienced the sixties, or at least the way he remembered that experience in 1974. But in his memoir Podhoretz does not accept Trilling's testimony at face value. He argues that Trilling avoided polemic in the sixties not because he was uncertain but because of a "venerability" complex. According to Podhoretz, Trilling wanted to end his days as "Professor Sir Lionel Trilling," an American equivalent of England's Isaiah Berlin. And to protect his reputation as a cultural elder he had to remain above the battle.

Certainly it is reasonable to have been disappointed with Trilling in the late sixties. But the disappointment might just as well have focused on his failure to oppose the Vietnam War rather than his failure to oppose the war's opponents. Writers on both the left and the right had reason to feel let down by Trilling. His remoteness saved him from the polemical excesses of intellectuals more deeply involved in the cultural debates of those years. But Trilling's coolness was purchased at too high a price. It now appears that Trilling's disengagement may have had less to do with a cowardly concern to protect his reputation than with a sense of bafflement.

I missed Trilling's leadership at the time and wrote about him with some bitterness in 1971.[1] I am not disposed to judge him as harshly now as I did fifteen years ago. Given the uncertainties Trilling had about nearly everything, it was right for him to turn to history for understanding rather than to trumpet opinions about which he was unsure simply because, in his intellectual milieu, everyone was supposed to have a ready opinion about everything. He may have intuited something wrong in the tone and the spirit of the neoconservatives, who would have liked his blessing. Certainly he distanced himself from their simplifications, like the notion that the new radicalism was a simple repetition of the old, corrupted leftism of the forties. It was better to be uncertain than to equate, for polemical purposes, the new adversary culture with the old Stalinism.[2]

In the late sixties Trilling was no longer the same kind of critic that he had been in the forties. If the younger Trilling had imitated the manner of Victorian men of letters like Arnold, the older man was moving toward a Central European mode of cultural criticism, a philosophical history of consciousness in the Hegelian mode. It is possible to appreciate the effort of re-creating the self implied in this groping for a new kind of writing while at the same time regretting the detachment and remoteness from immediate issues and events that made it necessary.

## Notes

[The numbered citation notes that appeared in the original have not been reproduced here.—Ed.]

1. See Mark Krupnick, "Lionel Trilling: Criticism and Illusion," in *Modern Occasions* 1 (Winter 1971): 282–87.

2. Most reviewers were irritated by Trilling's uncertainty. Graham Hough, who had praised Trilling's earlier books, spoke for many readers of *Beyond Culture* when he complained, in a review, that "to indulge so consistently in these hesitations, dissociations, and withdrawals is not, it seems to me, to stand beyond one's culture,

but simply to occupy a very indeterminate position within it." See Hough, " 'We' and Lionel Trilling," *Listener* (May 26, 1966): 93. But this negative appraisal should be balanced against Hough's very positive estimate of Trilling's career as a whole, in "Culture and Sincerity," *London Review of Books* (May 6–19, 1982): 6–7.

# 64

**Cornel West**

*"Lionel Trilling: Godfather of Neo-Conservatism,"* New Politics

*summer 1986*

Cornel West (1953– ), professor of religion and director of African American Studies at Princeton University, is the author of *The American Evasion of Philosophy: A Genealogy of Pragmatism* (1989), *Race Matters* (1993), *Keeping Faith: Philosophy and Race in America* (1993), and *Beyond Eurocentrism and Multiculturalism* (1993), among other books.

A Marxist cultural critic, Baptist minister, spellbinding orator, and prolific author, West is one of the leading intellectuals in America and probably the most visible representative of the new "black public intellectual." Often described by commentators as an intellectual son in the New York intellectuals' lineage, West is both a successor and opponent of Trilling's conservatized liberalism—though it is obvious in the following essay that West considers the enduring influence of New York intellectuals such as Trilling to be primarily due to "a nostalgia for a time when ideas really mattered." Influenced by Richard Rorty's neoliberal, Deweyan philosophy and pragmatist critique of metaphysics, West has developed his own distinctive version of pragmatism, which he terms "prophetic pragmatism."

In the essay below, West criticizes Trilling as "an intellectual dead end," given Trilling's relative inattention to issues of race and ethnicity and his moderate, allegedly regressive, political stance; in books such as *Race Matters*, West puts forth specific policy proposals to improve race relations, a form of social criticism both more radical and more politically engaged than Trilling's literary criticism. Nonetheless, the article also evidences West's admiration of Trilling as a stylist and critic of broad vision.

I shall focus on one of the major figures of the New York intellectuals: Lionel Trilling, the godfather of the contemporary neo-conservatives. I will suggest that though Trilling provides insights and blindnesses, he also leads to an intellectual dead-end.

Lionel Trilling is a thinker preeminently preoccupied with the circumstantial and the conditioned. He is obsessed both with the individual will and the need to curb it. Despite his apparent neglect of and distance from Emerson in his writings, Trilling is a thorough-going voluntarist who valorizes the act of thinking, the activity of consciousness. Yet Trilling also is highly suspicious of the freeplay of thought, the unregulated ideas of willful individuals and groups. Hence, like the New Humanists (e.g., Irving Babbit and Paul Elmer More) of the twenties without their rigid dogmatism and moral absolutism, Trilling highlights the social and biological constraints on the human quest for "pure spirit," the limits upon human efforts of individual and social transformation.

The fundamental impulse informing Trilling's writings, both fiction and nonfiction, was to provide a guide for the educated middle class of his day between the Scylla of Stalinist politics and the Charybdis of philistine culture. His basic aim was to curtail the angelic pretensions and utopian energies of the political left and to refine the basic instincts and gross tastes of the plebeian masses. Trilling's primary goal was to create, constitute and cultivate an intellectual class which inculcated the cult of complexity and promoted a liberal politics of moderation.

As an upwardly mobile son of a Jewish immigrant tailor, a rebel against his ethnic particularism, an adolescent with left-liberal sensibilities and a young adult with professional ambitions, Trilling attempted to carve out new intellectual space on the American cultural terrain. This space was to be occupied by his brand of "anxious humanism," bourgeois in content and liberal in character, regulated by "aliens" like himself who knew the pitfalls of left utopianism and the emptiness (and xenophobia!) of American conservatism.

In his first and best book, *Matthew Arnold* (1939), Trilling explicitly enunciated his literary and political allegiances to the emerging intellectual class in mid-century America. In a *Partisan Review* symposium in 1939 he wrote:

> My own literary interest . . . is in the tradition of humanistic thought and in the intellectual middle class which believes that it continues this tradition. Nowadays this is perhaps not properly pious; but however much I may acknowledge the historic role of the working class and the validity of Marxism, it would be only piety for me to say that my chief literary interest lay in this class and this tradition. What for me is so interesting in the intellectual middle class is the dramatic contradiction

of its living with the greatest possibility (call it illusion) of conscious choice, its believing itself the inheritor of the great humanist and rationalist tradition, and the badness and stupidity of its action. . . . it is for this intellectual class that I suppose I write.

From Arnold, Trilling constructed his conception of culture—a conception of values and sensibilities, of ways of life and ways of struggle that put a premium on order and hierarchy, authority and respectability. This Arnoldian understanding of culture promoted the intellectual values of engaged intelligence, civil tolerance and trans-ideological modulation. Trilling's project was to articulate and elaborate this conception of culture among the educated middle class in order to combat the encroachment of Stalinism and philistinism. Just as Arnold opposed the complacent materialism of the aristocracy and the vulgar anarchism of the working masses of his day, so Trilling exerted moral and cultural leadership to offset the simplistic catechism of the left and the crude hedonism of mass culture. In short, Trilling understood himself (quite early in his career) as a cosmopolitan intellectual emerging from a narrow ethnic parochialism involved in a fierce struggle for Arnoldian hegemony over the educated middle classes in mid-century America.

It is no accident that his major critique of Arnold was that Arnold had not adequately come to terms with the question of power. Arnold had not provided a feasible and concrete answer to the old question asked by Plato centuries ago, "how to place power and reason in the same agent, or how to make power reasonable, or how to endow reason with power?" Yet, in a gesture that both excuses Arnold's failure and uses Arnold's viewpoint to buttress a new American project, Trilling states:

We may best think of Arnold's effort as an *experimentum luciferum*, an experiment of light, rather than as an *experimentum fructiferum*, an experiment of fruit. . . .

Arnold, however, would not himself relish our leniency; he protested the practicability of his theory. His essentially mystic conception of the State reads almost like a Platonic myth. . . . The value of any myth cannot depend on its demonstration as a fact, but only on the value of the attitudes it embodies, the further attitudes it engenders and the actions it motivates. In these respects Arnold's myth is still fertile and valuable—and morally inescapable.

The effective articulation and elaboration of this American version of Arnoldian ideology depended upon Trilling's ability to acquire intellectual authority. He tried to do this in two ways. First, he worked carefully and cautiously within the anti-Semitic structures of the great Ivy League university, which greatly influenced public opinion (far more than Harvard and Yale at the time)—the Columbia University of John Dewey and president Nicholas Murray Butler.[1] Trilling served as an instructor from 1932 to 1939, assistant professor until 1945, associate professor from 1945 to 1948 and professor from 1948 to 1965. He was made the George Edward Woodberry Professor of Literature and Criticism in 1965 and he became a University Professor in 1970. Trilling left Columbia in 1974. As the first Jew to achieve such stature at Columbia University, Trilling understood well the politics of acquiring intellectual authority in the "objective and impartial" centers of American higher learning. In fact, a distinctive and enduring feature of Trilling's writings is that they acknowledge and accent the inescapable link between literature and society, culture and politics and, most importantly, literary criticism and power. In one of the more memorable passages in his most famous book, *The Liberal Imagination* (1950), Trilling writes,

> our fate, for better or worse, is political. It is therefore not a happy fate, even if it has an heroic sound, but there is no escape from it, and the only possibility of enduring it is to force into our definition of politics every human activity and every subtlety of every human activity. There are manifest dangers in doing this, but greater dangers in not doing it. Unless we insist that politics is imagination and mind, we will learn that imagination and mind are politics, and a kind that we will not like. *Partisan Review* has conceived its particular function to be the making of this necessary insistence. . . .

Yet Trilling's Arnoldian hegemonic struggle over the world views of the emerging intellectual class of his day was achieved not simply because of his academic status. Rather it was achieved principally by his style of writing, his form of presentation—the tone, nuance and attitude of his textual practice. Trilling is first and foremost a critic who mastered a unique form of literary style. He noted in his renowned essay "On the Teaching of Modern Literature" the need

> to see literary situations as cultural situations, and cultural situations as great elaborate fights about moral issues, and moral issues as having something to do with gratuitously chosen images of personal being, and images of personal being as having something to do with literary style.

Ironically, Trilling's preoccupation with his own style led him to downplay the role of form in the literary artists he examined. Yet, in retrospect, the indelible stamp Trilling leaves on the mind of his reader is less what he says than how he says it. For example, his defense of the value of moral realism in the great modern novels—like the critical realism of his Marxist counterpart, Georg Lukács[2]—was often unconvincing. And his loose readings of literary texts were usually irritating and frustrating. Instead, Trilling's authority and influence over his audience was acquired by his rhetorical strategies and the confident posture in his writings.

It is important to note that Trilling essentially gave up on the book as a form of presentation after 1943 (that is, after his book on E. M. Forster). Thereafter he worked exclusively in the genre of the essay—the occasional, non-academic essay or the introductory essays to a canonical literary text. Through the genre of the essay, Trilling tried to create an audience, a community of educated middle class people like himself who enshrined complexity, revelled in the felicities of the mind and thereby sidestepped the simple-mindedness of Stalinism and the kitsch of popular culture.

Trilling's ingenious use of the essay as a literary form gave his audience a sure guide through the cultural and political crisis of the times. This was so principally because his rhetorical strategies achieved two crucial aims. First, the conversational and elusive manner of his writings provided his world-weary audience an escape from the clichés and shibboleths predominant in mid-century American discourse. This version of literary escapism put him and them "above the fray" and created the illusion of superiority. Second, Trilling's interesting observations and stimulating suggestions could be put forward with little or no intellectual rigor or serious argumentation. His urbane style disarmed critical scrutiny and dispassionate objections. Instead, it solicited ideological readings and political replies—the very modes of discourse his style devalued and discredited. The response of Trilling was often to fall into the traps he had set. Hence, meaningful dialogue and substantive exchange deceptively appeared as an uncouth refusal to play by the rules of the refined parlance circumscribed by Trilling's Arnoldian ideology and rhetoric of "complexity, variousness and modulation."

As Jeffrey Cane Robinson[3] has noted in an uneven yet at times perceptive essay on Trilling,

> The essay presupposes an ideal community of intimates who know and share without essential dispute and disagreement, being drawn together by a common belief in the ultimate pleasures of mind. This high state of civilization assumed and addressed by the essayists may be what Keats envisions as a grand democracy in which all whisper results to their neighbors. The essay-as-idyll, to the extent that it generates in its reader a special degree of pleasure in the activity of his own mind and that of the

essayist and convincingly demonstrates that such shared activity is proof of health and attainment in a world which by and large does not encourage such activity, becomes the peculiar combative instrument of the self against society.

This description of a certain tradition of essay-writing indeed holds for Trilling. His style endows him and his audience—the peculiar and not-so-mysterious "we" sprinkled throughout his essays—with an unearned authority which sustained the critic and audience through various crises. This authority is unearned because no rational or moral case has been argued or defended, only asserted and assumed. Just as Reinhold Niebuhr's Augustinian interpretation of widely-accepted Christian myths imposed constraints upon the aggressive self-righteous impulses of educated middle-class WASPs that resulted in "ironic" and "sober" defenses of the American way of life,[4] so Lionel Trilling's version of agreed-upon Arnoldian myths stressed the limits of Promethean activity among secular middle-class intellectuals that yielded a tempered *rapprochement* with American social and political realities.

Trilling's comments in the renowned "Our Country and Our Culture" *Partisan Review* symposia of 1952 gave a direct reply to his earlier Platonic question to Arnold—of how power was to become reasonable. Trilling applauds the fact that intellectuals and the monied class have been brought together, that the educated middle class and the business elites are working cooperatively. This coincidence occurs when Trilling is near the height of his authority and influence; that is, just when he is associating the complex tragic vision of contemplative artistic achievement in his time with the curtailment of the political will to change the world.

Trilling's best essay, his powerful treatment of Keats, rejects this association but then goes on to conclude that the Keatsian link of tragic vision to redemptive political struggle is no longer available to us. Instead, Keats "stands as the last image of health at the very moment when the sickness of Europe began to be apparent." Accordingly, Trilling offers the "reasoned neutrality" and "intentional lack of glory" found in the quotidian explorations of William Dean Howells as a desirable replacement. Joseph Frank is indeed justified when he states in his well-known critique of this phase of Trilling's work:

> For it is one thing to make the experience of art—the experience of pleasure and beauty, of harmony and reconciliation—the *ideal* form of moral life. It is quite another to attribute the virtues of this aesthetic ideal to concrete social behavior which, quite independently of any relation-

ship with art, merely exhibits an abeyance or absence of the will. In other words, it is of the utmost importance not to confuse the boundaries of the ideal and the real, the aesthetic and the social; not to endow social passivity and quietism *as such* with the halo of aesthetic transcendence.

By the mid-'50s, Trilling's preoccupation with the circumstantial and the conditioned was deepened by his encounter with Sigmund Freud—the later Freud of *Beyond the Pleasure Principle* (1920) and *Civilization and Its Discontents* (1930). Although Trilling had written poignantly about death (as in his first story, "Impediments," in 1925, his best short story, "The Other Margaret" in 1945 and his only novel, *The Middle of the Journey* in 1947) and appreciatively of Freud ("Freud and Literature" and "Art and Neurosis" in *The Liberal Imagination*), his stress on cultural constraints upon the will took him beneath the recesses of the mind. And below the already fragile mind—that is, the middle-class world of refined manners, cultivated intelligence and social stability—lurked a frightening smoldering of rebellious impulses, base instincts and anarchic drives. Like Freud, Trilling viewed the ego as a delicate reed on the tempestuous seas of id. His world of "sincere" values was easy prey for "authentic" desires.

In his last texts, *Beyond Culture* (1965), *Sincerity and Authenticity* (1972), *Mind in the Modern World* (1972) and "Why We Read Jane Austen" (1976), Trilling senses that his project of consolidating educated middle-class hegemony will not last. With foreboding omens in his former student Allen Ginsberg's poetry, his Jewish *bête noire*, in Norman Mailer's "The White Negro" (1957) and in actual political action with the rise of the civil rights movement in the South, SDS in the North, the free speech movement in the West, the Black Power revolts in the cities and anti-war demonstrations in the streets and on college campuses (including those at Trilling's own Columbia!), the liberal consensus Trilling had helped create collapsed. And like most liberal establishmentarians, Trilling was horrified.

His famous conversational style became more frantic and shrill. His message more apocalyptic. And his brand of liberalism blurred into a tempered conservatism. In response to the turbulent decade of the '60s—much like his mentor, Arnold, did to the Hyde Park riots of 1866—Trilling shunned the cult of complexity (the old badge of refinement) and opted for Manichean thinking. He denounced dialectical dexterity and promoted categorical pronouncement. He even went as far as to link the transgressive aspects of the giants of high modernism—Joyce, Kafka, Proust—to the anarchic "modernism in the streets" of rebellious youth. His positive advice was a nostalgic return to the domestic tranquility of Jane Austen.

In his last major effort—his Charles Eliot Norton lectures at Harvard, *Sincerity and Authenticity*—Trilling's canvas became the *Bildung* of the self in the West since Shakespeare. Much like Max Horkheimer and Theodor Adorno's *Dialectic of Enlightenment* (1947) and Georg Lukács' *The Destruction of Reason* (1954), Trilling traces the decline of reason and the rise of irrationality; that is, the slide of the Western self down the slippery slope from the "sincere" Horatio to the "authentic" Kurtz, from the heights of Shakespeare to the depths of Conrad, reaching rockbottom with the id-applauding polymorphous self in Herbert Marcuse, Norman O. Brown and Ronald Laing. His nightmare had become a reality. The educated middle classes had become disaffected from their own bourgeois values. But instead of Stalinism and philistinism, there was the New Left and rock 'n' roll, drugs and free love. More pointedly, the new intellectual space Trilling had helped create—the space of liberal bourgeois humanist conversation and social intercourse above political polemics and mass culture—was eclipsed by an intensely polarized intellectual life in America, with Trilling clearly taking sides.

Trilling's Arnoldian project had reached a dead-end. His version of bourgeois humanism could find little place or potency after the end of the economic boom (1945–1973) in America and the need to restore "normalcy" by Republican Party conservative leadership. Those who attempted to remain true to Trilling's ideal of critical intelligence and moderation e.g. *Partisan Review*, *Salmagundi*, moved to the margins of American intellectual life—much like Alasdair MacIntyre's intellectual monks in the present dark ages as put forward in the last paragraphs of his influential book, *After Virtue* (1981). Those who lost patience with Trilling's cosmopolitanism (including his relative silence on the Holocaust) and garnered status and resources from the ascending conservatism in the country e.g. *Commentary*, *The American Scholar*, *The New Criterion*, moved to the forefront of the already polemicized and politicized intellectual life—only to further contribute to its debasement. The fact that so many of these neo-conservatives are fellow Jewish peers (cashing-in on late identity discoveries) who have transformed once exciting and pioneering intellectual periodicals into predictable, tendentious, ideological tracts would be quite disturbing to even the later Trilling.

And last, those who have tried to cling to a progressive version of the best of Trilling's project—his internationalism, his sense of history and his engaged role of the critic—tend to repeat his errors. For example, the internationalism of those around *Dissent* and *The New Republic* does not cut deep enough. They remain too elitist on cultural issues and, unlike Trilling, are often blinded by a sentimental attachment to and hence relatively uncritical of the state of Israel. Their sense of history remains too abstract and bookish. Therefore they are all too willing to see the present-day world through the lens of an earlier era and bygone ideological battles. So the ambiguous legacy of the New York intellectuals should cause us to pause in the rush to enshrine them.

Does the exemplary case of Lionel Trilling provide us with any enabling insights and directions in our times? I suggest that from Trilling we can learn Gramscian lessons; that is, that intellectuals are inescapably implicated in various social locations, ideological positions and historical situations. A major task of intellectuals, especially oppositional ones, is to become critical organic catalysts—namely, persons devoted to the production of critical perspectives linked to emerging insurgent counter-communities or, if possible, social movements. This holds for intellectual and political struggles inside and outside the academy. The case of Lionel Trilling exemplifies the workings of an effective critical organic catalyst within the confines of the educated middle class for liberal and conservative purposes. We need oppositional intellectual counterparts within the context of the labor, feminist, ecological, gay, lesbian, elderly, Latino, Native American and Black freedom struggles for revolutionary democracy and social freedom.

Left intellectuals must give up the self-image of perennial pariahs, without losing our individuality and critical consciousness. We must learn better how to constitute oppositional communities and how to function within counter-hegemonic movements. The coincidence of intense intellectual work and collective insurgent praxis is a precondition for the emergence of a new breed of potent cultural workers and powerful social movements in American life.

## Notes

1. Nicholas Murray Butler (1862–1947), American educator and 1931 Nobel Peace Prize co-winner, was a prominent Republican Party conservative who served as president of Columbia University from 1901 to 1945.—Ed.

2. Georg Lukács (1885–1971), Hungarian Marxist philosopher, developed a realistic aesthetic linking art, social struggle, and progressive politics.—Ed.

3. Jeffrey Cane Robinson (1943– ) is an American literary critic of English Romanticism.—Ed.

4. Niebuhr developed this interpretation most notably in *The Nature and Destiny of Man* (1941) and *The Children of Light and the Children of Darkness* (1944).—Ed.

## 65

## Lewis P. Simpson

## "Lionel Trilling and the Agency of Terror," Partisan Review

## winter 1987

One of the most significant critics of American literature of the South, as well as of American literature generally, Lewis P. Simpson (1916– ) is the author of *The Man of Letters in New England and the South: Essays on the History of the Literary Vocation in America* (1973), *The Dispossessed Garden: Pastoral and History in Southern Literature* (1975), *The Brazen Face of History: Studies in the Literary Consciousness in America* (1980), and *The Fable of the Southern Writer* (1994), among numerous other books.

Simpson's main preoccupation has been the fate of the South, especially its Civil War defeat and failure to grapple with the blood guilt associated with slavery and miscegenation. Chiefly a literary historian and essayist, Simpson has written extensively and edited books focused on the South's leading men of letters, including Thomas Jefferson, William Faulkner, Robert Penn Warren, Walker Percy, and Cleanth Brooks.

Simpson spent most of his academic career in the English department at Louisiana State University in Baton Rouge, where he is now professor emeritus. An influential figure in the development of the academic field of American literary studies generally and the cultural criticism of the American South in particular, he has served since 1963 as co-editor and advisory editor of *The Southern Review*, which was founded by Brooks and Warren. Simpson also served as general editor of the Library of Southern Civilization series during the 1960s and '70s.

Simpson respected Trilling's work and assigned it for review during his years as co-editor of the *Southern Review*. Although the two men were not close, theirs was a mutually respectful relationship of a senior to a junior man of letters. In works such as *Mind and the American Civil War: A Meditation on Lost Causes* (1989), Simpson shows his affinity with Trilling's thinking (in, e.g., *Mind in the Modern World*, 1973) by his use of the idea of "mind." Just as the concept of "mind" represents for Trilling a collective consciousness possessed by a people or era, the idea functions similarly in Simpson's work; typically it denotes the South's *Weltanschauung*, whereby Simpson links the South's "failure of mind" with its historical failure to overcome slavery and its legacy.

In the essay below, Simpson analyzes Trilling's "search for vocational identity." Using excerpts from Trilling's then-just-published journals, Simpson discusses Trilling's two opposing selves: the failed, would-have-been novelist vs. the successful man of letters and cultural critic. In a 1990 interview, Diana Trilling told me that Simpson's essay was the most insightful discussion of her husband's life and work that she had ever read. Her own assessment in her memoir, *The Beginning of the Journey* (1993), of her husband's self-image as a critic and writer bears some parallels to Simpson's conclusions about Trilling's vocational conflict.


My subject is a large and difficult one, Lionel Trilling's quest for vocation. If my remarks on it seem to bear an informal, even at times a personal quality, this is owing to two circumstances. One is that, although I did not know Trilling personally, for close to forty years he has been a part of my life as a teacher, historian, and editor in the field of American letters. The other circumstance is that I did know Trilling's older contemporary, Allen Tate (1889–1979), with whom I shall seek to bring Trilling (1905–1975) into a certain degree of relationship.[1] Assuming the privilege of personal interest, I should add, I will not consider the whole Trilling canon; omitting the famous study of Matthew Arnold (1939), my concern will be with the books that came in the 1950s and after. My sense of obligation to Trilling goes back to the time when, following my completion of the tedious and lengthy process of intimidation called getting a Ph.D., I began, though always to be confined to the campus, to try to get an education I might certify as my own. The books I think of most particularly are: *The Liberal Imagination* (1950); *The Opposing Self* (1955); *Beyond Culture* (1965); *Sincerity and Authenticity* (the Norton Lectures at Harvard in 1970, published in 1972); and *Mind in the Modern World* (the inaugural Jefferson Lecture of the National Endowment for the Humanities in 1972, published in pamphlet form the same year). But I shall here refer in any detail only to *The Liberal Imagination* and *The Opposing Self*. My orienting, if not altogether major, emphasis will be on a work by Trilling not until recently known publicly, the selection from his notebooks for the years 1927–1951, as compiled by Christopher Zinn and published in the fiftieth anniversary issue of *Partisan Review* (Vol. LI, #4, 1984). So far as I am aware I attribute a larger significance to the notebooks than other students of Trilling.

On the surface Tate and Trilling appear to be opposites: a Southerner who was one of the authors of the Agrarian manifesto *I'll Take My Stand* (a title, incidentally, that both Robert Penn Warren and Tate deplored, and for which Warren wanted to substitute "Tracts Against Communism"); a New York Jew, who in the time of the Agrarians was involved with the American Marxist movement. It is not surprising that, although Tate and Trilling had in common a connection with the Kenyon School of Letters in John Crowe Ransom's time at Kenyon College and as well engaged in some personal correspondence, there was no point in their careers when they had more than an incidental personal relationship. But the connection that exists between them in the literary and cultural history of their age is deeper. It goes back at least to the late 1930s, when Trilling's *Matthew Arnold* (1939) and Tate's novel *The Fathers* (1938) were, for American literary intellectuals anyway, current events. In March 1939 his close friend John Peale Bishop wrote to Tate that he was reading Trilling's *Matthew Arnold*, which, says Bishop, "stinks." A letter from Tate to Bishop a little later mentions a review Trilling had done of Tate's novel *The Fathers* (*Partisan Review*, Vol. VI, #1, 1938). Tate says he likes the comment "as well as I could like any Marxist view." Actually Tate did not so cavalierly dismiss the review. Among the most penetrating notices *The Fathers* received, it observes how Tate, "a traditionalist in his literary as well as his social preference," has created a "fable" of violence within "the limitations of strictest form" through his delicate control of the tone of his story and suggests a fundamental tension in Tate between a desire to refer social order to an explicit societal code—"under which people . . . live by a culture and not by a morality"—and his recognition of the possibility that the society of the Old South destroyed itself from "lack of mind." This interpretation hit home, getting at a problematic situation in Tate's vision of order that he not only failed effectively to refute in a reply to Trilling's review of *The Fathers* (*Partisan Review*, Vol. VI, #2, 1939), but would in fact never resolve. Tate might have been more convincing in his response if, in spite of his admission that Trilling's was the "ablest and most interesting" analysis of *The Fathers*, he had not had the fixed idea that Trilling was a doctrinaire Marxist. This, more than the merits of the subtle argument about the character of *The Fathers*, directed Tate's attitude toward Trilling. His unduly narrow perception of Trilling's politics was compounded, furthermore, by a rather acute disdain for the academic man of letters. In the same letter to Bishop in which he mentions Trilling's review, Tate also remarks on something Trilling had just written about Hemingway. That is, he declares, "foully written," adding "But when you get the English Department mentality combined with the Marxian dialectic, the result is a Y.M.C.A. secretary."

The bantering tone of Tate's depreciation of Trilling tends to mark an antipathy to English departments so firm (though not so inflexible as Edmund Wilson's) that for years only economic necessity forced Tate onto the campus for temporary stints of teaching; not until 1951 did Tate form a permanent association with a university, this with the English Department of the University of Minnesota, where he was eventually given tenure and the eminence of a chair.

Ironically Tate's objections to Trilling either on the political or academic counts were far wide of the mark. Compared, say, to the commitment of some of his associates who considered themselves to be "fellow travellers," Trilling's attraction to the New York brand of communism in the 1930s was superficial, marked more by his inability to become a true believer than by commitment to the cause. As a matter of fact, by the end of the first half of the decade of the thirties, as a notebook entry for June 13, 1936, shows, Trilling felt that he had freed himself from the "linear method that has irritated me in my reviewing for so long."

> Going through change of life and acquiring a new dimension. Principally a sense that I do not have to prove anything finally and ever-lastingly. A sense of life—of the past and present. Am no longer certain that the future will be a certain—Marxian—way. No longer measure all things by linear Marxian yardstick. But this is symbolic. A new emotional response to all things.

If anything, Trilling's commitment to the academic pursuit of letters and learning was less convinced than his subscription to a political doctrine. Although in outward appearance Trilling had a long lasting and harmonious connection with Columbia—where he acquired an awesome reputation as the occupant first of the George Edward Woodberry chair and later as the occupant of the still more distinguished seat of University Professor—and although he never seems to have imagined himself outside the academic life, or for that matter, outside Columbia, Trilling was always a doubting, at times recalcitrant, resident of the campus. In truth the published excerpts from his notebooks demonstrate that for a long time he was apprehensive that the university would be the damnation of his talent and that indeed he was never more than partially reconciled to the academic profession. For a number of years, the notebook entries indicate, he excused his employment as an instructor in English at Columbia on the basis of economic expediency: teaching was something he was doing "in order to get started on my work of writing." Yet as early as 1933 Trilling was bitterly accusing himself of violating his own motive. He records that he has seen a "crazy letter" Hemingway sent to Clifton Fadiman. Written when Hemingway "was drunk," Trilling says, the letter is "self-revealing, arrogant, scared, trivial, absurd." Nevertheless, he declares, it shows "how right such a man is compared to the 'good minds' of my university life—how he will produce and mean something to the world . . . how his life which he could expose without dignity and which is anarchic and 'childish' is a better life than anyone I know could live, and right for his job. And how far-far-far I am going from being a writer—how less and less I have the material and the mind and the will." The entry ends on a note of almost despairing prophecy: "A few—a very few—more years and the last chance will be gone." The pathos of his half-patronizing yet anguished jealousy of Hemingway's life as a freelance novelist is enhanced when we realize the force of the term "dignity" in Trilling's lament. Even though he was still in his twenties, Trilling did not have, and had never had, the Bohemian option of "exposing" his life "without dignity"—of writing a letter when he was drunk, or even of getting drunk. For one thing, he came from the discipline of the middle-class Jewish culture of New York City, a heritage not necessarily more repressive but far more closely structured than that of the boy from Oak Park, Illinois. Another, and, I conceive, more conclusive, reason why Trilling could not go with the Bohemian option was that the Trilling self who longed to identify with the Hemingway self—the self of the intense literary artist indifferent to or disdainful of society—was opposed by another, and dominant, Trilling self, a self that identified with the writer as man of letters and critic of society. This self was the proponent of the moral relevance, moral importance, and moral dignity of literature as a reality of human existence. In the service of this realm, the critic was responsible to literature even, if necessary, at the expense of becoming somewhat alienated from society. The dominant Trilling self—the man of letters and critic—existed in unhappy conjunction with Trilling the "creative" self. Indeed for years the critic self was under the reproachful censure of the "creative" self, which was, in its deliberate alienation from society, according to the value system of the modern literary culture spiritually the superior self.

Keeping in mind this postulation of a basic conflict in Trilling between the critic and the literary artist—the novelist, or in the generic sense of the term, the poet—let us move along by looking at some other moments in the notebooks when, as in the comment on Hemingway, Trilling either overtly or implicitly recognizes the unfolding inward history of his life. The initial moment I shall set down, from the year 1928, when Trilling was twenty-three years old, is a very succinct one, yet it is one that shadowed all the moments of his life: "Being a Jew is like walking in the wind or swimming: you are touched at all points and conscious everywhere." The second moment belongs to the year 1944: "I do not think of myself as a 'Jewish' writer: I do not have it in mind to serve by my writing any Jewish purpose. I would resent it if a critic of my work were to discover in it either faults or virtues which he called Jewish." The third moment goes back to the spring of 1936, when Trilling, who had by then been an instructor at Columbia for four years, heard that he would be dismissed: "The reason for dismissal is that as a Jew, Marxist, Freudian I am uneasy. This hampers my work and makes me unhappy."

Obviously some members of the professoriate at Columbia were as uneasy with the young Trilling as he was with them. Whether or not the fact that Trilling was a Jew entered in a primary way into his situation in 1936 (was more important, I mean, than his professed Marxism and Freudianism) is not clear, but in a time where anti-Semitism was still explicit in America—when at the more refined levels of American life, such as the Ivy League universities, Jews were kept in a segregated state by a "gentleman's agreement"—Trilling's Jewishness undoubtedly colored the attitude some of his senior colleagues took toward him. Their expression of dissatisfaction with his teaching because as a Marxist and a Freudian he violated academic decorum by allegedly presenting "literature as sociology and psychology" instead of as "literature" may well have cloaked an anti-Semitic attitude. Yet if so, it was a cover for something more subtle than simple racial prejudice. Trilling's real violation of academic decorum might well for some of his colleagues have consisted in their feeling that he had come into the academic halls to get out of the wind of his Jewishness. He was that disturbing presence, the outsider who would become an insider. Trilling had gone further than the two deracinated men of letters (and both may properly be so called), Marx and Freud, whom he had taken as his models. Choosing deracination, they had become high priests of modern culture; but in electing deracination, Trilling had identified himself primarily, as Marx and Freud did not, with the Western intellectual tradition as it is associated with the university, an institution that still substantially reflected its origin as the embodiment of the medieval ecumence of the Christian mind.

Yet, as we know, if Trilling, either directly or covertly, presented a Jewish problem at Columbia, he was not fired. Although it would be 1939 before he became an assistant professor and five more years before he reached the associate professor rank, Trilling presented more of a problem to himself than to his employer. Considering his commitment to the University to be nominal, insisting (though clearly concerned about his status on the faculty) that the academic profession was antithetical to his true vocation, he was yet unable to identify himself convincingly with a nonacademic, secular-spiritual literary community. He could not intimately experience a feeling of belonging to a literary priesthood redolent of the Christian faith—the order of Flaubert, Henry James, Proust, Joyce, and Hemingway (who expressed the ethos of the order perfectly when he said, "A writer should be of as great probity and honesty as a priest of God"). And, after an early association with a fraternity of liberal Jewish intellectuals represented by the *Menorah Journal*, he had—in spite of a deep and continuing feeling for the rabbinic tradition expressed in his notable essay on "Wordsworth and the Rabbis"—cut himself off from the possibility of belonging (like Malamud, Singer, and Bellow[2]) to a secularized priesthood of Jewish writers. Once, to be sure, Trilling began to doubt his association with the Marxist community of intellectuals, he in effect placed himself outside the available references for the literary life.

It was, I suspect, Trilling's realization that he did not have available to him a sustaining faith in the vocation to writing through an assumed relationship to a literary order that encouraged him to develop the affinity he early on sensed with the Victorians and eventually to choose Arnold for his dissertation subject at Columbia. A last embodiment of Renaissance Christian humanism, Arnold stressed the moralism of the classical writers as a necessary resource in carrying on a cultural program designed both to hold the Philistines at bay and assist in the moral progress of society. In highly principled Victorians like Arnold, Mill, Carlyle, and George Eliot, Trilling identified the literary vocation with a transcendent obligation, singularly and severely incumbent on the individual writer, always to make "duty" the preeminent rule of life. One of Trilling's favorite anecdotes was the story told by the Cambridge scholar F. W. H. Myers,[3] who, walking with George Eliot in the Fellows' Garden of Trinity College in the gathering gloom of a rainy May evening, heard this "austere sybil" pronounce the dictum that while God is inconceivable and immortality unbelievable, duty is "beyond question" the "preemptory and absolute" mandate of one's existence.

Yet the Victorians could not hold Trilling forever in their thrall. The self of the artist struggled against them. Whereas, to pick up with another moment in the notebooks, he had discovered at the beginning of the 1930s that John Stuart Mill is "enormously rich and exciting," fifteen years later, in 1945, he confided to his journal:

> The Victorians have lost all charm for me—they make my *parent* literature, the reading of with which I was most cosily at home—I could feel their warmth and seemed always to know my way among them—now they bore me utterly—I cannot read them—I cannot teach them with any conviction . . . Dickens is the exception—possibly Newman—

That Trilling might exclude Cardinal Newman from the charge of boredom does not, one feels sure, indicate any tendency toward a conversion to Christianity; it may intimate the drastic nature of Trilling's repudiation of his feeling of community with the social progressivism of the Victorians. Another notebook entry in 1945 makes this explicit.

> In three-four decades, the liberal progressive has not produced a single writer that it itself respects and reads with interest. A list of writers of our time shows that liberal-progressivism was a matter of contempt or indifference to every writer of large mind—Proust, Joyce, Lawrence, Eliot, Mann (early), Kafka, Yeats, Gide, Shaw—probably there is not a name to be associated with a love of liberal democracy or a hope for it.

Trilling solidifies his reactionary declaration by pointing to "the enormous breach" between the " 'serious' journalism of liberalism" and the "important works of the imagination in our time." It is well, he tells himself, that the breach exists, somewhat enigmatically implying that when, under compulsion of the "liberal-democratic ideal," the writer attempts to join imagination and action he contributes to the "spiritual collapse" of his age.

At this point Trilling was engaged with two books. One, a critical work, was to give him fame; the other, a work of the imagination, was to give him some credibility as a novelist but would likely have been little noticed save that it was taken to have been written by the critic, and is an exposé of the fallacy of his commitment to the radical politics of the 1930s. But intended by its author to be a "work of the imagination," *The Middle of the Journey* is at once more than an exposé, and less than a work of the imagination. Both works—*The Liberal Imagination* and *The Middle of the Journey*—are, it seems to me, fundamentally devoted to the same theme, which may be summed up as the illusion of a "continuity between imagination and action," and both seek the true relationship between criticism and fiction, or between ideas and poetry.

How much and at what depth the problem of the relationship between imagination and action preoccupied Trilling in the period from the middle 1940s to the 1950s—how it was a question that now presented itself to him as a most urgent crisis of vocation—cannot be dealt with fully here. But I think that the nature of Trilling's "career crisis" is presented in what may be the most intensely personal, the most dramatic, and it may be the most enigmatic, passage in the published notebook selections. This entry was made in 1946.

> I meant to write here a note that I had just got over a period of abt. 6–8 weeks of insatiable desire for praise & notice—nothing satisfied and the

more I got the more I wanted—grew by what it fed on—I had to make conscious effort to check this & not allow it to be publicly seen—I would *court* affirmation and flattery—also about this time a period of terrible sleeping, in which consciousness seemed increased in sleep & nightly problems were presented to me which *had* to be solved—I could see-smell-feel the aura of philosophy—the classroomy, textbooky aura of abstraction, terribly engaging, terribly repelling—life depended on solving the abstract problems presented to me—I would wake with a hideous sense of desolation and loss—absolutely hopeless—dominant in my thoughts the desire for children—one night near the end of this period a great sense of being on the point of *connection*—the connection between 2 things never before connected, which if reconciled would be of incalculable good—it all depended on my mental effort—but I could not do it—desolate—at the same time (end) a great sense that by not doing criticism, not using my "mind" I was losing all force and poetry whatever— giving myself only to the novel was making me go all soft and nothing— at the same time the novel was beginning to open up, but almost to seem too easy—this association of events came suddenly of itself & is almost too pat!—facing sexual scenes of novel—sexual fantasy in connection with them.

A "great sense of being on the point of *connection*—the connection between 2 things never before connected, which if reconciled would be of incalculable good": did Trilling—at a point when he was working with equal assiduity both as critic and novelist (or poet)—envision the possibility of resolving his divided career as writer? We are struck by the likelihood that this may be the import of the Freudian nightmare he records. Does the traumatic experience of his recurrent dream suggest a painful but blessed union of critic and poet? Whether or not we hear an echo of the Shakespearean imperative, "Let me not to the marriage of true minds admit impediment," we feel in Trilling's portrayal of his inner history a passion for the marriage of the mind of one self to that of the other. Trilling—is it too much to say?—sought a union in which the passion of the critic not only matches that of the poet but incorporates critic and poet. In a criticism of poetry that is a poetry of criticism—does he say?—he will become the embodiment of a whole and transcendent literary self? I am not prepared to argue that *The Middle of the Journey* in any precise way comes off as an attempt to unify criticism and poetry in the form of a novel. But both his novel and *The Liberal Imagination* suggest that in associating himself with the literature of social ideology promoted by the American "liberal progressivism" of the 1920s, while at the same time being drawn more and more to the "non-rational" literature of the great modern writers, Trilling became, like Allen Tate, the critic as both actor in and interpreter of the literary myth of modern history—I mean the story, the drama, of self and history that is so much the inward substance of modern history.

It would seem to have been at least partly through Tate that Trilling began to be aware of the broad, mythic context of the conflict he experienced between the rationalist literature of political persuasion and the works of the imagination in the twentieth century. In *The Liberal Imagination* Trilling, referring to Carlyle's observation that Shakespeare was "the product of medieval Catholicism *at the distance at which Shakespeare stood from it*" and that this had "much to do with the power of Shakespeare's intellect," says:

> Allen Tate has developed in a more particular way an idea that has much in common with what Carlyle here implies. Loosely put, the idea is that religion in its decline leaves a detritus of pieties, of strong assumptions, which afford a particularly fortunate condition for certain kinds of literature; these pieties carry a strong charge of intellect, or perhaps it would be more accurate to say that they tend to stimulate the mind in a powerful way.

Trilling has pointedly in mind here an essay on Emily Dickinson in Tate's *Reactionary Essays on Poetry and Ideas* (published in 1936), in which Tate, describing this eminently self-conscious descendant of the New England Puritans as "acting out her part in the history of her culture," asks: "What is the nature of a poet's culture?"

> A culture cannot be consciously created. It is an available source of ideas that are imbedded in a complete and homogeneous society. The poet finds himself balanced upon the moment when such a world is about to fall, when it threatens to run out into looser and less self-sufficient impulses. This world order [the Puritan world order] is assimilated in Miss Dickinson, as medievalism was in Shakespeare, to the poetic vision: it is brought down from abstraction to personal sensibility.

In Emily Dickinson, Tate says further, "There is no thought as such at all; nor is there feeling; there is that unique focus of experience which is at once neither and both." Like Shakespeare, she had no opinions but "had all the elements of a culture that has broken up." Her poetry comes from "an intellectual life towards which it feels no moral responsibility."

Trilling, it would seem likely, also read another essay in Tate's *Reactionary Essays*, "The Profession of Letters in the South." In this classic analysis Tate refers to the "peculiar historical consciousness" of the Southern writer, which he defines as "the curious burst of intelligence that we get at a crossing of the ways, not unlike, on an infinitesimal scale, the outburst of poetic genius at the beginning of the sixteenth century when commercial England had already begun to crush feudal England." Identifying the motive of the subject of the contemporary Southern writer with the seventeenth-century transition to modernity—the age that announced the effective destruction of the corporate community of Christendom by the forces of science, finance capitalism, and individualism—Tate suggests a parallel between the Southern writer and Marlowe or Shakespeare. In *Hamlet* or *Richard III* particularly Shakespeare dramatizes the psychic consequence of shifting the apprehension of existence from the traditionalist to the historical mode, and prophesies the results of the experience of individuation—comic, pathetic, tragic— that would occur as the society of assigned status fragmented. He not only intuits but establishes the subject of literature for the next five centuries: the modern self's emergence as a historical entity and its struggle to define its existence—pulled on the one hand by the will to autonomous meaning and on the other by its recollection of its origin in the dissolution of a hierarchical order.

Tate's depiction of Emily Dickinson impresses us as curiously ascribing to her ambivalent, even contradictory, character: on the one hand, being devoid of opinions, she is nonintellectual; on the other hand, she is intellectual in that her poetry derives from "an intellectual life." But the intellectual life Tate refers to is not of course her own life; it is what is still left of the "great idea" of puritanism—the necessity of absolutely purifying the relationship between God and the individual soul, which rested on a sophisticated theology devised by a highly learned body of Puritan theologians (or intellectuals). Tate's acute discernment of Emily Dickinson's situation, we judge, is not the greater because he is an intellectual and a critic than because he is a novelist and poet. We see in Tate the clear lineaments of that hybrid being who came into existence in the seventeenth century in response to the poet's need to explain his cultural situation to himself. I refer to the critic who defines the culture on the poet's terms. Abstracting the elements of the culture, he describes and explicates what the poet once assumed as given but now must seek to understand. In other words, he is a poet-critic, who makes poetry out of his search to understand the cultural situation. The line of poet-critics extends from Ben Jonson and Donne to Dryden, Pope, and Samuel Johnson; and on to Wordsworth, Coleridge, Shelley, Carlyle, Arnold, Poe, Whitman, Baudelaire, Henry James, Eliot, Edmund Wilson, and R. P. Blackmur. We can say, too, that the line extends to writers whose overt critical activity is incidental but whose critical sensibility—encompassed in their historical sensibility—is a primary governing force in their poetic accomplishment: among them, Flaubert, Yeats, Joyce,

Hemingway, and Faulkner. In fact, it is hardly too much to claim that all poetry—all work of the imagination—from the age of Donne on displays a tension between the critical and the poetic. The initial documentation of such a claim is Donne's magnificent poem, "Anatomy of the World," which is a direct critique of his culture—the culture of science and history—and is a more exact intimation than anything in Shakespeare of the subject of modern literature as defined by Trilling: "the selfhood which culture cherishes as its dearest gift." Donne's brutal metaphorical vision of the dissection of the anatomy of the medieval cosmology—exemplified by the work of Copernicus, Kepler, and Galileo—mirrors the disintegration of what had formerly seemed to be a divinely willed social structure.

> Prince, subject, father, son are things forgot,
> For every man alone thinks he hath got
> To be a phoenix, and that then can be
> None of that kind, of which he is, but he.

Yet, Donne suggests, in his new condition of being—in his sensitivity to the isolation of the self in history and the isolation of history in the self—the poet will find new force of being. Displaced from the bardic community of myth and tradition, he will, through his own will, relocate poetry in the dominion of the individual consciousness.

I become discursive. But in seeking to anticipate the result of Trilling's final rejection of programmatic liberalism and with it the programmatic pursuit of literature, Trilling, one realizes, is implicated in literary history as deeply as Eliot, Proust, Joyce, and the rest, who, in his estimation, are the authors of the "works of the imagination of our time."

A great easing of his struggle between the programmatic and the imaginative occurred when Trilling abandoned the notion that he must somehow interpret history as an ideological struggle. Another way to put this is to say that he came into the knowledge that literary power is never vested in ideas conceived as categorical concepts but in ideas conceived as emotions. I do not think we can uncover a wondrous epiphanic moment when the fallacy of rational constructs of history came to Trilling. The transformation of his vision of history, occurring uncertainly and slowly (and never completely) is most strikingly evidenced perhaps by his inner doubt and pain about his continuing affiliation with the academic world. In 1948 he appraised the meaning of his promotion to a full professor in terms not only of self-deprecation but almost of self-loathing, writing in his notebooks that he feared he was each year growing "weaker & weaker, more academic, less a person." He adds with unequivocal desperation: "Suppose I were to dare to believe that one could be a professor and a man! and a writer!—what arrogance and defiance of convention. Yet I deeply dare to believe that—and must learn to believe it on the surface." In 1951 Trilling took the most decisive gesture he ever made toward attaining freedom from the university system: he gave up his identification both with his major subject matter field, American literature, and his status as a graduate professor and went back to undergraduate lecturing. As any university teacher knows, a voluntary renunciation of one's status as a member of a graduate faculty—even though in Trilling's case it did not involve going back to freshman composition—is almost inconceivable. Even more than his resignation from the graduate school, Trilling's rejection of American literature as an academic subject can be taken as a last-ditch effort to separate the self of the critic from that of the imaginative writer. Contending with himself in the privacy of his notebooks, Trilling declares that he must get away from specializing in American literature because this "denies my being a part of it." This objection is juxtaposed with the somewhat incongruous idea that "as a subject" American literature cannot be dealt with in a systematic way through the study of its individual authors. It must be studied as a "history of culture." Yet Trilling reveals he is not thinking about an objective, systematic interpretation of American literature in its relation to cultural history. He has in mind, he says, an approach that is subjective—one that will require not only "subtlety & complexity" but "a total intellectual and emotional involvement." This, he protests, he cannot dedicate himself to. The ambiguity of his diagnosis of his connection with the literature of his own country suggests a genuine element of pathos in his situation. Had he not in truth reached the point when he must acknowledge that both the circumstances of his life and the limitations of his talent dictated that, though he was touched by the poet, his literary role would be largely that of the critic? Did he not want to obviate the pain of recognizing that he would never cut a figure as an American novelist? At the same time, did he not somehow understand that in his very attempt to fulfill his aspiration to be "a writer"—to be an author of works of the imagination, and thus a "part" of the literature of America— he had been living out the question put by Tate, "What is a poet's culture?" That, enmeshed in a detritus of pieties, he had been living his own version of the "crossing of the ways," participating in the repetitive experience of writers since Donne and discovering his own way what Tate says Poe and Hawthorne discovered a hundred years before, the essential modern subject, "the isolation and frustration of personality"?

By 1949, when he wrote "The Meaning of a Literary Idea" for a conference on American literature at the University of Rochester, Trilling had, I think, formulated a poetic, dramatic, and dynamic idea about the nature of literary ideas that would provide the foundation for a poetics of cultural criticism.

What comes into being when two contradictory emotions are made to confront each other and are required to have a relationship with each other is . . . quite properly called an idea. Ideas may also be said to be generated in the opposition of ideals, and in the felt awareness of the impact of new circumstances upon old forms of feeling and estimation, in the response to the conflict between new exigencies and old pieties. And it can be said that a work will have what I have been calling cogency in the degree that the confronting emotions go deep, or in the degree that the old pieties are firmly held and the new exigencies strongly apprehended.

At the end of the essay in which this definition of the "literary idea" is made ("The Meaning of a Literary Idea," which appears in *The Liberal Imagination*) Trilling says that when we learn to "think of ideas as living things, inescapably connected with our wills and desires, as suspectible of growth and development by their very nature, as showing their life by their tendency to change, as being liable, by this very tendency, to deteriorate and become corrupt and to work harm, then we shall stand in a relation to ideas which makes an active literature possible." During the years following the essay on "The Meaning of a Literary Idea," Trilling composed the series of compelling meditations on the idea of the modern self that constitutes his major achievement and—although he himself may never have quite known this—fulfills, as far as he could do so, his desire to be the author of works of the imagination. Significantly these meditations were composed in nearly all instances as occasional pieces—being written in response to an invitation to give a paper somewhere, provide an introductory comment for a new edition of a book, etcetera. Save, moreover, for *Sincerity and Authenticity*, a small volume composed of the Norton Lectures, Trilling wrote no more book-length works. Although leading the regular life of the classroom lecturer, he took on jobs like a freelance essayist, taking up topics as the literary demand arose; living apart from the academic tendency to deprecate the essay in favor of the book-length work, Trilling solidified his fame with two collections of essays published ten years apart. The first of these (the other is *Beyond Culture*, 1965), *The Opposing Self: Nine Essays in Criticism*, was published in 1955, the same year in which Tate brought out the volume that in the overall sense is his most significant collection of essays, *The Man of Letters in the Modern World*.

As this book is in Tate's career, *The Opposing Self* is, I take it, the crucial, the central, work in Trilling's career. Devoted to essays, or meditations, on Keats, Dickens, Tolstoy, Wordsworth, Orwell, Flaubert, and (in spite of his declaration about American literature) on two Americans, Howells and James, this volume, the author points out in a prefatory essay, deals with "episodes in the literature of the last century and a half." In the case of each writer he considers, Trilling says:

> I speak of the relation of the self to *culture* rather than to *society* because there is a useful ambiguity which attends the meaning of the word culture. It is the word by which we refer not only to a people's achieved works of intellect and imagination but also to its mere assumptions and unformulated valuations, to its habits, its manners, and its superstitions. The modern self is characterized by certain powers of indignant perception which, turned upon this unconscious portion of culture, have made it accessible to conscious thought.

In his declaration of the capacities of the modern self Trilling united the poet and the critic and by implication established the definition he had long sought of his own vocation to literature. But the cost of fulfilling this vocation—of obeying the self's powers of perception—is high, as the last essay in *The Opposing Self*, a disturbing meditation on *Mansfield Park*, makes clear; the expense is nothing less than the self's terrorizing of the self. I quote at some length from the key passage in the essay on Jane Austen's novel:

> It was Jane Austen who first represented the specifically modern personality and the culture in which it had its being. Never before had the moral life been shown as she shows it to be, never before had it been conceived to be so complex and difficult and exhausting. Hegel speaks of the "secularization of spirituality" as a prime characteristic of the modern epoch, and Jane Austen is the first to tell us what this involves. She is the first novelist to represent society, the general culture, as playing a part in the moral life, generating the concepts of "sincerity" and "vulgarity" which no earlier time would have understood the meaning of, and which for us are so subtle they defy definition, and are so powerful that none can escape their sovereignty. She is the first to be aware of the Terror which rules our [the writer's] moral situation, the ubiquitous anonymous judgment to which we respond, the necessity we feel to demonstrate the purity of our [the writer's] secular spirituality, whose dark and dubious places are more numerous and obscure than those of religious spirituality, to put our lives and styles to the question, making sure that not only in deeds but in *decor* they exhibit the signs of our belonging to the number of the secular-spiritual elect.
>
> She herself is an agent of the Terror—we learn from her what our lives should be and by what subtle and fierce criteria they will be judged, and how to pass upon the lives of our friends and fellows. Once we have comprehended her mode of judgment, the moral and spiritual lessons

of contemporary literature are easy—the metaphysics of "sincerity" and "vulgarity" once mastered, the modern teachers, Lawrence and Joyce, Yeats and Eliot, Proust and Gide, have but little to add save in the way of contemporary and abstruse examples.

In defining Jane Austen as the agent of the Terror of the secular spirituality that must serve the self of the modern writer—who having internalized history is imprisoned by it—as his only moral resource, we have the climactic moment (or so I would argue) in Trilling's search for vocational identity. It is the moment when his own power of indignant perception has become luminous to itself, and poet and critic have coalesced in a poetics of criticism; or, it may be said, in a poetics of the authorial self, which is characterized by the desperately precarious nature of the authorial self's authority over self.

In the remarkable prefatory essay to *The Man of Letters in the Modern World*, Allen Tate says we may scarcely hold that the moment of indignant perception bears a weight akin to that of the peripety of tragedy, the moment when the last seal on the tragic hero's ignorance of his condition is broken and the knowledge of his fate is fully revealed to him. Like Tate, Trilling would have been scornful of the idea that the modern critic qualifies as a tragic hero. But Tate may be said to have in a general sense spoken for Trilling as well as for himself in his conclusion that the "act of criticism . . . is a crisis of recognition always" and is not with a certain tragic ambience in that, for all the effort put into it, criticism yields no certain nor finally any knowledge at all. What the practice of criticism gives the critic in the end is the certain knowledge "that as literary critic one knows virtually nothing." By the time Tate said this he presumably knew a vision of existence beyond tragedy. He had been a Roman Catholic for five years, having formally accepted in 1959 what he had always believed to be true, namely that religion must be the condition of literature. Trilling could never believe other than that it is "an impropriety to try to guarantee literature by a religious belief." All that Trilling had to guarantee his vocation to literature was ultimately the quality of his devotion to it. On the basis of his witness to his vocation in his writings we can point to his literary commitment as being like that he attributes to Jane Austen when he speaks of her personality having answered to the demand of the modern secular-spiritual moral standard as described by Hegel: it requires that we not only put our deeds but the style of our lives to the question. Explicating Hegel in *The Opposing Self*, Trilling says that in the modern world moral and aesthetic standards are no longer joined "in the old way," one, that is, that makes "morality the criterion of the aesthetic"; the aesthetic is now the criterion of the moral," so that "not merely the deed itself . . . is . . . submitted to judgment," but the "entire nature, the *being*, of the agent." In the latter years of his life Trilling developed this notion about the quality of the agent still more intensely, elaborating in *Sincerity and Authenticity* an intricate distinction between the "sincere self" and the "authentic self." We may think with some assurance that he was impelled to elevate the concept of authenticity by his understanding of what disappears when religion is lost: this is, he says, nothing less than reality, "the imperative actuality of life." This observation occurs in *Sincerity and Authenticity* at a point when we might not expect it, in a discussion of Freud, for whom, as Trilling must insist, religion was an illusion. But Trilling read Freud as a great tragic poet, who in his youth, Trilling recalls, chose John Milton "as a favorite poet" because, "Although the idea of redemption could mean nothing to him," he shared "Milton's appalled elation . . . in the ordeal of man's life in history." For Trilling such an astringent but vividly dramatic, and immensely humanizing, attitude toward history guaranteed the continued meaning of literature. He had authenticated this attitude through his own experience of being a writer— his criticism at its best being, like the work of Jane Austen or D. H. Lawrence, an agency of the terror of the modern literary insight into the nature of history; he himself being a troubled, and compassionate, agent of the terror he beheld in our self-conscious existence in history.

## Notes

1. Allen Tate (1899–1979) belonged to the conservative literary circle of the 1920s called The Fugitives, which spurred the Southern Renaissance, and was also a member of the Southern Agrarians and an early major voice of the New Criticism.—Ed.

2. Bernard Malamud (1914–86) and Saul Bellow (1915– ) are American Jewish fiction writers; Isaac Bashevis Singer (1904–91), the most widely known Yiddish short-story writer and novelist, wrote a postwar trilogy of epic novels that trace the history of the Jews in Poland from the anti-Tsarist uprisings of 1863 to World War II.—Ed.

3. Frederic William Henry Myers (1843–1901) was a poet and essayist.—Ed.

# 66

*John Rodden*

*"Trilling's Homage to Orwell," adapted from* The Politics of

Literary Reputation

*1989*

John Rodden (1956– ) has taught at the University of Virginia and the University of Texas at Austin. He is the author of *The Politics of Literary Reputation: The Making and Claiming of "St. George" Orwell* (1989).

In the selection below, Rodden discusses Trilling's "homage to Orwell" in his moving, graceful introduction to Orwell's *Homage to Catalonia* (1952). Orwell and Trilling never met; it was "the man within the work," argues Rodden, with whom Trilling strongly identified. Trilling's introduction to *Homage to Catalonia* constituted "veiled autobiography," reflecting how deeply the life and work of Orwell, who had recently died in 1950, had "engaged Trilling's imagination and spirit."

> I hear on all sides of the extent of my reputation—which some even call "fame." In England it seems to be very considerable, and even in this country it is considerable, and in France there is some small trace, etc. . . . I contemplate this with astonishment. It is the thing I have most wanted since childhood on.–Lionel Trilling, notebook entry, 23 July 1952

In his 1952 introduction to the American edition of *Homage to Catalonia* Lionel Trilling characterized George Orwell, in an oft-quoted passage, as "a virtuous man," "a figure in our lives." "We," Trilling said, could be like him if only . . .

> if we but surrendered a little of the cant that comforts us, if for a few weeks we paid no attention to the little group with which we habitually exchange opinions, if we took our chance of being wrong or inadequate, if

we looked simply and directly. . . . He liberates us. . . . He frees us from the need for the inside dope. He implies that our job is not to be intellectual, certainly not intellectual in this sense or that, but merely to be intelligent according to our lights—he restores the old sense of the democracy of the mind. . . . He has the effect of making us believe that we can become full members of the society of thinking men. That is why he is a figure for us.

And yet, despite his graceful prose and elastic use of the first-person plural, the truth is that Trilling is expressing his private devotion to the image of "St. George." For it was Trilling's imagination and spirit that Orwell's life and work engaged. And it was Trilling's essay that elevated and secured Orwell's American reputation.[1]

Trilling's authority in New York intellectual circles accounted for the wide influence of his image of Orwell.[2] And that authority derived from Trilling's urbane personal manner and his rare gift for dramatizing his personality on paper. Trilling's fame, however, had to do not only with his intellectual authority, but also with his institutional authority in mid-century America, i.e., a range of affiliations that acted as professional bridges enabling his unusual, smooth traversing of the intellectual, academic, and publishing scenes in New York. For example, Trilling was the first tenured Jew in Columbia's English department. By the late 1940s, he sat on the editorial boards of *Partisan Review*, *Commentary*, and *Kenyon Review*; beginning in 1951, he headed the Reader's Subscription and Mid-Century book clubs. In the early 1950s Trilling also traveled to Europe as a cultural ambassador for the State Department and gained election to the National Institute of Arts and Letters and the Academy of Arts and Sciences; in the next decade he exercised growing influence over a younger generation of New York intellectuals, especially his former students at Columbia, among them editor-intellectuals such as Norman Podhoretz at *Commentary* and Jason Epstein at Anchor Books. During the 1950s and '60s, Trilling too was a "figure" on the Anglo-American intellectual scene, "a veritable version of the *PR* writer as a belated Matthew Arnold," in Leslie Fiedler's phrase.

And yet, despite the publication of numerous books on Orwell and a half-dozen on Trilling himself, it has gone unremarked that Trilling's oft-quoted view of Orwell as a "virtuous man" was a self-portrait of Trilling's own exalted position within the New York–*Partisan Review* intelligentsia. The background of Trilling's reception of Orwell—the intellectual-academic scene of postwar New York, especially the *Partisan Review* contributors and some Columbia university faculty—subtly conditioned Trilling's famous characterization of Orwell. And the impact of Trilling's essay on Orwell's reputation cannot be understood apart from Trilling's rise to international fame after the 1950 publication of *The Liberal Imagination*—or apart from his own struggle with the burdens of fame.

Indeed Trilling's essay on Orwell appeared at the moment when Trilling stood at the very peak of his reputation in informed intellectual circles. Given both that fact and Trilling's enduring status as the model American intellectual of his generation, it is illuminating to approach his Orwell essay autobiographically, sensitive to the "little group" with which Trilling "habitually exchanged opinions," to Trilling's fascination with Orwell's reputation, and to his self-confessed "astonishment" and perplexity at his own.

The passion of Trilling's prose, his choice of details about Orwell, and indeed the very title of his Orwell essay—"The Politics of Truth: Portrait of the Intellectual as a Man of Virtue"—make clear that Trilling saw Orwell as an intellectual ideal, the figure as intellectual hero. To Trilling, Orwell stood as a man of "truth" and "simple courage." By means of his remarkable "directness of relation to moral fact," Orwell seemed to have resolved the problem of political commitment and intellectual integrity, the liberal intellectual's—and Trilling's—agonized "politics of truth." First published in the March 1952 *Commentary*, edited by Trilling's friend and mentor Elliot Cohen, the essay reads like a wishful portrait of the first-generation New York intellectual as "man of virtue," "liberated" from his "little group," his comforting "cant," his "need for the inside dope," his intellectual "fashions"—indeed very much like a sketch of Trilling's ideal self.

To Trilling, Orwell was "the figure of not being a genius." An odd way of characterizing the keynote to a man's reputation. Since when is "not being a genius" a virtue in itself? And yet, approached from within the perspective of Trilling's situation in New York in the 1950s, the phrasing becomes comprehensible. "He is the figure of not being a genius, of fronting the world with nothing more than one's simple, direct, undeceived intelligence." Orwell was not a genius. ("What a relief. What an encouragement.") He was just an extraordinary ordinary man. He was the ordinary man's thinking man. He "stood" for "plainness of mind" and "telling the truth." And in this "he communicates to us the sense that what he has done, any one of us could do."

"Or could do if we but made up our minds to do it," Trilling added, as if to prick himself. For when Trilling the New York intellectual looked at Orwell the London intellectual, he saw a man who had renounced "intellectualizing" for plain, humble thinking. His Orwell had rejected respectable ideas, fashionable opinion, endless analysis, elaborate theoretical constructs—and stood instead for personal conviction and intuition, energy and nonconformity, open and nontechnical exchange, and intellectual freedom and passion. Orwell seemed to have achieved what Trilling was still struggling to achieve. The "great word" during his student days at Columbia, Trilling recalled in his memoir, "A Jew at Columbia," had been "*intelligence*," which "did not imply exceptional powers of abstract thought" but rather "a readiness to confront difficulty and complexity" and "an ability to bring thought cogently to bear upon all subjects to which thought might be appropriate." Trilling conceived "the intelligent man" as exemplified not by erudition and scholarship but by "an intelligence of the emotions and of task." His teacher John Erskine's[3] motto "The Moral Obligation to be Intelligent" became Trilling's too.

To Trilling, Orwell's "not being a genius" meant all this. It meant renouncing the image of the intellectual as a self-important "thinker" trafficking in lofty abstractions and disdainful of the daily, earthbound routines of "ordinary" people. It meant being "far removed from the Continental and American type of intellectual." Orwell was "an intellectual to his fingertips," said Trilling. But Orwell was no literary pedant or prima donna. For Orwell "implies that our job is not to be intellectual, at least not in this fashion or that, but as a man intelligent according to our lights." Trilling's Orwell, "the portrait of the intellectual as a man of virtue," was simply an honest, intelligent man.

Yet Trilling found Orwell exceptional. "It is hard to find personalities in the contemporary world who are analogous to Orwell." In him "there was indeed a quality of an earlier day," Trilling lamented, for Orwell was "an unusual kind of man, with a temper of heart and mind which is now rare." His student's characterization of Orwell as "a virtuous man" seemed to Trilling an archaism especially appropriate for describing Orwell. "Somehow to say that a man 'is good,' or even to speak of a man who 'is virtuous,' is not the same thing as saying, 'He is a virtuous man.'" That sentence's simple phrasing, by some quirk of the English language, thought Trilling, brought out "the private meaning of the word virtuous, which is not merely moral goodness but fortitude and strength." *Homage to Catalonia* was imbued with virtue in this most sturdy and old-fashioned sense, "a genuine moral triumph written in a tone uniquely simple and true." Orwell was no genius, just a man who renewed in one "a respect for the powers that tone does have, and the work one undertakes to do."

Indeed Trilling's own reputation was not founded on brilliance. By the early '50s, the younger generation saw him as an example of humanist-critical intelligence and instinctive good judgment. Like Orwell, he was regarded as a "different" sort of intellectual. Trilling belonged, said critic-friend Clifton Fadiman, not to "the party of the party" but to "the party of the Imagination." To observers critical of the *Partisan Review* writers for their parochialism and brashness, Trilling seemed a thinker independent of coteries, broadly humane and catholic in his tastes. Leslie Fiedler marveled at his "remarkable aura of respectability not granted to any of his colleagues." Unlike them, Trilling was "modesty itself," and yet he somehow also seemed to "embody and modify the *PR* spirit." Philip Toynbee noticed a strong resemblance between Orwell and Trilling as "liberal-democratic critics." Indeed the *Partisan Review* group considered the London-*Horizon* literary circle to be a virtual mirror image of their New York enclave. And they regarded Cyril Connolly's *Horizon*—to which Orwell and Trilling both contributed—as "*Partisan Review*'s English brother," in historian James Gilbert's phrase. Already by the early '50s, Trilling's name was associated with the subjects of his published and forthcoming books: Matthew Arnold, E. M. Forster, "The Liberal Imagination," and (opposed though the two concepts were in Trilling's vocabulary) "Sincerity and Authenticity."

One senses that these similarities in position and temper between Orwell and Trilling did not pass Trilling's eye unnoticed. In his obituary of Trilling, Steven Marcus closed by naming five authors whom his onetime teacher "most admired." Orwell was the only twentieth-century writer on the list. Significantly, of Orwell's many attributes, Trilling seized on Orwell's apparent "plainness of mind" and truth-telling. Trilling might well have focused on other attributes of Orwell, as so many other critics have done. But plainness and truth-telling were, of course, the very attributes that Trilling felt most Left intellectuals lacked—especially considering the Left's behavior during the Spanish civil war. And Trilling believed that the absence of these qualities had cut those Left intellectuals off from what Trilling called "the familial commonplace," "the stupidity of things." In Trilling's view, Orwell had never committed "the prototypical act of the modern intellectual" that marked the New York writers' own rise to cultural prominence and assimilation: "abstracting himself from the life of the family."

Of course, whatever his writings may suggest, Orwell was not fully integrated into the "life of the family," as his strained relations with his family over his struggles to become a writer suggest. Trilling was more accurate than he realized when he spoke of Orwell's "fronting the world" with his "simple, direct, undeceived intelligence." Orwell's literary persona was partly a front. But that is not to say it was deceptive. It was a carefully crafted projection of Orwell's literary ego ideal: the man of decency and simplicity. And the self-projection achieved its aim: Trilling, like others, *perceived* Orwell to be a "plain" man. In turn, Trilling's image of Orwell in his introduction to *Homage to Catalonia* was a moving, fully convincing portrait of a virtuous intellectual. Much of what made this portrait so convincing was Trilling's own passionate homage to Orwell. Trilling identified wholeheartedly with Orwell, not only with his situation and status, but also with his character and destiny.

And to some extent the two men ultimately realized a common destiny: Trilling's image of the "virtuous" Orwell came to prefigure the *Partisan* writers' image of Trilling himself. "He was, to use the old-fashioned term, a virtuous man," William Barrett wrote of Trilling in his 1982 autobiography, *Adventures Among the Intellectuals*, "and moreover, a virtuous man without any touch of the prig. And in the particular environment of New York in which we moved that was indeed an accomplishment."

Yet with special authority come special burdens. By 1952 Trilling felt the tensions of his singular place in New York intellectual life. His powerful attraction to Orwell was to a romanticized figure who seemed to occupy, posthumously, a similar place and to have resolved his own "politics of truth" in a way Trilling could not. In Trilling's case the politics were cultural and personal. Long after the battlelines of the 1930s had been drawn and erased, Trilling was still seeking to reconcile the dilemma of what Barrett called "the two M's," Marxism and Modernism, wanting to champion both, and yet ambivalent because he felt that the political tendency of modernism generally ran counter to progressive thought. How to have high art and "the old sense of the democracy of the mind"? Trilling saw that this dilemma was the form in which his century had chosen to represent the age-old question of the proper relations of the aesthetic, the political and the ethical. According to Barrett, Trilling "worried about this question for the rest of his life," "returning to it again and again, yet leaving it finally unsolved," except to recommend that one practice the openness of mind to consider the "possibilities" of both choices.

Inevitably for an intellectual leader like Trilling, such a question also posed a dilemma of personal action. And this quandary converged with another, apparently enduring worry of Trilling's: his own reputation. Podhoretz, who knew him intimately, suggests in *Breaking Ranks* (1979) that Trilling had two sides, one that unusually craved honor and another that yearned for action. What Trilling wanted all his life, and increasingly in his later years, Podhoretz judged, was "to achieve what might be called a position of venerability." In his 1978 autobiography, *New York Jew*, Alfred Kazin recalls Trilling's insistence in the 1940s that he would not write anything seeming to Kazin "to resemble an expensive picture on view. 'My reputation' was to be nursed along like money in a bank. It was capital." Trilling was carefully composing his own intellectual portrait, in both senses of the verb. He would squander no resources in the effort. "He seemed," concluded Kazin, "intent on not diminishing his career by a single word."[4]

However much he sought "venerability," Trilling did not want to remain above the political fray. Even in the early 1950s, a moment during which his authority was seldom questioned in print by the New York writers, these tensions between unsullied intellectual reputation and political action gripped him. Thereafter, in trying to criticize the Left from a liberal stand-point, Trilling found himself questioned by fellow liberals within and out-side the New York group. He found himself cast as an exponent of what Joseph Frank called "the conservative imagination." Trilling's prestige made him a target. His once-admired sensitivity to "the conditioned nature of life," his careful and deliberate "qualifications," and his constant reminders of how "complicated" everything was, were being interpreted by the mid-'50s, even within the *Partisan* circle, as indecisiveness, hair-splitting, and verbiage.[5] The New York group was breaking apart even as the *Catalonia* essay appeared, and members would split in the 1960s into rival political camps—liberal, radical, neoconservative, quietist—as stands on the Viet-nam War and communism divided Americans generationally and ideologi-cally. Trilling found it hard to take any firm stand at all.

Orwell thus symbolized for Trilling a man who had achieved renown yet had remained "authentic" and politically active—the type of the writer *and* man of action who "was what he wrote"—and was widely recognized for it. But whereas Orwell had won admiration by diving into the political muck and somehow remaining clean, Trilling had always seemed to rise up and transcend all local, internecine New York battles. By the early '50s, Trilling was finding this posture more and more difficult to maintain. Moreover, as he confided in a 1951 notebook entry, when he looked at his Columbia colleagues, he worried increasingly about becoming a "pale" and "timid" academic like them, "less and less a person."

At this crucial juncture in Trilling's life, Orwell and *Homage to Catalonia* stood before him. This was no accident. For Orwell combined in character and reputation the best of what Podhoretz described as "the two exemplary roles" Trilling saw immediately before him, in the reputations and political stances of his friends Isaiah Berlin and Sidney Hook. "If he had been En-glish," Podhoretz mused after Trilling's death, comparing him to Berlin, Trilling would have become known as "Professor Sir Lionel Trilling, resting on his laurels, admired by all, and already in his own lifetime seeming not for the age but for the ages." Trilling desired the eminence of Berlin without becoming like him a benevolent, apolitical, and even-handed friend to radicals and anti-radicals alike; at the same time, he wanted the exhilarating satisfactions and concrete political achievements of a feisty polemicist like Sidney Hook, without suffering like Hook the crude labeling and vilification that come with outspoken activism. Trilling sought both lasting and undisputed distinction and yet passionate engagement in the issues of his time.

Orwell as intellectual hero is therefore comprehensible, finally, as the type of a third model for Trilling: a Hook in life, a Berlin for posterity. But in the '60s Trilling could commit himself fully neither to his Berlin nor Hook role model—feeling "torn" between the two, in Podhoretz's view, "unable to become the one [Berlin] and afraid of becoming the other [Hook]."

For unlike Orwell, Trilling as "virtuous man" was not a figure of "plainness" and "fortitude and strength" to his contemporaries, but rather one of gracefulness, subtlety, and modesty. Trilling seized upon Orwell at a time when he needed precisely more strength, less subtlety. *Homage to Catalonia* had spoken to Trilling because it seemed to him a gutsy, daring book, written by "a man who tells the truth" and takes a stand.

To Trilling, whose mother was an English Jew and whose Anglophilia was exceptional among the *Partisan Review* intellectuals, Orwell stood forth as the last representative of a great nineteenth-century liberal tradition of English men of letters, an alternative tradition to both Marxism and anti-democratic modernism. Orwell had managed to be rooted in family values and to "praise such things as responsibility, order in one's personal life, fair play, physical courage"; yet he was also a relentlessly questioning "man of intelligence." Orwell had preserved his "love affair with the English language" and yet embodied "the old democracy of the mind." Looking from within and atop the New York intellectual world in 1952, Trilling understandably pointed to Orwell's example in *Homage to Catalonia* and felt, "He liberates us." "We" could be like him "if only . . ."

Almost a half century later, many American readers share Trilling's dream and lament. That we do so—my admiration for Trilling pluralizes my own pronouns here—has several reasons. It is attributable not only to Orwell's living voice on the page, but also to the quality of Trilling's prose and to his unrivaled intellectual authority at mid-century, all of which contributed to disseminate widely the image of "Trilling's Orwell." Indeed, if there is one thing we can say about the American Orwell, "the virtuous man," it is that Trilling's Orwell has become our own. Finally, to whatever extent Orwell became, or still remains, "a figure in our lives," it is due in no small part to the fact that he was once such in Lionel Trilling's.

# Notes

1. Reviewers have repeated Trilling's characterizations of Orwell (especially "virtuous man") almost ritually. Some critics have even argued that Trilling's introduction singlehandedly established Orwell's reputation in the United States.

In his 1952 review of *Homage to Catalonia*, Edmund Fuller concluded: "Without this interpretive help, the book probably would not carry its proper weight today." In *George Orwell: A Critical Heritage*, editor Jeffrey Meyers also calls Trilling's introduction "probably the most influential essay on Orwell."

2. What became, one wonders, of the class paper on Orwell that Trilling says his Columbia graduate student, who, as Trilling acknowledged, first had called Orwell "a virtuous man," was also writing at the time? The essay was never published, but the student has gone on to become an associate editor of *Partisan Review* and professor of English at Columbia University. The nameless student was Steven Marcus (letter to the author, 16 December 1986).

3. John Erskine (1879–1951), American educator, helped launch the Great Books movement while a Columbia University professor (1916–37) with works such as *The Moral Obligation To Be Intelligent* (1921).—Ed.

4. What Kazin failed to perceive was Trilling's anguish over how he was diminishing his life by this "insatiable desire for praise and notice," which "nothing satisfied," as Trilling confided in a journal entry (ca. 1947), and which only "grew by what it fed in." In a 1948 journal entry, written shortly after the appearance of *The Middle of the Journey*, Trilling accuses himself of overweening ambition—and implies that his aspiration to renown is doomed: "Suppose I were to believe that one could be a professor and a ???! and a writer!—what arrogance and defiance of convention" ("From the Notebooks of Lionel Trilling," in *Partisan Review: The Fiftieth Anniversary*, ed. William Phillips [New York: Stein and Day, 1984], pp. 24–25, 29).

5. Or, as Joseph Epstein once phrased it in a posthumous dig: "Trilling, that academic Demosthenes, his mouth filled not with pebbles but perpetual qualifications and hesitations."

67

*Bruno Bettelheim*

*"Notes on Lionel Trilling: Literature and Psychoanalysis," in*

Explorations: The Twentieth Century

*1989*

Bruno Bettelheim (1903–90), Viennese-born psychotherapist and educator, was professor of educational psychology at the University of Chicago and the author of *Love Is Not Enough—The Treatment of Emotionally Disturbed Children* (1950), *The Informed Heart* (1960), and *The Uses of Enchantment* (1982), among other books.

Both Bettelheim and Trilling were deeply influenced by and championed the work of Sigmund Freud, serving as important cultural mediators who introduced Freud's work beyond the specialist academy to American intellectuals. In the essay below, Bettelheim praises Trilling for explaining Freud to the American literary public and for defending him against psychoanalytic revisionists such as R. D. Laing and Norman O. Brown.

The work of Lionel Trilling, the great literary critic, was much influenced by Freud and psychoanalysis. But psychoanalysis also owes a great debt to Trilling because his writings brought Freud's true thoughts to the attention of American intellectuals, particularly during the 1950s when many misapprehensions about Freud and psychoanalysis abounded. Trilling promoted a correct view of Freud in many of his writings, but his book *The Liberal Imagination*, which appeared in 1950, was especially important. It was the book which firmly established him as the foremost literary critic of his generation.

Not only was Trilling's literary criticism informed by the thoughts of Freud, Trilling was also very impressed by Freud the person. And this long before he wrote in his 1962 introduction to the shortened version of Jones' biography of Freud: "Freud as a person stands before us with an exceptional distinctness and significance, and it is possible to say of him that there is no great figure of modern times who, seen as a developing mind and temperament, is of such singular interest" (vii).

He continues: "If we ask why this is so, the first answer must of course be the magnitude and nature of his achievement. The effect that psychoanalysis has had upon the life of the West is incalculable. Beginning as a theory of certain illnesses of the mind, it went on to become a radically new and momentous theory of mind itself. Of the intellectual disciplines that have to do with the nature and destiny of mankind, there is none that has not responded to the force of this theory. Its concepts have established themselves in popular thought, though often in crude and sometimes in perverted form, making not merely a new vocabulary but a new mode of judgment" (vii).

This "new mode of judgment" dominates much of Trilling's mature literary criticism. It is one of the yardsticks by which he measured literary and cultural achievement. Further, Trilling did his best to combat misunderstandings of Freud's ideas. He had nothing but contempt for the diluted and prettified manner in which Freud's teachings and that of psychoanalysis had been modified in the United States. He realized that such a dilution deprives Freud's teachings of their tragic implications for our understanding of man and his fate. He rejected strongly the efforts to distort Freud's teachings into an optimistic view of mankind.

As early as September 1942, when attempts to deprive psychoanalysis of its deep seriousness about the predicament of man were in their initial stage, Trilling wrote an article in *The Nation*, titled "The Progressive Psyche," in which he discussed Karen Horney's writings and severely criticized her deviation from Freud's teachings. He asserted that her views are "symptomatic of one of the great inadequacies of liberal thought, the need for optimism" (116). He contrasts Horney's facile optimism regarding the feasibility of self-analysis, by which she denied the strength of the forces of repression and neurotic defenses, with Freud's seriousness—he who "dared to present man with the truth about his own nature." Trilling particularly praised Freud for recognizing the "complex and passionate interplay between biology and nature" (117). In this article Trilling also strenuously objected to views which maintained that neurosis is due to nothing but the impact on man of culture in general and of society in particular.

It probably was not easy for Trilling to free himself of that need for optimism, which he came to scorn as one of the great inadequacies of liberal thought, and he shed it not without inner struggle because it ran counter to the convictions he had held in his earlier days when, in common with so many of the young left intellectuals of his generation, he had embraced Marxism. Thinking back to those earlier years, he wrote in his essay on Isaac Babel:

> In those days one still spoke of the "Russian experiment" and one might still believe that the light of dawn glowed on the test-tubes and crucibles of human destiny. And it was still possible to have very strange expectations of the new culture that would arise from the Revolution. I do not remember what my own particular expectations were, except that they involved a desire for an art that would have as little ambiguity as a proposition in logic. Why I wanted this I don't wholly understand. It was as if I hoped that the literature of the Revolution would realize some simple, inadequate notion of the "classical" which I had picked up at college; and perhaps I was drawn to this notion of the classical because I was afraid of the literature of modern Europe, because I was scared of its terrible intensities, ironies, and ambiguities. (*Beyond Culture*, 119–20).

Even as Trilling wrote this, he seems to have felt still a trace of nostalgia for the days when he could embrace certainties and avoid ambiguities, for he added: "If this is what I really felt, I can't say that I am now wholly ashamed of my cowardice" (120). But he resolutely freed himself of it, as he relinquished the need for optimism and easy certainties and embraced instead the complexities and the ambiguities of the Freudian concept of man.

Writing about Freud's *Civilization and its Discontents* in *Sincerity and Authenticity*, Trilling praises it as "a work of extraordinary power" and asserts that "for social thought in our time its significance is unique. It may be thought to stand like a lion in the path of all hopes of achieving happiness through the radical revision of social life" (151). Thus it was his making the psychoanalytic view of man his own which permitted him to free himself of his earlier belief in Marxism.

Even quite some time before Trilling said that psychoanalysis stood "like a lion" in the way of the belief that human happiness could be attained through radical changes in man's social life, Trilling stressed in various of his writings how important it was that Freud taught us to see the nature of man, and of his personality, as rooted not in society but in his biological inheritance. He based this conviction on what is popularly called Freud's "instinct theory," although Freud in his own writings seldom referred to instincts— rather, he spoke of drives. The use of the term *instinct* in the English editions of Freud's writings is due to an erroneous translation of the German word *Trieb* which Freud uses frequently throughout his writings, and which should have been translated correctly into English as *drive*.

What made these drives so important to Trilling's thought is the concept that our drives are rooted in man's biological inheritance, whether it is the sex drive, which Freud variously called the *libido* or *eros*, or destructive drives, which Freud conceptualized as the *death drive*, or *thanatos*. Eros, the first of these two opposite and opposing drives in man, is generally accepted as being of the greatest importance in man's make-up, since the continuation of our race is based on it. But the second, thanatos, the death drive, was and is still rejected by American psychoanalysis, an error which is emphatically decried by Trilling. He—in my opinion entirely correctly—thinks that in the United States the death drive is denied due to what he calls "the need for optimism."

While this is certainly so, I believe it is but part of an even more general tendency in the United States to avoid all thoughts of death. Witness the fact that in popular usage people don't die, but "pass on" and that after death, the corpse is arranged by the undertaker to appear most life-like. One speaks of visiting the corpse, as if to deny the fact that the person has died. Another aspect of this widespread desire to deny the ineluctability of death is that even non-believers wish to think a return from death is possible, as suggested by the accounts about persons who supposedly returned from death, while actually they never stopped living but only seemed to have done so.

So of Freud's drives theory, only one-half is generally accepted in the United States: the sex drive, or what is called the libido. But even the libido's tremendous importance in man's make-up is diminished by the liberal establishment, which emphasizes the belief that man is conditioned and shaped mainly by social and economic factors, rather than by his biological inheritance.

Trilling rejects the facile optimism of this position and points out that while the full implications of the role of biology in human existence—and of the death drive in particular—have been denied by optimistic social critics, the makers of literature have always been keenly aware of them. One of the essays in which Trilling deals most exhaustively with the relation between literature and psychoanalysis, as he saw it, is titled "Freud: Within and Beyond Culture." Here he wrote:

> Whether or not Freud's formulations of the death instinct stand up under scientific inquiry, I of course cannot venture to say. But certainly they confirm our sense of Freud's oneness with the tradition of literature. For literature has always recorded the impulse of the self to find affirmation even in its own extinction, even *by* its own extinction. When we read the great scene of the death of Oedipus at Colonus, we have little trouble, I think, in at least suspending our disbelief in Freud's idea. We do so the

more willingly because the impulse to death is, in this magnificent moment, expressed and exemplified by the most passionate of men, the man in whom the energy of will and intellect was greatest, the man, too, who at the moment of his desire for death speaks of his extraordinary power of love. (*Beyond Culture*, 98–99)

Trilling proposes that, far from being oppressive, a biological perspective, such as the one of Freud's system, actually may free us from the tyranny of culture:

Now Freud may be right or he may be wrong in the place he gives to biology in human fate, but I think we must stop to consider whether this emphasis on biology, correct or incorrect, is not so far from being a reactionary idea that it is actually a liberating idea. It proposes that culture is not all-powerful. It suggests that there is a residue of human quality beyond the reach of cultural control, and that this residue of human quality, elemental as it may be, serves to bring culture itself under criticism and keeps it from being absolute. (113)

If the relation between our common biological inheritance and culture is problematic, so too is the relation between the individual and culture. This conflict between the self and civilization plays a central role in the thought of Freud, who recognized that the conflict was an ancient one and one which had been chronicled for centuries in literature. For the student of literature, Trilling claims, this focus is a major accomplishment of Freud: "The great contribution he has made to our understanding of literature does not arise from what he says about literature itself but from what he says about the nature of the human mind: he showed us that poetry is indigenous to the very constitution of the mind; he saw the mind as being, in the greater part of its tendency, exactly of the poetry-making faculty. . . ." (92)

Trilling points out that Freud, in *Civilization and Its Discontents*, "had presented a paranoid version of the relation of the self to culture: he conceived of the self submitting to culture and being yet in opposition to it; he conceived of the self as being not wholly continuous with culture, as being not wholly created by culture, as maintaining a standing quarrel with its great benefactor" (117–18). The last paragraph of this essay, which contains one of the most complete discussions of Freudian thoughts by Trilling, reads:

I need scarcely remind you that in respect of this "paranoia" Freud is quite at one with literature. In its essence literature is concerned with the self; and the particular concern of the literature of the last two centuries has been with the self in its standing quarrel with culture. We cannot mention the name of any great writer of the modern period whose work has not in some way, and usually in a passionate and explicit way, insisted on this quarrel, who has not expressed the bitterness of his discontent with civilization, who has not said that the self made greater legitimate demands than any culture can hope to satisfy. This intense conviction of the existence of the self apart from culture is, as culture well knows, its noblest and most generous achievement. At the present moment it must be thought of as a liberating idea without which our developing ideal of community is bound to defeat itself. We can speak of no greater praise of Freud than to say that he placed this idea at the very center of his thought. (118)

Undoubtedly one's life history and personal development do play a role in being able to accept the insights of psychoanalysis and live with them. Mark Krupnik, in *Lionel Trilling and the Fate of Cultural Criticism*, points to some of Trilling's inner conflicts as having influenced his personal and intellectual development. He mentions in this respect particularly what he calls Trilling's "positive Jewishness," embraced in his youth and early years of adulthood, which conflicted with the ideal of the gentleman scholar and literary critic that became characteristic of Trilling's mature years. An equally problematic conflict was between what Krupnik calls "the downtown world of radical politics," to which Trilling belonged as part of the circle around *The Partisan Review*, and the "uptown world" of Columbia University with its ambience (36). Columbia certainly made its demands on Trilling, not the least because he was the first Jew to teach in its English Department. These inner conflicts, and possibly also others, probably convinced Trilling that only a view of man as torn by inner conflicts can permit a full understanding of him and his nature. That is, only what Freud called the unending battle between eternal eros and eternal thanatos, between id and superego, can provide us with that deeper understanding of man and his artistic creations which Trilling tries to convey to us in his literary criticisms.

There can be no doubt that as Trilling's mind matured, Freud's biologism replaced Marxism as his world view, or rather the view of man and his nature most congenial to his purposes and insights. From then on, the conflicts within man, rather than those between the classes, became the view which informed Trilling's understanding and appreciation of literature.

Trilling makes this world view explicit in many of his mature essays. For example, speaking of Henry James' fiction, specifically *The Bostonians*, Trilling writes that at the center of the novel is "the conflict of two principles, of which one is radical, the other conservative," and that this conflict can be thought of in terms of "energy and inertia . . . or force and form . . . or Libido and Thanatos" (*The Opposing Self*, 108).

Still, adherences to "the truth of the body, the truth of full sexuality, the truth of open aggressiveness have a high price," as Trilling asserts in his essay on Babel. It is a truth that particularly Jewish intellectuals—like Babel, and by implication, Trilling himself—often have to pay as the price of a true understanding of culture. Trilling mentions in this connection that Babel complained of being an intellectual "with spectacles on his nose and autumn in his heart": spectacles, one must assume, that interfere with seeing the truth of the body and of a full sexuality which stands at the center of Freud's system; while the autumn in the heart is the result of the realization that true happiness is hardly attainable to man (*Beyond Culture*, 136). The reason true happiness is unattainable, according to Freud, is that we are torn by inner conflicts, and in addition to the knowledge of our mortality, the omnipresence of the idea of death even in the midst of life, vitiates against full happiness in it.

I believe that what made the Freudian system so attractive to Trilling was Freud's conviction that the best we can gain out of life is to be able to love well and to work well, despite our inner conflicts and the knowledge that death is life's inescapable end. Witness the fact that in *The Liberal Imagination* he quotes with high approval Scott Fitzgerald's sentence "The test of a first-rate intelligence is the ability to hold two opposed ideas in the mind at the same time, and still retain the ability to function" (245–46). And one may think that the sentence from *Howards End*, "Death destroys a man but the idea of death is what saves him," which Trilling quotes, represents his idea of what makes for the truly moral and artistic life.

Despite these thoughts, Trilling's view of man and his culture is by no means a negative or joyless one. In his essay "William Dean Howells and the Roots of Modern Taste," he does me the honor of quoting me as follows: "A fight for the very survival of civilized mankind is actually a fight to restore man to a sensitivity toward the joys of life. Only in this way can man be liberated and the survival of civilized mankind be assured. Maybe a time has come in which our main efforts need no longer be directed toward modifying the pleasure principle. Maybe it is time we became concerned with restoring pleasure gratification to its dominant role in the reality principle; maybe society needs less a modification of the pleasure principle by reality, and more assertion of the pleasure principle against an overpowering pleasure-denying reality." After having quoted me in this way, Trilling continues, "It cannot be said of Howells' smiling aspects that they represent a very intense kind of pleasure; yet for most men they will at least serve, in Keats' phrase, to bind us to the earth, to prevent our being seduced by the godhead of disinte-gration" (*Opposing Self*, 102–03). It was Trilling's conviction that we must not permit ourselves to be seduced by the "godhead of disintegration" which accounted for his strong rejection of that anti-intellectualism which became the mode of the sixties.

In the same essay on Howells and the roots of modern taste, Trilling quotes Hannah Arendt that "to yield to the mere process of disintegration has become irresistible temptation, not only because it has assumed that spurious grandeur of 'historical necessity' but also because everything out-side it has begun to appear lifeless, bloodless, meaningless, and unreal" (99–100). This fascination with disintegration, with what Trilling calls the *charisma* of evil, is a danger of which he is keenly aware, maybe because in his Marxist days he was taken by the idea of a historical necessity which deter-mines the fate of man and of society.

It was Trilling's repudiation of this Marxist belief in a historical necessity and his conviction that the root of man is not in society but in himself which account for the Freudian concept of the self becoming ever more dominant in Trilling's thinking and writing. He chose *The Opposing Self* as the title of his 1955 collection of essays, and he came to see the affirmation of the self as the central theme of all great literature.

In the book *Sincerity and Authenticity*, Trilling is much concerned with the true self, both in literature and in culture. He states right at the beginning that "Sigmund Freud took the first steps toward devising a laborious disci-pline of research to discover where it [i.e., one's own self ] might be found" (5). Looking back at the beginning of psychoanalysis, Trilling comments: "When Freud's thought was first presented to a scandalized world, the recognition of unconditioned instinctual impulse which lies at its core was erroneously taken to mean that Freud wished to establish the dominion of impulse, with all that this implies of the negation of the socialized self. But then of course it became understood that the bias of psychoanalysis, so far from being Dionysian, is wholly in the service of the Apollonian principle, seeking to strengthen the 'honest soul' in the selfhood which is characterized by purposiveness and a clear-eyed recognition of limits" (56).

What seemed to have interested Trilling most in Freud and psycho-analysis was the parallel which he saw between their view of man and his world and what great literature conveys to us in different but analogous form. In his essay "Freud's Last Book," which he published in *A Gathering of Fugitives*, he discussed Freud's *An Outline of Psychoanalysis*. There Trilling wrote: "If we look for an analogue to Freud's vision of life, we find it, I think, in certain great literary minds. Say what we will about Freud's dealings with Shakespeare, his is the Shakespearean vision. And it is no mere accident that he levied upon Sophocles for the name of one of his central concepts." Elaborating on this analogy he continues:

> No doubt the thing we respond to in great tragedy is the implication of some meaningful relation between free will and necessity, and it is what we respond to in Freud. One of the common objections to Freud is that he grants too much to necessity, and that, in doing so, he limits the scope of man's possible development. There is irony in this accusation, in view of the whole intention of psychoanalysis, which is to free the soul from bondage to necessities that do not actually exist so that it may effectually confront those that do exist. Like any tragic poet, like any true moralist, Freud took it as one of his tasks to define the borders of necessity in order to establish the realm of freedom. (57–58)

After discussing how Freud sees man as being limited by his own nature, Trilling continues:

> Man as Freud conceives him makes his own limiting necessity by being man. This stern but never hopeless knowledge is precisely the vision of reality that we respond to in tragic art. . . . The tragic vision requires the full awareness of the limits which necessity imposes. But it deteriorates if it does not match this awareness with an idea of freedom. Freud under-took to provide such an idea—it was his life work. (58–59)

It is for these reasons, and in recognition of Freud's style, that Trilling says that this last work of Freud is the "occasion" of an "aesthetic experience" (56).

In his essay "Freud and Literature," which appeared in *The Liberal Imagination*, Trilling writes:

> The Freudian psychology is the only systematic account of the human mind which, in point of subtlety and complexity, of interest and tragic power, deserves to stand beside the chaotic mass of psychological insights which literature has accumulated through the centuries. To pass from the reading of a great literary work to a treatise of academic psychology is to pass from one order of perception to another, but the human nature of the Freudian psychology is exactly the stuff upon which the poet has always exercised his art. It is therefore not surprising that the psychoanalytical theory has had a great effect upon literature. Yet the relationship is reciprocal, and the effect of Freud upon literature has been no greater than the effect of literature upon Freud. (34)

This great effect that literature had on his thinking Freud always freely and gratefully acknowledged, as Trilling likewise acknowledged the effect of Freud's thinking and teaching on his literary criticism.

Trilling sees psychoanalysis as one of the culminations of Romanticist literature of the nineteenth century, because it was passionately devoted to research into the self. His prime example is Diderot's *Rameau's Nephew*, written in 1762, from which he quotes: "If the little savage," meaning the little child, "were left to himself, if he preserved all his foolishness and combined the violent passions of a man of thirty with the lack of reason of a child in the cradle, he'd wring his father's neck and go to bed with his mother" (36). Here, well over a century before Freud, the essence of the boy's oedipal wishes are spelled out and taken for granted by a great writer, insights which Freud attained only through laborious study of himself and of his patients. These are ideas which even now, despite Freud's teachings, are by no means generally accepted. It is also one illustration of the truth of Freud's claim, which he stated repeatedly, that he did not discover anything about the human psyche that the great poets and artists of past times had not known.

Trilling continues in the same essay,

> What, then, is the difference between, on the one hand, the dream and the neurosis, and, on the other hand, art? That they have certain common elements is of course clear; that unconscious processes are at work in both would be denied by no poet or critic; they share too, though in different degrees, the element of fantasy. But there is a vital difference between them which Charles Lamb saw so clearly in his defense of the sanity of genius: "The . . . poet dreams being awake. He is not possessed by his subject but he has dominion over it." This is the whole difference: the poet is in command of his fantasy, while it is exactly the mark of the neurotic that he is possessed by his fantasy. (45)

Despite this crucial difference, literature and psychoanalysis do have much in common. As Trilling points out in *Sincerity and Authenticity*, "psychoanalysis is a science which is based upon narration, upon telling. Its principle of explanation consists in getting the story told—somehow, anyhow—in order to discover how it begins. It presumes that the tale that is told will yield counsel" (140).

In *Beyond Culture* Trilling moves to consider the importance of the suspension of disbelief in literature and in psychoanalysis: "One of the best-known tags of literary criticism is Coleridge's phrase, 'the willing suspension of disbelief.' Coleridge says that the willing suspension of disbelief constitutes 'poetic faith.' . . . This Freud was able to do in a most extraordinary way, and not by the mere impulse of his temperament, but systematically, as an element of his science" (94). When his patients told him stories they invented, "he did not blame them, he did not say they were lying—he willingly suspended his disbelief in their fantasies, which they themselves believed, and taught himself how to find the truth that was really in them" (95).

Freud's capacity to suspend disbelief in his patients—in their fantasies, their dreams, their minds, and their selfhood—is, according to Trilling, analogous to the ability of the reader to suspend disbelief in the reality of a character in literature: "We must be reminded of that particular kind of understanding, that particular exercise of the literary intelligence by which we judge adversely the deeds of Achilles, but not Achilles himself, by which we do not blame Macbeth. . . ." (95)

Trilling goes on to point out another similarity between psychoanalysis and literature. Both explore the opposition between the "pleasure principle" and the "reality principle," which is also a recurring theme of literary criticism:

> Wordsworth speaks of the principle of pleasure—the phrase is his—as constituting the "naked and native dignity of man." He says, moreover, that it is the principle by which man not only "feels, and lives, and moves," but also "knows": the principle of pleasure was for Wordsworth the very ground of the principle of reality, and so of course it is for Freud, even though he seems to maintain the irreconcilability of the two principles. (97)

And in Keats' exploration of the self, Trilling also finds Freud's fundamental "pleasure principle" and the conflicts it engenders:

> When Keats said that beauty is truth, he was saying that the pleasure principle is at the root of existence, and of knowledge, and of the moral life. When he said that truth is beauty, he was putting in two words his enormously complex belief that the self can so develop that it may, in the intensity of art or meditation, perceive even very painful facts with a kind of pleasure, for it is one of the striking things about Keats that he represents so boldly and accurately the development of the self, and that, when he speaks of pleasure, he may mean—to use a language not his—sometimes the pleasure of the id, sometimes of the ego, and sometimes of the superego. (98)

From *Oedipus* to modern poetry Trilling traces the recurring themes that link psychoanalysis and literature, and he does so without vitiating the tragic oppositions that lie at the heart of Freud's vision of human nature and that find expression in a long literary tradition. In *Freud and the Crisis of Our Culture* Trilling writes about Freud that "we cannot fail to pronounce him one of the greatest humanistic minds" (93). In this respect Trilling was his equal, and in many other respects, too, as noted here, theirs were kindred minds. From Trilling's writings one can gain a better comprehension of Freud and psychoanalysis than from most other books written about them. Freud could not have wished for a better spokesman to tell about his contributions to our understanding of culture in general, and of literature in particular.

## Works Cited

Krupnick, Mark. *Lionel Trilling and the Fate of Cultural Criticism.* Evanston: Northwestern UP, 1986.

Trilling, Lionel. *Beyond Culture: Essays on Literature and Learning.* New York: Viking, 1968.

———. *Freud and the Crisis of Our Culture.* Boston: Beacon, 1955.

———. *A Gathering of Fugitives.* Boston: Beacon, 1956.

———. "Introduction." Ernest Jones. *The Life and Work of Sigmund Freud.* Abridged edition. New York: Basic Books, 1961.

———. *The Liberal Imagination: Essays on Literature and Society.* New York: Viking, 1950.

———. *The Opposing Self: Nine Essays in Criticism.* New York: Viking, 1955.

———. "The Progressive Psyche." *The Nation,* 12 Sept. 1942: 215–17.

## 68

*Gertrude Himmelfarb*

*Excerpts from* On Looking Into the Abyss *{adapted from "The*

*Abyss Revisited,"* The American Scholar*}*

*1994 {summer 1992}*

Gertrude Himmelfarb (1922– ) is Professor Emeritus of History at the Graduate School of the City University of New York, a notable scholar of British history (especially John Stuart Mill and Victorian England), and a frequent contributor to intellectual magazines. She is the author of *Victorian Minds: Essays on Nineteenth-Century Intellectuals* (1968), *On Liberty and Liberalism: The Case of John Stuart Mill* (1974), *The Idea of Poverty: England in the Industrial Age* (1984), *The New History and the Old* (1987), *Poverty and Compassion: The Moral Imagination of the Victorians* (1991), and *The De-Moralization of America: From Victorian Virtues to Modern Values* (1995), among other books. She has also edited works by Lord Acton, Thomas Malthus, and Mill.

Much of Himmelfarb's work focuses on historiographical issues, such as consensus-formation among historians, the rise and fall of cultural fashions, and the historical development of "the moral imagination" (a phrase of Trilling, of whom she is a strong admirer). A historian with a strong, conservatively toned revisionist sensibility, Himmelfarb is an outspoken defender of the leading values of Victorian morality. She is also opposed to the dominance within academic historiography of left-oriented social history (which she criticizes as a form of covert radical propaganda), preferring instead traditional historical approaches that emphasize politics and "high" culture.

A well-known neoconservative critic and scourge of "radical orthodoxy"—especially in the American academy—Himmelfarb views Trilling as a neoconservative forebear. In the following essay, originally titled "The Abyss Revisited," Himmelfarb returns to Trilling's famous essay, "On the Modern Element in Modern Literature" (1961)—collected in *Beyond Culture*

under the title "On the Teaching of Modern Literature"—arguing its significance and relevance to Right-Left academic debates of the 1990s. The revised version of this essay, which appears below, served as the opening
chapter to Himmelfarb's *On Looking into the Abyss: Untimely Thoughts on
Culture and Society* (1994). The volume is dedicated "to the memory of Lionel
Trilling"; Himmelfarb explains that "the spirit of Lionel Trilling hovers
over the book as a whole." The selection below begins with the opening of
Himmelfarb's introduction to the book, in which she discusses Trilling's
influence on her thinking and their friendship.

Nonetheless, in her memoir, *The Beginning of the Journey: The Marriage of
Diana and Lionel Trilling* (1993), Diana Trilling makes clear her view that an
abyss would separate the present-day political viewpoint of Lionel Trilling
from that of Himmelfarb and her husband Irving Kristol. Diana Trilling
laments the Kristols' embrace of a neoconservative "politics of self-interest"
and voices "enduring regret that our political disagreement has all but
ended the relationship." She adds: "Lionel did not live long enough to
witness the rise of the neoconservative movement, but I have little question
that if he had been alive and working in the eighties, he would have been
highly critical of this swing to the right by our old friends."

Only after completing this book did I realize how prominently Lionel Trilling figures in it. The title of the book (derived from the lead essay) is a
direct quotation from him. The title of another of the essays is an adaptation
from him. And most of the other essays cite him at crucial points of the
argument. In dedicating this book to him, I am discharging an intellectual
and personal debt that is long overdue.

I was never a student of Trilling's, but I was an admirer and a friend. (It
was one of his many virtues that his friendships knew no limits of age.) In
recent years I find myself returning to his writings more and more, not so
much for inspiration as for solace. The inspiration came many years ago
when I learned to appreciate a mode of thought that I now recognize—I did
not know this at the time—to be uniquely his: a seriousness about ideas that
was not "academic" (defying both the language of academia and the com-
partmentalization of disciplines); a seriousness about public affairs that
went beyond (or stopped short of) politics in the ordinary sense; a moral
*gravitas* that was surely unseemly when I was younger but that may be more
appropriate at my present age (and in the present time).

If I now find solace in Trilling, it is because he was able to resist the
insidious ideological and political fashions of his time without the coarsening of mind that often comes with doing battle, and also without the timid-

ity and equivocation that retreats from battle in an excess of fastidiousness. What I have come to realize more recently is that he was not only remarkably clearheaded about the threats to intellectual integrity and political liberty in his day; he was also remarkably prescient in recognizing the first signs of the new perils that have replaced the old.

In an earlier book, *Poverty and Compassion*, I adopted Trilling's much quoted phrase "the moral imagination" for the subtitle, and the passage in which that expression appears for the book's epigraph. Rereading that passage today, I am impressed once again by its wisdom. Nearly half a century ago, when the welfare state was young and "democratic socialism" was not yet the oxymoron it has become, Trilling foresaw the fallacy in what then seemed to be an enlightened, humane, and compassionate social policy. Almost in passing, in the course of discussing quite another subject, he made an observation that is of the greatest pertinence today:

> Some paradox of our nature leads us, when once we have made our fellow men the objects of our enlightened interest, to go on to make them the objects of our pity, then of our wisdom, ultimately of our coercion. It is to prevent this corruption, the most ironic and tragic that man knows, that we stand in need of the moral realism which is the product of the free play of the moral imagination.[1]

In the present book, I have had occasion again and again to draw upon the sense of "moral realism" that is so much a part of Trilling's "moral imagination": in the lead essay, where his image of the abyss invites us to reflect on the intellectual arrogance and spiritual impoverishment of some of the latest tendencies in literary criticism, philosophy, and history; in the essay on heroes, in which he is quoted as exposing the fatal weakness of structuralism long before it had even acquired that name; in the essay on nationalism, where the literary critic lectures the historian on the fallacies of the "long view," in which murder and torture seem not so terrible as they compose themselves into a "meaningful pattern."[2] Only by an oversight do the essays on Mill (his "one very simple principle" of liberty) and on Marx (his "standing Hegel on his head") fail to invoke Trilling, who repeatedly warned against the simplification, abstraction, and impoverishment of both liberalism and Marxism. . . .[3]

In a now classic essay, "On the Teaching of Modern Literature," Lionel Trilling described his students' response to his own course on modern literature:

> I asked them to look into the Abyss, and, both dutifully and gladly, they have looked into the Abyss, and the Abyss has greeted them with the

grave courtesy of all objects of serious study, saying: "Interesting, am I not? And *exciting*, if you consider how deep I am and what dread beasts lie at my bottom. Have it well in mind that a knowledge of me contributes materially to your being whole, or well-rounded, men."[4]

The subjects of that course were the modernist greats: Yeats, Eliot, Joyce, Proust, Kafka, Lawrence, Mann, Gide, Conrad. By way of background, Trilling had his students also read some of the seminal works that prepared the way for the modernists: Frazer's *Golden Bough*, Nietzsche's *Birth of Tragedy* and *Genealogy of Morals*, Freud's *Civilization and Its Discontents*, Diderot's *Rameau's Nephew*, Dostoyevsky's *Notes from Underground*, Tolstoy's *Death of Ivan Ilyitch*. Each of these, the literary and philosophical works alike, was profoundly subversive of culture, society, morality, conventional sexuality— of all that which was once confidently called "civilization." These were the "dread beasts" lurking at the bottom of the "Abyss." And it was this abyss that the students "dutifully and gladly"—and intelligently—looked into and found "interesting," even "exciting."

Trilling's point was that such a course, the teaching of such books, was self-defeating, for it transformed what should have been a profound spiritual and emotional experience into an academic exercise. Instead of hearing the writer's "wild cry" of terror, passion, mystery, rage, rapture, despair, the students heard themselves (and perhaps their professor) discoursing, seriously and sophisticatedly, about *Angst*, alienation, authenticity, sensibility. The result was to vitiate the works themselves and bring about precisely the opposite of their intended effect: "the socialization of the antisocial, or the acculturation of the anti-cultural, or the legitimization of the subversive."[5]

The image of the abyss haunted the most subversive author on Trilling's reading list, Nietzsche, and Nietzsche's most subversive hero, Zarathustra.

Man is a rope stretched between the animal and the Superman—a rope over an abyss.

Courage slayeth also giddiness at abysses: and where doth man not stand at abysses! Is not seeing itself—seeing abysses?

Ye are frightened: do your hearts turn giddy? Doth the abyss here yawn for you? Doth the hell-hound here yelp at you?

He who seeth the abyss, but with eagle's eyes—he who with eagle's talons *graspeth* the abyss: he hath courage.[6]

The same image is at the heart of *The Birth of Tragedy*, an account of the primal, tragic, "unnatural crime" epitomized by the myth of Oedipus and revealed by the "wisdom" of Dionysus. Because that crime is so monstrous, the wisdom that recognizes and embraces it is equally criminal, for "whoever, in pride of knowledge, hurls nature into the abyss of destruction, must himself experience nature's disintegration." Those who do not have the courage of a Dionysus, who lack the "divine frenzy" of the artist or poet, may take refuge in the serene philosophy of Apollo or in Sophocles' version of the myth, which superimposes upon it "the luminous afterimage which kind nature provides our eyes after a look into the abyss." Nietzsche, however, looking into that abyss with the open eyes of Dionysus, sees it as pure tragedy.

> Indeed, my friends, believe with me in this Dionysiac life and in the rebirth of tragedy! Socratic man has run his course; crown your heads with ivy, seize the thyrsus, and do not be surprised if tiger and panther lie down and caress your feet! Dare to lead the life of tragic man, and you will be redeemed.[7]

This is what Trilling's students were reading and what they glibly translated into the fashionable vocabulary of the time, thus domesticating the wild beasts and inuring themselves to the terrors of the abyss. This approach to the abyss, Trilling observed on another occasion, reminded him of a practical, responsible householder: "Having come to take nullity for granted, he wants to be enlightened and entertained by statements about the nature of nothing, what its size is, how it is furnished, what services the management provides, what sort of conversation and amusements can go on in it."[8] Nietzsche himself anticipated just this response when he mocked the aesthetes who engaged in "so much loose talk about art and [had] so little respect for it," who used "Beethoven and Shakespeare as subjects for light conversation."[9]

Nietzsche wrote more than a century ago; Trilling a few decades ago. Since then the abyss has grown deeper and more perilous, with new and more dreadful terrors lurking at the bottom. The beasts of modernism have mutated into the beasts of postmodernism—relativism into nihilism, amorality into immorality, irrationality into insanity, sexual deviancy into polymorphous perversity. And since then, generations of intelligent students under the guidance of their enlightened professors have looked into the abyss, have contemplated those beasts, and have said, "How interesting, how exciting."

Rereading Trilling's essay, I was struck by how pertinent it is to the present state of the academic culture; indeed, it is more pertinent now than it was in his own day. Trilling was troubled by the ease with which great books were emasculated (a word one hardly dares use today), the way passionate affirmations were reduced to rote formulas and subversive ideas made banal and respectable. But his students were at least reading those books and confronting those ideas. One cannot say that now with any confidence.

Today, students in some of the most distinguished departments of literature are all too often reading books about how to read books. Literary theory has replaced literature itself as the fashionable subject of study. Structuralism and deconstruction, gender theory and the new historicism, reader-response and speech-act theory—these are more hotly debated than the content and style of particular novels or poems. And when novels or poems are the ostensible subject of discussion, the theorists are so dominant ("hegemonic" or "privileged," as they would say), so insistent upon their superiority over author and work alike, that their comments on the latter are little more than commentaries on their own modes of criticism.

A book by one prominent theorist, Jonathan Culler, opens with a chapter entitled "Beyond Interpretation," suggesting that the interpretation of individual works is beneath the consideration of the serious theorist, is indeed an impediment to theory. "Formerly," Culler observes elsewhere, "the history of criticism was part of the history of literature . . . now the history of literature is part of the history of criticism."[10] Another eminent professor, Gerald Graff, reasons that since the various literary theories are irreconcilable, the only solution is to make them the focus of instruction, and this in undergraduate as well as graduate classes.[11] Lionel Trilling would have felt confirmed in his worst fears by this proposal, which elevates theory not only above the literary work but even above any interpretation of that work. He would also have savored the irony of the title of Graff's influential book *Professing Literature*—not reading or appreciating or understanding literature, but "professing" it; or, more ironic still, the former president of the Modern Language Association, Barbara Herrnstein Smith, who refers to the years in which she "professed" Shakespeare's sonnets.[12] (Trilling's own anthology of great literature is fittingly entitled *The Experience of Literature*.)

Moreover, the literature that is "professed," when theorists condescend to discuss actual works of literature, are "texts"—the very word denigrating both the idea of literature and the idea of greatness. As a text, Superman is as worthy of study as Shakespeare, or an obscure woman writer (obscure for good literary reasons) as meritorious as George Eliot (who is suspect not only because she assumed that male pseudonym but because she made a profession of being a writer rather than a feminist-writer). A graduate student at Louisiana State University, mindful of the grand tradition in that university epitomized by Cleanth Brooks, Robert Penn Warren, and *The Southern Review*, was dismayed to discover that their successors, determined to open the "canon" to women and black writers, have little concern with the literary merit of their books and no passion or even enthusiasm for the books them-selves. They are, she finds, more interested in making political statements than literary ones, and more interested in theory than in literature—any kind of literature. Given the assignment to "deconstruct something," one enterprising student chose to deconstruct the game "Trivial Pursuit," to the professor's delight.[13]

If literature is what theorists choose to call it, it is not surprising that interpretation (when they deign to interpret) is what they make of it. One of the gurus of this school, Stanley Fish, once said that the demise of objec-tivity "relieves me of the obligation to be right . . . and demands only that I be interesting."[14] He now regrets that statement, but he has not disavowed the sentiment. To be sure, what theorists regard as "interesting" may not be what a literate reader, unfamiliar with their arcane language and convoluted reasoning, would find intelligible, let along interesting. For theorists, what is interesting is what is outré, paradoxical, contradictory, opaque. Since there is no "right" interpretation, the opportunities to be "interesting," in this sense, are unlimited. And since novels and poems are simply "texts" (or "pretexts") that are entirely indeterminate and therefore totally malleable, they can be "textualized," "contextualized," "recontextualized," and "inter-textualized" at will. The result is a kind of free-floating verbal association, in which any word or idea can suggest any other (including, or especially, its opposite), and any text can be related in any fashion to any other.

Indeed, the very words of the text are recast, rearranged, and redefined. By the ingenious use of quotation marks, hyphens, diagonals, and paren-theses within and around words, by adding or subtracting syllables or letters and crossing out words while keeping them in the text, the critic can elicit the puns, double entendres, paradoxes, ambiguities, and antitheses that testify to the intrinsic "aporia" of language, the infinite play of "*différance.*" An English commentator has been moved to observe that ours is "the age of the inverted commas and the erased idea."[15]

In this Aesopian world, Jacques Derrida is free to transmute the philoso-pher Hegel into the word "Hegel," which evokes the French *aigle*, thus connoting "imperial or historic power."[16] This, in turn, inspires Geoffrey Hartman to identify *aigle* with Nietzsche's *Ekel*, meaning "disgust."[17] By such verbal gymnastics, the critic can engage in the most elaborate contor-tions and produce the most startling effects, unrestrained by anything but the limits of his own wit and audacity. It is an enviable position in which he finds himself, although not so enviable for the subject of this exercise, the philosopher Hegel, who is so readily reduced to an object of "disgust."

Not all of the practitioners of these arts identify themselves as decon-structionists. Geoffrey Hartman has described himself and Harold Bloom as "barely deconstructionists" compared with those "boa-deconstructors" Derrida, Paul de Man, and J. Hillis Miller.[18] Others have more prosaically distinguished between "soft" and "hard" deconstructionists. After the revelations about de Man's collaboration with the Nazis, some of the "softer" members of this school defected, denying that they are now, or ever have been, deconstructionists; some profess not to know any deconstructionists. Others stood firm, defending both deconstruction and de Man. Hartman himself took the occasion to offer so "soft" an interpretation of deconstruction—it was essentially, he said, a "defense of literature" and a "critique of German idealism"—that most literary critics might be regarded as unwitting deconstructionists.[19]

That deconstruction is not just a variant of the familiar modes of critical interpretation may be seen by examining one of the best known and most highly regarded examples of this genre: J. Hillis Miller's analysis of one of Wordsworth's "Lucy" poems, "A Slumber Did My Spirit Seal." This essay is especially noteworthy because Miller is one of the most influential figures of this school; because he is so enamored of his reading of this poem that he has repeated it on several occasions; because it has been taken as a model of deconstruction by deconstructionists themselves; and because it ventures to interpret a poem that has been admired by generations of readers and commented on by a host of scholars.[20] Moreover, the poem itself has the virtue of being so brief—only eight short lines—that one can easily keep it in mind as one reads the interpretation.

> A slumber did my spirit seal;
> I had no human fears;
> She seemed a thing that could not feel
> The touch of earthly years.
>
> No motion has she now, no force;
> She neither hears nor sees;
> Rolled round in earth's diurnal course,
> With rocks, and stones, and trees.

Traditionally the poem has been read as an elegy, a memorial to a girl who died at a tragically young age. Most commentators have dwelt upon what would be obvious to any thoughtful reader—the contrast, for example, between past and present, life and death, the innocence of youth and the tragic sense of mortality that comes with age. Miller finds in it a good many other contrasts, starting with "male as against female" and going on to "mother as against daughter or sister, or perhaps any female family member as against some woman from outside the family, that is, mother, sister, or daughter against mistress or wife, in short, incestuous desires against legitimate sexual feelings." He also brings to bear upon the poem—in accord with the principle that any text is relevant to any other, however far removed in time or subject—such authorities as Walter Benjamin, Paul de Man, Nietzsche, Wallace Stevens, Plato, Thales, and especially Heidegger. Thus Heidegger's play on the word "thing," in his commentary on Plato's *Theaetetus*, is applied to Wordsworth's use of that word. Where the "common reader" might assume that the poem's reference to the girl as a "thing" was meant to emphasize the fact that she was no longer alive, Miller, inspired by Heidegger explains that "a young girl" (presumably dead or alive) is a thing because "something is missing in her which men have."

But the poem is even "odder" than this, Miller says, as he proceeds to explicate the "obscure sexual drama" played out in it, a drama that has as its source the death of Wordsworth's own mother when he was eight. Lucy represents at the same time "the virgin child and the missing mother," a "virgin 'thing'" who is "sexually penetrated while still remaining virgin." The speaker in the poem is not only the opposite of Lucy—"male to her female, adult knowledge to her prepubertal innocence"; he is also "the displaced representative of both the penetrated and the penetrator." In fact Lucy and the speaker are "the same," though the poet is also "the perpetually excluded difference from Lucy, an unneeded increment, like an abandoned child." Since "Lucy" means ("of course") light, to "possess" Lucy would be to rejoin the "lost source of light"; thus Lucy is also the male principle, the "father sun as logos." To think about Lucy's death is to cause her death, for "thinking recapitulates in reverse mirror image the action of the earthly years in touching, penetrating, possessing, killing, encompassing, turning the other into oneself and therefore being left only with a corpse, an empty sign."

And so the interpretation goes on, becoming more and more convoluted, with Miller finally concluding that he has "seemingly" come far from the subject of his essay, "the state of contemporary literary study." But one might also conclude that he has come even further from those eight delicate lines of the poem.

This exercise in deconstruction recalls an image used by Trilling in another prophetic essay. While literary critics, he said, were endowing literature with "virtually angelic powers," they were also making it clear to the readers of literature that "the one thing you do not do when you meet an angel is wrestle with him."[21] What would he have said of critics today who tell their readers that when you meet an angel, not only do you not wrestle with him, you play with him—play word games with him, play fast and loose with his "text," play havoc with reason, common sense, and emotion? It is ironic, in view of the turgidity of their prose, to find deconstructionists solemnly invoking the principle of *jouissance* or *tromperie*, and to hear Geoffrey Hartman call them, not in criticism but in praise, "clowns or jongleurs."[22]

It is in this spirit, playfully and at the same time ponderously, that deconstructionists summon up the image of the abyss, an abyss that exists for them in language alone. Do we not all experience, Hartman observes, "the fear (a thrilling fear) of the abyss in all words whose resonance haunts us and must be appeased"?[23] The preface to a translation of one of Derrida's works explains: "The fall into the abyss of deconstruction inspires us with as much pleasure as fear. We are intoxicated with the prospect of never hitting bottom."[24] And Paul de Man is described as "the only man who ever looked into the abyss and came away smiling."[25] De Man came away smiling for the same reason that Hartman found the abyss thrilling and Derrida found it pleasurable—because his abyss is a purely linguistic one, constructed entirely out of words—indeed, out of a play on words. And having been so willfully constructed, it can be as willfully reconstructed and deconstructed.

Philosophy also has its abysses, and some philosophers are confronting them in the same way—playfully and irreverently, as a linguistic construct, having no "correspondence" with anything posing as "reality" or "truth." They quote Nietzsche's many maxims on this subject, such as his celebrated one on truth: "Truths are illusions of which one has forgotten that they *are* illusions; worn-out metaphors which have become powerless to affect the senses; coins which have their obverse effaced and now are no longer of account as coins but merely as metal."[26] But there is nothing illusory or metaphoric in Nietzsche's abyss, which is the primal, tragic fact of the human condition. Heidegger's abyss, on the other hand, is to be found in the sentence "Language speaks," and in that abyss one falls not downward but upward; indeed, there one can "become at home, . . . find a residence, a dwelling place for the life of man."[27]

Richard Rorty, one of America's most respected philosophers, calls himself a pragmatist, but so "light-mindedly," as he would say, that one can hardly recognize any kinship with his notably grave progenitor John Dewey. The main principle governing Rorty's philosophy is that there is no fixed or fundamental principle, no "essential" truth or reality. Indeed, philosophy, he says, no longer exists as an independent discipline. Marx promised to abolish philosophy by replacing it with "positive science"—that is, Marxism, which is deemed to be scientific rather than philosophical because it is simply the depiction of "reality."[28] Rorty would abolish philosophy by abolishing reality itself, which is nothing more than the arbitrary construct of the philosopher.

Unlike Marx, Rorty is confident that his revolution is already largely achieved. It is getting more and more difficult, Rorty good-humoredly observes, to locate "a real live metaphysical prig" who thinks there is a "reality" to be explored and a "truth" about reality to be discovered. There are, to be sure, a few such dodoes left.

> You can still find philosophy professors who will solemnly tell you that they are seeking *the truth*, not just a story or a consensus but an honest-to-God, down-home, accurate representation of the way the world is. A few of them will even claim to write in a clear, precise, transparent way, priding themselves on manly straightforwardness, on abjuring "literary" devices.[29]

Rorty himself has given up any such old-fashioned "philosophical machismo."[30] He has even gone so far in repudiating "machismo" as to apply the feminine pronoun to the "anti-essentialist" philosopher and the masculine pronoun to the "essentialist"—this after identifying himself as an "anti-essentialist."[31]

Rather than seek an essential truth, Rorty calls upon philosophers to "dream up as many new contexts as possible . . . to be as polymorphous in our adjustments as possible, to recontextualize for the hell of it."[32] They should, in fact, become philosophers-cum-poets, adopting a "light-minded aestheticism" to traditional philosophical questions, for only such an aestheticism can further the "disenchantment of the world." This disenchantment, moreover, must extend itself to morality as well as truth. Just because other people take moral issues seriously does not mean that philosophers should share that seriousness. On the contrary, they should "josh them out of the habit" of being serious and get them to look at moral issues aesthetically, playfully.[33]

"Taking philosophy seriously," Rorty explains, is not only philosophically naïve, positing a reality and a truth that do not exist, but politically dangerous, for essentialism encourages fundamentalism and fanaticism of the kind displayed by Shiites, Marxists, and Nazis. This is Heidegger's great fault. It is not his particular doctrines about the nature of man, reason, or history, that are "intrinsically fascistic." Nor are his doctrines invalidated by the fact that he himself was a Nazi, an anti-Semite, and altogether "a rather nasty piece of work." His mistake is rather in thinking that "philosophy must be taken seriously." Rorty warns us against this common mistake. An original philosopher is the product of a "neural kink," and one should no more look to him for wisdom or virtue than to an original mathematician, microbiologist, or chess master. Heidegger is an original in this sense, and one should take from him and make of him what one likes—which is not at all, Rorty admits, what Heidegger might have liked. The proper approach to Heidegger is "to read his books as he would not have wished them to be read: in a cool hour, with curiosity, and an open, tolerant mind."[34]

Or perhaps one should read them as novels. If Rorty finds no wisdom in philosophy, he does find it in fiction, which is not burdened by "transcultural notions of validity." Endorsing Milan Kundera's tribute to "the wisdom of the novel," Rorty announces that he happily joins him in "appealing to the novel against philosophy." To be sure, this may have unpleasant consequences, since the "realm of possibility," as revealed in the novel, is unlimited and uncontrolled. Might it not mean, for example, that "the wisdom of the novel encompasses a sense of how Hitler might be seen as in the right and the Jews in the wrong?" Yes, it does, and novels will surely be written that portray Hitler as he saw himself and that persuade readers to sympathize with him. Such novels will be written and *must* be written, Rorty insists, if we are to be faithful, as we should be, to "the wisdom of the novel."[35]

Kundera has not, in fact, written such a novel, and it is unlikely that he would. But Heidegger wrote books and delivered lectures that justified Nazism—and not only early in the Nazi regime but after the war, when the facts of the Holocaust were fully known. In 1948, rebuked by Herbert Marcuse for not recanting his support of the regime or denouncing the extermination of the Jews, Heidegger replied that Hitler's actions were comparable to the measures taken by the Allied forces against the East Germans. The following year he delivered a speech that may be the ultimate in "moral equivalency." "Agriculture," he declared, "is now a motorized food industry, in essence the same as the manufacturing of corpses in the gas chambers and extermination camps, the same as the blockade and starvation of the countryside, the same as the production of the hydrogen bombs."[36]

Looking into the abyss of philosophy, one might say, Heidegger saw the beasts of Nazism and found them tolerable. Rorty looks into the abyss of Heidegger—coolly, curiously, tolerantly—and sees not Heidegger as he saw himself, indeed, as he was, but an "original and interesting writer." Divorced from any "essential" truth, from any practical morality, and from the political consequences of his own philosophy, Heidegger can be readily assimilated into Rorty's philosophy—or non-philosophy. By the same token, we can look into Rorty and see him not as he sees himself—as the only sensible, pragmatic philosopher of liberal democracy—but as the proponent of a

relativism-cum-aestheticism that verges on nihilism and that may ultimately subvert liberal democracy together with all the other priggish metaphysical notions about truth, morality, and reality.

So too the discipline of history has more than its share of abysses and still
more historians prepared to make of them what they will. Like those literary
critics who recontextualize and deconstruct texts, or those philosophers who
abolish philosophy and aestheticize morality, so there are historians who
propose to "demystify" (and, some might say, "dehistoricize") history. This
is the intention behind some of the most fashionable schools of history: that
which explains everything in terms of race, class, and gender; that which
focuses entirely upon the daily lives of ordinary people ("history from below"); that which "structuralizes" history, displacing individuals, events,
and ideas by impersonal structures, forces, and institutions; and that which
"deconstructs" it, making all statements about the past aesthetic constructs
of the historian.[37]

The effect in each case is to mute the drama of history, to void it of
moral content, to mitigate evil and belittle greatness. It is ironic to find
these schools flourishing at a time when the reality of history has been all
too dramatic, when we have plumbed the depths of degradation and witnessed heroic efforts of redemption. Looking into the most fearsome abysses
of modern times, these historians see not beasts but faceless bureaucrats,
not corpses but statistics, not willful acts of brutality and murder but the
banal routine of everyday life, not gas chambers and gulags but military-
industrial-geopolitical complexes.

Of all these schools, history-from-below may seem most innocent. Yet
confronted with the abyss, it is as evasive and delusive as the others. If it
cannot take the measure of greatness, neither can it appreciate the enormity
of evil. *Alltagsgeschichte*, the history of everyday, workaday life, can tell us
much about the daily wartime life of ordinary Germans—the way they went
about their jobs, struggled to make ends meet, coped with the difficulties of
rationing and shortages, sent off husbands and fathers to die abroad, and
suffered injuries and deaths from air raids at home. All of this may be true,
but it is hardly the whole of the truth or even the most essential part of the
truth. Modeled on anthropology, this mode of history professes to be "value-
free." The result, one historian has pointed out, is that "workaday life in the
Third Reich could be remembered as no more than workaday life."[38] Another explains that it conveys "the normality of a 'normal' German living a
'normal' life," but tells us nothing about the uniqueness—indeed, abnor-
mality—of that time.[39]

Even in what it does tell us, it may be delusive. If ordinary people can give no evidence of the horrors of concentration camps or of deliberate, systematic, massive murders, they may give distorted evidence of those events that were within their daily experience—beatings on the street, children expelled from school, Jews forced from their homes and jobs. Such events may have impinged very little on the consciousness of people preoccupied with their own concerns or, it may be, prepared to ignore or belittle them because they themselves were not averse to them. The historian looking for evidence of anti-Semitism on the part of ordinary people may find only "mild," "passive" anti-Semitism, and will have no way of knowing the effect of such anti-Semitism in sanctioning and thus promoting official, virulent anti-Semitism. Or, finding evidence of a popular belief in eugenics, the historian may subsume that mild anti-Semitism under the larger, "functional" category of eugenics.

The effect of such a history would be to create "a Final Solution with no anti-Semitism; a Holocaust that is not unique."[40] It might even remove Hitler altogether from the social history of the Nazi period. And with Hitler gone, with nothing left but the normal and banal, *Alltagsgeschichte* becomes an "apologia" for Nazism.[41]

The most recent and modish way of demystifying the Holocaust is by "deconstructing" it. In principle, deconstruction is obliged to "problematize" the Holocaust as it does all historical "texts." Because of the sensitivity of the subject, however, and to avoid being identified with the "revisionist" school that denies the reality of the Holocaust, deconstructionists have trod warily.[42] But they have been less reticent when confronted with the revelation that one of their leading lights, Paul de Man, had written anti-Semitic articles in a pro-Nazi journal early in the war. Whether or not those writings by de Man—and, more important, his evasiveness and duplicity on this and related subjects throughout his life—may properly be taken as a reflection on deconstruction itself, there can be little doubt that the responses of his colleagues, some in the form of lengthy essays, are part of the literature of deconstruction. For in rallying to the defense of de Man, as most of them have, they have deconstructed his "texts" much as they might deconstruct any literary, philosophical, or historical text—and have deconstructed his critics as well.

Jacques Derrida's essay on de Man is a classic of this genre. De Man had said that it was a form of "vulgar anti-Semitism" to think that German culture could be identified with Judaism. Derrida interprets this to mean not what a reader of that pro-Nazi journal would surely have taken it to mean—that it was "vulgar" to identify German culture with Judaism—but rather that de Man was condemning "anti-Semitism *itself inasmuch as* [Derrida's italics] it is vulgar, always and essentially vulgar." Having thus absolved de Man of the charge of anti-Semitism, Derrida goes on to accuse de Man's critics (his "prosecutors," Derrida calls them) of being the real culprits—latter-day Nazis, in effect. It is they who reproduce the "exterminating gesture" ("gesture"!) of the Nazis by virtually "censuring [*sic*] or burning" de Man's books, and who speak of him as a "propagator," which is a code word for "censorship" [*sic*] and "denunciation" to the police. It is these critics who are guilty of an "ideologizing moralization" that is "immorality itself." And it is their "war," the war in the press, the war between de Man's critics and his friends, even the war within de Man himself, that is at issue as much as the war against the Nazis. After reading this exercise in deconstruction and apologetics, one can understand Derrida's remark that the overwhelming feeling produced in him by thinking about all this is one of "immense compassion"—not, as one might think, for the victims of Nazism, but for de Man's "enormous suffering" and "agony."[43]

Others have been less imaginative in their defense of de Man, excusing him on the grounds of youthful aberration, political expediency, and human frailty. One defender takes comfort in the fact that de Man proposed not the extermination of the Jews but only their expulsion from Europe;[44] another that he was not anti-Semitic but only "intellectually vulgar."[45] Still another reminds us that although many facts about the affair have emerged, facts in themselves are meaningless. "It is all a matter of interpretation, and each interpretation will probably reveal more about the interpreter than about de Man."[46]

Geoffrey Hartman, one of de Man's most devoted admirers (and himself, as he points out, a refugee from Nazi Germany), is pained by de Man's behavior, but finds "the American reaction, in its rush to judgment, as hard to take as the original revelations."[47] He also finds that those revelations, seen in perspective, are not quite so bad as we might think. De Man's writings were anti-Semitic, to be sure, but not a "vulgar" anti-Semitism, at least "not by the terrible standards of the day"; and his comments on the "Jewish problem" were "mild" compared with the "vicious" propaganda in other papers. De Man was only part of a larger problem. His "dirty secret" was the "dirty secret of a good part of civilized Europe," so that "once again," Hartman observes, speaking for all of us, "we feel betrayed by the intellectuals." And if de Man himself chose not to reveal that secret and never to acknowledge his past, it was because to do so would be an "effort of exculpation," thus a repetition of the original "error." What he did instead was to devote himself to his lifework, a critique of the "rhetoric of totalitarianism," the tendency to "totalize" language and literature. And this, Hartman concludes, "looks like a belated, but still powerful, act of conscience."[48]

If the defense of de Man often reads like a defense of deconstruction itself, it also resorts to arguments that clearly violate the principles of deconstruction. Thus his critics are taken to task for failing to consider his "authorial intentions," the historical and biographical context of his articles, even the testimony of his acquaintances. J. Hillis Miller invokes some of these arguments, going so far as to accuse the critics of doing great damage to "the possibilities of rational and informed discussion."[49] Similarly, Derrida, claiming to find factual errors in one critical article, "shudders to think that its author teaches history at a university."[50] If one is surprised to hear such conventional sentiments from theorists who normally deride "facticity" and rationality, "authorial intentions" and "extralinguistic" contexts, one may also recall their contempt for the "linear logic" that would preclude such inconsistency. (One may also sympathize with Miller, who was unfortunate enough to publish a book, the same year as the revelations about de Man appeared, predicting that "the millennium of universal justice and peace" would come "if all men and women became good readers in de Man's sense."[51]

The de Man case has many parallels to an earlier controversy about a book by David Abraham on the background of Nazism.[52] One of the points of criticism concerns the dedication, which reads, "For my parents—who at Auschwitz and elsewhere suffered the worst consequences of what I can merely write about."[53] A naïve reader might suppose that the "worst consequences" suffered by Abraham's parents, as by so many others at Auschwitz and elsewhere, was death. In fact, his parents were alive when the book was published. The historian Natalie Zemon Davis has analyzed the dedication, defending Abraham against any imputation of deception. In a thousand words she deconstructs and reconstructs the nineteen-word dedication so that it becomes a tribute not to dead parents but to live ones—and a tribute as well to the "survivors' son," the dedicator, who penetrated to a deeper truth than appears on the surface.[54]

Davis explains why the superficial reading of the dedication is erroneous. Few readers, she says, are likely to interpret it as a dedication to the dead, since one cannot dedicate anything to the dead, but only to their memory; moreover, the book jacket identifies the author as an assistant professor at Princeton, suggesting that he was too young to be the son of parents who perished in the camps. The dedication is properly read as an expression of thanks to the author's parents and as a reminder of "their special relation to his subject matter." While the book itself says almost nothing about anti-Semitism—it is a "structural analysis" of the roots of Nazism, Davis explains, and therefore deals with impersonal "social forces"—the last line of the book "circles round to the 'consequences' of the dedication" by referring to the German businessmen who "paved the road to serfdom" with "gold and blood." The dedication is thus a "strategy" by which the author reclaims the past. "So that's how it happened, says the survivors' son [or so Davis has him saying]; not the work of devils, but of historical forces and actors." This is the message of the dedication: "turn suffering into writing and figuring out, inform accusations with understanding, let the tragic endings of 'gold and blood' not be the last word."[55]

One's admiration for the creativity of this exercise is tempered by the realization of how far it has gone from the "text" itself—from the implied death of the author's parents to their resurrection as survivors; from the "worst consequences" inflicted by the Nazis in the death camps to the Weimar businessmen who "paved the road to serfdom" (as if "serfdom" is equivalent to the Holocaust); and from the Holocaust itself seen as deliberate, premeditated evil ("the work of devils") to an "understanding" of it as the product of "historical forces and actors." One may well be dismayed by the expenditure of so much ingenuity on a subject as solemn and unambiguous as this, an all too real abyss in which millions of people did in fact suffer the "worst consequences."

The implications of this mode of thought, exhibited in the writing and teaching of some of our most eminent literary critics, philosophers, and historians, have not been fully appreciated. (At least three of the writers who feature prominently in this essay—J. Hillis Miller, Richard Rorty, and Natalie Zemon Davis—have been presidents of their professional associations.) What happens to our passion for literature when any "text" qualifies as literature, when theory is elevated above poetry and the critic above the poet, and when literature, interpretation, and theory alike are said to be indeterminate and infinitely malleable? What happens to our respect for philosophy—the "love of wisdom," as it once was—when we are told that philosophy has nothing to do with either wisdom or virtue, that what passes as metaphysics is really linguistics, that morality is a form of aesthetics, and that the best thing we can do is not to take philosophy seriously? And what happens to our sense of the past when we are told that there is no past save that which the historian creates; or to our perception of the momentousness of history when we are assured that it is *we* who give moment to history; or to that most momentous historical event, the Holocaust, when it can be so readily "demystified" and "normalized," "structuralized" and "deconstructed"? And what happens when we look into the abyss and see no real beasts but only a pale reflection of ourselves—of our particular race, class, and gender; or, worse yet, when we see only the metaphorical, rhetorical, mythical, linguistic, semiotic, figurative, fictive simulations of our imaginations? And when, looking at an abyss so remote from reality, we are moved to say, like Trilling's students, "How interesting, how exciting."

When Nietzsche looked into the abyss, he saw not only real beasts but the beast in himself. "He who fights with monsters," he warned his reader, "should be careful lest he thereby become a monster. And if thou gaze long into an abyss, the abyss will also gaze into thee."[56] This was all too prophetic, for a few years later the abyss did gaze back at him and drew him down into the depths of insanity. Our professors look into the abyss secure in their tenured positions, risking nothing and seeking nothing save another learned article.

Nietzsche is now a darling of the academy. I have seen T-shirts emblazoned with the slogan "Nietzsche is Peachy." Nietzsche, who had no high regard for the academy but did have a highly developed sense of irony, would have enjoyed that sight.

## Notes

1. Lionel Trilling, "Manners, Morals, and the Novel" (1947), in *The Liberal Imagination: Essays on Literature and Society* (New York, 1950), pp. 221–22.

2. Trilling, "Tacitus Now" (1942), in *The Liberal Imagination: Essays on Literature and Society* (New York, 1950), p. 201.

3. See, for example, Trilling's preface to *The Liberal Imagination*, and his novel, *The Middle of the Journey.*

4. Lionel Trilling, "On the Teaching of Modern Literature" (1961), in *Beyond Culture: Essays on Literature and Learning* (New York, 1965), p. 27. The original title of Trilling's essay was "On the Modern Element in Modern Literature," a variation on Arnold's inaugural lecture, "On the Modern Element in Literature."

5. Ibid., p. 26.

6. Friedrich Nietzsche, *Thus Spake Zarathustra*, trans. Thomas Common, in *The Philosophy of Nietzsche* (Modern Library ed., New York, n.d.), p. 29 (prologue, ch. iv); p. 165 (part 3, ch. xlvi); p. 286 (part 4, ch. lxxiii, no. 2); p. 287 (part 4, ch. lxxiii, no. 4).

7. Nietzsche, *Birth of Tragedy*, trans. Francis Golffing (Anchor ed., New York, 1956), pp. 60–61 (ch. 9); p. 86 (ch. 14); p. 124 (ch. 21).

8. Trilling, "James Joyce in His Letters" (1968), in *The Last Decade: Essays and Reviews, 1965–75* (New York, 1978), p. 30.

9. Nietzsche, *Birth of Tragedy*, p. 135 (ch. 22).

10. Jonathan Culler, *The Pursuit of Signs: Semiotics, Literature, Deconstruction* (Ithaca, N.Y., 1981), ch. 1; Culler, *Framing the Sign: Criticism and Its Institutions* (Norman, Okla., 1988), p. 40.

11. Gerald Graff, *Professing Literature: An Institutional History* (Chicago, 1987), pp. 252ff. See also Graff, *Beyond the Culture Wars: How Teaching the Conflict Can Revitalize American Education* (New York, 1992).

12. Barbara Herrnstein Smith, *Contingencies of Value: Alternative Perspectives for Critical Theory* (Cambridge, Mass., 1988), p. 5.

13. Elizabeth Connell Fentress, "Why I Left Graduate School," *New Criterion*, June 1989, p. 78.

14. Stanley Fish, *Is There a Text in This Class?* (Cambridge, Mass., 1980), p. 180.

15. Richard King, "The Discipline of Fact / The Freedom of Fiction," *Journal of American Studies* (Cambridge, Eng.), 1991, p. 172.

16. Jacques Derrida, *Glas* (Paris, 1974), p. 7.

17. Geoffrey H. Hartman, *Criticism in Wilderness: The Study of Literature Today* (New Haven, 1980), pp. 138–41, 207–8, 210, 264.

18. Hartman et al., *Deconstruction and Criticism* (New York, 1990 [1st ed., 1979]), p. ix.

19. Hartman, "Blindness and Insight," *New Republic*, March 7, 1988, p. 29.

20. This account is based upon Miller's essay "On Edge: The Crossways of Contemporary Criticism," in *Romanticism and Contemporary Criticism*, ed. Morris Eaves and Michael Fischer (Ithaca, N.Y., 1986), pp. 102–11. For a summary of the traditional as well as deconstructionist interpretation of this poem, see David Lehman, *Signs of the Times: Deconstruction and the Fall of Paul de Man* (New York, 1991), pp. 125–29.

21. Trilling, "The Two Environments" (1965), in *Beyond Culture*, p. 231.

22. Hartman, "The State of the Art of Criticism," in *The Future of Literary Theory*, ed. Ralph Cohen (1989), p. 100.

23. Hartman, *Saving the Text: Literature/Derrida/Philosophy* (Baltimore, 1981), p. 151. Hartman speaks of "the abysm of words" in his introduction to *Deconstruction and Criticism*, p. ix.

24. Jacques Derrida, *Of Grammatology*, trans. Gayatri Chakravorty Spivak (Baltimore, 1976), p. lxxvii.

25. Lehman, pp. 155–56.

26. Nietzsche, "On Truth and Falsity in an Extra-Moral Sense," in *Early Greek Philosophy and Other Essays*, trans. M. A. Mügge, in *The Complete Works of Friedrich Nietzsche*, ed. Oscar Levy (New York, 1964), II, 180.

27. Martin Heidegger, *Poetry, Language, Thought*, trans. Albert Hofstadter (New York, 1971), pp. 191–92.

28. Karl Marx, *The German Ideology*, in Karl Marx and Friedrich Engels, *Basic Writings on Politics and Philosophy*, ed. Lewis S. Feuer (New York, 1959), p. 248.

29. Richard Rorty, *Essays on Heidegger and Others* (Philosophical Papers, vol. II) (Cambridge, Eng., 1991), p. 86. This is reminiscent of the much quoted passage in Derrida's "White Mythology," deriding the "metaphysical naivety of the wretched peripatetic" who does not realize that metaphysics is nothing more than mythology:

> A white mythology which assembles and reflects Western culture: the white man takes his own mythology (that is, Indo-European mythology), his *logos*— that is, the *mythos* of his idiom, for the universal form of that which it is still his inescapable desire to call Reason. (Derrida, "White Mythology: Metaphor in the Text of Philosophy," *New Literary History*, 1974, p. 11.)

30. Rorty, *Essays on Heidegger*, p. 86.

31. Rorty, *Objectivity, Relativism, and Truth* (Philosophical Papers, vol. I) (Cambridge, Eng., 1991), pp. 99–102.

32. Ibid., p. 110.

33. Ibid., p. 194.

34. Rorty, "Taking Philosophy Seriously," *New Republic*, April 11, 1988, pp. 31–34.

35. Rorty, "Truth and Freedom: A Reply to Thomas McCarthy," *Critical Inquiry*, Spring 1990, pp. 638–39.

36. Victor Farias, *Heidegger and Nazism*, ed. Joseph Margolis and Tom Rockmore; trans. Paul Burrell and Gabriel R. Ricci (Philadelphia, 1989 [1st ed., 1987]), pp. 283, 287.

37. For a discussion of structuralism and history, see Chapter II, "Of Heroes, Villains, and Valets"; and for deconstruction, see Chapter VII, "Postmodernist History."

38. Charles S. Maier, *The Unmasterable Past: History, Holocaust, and German National Identity* (Cambridge, Mass., 1988), pp. 36–37.

39. Dan Diner, "Between Aporia and Apology: On the Limits of Historicizing National Socialism," in *Reworking the Past: Hitler, the Holocaust, and the Historians' Debate*, ed. Peter Baldwin (Boston, 1990), p. 139.

40. Mary Nolan, "The *Historikerstreit* and Social History," in *Reworking the Past*, p. 243.

41. Diner, p. 140. See also David F. Crew, "*Alltagsgeschichte*: A New Social History 'from Below'?," *Central European History*, September/December 1989.

42. See Chapter VII, "Postmodernist History," pp. 142–46.

43. Derrida, "Like the Sound of the Sea Deep Within a Shell: Paul de Man's War," in *Responses on Paul de Man's Wartime Journalism*, ed. Werner Hamacher et al. (Lincoln, Nebr., 1989), pp. 129, 143, 149, 154, 157, 164 (n. 44). (This article appeared earlier in *Critical Inquiry*, Spring 1988.)

Derrida has responded to the revelations about Heidegger's Nazism in a similar spirit of compassion. Heidegger, he explains, had been briefly taken in by Nazism because of a philosophical error on his part, a misguided subjectivism and "metaphysical humanism." As for Heidegger's later silence on the Holocaust, this too Derrida finds defensible. Instead, Derrida reserves his criticism for those who are quick to condemn the silence; it is they who are "a bit indecent, even obscene."

Jean-François Lyotard, *Heidegger and "the jews,"* trans. Andreas Michel and Mark S. Roberts (Minneapolis, 1990), p. xxviii (interview by Jacques Derrida, quoted in the Foreword by David Carroll). See also Thomas Sheehan, "A Normal Nazi," *New York Review of Books*, January 14, 1993, p. 31.

44. Ortwin de Graef, "Aspects of the Context of Paul de Man's Earliest Publications," *Responses*, p. 113. It was de Graef, a young scholar and admirer of de Man, who first discovered these articles.

45. S. Heidi Krueger, "Opting to Know: On the Wartime Journalism of Paul de Man," ibid., p. 307.

46. David H. Hirsch, *The Deconstruction of Literature: Criticism After Auschwitz* (Hanover, N.H., 1991), pp. 108–9, quoting Leon S. Roudiez, "Searching for Achilles' Heel: Paul de Man's Disturbing Youth," *World Literature Today*, 1989, p. 439.

47. Hartman, *Minor Prophecies: The Literary Essay in the Culture Wars* (Cambridge, Mass., 1991), pp. 124–25.

48. Hartman, "Blindness and Insight," *New Republic*, p. 30. These and other points are developed at much greater length in Hartman's *Minor Prophecies*, pp. 123–48.

Another colleague and disciple of de Man, Shoshana Felman [Shoshana Felman (1932– ), author of *Literature and Psychoanalysis* (1982) and *Writing and Madness* (1985)], explains why his silence, his refusal to confess, was itself an ethical statement.

In the testimony of a work that performs actively an exercise of silence not as simple silence but as the absolute refusal of any trivializing or legitimizing discourse (of apology, of narrative, or of psychologizing explanation of recent history), de Man articulates . . . the incapacity of apologetic discourse to account for history as Holocaust, the ethical impossibility of a *confession that, historically and philosophically, cannot take place.* This complex articulation of the impossibility of concession embodies, paradoxically enough, not a denial of the author's guilt but, on the contrary, the most radical and irrevocable assumption of historical responsibility. Shoshana Felman, "Paul de Man's Silence," *Critical Inquiry*, Summer 1989, p. 733. (The italics are the author's.)

49. J. Hillis Miller, "An Open Letter to Professor Jon Wiener," *Responses*, p. 334; *Times Literary Supplement*, June 17–23, 1988, p. 685.

50. Derrida, *Responses*, p. 160 (n. 44).

51. Miller, *The Ethics of Reading* (New York, 1987), p. 58.

52. For a discussion of other aspects of this book, see Chapter VII, "Postmodernist History."

53. David Abraham, *The Collapse of the Weimar Republic: Political Economy and Crisis* (Princeton, 1981).

54. Natalie Zemon Davis, "About Dedications," *Radical History Review*, March 1985, pp. 94–96.

55. Ibid., pp. 95–96.

56. Nietzsche, *Beyond Good and Evil*, trans. Helen Zimmern (Modern Library ed., n.d.), p. 87 (ch. iv, no. 146).

## 69

*Diana Trilling*

*Excerpt from* The Beginning of the Journey: The Marriage of Diana and Lionel Trilling

*1993*

Diana Trilling (1905–96) was a literary-cultural critic and essayist. She was the author of three collections of prose and criticism, *Claremont Essays* (1964), *We Must March My Darlings* (1977), and *Reviewing the Forties* (1978), along with *Mrs. Harris: The Death of the Scarsdale Diet Doctor* (1981), a study of Jean Harris, the former girls' school headmistress convicted of murdering the well-known doctor Herman Tarnower. The book received a Pulitzer Prize nomination for nonfiction in 1982.

Diana Trilling was also known as a critic and editor of the work of D. H. Lawrence and especially as editor of the twelve-volume Uniform Edition of Lionel Trilling's complete works, published by Harcourt Brace Jovanovich (1977–80).

An important member of the elder generation of New York writers associated with *Partisan Review* and *Commentary* in the early postwar era, Diana Trilling was a prominent voice in the American intelligentsia for more than a half century. She first gained attention as a literary journalist and reviewer during her years as the fiction critic of *The Nation* (1942–49). A fierce critic of Stalinism even before World War II, Diana Trilling aroused controversy during the 1950s and '60s as an outspoken, self-described "liberal anti-Communist." Her anti-Communist politics were reflected in her work as a member of the American Committee for Cultural Freedom (which she chaired during 1955–57) and her regular columns for the anti-Stalinist *New Leader* (1957–59).

Like Lionel Trilling, Diana Trilling was a moral critic whose concerns revolved around political and cultural issues. Although the couple's positions on most major issues differed little, Diana Trilling was the more politically outspoken of the pair.

Diana Trilling's final major work was her autobiographical memoir of the early years with her husband, excerpted below. The book puzzled many readers and angered others, less because of Diana Trilling's surprising revelations about her own struggles in her youth and middle age than for her sharp revisionist portrait of Lionel Trilling, which emphasized a darker side to Trilling's life, at odds with his public image and well hidden from the view of friends and colleagues.

It was to decency that Lionel felt that he had sacrificed his hope of being a writer of fiction—conscience had not made a coward of him, it had made him a critic. Was I the only person in the world who knew this about Lionel? Did his friends and colleagues have no hint of how deeply he scorned the very qualities of character—his quiet, his moderation, his gentle reasonableness—for which he was most admired in his lifetime and which have been most celebrated since his death? . . . I could not have wished Lionel to be a drunkard in order to be a novelist. The power to write fiction does not lie in the bottle. But I could have wished him to have a thousand mistresses were this to have released him from the constraints upon him as a writer of fiction. I would willingly have been his female Leporello and sung his conquests.

## 70

**Tom Samet**

*" 'For That I Came': Lionel Trilling and the Self Now,"*

*unpublished essay*

**October 1997**

Tom Samet (1948– ) earned his Ph.D. in English and American Literature from Brown University, where for four years he served on the editorial staff of *Novel: A Forum on Fiction.* Samet began his teaching career at Rutgers University in 1977. In 1986 he accepted an administrative appointment with the University Scholars Program at Pennsylvania State University, returning to full-time teaching two years later as a charter member of the faculty of Louisiana Scholars' College, the state's designated honors program in the liberal arts, at Northwestern State University.

Samet has held fellowships from Brown University, the Rutgers University Research Council, and the American Council of Learned Societies. During 1989–90 he served as Fulbright Professor of American Literature at the University of Warsaw, in Poland. Samet's interests have centered on modern literature and literary criticism. His essays on Trilling, Edmund Wilson, Virginia Woolf, Hemingway, literary theory, and other topics have appeared in *Critical Inquiry, The New Republic, Criticism, The Centennial Review, Explorations, Novel*, and *Sewanee Review*.

In 1995 Samet was named vice president for academic affairs and dean of the faculty of Hood College in Frederick, Maryland, where he holds the rank of professor of English.

Each mortal thing does one thing and the same:
  Deals out that being indoors each one dwells;
  Selves—goes itself; *myself* it speaks and spells,

Crying *What I do is me: for that I came.*
–Gerard Manley Hopkins

There is a brief passage in *Sincerity and Authenticity* that takes us close to the center of Trilling's critical project. It occurs near the end of the fourth lecture—he has been discussing Wordsworth and Rousseau, having brought them together with his customary adroitness by way of reference to "the sentiment of being." That same phrase figures prominently elsewhere in Trilling's work; it appears, most notably, in an earlier essay on Wordsworth, where he associates it with a condition of stillness and repose, of wise passiveness and calm acceptance—with a kind of "elemental biological simplicity" that he then goes on to distinguish from a more strenuous, and a more militant, modern conception of being. The continuities and connections here are not hard to trace: the modes of selfhood posited in "Wordsworth and the Rabbis" and those divergent moral styles subsumed under the headings of "sincerity" and "authenticity" are situated along the same axis of inquiry. But before I go any further let me cite the passage that I have in mind: when they speak of the sentiment of being, Trilling argues, Rousseau and Wordsworth are concerned

> with such energy as contrives that the centre shall hold, that the circumference of the self keep unbroken, that the person be an integer, impenetrable, perdurable, and autonomous in being if not in action.[1]

I have said that this is central for the obvious reasons, for these are *Trilling's* allegiances and *Trilling's* intentions. No less than Rousseau and Wordsworth, he wants to preserve the sentiment of being, the sense of discrete and stable and coherent personal identity. He wants the center to hold, wants the self to be an integer, quite as much—and as desperately—as they do.

It is this commitment, more than anything else, that defines the contours of Trilling's work—defines not only its provenance and its purview, its major themes and abiding preoccupations, but the limits of its sympathetic engagement. The uneasiness that came increasingly to characterize Trilling's transactions with the literature of the modern period derives from his attachment to an ideal of autonomy and to a particular conception of the self. The aggravated selfhood of the Underground Man and the atrophied selves of Kafka and Beckett—these Trilling took to be indices of a profound "ontological crisis," of an enfeeblement and attenuation of the sentiment of being. Consider Trilling's commentary on the Kafkan self, that "I without a self"[2] to which Auden once referred: "For Kafka," Trilling writes,

the sense of evil is not contradicted by the sense of personal identity. . . .
In Kafka, long before the sentence is executed, even long before the
malign legal process is ever instituted, something terrible has been done
to the accused. We all know what that is—he has been stripped of all that
is becoming to a man except his abstract humanity, which, like his
skeleton, never is quite becoming to a man. He is without parents, home,
wife, child, commitment, or appetite; he has no connection with power,
beauty, love, wit, courage, loyalty, or fame, and the pride that may be
taken in these. So that we may say that Kafka's knowledge of evil exists
without the contradictory knowledge of the self in its health and validity.
(os, 34)

Appearing as they do in the great essay on Keats's letters, these remarks take
on added importance. For if Kafka dramatizes the self as it verges upon
extinction, it is Keats who stands for Trilling as the hero of secure identity,
the model of ontological wholeness. "The last image of health [so we are
told] at the very moment when the sickness of Europe began to be apparent"
(os, 43), Keats acknowledges the intractable "reality of circumstance" while
affirming "the creativity of the self that opposes circumstance, the self that is
imagination and desire" (os, 36). The argument is both moving and persuasive, and the essay—which is surely among Trilling's finest—deserves the
high praise that it has generally received. But there is an aspect of the Keatsian self that Trilling leaves wholly out of account. I have in mind the famous
letter to Richard Woodhouse of October 1818, in which Keats declares that
the poet "has no identity." "As to the poetical Character," he writes,

> it is not itself—it has no self—it is every thing and nothing—It has no
> character . . . not one word I ever utter can be taken for granted as an
> opinion growing out of my identical nature—how can it, when I have no
> nature?[3]

This sort of fluid, mobile, and indeterminate self had little appeal for Trilling. To one form of it he responded with intense distaste and misgiving: in
*Sincerity and Authenticity* he speaks in unusually caustic terms of the "trashi-
ness" of what David Reisman called the "other-directed" personality. Yet
Keats, in his letter to Woodhouse, would appear to be suggesting that something closely akin to other-direction is a part of his poetic equipment.
"When I am in a room with People," he notes, "if I ever am free from specu-
lating on creations of my own brain, then not myself goes home to myself:
but the identity of every one in the room begins so to press upon me that I
am in a very little time annihilated." At no point in his discussion of the
letters does Trilling consent to grapple with this issue. For all of his insis-

tence upon the political value of "uncertainties, mysteries, doubts," Trilling seems reluctant to confront the doubts that Keats expresses about the sentiment of his own being; and the unwillingness to reckon with *this form* of Negative Capability tells us a great deal about Trilling's commitment to his conception of the dense, weighty, fixed, and morally centered self.[4]

If we thus know pretty clearly what kind of self Trilling valued, we know also that such versions of selfhood are in general disrepute. "We have lost the *mystique* of the self," Trilling wrote in 1951, though he could hardly then have foreseen the systematic assault upon subjects and identities carried out in recent decades. That assault is formidably exemplified by a book completed in the year of Trilling's death—a moment, as it turned out, of intense ferment and debate about the politics of the self.

*A Future for Astyanax* undertakes to chart what its author, Leo Bersani, describes as "stages in the deconstruction of the self in modern literature."[5] He thus moves from an account of the "fear of desire" that is said to govern the formal and psychological structures of realistic fiction to an exploration of "alternatives to a psychology of stable centers of desire"—moves, that is to say, from prudential strategies for securing the "socially viable self" through a series of increasingly risky "adventures in psychic mobility." From the outset, Bersani champions what he calls the "scattered or disseminated self," arguing for an art "which mocks our faith in psychological coherence and in the civilizing value of sublimation." The book's polemical energy derives from an avowed political intention, for just as the "myth" of a "rigidly ordered self contributes to a pervasive cultural ideology of the self which serves the established order," so (Bersani maintains) the idea of the fragmented, discontinuous, "deconstructed" self strikes at the foundations of a "culture of repression and sublimation."

With its subtle readings of Flaubert, James, Stendhal, and others, *A Future for Astyanax* is at once finely nuanced and forcefully argued. Here I want only to consider its central premise, asking whether life in advanced capitalist societies is accurately reflected in the terms that Bersani proposes. Does it, in other words, usefully describe our contemporary situation to speak of "a culture of repression and sublimation"?

Two books contemporaneous with Bersani's, *The Cultural Contradictions of Capitalism* (1976) and *The Culture of Narcissism* (1978) give us reason to suppose that this may not be a satisfactory account.[6] Daniel Bell and Christopher Lasch are of course associated with significantly different political agendas; and Lasch, as regards the issue before us, provides testimony that is in some ways rather mixed. His analysis of the fierce, punitive superego that characterizes the contemporary narcissistic personality bears at least some resemblance to Bersani's discussion of the "suicidal melancholy" that threat-

ens modern civilization. But the *culture* in which this personality exists—
from which, Lasch insists, such a personality arises—is not to be understood
as repressive. Here Lasch and Bell are in fundamental agreement: our culture, they maintain, is one of impulse and gratification, of consumption,
display, and hedonistic indulgence; and it is a culture that sponsors not a
hardening or contraction of the boundaries of identity but a process of
disintegration.

There is a precursor document that may help to bring these matters still
more sharply into focus. A decade before the books of Bersani, Lasch, and
Bell, Robert Jay Lifton noted the emergence of a new kind of individual that
he called "protean man"—a type produced, he speculated, by unprecedented
disruptions of cultural tradition and by the "flooding of imagery" churned
out by the instruments of mass communication. Rejecting the language of
"character" and "personality" on the ground that it enshrines a notion of
fixity and permanence that is no longer applicable, Lifton used the term
"self-process" to define the new dynamics of identity. "The protean style of
self-process," he wrote, "is characterized by an interminable series of experiments and explorations—some shallow, some profound—each of which may
be readily abandoned in favor of still new psychological quests."[7] Lifton's
attitude toward these developments was not at all one of disapproval or
dismay; like Bersani, he wished to urge upon his readers the "extraordinary
range of possibility" contained in "the mode of transformation." His account of protean man, moreover, returns us to the question that I raised a
moment ago: in view of the "self-process" that he named and described, and
in view of the circumstances that have brought it about, does it really make
sense to propose what Bersani calls "psychic mobility" as a radical alternative to the dominance of the "coherently unified personality"? "An exuber-
ant indefiniteness about our own identity"—this, says Bersani, offers an
answer and antidote to "the tyrannical rigidities . . . of sublimated desire";
but Gerald Graff, writing three years later, seems closer to the mark in
suggesting that Bersani's style of "cultural radicalism . . . ignores the disappearance of the paternalistic repressions it seeks to dissolve."[8] Far from
enforcing "tyrannical rigidity" and "psychic immobility," our culture now
fosters and exploits an unlimited openness and pliancy, promoting them by
way of "protean" identities, transient relationships, fluid commitments,
shifting "lifestyles"; and far from threatening to undermine the restrictions
of the cultural status quo, the project of "deconstructing" the self may
finally be an act of unintended collaboration with our already decentered
and profoundly *deconstructive* social actuality.

Near the end of his life, Trilling had one last occasion to reflect upon these
questions, in a labored and dispirited essay, "On the Uncertain Future of the

Humanistic Educational Ideal." That uncertainty Trilling ascribed to none of the usual suspects. What threatened the traditions of "humanistic education" was neither the frenzy of acquisition and consumption, nor the narrow careerism of the young, nor economic anxieties trailing in the wake of the oil crisis of 1973, nor even the failure of the public schools (though of this last he took due note). Indeed, Trilling's diagnosis is all the stranger for its apparent indifference to these material facts, this "real foundation." The spectre haunting the "humanistic educational ideal" is instead an altered conception of the self: "If you set yourself to shaping a self," Trilling wrote,

> you limit yourself to that self and that life. You preclude any other kind of self remaining available to you. You close out other options, other possibilities which might have been yours. Such limitation, once acceptable, now goes against the cultural grain—it is almost as if the fluidity of the contemporary world demands an analogous limitlessness in our personal perspective. Any doctrine, that of the family, religion, the school, that does not sustain this increasingly felt need for a multiplicity of options and instead offers an ideal of a shaped self, a formed life, has the sign on it of a retrograde and depriving authority, which, it is felt, must be resisted. (LD, 175)

To the shaped self, the formed life, Trilling remained steadfastly committed. Nor, I think, should this allegiance be too readily dismissed as an impulse of reaction or retreat. Repudiating projects of liberation that mimic or accede to the derangements of the modern marketplace, he speaks to us on behalf of a sentiment of being—of the center that holds and the unbroken circumference—which may again be a radical and a redemptive idea.

## Notes

1. Lionel Trilling, *Sincerity and Authenticity* (Cambridge: Harvard University Press, 1972). All future citations from Trilling's work refer to the Uniform Edition (Harcourt Brace Jovanovich) and are noted parenthetically in the text: *The Opposing Self* (OS); *The Last Decade* (LD).

2. *The Dyer's Hand* (New York: Vintage Books, 1968), pp. 159–67.

3. *The Selected Letters of John Keats*, ed. Lionel Trilling (New York: Farrar, Straus and Young, 1951), p. 152.

4. In his essay on *Mansfield Park* Trilling does, in fact, associate Keats's phrase with that "negation" or evacuation of selfhood described in the correspondence with Woodhouse, and there Trilling makes clear his sympathetic response to the novel's indictment of "impersonation," its apparent allegiance to "fixity," "enclosure," and "stasis." See *The Opposing Self*, pp. 181–202.

5. Leo Bersani, *A Future for Astyanax: Character and Desire in Literature* (Boston: Little Brown, 1976).

6. Daniel Bell, *The Cultural Contradictions of Capitalism* (New York: Basic Books, 1976); Christopher Lasch, *The Culture of Narcissism* (New York: W.W. Norton, 1978).

7. Robert Jay Lifton, "Protean Man," *Partisan Review* (winter 1968), pp. 13–27. Just how thoroughly views like Lifton's have established themselves as a reigning form of cant is nicely demonstrated in recent remarks by Salman Rushdie, occasioned by the fiftieth anniversary of Indian independence (*Time Magazine*, 11 August 1997, p. 42). "In the modern age," writes Rushdie, "we have come to understand our own selves as composites, often contradictory, even internally incompatible. We have understood that each of us is many different people. Our younger selves differ from our older selves; we can be bold in the company of our lovers and timorous before our employers, principled when we instruct our children and corrupt when offered some secret temptation; we are serious and frivolous, loud and quiet, aggressive and easily abashed. The 19th century concept of the integrated self has been replaced by this jostling crowd of 'I's." Without wishing to erect a counter-abstraction to Rushdie's "19th century concept of the integrated self," I should note that our historical predecessors had quite as lively a sense of complexity as does Mr. Rushdie but tried not to confuse complexity with hypocrisy. Indeed, it may be that their allegiance to the "integrated" self helped to make them connoisseurs of hypocrisy—a virtue that we have lost—which they practiced resourcefully and diagnosed without mercy.

8. Gerald Graff, *Literature against Itself* (Chicago: University of Chicago Press, 1979), p. 95.

# For Further Reading

An excellent, comprehensive research tool for students of Lionel Trilling's work and life is Thomas Leitch, *Lionel Trilling: An Annotated Bibliography* (New York: Garland, 1993). Leitch's bibliography includes items through 1990 on Trilling, the New York intellectuals, and related topics. Accordingly, with the exception of citing the major books devoted to Trilling, this annotated selection of articles emphasizes sources either unaccountably omitted from Leitch's volume or published since 1991.

## Abbreviations

| | |
|---|---|
| BC | *Beyond Culture* |
| BJ | *The Beginning of the Journey* |
| DT | Diana Trilling |
| FCC | *Freud and the Crisis of Our Culture* |
| LD | *The Last Decade* |
| LI | *The Liberal Imagination* |
| LT | Lionel Trilling |
| MA | *Matthew Arnold* |
| OS | *The Opposing Self* |

Boyers, Robert. *Lionel Trilling: Negative Capability and the Wisdom of Avoidance* (Columbia: University of Missouri Press, 1977). This perceptive short monograph, which focuses on LT's short stories and his 1948 essay on James's *Princess Casamassima* (collected in *LI*), is the first substantial critical study of LT's work.

Budick, Emily Miller. "Lionel Trilling and the 'Being' of Culture." *Massachusetts Review: A Quarterly of Literature, the Arts, and Public Affairs* 35, no. 1 (spring 1994): 63–82. In LT's essay "Wordsworth and the Rabbis" (collected in *OS*), both LT and Wordsworth sympathize with rabbinic Judaism. LT's approach to Wordsworth was influenced by ideas at midcentury of American exceptionalism and high culture; his dialectical sensibility treats Wordsworth via a series of mediations between Jewish and Christian differences, secular and religious oppositions, and American and British cultures.

474 For Further Reading

Chace, William M. *Lionel Trilling: Criticism and Politics* (Stanford: Stanford University Press, 1980). A valuable close reading of LT's major works.

DeMott, Benjamin. "Rediscovering Complexity." *The Atlantic*, September 1988, 67–75. DeMott suggests that a renewed appreciation of LT's work, especially *LI*, is crucial to the task of revitalizing political liberalism in the 1980s. DeMott compares and contrasts LT's philosophy of liberalism with that of current figures such as Charles Murray and with LT's contemporaries such as Richard Hofstadter and Robert Merton.

Freedman, Jonathan. "Trilling, James, and the Uses of Cultural Criticism." *The Henry James Review* 14, no. 2 (spring 1993): 141–50. Assesses LT's debts to James and compares LT and James as critics and imaginative writers.

Glaberson, Eric. "The Literary Criticism of the New York Intellectuals: A Defense and Appreciation." *American Studies* 29, no. 1 (spring 1989): 71–95. Assesses LT and other leading New York intellectuals as writers who disdained theory and method for practical criticism.

Hart, Jeffrey. "Reality in America: Yet Once More." *Sewanee Review* 102, no. 4 (fall 1994): 631–41. The tendency of progressive literary academe to use race, gender, and class criteria—rather than literary merit—to judge literature calls for another book such as *LI*, which defended literary values against progressive ideology at midcentury.

Kriegel, Leonard. "*Partisan Review* and the New York Intellectuals: A Personal View." *The Gettysburg Review* 2, no. 2 (spring 1989): 227–37.

Krupnick, Mark. *Lionel Trilling and the Fate of Cultural Criticism* (Evanston IL: Northwestern University Press, 1986). The best study of LT's work and life, showing his evolution and the enduring value of his cultural criticism and life as a public intellectual.

Matthews, Fred. "Role Models? The Continuing Relevance of the 'New York Intellectuals.'" *Canadian Review of American Studies* 19, no. 1 (spring 1989): 69–99.

Nowlin, Michael E. "Lionel Trilling and the Institutionalization of Humanism." *Journal of American Studies* 25, no. 1 (April 1991): 23–38. Drawing primarily on a new analysis of *BC*, *LD*, and *MA*, Nowlin defends LT against charges from Cornel West and others that he was "a mandarin apologist for 'high culture.'" Nowlin regards one of LT's "great insights" to be his judgment that "the 'adversary' culture" is "essentially the dark mirror image of a frustrated humanistic enterprise" and suggests that LT's example shows how, even if one is "compromised" by "complicity with the established social order," this "complicity may be unavoidably the price one pays for 'speaking.'"

Nowlin, Michael E. "'Reality in America' Revisited: Modernism, the Liberal Imagination, and the Revival of Henry James." *Canadian Review of American Studies* 23, no. 3 (spring 1993): 1–29.

O'Hara, Dan. *Lionel Trilling: The Work of Liberation* (Madison: University of Wisconsin Press, 1988). LT is a "magnanimous" critic capable of "imaginative sympathy" with minds radically different from his own. Despite his conservatism and his status as a leading intellectual, this ability marks him as a "subversive patriarch" who undermined established ideological and literary orthodoxies.

Reising, Russell J. "Lionel Trilling, 'The Liberal Imagination,' and the Emergence of the Cultural Discourse of Anti-Stalinism." *boundary 2*, 10, no. 1 (spring 1993): 94–125. LT's literary criticism written between the 1940s and 1960s served as a critique of Stalinism and Soviet communism.

Rose, Jacqueline. "Freud and the Crisis of Our Culture." *Critical Quarterly* 37, no. 1 (spring 1995): 3–20. Rose contrasts LT in FCC with Freud himself and with views of the relation between self and culture offered by novelists such as Dorothy Richardson and Henry James. Rose suggests that these inadequate views of the relation between self and society can be enriched by the acceptance of multiculturalism.

Ross, T. J. "The Trillings and the Consolation of Criticism: *The Beginning of the Journey.*" *The Literary Review* 37, no. 4 (summer 1994): 724–25. Ross considers DT's efforts in BJ to portray the wilder side of LT's personality—to "rescue her husband from the goody-goody image of perfect gentle knight often laid on him"—not wholly successful and notes that the familiar image of the liberal, decent LT emerges from the memoir nonetheless.

Seed, David. "The Style of Politics in Lionel Trilling's *The Middle of the Journey.*" *Durham University Journal* 86, no. 55 (January 1994): 119–28.

Shapiro, Edward S. "Jewishness and the New York Intellectuals." *Judaism: A Quarterly Journal of Jewish Life and Thought* 39, no. 3 (summer 1989): 282–92.

Shoben, Edward Joseph, Jr. *Lionel Trilling: Mind and Character* (New York: Ungar, 1981). A perceptive study by a clinical psychologist of the relation between LT's work and character, including discussion about the role of teaching and fiction-writing for LT's criticism.

Stade, George. "Trilling and 'Ulysses.'" *Partisan Review* 59, no. 2 (spring 1992): 275–82. Drawing on LT's correspondence, Stade argues that LT regarded the portrayal of the uncensored human body and of bodily functions in *Ulysses* as Joyce's great achievement.

Strout, Cushing. "A Dark Wood in the Middle of the Journey: Willa Cather and Lionel Trilling." *Sewanee Review* 105, no. 3 (summer 1997): 381–95. Cather (1883–1947) and LT were ill-disposed toward each other. In a 1936 story, Cather described a hypothetical Jewish journalist who is not capable of appreciating a popular book. LT believed she meant him and criticized her understanding of the narrow, excessively spiritualized modern world. But Cather's *The Professor's House* (1925) and LT's *The Middle of the Journey* bear striking similarities in their attitudes toward the American academy.

Tanner, Stephen L. *Lionel Trilling* (Boston: Twayne, 1988). An illuminating chronological study of LT's career and his major and minor writings.

Weiland, Steven. "Looking for Lionel Trilling in All the Wrong Places, or Becoming a Land Grant Jew." *The Antioch Review* 52, no. 3 (summer 1994): 416–32. Weiland, a Jewish professor at Michigan State University, discusses the disparity between his youth and educational environment and his teaching at a Midwest land-grant institution. Weiland reflects on his presence in an institution very different from the intellectual culture of Columbia and New York, where LT spent his adult life, and on his learning from his undergraduate teachers, who were students of LT, to read *LI* as "the model of adult and academic discourse."

Weissman, Judith. "A Straight Back and an Arrogant Head." *The Georgia Review* 48, no. 1 (spring 1994), 1–8. DT's *BJ* defends liberalism, which is anathema to the contemporary literary academy, since literary theorists celebrate repressed voices and sexual/social perversions. By defending traditional liberalism, *BJ* champions "bourgeois" values that current literary theory opposes.

## Acknowledgments of Sources

Robert Morss Lovett, "The Mind of Matthew Arnold," is reprinted with permission from *The Nation* magazine, 11 March 1939, 297–98. © The Nation Company, L. P.

Jacques Barzun, "Trilling's Matthew Arnold," is reprinted from *Columbia University Quarterly* 31 (March 1939): 69–71.

Edmund Wilson, "Uncle Matthew," is reprinted from *The New Republic* 98 (22 March 1939): 194.

John Middleton Murry's piece is excerpted from "Lionel Trilling's Matthew Arnold," *Poets, Critics, Mystics: A Selection of Criticisms Written between 1919 and 1955 by John Middleton Murry*, ed. Richard Rees (Carbondale: Southern Illinois University Press, 1970), 69–77. Originally published as "Matthew Arnold Today," *Times Literary Supplement*, 11 March 1939, 148, 150.

William Phillip's piece is excerpted from "Whitman and Arnold," which first appeared in *Partisan Review* 6, no. 3 (spring 1939): 116–17.

Robert Penn Warren, "Arnold vs. the Nineteenth Century," was first published in *The Kenyon Review*, o.s. 1, no. 2 (spring 1939): 217–21. © 1939 by Kenyon College.

Edward Sackville-West, "The Modern Dilemma," is reprinted from *The Spectator*, 28 April 1939, 716.

T. Sturge Moore, review of *Matthew Arnold*, is reprinted from *English* 2 (summer 1939): 386–87.

John Peale Bishop, "Matthew Arnold Again," is reprinted from *Collected Essays of John Peale Bishop* (New York: Scribner's, 1948), 353–56.

David Daiches's review is reprinted from *Accent* 4 (spring 1943): 61–62.

Morton Dauwen Zabel, "A Forster Revival," is reprinted with permission from *The Nation* magazine, 7 August 1943, 158–59. © The Nation Company, L. P.

Clifton Fadiman, "E. M. Forster," originally appeared in *The New Yorker*, 14 August 1943, 68–69. Copyright © 1943, 1971 by Clifton Fadiman. This usage granted by permission.

George Mayberry, "The Forster Revival," is reprinted from *The New Republic* 109 (6 September 1943): 341.

Alan Pryce-Jones's review is reprinted from *The New Statesman and Nation*, 6 November 1943, 303. © New Statesman.

Irving Kristol, "The Moral Critic," is reprinted from *Enquiry*, April 1944, 20–23.

Kate O'Brien, "Refusal of Greatness," is reprinted from *The Spectator*, 1 December 1944, 509–10.

F. R. Leavis, "Meet Mr. Forster," is reprinted from *Scrutiny* 12, no. 1 (winter 1944): 308–9.

Michael Levenson, "Ernest Ironies: Trilling's Forster," is a previously unpublished essay, printed with the permission of the author.

Mark Schorer, "The Vexing Problem of Orientation," is reprinted from *The New York Times Book Review*, 12 October 1947, 4, 40. Copyright © 1947 by The New York Times. Reprinted by permission.

Robert Warshow's piece is excerpted from "The Legacy of the Thirties," which was originally published in *Commentary*, December 1947, 538–45; reprinted by permission; all rights reserved. It later appeared in *The Immediate Experience* (Garden City NY: Doubleday, 1962), 42–48.

Wylie Sypher, "The Political Imagination," first appeared in *Partisan Review* 15, no. 1 (January 1948): 125–27.

Leslie Fiedler, review of *The Middle of the Journey*, was first published in *The Kenyon Review*, o.s. 10, no. 3 (summer 1948): 524–25. © 1948 by Kenyon College.

John Bayley's piece is excerpted from "Middle-Class Futures," *Times Literary Supplement*, 11 April 1975, 399.

David Caute, "Summer People," is reprinted from *The New Statesman*, 11 April 1975, 486.

P. N. Furbank's piece is excerpted from "The Gravities of Grown-Upness," *Times Literary Supplement*, 21 August 1981, 951.

Ben Ray Redman, "Reality in Life and Literature," is reprinted from *Saturday Review of Literature*, 15 April 1950, 44–45.

Clifton Fadiman, "Lionel Trilling and the Party of the Imagination," originally appeared in *The New Yorker*, 22 April 1950, 115–18. Copyright © 1950, 1978 by Clifton Fadiman. This usage granted by permission.

R. W. B. Lewis, "Lionel Trilling and the New Stoicism," is reprinted by permission from *The Hudson Review* 3, no. 2 (summer 1950): 313–17. Copyright © 1950 by The Hudson Review, Inc.

Irving Howe, "Liberalism, History, and Mr. Trilling," is reprinted with permission from *The Nation* magazine, 27 May 1950, 529. © The Nation Company, L. P.

Stephen Spender, "Beyond Liberalism," is reprinted from *Commentary*, August 1950, 188–92, by permission; all rights reserved.

R. P. Blackmur, "The Politics of Human Power," is reprinted from and was first published in *The Kenyon Review*, 12 (autumn 1950): 663–73. © 1950 by Kenyon

College. It later appeared in *The Lion and the Honeycomb* (New York: Harcourt, Brace, 1955), 32–42.

Norman Podhoretz, "The Arnoldian Function in American Criticism," is reprinted from *Scrutiny* 18 (June 1951): 59–65, by permission of the author.

Delmore Schwartz's piece is excerpted from "The Duchess' Red Shoes," which first appeared in *Partisan Review* 20, no. 1 (January–February 1953): 55–73.

Quentin Anderson, "Reconsideration: Lionel Trilling," is reprinted by permission of *The New Republic*, 23 April 1977, 30–32. © 1977, The New Republic, Inc.

Harry Levin, "An Urgent Awareness," is reprinted from *The New York Times Book Review*, 13 February 1955, 3, 30. Copyright © 1955 by The New York Times. Reprinted by permission.

Paul Pickrel, "The Voice beyond Ideology," is reprinted from *Commentary*, April 1955, 398–400, by permission; all rights reserved.

Roy Fuller's piece is excerpted from review in *London Magazine*, November 1955, 87–90.

Angus Wilson, "To Know and Yet Not to Fear Reality," is reprinted from *Encounter* 5 (1955): 79–82.

Denis Donoghue, "The Critic in Reaction," is reprinted from *Twentieth Century* 158 (October 1955): 376–83.

Joseph Frank, "Lionel Trilling and the Conservative Imagination," was first published in the *Sewanee Review* 64, no. 2 (spring 1956): 296–309. Copyright 1956, 1984 by the University of the South. Reprinted with the permission of the editor and the author. It later appeared in *The Widening Gyre* (New Brunswick NJ: Rutgers UP, 1963), 253–74.

David Daiches, "The Mind of Lionel Trilling: An Appraisal," is reprinted from *Commentary*, July 1957, 66–69, by permission; all rights reserved.

E. B. Greenwood, "The Literary Criticism of Lionel Trilling," is reprinted from *Twentieth Century*, January 1958, 44–48.

George Steiner, "An Overture to Silence," is reprinted from *Book Week*, 31 October 1965, 4.

Robert Mazzocco, "Beyond Criticism," is reprinted from *The New York Review of Books*, 9 December 1965, 20–24.

Raymond Williams, "Beyond Liberalism," is reprinted from *The Manchester Guardian*, 21 April 1966, 10. © 1966 *The Guardian*.

Graham Hough, " 'We' and Lionel Trilling," is reprinted from *The Listener*, 26 May 1966, 760–61.

Denis Donoghue, "A Literary Gathering," is reprinted from *Commentary*, April 1968, 92–96, by permission; all rights reserved.

Mark Krupnick's piece is excerpted from "Lionel Trilling: Criticism and Illusion," *Modern Occasions* 1, no. 2 (winter 1971): 282–87.

Shirley Robin Letwin, "On the Birth and Death of the Individual," is reprinted from *The Spectator*, 21 October 1972, 624–26.

John Bayley, "The Last Honest Souls," is reprinted from *The Listener*, 26 October 1972, 543.

Geoffrey H. Hartman's piece is excerpted from a review of *Sincerity and Authenticity* and *Mind in the Modern World*, *The New York Times Book Review*, 4 February 1973, 1, 28–30.

Gerald Graff, "On Culture and Society," is reprinted from *Dissent* 20 (spring 1973): 230–34.

Irving Howe, "Lionel Trilling: Sincerity and Authenticity," is reprinted from "Reading Lionel Trilling," *Commentary*, August 1973, 68–71, by permission; all rights reserved. It later appeared in *Celebrations and Attacks* (New York: Horizon Press, 1979), 213–20.

Roger Sale, "Lionel Trilling," is reprinted from and was first published in *The Hudson Review* 26, no. 1 (spring 1973): 240–47. It later appeared in *On Not Being Good Enough* (New York: Oxford UP, 1979), 148–56.

John Holloway, "Sincerely, Lionel Trilling," is reprinted from *Encounter* 41, no. 3 (September 1973): 64–68.

Steven Marcus's piece is excerpted from "Lionel Trilling, 1905–75," *Art, Politics, and Will* (New York: Basic Books, 1976), 265–78; originally published in *The New York Times*, 13 November 1975, 1.

Irving Howe, "On Lionel Trilling: Continuous Magical Confrontation," is reprinted by permission of *The New Republic*, 13 March 1976, 29–31. © 1976, The New Republic, Inc.

Mark Shechner, "The Elusive Trilling," is reprinted from "The Elusive Trilling, Pt. II," *The Nation*, 24 September 1977, 278–80, with permission from *The Nation* magazine. © The Nation Company, L. P.

Richard Sennett, "On Lionel Trilling," is reprinted from *The New Yorker*, 5 November 1979, 204–17, by permission; © 1979 The New Yorker Magazine, Inc. All rights reserved.

Norman Podhoretz's excerpt is reprinted from *Breaking Ranks* (New York: Random House, 1979), 297–301, by permission of the author.

William Barrett, "Beginnings of Conservative Thought," is reprinted from "The Authentic Lionel Trilling," *Commentary*, February 1982, 36–47, by permission; all rights reserved. It later appeared in *The Truants: Adventures among the Intellectuals* (New York: Doubleday, 1982), 175–78.

Morris Dickstein, "The Critics Who Made Us: Lionel Trilling and *The Liberal Imagination*," was first published in the *Sewanee Review* 94, no. 2 (spring 1986): 323–34. Copyright 1986 by Morris Dickstein. Reprinted with the permission of the author.

Mark Krupnick, "The Neoconservatives," is reprinted from *Lionel Trilling and the Fate of Cultural Criticism* (Evanston, Ill.: Northwestern UP, 1986), 147–50. © 1986 by Mark Krupnick.

Cornel West, "Lionel Trilling: Godfather of Neo-Conservatism," is reprinted from *New Politics*, n.s., no. 1 (summer 1986): 233–42.

Lewis P. Simpson, "Lionel Trilling and the Agency of Terror," first appeared in *Partisan Review* 54, no. 1 (winter 1987): 18–35.

John Rodden, "Trilling's Homage to Orwell," is adapted from *The Politics of Literary Reputation* (New York: Oxford UP, 1989), 72–82.

Bruno Bettelheim, "Notes on Lionel Trilling: Literature and Psychoanalysis," is reprinted from *Explorations: The Twentieth Century* special series 3 (1989): 29–44, by permission of the Flora Levy Humanities Series.

Gertrude Himmelfarb's piece is excerpted from *On Looking Into the Abyss* (New York: Knopf, 1994), ix–xi, 1–26, 164–68, adapted from "The Abyss Revisited," *The American Scholar* 61, no. 3 (summer 1992): 337–49. Copyright © 1992 by the author.

Diana Trilling's piece is excerpted from *The Beginning of the Journey: The Marriage of Diana and Lionel Trilling* (New York: Harcourt Brace, 1993), 372–73.

Tom Samet, " 'For That I Came': Lionel Trilling and the Self Now," is a previously unpublished essay (October 1997), printed with permission of the author.

# Index